Random House Webster's
SPELL CHECKER
&
ABBREVIATIONS
DICTIONARY

Published by Ballantine Books:

RANDOM HOUSE WEBSTER'S DICTIONARY
RANDOM HOUSE ROGET'S THESAURUS
RANDOM HOUSE GUIDE TO GOOD WRITING
RANDOM HOUSE POWER VOCABULARY BUILDER
RANDOM HOUSE WEBSTER'S SPELL CHECKER &
    ABBREVIATIONS DICTIONARY
RANDOM HOUSE WORD MENU™
RANDOM HOUSE LATIN-AMERICAN SPANISH DICTIONARY
RANDOM HOUSE SPANISH-ENGLISH ENGLISH-SPANISH
    DICTIONARY
RANDOM HOUSE JAPANESE-ENGLISH ENGLISH-JAPANESE
    DICTIONARY
RANDOM HOUSE GERMAN-ENGLISH ENGLISH-GERMAN
    DICTIONARY
RANDOM HOUSE FRENCH-ENGLISH ENGLISH-FRENCH
    DICTIONARY

Random House Webster's
SPELL CHECKER
&
ABBREVIATIONS
DICTIONARY

BALLANTINE BOOKS • NEW YORK

Copyright © 1996 by Random House, Inc.

All rights reserved under International and Pan-American Copyright Conventions. Published in the United States by Ballantine Books, a division of Random House, Inc., New York, and simultaneously in Canada by Random House of Canada Limited, Toronto. Originally published as two works by Reference & Information Publishing, Random House, Inc., in 1996. No part of this publication may be reproduced in any form or by any means, electronic or mechanical, including photocopying, without permission, in writing, from the publisher. All inquiries should be addressed to Reference & Information Publishing, Random House, Inc., 201 East 50th Street, New York, NY 10022-7703.

A number of entered words in which we have reason to believe trademark, service mark, or other proprietary rights may exist have been designated as such by use of initial capitalization. However, no attempt has been made to designate as trademarks or service marks all personal computer words or terms in which proprietary rights might exist. The inclusion, exclusion, or definition of a word or term is not intended to affect, or express any judgment on, the validity or legal status of any proprietary rights which may be claimed in that word or term.

http://www.randomhouse.com

Library of Congress Catalog Card Number: 97-93538

ISBN 0-345-41440-3

Manufactured in the United States of America

First Ballantine Books Edition: August 1997

10 9 8 7 6 5 4 3 2

Table of Contents

How to Use this Book

Why a Spell Checker?

Dictionaries are most commonly used to look up spellings. But a dictionary offers a great wealth of information—meanings, pronunciations, syllable divisions, word origins, parts of speech, usage notes, and, frequently, illustrations, maps, tables, and charts. For exploring words in depth, nothing can take the place of a dictionary.

There are times, however, when a dictionary's very virtues, its richness, size, and complexity, make it a less than convenient reference choice. For looking up a spelling quickly or determining where to hyphenate a word, it is an advantage to be able to reach for something small and streamlined—a "speller-divider." The *Random House Webster's Spell Checker* offers that advantage.

Contents of this Book

In a single alphabetical list, this spell checker shows some 50,000 entries—common vocabulary words, names and places, and terms frequently encountered in the workplace, including the vocabularies of business and finance and the world of personal computers. Abbreviations and acronyms are also included in the list. Abbreviations shown for states are those recommended for use with ZIP codes.

The entry list also provides short definitions to distinguish between words that sound alike or look alike, or whose meanings are often confused. In most cases, all of the relevant definitions appear at each one of the entries involved. However, when confusable entries are close to one another, each shows only its own definition, and you can look nearby to find the entry with which it is being compared.

Word Division

In addition to dividing words into syllables, this book distinguishes between those syllable divisions that can appropriately be used for end-of-line hyphenation and those that cannot. Here are some general guidelines about word division:

- Do not divide a one-syllable word. This includes past tenses like *walked* and *dreamed,* which should never be split before the *-ed* ending.
- Do not divide a word so that a single letter is left at the end of a line, as in *a\bout,* or so that a single letter starts the following line, as in *cit\y.*
- Hyphenated compounds should preferably be divided only after the hyphen. If the first portion of the compound is a single letter, however, as in *D-day,* the word should not be divided.
- Word segments like *-ceous, -scious, -sial, -tion, -tious* should not be divided.

• The portion of a word left at the end of a line should not encourage a misleading pronunciation, as would be the case if *acetate*, a three-syllable word, were divided after the first e.

Symbols Used in this Book

All syllable divisions recommended for use as end-of-line hyphenation points are marked with a bold, centered dot, or bullet (•). This symbol is the one used most frequently in dictionaries to mark word divisions. The mark used in this book to divide syllables where end-of-line hyphenation is NOT recommended is the lightface backslash (\). The backslash character (recognizable to those who use the MS-DOS or Windows operating systems in their computers) was chosen for three reasons: (1) it is clearly distinct from the bullet; (2) it is not a character that can be perceived as part of an actual spelling; (3) it echoes the circle with a slash (○) commonly used to signal that something is forbidden, as in the "no smoking" sign.

Acknowledgments

The text of the *Random House Webster's Spell Checker* was derived from the large computerized database that is part of the Random House Living Dictionary Project. From inception to bound books, the Spell Checker has benefited from the support of the Reference Division staff. In addition, initial decisions about entry style were contributed by Anne D. Steinhardt, the text was compiled and edited by Chris Reid, and Connie Baboukis was responsible for the definitions. The book was copyedited by Trumbull Rogers. Roger Sperberg, this paperback edition's designer, set the book on a *PowerMac 8600* computer, using the Adobe Gill Sans typeface family.

> Enid Pearsons
> for the Editorial Staff
> Random House Reference Division

Introduction

English Spelling

The classic diatribe against the vagaries of English spelling is the one made famous by George Bernard Shaw, in which he claims that our spelling is so irregular (and so absurd!) that the common word *fish* could as well be spelled *ghoti*. The idea is as follows:

gh, *as in* cou**gh**, *equals the sound of* **f**
o, *as in* w**o**men, *equals the sound of* **i**
ti, *as in* na**ti**on, *equals the sound of* **sh**

The trouble with this analysis, amusing though it may be, is that it does not take into account the **phonotactics** of English, what might be called "the rules of the game." Without denying that in the English language we can have more than one sound for each spelling and more than one spelling for each sound, we can point to certain regularities regarding sound-spelling correspondences, among them rules of position. Taking these into account, we can see that Shaw's suggested spelling of *ghoti* for *fish* falls apart; *gh* NEVER equals the sound of *f* at the beginning of a word, only at the end, as in *rough, cough,* or *laugh*. The use of the letter *o* to represent the "short" *i* sound is even more restricted, appearing ONLY in the word *women*. Finally, *ti* produces the *sh* sound ONLY medially, typically in suffixes like *-tion* and *-tious*.

There are reasons for the sound-spelling irregularities in English; its history warrants them. For one thing, the number of sounds in the language is greater than the number of symbols available in our alphabet; some of these symbols must do double duty (as with "hard" and "soft" *c* and *g*) or must combine with other symbols in order to account for all the sounds. For another, English has borrowed heavily from other languages, retaining traces of their pronunciations with their spellings. In addition, spelling in general is conservative—it changes less readily than pronunciation. Modern English retains spellings that do not reflect the many changes in pronunciation that have occurred over the years, particularly during the Great Vowel Shift of the fifteenth century. Nor can any single set of spellings reflect the diversity of English dialects. English is a varied language that flourishes not only throughout North America and England, but over the entire globe. Add to this the fact that early printers were inconsistent and idiosyncratic in their spelling, and some of their misspellings have survived. All of these factors have led to the kinds of spelling irregularities that make the English language both frustrating and fascinating.

Nevertheless, for all its difficulties, English spelling is not entirely irrational. We return to "phonotactics." If certain letter combinations occur predominantly in certain portions of words, a growing familiarity with these patterns can increase your confidence in using and working with the

English language. And it can help to resolve an age-old problem:

Finding Spellings When You Know the Sounds

THE PROBLEM

Traditionally, there has been a fundamental difficulty with making efficient use of dictionaries and similar reference books: How can you look up a word if you don't know how to spell it? Where do you look? In what part of the alphabet?

THE SOLUTION

Although no complete solution exists, a "Table of Sound-Spelling Correspondences" like the one below can help. By listing alternative spellings for each of the sounds of English, and tying these sounds and spellings together, the table allows you to relate what you already know about a word—how to SAY it—with what you are trying to find out about the word—how to SPELL it.

Understanding the Table

CONTEXTS FOR GIVEN SPELLING PATTERNS

Tables showing the relationship between sounds and spellings can be found in most unabridged and desk dictionaries. The table in the *Random House Webster's Spell Checker* not only shows spelling patterns and the sounds they represent but indicates which part of a word (beginning, middle, or end) is likely to contain these patterns. For example, "-ag(m)," as in "diaphragm," is shown with a preceding hyphen and with parentheses around the *m*, as one of the patterns representing the "short"

a sound. This means that when the letters *ag* precede an *m* and the *agm* ends a word or syllable, *ag* is pronounced as a vowel, as if the *g* were not there. (In fact, when an *agm* combination is split between syllables, as in the word "syn•*tag*•*mat*\ic," so that the *g* ends one syllable and the *m* starts the next one, the *g* is NOT silent.)

From this example, you can see that parenthesized letters in the table indicate a CONTEXT for a given spelling pattern. Similarly, hyphens show where in a word or syllable that pattern is most likely to occur. A spelling pattern shown without any hyphens can occur in various parts of a word; some of these, like *air*, are also found as entire words.

KEY-WORD PATTERNS

For each sound, the table shows a large, boldface **key spelling**, followed by a familiar word (or words) in which that spelling typically occurs. This key word allows you, using your own English dialect, to fix the sound in your mind.

Following the key-word pattern is a list of other spellings for the same sound. Notice that you may pronounce some of the spellings in certain sections differently from the sound represented. Such spellings will probably be repeated at the sounds more appropriate for your dialect. Tables of this sort usually include unusual sound-spelling associations: some that are simply rare, like the *u* in *busy* or *business* as the short *i* sound, and others that are derived from languages other than English. French spellings standing for the "long" *o* sound, for example, might include *-eau, -eaux,* and *-ot.* Long lists of such spelling patterns, with no indication of which ones are frequent enough to be useful, can indeed be overwhelming. To simplify our table, we have marked the common spelling patterns for each sound with an asterisk.

Note that the combination of a vowel letter plus an ellipsis (three dots) and an e stands for any spelling in which that vowel and the e are separated by a single consonant. As a general rule, this "discontinuous vowel" pattern represents the long sound of that vowel. (Long *i*, for example, is frequently spelled with *i...e*, as in *ice*). But a discontinuous vowel can stand for other than long vowel sounds. In the word *have*, the *a...e* stands for a short *a* sound, and in the word *love*, *o...e* stands for the sound of short *u*.

Using the Table

To find a word, first sound it out. Say it out loud, if necessary. Determine especially how the first syllable is pronounced. In the table, find the various spelling equivalents for that pronunciation. Finally, look for each of those spellings in the *Random House Webster's Spell Checker* until you find the word you want.

AN INSTRUCTIVE EXAMPLE

If you say the words *persuade* and *pursue* aloud, you can hear that their initial syllables sound very much alike, something like the word *purr*, but not quite as strong. The *p* sound is fairly easy to spell; initial consonants usually are. The problem is with the following sound; it is not stressed and, depending on one's dialect of English, may either have a slight *r* "coloring" or be followed by an audible *r* sound. Among the spellings listed for that sound (for which the key word pattern is *-er*, as in father), you will find *ar-, ir-,* and *ur-*. If you then look in the Spell Checker for *p* followed by each of these spellings, you will eventually find both *persuade* (under *p* + *er*) and *pursue* (under *p* + *ur*). You will have discovered that although their initial syllables sound alike, the two words you were looking for are spelled differently.

Table of Sound–Spelling Correspondences

Vowels and diphthongs

*a- as in **a**t;
-a- as in h**a**t ("short" a)

-a'a-	ma'am
-ach(m)	drachm
-ag(m)	diaphragm
-ah-	dahlia
-ai-	plaid
-al-	half
-au-	laugh
-ua-	guarantor
-ui-	guimpe
i(n)-, -i(n)-	ingenue, lingerie
-i(m)-	timbre

*a...e as in **a**t**e**;
-a...e as in h**a**t**e** ("long" a)

-ae-	Gaelic
-ag(n)	champagne
*-ai-	rain
-aigh-	straight
-aig(n)	arraign
-ao-	gaol
-au-	gauge
-a(g)ue	vague
*-ay	ray
*é-	étude
-é	exposé
-e...e	suede
*-ea-	steak
-ee	matinee
eh	eh
*-ei-	veil
*-eig(n)	feign
*eigh-, -eigh-,	eight, weight
-eigh	weigh
-eilles	Marseilles
-er	dossier
-es(ne)	demesne
-et	beret
*-ey	obey

*air as in ch**air**

*-aire	doctrinaire
*-ar-	chary
*-are	dare
-ayer	prayer
*-ear	wear
-eer	Mynheer
e'er	ne'er
*-eir	their
-er	mal de mer
*-ere	there
-ey're	they're

*ah as in hurr**ah** ("broad" a)

*-a-	father
à	à la mode
-aa-	bazaar
*-al(f)	half
*-al(m)	calm
-as	faux pas
-at	éclat
-au	laugh
-e(r)-	sergeant
*-ea(r)-	hearth
-oi-	reservoir
-ua-	guard
i(n)-, -i(n)-	ingenue, lingerie

*e as in **e**bb ("short" e)

a-, -a-,	any, many
ae-	aesthete
-ai-	said
-ay-	says
*-ea-	leather
-eg(m)	phlegm
-ei-	heifer
-eo-	jeopardy
-ie-	friend
-oe-	foetid

*ee as in keep ("long" e)

ae-, -ae	Aesop, Caesar
-ay	quay
*e-, -e-	equal, secret
-e	strophe
*ea-, -ea-, -ea	each, team, tea
*-ea(g)ue	league
e'e-	e'en
*e...e	precede
*-ei	receive
-eip(t)	receipt
-eo	people
*-ey	key
-i	rani
*i...e	machine
*-ie-	field
-is	debris
*-i(g)ue	intrigue
*-i(q)ue	antique
-oe	amoeba
-uay	quay
*-y	city

*i as in if ("short" i)

*-a-	damage
-ae	anaesthetic
e-	England
-ee	been
*-ei	counterfeit
-ia	carriage
-ie	sieve
-o-	women
(b)u(s)-	business
-ui(l)-	build, guilt
*-y	sympathetic

*i...e as in ice ("long" i)

*-ai-	faille
ais-	aisle
-ay	kayak
aye	aye
*-ei	stein
-eigh-	height
eye	eye
*-ie	pie

*-igh	high
is-	island
*-uy	buy
*-y-, -y	cycle, sky
*-ye	lye

*o as in box

*(w)a-	wander
*-(u)a-	quadrant
-ach-	yacht
-au	astronaut
-eau	bureaucracy
-ou	cough
*ho-	honor

*o as in lo

*-au	mauve
-aut	hautboy
-aux	faux pas
-eau	beau
-eaux	Bordeaux
-eo	yeoman
-ew	sew
*o...e	rote
*-oa-	road
*-oe	toe
oh	oh
*-ol-	yolk
-oo-	brooch
-ot	depot
*-ou-	soul
*-ow	flow
*-owe	owe

*-aw as in paw

*-a-	tall
*(w)a(r)-	warrant
-ah	Utah
*-al-	walk
-as	Arkansas
*au-, -au-	author, vault
*-augh-	caught
*-o-	alcohol
*-oa-	broad
-oo-	floor
*-ough-	sought

*-oy as in b**oy**

-awy-	lawyer
-eu-	Freud
*-oi-	oil
-ois	Iriquois
-uoy	buoy

*-oo- as in l**oo**k

-o-	wolf
*-oul-	would
*-u-	pull

*oo-, *-oo-, *-oo as in **oo**ze, m**oo**d, ahch**oo**

-eu-	maneuver
*-ew	grew
-ieu	lieu
-o	who
o...e	move
-oe	canoe
-oeu-	manoeuvre
*-ou-	troup
*u...e	rule
*-ue	flue
-ug(n)	impugn
*-ui-	suit

*-ow as in br**ow**

au	Auschwitz
-au	landau
*ou-, *-ou-	out, shout
*-ough	bough

*u-, -u- as in **u**p, p**u**p

o-, *-o-	other, son
-oe	does
*o...e	love
-oo	blood
-ou(ble)	trouble

*ur-, *-ur- as in **ur**n, t**ur**n

*ear-, -ear-	eam, leam
*er-, -er-	ermine, term
err	err
-eur	poseur

her-	herb
*-ir-, -ir	thirsty, fir
(w)or-	work
-our-	scourge
-urr	purr
-yr-	myrtle

*u-, -u as in **u**tility, fut**u**re

-eau-	beauty
-eu-	feud
*-ew	few
*hu-	human
hu...e	huge
-ieu	purlieu
-iew	view
*u...e	use
*-ue	cue
-ueue	queue
yew-	yew
you	you
yu-	Yukon
yu...e	yule

*a as in **a**lone

*-e-	system
*-i-	easily
*-o-	gallop
*-u-	circus
à	tête-à-tête
-ai(n)	mountain
-ei(n)	mullein
-eo(n)	dungeon
-ia-	parliament
-io-	legion
-oi-	porpoise
*-ou-	curious
-y-	martyr

*-er as in fath**er**

*-ar	liar
*-ir	elixir
*-or	labor
*-our	labour
*-ur	augur
*-ure	future
-yr	martyr

Consonants

(Note that consonant spelling patterns such as -bb- and -tch-, shown with hyphens on either side, are frequently part of two adjacent syllables in a word, with part of the combination in one syllable and the rest in the next.)

*b-, *-b-, *-b as in **b**ed, am**b**er, ru**b**

*-bb-, *bb-	ho**bb**y, e**bb**
*-be	lo**b**e
bh-	**bh**eesty

*ch-, -ch-, *-ch as in **ch**ief, ah**ch**oo, ri**ch**

c-	**c**ello
*-che	ni**ch**e
*-tch-, *-tch	ha**tch**et, ca**tch**
-te	righ**t**eous
*-ti	ques**ti**on
*-tu	na**tu**ral

*d-, *-d-, *-d as in **d**o, o**d**or, re**d**

*-'d	we'**d**
*-dd-, *-dd	la**dd**er, o**dd**
*-de	fa**d**e
dh-	**dh**urrie
*-ed	pulle**d**
*-ld	shou**ld**

*f-, *-f-, as in **f**eed, sa**f**er

*-fe	li**f**e
*-ff-, *-ff	mu**ff**in, o**ff**
*-ft-	so**f**ten
*-gh	tou**gh**
*-lf	ca**lf**
pf-	**pf**ennig
*ph-	**ph**ysics
-ph-	sta**ph**ylococcus
-ph	sta**ph**

*g-, *-g-, *-g as in **g**ive, a**g**ate, fo**g**

*-gg	e**gg**
*gh-	**gh**ost
*gu-	**g**uard
*-gue	pla**gu**e

*h-, *-h- as in **h**it, a**h**oy

wh-	**wh**o

*wh- as in **wh**ere (like hw)

*hu- as in **hu**ge (like hyoo)

*j- as in **j**ust

-ch	Greenwi**ch**
*-d(u)	gra**d**uate
*-dg-	ju**dg**ment
*-dge	bri**dge**
*-di	sol**di**er
*-ge	sa**g**e
-gg	exa**gg**erate
*g(e)-, *-g(e)-	**g**em, a**g**ent
*g(i)-, *-g(i)-	**g**in, a**g**ile
-jj-	Ha**jj**i

*k-, *-k- as in **k**eep, ma**k**ing

*c-, *-c-	**c**ar, be**c**ome
*-cc-	a**cc**ount
-cch-	ba**cch**anal
*ch-	**ch**aracter
*-ck-	ba**ck**
-cq-	ac**q**uaint
-cqu-	la**cqu**er
-cque	sa**cque**
cu-	bis**c**uit
-gh	lou**gh**
*-ke	ra**k**e
-kh	Si**kh**
-lk	wa**lk**
q-	**q**adi
-q	Ira**q**
-qu-	li**qu**or
-que	pla**que**

*l-, *-l-, *-l as in **l**ive, a**l**ive, sai**l**

*-le	mi**le**
*-ll	ca**ll**
-lle	fai**lle**
-sl-	li**sl**e
-sle	ai**sle**

*m-, *-m-, *-m as in **m**ore, a**m**ount, ha**m**

-chm	cra**chm**
-gm	paradi**gm**
*-lm	ca**lm**
-mb	li**mb**
*-me	ho**me**
mh-	**mh**o
*-mm-	ha**mm**er
-mn	hy**mn**

*n-, *-n-, *-n as in **n**ot, ce**n**ter, ca**n**

*gn-	**gn**at
*kn-	**kn**ife
mn-	**mn**emonic
*-ne	do**ne**
*-nn-	ru**nn**er
*pn(eu)-	**pn**eumatic

*-ng-, *-ng as in ringi**ng**, ri**ng**

*-n(k)	pi**n**k
-ngg	mahjo**ngg**
-ngue	to**ngue**

*p-, *-p-, *-p as in **p**en, su**p**er, sto**p**

*-pe	ho**pe**
*-pp-	su**pp**er
-ppe	lagnia**ppe**

*r-, *-r-, *-r as in **r**ed, a**r**ise, fou**r**

*-re	pu**re**
*rh-	**rh**ythm
*-rr-	ca**rr**ot
-rrh	cata**rrh**
*wr-	**wr**ong

*s-, *-s-, *-s as in **s**ee, be**s**ide, ala**s**

*c(e)-, *-c(e)-,	**c**enter, ra**c**er
*c(i)-, *-c(i)-	**c**ity, a**c**id
*-ce	mi**ce**
*ps-	**ps**ychology
*sc-	**sc**ene
sch-	**sch**ism
*-se	mou**se**
*-ss-, *-ss	me**ss**enger, lo**ss**

*sh-, *-sh-, *-sh as in **sh**ip, a**sh**amed, wa**sh**

-ce	o**ce**an
ch-, *-ch-	**ch**aise, ma**ch**ine
-chs	fu**chs**ia
*-ci	spe**ci**al
psh-	**psh**aw
s(u)-	**s**ugar
sch-	**sch**ist
*-sci	con**sci**ence
-se	nau**se**ous
*-si	man**si**on
*-ss	ti**ss**ue
*-ssi	mi**ssi**on
*-ti	cap**ti**on

*t-, *-t-, *-t as in **t**oe, a**t**om, ha**t**

-bt	dou**bt**
-cht	ya**cht**
ct-	**ct**enophore
*-ed	talk**ed**
*-ght	bou**ght**
phth-	**phth**isic
'-t-	'**t**was
*-te	bi**te**
th-	**th**yme
*-tt-	bo**tt**om
tw-	**tw**o

*th-, *-th-, *-th as in **th**in, e**th**er, pa**th**

chth-	**chth**onian

*th-, *-th-, -th as in **th**en, o**th**er, smoo**th**

    *-the   ba**the**

*v-, *-v-, -v as in **v**isit, o**v**er, lu**v**

    -f   o**f**
    -ph-   Ste**ph**en
    *-ve   ha**ve**
    -vv-   fli**vv**er

*w-, *-w- as in **w**ell, a**w**ay

    -ju-   mari**ju**ana
    -o(i)-   ch**o**ir
    ou(i)-   **ou**ija
    (q)u-   q**u**iet
    *wh-   **wh**ere

*y- as in **y**et

    *-i-   un**i**on
    -j-   hallelu**j**ah
    -ll-   torti**ll**a

*z-, -z- as in **z**one, Bi**z**et

    *-s   ha**s**
    -sc-   di**sc**ern
    *-se   ri**se**
    x-   **x**ylem
    -ze   fu**ze**
    *-zz-, *-zz   bu**zz**ard, fu**zz**

-zi- as in bra**zi**er (like **zh**)

    *-ge   gara**ge**
    *-s(u)-   mea**s**ure
    *-si   divi**si**on
    *-z(u)-   a**z**ure

Words Commonly Misspelled

We have listed here some of the words that have traditionally proved difficult to spell. The list includes not only "exceptions," words that defy common spelling rules, but some that pose problems even while adhering to these conventions.

aberrant
abscess
absence
absorption
abundance
accede
acceptance
accessible
accidentally
accommodate
according
accordion
accumulate
accustom
achievement
acknowledge
acknowledgment
acoustics
acquaintance
acquiesce
acquire
acquittal
across
address
adequate
adherent
adjourn
admittance
adolescence
adolescent
advantageous
advertisement
affidavit
against

aggravate
aggression
aging
aisle
all right
alien
allegiance
almost
although
always
amateur
analysis
analytical
analyze
anesthetic
annual
anoint
anonymous
answer
antarctic
antecedent
anticipation
antihistamine
anxiety
aperitif
apocryphal
apostasy
apparent
appearance
appetite
appreciate
appropriate
approximate
apropos

arctic
arguing
argument
arouse
arrangement
arthritis
article
artificial
asked
assassin
assess
asthma
athlete
athletic
attorneys
author
authoritative
auxiliary

bachelor
balance
bankruptcy
barbiturate
barrette
basically
basis
beggar
beginning
belief
believable
believe
beneficial
beneficiary
benefit

benefited	cemetery	consequently
blizzard	census	consistent
bludgeon	certain	consummate
bologna	challenge	continuous
bookkeeping	chandelier	control
bouillon	changeable	controlled
boundaries	changing	controversy
breathe	characteristic	convalesce
brief	chief	convenience
brilliant	choir	coolly
broccoli	choose	copyright
bronchial	cinnamon	cornucopia
brutality	circuit	corollary
bulletin	civilized	corporation
buoy	clothes	correlate
buoyant	codeine	correspondence
bureau	collateral	correspondent
bureaucracy	colloquial	counselor
burglary	colonel	counterfeit
business	colossal	courageous
	column	courteous
cafeteria	coming	crisis
caffeine	commemorate	criticism
calisthenics	commission	criticize
camaraderie	commitment	culinary
camouflage	committed	curiosity
campaign	committee	curriculum
cancel	comparative	cylinder
cancellation	comparison	
candidate	competition	debt
cantaloupe	competitive	debtor
capacity	complaint	deceive
cappuccino	concede	decide
carburetor	conceivable	decision
career	conceive	decisive
careful	condemn	defendant
carriage	condescend	definite
carrying	conferred	definitely
casserole	confidential	dependent
category	congratulate	de rigueur
caterpillar	conscience	descend
cavalry	conscientious	descendant
ceiling	conscious	description
cellar	consensus	desiccate

desirable	ellipsis	fiftieth
despair	embarrass	finagle
desperate	encouraging	finally
destroy	endurance	financial
develop	energetic	foliage
development	enforceable	forcible
diabetes	enthusiasm	forehead
diaphragm	environment	foreign
different	equipped	forfeit
dilemma	erroneous	formally
dining	especially	forte
diocese	esteemed	fortieth
diphtheria	exacerbate	fortunately
disappear	exaggerate	forty
disappearance	exceed	fourth
disappoint	excel	friend
disastrous	excellent	frieze
discipline	except	fundamental
disease	exceptionally	furniture
dissatisfied	excessive	
dissident	executive	galoshes
dissipate	exercise	gauge
distinguish	exhibition	genealogy
divide	exhilarate	generally
divine	existence	gnash
doesn't	expense	government
dormitory	experience	governor
duly	experiment	graffiti
dumbbell	explanation	grammar
during	exquisite	grateful
	extemporaneous	grievance
easier	extraordinary	grievous
easily	extremely	guarantee
ecstasy		guard
effervescent	facilities	guidance
efficacy	fallacy	
efficiency	familiar	handkerchief
efficient	fascinate	haphazard
eighth	fascism	harass
eightieth	feasible	harebrained
electrician	February	hazard height
eligibility	fictitious	hemorrhage
eligible	fiend	hemorrhoid
eliminate	fierce	hereditary

heroes	intercede	management
hierarchy	interest	maneuver
hindrance	interfere	manufacturer
hoping	intermittent	maraschino
hors d'oeuvres	intimate	marital
huge	inveigle	marriage
humorous	irrelevant	marriageable
hundredth	irresistible	mathematics
hydraulic	island	mayonnaise
hygiene		meant
hygienist	jealous	medicine
hypocrisy	jeopardize	medieval
	journal	memento
icicle	judgment	mileage
identification	judicial	millennium
idiosyncrasy		miniature
imaginary	khaki	minuet
immediately	kindergarten	miscellaneous
immense	knowledge	mischievous
impresario		misspell
inalienable	laboratory	mistletoe
incident	laid	moccasin
incidentally	larynx	molasses
inconvenience	leery	molecule
incredible	leisure	monotonous
indelible	length	mortgage
independent	liable	murmur
indestructible	liaison	muscle
indictment	libel	mutual
indigestible	library	mysterious
indispensable	license	
inevitable	lieutenant	naive
inferred	likelihood	naturally
influential	liquefy	necessarily
initial	liqueur	necessary
initiative	literature	necessity
innocuous	livelihood	neighbor
innuendo	loneliness	neither
inoculation	losing	nickel
inscrutable	lovable	niece
installation		ninetieth
instantaneous	magazine	ninety
intellectual	maintenance	ninth
intelligence	manageable	noticeable

notoriety	peculiar	prescription
nuptial	penicillin	prevalent
	perceive	primitive
obbligato	perform	prior
occasion	performance	privilege
occasionally	peril	probability
occurred	permanent	probably
occurrence	permissible	procedure
offense	perpendicular	proceed
official	perseverance	professor
omission	persistent	proffer
omit	personnel	pronounce
omitted	perspiration	pronunciation
oneself	persuade	propagate
ophthalmology	persuasion	protégé(e)
opinion	persuasive	psychiatry
opportunity	petition	psychology
optimism	philosophy	pursuant
optimist	physician	pursue
ordinarily	piccolo	pursuit
origin	plaited	putrefy
original	plateau	
outrageous	plausible	quantity
	playwright	questionnaire
paean	pleasant	queue
pageant	plebeian	
paid	pneumonia	rarefy
pamphlet	poinsettia	recede
paradise	politician	receipt
parakeet	pomegranate	receivable
parallel	possess	receive
paralysis	possession	recipe
paralyze	possibility	reciprocal
paraphernalia	possible	recognize
parimutuel	practically	recommend
parliament	practice	reference
partial	precede	referred
participate	precedence	reign
particularly	precisely	relegate
pasteurize	predecessor	relevant
pastime	preference	relieve
pavilion	preferred	religious
peaceable	prejudice	remembrance
peasant	preparatory	reminisce

remiss	serviceable	submitted
remittance	seventieth	substantial
rendezvous	several	subtle
repetition	sheik	subtly
replaceable	shepherd	succeed
representative	sheriff	successful
requisition	shining	succession
resistance	shoulder	successive
responsibility	shrapnel	sufficient
restaurant	siege	superintendent
restaurateur	sieve	supersede
resuscitate	significance	supplement
reticence	silhouette	suppress
reveille	similar	surprise
rhyme	simultaneity	surveillance
rhythm	simultaneous	susceptible
riddance	sincerely	suspicion
ridiculous	sixtieth	sustenance
rococo	skiing	syllable
roommate	socially	symmetrical
	society	sympathize
	solemn	sympathy
sacrifice	soliloquy	synchronous
sacrilegious	sophomore	synonym
safety	sorority	syphilis
salary	sovereign	systematically
sandwich	spaghetti	
sarsaparilla	spatial	tariff
sassafras	special	temperament
satisfaction	specifically	temperature
scarcity	specimen	temporarily
scene	speech	tendency
scenery	sponsor	tentative
schedule	spontaneous	terrestrial
scheme	statistics	therefore
scholarly	statute	thirtieth
scissors	stevedore	thorough
secede	stiletto	thought
secrecy	stopped	thousandth
secretary	stopping	through
seize	strength	till
seizure	strictly	titillate
separate	studying	together
separately	stupefy	tonight
sergeant		

tournament	usable	Wednesday
tourniquet	usage	weird
tragedy	using	wherever
tragically	usually	whim
transferred	utilize	wholly
transient		whose
tries	vacancy	wield
truly	vacuum	woolen
twelfth	vague	wretched
twentieth	valuable	writing
typical	variety	written
tyranny	vegetable	wrote
	veil	wrought
unanimous	vengeance	
undoubtedly	vermilion	xylophone
unique	veterinarian	
unison	vichyssoise	yacht
unmanageable	village	yield
unnecessary	villain	
until		zealous
upholsterer	warrant	zucchini

Random House
Webster's
Spell Checker

aard•vark
a\back
ab\a•cus, pl. \a•cus\es or \a\ci
a\baft
ab\a•lo•ne
a•ban•don, •doned, •don•ing
a•ban•don•ment
a•base, a•based, a•bas•ing
a\bash
a\bashed
a•bate, a•bat\ed, a\bat•ing
a•bate•ment
ab•at•toir
ab•bé
ab•bess
ab•bey, pl. •beys
ab•bot
ab•bre•vi•ate, •at\ed, •at•ing
ab•bre•vi•a•tion
ab•di•cate, •cat\ed, •cat•ing
ab•di•ca•tion
ab•do•men
ab•dom•i•nal
ab•duct
ab•duc•tion
ab•duc•tor
a\beam
a\bed
ab•er•rance or ab•er•ran\cy
ab•er•rant
ab•er•ra•tion
a\bet, a•bet•ted, a•bet•ting
a•bet•tor or a•bet•ter
a•bey•ance
ab•hor, •horred, •hor•ring
ab•hor•rence
ab•hor•rent
a•bide, a•bode or a•bid\ed, a\bid•ing
a•bil•i•ty, pl. •ties
ab•ject
ab•ject\ly
ab•ject•ness
ab•ju•ra•tion

ab•jure (to renounce), •jured, •jur•ing [vs. ad•jure (to request)]
ab•la•tive
a\blaze
a\ble, a\bler, a\blest
a•ble-•bod\ied
a\ble•ism
a\bloom
ab•lu•tion
a\bly
ab•ne•gate, •gat\ed, •gat•ing
ab•ne•ga•tion
ab•nor•mal
ab•nor•mal•i\ty, pl. •ties
ab•nor•mal•ly
a\board
a\bode
a\bol•ish, •ished, •ish•ing
ab•o•li•tion
ab•o•li•tion•ism
ab•o•li•tion•ist
A-\bomb (atom bomb)
a\bom\i•na\ble
a\bom\i•na•bly
a\bom\i•na•tion
ab\o•rig\i•nal
aboriginal cost
ab\o•rig•i\ne
a\born•ing
a\bort, a\bort\ed, a\bort•ing
a\bor•tion
a\bor•tion•ist
a\bor•tive
a\bound, a\bound\ed, a\bound•ing
a\bout
a\bout-•face
a\bove
a\bove•board
a\bove•ground
a\bove•men•tioned
a\bove-•the-•line
ab•ra•ca•dab\ra
a\brade, a\brad\ed, a\brad•ing
a\bra•sion
a\bra•sive
ab•re•ac•tion

a\breast
a\bridge, a\bridged, a\bridg•ing
a\bridg•ment or a\bridge•ment
a\broad
ab•ro•gate, •gat\ed, •gat•ing
ab•ro•ga•tion
ab•rupt
ab•scess
ab•scessed
ab•scis\sa, pl. •sas or •sae
ab•scond, \ed, •ing
ab•scond\er
ab•sence
ab•sent, \ed, •ing
ab•sen•tee
ab•sen•tee•ism
ab•sen•tee man•age•ment
ab\sent-•mind\ed
ab•sinthe
ab•so•lute
ab•so•lute•ly
ab•so•lu•tion
ab•so•lut•ism
ab•so•lut•ist
ab•solve, •solved, •solv•ing
ab•sorb, •sorbed, •sorb•ing
ab•sorb•a•ble
absorbable risk
ab•sorb•en\cy
ab•sorb•ent
ab•sorp•tion
ab•sorp•tive
ab•stain, •stained, •stain•ing
ab•stain\er
ab•ste•mi•ous
ab•ste•mi•ous•ness
ab•sten•tion
ab•sti•nence
ab•sti•nent
ab•stract, •stract\ed, •stract•ing
ab•stract\ed
ab•strac•tion
ab•strac•tion•ism
ab•strac•tion•ist

ab•stract of ti•tle
ab•struse
ab•surd
ab•surd•i\ty, pl. •ties
a\bun•dance
a\bun•dant
a\buse, a\bused, a\bus•ing
a\bus\er
a\bu•sive
a\but, a\but•ted, a\but•ting
a\but•ment
a\bys•mal
a\byss
a\ca•cia
ac\a•deme
ac\a•de•mi\a
ac\a•dem\ic
ac\a•de•mi\cal\ly
ac\a•de•mi•cian
ac\a•de•mi•cism
a\cad•e\my, pl. •mies
a\can•thus, pl. •thus\es or •thi
a cap•pel\la
ac•cede (to consent), •ced\ed, •ced•ing [vs. ex•ceed (to surpass)]
ac•cel•er•ant
ac•cel•er•ate, •at\ed, •at\ing
accelerated de•pre•ci•a•tion
ac•cel•er\a•tion
acceleration clause
ac•cel•er\a•tive
ac•cel•er\a•tor
accelerator board
ac•cel•er•om\e•ter
ac•cent, \ed, •ing
ac•cen•tu\al
ac•cen•tu•ate, •at\ed, •at•ing
ac•cen•tu•a•tion
ac•cept (to receive), \ed, •ing [vs. ex•cept (to exclude)]
ac•cept•a•bil•i\ty
ac•cept•a\ble
ac•cept•a•bly
ac•cept•ance
ac•cep•ta•tion

ac•cept\ed
ac•cess (approach; to gain access to), •cessed, •cess•ing [vs. ex•cess (surplus)]
ac•ces•si•bil•i\ty
ac•ces•si\ble
ac•ces•sion
ac•ces•so\ry, pl. •ries
ac•cess time
ac•ci•dence
ac•ci•dent
ac•ci•den•tal
ac•ci•den•tal\ly
ac•ci•dent in•sur•ance
ac\ci\dent-•prone
ac•claim, •claimed, •claim•ing
ac•cla•ma•tion
ac•cli•mate, •mat\ed, •mat•ing
ac•cli•ma•ti•za•tion
ac•cli•ma•tize, •tized, •tiz•ing
ac•cliv•i\ty, pl. •ties
ac•co•lade
ac•com•mo•date, •dat\ed, •dat•ing
ac•com•mo•da•tion
ac•com•pa•ni•ment
ac•com•pa•nist
ac•com•pa\ny, •nied, •ny•ing
ac•com•plice
ac•com•plish
ac•com•plished
ac•com•plish•ment
ac•cord, •cord\ed, •cord•ing
ac•cord•ance
ac•cord•ing
ac•cord•ing\ly
ac•cor•di\on
ac•cor•di•on•ist
ac•cost, \ed, •ing
ac•count, \ed, •ing
ac•count•a•bil•i\ty
ac•count•a\ble
ac•count•an\cy
ac•count•ant
ac•count debt•or

account ex•ec\u•tive
ac•count•ing
ac•counts pay•a\ble
accounts re•ceiv•a\ble
ac•cou•ter•ment or ac•cou•tre•ment
ac•cred\it, •it\ed, •it•ing
ac•cred\i•ta•tion
ac•cre•tion
ac•cru\al
ac•crue, •crued, •cru•ing
accrued in•come
accrued li•a•bil•i\ty
ac•cul•tur•ate, •at\ed, •at•ing
ac•cul•tur•a•tion
ac•cu•mu•late, •lat\ed, •lat•ing
ac•cu•mu•la•tion
ac•cu•mu•la•tive
ac•cu•mu•la•tor
ac•cu•ra\cy
ac•cu•rate
ac•cu•rate\ly
ac•curs\ed
ac•cu•sa•tion
ac•cu•sa•tive
ac•cu•sa•to\ry
ac•cuse, •cused, •cus•ing
ac•cus\er
ac•cus•tom, •tomed, •tom•ing
ac•cus•tomed
a\cer•bic
a\cer•bi\ty
ac•et•al•de•hyde
ac\e\tate
a\ce•tic (of vinegar) [vs. as•cet\ic (austere)]
ac\e\tone
a\cet\y•lene
a\chieve, a\chieved, a\chiev•ing
a\chieve•ment
a\chiev\er
ach•ro•mat\ic
ac\id
a\cid•ic
a\cid\i•fi•ca•tion
a\cid•i\fy, •fied, •fy•ing
a\cid•i\ty

ac\i•do•sis

a\cid\u•la•tion

a\cid\u•lous

ack-•ack

ac•knowl•edge, •edged, •edg•ing

ac•knowl•edg•ment or ac•knowl•edge•ment

ac\me (*highest point*)

ac\ne (*skin eruption*)

ac\o•lyte

ac\o•nite

a\corn

a\cous•tic or a\cous•ti•cal

acoustic coup•ler

a\cous•ti•cal\ly

ac•ous•ti•cian

a\cous•tics

ac•quaint, \ed, •ing

acquaint•ance

ac•qui•esce, •esced, •esc•ing

ac•qui•es•cence

ac•qui•es•cent

ac•quire, •quired, •quir•ing

ac•quire•ment

ac•qui•si•tion

ac•quis\i•tive

ac•quit, •quit•ted, •quit•ting

ac•quit•tal

a\cre

a\cre•age

ac•rid

a\crid•i\ty

ac•ri•mo•ni•ous

ac•ri•mo•ni•ous\ly

ac•ri•mo•ni•ous•ness

ac•ri•mo\ny

ac•ro•bat

ac•ro•bat\ic

ac•ro•bat•ics

ac•ro•lect

ac•ro•lec•tal

ac•ro•nym

ac•ro•nym\ic or a\cron\y•mous

ac•ro•pho•bi\a

ac•ro•pho•bic

a\crop\o•lis

a\cross

a\cross-•the-•board

a\cros•tic

a\cryl•ic

act, \ed, •ing

act•ing

ac•tin\ic

ac•tin•i\um

ac•tion

ac•tion•a\ble

ac•ti•vate, •vat\ed, •vat•ing

ac•ti•va•tion

ac•ti•va•tor

ac•tive

ac•tive\ly

ac•tiv•ism

ac•tiv•ist

ac•tiv•i\ty, *pl.* •ties

activity ra•ti\o

ac•tor

ac•tress

acts (*deeds*) [*vs.* axe (*the tool*) *and* ask (*to inquire*)]

ac•tu\al

ac•tu•al•i\ty, *pl.* •ties

ac•tu•al•ize, •ized, •iz•ing

ac•tu•al\ly

ac•tu•ar•i\al

ac•tu•ar\y, *pl.* •ies

ac•tu•ate, •at\ed, •at•ing

a\cu•i\ty

a\cu•men

ac\u•punc•ture

a\cute

a\cute\ly

a\cute•ness

ad (*advertisement*) [*vs.* add (*to increase*)]

ad•age

a\da•gio, *pl.* •gios

ad\a•mant

ad\a•man•tine

a\dapt (*to modify*), \ed, •ing [*vs.* a\dept (*skilled*) *and* a\dopt (*to take as one's own*)]

a\dapt•a•bil•i\ty

a\dapt•a•ble

ad•ap•ta•tion

a\dapt\er or a\dap•tor

a\dap•tive

add (*to increase*), \ed, •ing [*vs.* ad (*advertisement*)]

ad•dend

ad•den•dum, *pl.* •den\da

add\er (*one that adds*)

ad•der (*snake*)

ad•dict

ad•dict\ed

ad•dic•tion

ad•dic•tive

add-•in

add-in pro•gram

ad•di•tion (*an adding*) [*vs.* e\di•tion (*a printing*)]

ad•di•tion\al

ad•di•tion•al\ly

ad•di•tive

ad•dle, •dled, •dling

add-•on

ad•dress, •dressed, •dress•ing

ad•dress•a\ble

ad•dress•ee

ad•duce (*to put evidence forward*), •duced, •duc•ing [*vs.* e\duce (*to draw out*)]

ad\e\nine

ad\e\noid

ad\e\noi•dal

a\dept (*skilled*) [*vs.* a\dapt (*to modify*) *and* a\dopt (*to take as one's own*)]

ad•ept (*an expert*)

a\dept\ly

a\dept•ness

ad\e•qua\cy

ad\e•quate

ad\e•quate\ly

ad•here, •hered, •her•ing

ad•her•ence

ad•her•ent

ad•he•sion

ad•he•sive

ad•he•sive•ness

ad hoc

ad ho•mi•nem

a\dieu (*good-bye*), *pl.* a\dieus or a\dieux [*vs.* a\do (*fuss*)]

ad in•fi•ni•tum

ad•i\os
ad\i•pose
ad\i•pos•i\ty
ad•ja•cen\cy
ad•ja•cent
ad•jec•ti•val
ad•jec•ti•val\ly
ad•jec•tive
ad•join
ad•join•ing
ad•journ, •journed,
 •journ•ing
ad•journ•ment
ad•judge, •judged,
 •judg•ing
ad•ju•di•cate, •cat•ed,
 •cat•ing
ad•ju•di•ca•tion
ad•ju•di•ca•tor
ad•junct
ad•ju•ra•tion
ad•jure (to request),
 •jured, •jur•ing [vs.
 ab•jure (to renounce)]
ad•just, •just•ed, •just•ing
ad•just•a•ble
ad\just\a\ble-•rate
ad•just\ed gross income
ad•just\er or ad•jus•tor
ad•just•ing en•try
ad•just•ment
ad•ju•tant
ad-•lib, •libbed, •lib•bing
ad-•lib\ber
ad•man, pl. •men
ad•min•is•ter, •tered,
 •ter•ing
ad•min•is•trate, •trat\ed,
 •trat•ing
ad•min•is•tra•tion
ad•min•is•tra•tive
ad•min•is•tra•tor
ad•mi•ra•ble
ad•mi•ra•bly
ad•mi•ral
ad•mi•ral\ty, pl. •ties
ad•mi•ra•tion
ad•mire, •mired, •mir•ing
ad•mir\er
ad•mir•ing\ly
ad•mis•si•bil•i\ty

ad•mis•si\ble
ad•mis•si•bly
ad•mis•sion
ad•mit, •mit•ted, •mit•ting
ad•mit•tance
ad•mit•ted\ly
ad•mix, •mixed or •mixt,
 •mix•ing
ad•mix•ture
ad•mon•ish, •ished,
 •ish•ing
ad•mon•ish•ment
ad•mo•ni•tion
ad•mon\i•to\ry
ad nau•se•am
a\do (fuss) [vs. a\dieu
 (good-bye)]
a\do•be
ad\o•les•cence
ad\o•les•cent
a\dopt (to take as one's
 own), \ed, •ing [vs. a\dapt
 (to modify) and a\dept
 (skilled)]
a\dopt•ee
a\dop•tion
a\dop•tive
a\dor•a•ble
a\do•ra•tion
a\dore, a\dored, a\dor•ing
a\dor•ing\ly
a\dorn, a\dorned,
 a\dorn•ing
a\dorn•ment
ADP (automatic data
 processing)
ad•re•nal
a\dren\a•line
a\drift
a\droit
a\droit\ly
a\droit\ness
ad•sorb (to gather on a
 surface), •sorbed,
 •sorb•ing [vs. ab•sorb
 (to take in)]
ad•sorb•ent
ad•sorp•tion
ad\u•late, •lat\ed, •lat•ing
ad\u•la•tion
ad\u•la•to\ry

a\dult
a\dul•ter•ant
a\dul•ter•ate, •at\ed,
 •at•ing
a\dul•ter\a•tion
a\dul•ter\er
a\dul•ter•ess
a\dul•ter•ous
a\dul•ter\y, pl. •ies
a\dult•hood
ad•um•brate, •brat\ed,
 •brat•ing
ad•um•bra•tion
ad va•lo•rem
ad•vance, •vanced,
 •vanc•ing
ad•vance•ment
ad•van•tage
ad•van•taged
ad•van•ta•geous
ad•van•ta•geous\ly
ad•vent
ad•ven•ti•tious
ad•ven•ture, •tured,
 •tur•ing
ad•ven•tur\er
ad•ven•ture•some
ad•ven•tur•ess
ad•ven•tur•ous
ad•verb
ad•ver•bi\al
ad•ver•bi\al\ly
ad•ver•sar\y, pl. •ies
ad•verse (opposing, as in
 "adverse opinions") [vs.
 a\verse (unwilling, as in
 "not averse to doing
 something")]
ad•verse\ly
ad•verse pos•ses•sion
ad•ver•si\ty, pl. •ties
ad•vert
ad•ver•tise, •tised,
 •tis•ing
ad•ver•tise•ment
ad•ver•tis\er
ad•vice (an opinion
 offered) [vs. ad•vise (to
 offer an opinion)]
ad•vis•a•bil•i\ty
ad•vis•a\ble

ad•vise (*to offer an opinion*), •vised, •vis•ing [*vs.* ad•vice (*an opinion offered*)]
ad•vis•ed\ly
ad•vise•ment
ad•vis\er *or* ad•vi•sor
ad•vi•so\ry, *pl.* •ries
ad•vo•ca\cy
ad•vo•cate, •cat\ed, •cat•ing
ae\gis
ae\on
aer•ate, •at\ed, •at•ing
aer•a•tion
aer\a•tor
aer•i\al
aer\i•al•ist
aer\ie (*bird's nest*) [*vs.* air\y (*like air*)]
aer\o•bat\ic
aer\o•bat•ics
aer•obe
aer\o•bic
aer\o•bics
aer\o•dy•nam\ic
aer\o•dy•nam•ics
aer\o•naut
aer\o•nau•ti•cal *or* aer\o•nau•tic
aer\o•nau•tics
aer\o•sol
aer\o•space
aes•thete *or* es•thete
aes•thet\ic *or* es•thet\ic
aes•thet\i•cal\ly *or* es•thet\i•cal\ly
aes•thet•ics *or* es•thet•ics
aes•ti•vate, •vat\ed, •vat•ing
aes•ti•va•tion
a\far
af•fa•bil•i\ty
af•fa\ble
af•fa•bly
af•fair
af•fect (*to act on*), \ed, •ing [*vs.* ef•fect (*a result; to bring about*)]
af•fec•ta•tion
•fect\ed
•fect•ing

af•fect•ing\ly
af•fec•tion
af•fec•tion•ate
af•fer•ent
af•fi•ance, •anced, •anc•ing
af•fi•da\vit
af•fil\i•ate, •at\ed, •at•ing
af•fil\i•a•tion
af•fin•i\ty, *pl.* •ties
af•firm, •firmed, •firm•ing
af•fir•ma•tion
af•firm\a•tive
af•fix, •fixed, •fix•ing
af•fix\a•tion
af•fla•tus
af•flict, •flict\ed, •flict•ing
af•flic•tion
af•flu•ence
af•flu•ent (*rich*) [*vs.* ef•flu•ent (*flowing*)]
af•ford, •ford\ed, •ford•ing
af•ford•a\ble
af•fray, •frayed, •fray•ing
af•fright
af•front, •front\ed, •front•ing
af•ghan
Af•ghan\i•stan
a\fi•cio•na\do, *pl.* •dos
a\field
a\fire
a\flame
AFL-•CIO (*labor union*)
a\float
a\flut•ter
a\foot
a\fore
a\fore•men•tioned
a\fore•said
a\fore•thought
a for\ti•o\ri
a\foul
a\fraid
a\fresh
Af•ri\ca
Af•ri•can
Af\ri•can-•A\mer\i•can
Af•ri•kaans
Af\ro, *pl.* •ros

Af\ro-•A\mer\i•can
af•ter
af•ter•birth
af•ter•burn\er
af•ter•care
af•ter cost
af•ter•deck
af•ter•ef•fect
af•ter•glow
af•ter-•hours
af•ter•life
af•ter•mar\ket
af•ter•math
af•ter•noon
af•ter•shave
af•ter•shock
af•ter•taste
af•ter•tax
af•ter•thought
af•ter•ward *or* af•ter•wards
af•ter•world
a\gain
a\gainst
a\gape
a\gar
ag•ate
a\ga\ve
a\gaze
age, aged (*did age*), ag•ing *or* age•ing
a\ged (*elderly*)
age•ism
age•ist
age•less
a\gen\cy, *pl.* •cies
a\gen\da, *pl.* •das *or* \da
a\gen•dum, *pl.* \da *or* •dums
a\gent
age-•old
ag•er\a•tum
ag•glom•er•ate, •at\ed, •at•ing
ag•glom•er•a•tion
ag•glu•ti•nate, •nat\ed, •nat•ing
ag•glu•ti•na•tion
ag•gran•dize, •dized, •diz•ing
ag•gran•dize•ment

ag•gra•vate, •vat\ed, •vat•ing
ag•gra•va•tion
ag•gre•gate
aggregate de•mand
aggregate sup•ply
ag•gre•ga•tion
ag•gres•sion
ag•gres•sive
ag•gres•sive\ly
ag•gres•sive•ness
ag•gres•sor
ag•grieve, •grieved, •griev•ing
a\ghast
ag•ile
a\gil•i\ty
ag\i•tate, •tat\ed, •tat•ing
ag\i•ta•tion
ag\i•ta•tor
a\gleam
a\glim•mer
a\glit•ter
a\glow
ag•nos•tic
ag•nos•ti•cism
a\go
a\gog
ag\o•nize, •nized, •niz•ing
ag\o•niz•ing\ly
ag\o\ny, pl. •nies
ag\o\ra, pl. •rae
ag\o•ra•pho•bi\a
ag\o•ra•pho•bic
a\gou\ti, pl. •tis or •ties
a\grar•i\an
a\gree, a\greed, a\gree•ing
a\gree•a\ble
a\gree•a•bly
a\gree•ment
ag•ri•busi•ness
ag•ri•cul•tur\al
ag•ri•cul•ture
ag•ri•cul•tur•ist
ag\ro-•e\co\nom\ic
ag\ro-•in\dus\tri\al
ag•ro•nom\ic or
    ag•ro•nom\i•cal
ag•ro•nom•ics
a\gron\o•mist
a\gron\o\my

a\ground
a\gue
a\head
a\hold
a\hoy
AI (artificial intelligence)
aid (to help)
aide (a helper)
aide-•de-•camp, pl. aides-
    •de-•camp
AIDS (acquired immune
    deficiency syndrome)
ai•grette
ail (to be ill), ailed, ail•ing
    [vs. ale (a beverage)]
ai•ler\on
ail•ment
aim•less
air (atmosphere; to air),
    aired, air•ing [vs. e'er
    (ever) and ere (before)
    and err (to do wrong)
    and heir (inheritor)]
air bag
air•borne
air•brush
air•bus
air-•con\di\tion
air conditioner
air-•cool, •cooled, •cool•ing
air•craft, pl. •craft
air•drome
air•drop, •dropped,
    •drop•ping
Aire•dale
air•field
air•flow
air•foil
air•glow
air•lift
air•line
air•lin•er
air•mail, •mailed, •mail•ing
air•man, pl. •men
air•plane
air•port
air•ship
air•sick
air•sick•ness
air•space
air•speed

air•stream
air•strip
air•tight
air-•to-•air
air-•to-•sur\face
air•waves
air•way
air•wor\thi\ness
air•wor\thy
air\y (like air), •i\er, •i•est
    [vs. aer\ie (bird's nest)]
aisle (passage) [vs. I'll
    (I will) and isle (island)]
a\jar
AK (Alaska)
a\kim\bo
a\kin
AL (Alabama)
Al\a•bam\a (AL)
Al\a•bam\i\an or
    Al\a•bam\an
al\a•bas•ter
à la carte
a\lac•ri\ty
à la king
à la mode
a\larm, a\larmed,
    a\larm•ing
a\larm•ing
a\larm•ist
a\las
A\las\ka (AK)
A\las•kan
al•ba•core
Al•ba•ni\a
Al•ba•ni\an
al•ba•tross
al•be\it
Al•ber\ta
Al•ber•tan
al•bi•nism
al•bi•no, pl. •nos
al•bum
al•bu•men (egg white)
al•bu•min (protein)
al•che•mist
al•che\my
al•co•hol
al•co•hol\ic
al•co•hol•ism
al•cove

al•de•hyde

al den\te

al•der

al•der•man, pl. •men

ale (a beverage) [vs. ail (to be ill)]

a\lee

ale•house, pl. •hous\es

a\lert, \ed, •ing

ale•wife, pl. •wives

al•ex•an•drine

a\lex•i\a

al•fal\fa

al•fres\co

al\ga, pl. •gae

al•gal

al•ge•bra

al•ge•bra\ic

Al•ge•ri\a

Al•ge•ri\an

ALGOL (programming language)

al•go•rithm

al•go•rith•mic

a\li\as

a\li•as•ing

al•i\bi

al•ien

al•ien•a\ble

al•ien•ate, •at\ed, •at•ing

al•ien•a•tion

al•ien cor•po•ra•tion

al•ien•ist

a\light, a\light\ed or a\lit, a\light•ing

a\lign, a\ligned, a\lign•ing

a\lign•ment

a\like

al\i•ment

al\i•men•ta\ry (digestive) [vs. el\e•men•ta\ry (basic)]

al\i•men•ta•tion

al\i•mo\ny, pl. •nies

al\i•quot

a\live

al•ka\li, pl. •lis or •lies

al•ka•line

al•ka•lin•i\ty

•ka•loid

•kyd

al•kyl

all (whole) [vs. awl (drill)]

Al•lah

all-•A\mer\i\can

all-•a\round

al•lay, •layed, •lay•ing

al•le•ga•tion

al•lege, •leged, •leg•ing

al•leg•ed\ly

al•le•giance

al•le•gor\i•cal

al•le•go\ry, pl. •ries

al•le•gret\to, pl. •tos

al•le•gro, pl. •gros

al•le•lu\ia

al•ler•gen

al•ler•gen\ic

al•ler•gic

al•ler•gist

al•ler\gy, pl. •gies

al•le•vi•ate, •at\ed, •at•ing

al•le•vi•a•tion

al•le•vi•a•tor

al•ley (street), pl. •leys [vs. al\ly (friend)]

al\ley•way

al•li•ance

al•lied

al•li•ga•tor

all-•im•por\tant

all-•in\clu\sive

al•lit•er•ate, •at\ed, •at•ing

al•lit•er•a•tion

al•lit•er\a•tive

al•lo•cate, •cat\ed, •cat•ing

al•lo•ca•tion

al•lo•morph

al•lo•mor•phic

al•lo•path\ic

al•lop\a•thy

al•lo•phone

al•lo•phon\ic

al•lot, •lot•ted, •lot•ting

al•lot•ment

all-•out

all•o\ver

al•low, •lowed, •low•ing

al•low•a\ble

al•low•ance

al•lowed (permitted) [vs. a\loud (with the voice)]

al•loy

all-•pow\er\ful

all-•pur\pose

all read\y (entirely ready) [vs. al•read\y (previously)]

all right

all-•round

all•spice

all-•star

all-•time

all to•geth\er (completely together) [vs. al•to•geth•er (wholly)]

al•lude (to refer), •lud\ed, •lud•ing [vs. e\lude (to avoid)]

al•lure, •lured, •lur•ing

al•lure•ment

al•lu•sion (reference) [vs. il•lu•sion (false idea)]

al•lu•sive (suggestive) [vs. e\lu•sive (evasive) and il•lu•sive (deceptive)]

al•lu•vi\al

al•lu•vi\um, pl. •vi•ums or •vi\a

al\ly (friend), pl. •lies [vs. al•ley (street)]

al\ly (to unite), •lied, •ly•ing

al\ma ma•ter

al•ma•nac

al•might\y

al•mond

al•mon\er

al•most

alms•house

al•ni\co

al\oe, pl. •oes

a\loft

a\lo\ha

a\lone

a\long

a\long•shore

a\long•side

a\loof

a\loof•ness

a\loud (with the voice) [vs. al•lowed (permitted)]

al•pac\a

al•pen•horn

al•pen•stock

al•pha
al•pha•bet
al•pha•bet\i•cal
al•pha•bet\i•cal\ly
al•pha•bet•ize, •ized,
 •iz•ing
al•pha•mer\ic
al•pha•nu•mer\ic
al•pha•nu•mer\i•cal\ly
al•pine
al•read\y (*previously*) [*vs.*
 all read\y (*entirely ready*)]
al\so
al\so-•ran
al•tar (*platform for
 worship*)
al•ter (*to change*), •tered,
 •ter•ing
al•ter\a•tion
al•ter•ca•tion
al•ter e\go
al•ter•nate, •nat\ed,
 •nat•ing
al•ter•nate\ly
al•ter•na•tion
al•ter•na•tive
al•ter•na•tive\ly
al•ter•na•tor
al•though
al•tim\e\ter
al•ti•tude (*height*) [*vs.*
 at•ti•tude (*manner*)]
al•to, *pl.* •tos
al•to•geth\er (*wholly*) [*vs.*
 all to•geth\er (*completely
 together*)]
al•tru•ism
al•tru•ist
al•tru•is•tic
ALU (*arithmetic logic unit*)
al•um
a\lu•mi\na
al\u•min\i\um (*Brit.*)
a\lu•mi•num (*Amer.*)
a\lum\na, *pl.* •nae
a\lum•nus, *pl.* \ni
al•ve•o•lar
al•ve•o•lus, *pl.* \li
al•ways
a\lys•sum
Alz•hei•mer's dis•ease

a\mah
a\main
a\mal•gam
a\mal•ga•mate, •mat\ed,
 •mat•ing
a\mal•ga•ma•tion
a\mal•ga•ma•tor
a\man\u•en•sis, *pl.* •ses
am\a•ryl•lis
a\mass
am\a•teur
am\a•teur•ish
am\a•teur•ism
am\a•to\ry
a\maze, a\mazed,
 a\maz\ing
a\maze•ment
a\maz•ing\ly
Am\a•zon
Am\a•zo•ni\an
am•bas•sa•dor
am•bas•sa•do•ri\al
am•bas•sa•dress
am•ber
am•ber•gris
am•bi•ance *or* am•bi•ence
am•bi•dex•trous
am•bi•ent
am•bi•gu•i\ty, *pl.* •ties
am•big\u•ous
(*unclear*) [*vs.*
 am•biv\a•lent (*uncer-
 tain*)]
am•bi•tion
am•bi•tious
am•biv\a•lence
am•biv\a•lent (*uncertain*)
 [*vs.* am•big\u•ous
 (*unclear*)]
am•ble, •bled, •bling
am•bly\o•pi\a
am•bro•sia
am•bro•sial
am•bu•lance
am•bu•lant
am•bu•la•to\ry
am•bush, •bushed,
 •bush•ing
a\me•ba *or* a\moe•ba, *pl.*
 •bas *or* •bae
a\me•bic *or* a\moe•bic

a\mel\io•rate, •rat\ed,
 •rat•ing
a\mel\io•ra•tion
a\mel\io•ra•tive
a\me•na•ble
a\mend (*to revise*), \ed,
 •ing [*vs.* e\mend (*to
 correct*)]
a\mend•ment
a\mends
a\men•i\ty, *pl.* •ties
A\mer\i\ca
A\mer\i•can
A\mer\i•ca\na
A\mer\i•can•ism
A\mer\i•can\i•za•tion
A\mer\i•can•ize, •ized,
 •iz•ing
am•er\i•ci\um
Am•er•ind *or*
 Am•er•in•di\an
am\e•thyst
AMEX (*American Stock
 Exchange*)
a\mi•a•bil•i\ty
a\mi•a•ble (*good-natured*)
 [*vs.* am\i•ca•ble (*peaceable*)]
a\mi•a•bly
am\i•ca•bil•i\ty
am\i•ca•ble (*peaceable*)
 [*vs.* a\mi•a•ble (*good-
 natured*)]
am\i•ca•bly
a\mid
a\mid•ships
a\midst
a\mi•go, *pl.* •gos
a\mi•no
A\mish
a\miss
am•i\ty (*friendship*) [*vs.*
 en•mi\ty (*hostility*)]
am•me•ter
am\mo
am•mo•nia
am•mo•nite
am•mo•ni\um
am•mu•ni•tion
am•ne•sia
am•ne•si\ac

am•nes\ty (*noun*), *pl.* •ties;
•tied, •ty•ing
am\ni\o•cen•te•sis
am•ni•on, *pl.* •ni•ons or
•ni\a
am•ni•ot\ic
a\moe\ba, *pl.* •bas or •bae
a\moe•bic
a\mok
a\mong
a\mongst
a\mon•til•la\do
a\mor\al (*without moral
standards*) [*vs.* im•mor\al
(*licentious*) *and*
im•mor•tal (*everlasting*)]
a\mo•ral•i\ty
am\o•rous
am\o•rous\ly
a\mor•phous
a\mor•phous•ness
am•or•ti•za•tion
am•or•tize, •tized, •tiz•ing
a\mount, \ed, •ing
a\mour
a\mour-•pro\pre
am•per•age
am•pere
am•pere-•hour
am•per•sand
am•phet\a•mine
am•phib•i\an
am•phib\i•ous
am•phi•the•a•ter
am•pho\ra, *pl.* •rae or •ras
am•ple, •pler, •plest
am•pli•fi•ca•tion
am•pli•fi\er
am•pli•fy, •fied, •fy•ing
am•pli•tude
am•ply
am•pule or am•poule
am•pu•tate, •tat\ed,
•tat•ing
am•pu•ta•tion
am•pu•tee
Am•trak
a\muck
am\u•let
a\muse, a\mused,
a\mus•ing

a\muse•ment
amusement tax
a\mus•ing\ly
am\yl
am\yl•ase
an\a•bol\ic
a\nach•ro•nism
a\nach•ro•nis•tic
an\a•con\da
a\nae•mi\a
a\nae•mic
an•aer•obe
an•aer\o•bic
an•aes•the•sia
an•aes•the•si\o•gist
an•aes•the•si•ol\o\gy
an•aes•thet\ic
an•aes•the•tist
an•aes•the•tize, •tized,
•tiz•ing
an\a•gram
a\nal
an•al•ge•si\a
an•al•ge•sic
an\a•log or an\a•logue
analog com•pu•ter
an\a•log\i•cal
an\a•log mon\i•tor
a\nal\o•gous
an\a•logue
a\nal\o\gy, *pl.* •gies
a\nal\y•sand
a\nal\y•sis, *pl.* •ses
an\a•lyst (*one who ana-
lyzes*) [*vs.* an•nal•ist (*historian*)])
an\a•lyt\ic or an\a•lyt\i•cal
an\a•lyze, •lyzed, •lyz•ing
an\a•phy•lac•tic
an\a•phy•lax\is
an•ar•chic
an•ar•chism
an•ar•chist
an•ar•chis•tic
an•ar•chy, *pl.* •chies
an•as•tig•mat\ic
a\nath\e•ma, *pl.* •mas
a\nath\e•ma•tize, •tized,
•tiz•ing
an\a•tom\i•cal or
an\a•tom\ic

a\nat\o•mist
a\nat\o•mize, •mized,
•miz•ing
a\nat\o•my, *pl.* •mies
an•ces•tor
an•ces•tral
an•ces•try, *pl.* •tries
an•chor, •chored,
•chor•ing
an•chor•age
an•cho•rite
an•chor•man, *pl.* •men
an\chor•per\son
an•chor store
an\chor•wom\an, *pl.*
•wom\en
an•cho\vy, *pl.* •vies
an•cient
an•cil•lar\y
an•dan\te
and•i\ron
and/•or
an•dro•gen
an•dro•gen\ic
an•drog\y•nous
an•droid
an•ec•dot\al
an•ec•dote (*short
narrative*) [*vs.* an•ti•dote
(*remedy*)]
a\ne•mi\a
a\ne•mic
an\e•mom\e•ter
a\nem\o\ne
a\nent
an•er•oid
an•es•the•sia or
an•aes•the•sia
an•es•the•si\ol\o•gist or
an•aes•the•si\ol\o•gist
an•es•the•si\ol\o\gy or
an•aes•the•si\ol\o\gy
an•es•thet\ic or
an•aes•thet\ic
an•es•the•tist or
an•aes•the•tist
an•es•the•tize or
an•aes•the•tize, •tized,
•tiz•ing
an•eu•rysm
a\new

an•gel (*heavenly spirit*) [vs.
  an•gle (*projecting corner;
  to fish*)]
an•gel•fish, *pl.* •fish or
  •fish•es
an•gel•ic
An•ge•lus
an•ger, •gered, •ger•ing
an•gi•na pec•to•ris
an•gi•o•gram
an•gi•o•sperm
an•gle (*projecting corner;
  to angle*) [vs. an•gel
  (*heavenly spirit*)]
an•gle (*to fish*), •gled,
  •gling [vs. an•gel
  (*heavenly spirit*)]
an•gler
an•gle•worm
An•gli•can
An•gli•can•ism
An•gli•cism
An•gli•ci•za•tion
An•gli•cize, •cized, •ciz•ing
an•gling
An•glo, *pl.* •glos
An\glo-•A\mer\i\can
An\glo•phile
An\glo•phil\i\a
An\glo•phobe
An\glo•pho•bi\a
An\glo•phone
An\glo-•Sax\on
An•go\ra
an•gri\ly
an•gry, •gri\er, •gri•est
angst
ang•strom
an•guish, •guished,
  •guish•ing
an•gu•lar
an•gu•lar•i\ty, *pl.* •ties
an•hy•dride
an•hy•drite
an•hy•drous
an\i•line
an\i•mad•ver•sion
an\i•mad•vert
an\i•mal
an\i•mal•cule
an\i•mal•ism

an\i•mal•like
an\i•mate, •mat•ed,
  •mat•ing
an\i•mat•ed\ly
an\i•ma•tion
an\i•ma•tor
an\i•mism
an\i•mist
an\i•mis•tic
an\i•mos•i\ty, *pl.* •ties
an\i•mus
an•i\on
an•i\on•ic
an•ise
an\i•seed
an\i•sette
an•kle
an•kle•bone
an•klet
an•nal•ist (*historian*) [vs.
  an\a•lyst (*one who ana-
  lyzes*)]
an•nals
an•neal, •nealed, •neal•ing
an•ne•lid
an•nex, •nexed, •nex•ing
an•nex•a•tion
an•ni•hi•late, •lat•ed,
  •lat•ing
an•ni•hi•la•tion
an•ni•hi•la•tor
an•ni•ver•sa\ry, *pl.* •ries
an\no Dom•i\ni
an•no•tate, •tat•ed,
  •tat•ing
an•no•ta•tion
an•no•ta•tor
an•nounce, •nounced,
  •nounc•ing
an•nounce•ment
an•nounc\er
an•noy, •noyed, •noy•ing
an•noy•ance
an•noyed
an•noy•ing
an•noy•ing\ly
an•nu\al
an•nu•al•ize, •ized, •iz•ing
an•nu•al\ly
an•nu\i•tant

an•nu•i\ty, *pl.* •ties
an•nul, •nulled, •nul•ling
an•nu•lar
an•nul•la•ble
an•nul•ment
an•nun•ci•a•tion
  (*announcement*) [vs.
  e\nun•ci•a•tion (*diction*)]
an•nun•ci•a•tor
an•ode
an\o•dize, •dized, •diz•ing
an\o•dyne
a\noint, , \ed, •ing
a\nom\a•lis•tic
a\nom\a•lous
a\nom\a\ly, *pl.* •lies
a\non
an\o•nym•i\ty
a\non\y•mous
a\noph\e•les
an\o•rak
an\o•rec•tic
an\o•rex\i\a
an\o•rex\ic
an•oth\er
an•ox\i\a
an•ox\ic
ANSI (*American National
  Standards Institute*)
an•swer, •swered,
  •swer•ing
an•swer•a•ble
an•swer-•on\ly mo•dem
ant (*the insect*) [vs. aunt
  (*the relative*)]
ant•ac\id
an•tag\o•nism
an•tag\o•nist
an•tag\o•nis•tic
an•tag\o•nize, •nized,
  •niz•ing
ant•arc•tic
Ant•arc•ti\ca
an•te (*to pay*), •ted or
  •teed, •te•ing [vs. an\ti
  (*one who is opposed*)]
an•te- (*before*) [vs. an\ti-
  (*against*)]
ant•eat\er
an•te•bel•lum
an•te•ced•ent

an•te•cham•ber
an•te•date, •dat•ed, •dat•ing
an•te•di•lu•vi•an
an•te•lope, *pl.* •lopes *or* •lope
an•te me•rid•i•em
an•ten•na, *pl.* •nas *or* •nae
an•te•pe•nult
an•te•pe•nul•ti•mate
an•te•ri•or
an•te•room
an•them
ant•hill
an•thol•o•gist
an•thol•o•gy, *pl.* •gies
an•thra•cite
an•thrax
an•thro\po•cen•tric
an•thro\po•cen•trism
an•thro•poid
an•thro•poi•dal
an•thro\po•log\i\cal
an•thro•pol•o•gist
an•thro•pol•o•gy
an•thro\po•met•ric
an•thro•pom\e•try
an•thro\po•mor\phic
an•thro\po•mor\phism
an\ti (*one who is opposed*), *pl.* •tis [*vs.* an\te (*to pay*)]
an\ti- (*against*) [*vs.* an\te- (*before*)]
an•ti•a•bor•tion
an•ti•air•craft
an•ti•a\li•as•ing
an•ti•bac•te•ri\al
an•ti•bal•lis•tic
an•ti•bi•ot\ic
an•ti•bod\y, *pl.* •ies
an•tic
an•ti•choice
An\ti•christ
an•tic\i•pate, •pat•ed, •pat•ing
an•tic\i•pa•tion
an•tic\i•pa•tor
an•tic\i•pa•to\ry
an•ti•cler\i•cal
an•ti•cler\i•cal•ism
an•ti•cli•mac•tic

an•ti•cli•max
an•ti•co•ag\u•lant
an•ti•cy•clone
an•ti•de•pres•sant
an•ti•dote (*remedy*) [*vs.* an•ec•dote (*short narrative*)]
an•ti•dump\ing
an•ti•freeze
an•ti•gen
an•ti•gen\ic
an•ti•ge•nic\i\ty
an•ti•his•ta•mine
an•ti-•in\tel\lec\tu•al
an•ti•knock
an•ti•log\a•rithm
an•ti•ma•cas•sar
an•ti•mag•net•ic
an•ti•mat•ter
an•ti•mis•sile
an•ti•mo\ny
an•ti•neu•tri\no, *pl.* •nos
an•ti•nu•cle\ar
an•ti•ox\i•dant
an•ti•par•ti•cle
an•ti•pas\to
an•ti•pa•thet•ic
an•tip\a•thy, *pl.* •thies
an•ti•per•son•nel
an•ti•per•spi•rant
an•tiph•o•nal
an•tiph•o\ny, *pl.* •nies
an•tip\o•dal
an•tip\o•des
an•ti•pol•lu•tion
an•ti•pro•ton
an•ti•py•ret•ic
an•ti•quar\i•an
an•ti•quar\y, *pl.* •ies
an•ti•quat•ed
an•tique, •tiqued, •tiqu•ing
an•tiq\ui\ty, *pl.* •ties
an\ti-•Sem\ite
an\ti-•Se\mit\ic
an\ti-•Sem\i\tism
an•ti•sep•sis
an•ti•sep•tic
an•ti•sep•ti•cal\ly
an•ti•slav•er\y
an•ti•so•cial

an\ti•stat\ic
an•tith\e•sis, *pl.* •ses
an\ti•thet\i\cal
an\ti•tox\in
an\ti•trust
an\ti•ven\in
an\ti•vi•rus pro•gram
ant•ler
ant•lered
an•to•nym
an•ton\y•mous
an\u•re•sis
an\u•ret\ic
a\nus
an•vil
anx\i\e\ty, *pl.* •ties
anx•ious
an\y
an\y•bod\y
an\y•how
an\y•more
an\y•one
an\y•place
an\y•thing
an\y•time
an\y•way
an\y•where
an\y•wise
a\or\ta, *pl.* •tas *or* •tae
a\or•tic
a\pace
a\part
a\part•heid
a\part•ment
ap\a•thet\ic
ap\a•thet\i•cal\ly
ap\a•thy
a\pé•ri•tif
ap•er•ture
a\pex, a\pex\es *or* a\pi•ces
a\pha•sia
a\pha•sic
a\phe•li\on, *pl.* •li\a
a\phid
aph\o•rism
aph\o•ris•tic
aph•ro•dis•i\ac
a\pi•ar\y, *pl.* •ies
a\piece
a\plen\ty
a\plomb

ap•ne\a
a\poc\a•lypse
a\poc\a•lyp•tic
a\poc•ry•pha
a\poc•ry•phal
ap\o•ge\an
ap\o•gee
a\po•lit\i•cal
a\pol\o•get\ic
a\pol\o•get\i•cal\ly
a\po\o•lo•gi\a
a\pol\o•gist
a\pol\o•gize, •gized,
•giz•ing
a\pol\o•gy, pl. •gies
ap\o•plec•tic
ap\o•plex\y
a\port
a\pos•ta\sy, pl. •sies
a\pos•tate
a pos•te•ri\o\ri
a\pos•tle
a\pos•to•late
ap•os•tol\ic
a\pos•tro•phe
a\pos•tro•phize, •phized,
•phiz•ing
a\poth\e•car\y, pl. •ies
ap\o•thegm (saying)
ap\o•them (geometric line)
a\poth\e•o•sis, pl. •ses
Ap•pa•la•chi\an
ap•pall, •palled, •pall•ing
ap•palled
ap•pall•ing
ap•pall•ing\ly
ap•pa•rat\us, pl. •rat\us or
•rat•us\es
ap•par\el, •eled or •elled,
•el•ing or •el•ling
ap•par•ent
ap•par•ent\ly
ap•pa•ri•tion
ap•peal, •pealed, •peal•ing
ap•peal•ing
ap•pear, •peared,
•pear•ing
ap•pear•ance
ap•pease, •peased,
•peas•ing
ap•pease•ment

ap•peas\er
ap•pel•lant
ap•pel•late
ap•pel•la•tion
ap•pel•lee
ap•pend, •ed, •ing
ap•pend•age
ap•pen•dec•to\my, pl.
•mies
ap•pen•di•ci•tis
ap•pen•dix, pl. •dix\es or
•di•ces
ap•per•cep•tion
ap•per•tain, •tained,
•tain•ing
ap•pe•stat
ap•pe•tite
ap•pe•tiz\er
ap•pe•tiz•ing
ap•pe•tiz•ing\ly
ap•plaud, •ed, •ing
ap•plause
ap•ple
ap\ple•jack
ap\ple•sauce
ap•pli•ance
ap•pli•ca•bil•i\ty
ap•pli•ca\ble
ap•pli•cant
ap•pli•ca•tion
applications soft•ware
ap•pli•ca•tor
ap•plied
applied cost
applied o\ver•head
ap•pli•qué
ap•ply, •plied, •ply•ing
ap•point, •ed, •ing
ap•point\ee
ap•poin•tive
ap•point•ment
ap•por•tion, •tioned,
•tion•ing
ap•por•tion•ment
ap•po•site (suitable) [vs.
op•po•site (facing)]
ap•po•si•tion
ap•prais\al
ap•praise (to evaluate),
•praised, •prais•ing [vs.
ap•prise (to inform)]

ap•prais\er
ap•pre•ci•a\ble
ap•pre•ci•a\bly
ap•pre•ci•ate, •at\ed,
•at•ing
ap•pre•ci•a•tion
ap•pre•cia•tive
ap•pre•hend, •ed, •ing
ap•pre•hen•sion
ap•pre•hen•sive
ap•pren•tice, •ticed,
•tic•ing
ap•pren•tice•ship
ap•prise (to inform),
•prised, •pris•ing [vs.
ap•praise (to evaluate)]
ap•proach, •proached,
•proach•ing
ap•proach•a•bil•i\ty
ap•proach•a\ble
ap•pro•ba•tion
ap•pro•pri•ate, •at\ed,
•at•ing
ap•pro•pri•ate\ly
ap•pro•pri•ate•ness
ap•pro•pri•a•tion
ap•pro•pri•a•tor
ap•prov\al
ap•prove, •proved,
•prov•ing
ap•prox\i•mate, •mat\ed,
•mat•ing
ap•prox\i•mate\ly
ap•prox\i•ma•tion
ap•pur•te•nance
ap•pur•te•nant
ap•ri•cot
A\pril
a pri•o\ri
a\pron
ap•ro•pos
ap•ti•tude
apt\ly
apt•ness
aq\ua
aq\ua•cade
Aq\ua-•lung
aq\ua•ma•rine
aq\ua•naut
aq\ua•plane, •planed,
•plan•ing

a\quar•i\um, •i•ums or \i\a

a\quat\ic

aq\ua•tint

aq\ue•duct

a\que•ous

aq\ui•line

a\quiv\er

AR (*Arkansas*)

Ar\ab

ar\a•besque

A\ra•bi\an

Ar\a•bic

ar•a•ble

a\rach•nid

Ar\a•ma\ic

ar•bi•tra•ble

ar•bi•trage, •traged, •trag•ing

ar•bi•trag\er or ar•bi•tra•geur

ar•bi•trar•i\ly

ar•bi•trar\i•ness

ar•bi•trar\y

ar•bi•trate, •trat\ed, •trat•ing

ar•bi•tra•tion

ar•bi•tra•tor

ar•bor

ar•bo•re\al

ar•bo•re•tum, *pl.* •tums or \ta

ar•bor•vi•tae

ar•bu•tus

arc (*curve; to arc*), arced or arcked, arc•ing or arck•ing [*vs.* ark (*boat*)]

ar•cade

ar•cane

ar•chae•o•log\i•cal or ar•che•o•log\i•cal

ar•chae•ol\o•gist

ar•chae•ol\o•gy

ar•chae•op•ter\yx

ar•cha\ic

ar•cha•i•cal\ly

ar•cha•ism

arch•an\gel

arch•bish\op

arch•dea•con

arch•di•oc\e•san

arch•di•o•cese

arch•duch•ess

arch•duke

arch•en\e\my, *pl.* •mies

ar•che•o•log\i•cal

ar•che•ol\o•gist

ar•che•ol\o\gy

arch\er

arch•er\y

ar•che•type

arch•fiend

ar•chi•pel•a\go, *pl.* •gos or •goes

ar•chi•tect

ar•chi•tec•ton\ic

ar•chi•tec•ton\ics

ar•chi•tec•tur\al

ar•chi•tec•tur•al\ly

ar•chi•tec•ture

ar•chi•trave

ar•chi•val

ar•chive

ar•chi•vist

arch\ly

arch•ness

arch•way

arc•tic

ar•dent

ar•dor

ar•du•ous

ar\e\la (*space*) [*vs.* a\ri\a (*song*)]

ar\e\a•way

a\re\na, *pl.* •nas

aren't (*are not*)

Ar•gen•ti\na

Ar•gen•tine

ar•gon

ar•go\sy, *pl.* •sies

ar•got

ar•gu•a•ble

ar•gu•a•bly

ar•gue, •gued, •gu•ing

ar•gu•ment

ar•gu•men•ta•tion

ar•gu•men•ta•tive

ar•gyle

a\ri\a (*song*) [*vs.* ar\e\la (*space*)]

ar\id

a\rid•i\ty

a\right

a\rise, a\rose, a\ris\en, a\ris•ing

ar•is•toc•ra\cy, *pl.* •cies

a\ris•to•crat

a\ris•to•crat\ic

ar•ith•met•ic (*noun*)

ar•ith•met\ic or ar•ith•met\i•cal (*adj.*)

ar•ith•met\ic log\ic u\nit (ALU)

Ar\i•zo\na (*AZ*)

Ar\i•zo•nan

ark (*boat*) [*vs.* arc (*curve*)]

Ar•kan•san

Ar•kan•sas (*AR*)

ar•ma\da

ar•ma•dil\lo, *pl.* •los

Ar•ma•ged•don

ar•ma•ment

ar•ma•ture

arm•band

arm•chair

Ar•me•ni\a

Ar•me•ni\an

arm•ful, *pl.* •fuls

arm•hole

ar•mi•stice

arm•let

arm•load

ar•moire

ar•mor

ar•mored

ar•mor\er

ar•mo•ri\al

ar•mor\y, *pl.* •ies

arm•pit

arm•rest

ar\my, *pl.* •mies

ar•ni\ca

a\ro\ma, *pl.* •mas

ar\o•mat\ic

ar\o•mat\i•cal\ly

a\round

a\rous\al

a\rouse, a\roused, a\rous•ing

ARPANET (*the computer network*)

ar•peg•gi\o, *pl.* •gi\os

ar•raign

ar•raign•ment

ar•range, •ranged,
 •rang•ing
ar•range•ment
ar•rang\er
ar•rant
ar•ras
ar•ray, •rayed, •ray•ing
ar•rears
ar•rest, \ed, •ing
ar•rest•ing
ar•ri•val
arrival rate
ar•rive, •rived, •riv•ing
ar•ro•gance
ar•ro•gant
ar•ro•gate, •gat\ed,
 •gat\ing
ar•row
ar\row•head
ar\row key
ar\row•root
ar•roy\o, pl. •roy\os
ar•se•nal
ar•se•nic (noun)
ar•sen\ic (adj.)
ar•son
ar•son•ist
ar•te•ri•al
ar•te•ri•o•gram
ar•te•ri•ole
ar•te•ri•o•scle•ro•sis
ar•ter\y, pl. •ies
ar•te•sian
art•ful
art•ful\ly
ar•thrit\ic
ar•thri•tis
ar•thro•pod
ar•ti•choke
ar•ti•cle
ar•tic\u•late, •lat\ed,
 •lat\ing
ar•tic\u•late\ly
ar•tic\u•la•tion
ar•tic\u•la•to\ry
ar•ti•fact
ar•ti•fice
ar•ti•fi•cial
artificial in•tel•li•gence
 (AI)
ar•ti•fi•ci•al•i\ty

ar•ti•fi•cial\ly
ar•til•ler\y
ar•ti•san
artisan's lien
art•ist
ar•tiste
ar•tis•tic
ar•tis•ti•cal\ly
art•less
art•work
art\y, •i\er, •i•est
Ar\y•an
as•bes•tos
as•bes•to•sis
as•cend, •cend\ed,
 •cend•ing
as•cend•an\cy or
as•cend•en\cy
as•cend•ant or
 as•cend•ent
as•cen•sion
as•cent (climb) [vs.
 as•sent (agreement)]
as•cer•tain, •tained,
 •tain•ing
as•cer•tain•a\ble
as•cet\ic (austere) [vs.
 a\ce•tic (of vinegar)]
as•cet\i•cism
ASCII (American Standard
 Code for International
 Interchange)
ASCII file
a\scor•bic
as•cot
as•crib•a\ble
as•cribe, •cribed, •crib•ing
as•crip•tion
a\sea
a\sep•sis
a\sep•tic
a\sex•u\al
a\shamed
a\sham•ed\ly
ash•can
ash\en
a\shore
ash•ram
ash•tray
A\sia•dol\lar

A\sian
A\si•at\ic
a\side
as\i•nine
as\i•nin•i\ty
ask (to inquire), asked,
 ask•ing [vs. acts (deeds)
 and axe (the tool)]
a\skance
a\skew
ask•ing price
a\slant
a\sleep
a\slope
a\so•cial
as•par\a•gus
as•par•tame
as•pect
as•pen
as•per•i\ty
as•perse, •persed,
 •pers•ing
as•per•sion
as•phalt
as•pho•del
as•phyx\i\a
as•phyx\i•ate, •at\ed,
 •at\ing
as•phyx\i•a•tion
as•phyx\i•a•tor
as•pic
as•pi•dis•tra
as•pir•ant
as•pi•rate, •rat\ed, •rat•ing
as•pi•ra•tion
as•pire, •pired, •pir•ing
as•pi•rin
as•sail, •sailed, •sail•ing
as•sail•a\ble
as•sail•ant
as•sas•sin
as•sas•si•nate, •nat\ed,
 •nat•ing
as•sas•si•na•tion
as•sault
as•say (to evaluate),
 •sayed, •say•ing [vs.
 es•say (to try;
 composition)]
as•sem•blage
as•sem•ble, •bled, •bling

as•sem•ble to or•der
as•sem•bler
as•sem•bly, *pl.* •blies
assembly lan•guage
as\sem\bly•man, *pl.* •men
as\sem\bly•wom\an, *pl.*
•wom\en
as•sent (*agreement*) [*vs.*
as•cent (*climb*)]
as•sert, •sert\ed, •sert•ing
as•ser•tion
as•ser•tive
as•sess, •sessed, •sess•ing
as•sess•ment
as•ses•sor
as•set
as•sev•er•ate, •at\ed,
•at•ing
as•sev•er•a•tion
as•si•du•i•ty
as•sid\u•ous
as•sign, •signed, •sign•ing
as•sig•na•tion
as•sign\ee
as•sign•ment
as•sign\or
as•sim\i•la•ble
as•sim\i•late, •lat\ed,
•lat•ing
as•sim\i•la•tion
as•sist, \ed, •ing
as•sis•tance (*help*) [*vs.*
as•sis•tants (*helpers*)]
as•sis•tant
as•siz\es
as•so•ci•ate, •at\ed, •at•ing
as•so•ci•a•tion
as•so•ci•a•tive
as•so•nance
as•so•nant
as•sort, \ed, •ing
as•sort\ed
as•sort•ment
assortment plan
as•suage, •suaged,
•suag•ing
as•suage•ment
as•sume, •sumed,
•sum•ing
as•sump•tion
as•sur•ance

as•sure, •sured, •sur•ing
as•sur•ed\ly
as•ta•tine
as•ter
as•ter•isk
as•ter•ism
a\stern
as•ter•oid
asth\ma
asth•mat\ic
as•tig•mat\ic
a\stig•ma•tism
a\stir
as•ton•ish, •ished, •ish•ing
as•ton•ish•ing
as•ton•ish•ment
as•tound, \ed, •ing
as•tound•ing
a\strad•dle
as•tra•khan
as•tral
a\stray
a\stride
as•trin•gent
as\tro•dome
as\tro•labe
as•trol\o•ger
as•trol\o•log\i•cal
as•trol\o•gist
as•trol\o\gy
as•tro•naut
as•tro•nau•ti•cal
as•tro•nau•tics
as•tron\o•mer
as•tro•nom\i•cal *or*
as•tro•nom\ic
as•tron\o•my
as\tro•phys\i•cist
as\tro•phys•ics
As\tro•turf
as•tute
a\sun•der
a\sy•lum
a\sym•met•ric *or*
a\sym•met•ri•cal
a\sym•me•try
a\syn•chro•nous
at\a•vism
at\a•vis•tic
ate (*did eat*) [*vs.* eight (*the
number*)]

at•el•ier
a\the•ism
a\the•ist
a\the•is•tic
ath\er\o•scle•ro•sis
ath\er\o•scle•rot\ic
a\thirst
ath•lete
ath•let\ic
ath•let\i•cal\ly
ath•let\i•cism
ath•let\ics
a\thwart
a\tilt
a\tin•gle
At•lan•tic
at•las
ATM (*automated teller
machine*)
at•mos•phere
at•mos•pher\ic
at•mos•pher\i•cal\ly
at•oll
at\om
a\tom•ic
at•om•ize, •ized, •iz•ing
at•om•iz\er
a\ton•al
a\to•nal•i•ty
a\ton•al\ly
a\tone, a\toned, a\ton•ing
a\tone•ment
a\top
at par
a\trem•ble
a\tri\um, *pl.* a\tri\a *or*
a\tri•ums
a\tro•cious
a\troc•i\ty, *pl.* •ties
at•ro•phy, •phied, •phy•ing
at•ro•pine
at•tach (*to fasten*),
•tached, •tach•ing
at•ta•ché (*embassy official*)
at•tached
at•tach•ment
at•tack, •tacked, •tack•ing
at•tack\er
at•tain, •tained, •tain•ing
at•tain•a•ble
at•tain•der

at•tain•ment
at•taint
at•tar
at•tempt, \ed, •ing
at•tend, \ed, •ing
at•tend•ance
at•tend•ant
at•ten•tion
at•ten•tive
at•ten\u•ate, •at\ed, •at•ing
at•ten\u•a•tion
at•test, \ed, •ing
at•tes•ta•tion
at-•the-•mar\ket
at•tic
at•tire, •tired, •tir•ing
at•ti•tude (*manner*) [vs. al•ti•tude (*height*)]
at•ti•tu•di•nize, •nized, •niz•ing
at•tor•ney, pl. •neys
at\tor\ney-•at-•law, pl. at\tor\neys-•at-•law
at•tract, •tract\ed, •tract•ing
at•trac•tion
at•trac•tive
at•trib•ut•a•ble
at•trib•ute (*verb*), •ut\ed, •ut•ing
at•tri•bute (*noun*)
at•tri•bu•tion
at•trib•u•tive
at•tri•tion
at•tune, •tuned, •tun•ing
a\typ\i•cal
a\typ\i•cal\ly
au•burn
au cou•rant
auc•tion, •tioned, •tion•ing
auc•tion•eer
au•da•cious
au•dac•i\ty
au•di•bil•i\ty
au•di\ble
au•di•bly
au•di•ence
au•di\o
au\di•ol\o•gist

au\di•ol\o\gy
au\di•om•e\ter
au\di\o•phile
au\di\o•tape
au•dit, \ed, •ing
audit com•mit•tee
au•dit o\pin•ion
au•di\tor
au•di•to•ri\um, pl. •ri•ums or •ri\a
au•di•to\ry
au•dit trail
au•ger (*a drill*) [vs. au•gur (*to predict*)]
aught (*zero*) [vs. ought (*should*)]
aug•ment
aug•men•ta•tion
au•gur (*to predict*), •gured, •gur•ing [vs. au•ger (*a drill*)]
au•gu\ry, pl. •ries
au•gust (*majestic*)
Au•gust (*the month*)
aunt (*the relative*) [vs. ant (*the insect*)]
au pair
au\ra, pl. au•ras or au•rae
au•ral (*of hearing*) [vs. o\ral (*spoken*)]
au•re•ate
au•re•ole
Au•re\o•my•cin
au re•voir
au•ri•cle (*outer ear*) [vs. or\a•cle (*shrine*)]
au•ric\u•lar
au•rif•er•ous
au•ro\ra bo•re•al\is
aus•cul•ta•tion
aus•pic\es
aus•pi•cious
aus•tere
aus•ter•i\ty
aus•tral
Aus•tral\ia
Aus•tral•ian
Aus•tri\a

Aus•tri\an
au•then•tic
au•then•ti•cal\ly
au•then•ti•cate, •cat\ed, •cat•ing
au•then•ti•ca•tion
au•then•tic•i\ty
au•thor, •thored, •thor•ing
au•tho•ri\al
au•thor\i•tar•i\an
au•thor\i•tar•i\an•ism
au•thor\i•ta•tive
au•thor•i\ty, pl. •ties
au•thor\i•za•tion
au•thor•ize, •ized, •iz•ing
authorized deal•er•ship
au\thor•ship
au•tism
au•tis•tic
au\to, pl. •tos
au\to•an\swer
au\to•bahn
au\to•bi\og•ra•pher
au\to•bi\o•graph\i•cal or au\to•bi\o•graph\ic
au\to•bi•og•ra•phy, pl. •phies
au\to•chang•er
au•toch•tho•nous
au\to•clave
au\to•cra•cy, pl. •cies
au\to•crat
au\to•crat•ic
au\to•crat\i•cal\ly
au\to•di\al•ing
au\to•di•dact
au\to•gi\ro, pl. •ros
au\to•graph, •graphed, •graph•ing
Au\to•harp
au\to•im•mune
au\to•in\tox\i•ca•tion
au\to•mate, •mat\ed, •mat•ing
au\to\mat\ed-•tell\er ma\chine (*ATM*)
au\to•mat•ic
au\to•mat\i•cal\ly
au\to•mat•ic da\ta proc•ess•ing (*ADP*)

automatic head park•ing

automatic mark•down

au•to•ma•tion (*automatic operation*)

au•tom\a•tize, •tized, •tiz•ing

au•tom\a•ton (*robot*), *pl.* •tons *or* \ta

au•to•mo•bile

au•to•mo•bil•ist

au•to•mo•tive

au•to•nom•ic

au•ton\o•mous

au•ton\o•my

au•top\sy, *pl.* •sies

au\to•re\peat

au\to•siz\ing

au\to•start

au\to•stra\da

au\to•sug•ges•tion

au\to•trace

au•tumn

au•tum•nal

aux•il•ia\ry, *pl.* •ries

a\vail, a\vailed, a\vail•ing

a\vail•a•bil•i\ty

a\vail•a•ble

av\a•lanche

a\vant-•garde

av\a•rice

av\a•ri•cious

a\vast

av\a•tar

a\venge, a\venged, a\veng•ing

a\veng\er

av\e•nue

a\ver, a\verred, a\ver•ring

av•er•age, •aged, •ag•ing

average cost

a\verse (*unwilling, as in "not averse to doing something"*) [vs. ad•verse (*opposing, as in "adverse opinions"*)]

a\ver•sion

a\ver•sive

a\vert, \ed, •ing

a\vi\an

a\vi•ar\y, *pl.* •ies

a\vi•a•tion

a\vi•a•tor

a\vi•a•trix

av\id

a\vid•i\ty

av\id\ly

a\vi•on•ic

a\vi•on•ics

av\o•ca•do, *pl.* •dos

av\o•ca•tion (*hobby*) [vs. vo•ca•tion (*career*)]

av\o•cet

a\void (*to shun*), \ed, •ing [vs. e\vade (*to elude*)]

a\void•a•ble

a\void•a•bly

a\void•ance

av\oir•du•pois

a\vouch, a\vouched, a\vouch•ing

a\vow, a\vowed, a\vow•ing

a\vow\al

a\vowed

a\vun•cu•lar

a\wait, \ed, •ing

a\wake, a\woke *or* a\waked, a\wak•ing

a\wak\en, •ened, •en•ing

a\wak•en•ing

a\ward

a\ware

a\ware•ness

a\wash

a\way (*apart*) [vs. a\weigh (*raised*)]

a\weigh (*raised*) [vs. a\way (*apart*)]

awe•some

awe•struck *or* awe•strick\en

aw•ful (*very bad*) [vs. of•fal (*garbage*)]

aw•ful\ly

a\while

a\whirl

awk•ward

awl (*drill*) [vs. all (*whole*)]

awn•ing

a\wry

ax *or* axe (*the tool*), *pl.* ax\es, axed, ax•ing [vs. acts (*deeds*) and ask (*to inquire*)]

ax•i\al

ax•i\om

ax\i•o•mat\ic

ax\is, *pl.* ax\es

ax\le

ax\le•tree

a\ya•tol•lah

aye (*yes*) [vs. I (*me*) and eye (*organ of sight*)]

AZ (*Arizona*)

a\zal\ea

az\i•muth

AZT (™, *the drug azidothymidine*)

Az•tec

az•ure

az•ur•ite

B

baa, baaed, baa•ing

Ba\al, *pl.* Ba•al\im

Bab•bitt

Bab•bitt\ry

bab•ble, •bled, •bling

babe

Ba•bel

babble (*to talk indistinctly*) [vs. bauble (*trinket*) and bubble (*globule of gas contained in a liquid*)]

ba•boon

ba•boon•er\y

ba•bush\ka, *pl.* •kas

ba\by, *pl.* •bies; •bied, •by•ing

ba\by•hood

ba\by•ish

ba\by•ish•ness

ba\by•like

Bab\y•lon

Bab\y•lo•ni\a

Bab\y•lo•ni\an

ba\by-•sit *or* ba\by•sit, •sat, •sit•ting

ba\by-•sit•ter *or* ba\by•sit•ter

bac•ca•lau•re•ate
bac•ca•rat or bac•ca•ra
bac•cha•nal
Bac•cha•na•li\a, pl. •li\a,
•li\as
bac•cha•na•li\an
Bac•chic
Bac•chus
Bach
bach\e•lor
bach\e•lor•hood
bach\e\lor's-•but\ton
ba•cil•lus, pl. ba•cil\li
back
back•ache
back•beat
back•bite, •bit, •bit•ten,
•bit•ing
back•bit\er
back•board
back•bone
back•break\er
back•break•ing
back•date, •dat\ed,
•dat•ing
back\er
back•field
back•fire, •fired, •fir•ing
back•gam•mon
back•ground
back•ground\er
back•hand
back•hand\ed
back-•haul allowance
back•ing
back•lash
back•less
back•log, •logged,
•log•ging
back of•fice (noun)
back-of•fice (adj.)
back or•der (noun)
back-•or\der (verb)
back•pack
back•pack\er
back-•ped\al, •ped\aled or
•ped\alled, •ped\al•ing or
•ped\al•ling
back•rest

back•seat driv\er
back•side
back•slap•per
back•slap•ping
back•slide, •slid,
•slid•ing
back•slid\er
back•space, •spaced,
•spac•ing
back•spin
back•stage
back•stairs or back•stair
back•stop, •stopped,
•stop•ping
back•stretch
back•stroke, •stroked,
•strok•ing
back•swept
back•swing
back talk (noun)
back-•talk (verb)
back•track
back\up
backup stock
back•ward
back\ward-•com\pat\i\ble
back•ward in•te•gra•tion
back•ward\ly
back•ward•ness
back•ward sched•ul•ing
back•wash
back•wa•ter
back•woods
back•yard
ba•con
bac•te•ri\a, pl. •te•ri\um
bac•te•ri\al
bac•te•ri•cid\al
bac•te•ri•cide
bac•te•ri•o•log\i•cal
bac•te•ri•ol\o•gist
bac•te•ri•ol\o\gy
bad (not good), worse,
worst; bad\der, bad\dest
[vs. bade (commanded)]
bade
badge
badg\er, •ered, •er•ing
bad\i•nage
bad•lands
bad\ly, worse, worst

bad•min•ton
bad-•mouth or
bad•mouth, •mouthed,
•mouth\ing or
•mouth•ing
baf•fle•ment
baf•fling\ly
bag, bagged, bag•ging
bag\a•telle
ba•gel
bag•gage
bag•gi\ly
bag•gi•ness
bag\gy, •gi\er, •gi•est
Bagh•dad or Bag•dad
bag•man, pl. •men
bag•pipe
bag•pip\er
bah
Ba•ha•mas, pl.
Ba•ha•mi\an
Bah•rain or Bah•rein
Bah•rain\i or Bah•rein\i
bail (security money) [vs.
bale (bundle)]
bail•iff
bail\i•wick
bail•ment
bail•out
bail•out pe•ri\od
bait (lure) [vs. bate (to
restrain)]
bait\er
baize
bake, baked, bak•ing
bak\er
Ba•kers•field
bak•er\y, pl. •ies
bal\a•lai•ka, pl. •kas
bal•ance, •anced,
•anc•ing
bal•ance of pay•ments
bal•ance sheet
bal•co•nied
bal•co\ny, pl. •nies
bald (hairless) [vs. balled
(shaped into a ball) and
bawled (cried)]
bal•der•dash
bald•ish
bald\ly

bald•ness

bale (*bundle*), baled, bal•ing [*vs.* bail (*security money*)]

bale•ful

bale•ful\ly

bale•ful•ness

Ba\li

Ba•li•nese, *pl.* •nese

balk

Bal•kan

balk•i\ly

balk\i•ness

balk\y, •i\er, •i•est

ball (*sphere*) [*vs.* bawl (*to wail*)]

bal•lad (*narrative poem*) [*vs.* bal•let (*dance form*) and bal•lot (*vote*)]

bal•lad•eer

bal•lad•like

bal•lad\ry

balled (*shaped into a ball*) [*vs.* bald (*hairless*) and bawled (*cried*)]

ball\er

bal•le•ri\na, *pl.* •nas

bal•let (*dance form*) [*vs.* bal•lad (*narrative poem*) and bal•lot (*vote*)]

bal•let\ic

bal•lis•tic

bal•lis•tics

bal•loon, •looned, •loon•ing

balloon pay•ment

bal•lot (*vote*) [*vs.* bal•lad (*narrative poem*) and bal•let (*dance form*)]

bal•lot\er

ball•park

ballpark pric•ing

ball•point

ball•room

bal•ly•hoo, *pl.* •hoos, •hooed, •hoo•ing

balm (*ointment*) [*vs.* bomb (*explosive device*)]

balm\i•ness

balm\y, •i\er, •i•est

ba•lo•ney (*nonsense*) [*vs.* bo•lo•gna (*cold cut sausage*) and Bo•lo•gna (*Italian city*)]

bal•sam

bal•sam\ic

Bal•tic

Bal•ti•more

bal•us•ter

bal•us•trade

Bal•zac

bam•boo, *pl.* •boos

bam•boo•zle, •zled, •zling

bam•boo•zle•ment

ban, banned, ban•ning

ba•nal

ba•nal•i\ty

ba•nal\ly

ba•nan\a, *pl.* •as

band (*strip; group*) [*vs.* banned (*barred*)]

band•age, •aged, •ag•ing

Band-•Aid (™)

ban•dan\na or ban•dan\a, *pl.* •dan•nas or •dan\as

ban•dan•naed

ban•di•ness

ban•dit, *pl.* ban•dits, ban•dit\ti

ban•dit\ry

band•lead\er

ban•do•leer or ban•do•lier

bands (*groups*) [*vs.* banns (*marriage notice*) and bans (*prohibits*)]

band•stand

band•wag\on

band•width

ban\dy, *pl.* •died, •dy•ing

ban\dy-•leg\ged

bane

bane•ful

bang, banged, bang•ing

Bang•kok

Ban•gla•desh

Ban•gla•desh\i

ban•gle

Ban•gui

bang-•up

ban•ish, •ished, •ish•ing

ban•ish•ment

ban•is•ter or ban•nis•ter

ban\jo, *pl.* •jos, •joes

ban\jo•ist

Ban•jul

bank, banked, bank•ing

bank•a\ble

bank account

bank•book

bank card

bank draft

bank\er

bank•er's ac•cept•ance

bank•note

bank•roll

bank•roll\er

bank•rupt, •rupt\ed, •rupt•ing

bank•rupt\cy, *pl.* •cies

ban•na\ble

banned (*barred*) [*vs.* band (*strip; group*)]

ban•ner

banns (*marriage notice*) [*vs.* bands (*groups*) and bans (*prohibits*)]

ban•quet

ban•quet\er or ban•que•teer

ban•quette

bans (*prohibits*) [*vs.* bands (*groups*) and banns (*marriage notice*)]

ban•shee

ban•tam

bantam store

ban\tam•weight

ban•ter, •tered, •ter•ing

ban•ter•ing\ly

Ban\tu, *pl.* •tus, \tu

ban•yan

ban•zai

ba•o•bab

bap•tism

bap•tis•mal

Bap•tist

bap•tize, •tized, •tiz•ing

bar, barred, bar•ring

barb

Bar•ba•di\an

Bar•ba•dos

bar•bar•i\an

bar•bar\ic
bar•bar\i•cal\ly
bar•ba•rism
bar•bar•i\ty, *pl.* •ties
bar•ba•rous
bar•ba•rous\ly
bar•be•cue *or* bar•be•que,
•cued *or* •qued, •cu•ing
or •qu•ing
barbed
bar•bell
bar•ber
bar•bi•tu•rate
Bar•ce\lo\na
bar code
bard (*poet*) [*vs.* barred
(*stopped*)]
bard\ic
bare (*uncovered; to bare*),
bar\er, bar•est; bare,
bared, bar•ing [*vs.* bear
(*to carry; the animal*)]
bare•back *or* bare•backed
bare•faced
bare•foot *or*
bare•foot\ed
bare•hand\ed
bare\ly
bare•ness
bar•gain, •gained, •gain•ing
bar•gain\er
bar•gain•ing u\nit
barge, barged, barg•ing
bar\i•tone
bar•i\um
bark (*tree covering; dog's
cry*) [*vs.* barque (*ship*)]
bark, barked, bark•ing
bark\er
bark•less
bar•ley
bar mitz•vah
barn
bar•na•cle
bar•na•cled
barn•like
barn•storm
barn•storm\er
barn•yard
ba•rom\e•ter
bar\o•met•ric

bar\on (*nobleman*) [*vs.*
bar•ren (*empty*)]
bar•on•ess
bar•on•et
ba•ro•ni\al
ba•roque (*ornate*)
bar•racks
bar•ra•cu\da, *pl.* \da, •das
bar•rage
barred (*stopped*) [*vs.* bard
(*poet*)]
bar•rel, •reled *or* •relled,
•rel•ing *or* •rel•ling
bar•ren (*empty*) [*vs.*
bar\on (*nobleman*)]
bar•ren•ness
bar•rette (*hair clasp*) [*vs.*
be•ret (*soft hat*)]
bar•ri•cade, •cad\ed,
•cad•ing
bar•ri\er
bar•ring
bar•ris•ter
bar•room
bar•row
bar•tend\er
bar•tend•ing
bar•ter
Bar•tók
bar\y\on
bar\y\on\ic
ba•sal
ba•salt
ba•sal•tic
base, based, bas•ing
base (*vile*), bas\er, bas•est
[*vs.* bass (*male singer; the
fish*)]
base•ball
base•band
base•board
base•less
base•less•ness
base•line *or* base line
base\ly
base•ment
base•ness
base pay
base-•point pric•ing

base-•stock meth\od
bash, bashed, bash•ing
bash\er
bash•ful
bash•ful\ly
bash•ful•ness
BASIC (*programming
language*)
ba•sic
ba•si•cal\ly
bas\il
ba•sil\i\ca, *pl.* •cas
ba•sin
ba•sis, *pl.* •ses
bask
bas•ket
bas\ket•ball
bas•ket pur•chase
bas•ket•work
Basque
Bas\ra
bas-•re\lief
bass, *pl.* bass *or* bass\es
(*fish*); bass\es (*male
singers*) [*vs.* base (*vile*)]
bas•set hound
bas•si•net
bass•ist
bas•so, *pl.* •sos, \si
bas•soon
bas•soon•ist
bas•tard
bas•tard\i•za•tion
bas•tard•ize, •ized
bas•tard\ly
baste, bast\ed, bast•ing
bas•tille
bas•tion
bat, bat•ted, bat•ting
batch
batch file
batch proc•ess•ing
bate, bat\ed, bat•ing
bath, *pl.* baths
bathe, bathed, bath•ing
bath\er
ba•thet\ic
bath•house
ba•thos (*anticlimax*) [*vs.*
pa•thos (*tender quality*)]
bath•robe

bath•room

bath•tub

ba•tik

ba•tiste

bat•like

ba•ton

Bat\on Rouge

bat•tal•ion

bat•ten, •tened, •ten•ing

bat•ter, •tered, •ter•ing

bat•ter•er

bat•ter\y, pl. •ies

bat•ting

bat•tle, •tled, •tling

bat\tle-•ax or
  bat\tle-•axe

bat\tle•field

bat\tle•ment

bat•tler

bat\tle•ship

bat\ty, •ti\er, •ti•est

bau•ble (trinket) [vs. babble (to talk indistinctly)
  and bubble (globule of
  gas contained in a liquid)]

baud, pl. baud

baux•ite

Ba•var\i\a

Ba•var\i\an

bawd•i\ly

bawd\i•ness

bawd\y, •i\er, •i•est

bawl (to wail) [vs. ball
  (sphere)]

bawled (cried) [vs. bald
  (hairless) and balled
  (shaped into a ball)]

bay

bay•ber\ry, pl. •ries

bay•o•net, •net\ed or
  •net•ted, •net•ing or
  •net•ting

bay\ou, pl. •ous

ba•zaar (marketplace) [vs.
  bi•zarre (strange)]

ba•zoo\ka, pl. •kas

BBB (Better Business
  Bureau)

BBS (bulletin board system)

be, am, are, is, are; was,
  were; been, be•ing

beach (shore) [vs. beech
  (the tree)]

beach, beached, beach•ing

beach•comb\er

beach•head

bea•con

bead

bead\ed

bea•dle

bea•gle

beak

beaked

beak\er

beam

bean (the vegetable) [vs.
  been (existed) and bin (box)]

bear (the animal), pl. bears
  or bear [vs. bare
  (uncovered)]

bear (to carry), bore,
  borne or born, bear•ing
  [vs. bare (uncovered)]

bear•a\ble

beard

bear\er bond

bear•ing

bear•ish

bear•like

bear mar•ket

beast

beast•li•ness

beast\ly, •li\er, •li•est

beat (to strike), beat,
  beat\en, beat•ing [vs.
  beet (the vegetable)]

beat•a\ble

be•a•tif\ic

be•a•tif\i•cal\ly

be•at\i•fi•ca\tion

be•at\i\fy (to make happy),
  •fied, •fy•ing [vs. beau•ti\fy
  (to make beautiful)]

beat•ing

be•at\i•tude

beat•nik

beat-•up

beau (sweetheart), pl.
  beaus or beaux [vs. bow
  (curve)]

Beau•mont

beaut

beau•te•ous

beau•ti•cian

beau•ti•fi•ca•tion

beau•ti•ful

beau•ti•ful\ly

beau•ti\fy (to make beau-
  tiful), •fied, •fy•ing [vs.
  be•at\i\fy (to make
  happy)]

beau\ty, pl. •ties

bea•ver, pl. •vers or •ver

be•calm

be•calmed

be•cause

beck and call

beck\on, •coned, •con•ing

be•cloud, •cloud\ed,
  •cloud•ing

be•come, •came, •come,
  •com•ing

be•com•ing\ly

bed, bed•ded, bed•ding

be•daub

be•daz•zle, •zled, •zling

bed•bug or bed bug

bed•clothes

bed•ding

be•deck

be•dev\il, •iled or •illed,
  •il•ing or •il•ling

be•dev•il•ment

bed•fel•low

bed•lam

Bed•ling•ton ter•ri•er

Bed•ou\in or Bed•u\in, pl.
  •ins or \in

bed•pan

bed•post

be•drag•gle, •gled, •gling

bed•rid•den

bed•rock

bed•roll

bed•room

bed•side

bed•sore

bed•spread

bed•spring

bed•time

bee

beech (the tree) [vs. beach
  (shore)]

beef, *pl.* beeves *or* beefs; beefed, beef•ing
beef•burg\er
beef•cake
beef\i•ness
beef•steak
beef\y, •i\er, •i•est
bee•hive
bee•keep\er
bee•keep•ing
bee•line
Be•el•ze•bub
been (*existed*) [*vs.* bean (*the vegetable*) *and* bin (*box*)]
beep
beep\er
beer (*the beverage*) [*vs.* bier (*coffin*)]
bees•wax
beet (*the vegetable*) [*vs.* beat (*to strike*)]
Bee•tho•ven
bee•tle, •tled, •tling
bee\tle-•browed
be•fall, •fell, •fall\en, •fall•ing
be•fit, •fit•ted, •fit•ting
be•fog, •fogged, •fog•ging
be•fore
be•fore•hand
be•foul, •fouled, •foul•ing
be•friend, •friend\ed, •friend•ing
be•fud•dle, •dled, •dling
be•fud•dle•ment
beg, begged, beg•ging
be•gan
be•get, be•got, be•got•ten, be•get•ting
be•get•ter
beg•gar
beg•gar\ly
be•gin, be•gan, be•gun, be•gin•ning
be•gin•ner
be•gone
be•go•nia, *pl.* •nias
be•grimed
be•grudge, •grudged, •grudg•ing

be•guile, •guiled, •guil•ing
be•gun
be•half
be•have, •haved, •hav•ing
be•hav•ior
be•hav•ior\al
be•head
be•held
be•he•moth
be•hest
be•hind
be•hind•hand
be•hold, •held, •hold•ing
be•hold\en
be•hold\er
be•hoove, •hooved, •hoov•ing
beige
Bei•jing *or* Pe•king
be•ing
Bei•rut
be•jew•eled *or* be•jew•elled
be•la•bor, •bored, •bor•ing
be•lat\ed
be•lat•ed\ly
be•lay, •layed, •lay•ing
bel can\to
belch, belched, belch•ing
be•lea•guer
Bel•fast
bel•fry, *pl.* •fries
Bel•gian
Bel•gium
Bel•grade
be•lie, •lied, •ly•ing
be•lief
be•liev•a•bil•i\ty
be•liev•a\ble
be•liev•a\ble•ness
be•liev•a\bly
be•lieve, •lieved, •liev•ing
be•liev\er
be•lit•tle, •tled, •tling
Be•lize
Be•li•ze\an
bell (*ringing instrument*)
bel•la•don\na
bell-•bot\tom
bell•boy

belle (*charming woman*)
belles-•let\tres
bell•hop
bel•li•cose
bel•li•cos•i\ty *or* bel•li•cose•ness
bel•lig•er•ent
bel•lig•er•ent\ly
bell-•less
bel•low (*to roar*) [*vs.* be•low (*under*)]
bel•lows
bell•weth\er
bel\ly, *pl.* •lies; •lied, •ly•ing
bel\ly•ache, •ached, •ach•ing
bel\ly•ach\er
bel\ly•but\ton *or* bel\ly but•ton
bel\ly•ful, *pl.* •fuls
be•long, •longed, •long•ing
Be•lo•rus•sia *or* Bye•lo•rus•sia
Be•lo•rus•sian *or* Bye•lo•rus•sian
be•lov\ed *or* be•loved (*adj.*)
be•lov\ed (*noun*)
be•low
be\low-•the-•line
belt, belt\ed, belt•ing
belt•less
belt•way
be•moan, •moaned, •moan•ing
be•mused
be•muse•ment
bench, benched, bench•ing
bench•mark *or* bench mark
bench press (*noun*)
bench-•press (*verb*), •pressed, •press\ing
bend, bent, bend•ing
bend•a\ble
bend\er
be•neath
ben•e•dic•tion
ben\e•dic•to•ry
ben\e•fac•tion

ben\e•fac•tor
ben\e•fac•tress
ben\e•fice
be•nef\i•cence
be•nef\i•cent
ben\e•fi•cial
beneficial in•ter•est
ben\e•fi•cial\ly
ben\e•fi•ci•ar\y, *pl.* •ar•ies
ben\e•fit, •fit\ed, •fit•ing
be•nev\o•lence
be•nev\o•lent
be•nev\o•lent\ly
Ben•gal
be•night\ed
be•nign
be•nig•nant
be•nig•nant\ly
be•nig•ni\ty
be•nign\ly
Be•nin
Be•ni•nese, *pl.* •nese
bent
be•numb, •numbed,
  •numb•ing
ben•zene (*chemical com-
  pound*)
ben•zine (*hydrocarbon
  mixture*)
be•queath, •queathed,
  •queath•ing
be•queath\al *or*
  be•queath•ment
be•quest
be•rate, •rat\ed, •rat•ing
Ber•ber
be•reave, •reaved *or* •reft,
  •reav•ing
be•reave•ment
be•ret (*soft hat*) [*vs.*
  bar•rette (*hair clasp*)]
berg
ber\i•ber\i
Ber•ing Strait
Berke•ley
ber•ke•li\um
Ber•lin
Ber•mu\da
Ber•mu•dan *or*
  Ber•mu•di\an
Bern *or* Berne

Ber•noul\li drive
ber\ry (*small fruit*), *pl.*
  •ries [*vs.* bur\y (*to
  conceal*)]
ber•serk
berth (*sleeping place*) [*vs.*
  birth (*being born*)]
ber\yl
ber•yl•ine
be•ryl•li\um
be•seech, •sought *or*
  •secched, •seech•ing
be•seech•ing\ly
be•set (*to attack*), •set,
  •set•ting [*vs.* besot (*to
  stupefy*)]
be•side (*near*)
be•sides (*moreover*)
be•siege, •sieged,
  •sieg•ing
be•sieg\er
be•smear, •smeared,
  •smear•ing
be•smirch, •smirched,
  •smirch•ing
be•sot (*to stupefy*) [*vs.*
  be•set (*to attack*)]
be•sot•ted
be•sought
be•spat•ter
be•speak, •spoke,
  •spo•ken, •speak•ing
be•spec•ta•cled
best
bes•tial
bes•tial\ly
bes•ti•ar\y, *pl.* •ar•ies
be•stir, •stirred, •stir•ring
be•stow, •stowed,
  •stow•ing
be•stow\al
be•stride, •strode *or*
  •strid, •strid•den,
  •strid•ing
best•sell\er
best•sell•er•dom
best-•sell\ing
bet, bet *or* bet•ted,
  bet•ting
be\ta, *pl.* •tas
beta fac•tor

be•take, •took, •tak\en,
  •tak•ing
be\ta test
be•tel
bête noire, *pl.* bêtes
  noires
be•think, •thought,
  •think•ing
Beth•le•hem
be•tide
be•times
be•to•ken, •kened,
  •ken•ing
be•tray, •trayed, •tray•ing
be•tray\al
be•tray\er
be•troth, •trothed,
  •troth•ing
be•troth\al
bet•ter (*superior*)
bet•ter•ment
bet•tor *or* bet•ter (*one
  who bets*)
be•tween
be•twixt
bev\el, •eled *or* •elled,
  •el•ing *or* •el•ling
bev•er•age
bev\y, *pl.* •ies
be•wail, •wailed, •wail•ing
be•ware
be•wigged
be•wil•der, •dered,
  •der•ing
be•wil•der•ing\ly
be•wil•der•ment
be•witch, •witched,
  •witch•ing
be•witch•ing\ly
be•witch•ment
bey, *pl.* beys
be•yond
bez\el
Bho•pal
Bhu•tan
Bhu•tan•ese *pl.* •ese
bi, *pl.* bis
bi•a\ly, *pl.* •lies
bi•an•nu\al (*twice a year*)
  [*vs.* bi•en•ni\al (*every two
  years*)]

bi•an•nu•al•ly

bi\as, bi•ased or bi•assed, bi•as•ing or bi•as•sing

bi•ath•lon

bib

Bi•ble

Bib•li•cal

Bib•li•cal•ly

bib•li•og•ra•pher

bib\li\o•graph\ic or bib•li•o•graph\i•cal

bib\li\o•graph\i•cal•ly

bib•li•og•ra•phy, pl. •phies

bib\li\o•phile

bib\u•lous

bi•cam•er\al

bi•car•bo•nate

bi•cen•ten•ni\al

bi•ceps, pl. •ceps or •ceps\es

bick\er, •ered, •er•ing

bi•con•cave

bi•con•vex

bi•cul•tur\al

bi•cul•tur•al•ism

bi•cus•pid

bi•cy•cle, •cled, •cling

bi•cy•cler or bi•cy•clist

bid, bade or bid, bid•den or bid, bid•ding

bid and asked

bid•der

bid\dy, pl. •dies

bide, bid\ed or bode, bid\ed, bid•ing

bi•det

bi•en•ni\al

bi•en•ni•al\ly

bier (coffin) [vs. beer (the beverage)]

bi•fo•cal

bi•fur•cate, •cat\ed, •cat•ing

bi•fur•ca•tion

big, big•ger, big•gest

big\a•mist

big\a•mous

big\a\my, pl. •mies

big bang the•o•ry

Big Board

big busi•ness

big•gie or big\gy, pl. •gies

big•gish

big•heart\ed

big•heart•ed•ness

big•horn, pl. •horns or •horn

bight (loop) [vs. bite (to cut with teeth) and byte (computer unit)]

big•mouth, pl. •mouths or •mouth

big•ness

big\ot

big-•tick\et

big•wig

bike, biked, bik•ing

bik\er

bike•way

bi•ki\ni, pl. •nis

bi•ki•nied

bi•lat•er\al

bi•lat•er•al•ism

bile

bilge

bi•lin•gual

bi•lin•gual•ism

bi•lin•gual\ly

bil•ious

bil•ious\ly

bil•ious•ness

bilk, bilked, bilk•ing

bill, billed, bill•ing

bill•board

bil•let

bil\let-•doux, pl. bil\lets-•doux

bill•fold

bil•liard

bil•liards

bill•ing

bil•lings•gate

bil•lion, pl. •lions or •lion

bil•lion•aire

bil•lionth

bill of ex•change

bill of lad•ing

bill of sale

bil•low, •lowed, •low•ing

bil\ly, pl. •lies

bim\bo, pl. •bos or •boes

bi•month\ly, pl. •lies

bin (box) [vs. bean (the vegetable) and been (existed)]

bi•na\ry, pl. •ries

bind, bound, bind•ing

bind•er\y, pl. •er•ies

bind•ing

binge, binged, bing•ing

bin\go

bin•na•cle

bin•oc\u•lar

bin•oc\u•lar•i\ty

bi•no•mi\al

bi\o, pl. bi\os

bi\o•chem\i•cal

bi\o•chem\i•cal\ly

bi\o•chem•ist

bi\o•chem•is•try

bi\o•cid\al

bi\o•cide

bi\o•de•grad•a•bil•i\ty

bi\o•de•grad•a•ble

bi\o•eth•ics

bi\o•feed•back

bi•og•ra•pher

bi\o•graph\i•cal

bi•og•ra•phy, pl. •phies

bi\o•log\i•cal

bi\o•log\i•cal•ly

bi•ol\o•gist

bi•ol\o\gy

bi\o•mass

bi\o•med\i•cal

bi\o•med\i•cine

bi•on\ic

bi\o•phys\i•cal

bi\o•phys\i•cal\ly

bi\o•phys\i•cist

bi\o•phys•ics

bi•op\sy, pl. •sies, •sied, •sy•ing

bi\o•rhythm

BIOS (basic input/output system)

bi\o•sci•ence

bi\o•sci•en•tist

bi\o•sphere

bi\o•tech•ni•cal

bi\o•tech•no•log\i•cal

bi\o•tech•nol\o•gist

bi\o•tech•nol\o\gy

bi•ot\ic
bi\o•tin
bi•par•ti•san
bi•par•ti•san•ship
bi•par•tite
bi•ped
bi•plane
bi•po•lar
bi•po•lar\i\ty
bi•po•lar\i•za•tion
bi•po•lar•ize, •ized, •iz•ing
bi•ra•cial
birch
bird
bird•bath
bird•brain
bird-•brained or
  bird•brained
bird•cage
bird\er
bird•house
bird\ie, •ied, •ie•ing
bird•like
bird•lime, •limed, •lim•ing
bird•seed
bird's-•eye, pl. •eyes
bi•ret\ta, pl. •tas
Bir•ming•ham
birth (act of being born)
  [vs. berth (sleeping
  place)]
birth, birthed, birth•ing
birth•day
birth•mark
birth•place
birth•rate
birth•right
birth•stone
bis•cuit
bi•sect
bi•sec•tion
bi•sex•u\al
bi•sex•u•al•i\ty
bi•sex•u•al\ly
bish\op
bish•op•ric
Bis•marck
bis•muth
bi•son, pl. •son
bisque
Bis•sau

bis•tro, pl. •tros
bit
bitch
bitch\i•ness
bitch\y, •i\er, •i•est
bite (to cut with teeth), bit,
  bit•ten, bit•ing [vs. bight
  (loop) and byte (computer unit)]
bit•ing
bit•ing\ly
bit-•mapped
bit•ter, •ter\er, •ter•est
bit•ter\ly
bit•tern
bit•ter•ness
bit•ters
bit\ter•sweet
bit\ter•sweet•ness
bi•tu•men
bi•tu•mi•nous
bi•va•lence or bi•va•len\cy
bi•va•lent
bi•valve
biv•ou\ac
bi•week\ly, pl. •lies
bi•year\ly
bi•zarre (strange) [vs.
  ba•zarre (marketplace)]
bi•zarre\ly
bi•zarre•ness
Bi•zet
blab or blab•ber, blabbed
  or blab•bered, blab•bing
  or blab•ber•ing
blab\ber•mouth
black, \er, •est
black-•and-•blue
black•ball, •balled, •ball•ing
black•ber\ry, pl. •ries
black•bird
black•board
black\en
black-•eyed Su•san
black•guard
black•head
black•ish
black•jack
black•list, •list\ed, •list•ing
black•mail, •mailed,
  •mail•ing

black•mail\er
black mar•ket
black•out
black•smith
black tie (noun)
black-•tie (adj.)
black•top, •topped,
  •top•ping
blad•der
blade
blam•a\ble or blame•a\ble
blame, blamed, blam•ing
blame•less
blame•less•ness
blame•wor•thy
blanch, blanched,
  blanch•ing
bland, \er, •est
blan•dish, •dished,
  •dish•ing
blan•dish•ment
bland\ly
bland•ness
blank, \er, •est
blank check
blank en•dorse•ment
blan•ket, •ket\ed, •ket•ing
blanket lien
blank\ly
blank•ness
blare, blared, blar•ing
blar•ney
bla\sé
blas•pheme, •phemed,
  •phem•ing
blas•phem\er
blas•phe•mous
blas•phe•mous\ly
blas•phe•my, pl. •mies
blast, blast\ed, blast•ing
blast\er
blast•off
bla•tant
bla•tant\ly
blath\er, •ered, •er•ing
blaze, blazed, blaz•ing
blaz\er
bla•zon, •zoned, •zon•ing
bleach, bleached,
  bleach•ing
bleach•a\ble

bleach\er

bleak, \er, •est

bleak\ly

bleak•ness

blear•i\ly

blear\i•ness

blear\y, •i\er, •i•est

bleat, bleat\ed, bleat•ing

bleed, bled, bleed•ing

bleed\er

bleep, bleeped, bleep•ing

blem•ish, •ished, •ish•ing

blench, blenched, blench•ing

blend, blend\ed, blend•ing

blend\er

bless, blessed or blest, bless•ing

bless\ed

bless•ed\ly

bless•ed•ness

bless•ing

blew (*did blow*) [*vs.* blue (*the color*)]

blight, \ed, •ing

blimp

blind, \er, •est; \ed, •ing

blind check

blind•fold, \ed, •ing

blind•ing\ly

blind\ly

blind•ness

blind•side, •sid\ed, •sid•ing

blind trust

blink, blinked, blink•ing

blink\er

blintz

blip, blipped, blip•ping

bliss

bliss•ful

bliss•ful\ly

blis•ter, •tered, •ter•ing

blithe, blith\er, blith•est

blithe\ly

blithe•ness

blitz, blitzed, blitz•ing

blitz\er

blitz•krieg

bliz•zard

bloat, bloat\ed, bloat•ing

blob

bloc (*political group*)

block (*solid mass; to obstruct*)

block•a\ble

block•ade, •ad\ed, •ad•ing

block•ad\er

block•age

block•bust\er

block•bust•ing

block\er

block•head

block•head\ed

block•house

bloke

blond, \er, •est

blond•ish

blond•ness

blood

blood•bath

blood•cur•dling

blood\ed

blood•hound

blood•i\ly

blood\i•ness

blood•less

blood•less\ly

blood•less•ness

blood•like

blood•line

blood•mo•bile

blood•shed

blood•shot

blood•stream

blood•suck\er

blood•suck•ing

blood•thirst\i•ness

blood•thirst\y

blood\y, •ied, \y•ing; •i\er, •i•est

bloom, bloomed, bloom•ing

bloom\er (*one that blooms; blunder*)

bloo•mers (*loose trousers*)

bloom•ing

bloop\er

blos•som

blot, blot•ted, blot•ting

blotch, blotched, blotch•ing

blotch\y, •i\er, •i•est

blot•ter

blouse, bloused, blous•ing

blouse•like

blous\on

blow, blew, blown, blow•ing

blow-•by-•blow

blow-•dry, •dried, •dry\ing, •dries

blow\er

blow fly or blow•fly

blow•gun

blow•out

blow•torch

blow\up

blow\y, •i\er, •i•est

blowz•i\ly or blows•i\ly

blowz\y or blows\y, •i\er, •i•est

BLS (*Bureau of Labor Statistics*)

blub•ber

bludg•eon, •eoned, •eon•ing

blue (*the color; to make blue*), blu\er, blu•est; blued, blu•ing or blue•ing [*vs.* blew (*did blow*)]

blue•bell

blue•ber\ry, *pl.* •ries

blue•bird

blue-•blood\ed

blue chip (*noun*)

blue-•chip (*adj.*)

blue-•col\lar

blue•gill

blue•grass

blue•jack\et

blue•ness

blue•nose

blue-•pen\cil, \ciled or \cilled, \cil\ing or \cil\ling

blue•point

blue•print

blue-•rinse or blue-•rinsed

blues

blue-•sky law

blue•stock•ing

bluff, \er, •est

bluff•a\ble

bluff\er
bluff\ly
bluff•ness
blu•ing or blue•ing
blu•ish or blue•ish
blun•der, •dered, •der•ing
blun•der•buss
blun•der•er
blun•der•ing\ly
blunt, \er, •est
blunt\ly
blunt•ness
blur, blurred, blur•ring
blurb
blur•red•ness
blur\ry, •ri\er, •ri•est
blurt, blurt\ed, blurt•ing
blush, blushed, blush•ing
blush\er
blush•ing\ly
blus•ter, •tered, •ter•ing
blus•ter•er
blus•ter•ing\ly
blus•ter\y
bo\a, pl. \as
boar (male swine) [vs.
    bore (dull person; to
    drill)]
board (lumber; to enter)
    [vs. bored (weary)]
board\er (lodger) [vs.
    bor•der (edge)]
board•ing•house or
    board•ing house
board of di•rec•tors
board•walk
boast, \ed, •ing
boast\er
boast•ful
boast•ful\ly
boast•ful•ness
boast•ing\ly
boat
boat\el
boat\er
boat•swain or bo's'n
bob, bobbed, bob•bing
bob•bin
bob•ble, •bled, •bling
bob\by, pl. •bies
bobby pin

bob•by•socks or
    bob•by•sox, pl.
bob•by•sox\er or bobby
    sox\er
bob•cat, pl. •cats, •cat
bob•sled, •sled•ded,
    •sled•ding
bob•sled•der
bob•tail
bob•white
Boc•cac•ci\o
boc•cie or boc\ci
bock beer
bode, bod\ed, bod•ing
bod•ice
bod•i\ly
bod•kin
bod\y, pl. •ies; •ied, \y•ing
bod\y•build\er or bod\y•
    •build\er
bod\y•build•ing or bod\y•
    •build\ing
bod\y•guard
Boer
bog, bogged, bog•ging
bo•gey (golf score; to
    bogey), pl. •geys; •geyed,
    •gey•ing [vs. bog•gy (of a
    bog) and bo\gy (hobgob-
    lin)]
bo•gey•man, pl. •men
bog•gle, •gled, •gling
bog\gy (of a bog)
Bo•go\tá
bo•gus
bo\gy (hobgoblin), pl. •gies
Bo•he•mi\a
Bo•he•mi\an
Bo•he•mi•an•ism
boil, boiled, boil•ing
boil\er
Boi\se
bois•ter•ous
bois•ter•ous\ly
bois•ter•ous•ness
bold (brave), \er, •est [vs.
    bowled (did bowl)]
bold\er (braver) [vs.
    boul•der (large rock)]
bold•face or bold•faced
bold\ly

bold•ness
bole (tree trunk) [vs. boll
    (seed pod) and bowl
    (dish)]
bo•le\ro, pl. •ros
Bol\í•var
bol\í•var or bol\í-•var, pl.
    bol\i•vars or bol\í•va•res
Bo•liv\i\a
Bo•liv•i\an
boll (seed pod)
boll wee•vil
bo\lo, pl. •los
bo•lo•gna (cold cut
    sausage) [vs. ba•lo•ney
    (nonsense)]
Bo•lo•gna (Italian city) [vs.
    ba•lo•ney (nonsense)]
Bol•she•vik, pl. •viks, •vik\i
Bol•she•vism
Bol•she•vist
bol•ster
bolt, \ed, •ing
bolt\er
bo•lus, pl. •lus\es
bomb (explosive device; to
    bomb), bombed,
    bomb•ing [vs. balm (oint-
    ment)]
bom•bard, \ed, •ing
bom•bar•dier
bom•bard•ment
bom•bast
Bom•bay
bomb\er
bomb•shell
bo\na fide or bo\na-•fide
bo•nan\za, pl. •zas
Bo•na•parte
bon ap•pé•tit
bon•bon
bond, \ed, •ing
bond•a\ble
bond•age
bond\ed ware•house
bond•hold\er
bond•hold•ing
bond•ing com•pa\ny
bond•man, pl. •men
bond rat•ing
bonds•man, pl. •men

bonds•wom\an, *pl.*
  •wom\en
bond•wom\an, *pl.*
  •wom\en
bone, boned, bon•ing
bone-•dry
bone•head
bone•head•ed•ness
bone•less
bone meal *or* bone•meal
bon\er
bon•fire
bong
bon\go, *pl.* •gos, •goes
bon\i•ness
bo•ni\to, *pl.* \to, •tos
bon•jour
bon mot, *pl.* bons mots
Bonn
bon•net, \ed, •ing
bon\ny, •ni\er, •ni•est
bon\ny•clab•ber *or*
  bon\ny•clap•per
bon•sai, *pl.* •sai
bon•soir
bo•nus, *pl.* •nus\es
bonus meth\od
bon vi•vant, *pl.* bons
  vi•vants
bon vo•yage
bon\y, •i\er, •i•est
boo, *pl.* boos; booed,
  boo•ing
boo-•boo, *pl.* •boos
boob tube
boo\by trap *(noun)*
boo\by-•trap *(verb)*
boo•dle
boog\ie, •ied, •ie•ing
book, booked, book•ing
book•case
book•end
book\ie
book•ing
book•ish
book•ish•ness
book in•ven•to\ry
book•keep\er
book•keep•ing
book•let
book•mak\er

book•mak•ing
book•mark
book•mo•bile
book•sell•er
book•sell•ing
book•shelf, *pl.* •shelves
book•store
book val\ue
book•worm
Bool•e\an log\ic
boom, boomed, boom•ing
boo•mer•ang
boom town *or*
  boom•town
boon
boon•docks
boon•dog•gle
boon•dog•gler
boor
boor•ish
boor•ish\ly
boost, \ed, •ing
boost\er
boost•er•ism
boot, \ed, •ing
boot•black
boot\ee *or* boot\ie *(baby
  shoe)* [*vs.* boo\ty *(plunder)*]
booth, *pl.* booths
boot•leg, •legged, •leg•ging
boot•leg•ger
boot•less
boot•less•ness
boot•lick\er
boo\ty *(plunder)* [*vs.*
  boot\ee *or* boot\ie *(baby
  shoe)*]
booze, boozed, booz•ing
booz\er
bop, bopped, bop•ping
bo•rax
Bor•deaux, *pl.* •deaux
bor•der *(edge)* [*vs.*
  board\er *(lodger)*]
bor•der, •dered, •der•ing
bor\der•land
bor\der•line
bore *(dull person; to drill)*,
  bored, bor•ing [*vs.* boar
  (male swine)]

bored *(weary)* [*vs.* board
  (lumber; to enter)]
bo\re\al
bore•dom
bo•ric ac\id
bor•ing
bor•ing\ly
born *(brought forth by
  birth)*
born-•a\gain
borne *(supported)*
Bor•ne\an
Bor•ne\o
bo•ron
bor•ough *(municipality)*
  [*vs.* bu•reau *(government
  department; chest of
  drawers)* and bur\ro
  (donkey) and bur•row
  (hole)]
bor•row, •rowed,
  •row\ing
bor•row\er
borscht *or* borsch
bor•zoi, *pl.* •zois
bosh
bo's'n *(boatswain)*
bos\om
bos•om\y
boss, bossed, boss•ing
bos\sa no\va, *pl.* bos\sa
  no•vas
boss•i\ly
boss\i•ness
boss•ism
boss\y, •i\er, •i•est
Bos•ton
Bos•to•ni\an
bo•sun
bo•tan\i•cal *or* bo•tan\ic
bot\a•nist
bot\a\ny
botch
both
both\er
both\er•some
Bot•swa\na
Bot•ti•cel\li
bot•tle, •tled, •tling
bot•tle•neck
bot•tler

bot•tom, •tomed,
•tom•ing

bot\tom•less

bot•tom line (*noun*)

bot\tom-line (*adj.*)

bot•tom man•age•ment

bot\u•lism

bou•doir

bouf•fant

bou•gain•vil•le\a, •le\as

bough (*tree branch*) [*vs.*
bow (*to bend*)]

bought

bouil•la•baisse

bouil•lon (*broth*) [*vs.*
bul•lion (*gold or silver*
ingots)]

boul•der (*large rock*) [*vs.*
bold\er (*braver*)]

boul\e•vard

bounce, bounced,
bounc•ing

bounc\er

bounc•ing

bounc\y

bound

bound\a\ry, *pl.* •ries

bound\en

bound\er

bound•less

boun•te•ous

boun•ti•ful

boun•ti•ful\ly

boun•ti•ful•ness

boun\ty, *pl.* •ties

bou•quet

Bour•bon

bour•geois, *pl.* •geois

bour•geoi•sie

bourse

bout

bou•tique

bou•ton•niere

bo•vine

bow (*to bend*) [*vs.* bough
(*tree branch*)]

bow (*curve*) [*vs.* beau
(*sweetheart*)]

bowd•ler\i•za•tion

bowd•ler•ize, •ized, •iz•ing

bowd•ler•iz\er

bow\el

bow\er

bow\ie knife

bow•knot

bowl (*dish*) [*vs.* bole (*tree*
trunk) *and* boll (*seed*
pod)]

bowled (*did bowl*) [*vs.*
bold (*brave*)]

bow•leg

bow•leg•ged

bow•leg•ged•ness

bowl\er

bowl•ing

bow•man, *pl.* •men

bow•sprit

box, boxed, box•ing

box•car

box\er

box•like

box of•fice (*noun*)

box-•of\fice (*adj.*)

boy (*male child*) [*vs.* buoy
(*floating marker*)]

boy•cott, \ed, •ing

boy•cott\er

boy•friend

boy•sen•ber\ry, *pl.* •ries

boy scout

bps (*bits per second*)

bra

brace, braced, brac•ing

brace•let

brack\en

brack\et, •et\ed, •et•ing

bracket creep

brack•ish

brack•ish•ness

bract

brac•te\al

brac•te•ate

bract\ed

bract•less

brad, brad•ded, brad•ding

brag, bragged, brag•ging

brag•ga•do•ci\o, *pl.* •ci\os

brag•gart

Brah\ma

Brah•man (*Hindu priest;*
cattle breed), *pl.* •mans

Brah•min (*cultured person*)

Brahms

braid, \ed, •ing

Braille

brain, brained, brain•ing

brain•child, *pl.* •chil•dren

brain-•dead *or* brain dead

brain\i•ness

brain•storm

brain•storm\er

brain•storm•ing

brain•wash

brain•wash\er

brain•wash•ing

brain\y, •i\er, •i•est

braise (*to cook by simmer-*
ing), braised, brais•ing
[*vs.* brays (*makes a harsh*
sound) *and* braze (*to*
make of brass)]

brake (*device for stopping;*
to stop), braked, brak•ing
[*vs.* break (*to shatter*)]

brake•man, *pl.* •men

bra•less

bram•ble

bram•bly

bran

branch, branched,
branch•ing

branch•less

brand, \ed, •ing

brand a\ware•ness

brand im•age

bran•dish, •dished,
•dish•ing

brand name

brand-•new

brand switch•ing

bran\dy, *pl.* •dies

brash, \er, •est

brash\ly

brash•ness

Bra•síl\ia

brass

bras•siere (*woman's*
undergarment) [*vs.*
bra•zier (*one who makes*
brass articles)]

brat

Bra•ti•sla\va

brat•tish *or* brat\ty

brat•wurst
Braun•schwei•ger
bra•va\do
brave, braved, brav•ing;
 brav\er, brav•est
brave\ly
brav•er\ly
bra\vo, *pl.* •vos, •voes;
 •voed, •vo•ing
bra•vu\ra, *pl.* •ras
brawl, brawled, brawl•ing
brawl\er
brawn
brawn\y, •i\er, •i•est
bray, brayed, bray•ing
braze (*to make of brass*),
 brazed, braz•ing [*vs.*
 braise (*to cook by sim-
 mering*) *and* brays
 (*makes a harsh sound*)]
bra•zen
bra•zen\ly
bra•zen•ness
bra•zier *or* bra•sier (*one
 who makes brass articles*)
 [*vs.* bras•siere (*woman's
 undergarment*)]
Bra•zil
Bra•zil•ian
Braz•za•ville
breach (*infraction; to
 breach*), breached,
 breach•ing [*vs.* breech
 (*rear part*)]
bread (*baked dough*) [*vs.*
 bred (*raised*)]
bread•bas•ket
bread•board
bread\ed
breadth (*width*) [*vs.*
 breath (*air inhaled and
 exhaled*) *and* breathe (*to
 inhale and exhale*)]
bread•win•ner
bread•win•ning
break (*to shatter*), broke,
 bro•ken, break•ing [*vs.*
 brake (*device for stop-
 ping; to stop*)]
break•a\ble
break•age

break•down
break\er
break-•e\ven point
break•fast, •fast\ed,
 •fast\ing
break•fast\er
break•front
break-•in
break•neck
break•out
break•through
break\up
break•wa•ter
breast, \ed, •ing
breast•bone
breast-•feed, •fed,
 •feed\ing
breast•plate
breast•stroke
breast•strok\er
breast•work
breath (*air inhaled and
 exhaled*) [*vs.* breadth
 (*width*)]
breathe (*to inhale and
 exhale*), breathed,
 breath•ing [*vs.* breadth
 (*width*)]
breath\er
breath•i\ly
breath•less
breath•less\ly
breath•tak•ing
breath•tak•ing\ly
breath\y, •i\er, •i•est
Brecht
Brecht•i\an
bred (*raised*) [*vs.* bread
 (*baked dough*)]
breech (*rear part*) [*vs.*
 breach (*infraction*)]
breech•cloth *or*
 breech•clout
breech\es
breed, bred, breed•ing
breed\er
breed•ing
breeze, breezed,
 breez•ing
breeze•less
breeze•way

Brem\en
breth•ren
breve
bre•vet, •vet•ted *or*
 •vet\ed, •vet•ting *or*
 •vet•ing
bre•vi•ar\y, *pl.* •ies
brev•i\ty
brew, brewed, brew•ing
brewed (*did brew*) [*vs.*
 brood (*offspring; to
 worry*)]
brew\er
brews (*makes beer*) [*vs.*
 bruise (*to injure*)]
brew•er\y, *pl.* •ies
Brezh•nev
bri\ar
bri•ar\y *or* bri•er\y
brib•a\ble *or* bribe•a\ble
bribe, bribed, brib•ing
brib\er
brib•er\y, *pl.* •er•ies
bric-•a-•brac *or* bric-•à-
 •brac
brick
brick•bat
bricked
brick•lay\er
brick•lay•ing
brid\al (*of a wedding*) [*vs.*
 bri•dle (*harness; to
 restrain*)]
bride
bride•groom
brides•maid
bridge, bridged, bridg•ing
bridge•a\ble
bridge•head
bridge loan
Bridge•port
bridge•work
bri•dle (*harness; to
 restrain*), •dled, •dling [*vs.*
 brid\al (*of a wedding*)]
Brie
brief, \er, •est
brief•case
brief•ing
brief\ly
brief•ness

bri\er or bri\ar

bri•er\y or bri•ar\y

brig

bri•gade, •gad\ed, •gad•ing

brig\a•dier

brig•and

brig•and•age

brig•an•tine

bright, \er, •est

bright\en, •ened, •en•ing

bright•en\er

bright\ly

bright•ness

bril•liance

bril•lian\cy

bril•liant

bril•lian•tine

bril•liant\ly

brim, brimmed, brim•ming

brim•ful

brim•stone

brin•dled

brine, brined, brin•ing

bring, brought, bring•ing

bring\er

brin\i•ness

brink•man•ship or
  brinks•man•ship

brin\y, •i\er, •i•est

bri•oche

bri•quette or bri•quet,
  •quet\ted, •quet•ting

Bris•bane

brisk, \er, •est

bris•ket

brisk\ly

brisk•ness

bris•ling

bris•tle, •tled, •tling

bris\tle•cone pine

bris•tly, •tli\er, •tli•est

Bris•tol

Brit

Brit•ain

britch\es

Brit\i•cism

Brit•ish

Brit•ish•ness

Brit\on

brit•tle, •tler, •tlest

brit•tle•ness

bro or Bro, pl. bros or
  Bros

broach (to mention),
  broached, broach•ing [vs.
  brooch (ornamental pin)]

broad, \er, •est

broad•band

broad•cast, •cast or
  •cast\ed, •cast•ing

broad•cast\er

broad•cloth

broad\en, •ened, •en•ing

broad-•form in•sur•ance

broad•ish

broad jump (noun)

broad-•jump (verb),
  •jumped, •jump•ing

broad•loom

broad\ly

broad-•mind\ed

broad-•mind\ed\ly

broad-•mind\ed\ness

broad•ness

broad•side, •sid\ed,
  •sid\ing

broad-•spec\trum

broad•sword

broad•tail

Broad•way

bro•cade, •cad\ed,
  •cad•ing

broc•co\li

bro•chette

bro•chure

bro•gan

brogue

broil, broiled, broil•ing

broil\er

broil•ing\ly

broke

bro\ken

bro\ken-•down

bro\ken•heart\ed

bro\ken•heart•ed\ly

bro\ken•heart•ed\ness

bro•ken lot

bro•ken\ly

bro•ker

bro•ker•age

bro•mide

bro•mine

bron•chi\al

bron•chi•tis

bron•chus, pl. •chi

bron\co•bust\er

bron\co•bust•ing

Bron\të

bron•to•saur

Bronx

bronze, bronzed,
  bronz•ing

brooch (ornamental pin)
  [vs. broach (to mention)]

brood (offspring; to worry),
  \ed, •ing [vs. brewed (did
  brew)]

brood\er

brook

Brook•lyn

broom•stick

broth

broth\el

broth\er, pl. broth•ers,
  breth•ren

broth\er•hood

broth\er-•in-•law, pl.
  broth\ers-•in-•law

brought

brou•ha\ha, pl. •has

brow

brow•beat, •beat,
  •beat\en, •beat•ing

brow•beat\er

brown, \er, •est

brown-•bag, •bagged,
  •bag\ging

brown-•bag\ger

brown\ie

Brown•ing

brown•ish

brown•ness

brown•out

brown•stone

Browns•ville

brows (foreheads)

browse (to read casually),
  browsed, brows•ing

brows\er

bru\in

bruise (to injure), bruised,
  bruis•ing [vs. brews
  (makes beer)]

bruis\er

bruit (to rumor), \ed, •ing [vs. brut (dry) and brute (beast)]

brunch

Bru•nei

Bru•nei\an

bru•nette

brunt

brush, brushed, brush•ing

brush-•off

brusque

brusque\ly

brusque•ness

Brus•sels

brut (dry) [vs. bruit (to rumor) and brute (beast)]

bru•tal

bru•tal\i•za•tion

bru•tal•ize, •ized, •iz•ing

bru•tal\ly

brute (beast) [vs. bruit (to rumor) and brut (dry)]

brut•ish

brut•ish•ness

bub•ble (globule of gas contained in a liquid), •bled, •bling [vs. bab•ble (to talk indistinctly) and bau•ble (trinket)]

bub•ble•gum

bub\ble mem\o\ry

bub\ble•top or bub\ble-•top

bub•bling\ly

bu\bo, pl. •boes

bu•bon\ic plague

buc•ca•neer

Bu•chan\an

Bu•cha•rest

buck, bucked, buck•ing

buck•board

buck\et

bucket shop

buck•eye, pl. •eyes

buck\le, •led, •ling

buck•ler

buck•ram

buck•saw

buck•shot

buck•skin

buck•tooth, pl. •teeth

buck•toothed

buck•wheat

bu•col\ic

bud, bud•ded, bud•ding

Bu•da•pest

Bud•dha, pl. •dhas

Bud\dha•hood

Bud•dhism

Bud•dhist

bud\dy, pl. •dies; •died, •dy•ing

budge, budged, budg•ing

budg•er\i•gar

budg\et, •et\ed, •et•ing

budg•et•ar\y

budg•et•er

budg\ie

Bue•nos Ai•res

buff, buffed, buff•ing

buf•fa\lo, pl. •loes, •los, \lo; •loed, •lo•ing

buff\er, •ered, •er•ing

buffer stock

buf•fet (self-service meal)

buf\fet (strike repeatedly)

buf•foon

buf•foon•er\y

buf•foon•ish

bug, bugged, bug•ging

bug•bear

bug-•eyed

bug-•free

bug\gy, pl. •gies

bu•gle, •gled, •gling

bu•gler

build, built, build•ing

build\er

build•ing

building and loan as•so•ci•a•tion

build\up or build-•up

built-•in

built-•up

Bu•jum•bu\ra

bulb

Bul•gar\i\a

Bul•gar•i\an

bulge, bulged, bulg•ing

bulg\y, •i\er, •i•est

bulk, bulked, bulk•ing

bulk dis•count

bulk freight

bulk•head

bulk\y, •i\er, •i•est

bull, bulled, bull•ing

bull•dog, •dogged, •dog•ging

bull•doze, •dozed, •doz•ing

bull•doz\er

bul•let

bul•le•tin

bulletin board

bul\let•proof

bull•fight

bull•fight\er

bull•fight•ing

bull•finch

bull•frog

bull•head\ed

bull•head•ed\ly

bull•head•ed•ness

bull•horn or bull horn

bul•lion (gold or silver ingots) [vs. bouil•lon (broth)]

bull•ish

bull-•like

bull mar•ket

bul•lock

bull pen or bull•pen

bull•ring

bull's-•eye, pl. •eyes

bul\ly, pl. •lies; •lied, •ly•ing

bul•rush

bul•wark

bum, bummed, bum•ming

bum•ble, •bled, •bling

bum\ble•bee or bum•ble bee

bum•bler

bum•mer

bump, bumped, bump•ing

bump\er

bump•kin

bump•tious

bump•tious•ness

bump\y, •i\er, •i•est

bun

bunch, bunched, bunch•ing

bun•dle, •dled, •dling

bung, bunged, bung•ing

bun•ga•low

bun•gee cord

bung•hole

bun•gle, •gled, •gling

bun•gler

bun•ion

bunk (nonsense)

bunk (bed; to bed down), bunked, bunk•ing

bun•ker

bunk•house

bun\ko or bun\co, pl. •kos or •cos

bun•kum or bun•combe

bun\ny, pl. •nies

Bun•sen burn\er

bunt, \ed, •ing

bunt\er

bun•ting

bu\oy (floating marker) [vs. boy (male child)]

buoy•an\cy

buoy•ant

buoy•ant\ly

bur•den, •dened, •den•ing

bur•dock

bu•reau (government department; chest of drawers), pl. bu•reaus, bu•reaux [vs. bor•ough (municipality)]

bu•reauc•ra\cy, pl. •cies

bu•reau•crat

bu•reau•crat\ic

bu•reau•crat\i•cal\ly

bu•reauc•ra•ti•za•tion

bu•reauc•ra•tize, •tized, •tiz•ing

bu•rette or bu•ret

burg

bur•geon

burg\er (hamburger)

burgh\er (townsperson)

bur•glar

bur•glar•ize, •ized, •iz•ing

bur•gla\ry, pl. •ries

bur•gle, •gled, •gling

bur•go•mas•ter

Bur•gun\dy, pl. •dies

bur•i\al

Bur•ki\na Fa\so

bur•lap

bur•lesque, •lesqued, •les•quing

bur•li•ness

bur\ly, •li\er, •li•est

Bur\ma

Bur•mese, pl. Bur•mese

burn, burned or burnt, burn•ing

burn•a\ble

burn\er

burn-•in (noun)

bur•nish

bur•noose or bur•nous

bur•noosed or bur•noused

burn•out

burn rate

burnt

burp, burped, burp•ing

burr

bur\ro (donkey), pl. •ros

bur•row (hole; to dig), •rowed, •row•ing

bur\sa, pl. •sae, •sas

bur•sal

bur•sar

bur•si•tis

burst, burst, burst•ing

Bu•run\di

Bu•run•di\an

bur\y (to conceal), •ied, \y•ing [vs. ber\ry (small fruit)]

bus (the vehicle), pl. bus\es or bus•ses; bused or bussed, bus•ing or bus•sing [vs. buss (the kiss)]

bus•boy or bus boy

bus\by, pl. •bies

bush

bushed

bush\el

bush•ing

bush•man, pl. •men

bush•mas•ter

bush\y, •i\er, •i•est

bus•i\ly

busi•ness

business col•lege

business cy•cle

busi•ness•like

busi•ness•man, pl. •men

busi•ness•per•son

busi•ness•wo•man, pl. •wo•men

bus•kin

bus mouse

bus to•pol\o\gy

buss (the kiss), bussed, buss•ing [vs. bus (the vehicle)]

bust, bust\ed, bust•ing

bus•tle, •tled, •tling

bus\y, bus•ied, bus\y•ing; bus•i\er, bus•i•est

bus\y•bod\y, pl. •bod•ies

bus\y•ness

bus\y•work

but (on the contrary) [vs. butt (end; to push)]

bu•tane

butch

butch\er

butch•er\y

but•ler

butt (end; to push) [vs. but (on the contrary)]

butte (hill)

but•ter, •tered, •ter•ing

but\ter•cup

but\ter•fat

but\ter•fin•gered

but\ter•fin•gers, pl. •gers

but\ter•fish, pl. •fish\es, •fish

but\ter•fly, pl. •flies

but\ter•less

but\ter•milk

but\ter•nut

but\ter•scotch

but•ter\y

but•tock

but•ton, •toned, •ton•ing

but\ton-•down

but\ton•hole, •holed, •hol•ing

but\ton•less

but•tress, •tressed, •tress•ing

bux\om

bux•om•ness

buy (to purchase), bought, buy•ing [vs. by (near) and bye (good-bye)]

buy•back

buy\er

buy•ers' mar•ket

buy•ing pow\er

buy•out

buzz, buzzed, buzz•ing

buz•zard

buzz\er

buzz•word

by (near) [vs. buy (to purchase) and bye (good-bye)]

by-•and-•by

bye (good-bye) [vs. buy (to purchase) and by (near)]

bye-•bye

by-•elec\tion

Bye•lo•rus•sia

Bye•lo•rus•sian (Belorussia)

by•gones

by•law

by•line or by-•line, •lined, •lin•ing, or •lined, •lin\ing

by•pass or by-•pass,

•passed, •pass•ing, or •passed, •pass\ing

by-•path or by•path, pl. •paths

by•play or by-•play

by-•prod\uct

by-•road or by•road

By•ron

By•ron•ic

by•stand\er

byte (computer unit) [vs. bight (loop) and bite (to cut with teeth)]

by•way

by•word

Byz•an•tine

C

CA (California)

cab, cabbed, cab•bing

ca•bal, •balled, •bal•ling

cab•a\la or cab•ba\la, pl. •las

ca•bal•le•ro, pl. •ros

ca•ban\a, pl. •ban\as

cab\a•ret

cab•bage

cab\by or cab•bie, pl. •bies

cab\in

cab\i•net

cab\i•net•mak\er

cab\i•net•mak•ing

cab\i•net•work

ca•ble, •bled, •bling

ca•ble car or ca•ble•car

ca\ble•cast, •cast, •cast, •cast\ed, •cast•ing

ca\ble•gram

ca\ble-read\y

ca•boo•dle

ca•boose

cab•ri•o•let

ca•ca\o, pl. •ca\os

cac•cia•to\re

cache (hiding place; computer accelerator; to cache), cached, cach•ing [vs. cash (money)]

ca•chet

cack\le, •led, •ling

ca•coph\o•nous

ca•coph\o•nous\ly

ca•coph\o•ny, pl. •nies

cac•tus, pl. •ti or •tus\es or •tus

CAD (computer-aided design)

cad

CAD/CAM (computer-aided design/computer-aided manufacturing)

ca•dav\er

ca•dav•er•ous

cad•die (golf attendant; to caddie), •died, •dy•ing

cad•dy (container), pl. •dies

ca•den\za, pl. •zas

ca•det

Ca•dette

cadge, cadged, cadg•ing

cad•mi•um

ca•dre

ca•du•ce\us, pl. •ce\i

Cae•sar

Cae•sar\e\an or Cae•sar•i\an

cae•su\ra or ce•su\ra, pl. cae•su•ras or ce•su•ras or cae•su•rae

ca•fé or ca\fe, pl. •fés or •fes

café au lait

caf\e•te•ri\a, pl. •ri\as

cafeteria plan

caf•feine

caf•tan or kaf•tan

cage, caged, cag•ing

cag\ey or cag\y, cag•i\er, cag•i•est

cag•i\ly

cag•i•ness

ca•hoots

CAI (computer-assisted instruction)

Cain

Cai\ro

cais•son

ca•jole, •joled, •jol•ing

ca•jol•er\y

Ca•jun

cake, caked, cak•ing

cal\a•bash

cal\a•boose

cal\a•mine

ca•lam\i•tous

ca•lam\i•tous\ly

ca•lam\i•ty, pl. •ties

cal•car\e•ous

cal•cif•er•ous

cal•ci•fi•ca•tion

cal•ci•fy, •fied, •fy•ing

cal•ci•mine or kal•so•mine, •mined, •min•ing

cal•cine, •cined, •cin•ing

cal•cite

cal•ci\um
cal•cu•la\ble
cal•cu•late, •lat\ed, •lat•ing
cal•cu•lat\ed
cal•cu•lat•ing
cal•cu•la•tion
cal•cu•la•tor
cal•cu•lus, pl. \li or •lus\es
Cal•cut\ta
cal•dron
cal•en•dar (table of dates) [vs. col•an•der (strainer)]
cal•en•der (pressing machine)
calf, pl. calves
calf•less
calf•like
calf•skin
Cal•ga\ry
cal\i•ber
cal\i•brate, •brat\ed, •brat•ing
cal\i•bra•tion
cal\i\co, pl. •coes or •cos
Cal\i•for•nia (CA)
Cal\i•for•nian
cal\i•for•ni\um
cal\i•per or cal•li•per
ca•liph or ca•lif
cal•is•then\ic
cal•is•then•ics or cal•lis•then•ics
calk, calked, calk•ing
call, called, call•ing
cal\la, pl. •las
call•a•ble bond
call•back or call-•back
call\er
caller ID
call girl
cal•lig•ra•pher
cal•li•graph\ic
cal•lig•ra•phy
call•ing
cal•li•o\pe
call op•tion
cal•lous (insensitive) [vs. cal•lus (hardened skin)]
cal•lous\ly
cal•lous•ness
cal•low

cal•low•ness
call-•up
cal•lus (hardened skin), pl. •lus\es [vs. cal•lous (insensitive)]
calm (still; to make calm), \er, •est; calmed, calm•ing [vs. cam (round machine part)]
calm\ly
calm•ness
ca•lor\ic
cal\o•rie or cal\o\ry, pl. •ries
cal\o•rif\ic
cal\u•met
ca•lum•ni•ate, •at\ed, •at•ing
ca•lum•ni•a•tion
ca•lum•ni•a•tor
ca•lum•ni•ous
cal•um\ny, pl. •nies
Cal•va\ry (biblical place) [vs. cav•al\ry (troops on horseback)]
calve, calved, calv•ing
calves
Cal•vin
Cal•vin•ism
Cal•vin•ist
Cal•vin•is•tic
Ca•lyp\so, pl. •sos
ca•lyx, pl. ca•lyx\es or cal\y•ces
CAM (computer-aided manufacturing)
cam (round machine part) [vs. calm (still)]
ca•ma•ra•de•rie
cam•bi•um, pl. •bi•ums or •bi\a
Cam•bo•di\a
Cam•bo•di\an
Cam•bri\an
cam•bric
Cam•bridge
came
cam\el
ca•mel•lia, pl. •lias
Cam•em•bert
cam\e\o, pl. cam•e\os

cam•er\a, pl. •er\as
cam•er\a•man, pl. •men
Cam\e\roon
cam\i•sole
cam\o•mile
cam•ou•flage, •flaged, •flag•ing
camp, camped, camp•ing
cam•paign
cam•paign\er
camp\er
camp•fire
cam•phor
camp•site or camp-•site
cam•pus, pl. •pus\es
camp\y, camp•i\er, camp•i•est
cam•shaft
can (be able to), could
can (preserve), canned, can•ning
Ca•naan
Can\a\da
Ca•na•di\an
Canadian ba•con
Ca•na•di•an•ism
ca•nal
can\a\pé (appetizer), pl. •pés [vs. can\o\py (awning)]
ca•nard
ca•nar\y, pl. •nar•ies
ca•nas\ta
Can•ber\ra
can•can
can•cel, •celed or •celled, •cel•ing or •cel•ling
can•cel•a•ble
can•cel•la•tion
can•cer (malignant tumor) [vs. can•ker (ulcerous sore)]
can•cer•ous
Can•cún
can•de•la•bra, pl. •bras
can•de•la•brum, pl. •bra or •brums
can•did (frank) [vs. can•died (sugared)]
can•di•da•cy
can•di•date

can•did\ly

can•did•ness

can•died (*sugared*) [vs. can•did (*frank*)]

can•dle

can•dle•stick

can•dor

can\dy, *pl.* •dies; •died, •dy•ing

can•dy•like

can\dy strip\er

cane, caned, can•ing

cane•brake

ca•nine

can•is•ter

can•ker (*ulcerous sore*) [vs. can•cer (*malignant tumor*)]

can•ker•ous

can•na•bis

canned

can•ner\y, *pl.* •ies

can•ni•bal

can•ni•bal•ism

can•ni•bal•is•tic

can•ni•bal•ize, •ized, •iz•ing

can•ni\ly

can•ni•ness

can•non (*mounted gun*), *pl.* •nons *or* •non [vs. can\on (*law*) and can•yon (*valley*)]

can•non•ade, •ad\ed, •ad•ing

can•not

can\ny, •ni\er, •ni•est

ca•noe, •noed, •noe•ing

ca•noe•ist

can\on (*law*) [vs. can•non (*mounted gun*) and can•yon (*valley*)]

ca•ñon (*canyon*)

ca•non\i•cal *or* ca•non\ic

can•on\i•za•tion

can•on•ize, •ized, •iz•ing

can\o\py (*awning*), *pl.* •pies [vs. can\a\pé (*appetizer*)]

can't (*cannot*)

cant (*jargon; angle*)

can•ta•bi\le

can•ta•loupe *or* can•ta•loup

can•tan•ker•ous

can•tan•ker•ous•ness

can•ta\ta, *pl.* •tas

can•teen

can•ter (*slow gallop*), •tered, •ter•ing [vs. can•tor (*singer*)]

can•ti•le•ver

can\to, *pl.* •tos

can•ton

can•ton\al

Can•ton•ese, *pl.* •ese

can•tor (*singer*) [vs. can•ter (*slow gallop*)]

can•to•ri\al

can•vas (*cloth*)

can•vas•back, *pl.* •backs *or* •back

can•vass (*to solicit*), •vassed, •vass•ing

can•vass\er

can•yon (*valley*) [vs. can•non (*mounted gun*) and can\on (*law*)]

cap, capped, cap•ping

ca•pa•bil•i\ty

ca•pa\ble

ca•pa•bly

ca•pa•cious

ca•pa•cious\ly

ca•pa•cious•ness

ca•pac\i•tance

ca•pac\i•tor

ca•pac•i\ty, *pl.* •ties

ca•par\i•son, •soned, •son•ing

cape

caped

ca•per, •pered, •per•ing

Cape Verde

cap•il•lar\y, *pl.* •lar•ies

cap\i•tal (*principal; official city*) [vs. Cap\i•tol (*building*)]

capital as•set

capital gain

capital goods

cap\i\tal-•in\ten\sive

cap\i•tal•ism

cap\i•tal•ist

cap\i•tal•is•tic

cap\i•tal\i•za•tion

capitalization rate

cap\i•tal•ize, •ized, •iz•ing

cap\i•tal stock

Cap\i•tol (*building*) [vs. cap\i•tal (*principal; official city*)]

ca•pit\u•late, •lat\ed, •lat•ing

ca•pit\u•la•tion

cap•let

ca•pon

cap•puc•ci\no

ca•pric•ci\o, *pl.* •ci\os *or* \ci

ca•price

ca•pri•cious

ca•pri•cious\ly

ca•pri•cious•ness

Cap•ri•corn

caps

cap•siz•a\ble

cap•size, •sized, •siz•ing

cap•stan

cap•stone

cap•su•lar

cap•sule

cap•tain

cap•tain\cy

cap•tion, •tioned, •tion•ing

cap•tious

cap•tious\ly

cap•tious•ness

cap•ti•vate, •vat\ed, •vat•ing

cap•ti•va•tion

cap•tive

cap•tiv•i\ty

cap•tor

cap•ture, •tured, •tur•ing

car

Ca•ra•cas

car\a•cul

ca•rafe

car\a•mel

car\a•mel•ize, •ized, •iz•ing

car\a•pace

car\at (*gem weight*) [vs. car\et (*insert mark*) and car•rot (*the vegetable*) and kar\at (*gold weight*)]
car\a•van, •vaned or •vanned, •van•ing or •van•ning
car\a•van•sa\ry or car\a•van•se\rai, *pl.* •sa•ries *or* se•rais
car\a•way
car•bide
car•bine
car•bo•hy•drate
car•bol\ic ac\id
car•bo-•load\ing
car•bon
carbon 14
car•bon•ate, •at\ed, •at•ing
car•bon•a•tion
car•bon di•ox•ide
Car•bon•if•er•ous
car•bon mon•ox•ide
car•bon tet•ra•chlo•ride
Car•bo•run•dum (™)
car•boy
car•bun•cle
car•bu•re•tor
car•cass
car•cin\o•gen
car•cin\o•gen•ic
car•ci•no•ge•nic•i\ty
car•ci•no\ma, *pl.* •mas *or* •ma\ta
card
card•board
card-•car\ry\ing
car•di\ac
car•di•gan
car•di•nal
car\di\o•gram
car\di\o•graph
car\di\o•graph\ic
car\di•og•ra•phy
car\di\o•log\i•cal
car•di•ol\o•gist
car•di•ol•o•gy
car\di\o•pul•mo•nar\y
car\di\o•vas•cu•lar
card•sharp or card•sharp\er

care, cared, car•ing
CARE (*Cooperative for American Relief Everywhere*)
ca•reen, •reened, •reen•ing
ca•reer, •reered, •reer•ing
care•free
care•ful
care•ful\ly
care•ful•ness
care•giv\er
care•less
care•less•ly
care•less•ness
ca•ress, •ressed, •ress•ing
car\et (*insert mark*) [vs. car\at (*gem weight*) and car•rot (*the vegetable*) and kar\at (*gold weight*)]
care•tak\er
care•worn
car•fare
car\go, *pl.* •goes *or* •gos
car•hop
Car•ib•be•an Sea
car\i•bou, *pl.* •bous *or* •bou
car\i•ca•ture, •tured, •tur•ing
car\i•ca•tur•ist
car•ies (*decay*), *pl.* •ies [vs. car•ries (*does carry*)]
car•il•lon
car\i•ous
car•load
carload lot
car•mine
car•nage
car•nal
car•na•tion
car•ni•val
car•ni•vore
car•niv\o•rous
car\ny, *pl.* •nie
car\ol (*song; to carol*), •oled *or* •olled, •ol•ing *or* •ol•ling [vs. car•rel (*study nook*)]
car•ol\er *or* car•ol•ler
car\om, •omed, •om•ing
car\o•tene

ca•rot\id
ca•rous\al
ca•rouse, •roused, •rous•ing
car•ou•sel *or* car•rou•sel
carp, *pl.* carp *or* carps
carp, carped, carp•ing
car•pal (*of the wrist*)
carpal tun•nel syn•drome
car•pel (*flower part*)
car•pen•ter
car•pen•try
car•pet, •pet\ed, •pet•ing
car•pet•bag
car•pet•bag•ger
car•pet•ing
car•pool, •pooled, •pool•ing
car•port
car•rel (*study nook*) [vs. car\ol (*song; to carol*)]
car•pus, *pl.* \pi
car•r\age
carriage re•turn (*CR*)
car•ri\er
carrier pig•eon
car•ri•er's lien
car•ries (*does carry*) [vs. car•ies (*decay*)]
car•ri\on
Car•roll
car•rot (*the vegetable*) [vs. car\at (*gem weight*) and car\et (*insert mark*) and kar\at (*gold weight*)]
car•rou•sel
car\ry, *pl.* •ries; •ried, •ry•ing
car\ry•all
car\ry-•back
car\ry-•for\ward
car•rying charge
car\ry-•on
car\ry•o\ver
car•sick
car•sick•ness
Car•son Cit\y
cart, cart\ed, cart•ing
cart•age
carte blanche, *pl.* cartes blanches

car•tel
Car•ter
cart\er
Car•te•sian
car•ti•lage
car•ti•lag\i•nous
car•tog•ra•pher
car•to•graph\ic
car•tog•ra•phy
car•ton
car•toon
car•toon•ist
car•tridge
cart•wheel
carve, carved, carv•ing
Car•ver
carv\er
car wash or car•wash
car\y•at\id, pl. •ids or •i\des
ca•sa\ba or cas•sa\ba, pl. •bas
Cas\a•blan\ca
Cas\a•no\va
cas•cade, •cad\ed, •cad•ing
cascading men\u
case, cased, cas•ing
ca•sein
case•load
case•ment
case•work
case•work\er
cash (money; to cash), cashed, cash•ing [vs. cache (hiding place; computer accelerator; to cache)]
cash ac•count•ing
cash-•and-•car\ry
cash•book
cash budg\et
cash cow
cash\ew
cash flow
cash•ier
cashier's check
cash•less
cash machine
cash•mere or kash•mir
cash•point
cash reg•is•ter

cas•ing
ca•si\no (amusement hall), pl. •nos [vs. cas•si\no (card game)]
cask (container)
cas•ket (coffin) [vs. gas•ket (sealing ring)]
Cas•pi\an Sea
casque (helmet)
Cas•san•dra, pl. •dras
cas•sa•va, pl. •vas
cas•se•role
cas•sette
cas•sia, pl. •sias
cas•si\no (card game) [vs. ca•si\no (amusement hall)]
cas•sock
cas•so•war\y, pl. •war•ies
cast (to throw), cast, cast•ing
cas•ta•net
cast•a•way
caste (social class)
cast\er
cas•ti•gate, •gat\ed, •gat•ing
cas•ti•ga•tion
cast iron (noun)
cast-•i\ron (adj.)
cas•tle
cast•off
cas•tor oil
cas•trate, •trat\ed, •trat•ing
cas•tra•tion
Cas•tro
cas\u\al (offhand) [vs. caus\al (of a cause)]
cas\u•al\ly
cas\u•al•ness
cas\u•al\ty, pl. •ties
cat
CAT (computerized axial tomography)
cat\a•clysm
cat\a•clys•mic
cat\a•comb
cat\a•falque
cat\a•lep\sy
cat\a•lep•tic

cat\a•log or cat\a•logue, •loged or •logued, •log\ing or •logu•ing
cat\a•lyst
cat\a•lyt\ic
cat\a•lyze, •lyzed, •lyz•ing
cat\a•ma•ran
cat\a•pult, •pult\ed, •pult•ing
cat\a•ract
ca•tarrh
ca•tas•tro•phe
cat\a•stroph\ic
cat\a•to•ni\a
cat\a•ton\ic
cat•bird
cat•boat
cat•call
catch, caught, catch•ing
Catch-•22, pl. Catch-•22s or Catch-•22's
catch•all
catch\er
catch\i•ness
catch•ing
catch•ment
catch\up
catch•word
catch\y, •i\er, •i•est
cat\e•chism
cat\e•chist
cat\e•chize, •chized, •chiz•ing
cat\e•gor\i•cal
cat\e•gor\i•cal\ly
cat\e•go•rize, •rized, •riz•ing
cat\e•go\ry, pl. •ries
ca•ter, •tered, •ter•ing
cat\er-•cor\nered or cat•er-•cor\ner
cat•er•pil•lar
cat•er•waul, •wauled, •waul•ing
cat•fish, cat•fish, pl. •fish or •fish\es
cat•gut
ca•thar•sis, pl. •ses
ca•thar•tic
ca•the•dral
cath\e•ter

cath\e•ter•ize, •ized,
•iz\ing

cath•ode

cath\ode-•ray tube

Cath\o•lic

cath\o•lic

Ca•thol\i•cism

cath\o•lic•i\ty

cat•i\on

cat•nap, •napped,
•nap•ping

cat•nip

cat•o'-•nine-•tails, pl.
•tails

CAT scan (computerized
axial tomography scan)

CAT scan•ner

Cats•kill Moun•tains

cat's-•paw or cats•paw

cat•sup (ketchup)

cat•tail

cat•ti\ly

cat•ti•ness

cat•tle

cat•tle•man, pl. •men

cat\ty, •ti\er, •ti•est

cat\ty-•cor\nered or
cat\ty-•cor\ner

CATV (community
antenna television)

cat•walk

Cau•ca•sian

Cau•ca•sus, the

cau•cus, pl. •cus\es

cau•dal

caught

caul•dron or cal•dron

cau•li•flow\er

caulk or calk, caulked or
calked, caulk•ing or
calk•ing

caus\al (of a cause) [vs.
cas\u\al (offhand)]

caus•al•i\ty

cau•sa•tion

caus\a•tive

cause, caused, caus•ing

cau•se•rie

cause•way

caus•tic

caus•ti•cal\ly

cau•ter\i•za•tion

cau•ter•ize, •ized, •iz•ing

cau•tion, •tioned,
•tion•ing

cau•tion•ar\y

cau•tious

cau•tious\ly

cau•tious•ness

cav•al•cade

cav\a•lier

cav\a•lier\ly

cav•al\ry (troops on horseback), pl. •ries [vs.
Cal•va\ry (biblical place)]

cav•al•ry•man, pl. •men

cave, caved, cav•ing

ca•ve\at

caveat emp•tor

caveat ven•di•tor

cave-•in

cave man

cav•ern

cav•ern•ous

cav\i\ar or cav\i•are

cav\il, •iled or illed, •il•ing
or •il•ling

cav\i\ty, pl. •ties

ca•vort, •vort\ed,
•vort•ing

caw, cawed, caw•ing

cay (island) [vs. key (lock
opener) and quay (wharf)]

cay•enne

cay•use

CD (compact disc)

CD (certificate of deposit)

CD-\ROM (compact disc
read-only memory)

cease, ceased, ceas•ing

cease-•fire

cease•less

cease•less\ly

ce•cum or cae•cum, pl. \ca

ce•dar

cede (to give up), ced\ed,
ced\ing [vs. seed (plant
ovule)]

ce•dil\la, pl. •las

ceil•ing (top of room) [vs.
seal•ing (closing tightly)]

cel\e•brant

cel\e•brate, •brat\ed,
•brat•ing

cel\e•brat\ed

cel\e•bra•tion

ce•leb•ri\ty, pl. •ties

ce•ler•i\ty

cel•er\y

ce•les\ta or ce•leste, pl.
•les•tas or •lestes

ce•les•tial

cel\i•ba\cy

cel\i•bate

cell (small compartment)
[vs. sell (to offer for
money)]

cel•lar (basement) [vs.
sell\er (one who sells)]

cell•block

celled

Cel•li\ni

cel•list

cel\lo, pl. •los

cel•lo•phane

cel•lu•lar

cellular phone

cel•lu•lite

cel•lu•loid

cel•lu•lose

Cel•si\us

Celt or Kelt

Celt\ic or Kelt\ic

ce•ment, •ment\ed,
•ment•ing

cem\e•ter\y, pl. •ter•ies

ce•no•bite or coe•no•bite

cen\o•taph

Ce•no•zo\ic

cen•ser (container for
incense)

cen•sor (official overseer)

cen•so•ri•ous

cen•sor•ship

cen•sur•a\ble

cen•sure (disapproval),
•sured, •sur•ing

cen•sus (population count),
pl. •sus\es [vs. sens\es
(faculties)]

cent (penny) [vs. scent
(odor) and sent (did
send)]

cen•taur
cen•ta\vo, *pl.* •vos
cen•te•nar•i•an
cen•ten•ar\y, *pl.* •ar•ies
cen•ten•ni•al
cen•ter, •tered, •ter•ing
cen•ter•board
cen•ter•fold
cen•ter•piece
cen\ti•grade
cen•time, *pl.* •times
cen•ti•me•ter
cen\ti\me\ter-•gram-
•sec\ond
cen•tip\e•dal
cen•ti•pede
cen•tral
cen•tral•i\ty
cen•tral\i•za•tion
cen•tral•ize, •ized,
•iz•ing
cen•tral\ly
cen•tral proc•ess\ing u\nit
(*CPU*)
cen•tre, •tred, •tring
cen•trif\u•gal
cen•trif\u•gal\ly
cen•tri•fuge, •fuged,
•fug•ing
cen•trip\e•tal
cen•trip\e•tal\ly
cen•trist
cents (*pennies*) [*vs.* scents
(*odors*) and sense
(*faculty*)]
cents-•off
cen•tu•ri\on
cen•tu\ry, *pl.* •ries
CEO *or* C.E.O. (*chief
executive officer*)
ce•phal\ic
ce•ram\ic
ce•ram•ics
ce•ram•ist
ce•re\al (*grain*) [*vs.* se•ri\al
(*story in installments; of a
sequence*)]
cer\e•bel•lum, *pl.*
•bel•lums *or* •bel\la
ce•re•bral
cer\e•bra•tion

ce•re•brum, *pl.* •brums *or*
•bra
cer\e•mo\ni•al
cer\e•mo•ni•ous
cer\e•mo•ni•ous\ly
cer\e•mo\ny, *pl.* •nies
ce•rise
ce•ri\um
cer•met
cer•tain
cer•tain\ly
cer•tain\ty, *pl.* •ties
cer•tif\i•a•ble
cer•tif\i•cate, •cat\ed,
•cat•ing
certificate of de•pos\it
(*CD*)
cer•ti•fi•ca•tion
cer•ti•fied check
certified pub•lic
ac•count•ant (*CPA*)
cer•ti\fy, •fied, •fy•ing
cer•ti•tude
Cer•van•tes
cer•vi•cal
cer•vix, *pl.* cer•vix\es *or*
cer•vi•ces
Ce•sar•e\an
ce•si\um
ces•sa•tion
ces•sion (*yielding*) [*vs.*
ses•sion (*meeting*)]
cess•pool
ce•ta•cean
ce•ta•ceous
Cey•lon
Cey•lon•ese, *pl.* •ese
Cé•zanne
CFO *or* C.F.O. (*chief
financial officer*)
Cha•blis
cha-•cha, *pl.* •chas; •chaed,
•cha•ing
Chad
Chad•i\an
chafe (*to rub*), chafed,
chaf•ing
chaff (*husks; to chaff*),
chaffed, chaff•ing
chaf•finch
chaff•ing\ly

Cha•gall
cha•grin
cha•grined *or* cha•grinned
chain
chain-•re\act, •re\act•ed,
•re\act\ing
chain saw (*noun*)
chain-•saw (*verb*), •sawed,
•saw\ing
chain-•smoke, •smoked,
•smok\ing
chain store
chair, chaired, chair•ing
chair•lift
chair•man , *pl.* •men
chairman of the board
chair•man•ship
chair•per•son
chair•per•son•ship
chair•wom\an, *pl.*
•wom\en
chair•wom•an•ship
chaise longue, *pl.* chaise
longues *or* chaises
longues
chal•ced•o\ny
cha•let
chal•ice (*wine cup*) [*vs.*
chal•lis (*the fabric*)]
chalk, chalked, chalk•ing
chalk•board
chal•lah
chal•lenge, •lenged,
•leng•ing
chal•leng•er
chal•lis (*the fabric*) [*vs.*
chal•ice (*wine cup*)]
cham•ber
cham•bered
cham•ber•lain
cham•ber•maid
cham•ber of commerce
cha•me•le\on
cham•ois, *pl.* cham•ois
cham\o•mile *or*
cam\o•mile
champ (*champion*)
champ *or* chomp (*chew*),
champed, champ•ing *or*
chomped, chomp•ing
cham•pagne

cham•pi\on, •oned,
•on•ing

chance, chanced,
chanc•ing

chan•cel•ler\y, pl. •ler•ies

chan•cel•lor

chan•cel•lor•ship

chan•cer\y, pl. •cer•ies

chanc\i•ness

chan•cre

chan•croid

chanc\y

chan•de•lier

chan•dler

change, changed,
chang•ing

change•a\ble

change•less

change•ling

change•o\ver

chang\er

chan•nel, •neled or
•nelled, •nel•ing or
•nel•ling

chan•nel•ize, •ized, •iz•ing

chan•son, pl. •sons

chant, chant\ed, chant•ing

chan•teuse, pl. •teuses

chan•tey (sailor's song) [vs.
shan\ty (hut)]

Cha•nu•kah (Hanukkah)

cha\os

cha•ot\ic

chap

chap, chapped, chap•ping

chap•ar•ral

cha•peau, pl. •peaux or
•peaus

chap\el

chap•er\on or
chap•er•one, •oned,
•on•ing

chap•fall\en or
chop•fall\en

chap•lain

chap•lain\cy

chap•lain•ship

chap•let

Chap•lin

chap•ter

Chapter 11

char, charred, char•ring

char•ac•ter

character-•based

char•ac•ter•is•tic

char•ac•ter•is•ti•cal\ly

char•ac•ter•i\za•tion

char•ac•ter•ize, •ized,
•iz•ing

char•ac•ter string

cha•rade

char•broil, •broiled,
•broil•ing

char•coal

chard

Char•don•nay

charge, charged,
charg•ing

charge•a\ble

charge account

charge card

char\gé d'af•faires, pl.
char•gés d'af•faires

charg\er

char•l\ot

cha•ris\ma, pl. •ma\ta

char•is•mat\ic

char\i•ta\ble

char\i•ta\ble•ness

char\i•ta•bly

char•i\ty, pl. •ties

char•la•tan

Char•le•magne

Charles•ton (the city)

Charles•ton (the dance; to
do the Charleston),
•toned, •ton•ing

char•ley horse

char•lotte russe

Char•lotte•town

charm, charmed,
charm•ing

charm\er

charm•ing

charm•ing\ly

char•nel

Char\on

chart, chart\ed, chart•ing

char•ter (to authorize),
•tered, •ter•ing

chart\er (one who charts)

Char•treuse (™)

char•wom\an, pl.
•wom\en

char\y (cautious), •i\er,
•i•est [vs. cher\ry (the
fruit)]

chase, chased (pursued),
chas•ing [vs. chaste
(pure)]

chas\er

chasm

chas•sis, pl. chas•sis

chaste (pure) [vs. chased
(pursued)

chaste\ly

chas•ten, •tened, •ten•ing

chas•tise, •tised, •tis•ing

chas•tise•ment

chas•ti\ty

chat, chat•ted, chat•ting

châ•teau or cha•teau, pl.
•teaus or •teaux

chat\e•laine

Chat•ta•noo\ga

chat•tel

chattel mort•gage

chat•ter, •tered, •ter•ing

chat•ter•box

chat•ti•ness

chat\ty, •ti\er, •ti•est

Chau•cer

chauf•feur

chau•vin•ism

chau•vin•ist

chau•vin•is•tic

cheap (inexpensive), \er,
•est [vs. cheep (chirp)]

cheap\en

cheap\ly

cheap•ness

cheap•skate

cheat, cheat\ed, cheat•ing

cheat\er

check (order for money; to
verify), checked,
check•ing [vs. Czech
(the people and lan-
guage)]

check•book

check\er

check•er•board

check•ing account

check•list
check•mate, •mat\ed, •mat•ing
check•off
check•out or check-•out
check•point
check•room
check•sum
check\up
check•writ\er
ched•dar
cheek
cheek•bone
cheek\i•ness
cheek\y, cheek•i\er, cheek•i•est
cheep (*chirp; to cheep*), cheeped, cheep•ing [vs. cheap (*inexpensive*)]
cheer, cheered, cheer•ing
cheer•ful
cheer•ful\ly
cheer•ful•ness
cheer•i\ly
cheer\i•ness
cheer\i\o
cheer•lead\er
cheer•less
cheer•less\ly
cheer•less•ness
cheer\y, •i\er, •i•est
cheese
cheese•burg\er
cheese•cake
cheese•cloth
chees\y, •i\er, •i•est
chee•tah
chef
Che•khov
Che•kho•vi\an
chem
chem\i•cal
chem\i•cal\ly
che•mise
chem•ist
chem•is•try
che\mo•ther\a\py
chem•ur\gy
che•nille
cheque

cher•ish, •ished, •ish•ing
Cher\o•kee, pl. •kees or •kee
che•root
cher\ry (*the fruit*), pl. •ries [vs. char\y (*cautious*)]
cher•ry•stone
chert
cher\ub, pl. cher•ubs or cher\u•bim
che•ru•bic
cher•vil
Ches\a•peake
chess
chess•board
chess•man, pl. •men
chest
ches•ter•field
chest•nut
Che•va•lier
chev\a•lier
chev•ron
chew, chewed, chew•ing
chews (*masticates*) [vs. choose (*to select*)]
chew\y, •i\er, •i•est
Chey•enne, pl. •ennes or •enne
Chi•an\ti
chi\a•ro•scu\ro, pl. •ros
chic (*stylish*) [vs. chick (*baby chicken*) and sheik (*Arab chief*)]
Chi•ca\go
chi•can•er\y, pl. •er•ies
Chi•ca\no, pl. •nos
chi•chi
chick (*baby chicken*) [vs. chic (*stylish*) and sheik (*Arab chief*)]
chick\a•dee
Chick\a•saw, pl. •saws or •saw
chick\en
chick\en feed
chick\en-•heart\ed
chick\en•pox or chick\en pox
chick•pea
chic\le
chic\o•ry, pl. •ries

chide, chid\ed, chid, chid•ing
chief
chief ex•ec\u•tive of•fi•cer (*CEO*)
chief fi•nan•cial officer (*CFO*)
chief\ly
chief op•er•at•ing officer (*COO*)
chief•tain
chif•fon
chig•ger
chi•gnon
Chi•hua•hua
chil•blain
child, pl. chil•dren
child•bear•ing
child•birth
child•hood
child•ish
child•ish\ly
child•ish•ness
child•less
child•like
chil•dren
Chil\e (*the country*)
Chil•e\an
chil\i or chil\e (*pepper*), pl. chil•ies or chil\es
chill, chilled, chill•ing
chill\i•ness
chill\y (*cold*), •i\er, •i•est
chime, chimed, chim•ing
chi•me\ra
chi•mer\i•cal or chi•mer\ic
chim•ney, pl. •neys
chimp
chim•pan•zee
chin, chinned, chin•ning
chi\na
chinch bug
chin•chil\la, pl. •las
Chi•nese, pl. •nese
chink, chinked, chink•ing
chi\no, pl. •nos
Chi•nook, pl. •nooks or •nook
chintz
chintz\y, •i\er, •i•est
chip, chipped, chip•ping

chip•munk

chip•per

Chip•pe\wa, *pl.* •was or \wa

chi•rop\o•dist

chi•ro•prac•tic

chi\ro•prac•tor

chirp, chirped, chirp•ing

chir•rup, •ruped, •rup•ing

chis\el, •eled or •elled, •el•ing or •el•ling

chis•el\er or chis•el•ler

chit

chit•chat

chit•ter•lings or chit•lings

chiv•al•rous

chiv•al•rous\ly

chiv•al\ry

chive

chlo•ral

chlo•ride

chlo•ri•nate, •nat\ed, •nat•ing

chlo•ri•na•tion

chlo•rine

chlo•ro•form

chlo•ro•phyll

chock

chock-•full

choc\o•hol\ic

choc\o•late

choice, choic\er, choic•est

choir (*chorus*) [*vs.* quire (*24 sheets*)]

choke, choked, chok•ing

chok\er

chol\er (*anger*) [*vs.* col•lar (*neck of garment*) and col\or (*hue*)]

chol•er\a

chol•er\ic

cho•les•ter\ol

chomp, chomped, chomp•ing

Chong•qing or Chung•king

choose (*to select*), chose, cho•sen, choos•ing [*vs.* chews (*masticates*)]

choos\er

choos\i•ness

choos\y, choos•i\er, choos•i•est

chop, chopped, chop•ping

Cho•pin

chop•per

chop•pi•ness

chop\py, •pi\er, •pi•est

chop•stick

chop su\ey

cho•ral (*of a chorus*) [*vs.* cor\al (*marine skeleton*) and cor•ral (*enclosure*)]

cho•rale (*hymn*)

chord (*musical tones*) [*vs.* cord (*string*)]

chore

cho•re\a

cho\re\o•graph, •graphed, •graph•ing

cho•re•og•ra•pher

cho\re\o•graph\ic

cho•re•og•ra•phy

chor•tle, •tled, •tling

cho•rus, *pl.* •rus\es

chose

cho•sen

chow

chow•der

chow mein

chrism

Christ

chris•ten, •tened, •ten•ing

Chris•ten•dom

chris•ten•ing

Chris•tian

Chris•ti•an•i\ty

Chris•tian•ize, •ized, •iz•ing

Christ•mas

chro•mat\ic

chro•mat\i•cal\ly

chrome

chro•mi\um

chro\mo•so•mal

chro\mo•some

chron\ic

chron\i•cal\ly

chron\i•cle, •cled, •cling

chron\i•cler

chron\o•log\i•cal

chron\o•log\i•cal\ly

chro•nol\o\gy, *pl.* •gies

chro•nom\e•ter

chrys\a•lis, *pl.* chrys\a•lis\es or chry•sal\i•des

chry•san•the•mum

chub•bi•ness

chub\by, •bi\er, •bi•est

chuck

chuck\le, chuck•led, chuck•ling

chug, chugged, chug•ging

chum, chummed, chum•ming

chum\my, •mi\er, •mi•est

chump

Chung•king

chunk

chunk\i•ness

chunk\y, •i\er, •i•est

church

church•go\er

Church•ill

church•man *pl.* •men

church•wom\an, *pl.* •wom\en

church•ward\en

church•yard

churl•ish

churn, churned, churn•ing

chute (*inclined channel*) [*vs.* shoot (*to fire a gun*)]

chut•ney

chutz\pa or chutz•pah

CIA or C.I.A. (*Central Intelligence Agency*)

ciao

ci•ca\da, *pl.* •das or •dae

cic\a•trix or cic\a•trice, *pl.* cic\a•tri•ces

Cic\e\ro

ci•der

Cie. or cie. (*company*)

CIF (*cost, insurance, and freight included*)

ci•gar

cig\a•rette or cig\a•ret

cig\a•ril\lo, *pl.* •los

cil\i\a, *pl.* cil•i\um

cinch

cin•cho\na

Cin•cin•nat\i
cin•der
cin\e\ma, *pl.* •mas
cin\é\ma vé•ri\té
cin\e•mat\ic
cin\e\ma•tog•ra•pher
cin\e\ma•tog•ra•phy
cin•na•bar
cin•na•mon
ci•pher, •phered, •pher•ing
cir\ca
cir•ca•di\an
cir•cle, •cled, •cling
cir•clet
cir•cuit
circuit board
cir•cu•i•tous
cir•cu•i•tous\ly
cir•cu•i•tous•ness
cir•cuit\ry
cir\cuit-•switched
cir•cu•lar
cir•cu•lar•i\ty
cir•cu•late, •lat\ed, •lat•ing
cir•cu•la•tion
cir•cu•la•to\ry
cir•cum•cise, •cised,
 •cis•ing
cir•cum•ci•sion
cir\cum•fer•ence
cir•cum•flex
cir\cum•lo•cu•tion
cir\cum•nav\i•gate,
 •gat\ed, •gat•ing
cir\cum•nav\i•ga•tion
cir•cum•scribe, •scribed,
 •scrib•ing
cir•cum•scrip•tion
cir•cum•spect
cir•cum•spec•tion
cir•cum•stance
cir•cum•stan•tial
cir•cum•vent, •vent\ed,
 •vent•ing
cir•cum•ven•tion
cir•cus, *pl.* •cus\es
cir•rho•sis
cir•rus, *pl.* cir\ri
CISC (*complex instruction
 set computer*)
cis•tern

cit\a•del
ci•ta•tion
cite (*to refer to*), cit\ed,
 cit•ing [*vs.* sight (*vision*)
 and site (*location*)]
cit\i•fied *or* cit\y•fied
cit\i•zen
cit\i•zen\ry
cit\i•zen•ship
cit•ric ac\id
cit•ron
cit•ron•el\la
cit•rus fruit
cit\y, *pl.* cit•ies
cit\y-•state
civ\et
civ\ic
civ•ics
civ\il
ci•vil•ian
ci•vil•i\ty, *pl.* •ties
civ\i•li•za•tion
civ\i•lize, •lized, •liz•ing
civ•vies *or* civ•ies
clack (*to make a sharp
 sound*) [*vs.* claque (*hired
 audience*)]
clad
claim, claimed, claim•ing
claim•ant
clair•voy•ance
clair•voy•ant
clam, clammed, clam•ming
clam•bake
clam•ber, •bered, •ber•ing
clam•mi•ness
clam\my, •mi\er, •mi•est
clam•or, •ored, •or•ing
clam•or•ous
clamp, clamped, clamp•ing
clam•shell com•put\er
clan
clan•des•tine
clan•des•tine•ly
clang, clanged, clang•ing
clang\or
clank, clanked, clank•ing
clan•nish
clan•nish•ness
clans•man, *pl.* •men
clans•wom\an, *pl.* •wom\en

clap, clapped, clap•ping
clap•board
clap•per
clap•trap
claque (*hired audience*)
 [*vs.* clack (*to make a
 sharp sound*)]
clar\et
clar\i•fi•ca•tion
clar•i\fy, •fied, •fy•ing
clar\i•net
clar\i•net•ist
clar\i•net•tist
clar•i\on call
clar•i\ty
clash, clashed, clash•ing
clasp, clasped, clasp•ing
class, classed, class•ing
clas•sic
clas•si•cal
clas•si•cism
clas•si•fi•ca•tion
clas•sified ad
clas•sified ad•vertising
clas•si\fy, •fied, •fy•ing
class•less
class•mate
class•room
class\y, class•i\er,
 class•i•est
clat•ter, •tered, •ter•ing
clause (*part of sentence*)
 [*vs.* claws (*animal nails*)]
claus•tro•pho•bi\a
claus•tro•pho•bic
clav\i•chord
clav\i•cle
cla•vier
claw, clawed, claw•ing
claws (*animal nails*) [*vs.*
 clause (*part of sentence*)]
clay
clean, clean\er, clean•est;
 cleaned, clean•ing
clean-•cut
clean\er
clean•li•ness
clean\ly, •li\er, •li•est
clean•ness
cleanse, cleansed,
 cleans•ing

cleans\er

clean\up

clear, clear\er, clear•est; cleared, clear•ing

clear•ance

clear-•cut

clear•ing

clearing ac•count

clear•ing•house or clear•ing house, pl. •hous\es

clear\ly

clear•ness

cleat

cleav•age

cleave, cleft or cleaved, clove or clo•ven, cleav•ing

cleav\er

clef

cleft

clem\a•tis

clem•en\cy

Clem•ens

clem•ent

clench (to close tightly), clenched, clench•ing [vs. clinch (to settle)]

Cle•o•pa•tra

cler\gy

cler•gy•man, pl. •men

cler•gy•wom\an, pl. •wom\en

cler\ic

cler\i•cal

cler\i•cal•ism

clerk

Cleve•land

clev\er, •er\er, •er•est

clev•er\ly

clev•er•ness

cli•ché

cli•chéd

click (sharp sound; to click), clicked, click•ing [vs. clique (exclusive group)]

cli•ent

cli•en•tele

cli\ent/•serv\er

cliff

cliff-•hang\er or cliff•hang\er

cli•mac•ter\ic

cli•mac•tic (of a climax)

cli•mate

cli•mat\ic (of climate)

cli•max

climb (to ascend), climbed, climb•ing

climb•a\ble

climb\er

clime (climate)

clinch (to settle), clinched, clinch•ing [vs. clench (to close tightly)]

clinch\er

cling, clung, cling•ing

clin\ic

clin\i•cal

clin\i•cal\ly

cli•ni•cian

clink, clinked, clink•ing

clink\er

cli•o•met•rics

clip, clipped, clip•ping

clip art

clip•board

clip•per

clip•ping

clique (exclusive group) [vs. click (sharp sound)]

cli•quish

clit\o•ral

clit\o•ris, pl. clit\o•ris\es or cli•to•ri•des

cloak, cloaked, cloak•ing

cloak-•and-•dag\ger

cloak•room

clob•ber, •bered, •ber•ing

cloche

clock, clocked, clock•ing

clock speed

clock•wise

clock•work

clod

clod•dish

clod•hop•per

clog, clogged, clog•ging

cloi•son\né

clois•ter

clomp, clomped, clomp•ing

clone, cloned, clon•ing

clop, clopped, clop•ping

close (to shut), closed, clos•ing; clos\er, clos•est [vs. clothes (garments) and cloths (pieces of fabric)]

closed-•cap\tioned

closed-•cir\cuit

closed cor•po•ra•tion

closed dis•play

closed-•end

close•fist\ed

close-•fit\ting

close-•knit

close\ly

close•mouthed

close•ness

close•out

clos\et, •et\ed, •et•ing

close\up

clo•sure

clot, clot•ted, clot•ting

cloth

clothe, clothed, clad, cloth•ing

clothes (garments) [vs. close (to shut) and cloths (pieces of fabric)]

clothes•horse

clothes•pin

cloth•ier

cloth•ing

cloths (pieces of fabric)

clo•ture

cloud, cloud\ed, cloud•ing

cloud•burst

cloud•less

cloud\y, •i\er, •i•est

clout

clove

clo•ven

clo•ver, pl. •vers or •ver

clo\ver•leaf, pl. •leafs or •leaves

clown, clowned, clown•ing

clown•ish

clown•ish\ly

cloy, cloyed, cloy•ing
club, clubbed, club•bing
club•foot, pl. •feet
club•foot\ed
club•house, pl. •hous\es
cluck, clucked, cluck•ing
clue, clued, clu•ing
clump, clumped,
  clump•ing
clum•si\ly
clum•si•ness
clum\sy, •si\er, •si•est
clung
clunk\er
clunk\y, •i\er, •i•est
clus•ter, •tered, •ter•ing
clutch, clutched,
  clutch•ing
clut•ter, •tered, •ter•ing
CMOS (complementary
  metal oxide semi-
  conductor)
CO (Colorado)
Co. (company)
C/o or c/o ("in care of" on
  mail)
coach, coached, coach•ing
coach•man, pl. •men
co•ag\u•lant
co•ag\u•late, •lat\ed,
  •lat•ing
co•ag\u•la•tion
coal (the mineral) [vs. kohl
  (black powder)]
co•a•lesce, •lesced,
  •lesc•ing
co•a•les•cence
co•a•les•cent
co•a•li•tion
coarse (rough), coars\er,
  coars•est [vs. course
  (class; route)]
coarse\ly
coars\en, •ened, •en•ing
coarse•ness
coast
coast\al
coast\er
coast•line
coat (outer garment) [vs.
  cote (coop)]

coat•tail
co•au•thor
coax
co•ax•i\al
coax•ing\ly
cob
co•balt
cob•ble, •bled, •bling
cob•bler
cob•ble•stone
COBOL (programming
  language)
co•bra, pl. •bras
cob•web
cob•webbed
co•caine
coc•cus, pl. \ci
coc•cyx, pl. coc•cy•ges
coch\i•neal
coch•le\a, pl. •le\ae or •le\as
coch•le\ar
cock
cock•ade
cock\a•ma•mie or
  cock\a•ma\my
cock-•and-•bull sto\ry
cock\a•too, pl. •toos
cock•crow
cock•er\el
cock\er span•iel
cock•eyed
cock•fight
cock•fight•ing
cock•horse
cock•i\ly
cock\i•ness
cock\le
cock•le•shell
cock•ney, pl. •neys
cock•pit
cock•roach
cocks•comb
cock•sure
cock•tail
cock\y, cock•i\er,
  cock•i•est
co•coa
co•co•nut or co•coa•nut
co•coon
C.O.D. or c.o.d. (cash on
  delivery)

cod, pl. cod or cods
co\da, pl. •das
cod•dle, •dled, •dling
code, cod\ed, cod•ing
co•deine
co•de\pend•ent
co•dex, pl. co•di•ces
cod•fish, pl. •fish or
  •fish\es
codg\er
cod\i•cil
cod\i•fi•ca•tion
cod•i\fy, •fied, •fy•ing
co•don
co\ed or co-•ed
co•ed\u•ca•tion
co•ed\u•ca•tion\al
co•ef•fi•cient
coe•len•ter•ate
co•e\qual
co•e\qual\ly
co•erce, •erced, •erc•ing
co•er•cion
co•er•cive
co•e\val
co•ex•ist, •ist\ed, •ist•ing
co•ex•ist•ence
co•ex•ist•ent
co•ex•ten•sive
cof•fee
cof\fee•cake
cof\fee•house, pl.
  •hous\es
cof\fee•pot
cof•fer
cof•fin
cog
c.o.g. (customer-owned
  goods)
co•gen\cy
co•gent
co•gent\ly
cog\i•tate, •tat\ed, •tat•ing
cog\i•ta•tion
cog\i•ta•tor
co•gnac
cog•nate
cog•ni•tion
cog•ni•za\ble
cog•ni•zance
cog•ni•zant

cog•no•men, *pl.* •no•mens
  or •nom\i\na
co•gno•scen\ti, *pl.* \te
cog•wheel
co•hab\it
co•hab•it•ant
co•hab\it, •it\ed, •it•ing
co•hab\i•ta•tion
co•heir
co•here, •hered, •her•ing
co•her•ence
co•her•ent
co•her•ent\ly
co•he•sion
co•he•sive
co•hort
coif (*hair style*), coifed,
  coif•ing [*vs.* quaff (*to
  drink*)]
coif•feur (*hairdresser*)
coif•fure (*hair style*)
coil, coiled, coil•ing
coin, coined, coin•ing
coin•age
co•in•cide, •cid\ed,
  •cid•ing
co•in•ci•dence
co•in•ci•den•tal
co•in\ci•den•tal\ly
co•i•tal
co•i•tus
coke, coked, cok•ing
COLA (*cost of living
  adjustment*), *pl.* COLAs
  or COLA's [*vs.* co\la
  (*soft drink*) and ko\la
  (*nut*)]
col•an•der (*strainer*) [*vs.*
  cal•en•dar (*table of
  dates*) and cal•en•der
  (*pressing machine*)]
cold, \er, •est
cold-•blood\ed or
  cold•blood\ed
cold boot
cold call
cold\ly
cold•ness
cold shoul•der (*noun*)
cold-•shoul\der (*verb*)
cold-•tur\key (*adj.*)

cole•slaw
co•le\us, *pl.* •us\es
col\ic
col•ick\y
col•i•se\um (*stadium*) [*vs.*
  Col•os•se\um (*Roman
  amphitheater*)]
co•li•tis
col•lah\o•rate, •rat\ed,
  •rat•ing
col•lab\o•ra•tion
col•lab\o•ra•tor
col•lage (*art form*) [*vs.*
  col•lege (*school*)]
col•lag•ist
col•lapse, •lapsed,
  •laps•ing
col•laps\i•ble
col•lar (*neck of garment*),
  •lared, •lar•ing [*vs.*
  chol\er (*anger*) and
  col\or (*hue*)]
col•lar•bone
col•lard
col•lar•less
col•late, •lat\ed, •lat•ing
col•lat•er•al
col•la•tion
col•la•tor
col•league
col•lect, •lect\ed, •lect•ing
col•lect•a\ble or
  col•lect•i\ble
col•lect\ed
col•lect•i\ble
col•lec•tion
col•lec•tive
collective bar•gain•ing
col•lec•tive\ly
col•lec•tiv•ism
col•lec•tiv•ist
col•lec•ti•vi•za•tion
col•lec•ti•vize, •vized,
  •viz•ing
col•lec•tor
col•leen
col•lege (*school*) [*vs.*
  col•lage (*art form*)]
col•le•gial
col•le•gian
col•le•giate

col•lide, •lid\ed, •lid•ing
col•lie
col•lier
col•lier\y, *pl.* •lier•ies
col•li•sion (*crash*) [*vs.*
  col•lu•sion (*conspiracy*)]
col•lo•cate, •cat\ed,
  •cat•ing
col•lo•ca•tion
col•loid
col•loi•dal
col•lo•qui\al
col•lo•qui•al•ism
col•lo•qui•al\ly
col•lo•qui•um, *pl.*
  •qui•ums or •qui\a
col•lo•quy, *pl.* •quies
col•lude, •lud\ed, •lud•ing
col•lu•sion (*conspiracy*)
  [*vs.* col•li•sion (*crash*)]
col•lu•sive
co•logne
Co•lom•bi\a
Co•lom•bi\an (*of the
  country Colombia*) [*vs.*
  Co•lum•bi\an (*of the
  explorer Columbus*)]
Co•lom•bo
co•lon, *pl.* •lons
colo•nel (*military officer*)
  [*vs.* ker•nel (*seed*)]
co•lo•ni•al
co•lo•ni•al•ism
co•lo•ni•al•ist
col\o•nist
col\o•ni•za•tion
col\o•nize, •nized, •niz•ing
col\o•niz\er
col•on•nade
col•on•nad\ed
col\o\ny, *pl.* •nies
col\o•phon
col\or (*hue; to color*),
  •ored, •or•ing [*vs.*
  chol\er (*anger*) and
  col•lar (*neck of gar-
  ment*)]
Col\o•rad\an
Col\o•rad\o (*CO*)
col\o•ra•tion
col\o•ra•tu\ra, *pl.* •ras

col\or•blind

col•or•cast, •cast, •cast•ing

col•ored

col•or•fast

col•or•ful

col•or•ful\ly

col•or•ful•ness

col•or•ing

col•or\i•za•tion

col•or•ize, •ized, •iz•ing

col•or•less

col•or•less\ly

col•or•less•ness

col•or mon•i•tor

co•los•sal

co•los•sal\ly

Col•os•se•um (*Roman amphitheater*) [vs. col\i•se•um (*stadium*)]

co•los•sus, pl. •los\si or •los•sus\es

co•los•to\my, pl. •mies

co•los•trum

col•our, •oured, •our•ing

colt

colt•ish

Co•lum•bi\a

Co•lum•bi\an (*of the explorer Columbus*) [vs. Co•lom•bi\an (*of the country Colombia*)]

col•um•bine

Co•lum•bus

col•umn

co•lum•nar

col•um•nist

co\ma (*unconscious state*), pl. •mas [vs. com\ma (*punctuation mark*)]

co•mak\er

com\a•tose

comb, combed, comb•ing

com•bat, •bat\ed, •bat•ing, •bat•ted, •bat•ting

com•bat•ant

com•bat•ive

com•bi•na•tion

com•bine, •bined, •bin•ing

comb•ings

com\bo, pl. •bos

com•bus•ti•bil•i\ty

com•bus•ti\ble

com•bus•tion

come, came, come, com•ing

come•back

co•me\di\an

co•me\di•enne

come•down

com•e\dy, pl. \dies

come•li•ness

come\ly, •li\er, •li•est

come-•on (*noun*)

com\er

co•mes•ti\ble

com\et

com•et•ar\y

come-up•pance

COMEX (*Commodity Exchange, New York*)

com•fort, •fort\ed, •fort•ing

com•fort•a\ble

com•fort\er

com•fort let•ter

com\fy, •fi\er, •fi•est

com\ic (*funny*) [vs. kar•mic (*of fate*)]

com\i•cal

com\i•cal\ly

com•ing

com•i\ty, pl. •ties

com•ma (*punctuation mark*), pl. •mas [vs. co\ma (*unconscious state*)]

com•mand (*to order*) [vs. com•ment (*to recom-mend*)]

com•man•dant

com•man•deer, •deered, •deer•ing

com•mand driv\en

com•mand\er

com•mand•ment

com•man\do, pl. •dos or •does

com•mand shell

com•mem\o•rate, •rat\ed, •rat•ing

com•mem\o•ra•tion

com•mem\o•ra•tive

com•mence, •menced, •menc•ing

com•mence•ment

com•mend (*to recommend*), •mend\ed, •mend•ing [vs. com•mand (*to order*)]

com•mend•a\ble

com•mend•a•bly

com•men•da•tion (*praise*) [vs. con•dem•na•tion (*denunciation*)]

com•mend\a•to\ry

com•men•su•ra•bil•i\ty

com•men•su•ra\ble

com•men•su•rate

com•ment, •ment\ed, •ment•ing

com•men•tar\y, pl. •tar•ies

com•men•ta•tor

com•merce

com•mer•cial

commercial bank

com•mer•cial•ism

com•mer•cial\i•za•tion

com•mer•cial•ize, •ized, •iz•ing

com•mer•cial\ly

com•mer•cial pa•per

com•min•gle, •gled, •gling

com•mis•er•ate, •at\ed, •at•ing

com•mis•er•a•tion

com•mis•sar

com•mis•sar•i\at

com•mis•sar\y, pl. •sar•ies

com•mis•sion, •sioned, •sion•ing

com•mis•sion\er

com•mit, •mit•ted, •mit•ting

com•mit•ment

com•mit•tee

com•mit•tee•man, pl. •men

com•mit•tee•wom\an, pl. •wom\en

com•mode

com•mo•di•ous
com•mod•i•ty, pl. •ties
commodity ex•change
com•mo•dore
com•mon, \er, •est
com•mon•al•ty, pl. •ties
common car•ri\er
com•mun\er
com•mon\ly
Com\mon Mar•ket
com\mon•place
com•mon sense (noun)
com\mon•sense (adj.)
com\mon•sen•si•cal
com\mon-•size
   state•ment
com•mon stock
com\mon•weal or
   com•mon weal
com\mon•wealth
com•mo•tion
com•mu•nal
com•mune, •muned,
   •mun•ing
com•mu•ni•ca•bil•i\ty
com•mu•ni•ca\ble
com•mu•ni•cant
com•mu•ni•cate, •cat\ed,
   •cat•ing
com•mu•ni•ca•tion
communications
   pro•to•col
com•mu•ni•ca•tive
com•mu•ni•ca•tor
com•mun•ion
com•mu•ni•qué
com•mu•nism
com•mu•nist
com•mu•ni\ty, pl. •ties
community chest
com•mu•ta•tion
com•mu•ta•tive
com•mute, •mut\ed,
   •mut•ing
com•mut\er
Com\o•ros
comp
com•pact, \ed, •ing
compact disc (CD)
com•pact\ly
com•pact•ness

com•pac•tor
com•pan•ion
com•pan•ion•a\ble
com•pan•ion•ship
com•pan•ion•way
com•pa\ny, pl. •nies
company loan
com•pa•ra•bil•i\ty
com•pa•ra\ble
com•pa•ra•bly
com•par\a•tive
com•par\a•tive\ly
com•pare, •pared,
   •par•ing
com•par\i•son
com•part•ment,
   •ment\ed, •ment•ing
com•part•men•tal
com•part•men•tal\i•za•tion
com•part•men•tal•ize,
   •ized, •iz•ing
com•pass, •passed,
   •pass•ing
com•pas•sion
com•pas•sion•ate
com•pas•sion•ate\ly
com•pat\i•bil•i\ty
com•pat\i•ble
com•pat\i•ble•ness
com•pa•tri\ot
com•peer
com•pel, •pelled, •pel•ling
com•pen•di\um, pl.
   •di•ums or •di\a
com•pen•sate, •sat\ed,
   •sat•ing
com•pen•sa•tion
com•pen•sa•to\ry
com•pete, •pet\ed,
   •pet•ing
com•pe•tence
com•pe•tent
com•pe•tent\ly
com•pe•ti•tion
com•pet\i•tive
competitive mar•ket
com•pet\i•tor
com•pi•la•tion
com•pile, •piled, •pil•ing
com•pil\er
com\pile-•time er•ror

com•pla•cen\cy or
   com•pla•cence
com•pla•cent (self-
   satisfied) [vs.
   com•plai•sant
   (agreeable)]
com•plain, •plained,
   •plain•ing
com•plain•ant
com•plain\er
com•plaint
com•plai•sance
com•plai•sant (agreeable)
   [vs. com•pla•cent (self-
   satisfied)]
com•plai•sant\ly
com•pleat
com•plect\ed
com•ple•ment (completing
   part), •ment\ed,
   •ment•ing [vs.
   com•pli•ment (praise)]
com•ple•men•ta\ry
com•plete, •plet\ed,
   •plet•ing
com•plete\ly
com•plete•ness
com•ple•tion
com•plex
com•plex•ion
com•plex•i\ty
com•pli•ance
com•pli•ant
com•pli•cate, •cat\ed,
   •cat•ing
com•pli•ca•tion
com•plic•i\ty
com•pli•ment (praise),
   •ment\ed, •ment•ing [vs.
   com•ple•ment (complet-
   ing part)]
com•pli•men•ta\ry
com•ply, •plied, •ply•ing
com•po•nent
com•port, •port\ed,
   •port•ing
com•port•ment
com•pose (to make up),
   •posed, •pos•ing [vs.
   com•prise (to contain)]
com•posed

com•pos•ed\ly
com•pos\er
com•pos•ite
com•po•si•tion
com•pos\i•tor
com•post, •post\ed,
•post•ing
com•po•sure
com•pote
com•pound, •pound\ed,
•pound•ing
compound in•ter•est
com•pre•hend, •hend\ed,
•hend•ing
com•pre•hen•si\ble
(intelligible)
com•pre•hen•sion
com•pre•hen•sive
(inclusive)
comprehensive
in•sur•ance
com•pre•hen•sive\ly
com•pre•hen•sive•ness
com•press, •pressed,
•press•ing
com•pres•sion
com•prise (to contain),
•prised, •pris•ing [vs.
com•pose (to make up)]
com•pro•mise, •mised,
•mis•ing
comp•trol•ler
com•pul•sion (coercion)
com•pul•sive
com•pul•sive\ly
com•pul•sive•ness
com•pul•so\ry
compulsory ar•bi•tra•tion
com•punc•tion (remorse)
com•pu•ta•tion
com•pute, •put\ed,
•put•ing
com•put\er
com•put\er-•aid\ed
com•put\er•ese
com•put\er graph•ics
com•put•er\i•za•tion
com•put•er•ize, •ized,
•iz•ing
com•put•er•ized ax•i\al
to•mog•ra•phy (CAT)

com•put\er lan•guage
computer lit•er\a\cy
com•put\er•ma•ni\a
com•put\er•pho•bi\a
com•put\er vi•rus
computer worm
com•rade
com•rade•ship
con, conned, con•ning
con•cat\e•nate, •nat\ed,
•nat•ing
con•cat\e•na•tion
con•cave (curved inward)
[vs. con•vex (curved
outward)]
con•ceal, •cealed, •ceal•ing
con•ceal\er
con•ceal•ment
con•cede, •ced\ed, •ced•ing
con•ceit
con•ceit\ed
con•ceiv•a\ble
con•ceiv•a\bly
con•ceive, •ceived,
•ceiv•ing
con•cen•trate, •trat\ed,
•trat•ing
con•cen•tra•tion
con•cen•tric
con•cept
con•cep•tion
con•cep•tu\al
con•cep•tu•al•ize, •ized,
•iz•ing
con•cep•tu•al\ly
con•cern
con•cerned
con•cern•ing
con•cert
con•cert\ed
con•cert•ed\ly
con•cer•ti•na
con\cert•mas•ter
con•cer\to, pl. •tos or \ti
con•ces•sion
con•ces•sion•aire or
con•ces•sion\er
conch (marine mollusk), pl.
conchs or con•ches [vs.
conk (to hit on the
head)]

con•cierge, pl. •cierges
con•cil•i•ate, •at\ed,
•at•ing
con•cil•i•a•tion
con•cil•i•a•tor
con•cil•i•a•to\ry
con•cise
con•cise\ly
con•cise•ness
con•clave
con•clude, •clud\ed,
•clud•ing
con•clu•sion
con•clu•sive
con•clu•sive\ly
con•clu•sive•ness
con•coct, •coct\ed,
•coct•ing
con•coc•tion
con•com\i•tant
con•cord
con•cord•ance
con•cord•ant
con•cor•dat
con•course
con•crete
con•crete\ly
con•crete•ness
con•cu•bine
con•cu•pis•cence
con•cu•pis•cent
con•cur, •curred, •cur•ring
con•cur•rence
con•cur•rent
con•cur•rent\ly
con•cus•sion
con•demn (to censure),
•demned, •demn•ing [vs.
con•temn (to dispise)]
con•dem•na•tion (denun-
ciation) [vs.
com•men•da•tion
(praise)]
con•dem•na•to\ry
con•den•sa•tion
con•dense, •densed,
•dens•ing
con•dens\er
con•de•scend, •scend\ed,
•scend•ing
con•de•scend•ing\ly

con•de•scen•sion
con•dign
con•di•ment
con•di•tion, •tioned,
 •tion•ing
con•di•tion\al
con•di•tion•al\ly
con•di•tion\al sale
con•di•tioned
con•di•tion\er
con\do, pl. •dos
con•dole, •doled, •dol•ing
con•do•lence
con•dom
con•do•min•i\um
con•done, •doned,
 •don•ing
con•dor
con•duce, •duced,
 •duc•ing
con•du•cive
con•duct, •duct\ed,
 •duct•ing
con•duct•ance
con•duc•tion
con•duc•tive
con•duc•tiv•i\ty, pl. •ties
con•duc•tor
con•duit
cone, coned, con•ing
co•ney, pl. •neys
con•fab, •fabbed, •fab•bing
con•fab\u•late, •lat\ed,
 •lat•ing
con•fab\u•la•tion
con•fec•tion
con•fec•tion\er
con•fec•tion•er\y, pl.
 •er•ies
con•fed•er•a\cy, pl. •cies
con•fed•er•ate, •at\ed,
 •at•ing
con•fed•er•a•tion
con•fer, •ferred, •fer•ring
con•fer\ee
con•fer•ence, •enced,
 •enc•ing
con•fer•ment
con•fess, •fessed, •fess•ing
con•fess•ed\ly
con•fes•sion

con•fes•sion\al
con•fes•sor
con•fet\ti
con•fi•dant or •dante
con•fide, •fid\ed, •fid•ing
con•fi•dence
con•fi•dent
con•fi•den•tial
con•fi•den•ti•al•i\ty
con•fi•den•tial\ly
con•fi•dent\ly
con•fig\u•ra•tion
con•fine, •fined, •fin•ing
con•fine•ment
con•firm, •firmed,
 •firm•ing
con•fir•ma•tion
con•firmed
con•fis•cate, •cat\ed,
 •cat•ing
con•fis•ca•tion
con•fis•ca•to\ry
con•fla•gra•tion
con•flate, •flat\ed, •flat•ing
con•fla•tion
con•flict, •flict\ed, •flict•ing
con•flict of in•ter•est
con•flic•to\ry
con•flu•ence
con•flu•ent
con•form, •formed,
 •form•ing
con•form•a\ble
con•for•ma•tion
con•form\er
con•form•ism
con•form•ist
con•form•i\ty, pl. •ties
con•found, •found\ed,
 •found•ing
con•fra•ter•ni\ty, pl. •ties
con•frere
con•front, •front\ed,
 •front•ing
con•fron•ta•tion
con•fron•ta•tion\al
Con•fu•cian
Con•fu•cian•ism
Con•fu•cius
con•fuse, •fused, •fus•ing
con•fus•ed\ly

con•fus•ing\ly
con•fu•sion
con•fute, •fut\ed, •fut•ing
con\ga, •gas; •gaed, •ga•ing
con•geal, •gealed,
 •geal•ing
con•geal•ment
con•gen•ial
con•ge•ni•al•i\ty
con•gen•ial\ly
con•gen\i•tal
con•gen\i•tal\ly
con•ger
con•ge•ries
con•gest
con•gest\ed
con•ges•tion
con•ges•tive
con•glom•er•ate, •at\ed,
 •at•ing
con•glom•er•a•tion
Con\go
con•grat\u•late, •lat\ed,
 •lat•ing
con•grat\u•la•tion
con•grat\u•la•to\ry
con•gre•gate, •gat\ed,
 •gat•ing
con•gre•ga•tion
con•gre•ga•tion\al
con•gre•ga•tion•al•ism
con•gre•ga•tion•al•ist
con•gress
con•gres•sion\al
con•gress•man, pl. •men
con•gress•per•son
con•gress•wom\an, pl.
 •wom\en
con•gru•ence
con•gru•ent
con•gru•i\ty
con•gru•ous
con\ic or con\i•cal
con\i•cal\ly
co•ni•fer
co•nif•er•ous
con•jec•tur\al
con•jec•ture, •tured,
 •tur•ing
con•join, •joined,
 •join•ing

con•joint
con•ju•gal
con•ju•gate, •gat\ed,
•gat•ing
con•ju•ga•tion
con•junc•tion
con•junc•ti•va, *pl.* •vas or
•vae
con•junc•ti•vi•tis
con•jur•a•tion
con•jure, •jured, •jur•ing
con•jur\er or con•ju•ror
conk, conked, conk•ing
(to hit on the head) [vs.
conch (marine molusk)]
con•nect, •nect\ed,
•nect•ing
Con•nect\i•cut (CT)
con•nec•tion
con•nec•tive
con•nip•tion
con•niv•ance
con•nive, •nived, •niv•ing
con•niv\er
con•nois•seur
con•no•ta•tion
con•no•ta•tive
con•note, •not\ed,
•not•ing
con•nu•bi\al
con•quer, •quered,
•quer•ing
con•quer•a\ble
con•quer\or
con•quest
con•quis•ta•dor, *pl.* •dors
or •do•res
con•san•guin\e•ous or
con•san•guine
con•san•guin•i\ty
con•science
con•science•less
con•sci•en•tious (meticu-
lous)
con•sci•en•tious\ly
con•sci•en•tious•ness
con•sci•en•tious
ob•jec•tor
con•scious (aware)
con•scious\ly
con•scious•ness

con•script, •script\ed,
•script•ing
con•scrip•tion
con•se•crate, •crat\ed,
•crat•ing
con•se•cra•tion
con•sec\u•tive
con•sec\u•tive\ly
con•sen•sus
con•sent, •sent\ed,
•sent•ing
consent or•der
con•se•quence
con•se•quent
con•se•quen•tial
con•se•quent\ly
con•serv•an\cy, *pl.* •cies
con•ser•va•tion
con•ser•va•tion•ist
con•serv\a•tism
con•serv\a•tive
con•serv\a•tive\ly
con•serv\a•tor
con•serv\a•to\ry, *pl.* •ries
con•serve, •served,
•serv•ing
con•sid\er, •ered, •er•ing
con•sid•er•a\ble
con•sid•er•a\bly
con•sid•er•ate
con•sid•er•ate\ly
con•sid•er•a•tion
con•sid•er•ing
con•sign, •signed,
•sign•ing
con•sign•ee
con•sign•ment
con•sign•or
con•sist, •sist\ed, •sist•ing
con•sist•en\cy or
con•sist•ence, *pl.* •cies
con•sist•ent
con•sist•ent\ly
con•sis•to\ry, *pl.* •ries
con•so•la•tion
con•sol\a•to\ry
con•sole, •soled, •sol•ing
con•sol\i•date, •dat\ed,
•dat•ing
con•sol\i•da•tion
con•sol•ing\ly

con•som\mé
con•so•nance
con•so•nant
con•so•nan•tal
con•so•nant\ly
con•sort, •sort\ed,
•sort•ing
con•sor•ti\um, *pl.* •ti\a
con•spic\u•ous
con•spic\u•ous\ly
con•spic\u•ous•ness
con•spir•a\cy, *pl.* •cies
con•spir\a•tor or
con•spir\er
con•spir\a•to•ri\al
con•spire, •spired,
•spir•ing
con•sta•ble
con•stan\cy
con•stant
constant dol•lars
Con•stan•ti•no•ple
con•stant\ly
con•stel•la•tion
con•ster•na•tion
con•sti•pate, •pat\ed,
•pat•ing
con•sti•pa•tion
con•stit\u•en\cy, *pl.* •cies
con•stit\u•ent
con•sti•tute, •tut\ed,
•tut•ing
con•sti•tu•tion
con•sti•tu•tion•al
con•sti•tu•tion•al•i\ty
con•sti•tu•tion•al\ly
con•strain, •strained,
•strain•ing
con•straint
con•strict, •strict\ed,
•strict•ing
con•stric•tion
con•stric•tive
con•stric•tor
con•stru•a\ble
con•struct, •struct\ed,
•struct•ing
con•struc•tion
con•struc•tion•ist
con•struc•tive
con•struc•tive\ly

con•strue, •strued, •stru•ing
con•sub•stan•ti•a•tion
con•sul (*diplomat*) [vs. coun•cil (*assembly*) and coun•sel (*advice*)]
con•su•lar
con•su•late
con•sult, •sult\ed, •sult•ing
con•sult•ant
con•sul•ta•tion
con•sum•a•ble
con•sume, •sumed, •sum•ing
con•sum\er
consumer cred\it
con•sum•er•ism
con•sum\er price index (*CPI*)
con•sum•mate, •mat\ed, •mat•ing
con•sum•mate\ly
con•sum•ma•tion
con•sump•tion
con•sump•tive
con•tact, •tact\ed, •tact•ing
con•ta•gion
con•ta•gious
con•ta•gious\ly
con•ta•gious•ness
con•tain, •tained, •tain•ing
con•tain\er
con•tain•er\i•za•tion
con•tain•er•ize, •ized, •iz•ing
con•tain•er•ship
con•tain•ment
con•tam\i•nant
con•tam\i•nate, •nat\ed, •nat•ing
con•tam\i•na•tion
con•temn (*to despise*), •temned, temn•ing [vs. condemn (*to censure*)]
con•tem•plate, •plat\ed, •plat•ing
con•tem•pla•tion
con•tem•pla•tive
con•tem•po•ra•ne•ous

con•tem•po•rar\y, *pl.* •rar•ies
con•tempt•i\ble
con•tempt•i•bly
con•temp•tu•ous
con•temp•tu•ous\ly
con•tend, •tend\ed, •tend•ing
con•tend\er
con•tent
con•tent\ed
con•tent•ed\ly
con•ten•tion
con•ten•tious
con•tent•ment
con•test, •test\ed, •test•ing
con•test•a\ble
con•test•ant
con•text
con•text-•sen\si\tive
con•tex•tu\al
con•ti•gu•i\ty
con•tig\u•ous
con•ti•nence
con•ti•nent
con•ti•nen•tal
con•tin•gen\cy, *pl.* •cies
con•tin•gent
contingent li\a•bil•i\ty
con•tin\u•al (*intermittent*) [vs. con•tin\u•ous (*uninterrupted*)]
con•tin\u•al\ly
con•tin\u•ance
con•tin\u•a•tion
con•tin•ue, •ued, •u•ing
con•ti•nu•i\ty
con•tin\u•ous (*uninterrupted*) [vs. con•tin\u•al (*intermittent*)]
con•tin\u•ous\ly
con•tin\u•ous speech sys•tem
con•tin\u•um, *pl.* •tin\u\a
con•tort
con•tor•tion
con•tor•tion•ist
con•tour
con•tra, *pl.* •tras
contra ac•count

con•tra•band
con•tra•cep•tion
con•tra•cep•tive
con•tract, •tract\ed, •tract•ing
contract car•ri\er
con•trac•tile
con•trac•tion
con•trac•tor
con•trac•tu\al
con\tra•dict, •dict\ed, •dict•ing
con\tra•dic•tion
con\tra•dic•to\ry
con•trail
con\tra•in\di•cate, •cat\ed, •cat•ing
con\tra\in•di•ca•tion
con•tral\to, *pl.* •tos
con•trap•tion
con•tra•pun•tal
con•trar\i•ness
con•trar\i•wise
con•trar\y, *pl.* •trar•ies
con•trast, •trast\ed, •trast•ing
con\tra•vene, •vened, •ven•ing
con\tra•ven•tion
con•tre•temps, *pl.* •temps
con•trib•ute, •ut\ed, •ut•ing
con•tri•bu•tion
con•trib\u•tor
con•trib\u•to\ry
con•trite
con•trite\ly
con•tri•tion *or* con•trite•ness
con•triv•ance
con•trive, •trived, •triv•ing
con•trol, •trolled, •trol•ling
control char•ac•ter
con•trol•la\ble
con•trol•ler
controller board
con•tro•ver•sial
con•tro•ver\sy, *pl.* •sies
con•tro•vert, •vert\ed, •vert•ing

con•tu•ma•cious
con•tu•ma•cy
con•tu•me•li•ous
con•tu•me•ly
con•tuse, •tused, •tus•ing
con•tu•sion
co•nun•drum
con•ur•ba•tion
con•va•lesce, •lesced,
•lesc•ing
con•va•les•cence
con•va•les•cent
con•vec•tion
con•vene, •vened,
•ven•ing
con•ven•ience
convenience goods
con•ven•ient
con•ven•ient\ly
con•vent
con•ven•ti•cle
con•ven•tion
con•ven•tion•al
con•ven•tion•al•i•ty
con•ven•tion•al\ly
con•ven•tion•al mem•o\ry
con•verge, •verged,
•verg•ing
con•ver•gence
con•ver•gent
con•ver•sant
con•ver•sa•tion
con•ver•sa•tion\al
con•ver•sa•tion•al•ist
con•verse
con•verse, •versed,
•vers•ing
con•verse\ly
con•ver•sion
con•vert, •vert\ed,
•vert•ing
con•vert\er
con•vert•i\ble
convertible bond
con•vex (curved outward)
[vs. con•cave (curved
inward)]
con•vex•i\ty
con•vey, •veyed, •vey•ing
con•vey•ance
con•vey\er or con•vey\or

con•vict, •vict\ed, •vict•ing
con•vic•tion
con•vince, •vinced,
•vinc•ing
con•vinc•ing
con•vinc•ing\ly
con•viv•i\al
con•viv•i•al•i\ty
con•vo•ca•tion
con•voke, •voked,
•vok•ing
con•vo•lut\ed
con•vo•lu•tion
con•voy, •voyed, •voy•ing
con•vulse, •vulsed,
•vuls•ing
con•vul•sion
con•vul•sive
con•vul•sive\ly
coo, cooed, coo•ing
COO (chief operating
officer)
cook, cooked, cook•ing
cook•book
cook\er
cook•er\y, pl. •er•ies
cook\ie or cook\y (flat
cake), pl. cook•ies [vs.
kook\y (eccentric)]
cook•out
cool, cool\er, cool•est;
cooled, cool•ing
cool•ant
cool\er
Cool•idge
coo•lie (laborer) [vs.
cool\ly (calmly) and
cou•lee (ravine)]
cool\ing-•off law
cooling-off pe•ri\od
cool\ly (calmly)
cool•ness
coon
coon•hound
coon•skin
co-•op (cooperative
enterprise), co-•oped,
co-op\ing
coop (enclosure) [vs. coup
(daring act) and coupe
(two-door car)]

Coo•per
coop\er
co-op\er•ate or co-
•op\er•ate, •at\ed or
\at\ed, •at•ing or \at\ing
co•op\er•a•tion or
co-•op\er•a\tion
co•op\er•a•tive or
co-•op\er•a\tive
co-•opt, •opt\ed,
•opt\ing
co•or•di•nate or
co•or\di•nate, •nat\ed or
\nat\ed, •nat•ing or
\nat\ing
co•or•di•na•tion or
co-•or\di\na\tion
co•or•di•na•tor or
co-•or\di\na\tor
coot
coot\ie
cop, copped, cop•ping
cope, coped, cop•ing
Co•pen•ha•gen
Co•per•ni•can
Co•per•ni•cus
cop•i\er
co•pi•lot
cop•ing
co•pi•ous
co•pi•ous\ly
co•pi•ous•ness
Cop•land
co•pol\y•mer
cop-•out
cop•per
cop•per•head
cop•per\y
cop\ra
co•proc•es•sor
copse or cop•pice
cop•ter
cop\u\la, pl. •las or •lae
cop•u•late, •lat\ed,
•lat•ing
cop•u•la•tion
cop•u•la•tive
cop\y, pl. cop•ies; cop•ied,
cop\y•ing
cop\y•board scan•ner
cop\y•book

cop\y•cat
cop\y•ed\it or cop\y-
•ed\it, •ed•it\ed or
•ed\it\ed, •ed•it•ing or
•ed\it\ing
cop\y•ed\i•tor
cop\y pro•tec\tion
cop\y•right, •right\ed,
•right•ing
cop\y•writ\er
co•quet, •quet•ted,
•quet•ting
co•quet\ry
co•quette
co•quet•tish
cor\al (*marine skeleton*)
[*vs.* cho•ral (*of a chorus*)
and cho•rale (*hymn*) and
cor•ral (*enclosure*)]
cord (*string*) [*vs.* chord
(*musical tones*)]
cor•dial
cor•dial•i\ty
cor•dial\ly
cor•dil•le\ra
cord•less
cor•don, •doned, •don•ing
Cor•do•van
cor•du•roy
core (*center; to remove the
core of*), cored, cor•ing
[*vs.* corps (*organization*)
and corpse (*dead body*)]
co•re\spond•ent (*joint
defendant*) [*vs.*
cor•re•spond•ent
(*writer*)]
co•ri•an•der
Co•rin•thi\an
cork
cork\er
cork•screw
cor•mo•rant
corn
corn•ball
corn bread or corn•bread
corn•cob
cor•ne\a, *pl.* •ne\as
cor•ne\al
corned
cor•ner, •nered, •ner•ing

cor•ner•stone
cor•net
corn•flow\er
cor•nice
corn•meal
corn pone
corn•row
corn•starch
cor•nu•co•pi\a, *pl.* •pi\as
corn\y, corn•i\er,
corn•i•est
co•rol\la, *pl.* •las
co•rol•lar\y, *pl.* •lar•ies
co•ro\na, *pl.* •nas or •nae
cor\o•nar\y, *pl.* •nar•ies
cor\o•na•tion
cor\o•ner
cor\o•net
Corp. (*corporation*)
cor•po\ra
cor•po•ral (*of the body;
military officer*)
cor•po•rate
corporate bond
corporate raid\er
cor•po•ra•tion
cor•po•re\al (*material*)
corps (*organization*), *pl.*
corps [*vs.* core (*center*)]
corpse (*dead body*)
corps•man, *pl.* •men
cor•pu•lence
cor•pu•lent
cor•pus, *pl.* •po\ra or
•pus\es
Cor•pus Chris\ti
cor•pus•cle
cor•pus de•lic\ti, *pl.*
cor•po\ra de•lic\ti
cor•ral (*enclosure; to
corral*), •ralled, •ral•ling
[*vs.* chor\al (*of a chorus*)
and cho•rale (*hymn*) and
cor\al (*marine skeleton*)]
cor•rect, •rect\ed,
•rect•ing
cor•rec•tion
cor•rec•tion\al
cor•rec•tive
cor•rect\ly
cor•rect•ness

cor•re•late, •lat\ed,
•lat•ing
cor•re•la•tion
cor•rel\a•tive
cor•re•spond, •spond\ed,
•spond•ing
cor•re•spond•ence
cor•re•spond•ent (*writer*)
[*vs.* co•re\spond•ent
(*joint defendant*)]
correspondent bank
cor•re•spond•ing\ly
cor•ri•dor
cor•rob\o•rate, •rat\ed,
•rat•ing
cor•rob\o•ra•tion
cor•rob\o•ra•tive
cor•rob\o•ra•tor
cor•rode, •rod\ed,
•rod•ing
cor•ro•sion
cor•ro•sive
cor•ru•gate, •gat\ed,
•gat•ing
cor•ru•ga•tion
cor•rupt, •rupt\ed,
•rupt•ing
cor•rupt•i\ble
cor•rup•tion
cor•rupt\ly
cor•sage
cor•sair
cor•set, •set\ed, •set•ing
cor•tege or cor•tège
cor•tex, *pl.* •ti•ces
cor•ti•cal
cor•ti•sone
co•run•dum
cor•us•ca•tion
cor•vette
co•sign, •signed,
•sign•ing
co•sign\er
cos•met•ic
cos•met\i•cal\ly
cos•me•tol\o•gist
cos•me•tol\o•gy
cos•mic
cos•mog\o•ny, *pl.* •nies
cos\mo•log\i•cal
cos•mol\o•gy

cos\mo•naut
cos\mo•pol\i•tan
cos\mo•pol\i•tan•ism
cos•mos, pl. •mos or
•mos\es
Cos•sack
cost, cost, cost\ed,
cost•ing
cost ac•count•ing
co•star or co-•star,
•starred, •star•ring or
•star\ring
Cos\ta Ri\ca
Cos\ta Ri•can
cost-•ben\e\fit a\nal\y•sis
cost-•ef\fec•tive
cos•tive
cost•li•ness
cost\ly, •li\er, •li•est
cost of liv•ing
cost o\ver•run
cost-•plus
cost-•push
cos•tume, •tumed,
•tum•ing
cos•tum\er
co\sy, pl. •sies; •sied,
•sy•ing; •si\er, •si•est
cot
cote (coop) [vs. coat
(outer garment)]
Côte d'I\voire
co•te•rie
co•ter•mi•nous or
co•ter•mi•nal
co•til•lion
cot•tage
cottage in•dus•try
cot•ter pin
cot•ton
cot\ton•mouth, pl.
•mouths
cot\ton•seed, pl. •seeds or
•seed
cot\ton•tail
cot\y•le•don
couch, couched,
couch•ing
cou•gar, pl. •gars or •gar
cough, coughed,
cough•ing

could
cou•lee (ravine) [vs.
coo•lie (laborer) and
cool\ly (calmly)]
cou•lomb
coun•cil (assembly) [vs.
con•sul (diplomat) and
coun•sel (advice)]
coun•cil•man, pl. •men
coun•cil•per•son
coun•cil•wom\an, pl.
•wom\en
coun•ci•lor or
coun•cil•lor (member of
a council)
coun•sel (advice; to
advise), pl. •sel; •seled or
•selled, •sel•ing or
•sel•ling [vs. con•sul
(diplomat) and coun•cil
(assembly)]
coun•se•lor (adviser)
count, count\ed,
count•ing
count•down
coun•te•nance, •nanced,
•nanc•ing
coun•ter (against; long,
narrow table)
count\er (one who counts)
coun\ter•act, •act\ed,
•act•ing
coun•ter•ac•tion
coun\ter•at•tack, •tacked,
•tack•ing
coun\ter•bal•ance, •anced,
•anc•ing
coun•ter•claim, •claimed,
•claim•ing
coun•ter•clock•wise
coun•ter•cul•ture
coun•ter•es•pi•o•nage
coun•ter•feit, •feit\ed,
•feit•ing
coun•ter•feit\er
coun\ter•in•sur•gen\cy, pl.
•cies
coun\ter•in•tel•li•gence
count•er•man, pl. •men
coun\ter•mand, •mand\ed,
•mand•ing

coun\ter•meas•ure
coun\ter•of•fen•sive
coun\ter•pane
coun\ter•part
coun\ter•point
coun\ter•poise
coun\ter•pro•duc•tive
coun\ter•rev\o•lu•tion
coun\ter•rev\o•lu•tion•ar\y
coun\ter•sign, •signed,
•sign•ing
coun\ter•sink, •sank,
•sunk, •sink•ing
coun\ter•spy, pl. •spies
coun\ter•ten\or
coun\ter•vail, •vailed,
•vail•ing
count•ess
count•ing house
count•less
coun•tri•fied
coun•try, pl. •tries
coun\try-•and-•west\ern
coun•try•man, pl. •men
coun\try•side
coun•try•wom\an, pl.
•wom\en
coun\ty, pl. •ties
coup (daring act), pl.
coups [vs. co-\op
(cooperative enterprise)
and coop (enclosure)
and coupe (two-door
car)]
coup de grâce, pl. coups
de grâce
coup d'é\tat, pl. coups
d'é\tat
coupe (two-door car)
cou\pé
cou•ple, •pled, •pling
cou•plet
cou•pling
cou•pon
coupon bond
cou•pon•ing
coupon rate
cour•age
cou•ra•geous
cou•ra•geous\ly
cour•i\er

course (*class; route; to course*), coursed, cours•ing [*vs.* coarse (*rough*)]
course•ware
court, court\ed, court•ing
cour•te•ous
cour•te•ous\ly
cour•te•san
cour•te\sy (*politeness*) [*vs.* curt\sy (*bow*)]
court•house, *pl.* •hous\es
cour•ti\er
court•li•ness
court\ly, •li\er, •li•est
court-•mar\tial, *pl.* courts-•mar\tial *or* court-•mar\tials; •tialed *or* •tialled, •tial\ing *or* •tial\ling
court•room
court•ship
court•yard
cous•cous
cous\in
cou•ture
cou•tu•ri\er *or* •tu•ri•ère
cove
cov\en
cov\e\nant
Cov•en•try
cov\er, •ered, •er•ing
cov•er•age
cov\er•all
cov\er•let
co•vert
co•vert\ly
cov\er-•up
cov\et, •et\ed, •et•ing
cov•et•ous
cov•et•ous•ness
cov\ey, *pl.* •eys
cow, cowed, cow•ing
cow•ard (*one who lacks courage*) [*vs.* cow•ered (*crouched*)]
cow•ard•ice
cow•ard•li•ness
cow•ard\ly
cow•bird
cow•boy *or* •girl

cow\er
cow•ered (*crouched*), •ered, •er•ing [*vs.* cow•ard (*one who lacks courage*)]
cow•hand
cow•hide
cowl
cow•lick
cowl•ing
co•work\er
cow•poke
cow•pox
cow•punch\er
cow•slip
cox•comb
cox•swain
coy, \er, •est
coy\ly
coy•ness
coy•o\te, *pl.* •tes *or* \te
co•zi\ly
co•zi•ness
co\zy, *pl.* •zies; •zied, •zy•ing; •zi\er, •zi•est
CPA *or* C.P.A. (*certified public accountant*)
CPI (*consumer price index*)
CPU (*central processing unit*)
CR (*carriage return*)
crab, crabbed, crab•bing
crab•bed
crab\by
crack, cracked, crack•ing
crack•down
cracked
crack\er
crack•er•jack
crack\le, •led, •ling
crack•pot
crack\up
cra•dle, •dled, •dling
craft, *pl.* crafts *or* craft; craft\ed, craft•ing
crafts•man, *pl.* •men
crafts•man•ship
crafts•wom\an, *pl.* crafts•wom\en
crafts•wom•an•ship
craft un•ion

craft\y, •i\er, •i•est
crag
crag\gy, •gi\er, •gi•est
cram, crammed, cram•ming
cramp
cramped
cran•ber\ry, *pl.* •ries
crane, craned, cran•ing
cra•ni\al
cra•ni\um, *pl.* •ni•ums *or* •ni\a
crank, cranked, crank•ing
crank•case
crank\i•ness
crank•shaft
crank\y, •i\er, •i•est
cran\ny, *pl.* •nies
crap, crapped, crap•ping
crape
crap\py, •pi\er, •pi•est
craps
crap•shoot\er
crash, crashed, crash•ing
crash-•land, crash-•land, •land\ed, •land\ing
crass
crass\ly
crass•ness
crate, crat\ed, crat•ing
Cra•ter
cra•ter (*depression*)
crat\er (*one who crates*)
cra•vat
crave, craved, crav•ing
cra•ven
cra•ven\ly
crav•ing
craw
craw•fish, *pl.* •fish *or* •fish\es
crawl, crawled, crawl•ing
crawl\er
crawl•space *or* crawl space
cray•fish *or* craw•fish, *pl.* •fish *or* •fish\es
cray\on
craze
crazed

cra•zi\ly

cra•zi•ness

cra\zy, pl. •zies; •zi\er, •zi•est

creak (to squeak), creaked, creak•ing [vs. creek (stream)]

creak\ly, •i\er, •i•est

cream, creamed, cream•ing

cream\er

cream•er\ly, pl. •er•ies

cream\i•ness

cream\ly, •i\er, •i•est

crease, creased, creas•ing

crease•less

cre•ate, •at\ed, •at•ing

cre•a•tion

cre•a•tion•ism

cre•a•tion•ist

cre•a•tive

cre•a•tive\ly

cre•a•tiv•i\ty

cre•a•tor

crea•ture

crèche

cre•dence

cre•den•tial

cre•den\za, pl. •zas

cred•i•bil•i\ty

cred•i•ble (trust-worthy)

cred•i•bly

cred\it, •it\ed, •it•ing

cred•it•a\ble (praiseworthy)

cred•it•a•bly

cred\it card

cred\i•tor

cred\it rat•ing

credit un•ion

cred•it•wor•thy

cre\do, pl. •dos

cre•du•li\ty

cred\u•lous

cred\u•lous\ly

Cree, pl. Crees or Cree

creed

creek (stream) [vs. creak (to squeak)]

Creek, pl. Creeks or Creek

creel

creep, crept or creeped, creep•ing

creep\er

creep•i\ly

creep\i•ness

creep\ly, •i\er, •i•est

cre•mate, •mat\ed, •mat•ing

cre•ma•tion

cre•ma•to\ry or cre•ma•to•ri\um, pl. •ries or •ri•ums

crème de menthe

cren•el•a•tion

Cre•ole

cre•o•sote

crepe

crept

cre•pus•cu•lar

cre•scen\do, pl. •dos or \di; •doed

cres•cent

cress

crest, crest\ed, crest•ing

crest•fall\en

Cre•ta•ceous

Cre•tan (of Crete)

Crete

cre•tin (deformed person)

cre•tin•ism

cre•tonne

cre•vasse

crev•ice

crew

crews (groups) [vs. cruise (to sail) and cruse (earthen container)]

crew\el (yarn) [vs. cru\el (causing pain)]

crew•el•work

crew•man, pl. crew•men

crib, cribbed, crib•bing

crib•bage

crick

crick\et

crick•et\er

cried

cri\er

crime

Cri•me\a

Cri•me\an

crim\i•nal

crim\i•nal•i\ty

crim\i•nal\ly

crim\i•nol\o•gist

crim\i•nol\o\gy

crimp, crimped, crimp•ing

crim•son

cringe, cringed, cring•ing

crin•kle, •kled, •kling

crin•kly, •kli\er, •kli•est

crin\o•line

crip•ple, •pled, •pling

cri•sis, pl. •ses

crisp, crisped, crisp•ng; crisp\er, crisp•est

crisp\ly

crisp•ness

crisp\ly, •i\er, •i•est

criss•cross, •crossed, •cross•ing

cri•te•ri\on, pl. •te•ri\a or •te•ri•ons

crit\ic (one who evaluates) [vs. cri•tique (review)]

crit\i•cal

crit\i•cal\ly

crit\i•cal path

crit\i•cism

crit\i•cize, •cized, •ciz•ing

crit\i•ciz\er

cri•tique (review), •tiqued, •ti•quing [vs. crit\ic (one who evaluates)]

crit•ter

croak, croaked, croak•ing

Cro•a•tia

cro•chet (needlework), •cheted, •chet•ing [vs. crotch\et (whim)]

crock

crocked

crock•er\y

Crock•pot (™)

croc\o•dile

cro•cus, pl. •cus\es

crois•sant, pl. •sants

Crom•well

crone

cro\ny, pl. •nies

crook

crooked (did bend)

crook\ed (*not straight*)
crook•ed\ly
crook•ed•ness
crook•neck
croon, crooned, croon•ing
croon\er
crop, cropped, crop•ping
crop-•dust, •dust\ed,
 •dust\ing
crop-•dust\er
crop•land
crop•per
cro•quet (*the game*)
cro•quette (*ball of minced food*)
cross, crossed, cross•ing;
 cross\er, cross•est
cross•bar
cross•beam
cross•bones
cross•bow
cross•breed, •bred,
 •breed•ing
cross-•coun\try
cross-cut, •cut, •cut•ting
cross-•e\las\tic\l\ty
cross-•ex\am\i\na\tion
cross-•ex\am•ine, \ined,
 \in\ing
cross-•eye
cross-•eyed
cross fire *or* cross•fire
cross•hatch, •hatched,
 •hatch•ing
cross•ing
cross\ly
cross•o\ver
cross•piece
cross-•pol\li\nate,
 •pol\li\nat\ed,
 •pol\li\nat\ing
cross-•pol\li\na\tion
cross•road
cross•ruff
crossruff pro•mo•tion
cross-•sec\tion\al
cross•town
cross•walk
cross•wise *or* cross•ways
cross•word puz•zle
crotch

crotch\et (*whim*) [vs.
 cro•chet (*needlework*)]
crotch•et\y
crouch, crouched,
 crouch•ing
croup
crou•pi\er
croup\y, croup•i\er,
 croup•i•est
crou•ton
crow, crowed (*did crow*)
 or crew, crowed, crow•ing
crow•bar
crowd (*large group*)
crowd\ed
crow•foot, *pl.* •foots *or*
 •feet
crown, crowned,
 crown•ing
crow's-•foot, *pl.* •feet
crow's-•nest *or* crow's
 nest
CRT (*cathode-ray tube*)
cru•cial
cru•cial\ly
cru•ci•ble
cru•ci•fix
cru•ci•fix•ion
cru•ci•form
cru•ci•fy, •fied, •fy•ing
crude, crud\er, crud•est
crude\ly
crude•ness
cru•di•tés (*raw vegetables*)
crud•i\ty (*crudeness*)
cru•el (*causing pain*), \er,
 •est [*vs.* crew\el (*yarn*)]
cru•el\ly
cru•el\ty
cru•et
cruise (*to sail*), cruised,
 cruis•ing [vs. crews
 (*groups*) *and* cruse
 (*earthen container*)]
cruis\er
crul•ler
crumb
crum•ble, •bled, •bling
crum•bly, •bli\er, •bli•est
crumb\y, •i\er, •i•est
crum\my, •mi\er, •mi•est

crum•pet
crum•ple, •pled, •pling
crunch, crunched,
 crunch•ing
crunch\y, •i\er, •i•est
crup•per
cru•sade, •sad\ed, •sad•ing
cru•sad\er
cruse (*earthen container*)
 [*vs.* crews (*groups*) *and*
 cruise (*to sail*)]
crush, crushed, crush•ing
crush\er
crust, crust\ed, crust•ing
crus•ta•cean
crust\y, •i\er, •i•est
crutch
crux, *pl.* crux\es *or*
 cru•ces
cry, *pl.* cries; cried, cry•ing
cry•ba\by, *pl.* •bies
cry\o•gen\ic
cry\o•gen•ics
cry\o•sur•ger\y
crypt
cryp•tic
cryp•ti•cal\ly
cryp\to•gram
cryp•tog•ra•pher
cryp•tog•ra•phy
crys•tal
crys•tal•line
crys•tal•li•za•tion
crys•tal•lize, •lized, •liz•ing
crys•tal•log•ra•phy
C-\sec\tion
CT (*Connecticut*)
cub
Cu\ba
Cu•ban
cub\by•hole
cube, cubed, cub•ing
cu•bic
cu•bi•cle
cub•ism
cub•ist
cu•bit
cub scout
cuck•old
cuck\oo, *pl.* •oos; •ooed,
 •oo•ing

cu•cum•ber
cud
cud•dle, •dled, •dling
cud•dle•some
cud•dly, •dli\er, •dli•est
cudg\el, •eled or •elled, •el•ing or •el•ling
cue (signal), cued, cu•ing [vs. queue (line; sequence)]
cuff, cuffed, cuff•ing
cuff link or cuff•link
Cui•si•nart (™)
cui•sine
cul•de•sac, pl. culs•de•sac
cu•li•nar\y
cull, culled, cull•ing
cul•mi•nate, •nat\ed, •nat•ing
cul•mi•na•tion
cu•lottes or cu•lotte
cul•pa•bil•i\ty
cul•pa•ble
cul•pa•bly
cul•prit
cult
cult•ist
cul•ti•va\ble or cul•ti•vat\a•ble
cul•ti•vate, •vat\ed, •vat•ing
cul•ti•va•tion
cul•tur\al
cul•tur•al\ly
cul•ture, •tured, •tur•ing
cul•vert
cum•ber•some
cum div\i•dend
cum\in
cum•mer•bund
cu•mu•la•tive
cu•mu•la•tive\ly
cu•mu•lus, pl. \li
cu•ne•i•form
cun•ning
cun•ning\ly
cup, cupped, cup•ping
cup•board
cup•cake

cup•ful, pl. •fuls
Cu•pid
cu•pid•i\ty
cu•po\la, pl. •las
cur
cur•a\ble
cu•ra\re
cu•rate
cur\a•tive
cu•ra•tor
curb, curbed, curb•ing
curd (cheese) [vs. Kurd (member of Asian people)]
cur•dle, •dled, •dling
cure, cured, cur•ing
cu\ré, pl. •rés
cure-•all
cu•ret•tage
cu•rette, •ret•ted, •ret•ting
cur•few
cu•ri\a, pl. cu•ri\ae
cu•rie
cu•ri\o, pl. •ri\os
cu•ri•os•i\ty, pl. •ties
cu•ri•ous
cu•ri•ous\ly
cu•ri\um
curl, curled, curl•ing
curl\er
cur•lew
curl\i•cue
curl\y, •i\er, •i•est
cur•mudg•eon
cur•rant (the fruit)
cur•ren\cy, pl. •cies
currency ex•change
cur•rent (present; flow)
cur•rent\ly
cur•rent val\ue
cur•ric\u•lar
cur•ric\u•lum, pl. \la or •lums
cur\ry, pl. •ries; •ried, •ry•ing
cur•ry•comb
curse, cursed (did curse), curs•ing
curs\ed (deserving a curse)
cur•sive
cur•sor

cursor con•trol mode
cur•so•ri\ly
cur•so\ry
curt, \er, •est
cur•tail, •tailed, •tail•ing
cur•tail•ment
cur•tain
cur•tained
curt\ly
curt•ness
curt\sy (bow), pl. •sies; •sied, •sy•ing [vs. cour•te\sy (politeness)]
cur•va•ceous
cur•va•ture
curve, curved, curv•ing
curv\y, •i\er, •i•est
cush•ion, •ioned, •ion•ing
cush\y, •i\er, •i•est
cusp
cus•pid
cus•pi•dor
cuss, cussed, cuss •ing
cus•tard
Cus•ter
cus•to•di\an
cus•to\dy
cus•tom
cus•tom•ar•i\ly
cus•tom•ar\y
cus•tom-•built
cus•tom•er
customer serv•ice
cus•tom•er's man
cus\tom•house, pl. •hous\es
cus•tom•i•za•tion
cus•tom•ize, •ized, •iz•ing
cus\tom-•made
cus•toms un•ion
cut, cut, cut•ting
cut-•and-•dried
cu•ta•ne•ous
cut•a\way
cut•back
cute, cut\er, •cut•est
cute•ness
cute\sy
cu•ti•cle

cut\ie
cut•lass
cut•ler\y
cut•let
cut•off
cutoff test
cut•out
cut-•rate
cut-•sheet feed\er
cut•ter
cut•throat
cut•ting
cut•ting\ly
cut•tle•fish, *pl.* •fish or •fish\es
CVP (*cost-volume-profit analysis*)
cy•a•nide
cy\ber•na•tion
cy\ber•net•ics
cy\ber•punk
cy\ber•space

cy•cla•men
cy•cle, •cled, •cling
cycle bill•ing
cy•clic\al or cy•clic
cyclical un•em•ploy•ment
cy•cli•cal\ly
cy•clist or cy•cler
cy•clom\e•ter
cy•clone
cy•clon\ic
Cy•clops
cy•clo•spo•rine or cy•clo•spo•rin
cy•clo•tron
cyg•net (*young swan*) [vs. sig•net (*small seal*)]
cyl•in•der
cy•lin•dri•cal
cym•bal (*percussion instrument*) [vs. sym•bol (*sign*)]
cym•bal•ist
cyn\ic

cyn\i•cal
cyn\i•cal\ly
cyn\i•cism
cy•no•sure
cy•pher
cy•press (*the tree*)
Cyp•ri\ot
Cy•prus (*the country*)
cyst
cys•tic fi•bro•sis
cy•tol\o\gy
cy•to•plasm
cy•to•sine
czar or tsar
cza•ri\na or tsa•ri\na, *pl.* •nas
Czech (*the people and language*) [vs. check (*order for money; to verify*)]
Czech\o•slo•va•ki\a
Czech\o•slo•va•ki\an
Czech Repub•lic

D

dab, dabbed, dab•bing
dab•ble, •bled, •bling
dab•bler
Dac\ca
da•cha
dachs•hund
Da•cron (™)
dac•tyl
dad
da\da
da\da•ism
da\da•ist
dad\dy, *pl.* •dies
dad\dy-•long\legs or dad\dy long•legs, *pl.* •long\legs or •long•legs
da\do, *pl.* •does, •dos
dae•mon
dae•mon\ic
daf•fi•ness
daf•fo•dil
daf\fy, •fi\er, •fi•est
daft
dag•ger
da•guerre•o•type
dah\lia, *pl.* •ias
Da•ho•man or Da•ho•me\an

Da•ho•mey
dai\ly, *pl.* •lies
dain•ties
dain•ti\ly
dain•ti•ness
dain\ty, •ti\er, •ti•est
dai•qui\ri, *pl.* •ris
dair\y (*milk farm*), *pl.* dair•ies [vs. di•a\ry (*journal*)]
dair\y•ing
dair\y•maid
dair\y•man or •wom\an, *pl.* •men or •wom\en
da\is
dai\sy, *pl.* •sies
dai\sy-•wheel print\er
Da•kar
Da•ko\ta, *pl.* •tas, \ta
Da•ko•tan
dale
Da\li
Da•li•esque
Dal•las
dal•li•ance
dal\ly, •lied, •ly•ing
Dal•ma•tian

dam (*obstruct*), dammed, dam•ming [vs. damn (*to condemn*)]
dam•age, •aged, •ag•ing
dam•age con•trol (*noun*)
dam\age-•con\trol (*adj.*)
Da•mas•cus
dam•ask
dame
damn (*to condemn*), damned, damn•ing [vs. dam (*to obstruct*)]
dam•na•ble
dam•na•bly
dam•na•tion
damned, damned•est or damnd•est
Dam\o•cles
damp, damp\er, damp•est
damp-•dry, •dried, •dry\ing
damp\en, •ened, •en•ing
damp•en\er
damp\er
damp•ness
dam•sel
dam•sel•fly, *pl.* •flies

dam•son

dance, danced, danc•ing

danc\er

danc•er•cise

D and C (*dilation and curetage, uterine surgery*)

dan•de•li\on

dan•der

dan•druff

dan•dy, *pl.* •dies; •di•est

dan•dy•ish

Dane

dan•ger

dan•ger•ous

dan•ger•ous\ly

dan•gle, •gled, •gling

Dan•iel

Dan•ish

dank

dank\ly

dan•seur

dan•seuse, *pl.* •seuses

Dan\te

Dan•ube

Dan\u•bi\an

dap•per

dap•pled

Dar•da•nelles

dare, dared, dar•ing, dares or dare

dare•dev\il

dare•dev•il\ry or dare•dev•il•try

dar•ing

dar•ing\ly

dark, dark\er, dark•est

dark\en, •ened, •en•ing

dark\ly

dark•ness

dark•room

dar•ling

darn, darned, darn•ing

darned

dart, dart\ed, dart•ing

dart•ing\ly

Dar•von (™)

Dar•win

Dar•win•ism

dash, dashed, dash•ing

dash•board

da•shi\ki, *pl.* •kis

dash•ing

dash•ing\ly

das•tard\ly

DAT (*digital audiotape*)

da\ta

data bank or da\ta•bank

da\ta•base or da\ta base

da\ta•base man•age•ment sys•tem (*DBMS*)

database serv\er

da\ta bus

data com•pres•sion

data proc•ess•ing

data proc•es•sor

data type

date, dat\ed, dat•ing

dat•ed•ness

date•line

date•lined

date rape

da•tive

da•tum, *pl.* da\ta, da•tums

daub, daubed, daub•ing

daub\er

daugh•ter

daugh•ter•board

daugh•ter-•in-•law, *pl.* daugh•ters-•in-•law

daunt, \ed, •ing

daunt•ing\ly

daunt•less

daunt•less\ly

daunt•less•ness

dau•phin

dav•en•port

Da•vid

da Vin\ci

Da•vis

dav\it

daw•dle, •dled, •dling

daw•dler

dawn, dawned, dawn•ing

day

day•bed

day•break

day care (*noun*)

day-•care (*adj.*)

day•dream, •dreamed, •dream•ing

day•dream\er

Day-•Glo (™)

day•light

day\light-•sav\ing time or day•light sav•ing time (*DST*)

day•time

day-•to-•day

Day•ton

Day•to\na Beach

daze

dazed

daz•ed\ly

daz•zle, •zled, •zling

daz•zler

d/b/a (*doing business as*)

DBMS (*database management system*)

DC or D.C. (*District of Columbia*)

D-\day or D-\Day

DDT (*insecticide*)

DE (*Delaware*)

dea•con

de•ac•ti•vate, •vat\ed, •vat•ing

de•ac•ti•va•tion

dead, \er, •est

dead•beat

dead•bolt

dead\en, •ened, •en•ing

dead end (*noun*)

dead-•end (*adj.*)

dead•line

dead•li•ness

dead•lock, •locked, •lock•ing

dead\ly, •li\er, •li•est

dead•pan, •panned, •pan•ning

dead•wood

deaf, \er, •est

deaf\en, •ened, •en•ing

deaf-•mute

deaf•ness

deal, dealt, deal•ing

deal\er

deal•er•ship

deal\er tie-•in

dean

dear (*beloved*), \er, •est [vs. deer (*animal*)]

dear\ly

dear•ness
dearth
death
death•bed
death ben\e•fit
death•blow
death•less
death•like
death\ly
death•trap
deb
de•ba•cle
de•bar, •barred, •bar•ring
de•bark, •barked, •bark•ing
de•bar•ka•tion
de•bar•ment
de•base, •based, •bas•ing
de•base•ment
de•bat•a\ble
de•bate, •bat\ed, •bat•ing
de•bat\er
de•bauch, •bauched,
•bauch•ing
deb•au•chee
de•bauch•er\y
de•ben•ture
de•bil\i•tate, •tat\ed, •tat•ing
de•bil\i•ta•tion
de•bil•i\ty
deb\it (*bookkeeping entry*)
[vs. debt (*obligation*)]
deb\it, •it\ed, •it•ing
deb\it bal•ance
deb\it card
deb\o•nair
de•brief, •briefed,
•brief•ing
de•bris or dé•bris
debt (*obligation*) [vs. deb\it
(*bookkeeping entry*)]
debt-•eq\ui\ty
deb•tor
de•bug, •bugged, •bug•ging
de•bug•ger
de•bunk, •bunked,
•bunk•ing
De•bus\sy
de•but or dé•but, •buted,
•but•ing
deb\u•tante or
déb\u•tante

dec•ade
dec\a•dence
de•caf•fein•at\ed
de•cal
Dec\a•logue or Dec\a•log
de•camp, •camped,
•camp•ing
de•cant, •cant\ed,
•cant•ing
de•cant\er
de•cap\i•tal•ize
de•cap\i•tate, •tat\ed,
•tat•ing
de•cap\i•ta•tion
de•cath•lon
de•cay, •cayed, •cay•ing
de•cease, •ceased,
•ceas•ing
de•ceased (*dead*) [vs.
dis•eased (*sick*)]
de•ce•dent
de•ceit
de•ceit•ful
de•ceit•ful\ly
de•ceit•ful•ness
de•ceive, •ceived,
•ceiv•ing
de•ceiv\er
de•ceiv•ing\ly
de•cel•er•ate, •at\ed,
•at•ing
de•cel•er•a•tion
de•cel•er\a•tor
De•cem•ber
de•cen\cy, *pl.* •cies
de•cen•ni•al
de•cen•ni•al\ly
de•cent (*proper*) [vs.
de•scent (*downward
movement*) and dis•sent
(*disagreement*)]
de•cent\ly
de•cen•tral\i•za•tion
de•cen•tral•ize, •ized,
•iz•ing
de•cep•tion
de•cep•tive
de•cer•ti•fi•ca•tion
dec\i•bel
de•cide, •cid\ed, •cid•ing
de•cid•ed\ly

de•cid\u•ous
dec\i•mal
dec\i•mate, •mat\ed,
•mat•ing
dec\i•ma•tion
de•ci•pher, •phered,
•pher•ing
de•ci•pher•a\ble
de•ci•sion
de•ci•sion mak•ing (*noun*)
decision-•mak\ing (*adj.*)
de•ci•sive
de•ci•sive\ly
de•ci•sive•ness
deck, decked, deck•ing
de•claim, •claimed,
•claim•ing
dec•la•ma•tion
de•clam\a•to\ry
de•clar•a\ble
de•clar\a•tive
de•clare, •clared, •clar•ing
de•clas•si•fy, •fied, •fy•ing
dec•len•sion
dec•li•na•tion
de•cline, •clined, •clin•ing
de•clin•ing bal•ance
de•cliv•i\ty, *pl.* •ties
de•code, •cod\ed,
•cod•ing
dé•col•le•tage or
de•col•le•tage
dé•col•le•té or
de•col•le•te
de•col\o•ni•za•tion
de•col\o•nize, •nized,
•niz•ing
de•com•mis•sion, •sioned,
•sion•ing
de•com•pose, •posed,
•pos•ing
de•com•po•si•tion
de•com•press, •pressed,
•press•ing
de•com•pres•sion
de•con•ges•tant
de•con•struct, •struct\ed,
•struct•ing
de•con•struc•tion
de•con•tam\i•nate,
•nat\ed, •nat•ing

de•con•tam\i•na•tion
dé•cor or de•cor
dec\o•rate, •rat\ed, •rat•ing
dec\o•ra•tion
dec\o•ra•tive
dec\o•ra•tor
dec\o•rous
dec\o•rous\ly
de•co•rum
de•cou•page or dé•cou•page
de•coy, •coyed, •coy•ing
de•crease, •creased, •creas•ing
de•cree (law) [vs. de•gree (step; academic title)]
de•cree, •creed, •cree•ing
de•crep\it
de•crep\i•tude
de•cre•scen\do, pl. •dos, \di
de•crim\i•nal•ize, •ized, •iz•ing
de•cry, •cried, •cry•ing
de•cryp•tion
ded\i•cate, •cat\ed, •cat•ing
dedicated serv\er
de•duce, •duced, •duc•ing
de•duc•i\ble
de•duct, •duct\ed, •duct•ing
de•duct•i\ble
de•duc•tion
de•duc•tive
deed, deed\ed, deed•ing
deed of trust
dee•jay
deem, deemed, deem•ing
de–•em\pha\sis
de–•em\pha•size, \sized, \siz\ing
deep, deep\er, deep•est
deep e\col\o\gy
deep\en, •ened, •en•ing
deep freeze (noun)
deep–•freeze (verb), •freezed or •froze, •freezed or •fro\zen, •freez\ing

deep–•fry, •fried, •fry\ing
deep\ly
deep•ness
deep pock•ets
deep–•root\ed
deep–•sea
deep–•seat\ed
deep six (noun)
deep–•six (verb), •sixed, •six\ing
deep space (noun)
deep–•space (adj.)
deer (animal), pl. deer, deers [vs. dear (beloved)]
de–•es\ca\late or de–•es\ca•late, •lat\ed, \lat•ing or •lat•ing
de–•es\ca\la\tion
de•face, •faced, •fac•ing
de•face•ment
de fac\to
de•fal•ca•tion
def\a•ma•tion
de•fam\a•to\ry
de•fame, •famed, •fam•ing
de•fault, •fault\ed, •fault•ing
de•fault•er
def\e•cate, •cat\ed, •cat•ing
def\e•ca•tion
de•fect, •fect\ed, •fect•ing
de•fec•tion
de•fec•tive
de•fend, •fend\ed, •fend•ing
de•fend•ant
de•fend•er
de•fense
de•fense•less
de•fen•si\ble
de•fen•sive
de•fer (to postpone), •ferred, •fer•ring [vs. dif•fer (to disagree)]
def•er•ence (respect) [vs. dif•fer•ence (unlikeness)]

def•er•en•tial
de•fer•ment
de•ferred an•nu•i\ty
deferred com•pen•sa•tion
de•fi•ance
de•fi•ant
de•fi•ant\ly
de•fi•cien\cy
de•fi•cient
def\i•cit
def\i•cit spend•ing
de•file, •filed, •fil•ing
de•file•ment
de•fine, •fined, •fin•ing
de•fin\er
def\i•nite (precise) [vs. de•fin\i•tive (final)]
def\i•nite\ly
def\i•nite•ness
def\i•ni•tion
de•fin\i•tive (final) [vs. def\i•nite (precise)]
de•flate, •flat\ed, •flat•ing
de•fla•tion
de•fla•tion•ar\y
de•flect, •flect\ed, •flect•ing
de•flec•tion
de•flec•tor
De•foe
de•fog, •fogged, •fog•ging
de•fog•ger
de•fo•li•ant
de•fo•li•ate, •at\ed, •at•ing
de•fo•li•a•tion
de•for•est, •est\ed, •est•ing
de•for•est•a•tion
de•form, •formed, •form•ing
de•for•ma•tion
de•formed
de•form•i\ty, pl. •ties
de•frag•ment
de•frag•men•ta•tion
de•fraud, •fraud\ed, •fraud•ing
de•fray, •frayed, •fray•ing
de•frost, •frost\ed, •frost•ing
de•frost•er

deft, \er, •est

deft\ly

de•funct

de•fuse (to make harmless), •fused, •fus•ing [vs. dif•fuse (widely spread)]

de\fy, pl. •fies; •fied, •fy•ing

De•gas

de•gas, •gassed, •gas•sing

de Gaulle

de•gen•er•a•cy

de•gen•er•ate, •at\ed, •at•ing

de•gen•er•a•tion

de•gen•er\a•tive

de•grade, •grad\ed, •grad•ing

de•gree (step; academic title) [vs. de•cree (law)]

de•hire

de•hu•man\i•za•tion

de•hu•man•ize, •ized, •iz•ing

de•hu•mid\i•fi•er

de•hu•mid\i\fy, •fied, •fy•ing

de•hy•drate, •drat\ed, •drat•ing

de•hy•dra•tion

de•hy•dra•tor

de•hy•dro•gen•ate, •at\ed, •at•ing

de•ice or de-•ice, •iced, •ic\ing

de-•ic\er or de•ic\er

de•i•fi•ca•tion

de•i\fy, •fied, •fy•ing

deign, deigned, deign•ing

de•ism

de•i\ty, pl. •ties

dé\jà vu

de•ject\ed

de•jec•tion

Del\a•ware, pl. •wares, •ware (DE)

Del\a•war•e\an

de•lay, •layed, •lay•ing

de•lec•ta\ble

de•lec•ta•tion

del\e•gate, •gat\ed, •gat•ing

del\e•ga•tion

de•lete, •let\ed, •let•ing

del\e•te•ri•ous

de•le•tion

delft (pottery)

Delft (the city)

Del\hi

del\i, pl. del\is

de•lib•er•ate, •at\ed, •at•ing

de•lib•er•ate\ly

de•lib•er•a•tion

del\i•ca•cy, pl. •cies

del\i•cate

del\i•cate\ly

del\i•cate•ness

del\i•ca•tes•sen

de•li•cious

de•li•cious\ly

de•li•cious•ness

de•light, •light\ed, •light•ing

de•light\ed

de•light•ful

de•light•ful\ly

de•lim•it, •it\ed, •it•ing

de•lim\i•ta•tion

de•lim\i•ta•tive

de•lim•it\er

de•lin\e•ate, \at\ed, \at•ing

de•lin•e•a•tion

de•lin•quen\cy

de•lin•quent

del\i•quesce, •quesced, •quesc•ing

del\i•ques•cent

de•lir\i•ous

de•lir\i•ous\ly

de•lir\i•ous•ness

de•lir•i\um, pl. •lir•i•ums, •lir\i\a

de•list, •list\ed, •list•ing

de•liv•er, •ered, •er•ing

de•liv•er•ance

de•liv•ered cost

de•liv•er\y, pl. •er•ies

dell

Del•phi

del•phin•i\um, pl. •i•ums, \i\a

del\ta, pl. •tas

del•toid

delts, pl.

de•lude, •lud\ed, •lud•ing

de•luge, •uged, •ug•ing

de•lu•sion

de•lu•sive

de•luxe or de luxe

delve, delved, delv•ing

delv\er

de•mag•net\i•za•tion

de•mag•net•ize, •ized, •iz•ing

dem\a•gogue

dem\a•gogu•er\y

dem\a•go\gy

de•mand, •mand\ed, •mand•ing

demand curve

demand de•pos\it

de•mand•ing\ly

de•mand loan

demand note

de\mand-•pull

de\mand-•side

de•mar•cate, •cat\ed, •cat•ing

de•mar•ca•tion

de•mean, •meaned, •mean•ing

de•mean\or

de•ment\ed

de•men•tia

de•mer\it

de•mesne

De•me•ter

dem\i•god

dem\i•john

de•mil\i•ta•rize, •rized, •riz•ing

dem\i•mon•daine

dem\i•monde

de•mise, •mised, •mis•ing

dem\i•tasse

dem\o, pl. dem\os

de•mo•bi•li•za•tion

de•mo•bi•lize, •lized, •liz•ing

de•moc•ra\cy, pl. •cies

dem\o•crat

dem\o•crat\ic

dem\o•crat\i•cal\ly

Dem\o•crat\ic Par\ty

de•moc•ra•ti•za•tion

de•moc•ra•tize, •tized,
•tiz•ing

de•mod\u•late, •lat\ed,
•lat•ing

de•mod\u•la•tion

de•mod\u•la•tor

dem\o•graph\ic

dem\o•graph\ics, pl.

de•mol•ish, •ished,
•ish•ing

dem\o•li•tion

de•mon

de•mon\e•tize, •tized,
•tiz•ing

de•mo•ni\ac or
de•mo•ni•a•cal

de•mo•ni•a•cal•ly

de•mon\ic

de•mon\stra\ble

de•mon\stra•bly

dem•on\strate, •strat\ed,
•strat•ing

dem•on\stra•tion

de•mon\stra•tive

de•mor•al\i•za•tion

de•mor•al•ize, •ized,
•iz•ing

dem\os (demonstrations)

de•mos (populace)

De•mos•the•nes

de•mote, •mot\ed,
•mot•ing

de•mo•tion

de•mur (to object),
•murred, •mur•ring

de•mure (modest),
•mur\er, •mur•est

de•mure\ly

de•mur•rage

de•mur•rer

den

de•na•tured

den•drite

Deng Xiao•ping

de•ni•a•bil•i\ty

de•ni•a•ble

de•ni\al

de•nier (weight unit)

de•ni•er (one who denies)

den\i•grate, •grat\ed,
•grat•ing

den\i•gra•tion

den\im

den\i•zen

Den•mark

de•nom\i•nate, •nat\ed,
•nat•ing

de•nom\i•na•tion

de•nom\i•na•tion\al

de•nom\i•na•tor

de•no•ta•tion

de•note, •not\ed, •not•ing

de•noue•ment or
dé•noue•ment

de•nounce, •nounced,
•nounc•ing

dense, dens\er, dens•est

dense\ly

dense•ness

den•si\ty, pl. •ties

dent, dent\ed, dent•ing

den•tal

dental floss

den•ti•frice

den•tin or den•tine

den•tist

den•tist\ry

den•ture

de•nu•cle•ar•ized

de•nude, •nud\ed,
•nud•ing

de•nun•ci•a•tion

Den•ver

de\ny, •nied, •ny•ing

de•o•dor•ant

de•o•dor•ize, ized, •iz•ing

de•o•dor•iz•er

de•ox\y•ri•bo•nu•cle\ic
ac\id

de•part, •part\ed,
•part•ing

de•part•ment

de•part•men•tal

de•part•men•tal\i•za•tion

de•part•men•tal•ize,
•ized, •iz•ing

de•part•ment store

de•par•ture

de•pend, •pend\ed,
•pend•ing

de•pend•a•bil•i\ty

de•pend•a•ble

de•pend•ence

de•pend•en\cy, pl. •cies

de•pend•ent

dependent de•mand

de•per•son•al•ize, •ized,
•iz•ing

de•pict, •pict\ed, •pict•ing

de•pic•tion

de•pil\a•to\ry, pl. •ries

de•plane, •planed,
•plan•ing

de•plete, •plet\ed,
•plet•ing

de•ple•tion

depletion al•low•ance

de•plor•a•ble

de•plore, •plored,
•plor•ing

de•ploy, •ployed,
•ploy•ing

de•ploy•ment

de•po•lar\i•za•tion

de•po•lar•ize, •ized,
•iz•ing

de•po•lit\i•cize, •cized,
•ciz•ing

de•po•nent

de•pop\u•late, •lat\ed,
•lat•ing

de•pop\u•la•tion

de•port, •port\ed,
•port•ing

de•por•ta•tion

de•port•ment

de•pose, •posed, •pos•ing

de•pos\it, •it\ed, •it•ing

dep\o•si•tion (testimony)
[vs. dis•po•si•tion
(temperament)]

de•pos\i•tor

de•pos\i•to\ry, pl. •ries

de•pot

de•praved (corrupt) [vs.
de•prived (lacking
necessities)]

de•prav•i\ty

dep•re•cate (*to belittle*), •cat\ed, •cat•ing [*vs.* de•pre•ci•ate (*to lessen in value*)]

dep•re•ca•tion

dep•re•ca•to\ry

de•pre•ci•a\ble

de•pre•ci•ate (*to lessen in value*), •at\ed, •at•ing [*vs.* dep•re•cate (*to belittle*)]

de•pre•ci•a•tion

dep•re•da•tion

de•press, •pressed, •press•ing

de•pres•sant

de•pressed

de•pres•sion

de•press•ive

dep•ri•va•tion

de•prive, •prived, •priv•ing

de•prived (*lacking necessities*) [*vs.* de•praved (*corrupt*)]

de•pro•gram, •grammed *or* •gramed, •gram•ming *or* •gram•ing

de•pro•gram\er *or* de•pro•gram•mer

dept. (*department*)

depth

dep\u•ta•tion

de•pute, •put\ed, •put•ing

dep\u•tize, •tized, •tiz•ing

dep\u•ty, *pl.* •ties

de•rail, •railed, •rail•ing

de•rail•leur

de•rail•ment

de•range, •ranged, •rang•ing

de•range•ment

der\by, *pl.* •bies

de•reg\u•late, •lat\ed, •lat•ing

de•reg\u•la•tion

der\e•lict

der\e•lic•tion

de•ride, •rid\ed, •rid•ing

de•ri•sion

de•ri•sive

de•ri•sive\ly

der\i•va•tion

de•riv\a•tive

de•rive, •rived, •riv•ing

derived de•mand

der•ma•ti•tis

der•ma•to•log\i•cal

der•ma•tol\o•gist

der•ma•tol\o•gy

der•mis

der\o•gate, •gat\ed, •gat•ing

der\o•ga•tion

de•rog\a•to\ry

der•rick

der•ri•ère *or* der•ri•ere

der•rin•ger

der•vish

DES (*diethylstilbestrol*)

de•sal\i•nate, •nat\ed, •nat•ing

de•sal\i•na•tion

des•cant *or* dis•cant, •cant\ed, •cant•ing

Des•cartes

de•scend, •scend\ed, •scend•ing

de•scend•ant (*offspring*)

de•scend•ent (*falling*)

de•scend\er (*part of lowercase letter*)

de•scent (*downward movement*) [*vs.* de•cent (*proper*) *and* dis•sent (*disagreement*)]

de•scribe, •scribed, •scrib•ing

de•scrip•tion

de•scrip•tive

de•scry, •scried, •scry•ing

des\e•crate, •crat\ed, •crat•ing

des\e•cra•tion

de•seg•re•gate, •gat\ed, •gat•ing

de•seg•re•ga•tion

de•sen•si•ti•za•tion

de•sen•si•tize, •tized, •tiz•ing

des•ert (*dry place*)

de•sert (*to run away*), •sert\ed, •sert•ing [*vs.* des•sert (*sweet food*)]

de•sert\er

de•serve, •served, •serv•ing

de•serv•ed\ly

des•ic•cate, •cat\ed, •cat•ing

des•ic•ca•tion

de•sid•er•a•tum, *pl.* \ta

de•sign, •signed, •sign•ing

des•ig•nate, •nat\ed, •nat•ing

des•ig•na•tion

de•sign\er

de•sign•ing

de•sir•a•bil•i\ty

de•sir•a\ble

de•sir•a•bly

de•sire, •sired, •sir•ing

de•sir•ous

de•sist, •sist\ed, •sist•ing

desk

desk•top

desktop com•put\er

desktop con•fig\u•ra•tion

desktop pub•lish\er

desktop pub•lish•ing (*DTP*)

Des Moines

des\o•late (*forlorn*) [*vs.* dis•so•lute (*immoral*)]

des\o•lat\ed

des\o•late\ly

des\o•la•tion

de•spair, •spaired, •spair•ing

des•patch, •patched, •patch•ing

des•per\a\do, *pl.* •does, •dos

des•per•ate (*hopeless*) [*vs.* dis•pa•rate (*different*)]

des•per•ate\ly

des•per•a•tion

de•spi•ca\ble

de•spise, •spised, •spis•ing

de•spite

de•spoil, •spoiled, •spoil•ing

de•spond•en\cy *or* de•spond•ence

de•spond•ent

des•pot

des•pot\ic
des•pot\i•cal\ly
des•pot•ism
des•sert (*sweet food*) [vs. de•sert (*to run away*)]
des•ti•na•tion
destination di•rec•to\ry
des•tine, •tined, •tin•ing
des•ti\ny, pl. •nies
des•ti•tute
des•ti•tut\ed
des•ti•tu•tion
de•stroy, •stroyed, •stroy•ing
de•stroy\er
de•struct, •struct\ed, •struct•ing
de•struc•tion
de•struc•tive
de•struc•tive\ly
de•struc•tive•ness
des•ue•tude
des•ul•to\ry
de•tach, •tached, •tach•ing
de•tach•a\ble
de•tached
de•tach•ment
de•tail, •tailed, •tail•ing
de•tain, •tained, •tain•ing
de•tect, •tect\ed, •tect•ing
de•tect•a\ble or de•tect•i\ble
de•tec•tion
de•tec•tive
de•tec•tor
dé•tente or de•tente
de•ten•tion
de•ter, •terred, •ter•ring
de•ter•gent
de•te•ri•o•rate, •rat\ed, •rat•ing
de•te•ri•o•ra•tion
de•ter•mi•na\ble
de•ter•mi•nant
de•ter•mi•nate
de•ter•mi•na•tion
de•ter•mine, •mined, •min•ing
de•ter•rence
de•ter•rent
de•test, •test\ed, •test•ing

de•test•a\ble
de•tes•ta•tion
de•throne, •throned, •thron•ing
det\o•nate, •nat\ed, •nat•ing
det\o•na•tion
det\o•na•tor
de•tour, •toured, •tour•ing
de•tox, •toxed, •tox•ing
de•tox\i•fi•ca•tion
de•tox\i\fy, •fied, •fy•ing
de•tract (*to take away*), •tract\ed, •tract•ing [vs. dis•tract (*to divert*)]
de•trac•tion
de•trac•tor
det\ri•ment
det•ri•men•tal
de•tri•tus
De•troit
deuce
deu•te•ri\um
Deut•sche mark
de•val•u•a•tion
de•val•ue, •val•ued, •val\u•ing
dev•as•tate, •tat\ed, •tat•ing
dev•as•ta•tion
de•vel•op, •oped, •op•ing
de•vel•op\er
de•vel•op•ment
de•vi•ance
de•vi•ant
de•vi•ate, •at\ed, •at•ing
de•vi•a•tion
de•vi•a•tor
de•vice (*contrivance*) [vs. de•vise (*to work out*)]
de•vice-•de•pend\ent
de•vice driv\er
dev\il, •iled or •illed, •il•ing or •il•ling
dev•il•ish
dev\il•may-•care
dev•il•ment
dev•il•try, pl. •tries
de•vi•ous
de•vi•ous•ness

de•vise (*to work out*), •vised, •vis•ing [vs. de•vice (*contrivance*)]
de•vi•see
de•vi•sor
de•vi•tal•ize, •ized, •iz•ing
de•void
de•volve, •volved, •volv•ing
de•vote, •vot\ed, •vot•ing
de•vot•ed\ly
dev\o•tee
de•vo•tion
de•vo•tion\al
de•vour, •voured, •vour•ing
de•vout, •er, •est
de•vout\ly
dew (*moisture*) [vs. do (*to act*) and due (*owed*)]
dew•drop
dew•lap
dew\y, •i\er, •i•est
dex•ter•i\ty
dex•ter•ous
dex•trose
Dha\ka or Dac\ca
dho\ti, pl. •tis
di\a•be•tes
di\a•bet\ic
di\a•bol\ic or di\a•bol\i•cal
di\a•bol\i•cal\ly
di\a•crit\ic
di•a•dem
di•ag•nose, •nosed, •nos•ing, •nos\es
di•ag•no•sis, pl. •ses
di•ag•nos•tic
di•ag•nos•ti•cian
di•ag\o•nal
di•ag\o•nal\ly
di\a•gram, •gramed or •grammed, •gram•ing or •gram•ming
di\al, di•aled or di•alled, di•al•ing or di•al•ling
di\a•lect
di\a•lec•tal (*of a dialect*)
di\a•lec•tic (*logical debate*)
di\a•lec•ti•cal
di\a•logue or di\a•log

dialogue box
di•al\y•sis, pl. •ses
di•am\e•ter
di\a•met•ri•cal or
  di\a•met•ric
di\a•met•ri•cal\ly
dia•mond
dia•mond•back
Di•an\a
di•a•pa•son
dia•per, •percd, •per•ing
di•aph\a•nous
di\a•phragm
di\a•phrag•mat•ic
di•a•rist
di•ar•rhe\a or
  di•ar•rhoe\a
di•a\ry (journal), pl. •ries
  [vs. dair\y (milk farm)]
Di•as•po\ra
di•as•to\le
di•as•tol\ic
di•a•tom
di•a•ton\ic
di•a•tribe
di•az\e•pam
dice, sing. die; diced,
  dic•ing
di•chot\o\my, pl. •mies
dick
Dick•ens
dick\er, •ered, •er•ing
Dick•in•son
di•cot\y•le•don
di•cot\y•le•don•ous
Dic•ta•phone (™)
dic•tate, •tat\ed, •tat•ing
dic•ta•tion
dic•ta•tor
dic•ta•to•ri\al
dic•ta•tor•ship
dic•tion
dic•tion•ar\y, pl. •ar•ies
dic•tum, pl. \ta, •tums
did
di•dac•tic
did•dle, •dled, •dling
di\do, pl. •dos, •does
die (cube), pl. dice
die (device for forming or
  cutting material), pl. dies

die (to cease living), died,
  dy•ing [vs. dye (to color)]
die-•hard or die\hard
di•e•lec•tric
di•er\e•sis or di•aer\e•sis,
  pl. •ses
di•e\ret\ic (of a dieresis)
  [vs. di-•u\ret\ic (increasing urine volume)]
die•sel
di\et, •et\ed, •et•ing
di•e\tar\y
di•et\er
di•e\tet\ic
di•eth\yl•stil•bes •trol
  (DES)
di•e•ti•tian or di•e•ti•cian
dif•fer (to disagree),
  •fered, •fer•ing [vs.
  de•fer (to postpone)]
dif•fer•ence (unlikeness)
  [vs. def•er•ence
  (respect)]
dif•fer•ent
dif•fer•en•tial
differential cost
dif•fer•en•ti•ate, •at\ed,
  •at•ing
dif•fer•en•ti•a•tion
dif•fer•ent\ly
dif•fi•cult
dif•fi•cul\ty, pl. •ties
dif•fi•dence
dif•fi•dent
dif•frac•tion
dif•fuse, •fused, •fus•ing
dif•fuse (widely spread)
  [vs. de•fuse (to make
  harmless)]
dif•fuse\ly
dif•fuse•ness
dif•fu•sion
dig, dug, dig•ging
di•gest, •gest\ed, •gest•ing
di•gest•i•ble
di•ges•tion
di•ges•tive
dig•ger
dig\it
dig•it\al
digital au\di•o•tape (DAT)

digital com•put\er
dig\i•tal\is
dig•it•al\ly
dig•it\al mon\i•tor
dig\i•tize, •tized, •tiz•ing
dig\i•tiz\er
dlg\i•tiz•ing tab•let
dig•ni•fied
dig•ni•fy, •fied, •fy•ing
dig•ni•tar\y, pl. •tar•ies
dig•ni\ty, pl. •ties
di•graph
di•gress, •gressed,
  •gress•ing
di•gres•sion
dike
di•lap\i•dat\ed
di•lap\i•da•tion
di•late, •lat\ed, •lat•ing
di•la•tion
dil\a•to\ry
di•lem\ma, pl. •mas
dil•et•tante, pl. •tantes or
  •tan\ti
dil•et•tant•ism
dil\i•gence
dil\i•gent
dil\i•gent\ly
dill
dil\ly, pl. •lies
dil\ly•dal\ly, •lied, •ly•ing
di•lute, •lut\ed, •lut•ing
di•lu•tion
dim, dimmed, dim•ming;
  dim•mer, dim•mest
dime
di•men•sion
di•men•sion\al
di•min•ish, •ished, •ish•ing
di•min•u•en\do, pl. •does
dim\i•nu•tion
di•min\u•tive
dim\i\ty
dim\ly
dim•mer
dim•ness
dim•ple, •pled, •pling
dim sum
dim•wit
dim•wit•ted
din, dinned, din•ning

di•nar
dine, dined, din•ing
din\er (*person eating*) [*vs.* din•ner (*meal*)]
di•nette
ding, dinged, ding•ing
ding-•a-•ling
din•ghy (*boat*), pl. •ghies [*vs.* din\gy (*dull*)]
din\gi•ness
din\go, pl. •goes
din\gy (*dull*), •gi\er, •gi\est [*vs.* din•ghy (*boat*)]
dink\y
din•ner (*meal*) [*vs.* din\er (*person eating*)]
din•ner•ware
di•no•saur
dint
di•oc\e•san
di•o•cese
di•ode
Di•og\e•nes
Di•o•ny•sus or Di•o•ny•sos
di•o•ram\a, pl. •ram\as
di•ox\in
dip, dipped, dip•ping
diph•the•ri\a
diph•thong
dip•loid
di•plo\ma, pl. •mas
di•plo•ma\cy
dip•lo•mat
dip•lo•mat\ic
dip•lo•mat\i•cal\ly
di•pole
dip•per
dip\py, •pi\er, •pi•est
dip•so•ma•ni\a
dip•so•ma•ni\ac
dip•stick
DIP switch (*dual in-line package switch*)
dip•tych
dire
di•rect, •rect\ed, •rect•ing
di\rect-•con\nect mo\dem
di•rect cost
direct cost•ing

direct de•pos\it
di•rec•tion
di•rec•tion\al
di•rec•tive
di•rect\ly
di•rect mail
direct mar•ket•ing
direct mem\o\ry ac•cess (*DMA*)
di•rect•ness
di•rec•tor
di•rec•to•rate
di•rec•tor•ship
di•rec•to\ry, pl. •ries
di•rect tax
dirge
dir\i•gi\ble
dirk
dirn\dl
dirt
dirt-•cheap
dirt\i•ness
dirt\y, dirt•ied, dirt\y•ing; dirt•i\er, dirt•i•est
dis•a•bil•i\ty, pl. •ties
disability ben\e•fit
disability in•sur•ance
dis•a•ble, \bled, \bling
dis•ad•van•tage
dis•ad•van•taged
dis•ad•van•ta•geous
dis•af•fect\ed
dis•af•fec•tion
dis•af•fil\i•ate, •at\ed, •at•ing
dis•af•fil\i•a•tion
dis•a\gree, \greed, \gree•ing
dis•a•gree•a\ble
dis•a•gree•a•bly
dis•a•gree•ment
dis•al•low, •lowed, •low•ing
dis•ap•pear, •peared, •pear•ing
dis•ap•pear•ance
dis•ap•point, •point\ed, •point•ing
dis•ap•point•ment

dis•ap•pro•ba•tion
dis•ap•prov\al
dis•ap•prove (*to condemn*), •proved, •prov•ing [*vs.* dis•prove (*to refute*)]
dis•ap•prov•ing\ly
dis•arm, •armed, •arm•ing
dis•ar•ma•ment
dis•arm•ing
dis•arm•ing\ly
dis•ar•range, •ranged, •rang•ing
dis•ar•range•ment
dis•ar•ray
dis•as•sem•ble (*to take apart*), •bled, •bling [*vs.* dis•sem•ble (*to disguise*)]
dis•as•so•ci•ate, •at\ed, •at•ing
dis•as•ter
dis•as•trous
dis•a•vow, \vowed, \vow•ing
dis•a\vow\al
dis•band, •band\ed, •band•ing
dis•bar, •barred, •bar•ring
dis•bar•ment
dis•be•lief
dis•be•lieve, •lieved, •liev•ing
dis•burse (*to pay out*), •bursed, •burs•ing [*vs.* dis•perse (*to scatter*)]
dis•burse•ment
disc or disk
dis•card, •card\ed, •card•ing
dis•cern, •cerned, •cern•ing
dis•cern•a\ble or dis•cern•i\ble
dis•cern•ment
dis•charge, •charged, •charg•ing
dis•ci•ple
dis•ci•pli•nar\i\an
dis•ci•pli•nar\y
dis•ci•pline, •plined, •plin•ing

dis•claim, •claimed,
•claim•ing
dis•claim\er
dis•close, •closed,
•clos•ing
dis•clo•sure
disclosure a\gree•ment
dis•co, pl. •cos; •coed,
•co•ing
dis•col•or, •ored, •or•ing
dis•col•or•a•tion
dis•com•fit (to frustrate),
•fit\ed, •fit•ing
dis•com•fort (uneasiness)
dis•com•mode, •mod\ed,
•mod•ing
dis•com•pose, •posed,
•pos•ing
dis•com•po•sure
dis•con•cert, •cert\ed,
•cert•ing
dis•con•nect, •nect\ed,
•nect•ing
dis•con•nec•tion
dis•con•so•late
dis•con•so•late\ly
dis•con•tent, •tent\ed,
•tent•ing
dis•con•tent•ed
dis•con•tin\u•ance
dis•con•tin\u•a•tion
dis•con•tin•ue, •tin•ued,
•tin\u•ing
dis•con•ti•nu•i\ty, pl. •ties
dis•cord
dis•cord•ant
dis•co•theque or
dis•co•thèque
dis•count, •count\ed,
•count•ing
dis•coun•te•nance,
•nanced, •nanc•ing
dis•count house
discount store
dis•cour•age, •aged,
•ag•ing
dis•cour•age•ment
dis•cour•ag•ing\ly
dis•course, •coursed,
•cours•ing
dis•cour•te•ous

dis•cour•te\sy, pl. •sies
dis•cov\er, •ered, •er•ing
dis•cov•er\er
dis•cov•er\y, pl. •er•ies
dis•cred\it, •it\ed, •it•ing
dis•cred•it•a\ble
dis•creet (prudent) [vs.
dis•crete (separate)]
dis•creet\ly
dis•crep•an\cy, pl. •cies
dis•crep•ant
dis•crete (separate) [vs.
dis•creet (prudent)]
discrete speech sys•tem
dis•cre•tion
dis•cre•tion•ar\y
discretionary ac•count
dis•crim\i•nate, •nat\ed,
•nat•ing
dis•crim\i•nat•ing
dis•crim\i•na•tion
dis•crim\i•na•tor\y
dis•cur•sive
dis•cus, pl. dis•cus\es
dis•cuss, •cussed, •cuss•ing
dis•cus•sant
dis•cus•sion
dis•dain, •dained, •dain•ing
dis•dain•ful
dis•ease
dis•eased (sick) [vs.
de•ceased (dead)]
dis•em•bark, •barked,
•bark•ing
dis•em•bar•ka•tion
dis•em•bod\i•ment
dis•em•bod•ied
dis•em•bow•el, •eled or
•elled, •el•ing or •el•ling
dis•en•chant, •chant\ed,
•chant•ing
dis•en•chant•ment
dis•en•cum•ber, •bered,
•ber•ing
dis•en•gage, •gaged,
•gag•ing
dis•en•gage•ment
dis•en•tan•gle, •gled, •gling
dis•es•tab•lish, •lished,
•lish•ing
dis•es•tab•lish•ment

dis•fa•vor, •vored, •vor•ing
dis•fig•ure, •ured, •ur•ing
dis•fig•ure•ment
dis•fran•chise or
dis•en•fran•chise,
•chised, •chis•ing
dis•fran•chise•ment
dis•gorge, •gorged,
•gorg•ing
dis•grace, •graced,
•grac•ing
dis•grace•ful
dis•grace•ful\ly
dis•grun•tled
dis•guise, •guised,
•guis•ing
dis•gust
dis•gust\ed
dis•gust•ing
dish, dished, dish•ing
dis•ha•bille or des•ha•bille
dis•har•mo•ny, pl. •nies
dish•cloth
dis•heart•en, •ened,
•en•ing
di•shev•eled or
di•shev•elled
di•shev•el•ment
dis•hon•est
dis•hon•est\ly
dis•hon•es\ty
dis•hon•or, •ored, •or•ing
dis•hon•or•a\ble
dish•pan
dish•rag
dish•tow\el
dish•wash\er
dis•il•lu•sion, sioned,
•sion•ing
dis•il•lu•sion•ment
dis•in•clined
dis•in•fect, •fect\ed,
•fect•ing
dis•in•fect•ant
dis•in•flate, •flat\ed,
•flat•ing
dis•in•fla•tion
dis•in•gen\u•ous
dis•in•her\it, •it\ed, •it•ing
dis•in•te•grate, •grat\ed,
•grat•ing

dis•in•te•gra•tion

dis•in•ter, •terred,
•ter•ring

dis•in•ter•est\ed

dis•in•vest•ment

dis•joint\ed

disk

disk cache

disk crash

disk drive

disk•ette

disk jock\ey (*D.J.*)

disk op•er•at•ing sys•tem
(*DOS*)

disk op•ti•miz\er

disk pack

dis•like, •liked, •lik•ing

dis•lo•cate, •cat\ed,
•cat•ing

dis•lo•ca•tion

dis•lodge, •lodged,
•lodg•ing

dis•loy\al

dis•loy•al\ty

dis•mal

dis•mal\ly

dis•man•tle, •tled, •tling

dis•may, •mayed, •may•ing

dis•mem•ber, •bered,
•ber•ing

dis•mem•ber•ment

dis•miss, •missed,
•miss•ing

dis•miss\al

dis•mount, •mount\ed,
•mount•ing

dis•o•be•di•ence

dis•o•be•di•ent

dis•o•bey, \beyed, \bey•ing

dis•o•blige, \bliged,
\blig•ing

dis•or•der, •dered,
•der•ing

dis•or•der•li•ness

dis•or•der\ly

dis•or•gan\i•za•tion

dis•or•gan•ize, •ized,
•iz•ing

dis•o•ri•ent, •ent\ed,
•ent•ing

dis•o•ri•en•ta•tion

dis•own, •owned,
•own•ing

dis•par•age, •aged, •ag•ing

dis•par•age•ment

dis•par•ag•ing

dis•pa•rate (*different*) [vs.
des•per•ate (*hopeless*)]

dis•par•i\ty

dis•pas•sion•ate

dis•pas•sion•ate\ly

dis•patch, •patched,
•patch•ing

dis•patch\er

dis•pel, •pelled, •pel•ling

dis•pen•sa\ble

dis•pen•sa\ry, *pl.* •ries

dis•pen•sa•tion

dis•pense, •pensed,
•pens•ing

dis•pens\er

dis•per•sal

dis•perse (*to scatter*),
•persed, •pers•ing [vs.
dis•burse (*to pay out*)]

dis•per•sion

dis•pir•it\ed

dis•pir•it•ing

dis•place, •placed,
•plac•ing

dis•place•ment

dis•play, •played, •play•ing

display ad

dis•please, •pleased,
•pleas•ing

dis•pleas•ure

dis•port, •port\ed,
•port•ing

dis•pos•a•bil•i\ty

dis•pos•a\ble

disposable in•come

dis•pos\al

dis•pose, •posed, •pos•ing

dis•po•si•tion (*tempera-
ment*) [vs. dep\o•si•tion
(*testimony*)]

dis•pos•sess, •sessed,
•sess•ing

dis•pro•por•tion

dis•pro•por•tion•ate

dis•pro•por•tioned

dis•prov•a\ble

dis•prove (*to refute*),
•proved, •prov•ing [vs.
dis•ap•prove (*to con-
demn*)]

dis•put•a\ble

dis•pu•tant

dis•pu•ta•tion

dis•pu•ta•tious or
dis•put\a•tive

dis•pu•ta•tious\ly

dis•pute, •put\ed, •put•ing

dis•qual\i•fi•ca•tion

dis•qual\i\fy, •fied, •fy•ing

dis•qui\et, •et\ed, •et•ing

dis•qui•si•tion

dis•re•gard, •gard\ed,
•gard•ing

dis•re•pair

dis•rep\u•ta\ble

dis•re•pute

dis•re•spect, •spect\ed,
•spect•ing

dis•re•spect•ful

dis•robe, •robed, •rob•ing

dis•rupt, •rupt\ed,
•rupt•ing

dis•rup•tion

dis•rup•tive

dis•sat•is•fac•tion

dis•sat•is•fied

dis•sect, •sect\ed,
•sect•ing

dis•sec•tion

dis•sem•ble (*to disguise*),
•bled, •bling [vs.
dis•as•sem•ble (*to take
apart*)]

dis•sem•bler

dis•sem\i•nate, •nat\ed,
•nat•ing

dis•sem\i•na•tion

dis•sen•sion

dis•sent (*disagreement*)
[vs. de•cent (*proper*) and
de•scent (*downward
movement*)]

dis•sent, •sent\ed,
•sent•ing

dis•sent\er

dis•ser•ta•tion

dis•serv•ice

dis•si•dence
dis•si•dent
dis•sim\i•lar
dis•sim\u•late, •lat\ed, •lat•ing
dis•sim\u•la•tion
dis•si•pate, •pat\ed, •pat•ing
dis•si•pa•tion
dis•so•ci•ate, •at\ed, •at•ing
dis•so•ci•a•tion
dis•so•lute (*immoral*) [vs. des\o•late (*forlorn*)]
dis•so•lute•ness
dis•so•lu•tion
dis•solve, •solved, •solv•ing
dis•so•nance
dis•so•nant
dis•suade, •suad\ed, •suad•ing
dis•taff
dis•tal
dis•tance, •tanced, •tanc•ing
dis•tant
dis•tant\ly
dis•taste
dis•taste•ful
dis•tem•per
dis•tend, •tend\ed, •tend•ing
dis•ten•tion
dis•till, •tilled, •till•ing
dis•til•late
dis•til•la•tion
dis•till\er
dis•till\er\y, pl. •er•ies
dis•tinct
dis•tinc•tion
dis•tinc•tive
dis•tinc•tive\ly
dis•tinc•tive•ness
dis•tinct\ly
dis•tin•guish, •guished, •guish•ing
dis•tin•guish•a•ble
dis•tin•guished
dis•tort, •tort\ed, •tort•ing

dis•tor•tion
dis•tract (*to divert*), •tract\ed, •tract•ing [vs. de•tract (*to take away*)]
dis•trac•tion
dis•trait
dis•traught
dis•tress, •tressed, •tress•ing
distress sale
dis•trib•ute, •ut\ed, •ut•ing
distributed da\ta•base
distributed proc•ess•ing
dis•tri•bu•tion
distribution ex•pense
dis•trib\u•tor
dis•trict
Dis•trict of Colum•bia (*D.C.*)
dis•trust, •trust\ed, •trust•ing
dis•trust•ful
dis•turb, •turbed, •turb•ing
dis•turb•ance
dis•u\nite, •nit\ed, •nit•ing
dis•u•ni\ty
dis•use
ditch, ditched, ditch•ing
dith\er, •ered, •er•ing
dit\to, pl. •tos; •toed, •to•ing
dit\ty, pl. •ties
ditz
di•u\ret\ic (*increasing urine volume*) [vs. di•e\ret\ic (*of a dieresis*)]
di•ur•nal
di•ur•nal\ly
di\va, pl. •vas
di•va•lent
di•van
dive, dived or dove, dived, div•ing, dives (*plunges*)
div\er
di•verge, •verged, •verg•ing
di•ver\gence
di•ver\gent
di•vers (*several*)

di•verse (*unlike*)
di•verse\ly
di•ver\si•fi•ca•tion
di•ver\si•fy, •fied, •fy•ing
di•ver\sion
di•ver\sion•ar\y
di•ver\si\ty
di•vert, •vert\ed, •vert•ing
di•ver\tic•u•li•tis
Di•ves (*rich man*)
di•vest, •vest\ed, •vest•ing
di•vest\i•ture
di•vid•a\ble
di•vide, •vid\ed, •vid•ing
div\i•dend
div\id\er
div\i•na•tion
di•vine, •vined, •vin•ing; •vin\er, •vin•est
di•vine\ly
di•vin\er
di•vin•i\ty, pl. •ties
di•vis•i•bil•i\ty
di•vis•i\ble
di•vi•sion
di•vi•sion\al
di•vi•sive
di•vi•sive\ly
di•vi•sive•ness
di•vi•sor
di•vorce (*dissolution of marriage*), •vorced, •vorc•ing
di•vor•cé (*divorced man*)
di•vor•cée or di•vor•cee (*divorced woman*)
div\ot
di•vulge, •vulged, •vulg•ing
div\vy, •vied, •vy•ing, •vies
Dix\ie
Dix\ie•land
diz•zi\ly
diz•zi•ness
diz\zy, •zi\er, •zi•est
diz•zy•ing
D.J. (*disk jockey*)
djel•la•bah or djel•la\ba, pl. •bahs or •bas
Dji•bou\ti
DMA (*direct memory access*)

DNA (carrier of genes)
Dnie•per or Dne\pr
do (musical tone), pl. dos [vs. doe (deer) and dough (bread mixture)]
do (party), pl. dos, do's
do (to act), did, done, do•ing, does [vs. dew (moisture) and due (owed)]
do•a\ble
Do•ber•man pin•scher
doc
do•cent
doc•ile
do•cil•i\ty
dock, docked, dock•ing
dock\et, •et\ed, •et•ing
dock•yard
doc•tor, •tored, •tor•ing
doc•tor\al
doc•tor•ate
doc•tri•naire
doc•tri•nal
doc•trine
doc\u•dra\ma
doc\u•ment, •ment\ed, •ment•ing
doc\u•men•ta\ry, pl. •ries
doc\u•men•ta•tion
dod•der•ing
dodge, dodged, dodg•ing
Dodg\ers
do\do, pl. •dos, •does
doe (deer), pl. does, doe [vs. do (musical tone) and dough (bread mixture)]
do\er
does
doe•skin
does\n't
doff, doffed, doff•ing
dog, dogged (did dog), dog•ging
dog•catch\er
dog•eared
dog•fight
dog•fish, pl. •fish or •fish\es
dog•ged (stubborn)
dog•ged\ly

dog•ger\el
dog•gone, •gon•est
dog•goned
dog\gy or dog•gie (small dog), pl. •gies
dog\gy bag
dog•house, pl. •hous\es
do•gie or dog•gey (motherless calf), pl. •gies or •geys
dog•leg
dog\ma, pl. •mas
dog•mat\ic or dog•mat\i•cal
dog•mat\i•cal\ly
dog•ma•tism
do-•good\er
dog-•tired
dog•trot, •trot•ted, •trot•ting
dog•wood
doi\ly, pl. •lies
do•ing
do-•it-•your\self
do-•it-•your\self•er
Dol\by (™)
dol•drums, pl.
dole, doled, dol•ing
dole•ful
dole•ful\ly
doll
dol•lar
dol\lar-•a-•year man
dol•lar day
dol•lop
dol\ly, pl. dol•lies; dol•lied, dol\ly •ing
do•lor•ous
do•lor•ous\ly
dol•phin
dolt
dolt•ish
do•main
dome
do•mes•tic
do•mes•ti•cal\ly
do•mes•ti•cate, •cat\ed, •cat•ing
do•mes•ti•ca•tion
do•mes•tic
cor•po•ra•tion

do•mes•tic•i\ty
dom\i•cile
dom\i•nance
dom\i•nant
dom\i•nate, •nat\ed, •nat•ing
dom\i•na•tion
dom\i•neer
dom\i•neer•ing
Dom\i•ni\ca
Do•min\i•can Re•pub\lic
do•min•ion
dom\i•no, pl. •noes
don, donned, don•ning
do\na, pl. •nas
do\ña, pl. •ñas
do•nate, •nat\ed, •nat•ing
do•na•tion
done (finished) [vs. dun (to demand payment)]
don•key, pl. •keys
Donne
don\ny•brook
do•nor
Don Quix\o\te
don't
do•nut
doo•dad
doo•dle, •dled, •dling
doom, doomed, doom•ing
dooms•day
door
door•bell
door•man, pl. •men
door•mat
door•step
door•way
door•yard
dope, doped, dop•ing
dope\y or dop\y, dop•i\er, dop•i•est
Dor•ic
dorm
dor•man\cy
dor•mant
dor•mer
dor•mi•to\ry, pl. •ries
dor•mouse, pl. •mice
dor•sal
Dort•mund
do\ry, pl. •ries

DOS (*disk operating system*)
dos•age
dos *and* don'ts
dose, dosed, dos•ing
do•sim\e•ter
dos•si\er
dost
Dos•to•ev•sky *or* Dos•to•yev•sky
dot, dot•ted, dot•ting
dot•age
dote, dot\ed, dot•ing
doth
dot•ing
dot•ing\ly
dot-•ma\trix print\er
dot pitch
dot prompt
dot\ty, •ti\er, •ti•est
Dou\ay Bi•ble
dou•ble, •bled, •bling
dou\ble-•bar\reled
dou\ble-•blind
dou\ble-•breast\ed
dou\ble-•click
dou\ble-•cross, •crossed, •cross\ing
dou\ble-•cross\er
dou•ble date (*noun*)
dou\ble-•date (*verb*), •dat\ed, •dat\ing
dou\ble-•deal\ing
dou\ble-•deck\er
dou\ble-•den\si\ty
dou\ble-•dip\ping
dou•ble en•ten•dre, *pl.* dou•ble en•ten•dres
dou\ble-•en\try
dou•ble•head\er
dou•ble in•dem•ni\ty
dou\ble-•joint\ed
dou•ble knit (*noun*)
dou\ble-•knit (*adj.*)
dou•ble- •pre\ci\sion
dou\ble-•reed
dou\ble-•sid\ed
dou\ble-•space, •spaced, •spac\ing
dou•blet
dou\ble-•talk

dou•ble tax•a•tion
dou•bloon
dou•bly
doubt, doubt\ed, doubt•ing
doubt\er
doubt•ful
doubt•ful\ly
doubt•less
doubt•less\ly
douche, douched, douch•ing
dough (*bread mixture*) [*vs.* do (*musical tone*) *and* doe (*deer*)]
dough•nut *or* do•nut
dough\ty, •ti\er, •ti•est
Doug•las fir
dour
dour•ness
douse *or* dowse, doused *or* dowsed, dous•ing *or* dows•ing
dove
Do•ver
dove•tail, •tailed, •tail•ing
dow\a\ger
dow•di•ness
dow\dy, *pl.* •di\er, •di•est
dow\el
dow•eled *or* dow•elled
dow\er, •ered, •er•ing
Dow Jones
down
down, downed, down•ing
down-•and-•dirt\y
down•beat
down•cast
down\er
down•fall
down•grade, •grad\ed, •grad•ing
down•heart\ed
down•hill
down-•home
down•load
down•load•a\ble
down•mar•ket
down pay•ment
down•pour

down•right
down•scale, •scaled, •scal•ing
Down's syn•drome
down•stage
down•stairs
down•state
down•stream
down•swing
down•tick
down-•to-•earth
down•town
down•trod•den
down•turn
down•ward
down\ward-•com\pat\i\ble
down•wind
down\y, •i\er, •i•est
dow\ry, *pl.* •ries
dowse, dowsed, dows•ing
dox•ol\o\gy, *pl.* •gies
doy\en, *pl.* doy•ens
Doyle
doze, dozed, doz•ing
doz\en, *pl.* doz•ens, doz\en
dpi (*dots per inch*)
Dr. (*doctor*), *pl.* Drs.
drab, drab•ber, drab•best
drab•ness
drach\ma, *pl.* •mas, •mae
draft (*plan*) [*vs.* draught (*drink*) *and* drought (*dry period*)]
draft, draft\ed, draft•ing
draft\ee
draft\i•ness
draft mode
drafts•man, *pl.* •men
drafts•man•ship
draft\y, draft•i\er, draft•i•est
drag, dragged, drag•ging
drag\gy, •gi\er, •gi•est
drag•net
drag\o•man, *pl.* •mans, •men
drag\on
drag•on•fly, *pl.* •flies
dra•goon, •gooned, •goon•ing

drain, drained, drain•ing

drain•age

drain\er

drain•pipe

drake

DRAM (*dynamic random access memory*)

dram

dra\ma, *pl.* •mas

Dram\a•mine (™)

dra•mat•ic

dra•mat•ics

dram\a•tist

dram\a•ti•za•tion

dram\a•tize, •tized, •tiz•ing

drank

drape, draped, drap•ing

drap\er

dra•per\y, *pl.* •per•ies

dras•tic

dras•ti•cal\ly

draught (*drink*) [*vs.* draft (*plan*) and drought (*dry period*)]

draw, drew, drawn, draw•ing

draw•back

draw•bridge

draw\ee

draw\er

draw•ing

drawing ac•count

drawl, drawled, drawl•ing

drawn

draw pro•gram

draw•string *or* draw string

dray

dread, dread\ed, dread•ing

dread•ful

dread•locks, *pl.*

dread•nought *or* dread•naught

dream, dreamed *or* dreamt, dream•ing

dream\er

dream•i\ly

dream•land

dream•less

dream•like

dream\y, •i\er, •i•est

dredge, dredged, dredg•ing

dregs, *pl.*

Drei•ser

drench, drenched, drench•ing

Dres•den

dress, dressed, dress•ing

dress\er

dress\i•ness

dress•ing

dress\ing-•down

dress•mak\er

dress•mak•ing

dress\y, •i\er, •i•est

drew

drib•ble, •bled, •bling

drib•bler

drib•let

dried

dri\er

dri•est

drift, drift\ed, drift•ing

drift\er

drift•wood

drill, drilled, drill•ing

drill•mas•ter

dri\ly

drink, drank, drunk, drink•ing

drink•a\ble

drink\er

drip, dripped, drip•ping

drip-•dry, *pl.* •dried, •dry\ing, •dries

drip•ping

drive, drove, driv\en, driv•ing

drive-•in

driv\el, •eled *or* •elled, •el•ing *or* •el•ling

driv\er

drive•way

driz•zle, •zled, •zling

driz•zly

drogue

droll, droll\er, droll•est

droll•er\y, *pl.* •er•ies

drom\e•dar\y, *pl.* •dar•ies

drone, droned, dron•ing

drool, drooled, drool•ing

droop, drooped, droop•ing

droop\i•ness

droop\y, •i\er, •i•est

drop, dropped, drop•ping

drop kick (*noun*)

drop-•kick (*verb*), •kicked, •kick\ing

drop-•kick\er

drop•let

drop-•off

drop•out *or* drop-•out

drop•per

drop ship•per

drop•si•cal

drop\sy

dross

drought (*dry period*) [*vs.* draft (*plan*) and draught (*drink*)]

drove

drown, drowned, drown•ing

drowse, drowsed, drows•ing

drow•si•ness

drow\sy, •si\er, •si•est

drub, drubbed, drub•bing

drudge, drudged, drudg•ing

drudg•er\y

drug, drugged, drug•ging

drug•gie *or* drug\gy, *pl.* •gies

drug•gist

drug•store *or* drug store

dru\id

dru•id•ism

drum, *pl.* drums; drummed, drum•ming

drum ma•jor•ette

drum•mer

drum•stick

drunk

drunk•ard

drunk\en

drunk•en\ly

drunk•en•ness

drupe

dry, *pl.* drys or dries; dried, dry•ing; dri\er, dri\est

dry\ad

dry-•clean, •cleaned, •clean\ing

dry\er

dry\ly

dry•ness

DTP (*desktop publishing*)

DST or D.S.T. (*daylight-saving time*)

du\al (*double*) [*vs.* du\el (*fight*)]

du•al•ism

du•al•i\ty

dub, dubbed, dub•bing

Du•bai

dub•ber

du•bi•ous

du•bi•ous\ly

Dub•lin

du•cal

duc\at

duch•ess

duch\y, *pl.* duch•ies

duck, *pl.* ducks or duck

duck, ducked, duck•ing

duck•bill

duck•ling

duct

duc•tile

duc•til•i\ty

duct•less

dud

dude

dudg•eon (*indignation*) [*vs.* dun•geon (*prison*)]

due (*owed*) [*vs.* dew (*moisture*) and do (*to act*)]

due bill

due date

du\el (*fight*), •eled or •elled, •el•ing or •el•ling [*vs.* du\al (*double*)]

du•el•ist

du\et

duf•fel bag

duff\er

dug

dug•out

du jour

duke

duke•dom

dul•cet

dul•ci•mer

dull, dulled, dull•ing; dull\er, dull•est

dull•ard

dull•ness

dul\ly

Du•luth

du\ly

Du•mas

dumb, \er, •est

dumb•bell

dumb•found, •found\ed, •found•ing

dumb\ly

dumb•ness

dumb ter•mi•nal

dumb•wait\er

dum•dum

dum\my, *pl.* •mies; •mied, •my•ing

dump, dumped, dump•ing

dump•ling

dumps, *pl.*

Dump•ster (™)

dump\y, •i\er, •i•est

dun (*to demand payment*), dunned, dun•ning [*vs.* done (*finished*)]

dunce

dune

dung

dun•ga•ree

dun•geon (*prison*) [*vs.* dudg•eon (*indignation*)]

dung•hill

dunk, dunked, dunk•ing

Dun•kirk

du\o, *pl.* du\os

du\o•de•nal

du\o•de•num, *pl.* du\o•de\na, du\o•de•nums

du•op\o\ly, *pl.* •lies

dupe, duped, dup•ing

du•ple

du•plex

du•pli•cate, •cat\ed, •cat\ing

du•pli•ca•tion

du•pli•ca•tor

du•plic•i\ty, *pl.* •ties

du•ra•bil•i\ty

du•ra•ble

durable goods

du•ra•bly

du\ra ma•ter

dur•ance

du•ra•tion

Dur•ban

du•ress

Dur•ham

dur•ing

du•rum wheat

dusk

dusk\y, •i\er, •i•est

Düs•sel•dorf

dust, dust\ed, dust•ing

dust\er

dust\i•ness

dust•pan

dust\y, dust•i\er, dust•i•est

Dutch

Dutch auc•tion

du•te•ous

du•ti•a\ble

du•ti•ful

du•ti•ful\ly

du\ty, *pl.* •ties

du\ty-•free

du•vet

Dvo• řák (*the composer*)

Dvo•rak (*keyboard*)

dwarf, *pl.* dwarfs or dwarves dwarfed, dwarf•ing

dwarf•ish

dwarf•ism

dwell, dwelt or dwelled, dwell•ing

dwell\er

dwell•ing

DWI (*driving while intoxicated*)

dwin•dle, •dled, •dling

dyb•buk
dye (*to color*), dyed,
  dye•ing [*vs.* die (*to cease
  living*)]
dyed-•in-•the-•wool
dye•stuff
dy•ing
dy\na•book

dy•nam\ic
dynamic var•i•a\ble
dy•nam\i•cal\ly
dy•nam•ics
dy•na•mism
dy•na•mite, •mit\ed,
  •mit•ing
dy•na\mo, *pl.* •mos

dy•nas•tic
dy•nas\ty, *pl.* •ties
dys•en•ter\y
dys•func•tion
dys•lex\i\a
dys•lex\ic
dys•pep•sia
dys•pep•tic

E

each
each oth\er
ea•ger
ea•ger\ly
ea•ger•ness
ea•gle
ea\gle-•eyed
ea•glet
ear
ear•ache
ear•drum
earl
earl•dom
ear•less
ear•li•ness
ear•lobe *or* ear lobe
ear\ly, •li\er, •li•est
early re•tire•ment
ear•mark, •marked,
  •mark•ing
ear•muff
earn (*to gain*), earned,
  earn•ing [*vs.* urn (*vase*)]
earned in•come
earn\er
ear•nest
ear•nest\ly
ear•nest•ness
earn•ings, *pl.*
earnings per share
ear•phone
ear•plug
ear•ring
ear•shot
ear•split•ting
earth, earthed, earth•ing
earth\en
earth•en•ware
earth\i•ness
earth•li•ness
earth•ling

earth\ly
earth•quake
earth•shak•ing
earth•ward
earth•work
earth•worm
earth\y, •i\er, •i•est
ear•wax
ear•wig
ease, eased, eas•ing
ea•sel
ease•ment
eas\i\ly
eas\i•ness
east
Eas•ter
east•er\ly, *pl.* •lies
east•ern
east•ern\er
east•ward
eas\y, eas•i\er, eas•i•est
eas\y chair
eas\y•go•ing
eat, ate, eat\en, eat•ing
eat•er\y, •er•ies
eats, *pl.*
eau de Co•logne
eave
eaves•drop, •dropped,
  •drop•ping
eaves•drop•per
ebb, ebbed, ebb•ing
EBCDIC (*Extended Binary-
  Coded Decimal
  Interchange Code*)
eb•on\y
e\bul•lience
e\bul•lient
e\bul•lient\ly
eb•ul•li•tion
EC (*European Community*)

dy•nas•tic
ec•cen•tric
ec•cen•tri•cal\ly
ec•cen•tric•i\ty
Ec•cle•si•as•tes
ec•cle•si•as•tic
ECG (*electrocardiogram;
  electrocardiograph*)
ech\o, *pl.* ech•oes;
  ech•oed, ech\o•ing
e\cho\ic
ech\o•lo•ca•tion
é\clair
é\clat
ec•lec•tic
ec•lec•ti•cal\ly
ec•lec•ti•cism
e\clipse, e\clipsed,
  e\clips•ing
e\clip•tic
ec•logue
ec\o•cide
ec\o•log\i•cal
ec\o•log\i•cal\ly
e\col\o•gist
e\col\o•gy
e\con\o•met•rics
ec\o•nom\ic
ec\o•nom\i•cal
ec\o•nom\i•cal\ly
ec\o•nom\ic in•di•ca•tor
economic rent
ec\o•nom•ics
e\con\o•mist
e\con\o•mize, •mized,
  •miz•ing
e\con•o\my, *pl.* •mies
economy of scale
ec\o•sys•tem
ec\ru *or* éc\ru•
ec•sta\sy, *pl.* •sies
ec•stat\ic

ec•stat\i•cal\ly
ec\to•plasm
ECU (*currency of European Community*)
Ec•ua•dor
Ec•ua•do•ran or Ec•ua•do•re\an or Ec•ua•do•ri\an
ec\u•men\i•cal or ec\u•men\ic
ec\u•men\i•cal\ly
ec\u•me•nism or ec\u•men\i•cism
ec\u•me•nist
ec•ze\ma
E\dam
ed\dy, pl. •dies; •died, •dy•ing
e\del•weiss
e\de\ma, pl. •mas, •ma\ta
E\den
E\den\ic
edge, edged, edg•ing
edge con•nec•tor
edg\er
edge•wlse or edge•ways
edg\i•ness
edg•ing
edg\y, •i\er, •i•est
ed•i•bil\i•ty
ed•i\ble
ed•i\ble•ness
e\dict
ed\i•fi•ca•tion
ed\i•fice
ed\i\fy, •fied, •fy•ing
Ed•in•burgh
Ed\i•son
ed\it, •it\ed, •it•ing
e\di•tion (*a printing*) [*vs.* ad•di•tion (*an adding*)]
ed\i•tor
ed\i•to•ri\al
ed\i•to•ri•al•ize, •ized, •iz•ing
Ed•mon•ton
EDP (*electronic data processing*)
EDT or E.D.T. (*Eastern daylight-saving time*)
ed\u•ca•bil•i•ty

ed\u•ca\ble or ed\u•cat•a\ble
ed\u•cate, •cat\ed, •cat•ing
ed\u•ca•tion
ed\u•ca•tion\al
ed\u•ca•tor
e\duce (*to draw out*), e\duced, e\duc•ing [*vs.* ad•duce (*to put evidence forward*)]
Ed•ward•i\an
Ed•ward•i\an•ism
EEC (*European Economic Community*)
EEG (*electroencephalogram*)
eel, pl. eel, eels
EEPROM (*electrical erasable programmable read-only memory*)
e\'er (*ever*) [*vs.* air (*atmosphere*) and ere (*before*) and heir (*inheritor*)]
ee•rie (*ghostly*), •ri\er, •ri•est [*vs.* Eir\e (*Ireland*) and E\rie (*member of American Indian people*)]
ee•ri\ly
ee•ri•ness
ef•face, •faced, •fac•ing
ef•face•ment
ef•fect (*a result; to bring about*), •fect\ed, •fect•ing [*vs.* af•fect (*to act on*)]
ef•fec•tive
ef•fec•tive\ly
ef•fec•tive•ness
ef•fects, pl.
ef•fec•tu\al
ef•fec•tu•al\ly
ef•fec•tu•ate, •at\ed, •at•ing
ef•fem•i•na•cy
ef•fem•i•nate
ef•fer•ent
ef•fer•vesce, •vesced, •vesc•ing
ef•fer•ves•cence
ef•fer•ves•cent
ef•fete
ef•fete•ness

ef•fi•ca•cious
ef•fi•ca•cious\ly
ef•fi•ca\cy
ef•fi•cien\cy
efficiency ex•pert
ef•fi•cient
ef•fi•cient\ly
ef•fi\gy, pl. •gies
ef•flo•res•cence
ef•flo•res•cent
ef•flu•ence
ef•flu•ent (*flowing*) [*vs.* af•flu•ent (*rich*)]
ef•flu•vi\um, pl. •vi\a, •vi•ums
ef•fort
ef•fort•less
ef•fort•less\ly
ef•fron•ter\y
ef•ful•gence
ef•ful•gent
ef•fu•sion
ef•fu•sive
ef•fu•sive\ly
ef•fu•sive•ness
EFT (*electronic funds transfer*)
eft
e.g. (*for example*) [*vs.* i.e. (*that is*)]
e\gad or e\gads
e\gal•i•tar•i\an
e\gal•i•tar•i\an•ism
egg, egged, egg•ing
egg•beat\er
egg foo (*or* fu) yung
egg•head
egg•nog
egg•plant
egg•shell
e\gis
eg•lan•tine
e\go (*self*), pl. e\gos [*vs.* er\go (*therefore*)]
e\go•cen•tric
e\go•cen•tric•i\ty
e\go•ism
e\go•ist
e\go•is•tic
e\go•tism
e\go•tist

e\go•tis•tic
e\go•tis•ti•cal
e\go•tis•ti•cal\ly
e\go trip
e\go-•trip\per
e\gre•gious
e\gre•gious\ly
e\gre•gious•ness
e\gress
e\gret
E\gypt
E\gyp•tian
eh
ei•der•down
eight (number) [vs. ate (did eat)]
eight•ball
eight•een
eight•eenth
eighth
eight\i•eth
eight\y, pl.
Ein•stein
Ein•stein•i\an
ein•stein•i•um
Eir\e (Ireland) [vs. ee•rie (ghostly) and E\rie (member of American Indian people)]
Ei•sen•how\er
ei•ther (one of two) [vs. e\ther (anesthetic drug)]
e\jac\u•late, •lat\ed, •lat•ing
e\jac\u•la•tion
e\jac\u•la•to\ry
e\ject, e\ject\ed, e\ject•ing
e\jec•tion
eke, eked, ek•ing
EKG (electrocardiogram; electrocardiograph)
e\lab\o•rate, •rat\ed, •rat•ing
e\lab\o•rate\ly
e\lab\o•rate•ness
e\lab\o•ra•tion
e\lan
e\land, pl. e\lands, e\land
e\lapse (to pass), e\lapsed, e\laps•ing [vs. lapse (to subside; error)]

e\las•tic
e\las•tic•i\ty
e\las•ti•cize, •cized, •ciz•ing
e\lat\ed
e\la•tion
el•bow, •bowed, •bow•ing
el\bow•room
ELD (electroluminescent display)
eld\er (older person; older) [vs. old\er (having greater age)]
el•der (tree)
el•der•ber\ry, pl. •ries
eld•er\ly
eld•est
El Do•ra\do
e\lect, e\lect\ed, e\lect•ing
e\lec•tion (selection by vote) [vs. el\o•cu•tion (public speaking)]
e\lec•tion•eer, •eered, •eer•ing
e\lec•tive
e\lec•tor
e\lec•tor\al
e\lec•tor•ate
e\lec•tric
e\lec•tri•cal\ly
e\lec•tri•cian
e\lec•tric•i\ty
e\lec•tri•fi•ca•tion
e\lec•tri•fi\er
e\lec•tri•fy, •fied, •fy•ing
e\lec\tro•car\di•o•gram (ECG; EKG)
e\lec\tro•car\di•o•graph (ECG; EKG)
e\lec\tro•con•vul•sive ther•a\py
e\lec\tro•cute, •cut\ed, •cut•ing
e\lec\tro•cu•tion
e\lec•trode
e\lec\tro•en\ceph\a\lo•gram (EEG)
e\lec\tro•en\ceph\a\lo•graph
e\lec•trol\o•gist
e\lec•trol\y•sis

e\lec\tro•lyte
e\lec\tro•lyt\ic
e\lec\tro•mag•net
e\lec\tro•mag•net•ic
e\lec\tro•mag•net•i•cal\ly
e\lec\tro•mag•net•ism
e\lec\tro•mo\tive
e\lec•tron
e\lec•tron\ic
e\lec•tron\i•cal\ly
e\lec•tron\ic bank•ing
electronic da\ta processing (EDP)
electronic mail
electronic mail•box
e\lec•tron\ics
e\lec•tron\ic tab•let
e\lec•tron mi\cro•scope
e\lec\tro•plate, •plat\ed, •plat•ing
e\lec\tro•scope
e\lec\tro•scop\ic
e\lec\tro•shock
e\lec\tro•stat\ic
e\lec\tro•stat•ics
e\lec\tro•type, •typed, •typ•ing
el•ee•mos\y•nar\y
el\e•gance
el\e•gant
el\e•gant\ly
el\e•gi\ac
el\e•gy (poem of lament), pl. •gies [vs. eu•lo\gy (speech of praise)]
el\e•ment
el\e•men•tal
el\e•men•ta\ry (basic) [vs. al\i•men•ta\ry (digestive)]
el\e•phant, pl. •phants, •phant
el\e•phan•ti•a•sis
el\e•phan•tine
el\e•vate, •vat\ed, •vat•ing
el\e•va•tion
el\e•va•tor
e\lev\en
e\lev•enth
ELF or elf (extremely low frequency)
elf, pl. elves

El Gre\co

e\lic\it (*to bring forth*),
•it\ed, •it•ing [*vs.* il•lic\it
(*illegal*)]

e\lic\i•ta•tion

e\lide, e\lid\ed, e\lid•ing

el\i•gi•bil•i•ty

el\i•gi•ble (*qualified*) [*vs.*
il•leg•i\ble (*hard to read*)]

E\li•jah

e\lim\i•nate, •nat\ed,
•nat•ing

e\lim\i•na•tion

El\i•ot

e\li•sion

e\lite *or* é\lite

e\lit•ism

e\lit•ist

e\lix\ir

E\liz\a•beth

E\liz\a•be•than

elk, *pl.* elks, elk

ell

el•lipse (*curve*), *pl.* •lips\es

el•lip•sis (*omission of
word*), *pl.* •ses

el•lip•ti•cal *or* el•lip•tic

el•lip•ti•cal\ly

elm

El Ni\ño

el\o•cu•tion (*public speaking*) [*vs.* e\lec•tion (*selection by vote*)]

e\lon•gate, •gat\ed,
•gat•ing

e\lon•ga•tion

e\lope, e\loped, e\lop•ing

e\lope•ment

el\o•quence

el\o•quent

el\o•quent\ly

El Pas\o

El Sal•va•dor

else

else•where

e\lu•ci•date, •dat\ed,
•dat•ing

e\lu•ci•da•tion

e\lude (*to avoid*), e\lud\ed,
e\lud•ing [*vs.* al•lude (*to
refer*)]

e\lu•sive (*evasive*) [*vs.*
al•lu•sive (*suggestive*) and
il•lu•sive (*deceptive*)]

e\lu•sive•ness

elves

E\ly•sian

E\ly•si\um

e\ma•ci•at\ed

e\ma•ci•a•tion

E-\mail *or* e-\mail

em\a•nate, •nat\ed,
•nat•ing

em\a•na•tion

e\man•ci•pate, •pat\ed,
•pat•ing

e\man•ci•pa•tion

e\man•ci•pa•tor

e\mas•cu•late, •lat\ed,
•lat•ing

e\mas•cu•la•tion

em•balm, •balmed,
•balm•ing

em•balm\er

em•bank•ment

em•bar•go, *pl.* •goes;
•goed, •go•ing

em•bark, •barked,
•bark•ing

em•bar•ka•tion

em•bar•rass, •rassed,
•rass•ing

em•bar•rass•ing\ly

em•bar•rass•ment

em•bas\sy, *pl.* •sies

em•bat•tled

em•bed, •bed•ded,
•bed•ding

embedded com•mand

em•bel•lish, •lished,
•lish•ing

em•bel•lish•ment

em•ber

em•bez•zle, •zled, •zling

em•bez•zle•ment

em•bez•zler

em•bit•ter, •tered,
•ter•ing

em•bla•zoned

em•blem

em•blem•at\ic

em•bod\i•ment

em•bod\y, •bod•ied,
•bod\y•ing

em•bold\en, •ened,
•en•ing

em•bo•lism

em•boss, •bossed,
•boss•ing

em•bou•chure

em•brace, •braced,
•brac•ing

em•brace•a\ble

em•bra•sure

em•bro•ca•tion

em•broi•der, •dered,
•der•ing

em•broi•der\y, *pl.* •der•ies

em•broil, •broiled,
•broil•ing

em•broil•ment

em•bry\o, *pl.* \os

em\bry\o•log\i•cal

em•bry•ol\o•gist

em•bry•ol\o\gy

em•bry•on\ic

em•cee, •ceed, •cee•ing

e\mend, e\mend\ed,
e\mend•ing

e\men•da•tion

em•er•ald

e\merge, e\merged,
e\merg•ing

e\mer•gence

e\mer•gen\cy, *pl.* •cies

e\mer•gent

e\mer\i•tus, *pl.* \ti

Em•er•son

em•er\y

e\met\ic

em\i•grant

em\i•grate (*to leave one's
country*), •grat\ed,
•grat•ing [*vs.*
im•mi•grate (*to come to
a new country*)]

em\i•gra•tion

é\mi•gré

em\i•nence

em\i•nent (*renowned*) [*vs.*
im•ma•nent (*inherent*)
and im•mi•nent
(*impending*)]

e\mir
em•ir•ate
em•is•sar\y, *pl.* •sar•ies
e\mis•sion
e\mit, e\mit•ted, e\mit•ting
e\mit•ter
e\mol•lient (*softening*)
e\mol\u•ment (*salary*)
e\mote, e\mot•ed, e\mot•ing
e\mo•tion
e\mo•tion•al
e\mo•tion•al•ism
e\mo•tion•al\ly
em•path•ic (*sharing another's feelings*) [*vs.* em•phat•ic (*uttered strongly*)]
em•pa•thize, •thized, •thiz•ing
em•pa•thy
em•per\or
em•pha•sis, *pl.* •ses
em•pha•size, •sized, •siz•ing
em•phat•ic (*uttered strongly*) [*vs.* em•path•ic (*sharing another's feelings*)]
em•phat\i•cal\ly
em•phy•se\ma
em•pire (*domain*) [*vs.* um•pire (*referee*)]
em•pir\i•cal
em•pir\i•cal\ly
em•pir\i•cism
em•pir\i•cist
em•place•ment
em•ploy, •ployed, •ploy•ing
em•ploy•a•ble
em•ploy\ee
em•ploy\er
em•ploy•ment
employment a\gen\cy
em•po•ri\um, *pl.* •ri•ums, •ri\a
em•pow\er, •ered, •er•ing
em•pow•er•ment
em•press
emp•ti\ly

emp•ti•ness
emp\ty, *pl.* •ties; •tied, •ty•ing; •ti\er, •ti•est
emp\ty-•hand\ed
emp\ty nest\er
em•py•re\an
e\mu, *pl.* e\mus
em•u•late, •lat\ed, •lat•ing
em•u•la•tion
em•u•la•tive
em•u•la•tor
e\mul•si•fi•ca•tion
e\mul•si\fy, •fied, •fy•ing
e\mul•sion
en•a•ble (*to give power*), \bled, \bling [*vs.* un•a•ble (*not able*)]
en•a•bler
en•act, •act\ed, •act•ing
en•act•ment
e\nam\el, •eled *or* •elled, •el•ing *or* •el•ling
e\nam•el•ware
en•am\or, •ored, •or•ing
en bloc
en•camp, •camped, •camp•ing
en•camp•ment
en•cap•su•late, •lat\ed, •lat•ing
en•cap•su•la•tion
en•case, •cased, •cas•ing
en\ceph\a•lit\ic
en\ceph\a•li•tis
en\ceph\a•lo•my•e•li•tis
en\ceph\a•lon, *pl.* •lons, \la
en•chain, •chained, •chain•ing
en•chant, •chant\ed, •chant•ing
en•chant•ing\ly
en•chi•la\da, *pl.* •das
en•ci•pher, •phered, •pher•ing
en•ci•pher•ment
en•cir•cle, •cled, •cling
en•cir•cle•ment
en•clave
en•close, •closed, •clos•ing
en•clo•sure

en•code, •cod\ed, •cod•ing
en•co•mi\um, *pl.* •mi•ums, •mi\a
en•com•pass, •passed, •pass•ing
en•core, •cored, •cor•ing
en•coun•ter, •tered, •ter•ing
en•cour•age, •aged, •ag•ing
en•cour•age•ment
en•cour•ag•ing\ly
en•croach, •croached, •croach•ing
en•croach•ment
en•crust, •crust\ed, •crust•ing
en•crus•ta•tion
en•cryp•tion
en•cum•ber, •bered, •ber•ing
en•cum•brance
en•cyc•li•cal
en•cy•clo•pe•di\a *or* en•cy•clo•pae•di\a
en•cy•clo•pe•dic
en•cyst, •cyst\ed, •cyst•ing
end, end\ed, end•ing
en•dan•ger, •gered, •ger•ing
en•dan•gered spe•cies
en•dan•ger•ment
en•dear, •deared, •dear•ing
en•dear•ing\ly
en•dear•ment
en•deav\or, •ored, •or•ing
en•dem•ic
end•ing
ending in•ven•to\ry
en•dive
end•less
end•less\ly
end•less•ness
end•most
en\do•crine
en\do•cri•nol\o•gist
en\do•cri•nol\o\gy
end-•of-•file (*EOF*)
end-•of-•line (*EOL*)

en•dog\e•nous
en•dorse, •dorsed,
•dors•ing
en•dorse•ment
en•dors\er
en\do•scope
en\do•scop\ic
en•dos•co\py
en\do•ther•mic or
en\do•ther•mal
en•dow, •dowed,
•dow•ing
en•dow•ment
endowment in•sur•ance
en•due (to provide), •dued,
•du•ing [vs. un•do (to
reverse) and un•due
(excessive)]
en•dur•a\ble
en•dur•ance
en•dure, •dured, •dur•ing
en•dur•ing\ly
end us\er
end•ways or end•wise
en\e\ma, pl. •mas
en\e\my, pl. •mies
en•er•get\ic
en•er•get\i•cal\ly
en•er•gize, •gized, •giz•ing
en•er•giz\er
en•er•gy, pl. •gies
en•er•vate (to weaken),
•vat\ed, •vat•ing [vs.
in•ner•vate (to
invigorate)]
en•er•va•tion
en•er•va•tor
en•fee•ble, •bled, •bling
en•fee•ble•ment
en•fi•lade, •lad\ed, •lad•ing
en•fold (to wrap), •fold\ed,
•fold•ing [vs. un•fold (to
lay open)]
en•force, •forced,
•forc•ing
en•force•a\ble
en•force•ment
en•forc\er
en•fran•chise, •chised,
•chis•ing
en•fran•chise•ment

en•gage, •gaged, •gag•ing
en•gage•ment
en•gag•ing
en•gag•ing\ly
En•gels
en•gen•der, •dered,
•der•ing
en•gine
en•gi•neer, •neered,
•neer•ing
Eng•land
Eng•lish
Eng•lish•man or •wom\an,
pl. •men or •wom\en
en•gorge, •gorged,
•gorg•ing
en•grave, •graved,
•grav•ing
en•grav\er
en•grav•ing
en•gross, •grossed,
•gross•ing
en•gross•ing
en•gulf, •gulfed, •gulf•ing
en•hance, •hanced,
•hanc•ing
enhanced key•board
en•hance•ment
e\nig\ma
en•ig•mat\ic
en•join, •joined, •join•ing
en•joy, •joyed, •joy•ing
en•joy•a\ble
en•joy•ment
en•large, •larged, •larg•ing
en•large•ment
en•larg\er
en•light\en, •ened, •en•ing
en•light•en•ment
en•list, •list\ed, •list•ing
en•list•ee
en•list•ment
en•liv\en, •ened, •en•ing
en masse
en•mesh, •meshed,
•mesh•ing
en•mi\ty (hostility), pl. •ties
[vs. am•i\ty (friendship)]
en•no•ble, •bled, •bling
en•no•ble•ment
en•nui

e\nor•mi\ty, pl. •ties
e\nor•mous
e\nor•mous\ly
e\nor•mous•ness
e\nough
en•plane or emplane,
•planed, •plan•ing
en•quire, •quired,
•quir•ing
en•quir\y, pl. •quir•ies
en•rage, •raged, •rag•ing
en•rap•ture, •tured,
•tur•ing
en•rich, •riched, •rich•ing
en•rich•ment
en•roll or en•rol (to
enlist), •rolled, •roll•ing
or •rol•ling [vs. un•roll
(to display)]
en•roll•ment
en route
en•sconced
en•sem•ble
en•shrine, •shrined,
•shrin•ing
en•shroud, •shroud\ed,
•shroud•ing
en•sign
en•slave, •slaved, •slav•ing
en•slave•ment
en•snare, •snared,
•snar•ing
en•sue, •sued, •su•ing
en•sure, •sured,
•sur•ing
en•tail, •tailed, •tail•ing
en•tail•ment
en•tan•gle, •gled, •gling
en•tan•gle•ment
en•tente
en•ter, •tered, •ter•ing
en•ter\i•tis
En•ter key
en•ter•prise
en•ter•pris•ing
en•ter•tain, •tained,
•tain•ing
en•ter•tain\er
en•ter•tain•ment
en•thrall, •thralled,
•thrall•ing

en•throne, •throned,
•thron•ing
en•throne•ment
en•thuse, •thused,
•thus•ing
en•thu•si•asm
en•thu•si•ast
en•thu•si•as•tic
en•thu•si•as•ti•cal\ly
en•tice, •ticed, •tic•ing
en•tice•ment
en•tic•ing\ly
en•tire
en•tire\ly
en•tire\ty
en•ti•tle, •tled, •tling
en•ti•tle•ment
en•ti\ty, pl. •ties
en•tomb, •tombed,
•tomb•ing
en•to•mol\o•gist
en•to•mol\o\gy (study
of insects) [vs.
et\y•mol\o\gy (study of
words)]
en•tou•rage
en\tr'acte
en•trails, pl.
en•train, •trained,
•train•ing
en•trance (noun)
en•trance (verb), •tranced,
•tranc•ing
en•tranc•ing\ly
en•trant
en•trap, •trapped,
•trap•ping
en•trap•ment
en•treat, •treat\ed,
•treat•ing
en•treat•ing\ly
en•treat\ly, pl. •ies
en•trée or en•tree
en•trench, •trenched,
•trench•ing
en•trench•ment
en•tre•pre•neur
en•tre•pre•neur•i\al
en•tro\py
en•trust, •trust\ed,
•trust•ing

en•try, pl. •tries
entry lev\el
entry val\ue
en•twine, •twined,
•twin•ing
e\nu•mer•ate, •at\ed,
•at•ing
e\nu•mer•a•tion
e\nun•ci•ate, •at\ed, •at•ing
e\nun•ci•a•tion (diction)
[vs. an•nun•ci•a•tion
(announcement)]
en•vel\op (to wrap),
•oped, •op•ing
en•ve•lope (covering)]
en•vel•op•ment
en•ven\om, •omed,
•om•ing
en•vi•a•ble
en•vi•a•bly
en•vi•ous
en•vi•ous\ly
en•vi•ous•ness
en•vi•ron•ment
en•vi•ron•men•tal
en•vi•ron•men•tal•ism
en•vi•ron•men•tal•ist
en•vi•ron•men•tal\ly
en•vi•rons, pl.
en•vis•age, •aged, •ag•ing
en•vi•sion, •sioned,
•sion•ing
en•voy
en\vy, pl. •vies; •vied,
•vy•ing
en•zyme
EO (erasable optical disk)
E\o•cene
EOF (end-of-file)
EOL (end-of-line)
E\o•li\an
e.o.m. or E.O.M. (end-of-
month)
e.o.m. dat•ing
e\on or ae\on
EPA (Environmental
Protection Agency)
ep•au•let or ep•au•lette
é\pée or e\pee
e\phed•rine

e\phem•er\a, pl. •er\as
e\phem•er\al
ep\ic (heroic poem) [vs.
ep•och (era)]
ep\i•cene
ep\i•cen•ter
ep\i•cure
ep\i•cu•re\an
ep\i•dem\ic
ep\i•de•mi•ol\o•gist
ep\i•de•mi•ol\o\gy
ep\i•der•mal or
ep\i•der•mic
ep\i•der•mis
ep\i•glot\tis, pl.
•glot•tis\es, •glot•ti•des
ep\i•gram (pointed
statement) [vs.
ep\i•graph (motto)]
ep\i•gram•mat\ic
ep\i•graph (motto) [vs.
ep\i•gram (pointed
statement)]
ep\i•lep\sy
ep\i•lep•tic
ep\i•logue or ep\i•log
ep\i•neph•rine or
ep\i•neph•rin
e\piph\a\ny, pl. •nies
e\pis•co•pa\cy, pl. •cies
e\pis•co•pal
E\pis•co•pa•lian
e\pis•co•pate
ep\i•sode
ep\i•sod\ic
e\pis•te•mol\o\gy
e\pis•tle
e\pis•to•lar\y
ep\i•taph (inscription) [vs.
ep\i•thet (curse)]
ep\i•the•li\al
ep\i•the•li\um, pl. •li•ums,
•li\a
ep\i•thet (curse) [vs.
ep\i•taph (inscription)]
e\pit\o•me
e\pit\o•mize, •mized,
•miz•ing
e plu•ri•bus u\num
ep•och (era) [vs. ep\ic
(heroic poem)]

ep•och\al

ep•ox\y, *pl.* •ox•ies

EPROM (*erasable programmable read-only memory*)

ep•si•lon

Ep•som salt

Ep\stein-•Barr vi•rus

eq•ua\ble (*uniform*) [*vs.* eq•ui•ta\ble (*just*)]

eq•ua•bly

e\qual, e\qualed *or* e\qualled, e\qual•ing *or* e\qual\ling

e\qual•i\ty

e\qual\i•za\tion

e\qual•ize, •ized, •iz•ing

e\qual•iz\er

e\qual\ly

e\qua•nim•i\ty

e\quat•a\ble

e\quate, e\quat\ed, e\quat•ing

e\qua•tion

e\qua•tor

E\qua•to•ri\al Guin\ea

eq•uer\ry, *pl.* •ries

e\ques•tri\an

e\ques•tri•enne

e\qui•dis•tant

e\qui•lat•er\al

e\qui•lib•ri\um, *pl.* •ri•ums, •ri\a

e\quine

e\qui•noc•tial

e\qui•nox

e\quip, e\quipped, e\quip•ping

eq•ui•page

e\quip•ment

e\qui•poise, •poised, •pois•ing

eq•ui•ta\ble (*just*) [*vs.* eq•ua\ble (*uniform*)]

eq•ui•ta•bly

eq•ui\ty, *pl.* •ties

equity cap\i•tal

e\quiv\a•lence *or* e\quiv\a•len\cy

e\quiv\a•lent

e\quiv\o•cal

e\quiv\o•cal\ly

e\quiv\o•cate, •cat\ed, •cat•ing

e\quiv\o•ca•tion

e\quiv\o•ca•tor

e\ra (*age*), *pl.* e\ras [*vs.* er•ror (*mistake*)]

e\rad\i•ca\ble

e\rad\i•cate, •cat\ed, •cat•ing

e\rad\i•ca•tion

e\rad\i•ca•tor

e\ras•a\ble (*removable*) [*vs.* i\ras•ci\ble (*easily angered*)]

erasable op•ti•cal disk (*EO*)

e\rase, e\rased, e\ras•ing

e\ras\er

E\ras•mus

e\ra•sure

er•bi\um

ere (*before*) [*vs.* air (*atmosphere*) and e'er (*ever*) and heir (*inheritor*)]

e\rect (*to build*), e\rect\ed, e\rect•ing [*vs.* e\ruct (*to belch*)]

e\rec•tile

e\rec•tion

e\rect\ly

e\rect•ness

e\rec•tor

ere•long

er\e•mite

erg

er\go (*therefore*) [*vs.* e\go (*self*)]

er\go•nom\ic

er\go•nom\i•cal\ly

er\go•nom•ics

er•gos•ter\ol

er•got

E\rie (*member of American Indian people*), *pl.* E\ries, E\rie [*vs.* ee•rie (*ghostly*) and Eir\e (*Ireland*)]

Er\in

ERISA (*Employee Retirement Income Security Act*)

er•mine, *pl.* •mines, •mine

e\rode, e\rod\ed, e\rod•ing

e\rog\e•nous

E\ros

e\ro•sion

e\ro•sive

e\rot\ic (*sexy*) [*vs.* er•rat\ic (*unpredictable*)]

e\rot\i•ca

e\rot\i•cal\ly

e\rot\i•cism

err, erred, err•ing

er•rand (*excursion for a task*)

er•rant (*roving*)

er•rat\ic (*unpredictable*) [*vs.* e\rot\ic (*sexy*)]

er•rat\i•cal\ly

er•ra•tum, *pl.* \ta

er•ro•ne•ous

er•ro•ne•ous\ly

er•ror (*mistake*) [*vs.* e\ra (*age*)]

error de•tec•tion

er•ror•less

er•satz

erst

erst•while

ERT (*estrogen replacement therapy*)

e\ruct (*to belch*), e\ruct\ed, e\ruct•ing [*vs.* e\rect (*to build*)]

er\u•dite

er\u•dite\ly

er\u•di•tion

e\rupt, e\rupt\ed, e\rupt•ing

e\rup•tion

er\y•sip\e•las

e\ryth•ro•cyte

es•ca•late, •lat\ed, •lat•ing

es•ca•la•tion

es•ca•la•tor

escalator clause

es•cal•lop, •loped, •lop•ing

es•ca•pade

es•cape, •caped, •cap•ing

escape char•ac•ter

es•cape clause
es•cap\ee
es•cape•ment
es•cape se•quence
es•cap•ism
es•cap•ist
es•ca•role
es•carp•ment
es•chew, •chewed, •chew•ing
es•cort, •cort\ed, •cort•ing
es•cri•toire
es•crow, •crowed, •crow•ing
es•cu•do, pl. •dos
es•cutch•eon
Es•ki•mo, pl. •mos, \mo
ESL (English as a second language)
ESOP (employee stock ownership plan)
e\soph\a•ge\al
e\soph\a•gus, pl. \gi
es\o•ter•ic
es\o•ter\i•cal\ly
es•pa•drille
es•pe•cial
es•pe•cial\ly
Es•pe•ran\to
es•pi•o•nage
es•pla•nade
es•pous\al
es•pouse, •poused, •pous•ing
es•pres\so
es•prit
es•prit de corps
es•py, •pied, •py•ing
Esq. or Esqr. (esquire)
es•quire
es•say (to try; composition), •sayed, •say•ing [vs. as•say (to evaluate)]
es•say•ist
es•sence
Es•sene
es•sen•tial
es•sen•tial\ly
EST or E.S.T. (Eastern Standard Time)

es•tab•lish, •lished, •lish•ing
es•tab•lish•ment
es•tate
estate tax
es•teem, •teemed, •teem•ing
es•ter
es•thete
es•thet\ic
es•thet•ics
es•ti•ma\ble
es•ti•mate, •mat\ed, •mat•ing
es•ti•ma•tion
Es•to•ni\a
Es•to•ni\an
es•trange, •tranged, •trang•ing
es•trange•ment
es•tro•gen
estrogen re•place•ment ther•a\py (ERT)
es•trous
es•trus
es•tu•ar\y, pl. •ar•ies
ETA or E.T.A. (estimated time of arrival)
é\ta•gère or e\ta•gere
et al. (and others)
etc. (et cetera)
etch, etched, etch•ing
etch\er
etch\ing
e\ter•nal
e\ter•nal\ly
e\ter•ni\ty, pl. •ties
eth•ane
eth\a•nol
e\ther (anesthetic drug) [vs. ei•ther (one of two)]
e\the•re\al
e\the•re\al\ly
eth\ic (principle) [vs. eth•nic (cultural)]
eth\i•cal
eth\i•cal\ly
eth\i•cal pric•ing
eth•ics

eth•nic (cultural) [vs. eth\ic (principle)]
eth•ni•cal\ly
eth•nic•i\ty
eth\no•cen•tric
eth\no•cen•trism
eth•nol\o\gy
e\thol\o\gy
e\thos
eth\yl
eth\yl•ene
e\ti•ol•o\o\gy, pl. •gies
et\i•quette
E\tru•ri\a
E\trus•can
é\tude
ETV (educational television)
et\y•mo•log\i•cal
et\y•mol\o•gist
et\y•mol\o\gy (study of words), pl. •gies [vs. en•to•mol\o\gy (study of insects)]
eu•ca•lyp•tus, pl. \ti, •tus\es
Eu•cha•rist
Eu•cha•ris•tic
eu•chre, •chred, •chring
Eu•clid
Eu•clid•e\an or Eu•clid•i\an
Eu•gene
eu•gen\ic
eu•gen\i•cal\ly
eu•gen•ics
eu•lo•gist
eu•lo•gis•tic
eu•lo•gize, •gized, •giz•ing
eu•lo\gy (speech of praise), pl. •gies [vs. el\e\gy (poem of lament)]
eu•nuch
eu•phe•mism (mild substitution for offensive expression) [vs. eu•phu•ism (affected literary style)]
eu•phe•mis•tic
eu•phe•mis•ti•cal\ly
eu•pho•ni•ous
eu•pho•ni•ous\ly

eu•pho\ny, *pl.* •nies
eu•pho•ri\a
eu•phor\ic
Eu•phra•tes
eu•phu•ism (*affected literary style*) [vs. eu•phe•mism (*mild substitution for offensive expression*)]
Eur•a\sia
Eur•a\sian
eu•re\ka
Eu•rip\i•des
Eu\ro•bond
Eu\ro•cur•ren\cy, *pl.* •cies
Eu\ro•dol•lar
Eu•rope
Eu\ro•pe\an
European Ec\o•nom\ic Com•mu•ni\ty (*EEC*)
eu•ro•pi\um
Eu•sta•chian tube
eu•tha•na•sia
eu•troph\i•ca•tion
e\vac\u•ate, •at\ed, •at•ing
e\vac\u•a•tion
e\vac\u\ee
e\vade (*to elude*), e\vad\ed, e\vad•ing [vs. a\void (*to shun*)]
e\vad\er
e\val\u•ate, •at\ed, •at•ing
e\val\u•a•tion
e\val\u•a•tor
ev\a•nes•cence
ev\a•nes•cent
e\van•gel•i\cal
e\van•gel\i\cal•ism
e\van•ge•lism
e\van•ge•list
e\van•ge•lis•tic
Ev•ans•ville
e\vap\o•rate, •rat\ed, •rat•ing
e\vap\o•ra•tion
e\va•sion
e\va•sive
e\va•sive\ly
e\va•sive•ness
eve

e\ven, e\vened, e\ven•ing (*making even*)
even foot\er
e\ven•hand\ed
e\ven•hand•ed\ly
e\ven•hand•ed•ness
eve•ning (*night*)
e\ven\ly
e\ven•ness
E\ven•song
e\vent
event-•driv\en
e\ven-•tem\pered
e\vent•ful
e\vent•ful\ly
e\ven•tide
e\ven•tu\al
e\ven•tu•al•i\ty, *pl.* •ties
e\ven•tu•al\ly
e\ven•tu•ate, •at\ed, •at•ing
ev\er
Ev•er•est
Ev\er•glades
ev\er•green
ev\er•last•ing
ev\er•last•ing\ly
ev\er•more
eve\ry
eve\ry•bod\y
eve\ry•day
eve\ry•one
eve\ry•place
eve\ry•thing
eve\ry•where
e\vict, e\vict\ed, e\vict•ing
e\vic•tion
ev\i•dence, •denced, •denc•ing
ev\i•dent
ev\i•dent\ly
e\vil
e\vil•do\er
e\vil•do•ing
e\vil\ly
e\vil-•mind\ed
e\vince, e\vinced, e\vinc•ing
e\vis•cer•ate, •at\ed, •at•ing
e\vis•cer•a•tion

ev\o•ca•tion
e\voc\a•tive
e\voc\a•tive\ly
e\voc\a•tive•ness
e\voke, e\voked, e\vok•ing
ev\o•lu•tion
ev\o•lu•tion•ar\y
ev\o•lu•tion•ism
ev\o•lu•tion•ist
e\volve, e\volved, e\volv•ing
ewe (*female sheep*) [vs. yew (*tree*) and you (*person addressed*)]
ew\er
ex
ex•ac•er•bate, •bat\ed, •bat•ing
ex•ac•er•ba•tion
ex•act, •act\ed, •act•ing
ex•act•ing\ly
ex•ac•tion
ex•ac•ti•tude
ex•act\ly
ex•act•ness
ex•ag•ger•ate, •at\ed, •at•ing
ex•ag•ger•at•ed\ly
ex•ag•ger•a•tion
ex•alt (*glorify*), •alt\ed, •alt•ing [vs. ex•ult (*rejoice*)]
ex•al•ta•tion
ex\am
ex•am\i•na•tion
ex•am•ine, •ined, •in•ing
ex•am•in\er
ex•am•ple, •pled, •pling
ex•as•per•ate, •at\ed, •at•ing
ex•as•per•a•tion
ex•ca•va•te, •vat\ed, •vat•ing
ex•ca•va•tion
ex•ca•va•tor
ex•ceed (*to surpass*), •ceed\ed, •ceed•ing [vs. ac•cede (*to consent*)]
ex•ceed•ing\ly
ex•cel, •celled, •cel•ling
ex•cel•lence

Ex•cel•len\cy, *pl.* •cies

ex•cel•lent

ex•cel•lent\ly

ex•cel•si\or

ex•cept (*to exclude*), •cept\ed, •cept•ing [*vs.* ac•cept (*to receive*)]

ex•cep•tion

ex•cep•tion•a\ble (*objectionable*)

ex•cep•tion\al (*outstanding*)

ex•cep•tion•al\ly

ex•cerpt, •cerpt\ed, •cerpt•ing

ex•cess (*surplus*) [*vs.* ac•cess (*approach*)]

ex•ces•sive

ex•ces•sive\ly

ex•change, •changed, •chang•ing

ex•change•a\ble

exchange con•trol

exchange rate

ex•cheq•uer

ex•cis•a\ble

ex•cise, •cised, •cis•ing

excise tax

ex•ci•sion

ex•cit•a•bil•i\ty

ex•cit•a\ble

ex•ci•ta•tion

ex•cite, •cit\ed, •cit•ing

ex•cit•ed\ly

ex•cite•ment

ex•cit•ing

ex•cit•ing\ly

ex•claim, •claimed, •claim•ing

ex•cla•ma•tion

ex•clam\a•to\ry

ex•clude, •clud\ed, •clud•ing

ex•clu•sion

ex•clu•sive

ex•clu•sive\ly

ex•clu•sive•ness

ex•com•mu•ni•cate, •cat\ed, •cat•ing

ex•co•ri•ate, •at\ed, •at•ing

ex•co•ri•a•tion

ex•cre•ment

ex•cre•men•tal

ex•cres•cence

ex•cres•cent

ex•cre\ta

ex•crete, •cret\ed, •cret•ing

ex•cre•tion

ex•cre•to\ry

ex•cru•ci•at•ing

ex•cru•ci•at•ing\ly

ex•cul•pate, •pat\ed, •pat•ing

ex•cul•pa•tion

ex•cur•sion

ex•cus•a\ble

ex•cus•a\bly

ex•cuse, •cused, •cus•ing

ex div\i•dend

ex\e•cra\ble

ex\e•crate, •crat\ed, •crat•ing

ex\e•cra•tion

ex\e•cut•a\ble file

ex\e•cute, •cut\ed, •cut•ing

ex\e•cu•tion

ex\e•cu•tion\er

ex•ec\u•tive

executive of•fi•cer

executive sec•re•tar\y

ex•ec\u•tor

ex•ec\u•trix, *pl.* •tri•ces, •trix\es

ex\e•ge•sis, *pl.* •ses

ex\e•get\ic

ex•em•plar

ex•em•pla\ry

ex•em•pli•fi•ca•tion

ex•em•pli\fy, •fied, •fy•ing

ex•empt, •empt\ed, •empt•ing

ex•emp•tion

ex•empt per•son•nel

ex•er•cise (*to use; activity*), •cised, •cis•ing [*vs.* ex•or•cise (*to expel*)]

ex•er•cis\er

ex•ert, •ert\ed, •ert•ing

ex•er•tion

ex•ha•la•tion

ex•hale, •haled, •hal•ing

ex•haust, •haust\ed, •haust•ing

ex•haus•tion

ex•haus•tive

ex•hib\it, •it\ed, •it•ing

ex•hi•bi•tion

ex•hi•bi•tion•ism

ex•hi•bi•tion•ist

ex•hi•bi•tion•is•tic

ex•hib\i•tor

ex•hil\a•rate, •rat\ed, •rat•ing

ex•hil\a•rat•ing\ly

ex•hil\a•ra•tion

ex•hort, •hort\ed, •hort•ing

ex•hor•ta•tion

ex•hu•ma•tion

ex•hume, •humed, •hum•ing

ex\i•gen\cy, *pl.* •cies

ex\i•gent

ex•ile, •iled, •il•ing

ex•ist, •ist\ed, •ist•ing

ex•ist•ence

ex•ist•ent

ex•is•ten•tial

ex•is•ten•tial•ism

ex•is•ten•tial•ist

ex•is•ten•tial\ly

ex\it, •it\ed, •it•ing

ex\o•bi•ol\o•gy

ex\o•crine

ex\o•dus

ex of•fi•ci\o

ex•on•er•ate, •at\ed, •at•ing

ex•on•er•a•tion

ex•or•bi•tance

ex•or•bi•tant

ex•or•bi•tant\ly

ex•or•cise (*to expel*), •cised, •cis•ing [*vs.* ex•er•cise (*to use; activity*)]

ex•or•cism

ex•or•cist

ex\o•sphere

ex•ot\ic

ex•ot\i•cism

ex•pand (*to increase*),
  •pand\ed, •pand•ing [*vs.*
  ex•pend (*to use up*)]

ex•pand\ed mem•o\ry

ex•panse

ex•pan•si•ble

ex•pan•sion

expansion board

expansion bus

expansion card

ex•pan•sion•ism

ex•pan•sion•ist

ex•pan•sion slot

ex•pan•sive (*extensive*) [*vs.*
  ex•pen•sive (*costly*)]

ex•pan•sive\ly

ex•pan•sive•ness

ex par\te

ex•pa•ti•ate, •at\ed,
  •at•ing

ex•pa•ti•a•tion

ex•pa•tri•ate

ex•pa•tri•a•tion

ex•pect, •pect\ed,
  •pect•ing

ex•pect•an\cy, *pl.* •cies

ex•pect•ant

ex•pect•ant\ly

ex•pec•ta•tion

ex•pect\ed yield

ex•pec•to•rant

ex•pec•to•rate, •rat\ed,
  •rat•ing

ex•pec•to•ra•tion

ex•pe•di•en\cy

ex•pe•di•ent

ex•pe•dite, •dit\ed,
  •dit•ing

ex•pe•dit\er *or*
  ex•pe•di•tor

ex•pe•di•tion

ex•pe•di•tion•ar\y

ex•pe•di•tious

ex•pe•di•tious\ly

ex•pe•di•tious•ness

ex•pe•di•tor

ex•pel, •pelled, •pel•ling

ex•pend (*to use up*),
  •pend\ed, •pend•ing [*vs.*
  ex•pand (*to increase*)]

ex•pend•a\ble

ex•pend\i•ture

ex•pense, •pensed,
  •pens•ing

expense ac•count

ex•pen•sive (*costly*) [*vs.*
  ex•pan•sive (*extensive*)]

ex•pen•sive\ly

ex•pe•ri•ence, •enced,
  •enc•ing

ex•per\i•ment, •ment\ed,
  •ment•ing

ex•per\i•men•tal

ex•per\i•men•tal\ly

ex•per\i•men•ta•tion

ex•per\i•ment\er

ex•pert

ex•per•tise

ex•pert\ly

ex•pert•ness

ex•pert sys•tem

ex•pi•ate, •at\ed, •at•ing

ex•pi•a•tion

ex•pi•ra•tion

ex•pire, •pired, •pir•ing

ex•plain, •plained,
  •plain•ing

ex•pla•na•tion

ex•plan\a•to\ry

ex•ple•tive

ex•pli•ca•ble

ex•pli•cate, •cat\ed,
  •cat•ing

ex•pli•ca•tion

ex•plic\it

ex•plic•it\ly

ex•plic•it•ness

ex•plode, •plod\ed,
  •plod•ing

ex•ploit, •ploit\ed,
  •ploit•ing

ex•ploi\ta•tion

ex•ploit\a•tive *or*
  ex•ploit•ive

ex•ploit\er

ex•plo•ra•tion

ex•plor\a•to\ry

ex•plore, •plored,
  •plor•ing

ex•plor\er

ex•plo•sion

ex•plo•sive

ex•plo•sive\ly

ex•plo•sive•ness

ex\po, *pl.* •pos

ex•po•nent

ex•po•nen•tial

ex•po•nen•tial\ly

ex•port, •port\ed,
  •port•ing

ex•por•ta•tion

ex•port\er

ex•pose (*to uncover*),
  •posed, •pos•ing

ex•po\sé (*public
  disclosure*)

ex•po•si•tion

ex•pos\i•tor

ex•pos\i•to\ry

ex post fac\to

ex•pos•tu•late, •lat\ed,
  •lat•ing

ex•pos•tu•la•tion

ex•po•sure

ex•pound, •pound\ed,
  •pound•ing

ex•pound\er

ex•press, •pressed,
  •press•ing

ex•press•age

ex•press•i\ble

ex•pres•sion

ex•pres•sion•ism

ex•pres•sion•ist

ex•pres•sion•is•tic

ex•pres•sion•less

ex•pres•sive

ex•pres•sive\ly

ex•pres•sive•ness

ex•press\ly

ex•press war•ran\ty

ex•press•way

ex•pro•pri•ate, •at\ed,
  •at•ing

ex•pro•pri•a•tion

ex•pul•sion

ex•punge, •punged,
  •pung•ing

ex•pur•gate, •gat\ed,
  •gat•ing

ex•pur•ga•tion

ex•quis•ite

ex•quis•ite\ly
ex•quis•ite•ness
ex•tant (*existing*) [*vs.*
ex•tent (*scope*)]
ex•tem•po•ra•ne•ous
ex•tem•po\re
ex•tem•po•rize, •rized,
•riz\ing
ex•tend, •tend\ed,
•tend•ing
extended ASCII
extended fam•i\ly
extended mem•o\ry
ex•tend\er
ex•ten•si\ble
ex•ten•sion
ex•ten•sive
ex•ten•sive\ly
ex•tent (*scope*) [*vs.*
ex•tant (*existing*)]
ex•ten\u•ate, •at\ed,
•at•ing
ex•ten\u•a•tion
ex•te•ri\or
ex•ter•mi•nate, •nat\ed,
•nat•ing
ex•ter•mi•na•tion
ex•ter•mi•na•tor
ex•tern
ex•ter•nal
external au•di•tor
external com•mand
ex•ter•nal\ly
ex•ter•nal mo•dem
ex•tinct
ex•tinc•tion
ex•tin•guish, •guished,
•guish•ing
ex•tin•guish\er
ex•tir•pate, •pat\ed,
•pat•ing
ex•tir•pa•tion
ex•tol, •tolled, •tol•ling
ex•tort, •tort\ed, •tort•ing
ex•tor•tion•ate
ex•tra, *pl.* •tras

ex•tract, •tract\ed,
•tract•ing
ex•trac•tion
ex•trac•tor
ex•tra•cur•ric\u•lar
ex•tra•dit•a\ble
ex•tra•dite, •dit\ed, •dit•ing
ex•tra•di•tion
ex•tra div•i\dend
ex•tra-•high-•den\si\ty
ex•tra•le\gal
ex•tra•mar\i•tal
ex•tra•mu•ral
ex•tra•ne•ous
ex•tra•ne•ous\ly
ex•traor•di•nar\i•ly
ex•traor•di•nar\y
extraordinary i\tem
extraordinary re•pair
ex•trap\o•late, •lat\ed,
•lat•ing
ex•trap\o•la•tion
ex•tra•sen•so\ry
ex•tra•ter•res•tri\al
ex•tra•ter•ri•to•ri\al
ex•tra•ter•ri•to•ri•al•i\ty
ex•trav\a•gance
ex•trav\a•gant
ex•trav\a•gant\ly
ex•trav\a•gan\za, *pl.* •zas
ex•tra•ve\hic\u•lar
ex•tra•vert
ex•treme
ex•treme\ly
ex•trem•ism
ex•trem•ist
ex•trem•i\ty, *pl.* •ties
ex•tri•cate, •cat\ed,
•cat•ing
ex•tri•ca•tion
ex•trin•sic
ex•trin•si•cal\ly
ex•tro•ver•sion
ex•tro•vert
ex•trude, •trud\ed,
•trud•ing

ex•tru•sion
ex•tru•sive
ex\u\ber•ance
ex\u\ber•ant
ex\u\ber•ant\ly
ex\u•da•tion
ex•ude, •ud\ed, •ud•ing
ex•ult (*rejoice*), •ult\ed,
•ult•ing [*vs.* ex•alt
(*glorify*)]
ex•ult•ant
ex•ul•ta•tion
ex•ult•ing\ly
ex•ur•ban
ex•ur•bi\a
eye (*organ of sight*) [*vs.*
aye (*yes*) *and* I (*me*)]
eye, eyed, ey•ing *or*
eye•ing
eye•ball, •balled, •ball•ing
eye•brow
eye-•catch\ing
eyed
eye•drop•per
eye•ful, *pl.* •fuls
eye•glass
eye•lash
eye•less
eye•let (*small hole*) [*vs.*
is•let (*small island*)]
eye•lid
eye•lin\er
eye•o\pen\er
eye•o\pen•ing
eye•piece
eye•shade
eye shad\ow
eye•sight
eye•sore
eye•strain
eye•tooth, *pl.* •teeth
eye•wash
eye•wit•ness, •nessed,
•ness•ing
ey•rie *or* ey\ry, *pl.* •ries
E\ze•ki\el

F

fa•ble
fa•bled
fab•ric

fab•ri•cate, •cat\ed,
•cat•ing
fab•ri•ca•tion

fab•ri•ca•tor
fab\u•lous
fab\u•lous\ly

fa•cade or fa•çade

face, faced, fac•ing

faced

face•less

face-•lift

face-•off

face-•sav\ing

fac\et (gem surface) [vs. fau•cet (flow control valve)]

fa•ce•tious

fa•ce•tious\ly

fa•ce•tious•ness

fa•cial

fac•ile

fac•ile\ly

fa•cil\i•tate, •tat\ed, •tat•ing

fa•cil\i•ta•tion

fa•cil\i•ta•tor

fa•cil\i•ty (ease), pl. •ties [vs. fe•lic•i•ty (happiness)]

fac•ing

fac•sim\i\le, •led, •le•ing

fact

fac•tion

fac•tion\al

fac•tion•al•ism

fac•tious (contentious) [vs. fac•ti-•tious (artificial) and fic•ti•tious (imaginary)]

fac•tious•ness

fac•ti•tious (artificial) [vs. fac•tious (contentious) and fic•ti•tious (imaginary)]

fac•tor, •tored, •tor•ing

fac•tor•age

fac•to\ry, pl. •ries

fac•to•tum

fact sheet

fac•tu\al

fac•tu•al\ly

fac•ul\ty, pl. •ties

fad

fad•dish

fad•dist

fade, fad\ed, fad•ing

fae•cal

fae•ces

fa•er\ie or fa•er\y, pl. •er•ies

fag•got (disparaging term for homosexual)

fag\ot (bundle of twigs)

Fahr•en•heit

fa•ience or fa•ience

fail, failed, fail•ing

faille (ribbed fabric) [vs. file (folder; tool)]

fail-•safe

fail•ure

fain

faint, \er, •est

faint (to lose conscious-ness), \ed, •ing [vs. feint (to deceive)], \ed, •ing

faint•heart\ed

faint\ly

faint•ness

fair (impartial), \er, •est [vs. fare (transportation charge; food)]

fair em•ploy•ment

fair•ground

fair-•haired

fair\ly

fair mar•ket val\ue

fair•ness

fair trade (noun)

fair-•trade (adj.)

fair•way

fair\y, pl. fair•ies

fair\y•land

fair\y tale

fait ac•com•pli, pl. faits ac•com•plis

faith

faith•ful

faith•ful\ly

faith•ful•ness

faith•less

faith•less\ly

faith•less•ness

fake, faked, fak•ing

fak\er (one who pretends)

fa•kir (Muslim or Hindu monk)

fal•con

fal•con\er

fal•con\ry

fall, fell, fall\en, fall•ing

fal•la•cious

fal•la•cious\ly

fal•la\cy, pl. •cies

fal•li•bil•i\ty

fal•li\ble

fall\ing-•out, pl. fall\ings-•out

fall•off

fal•lo•pi\an or Fal•lo•pi\an

fall•out or fall-•out

fal•low

false, fals\er, fals•est

false drop

false•hood

false\ly

false•ness

fal•set\to, pl. •tos

fals\ie

fal•si•fi•ca•tion

fal•si\fy, •fied, •fy•ing

fal•si\ty

fal•ter, •tered, •ter•ing

fal•ter•ing\ly

fame

famed

fa•mil•ial

fa•mil•iar

fa•mil\i•ar•i\ty, pl. •ties

fa•mil•iar•ize, •ized, •iz•ing

fa•mil•iar\ly

fam•i\ly, pl. •lies

fam•ine

fam•ish, •ished, •ish•ing

fa•mous

fa•mous\ly

fan, fanned, fan•ning

fa•nat\ic

fa•nat\i•cal\ly

fa•nat\i•cism

fan•ci\er

fan•ci•ful

fan•ci•ful\ly

fan\cy, pl. •cies; •cied, •cy•ing; •ci\er, •ci•est

fan\cy-•free

fan\cy•work

fan•dan\go, pl. •gos

fan•dom

fan•fare

fang

fanged

fan•jet or fan jet

fan•light

Fan•nie Mae (*Federal National Mortgage Association*)

fan\ny, *pl.* •nies

fan\ny pack

fan•ta•sia, *pl.* •sias

fan•ta•size, •sized, •siz•ing

fan•tas•tic

fan•tas•ti•cal\ly

fan•ta\sy or phan•ta\sy, *pl.* •sies, •sied, •sy•ing

far, far•ther or fur•ther, far•thest or fur•thest

far\ad

far•a\way

farce

fare (*transportation charge; food*), fared, far•ing [*vs. fair (impartial)*]

fare•well

far-•fetched or far•fetched

far-•flung

fa•ri\na

far\i•na•ceous

farm, farmed, farm•ing

Far•mer

farm\er

farm•hand or farm hand

farm•house, *pl.* •hous\es

farm•land

farm•stead

farm•yard

far\o

far-•off

far-•out

far•ra\go, *pl.* •goes

far-•reach\ing

far•row

far•sight\ed

far•sight•ed•ness

far•ther (*to a greater distance*) [*vs. fur•ther (to a greater extent)*]

far•ther•most

far•thest

far•thing

F.A.S. (*free alongside ship*)

fas•ci•cle

fas•ci•nate, •nat\ed, •nat•ing

fas•ci•na•tion

fas•cism

fas•cist

fa•scis•tic

fash•ion, •ioned, •ion•ing

fash•ion•a\ble

fash•ion•a•bly

fast, \er, •est

fast, \ed, •ing

fast•back

fas•ten, •tened, •ten•ing

fas•ten\er

fast food (*noun*)

fast-•food (*adj.*)

fas•tid\i•ous

fas•tid\i•ous\ly

fas•tid\i•ous•ness

FAT (*file allocation table*)

fat, fat•ter, fat•test

fa•tal

fatal er•ror

fa•tal•ism

fa•tal•ist

fa•tal•is•tic

fa•tal\i•ty, *pl.* •ties

fa•tal\ly

fat•back

fate (*destiny*) [*vs. fete or fête (celebration)*]

fat\ed

fate•ful

fate•ful\ly

fat•head\ed

fa•ther, •thered, •ther•ing

fa•ther•hood

fa\ther-•in-•law, *pl.* fa\thers-•in-•law

fa•ther•land

fa•ther•less

fa•ther\ly

fath\om, *pl.* •oms or \om; •omed, •om•ing

fa•tigue, •tigued, •ti•guing

fat•ness

fat•ten, •tened, •ten•ing

fat•ti•ness

fat\ty, *pl.* •ties; •ti\er, •ti•est

fa•tu•i\ty

fat\u•ous

fat\u•ous\ly

fat\u•ous•ness

fau•cet (*flow control valve*) [*vs.* fac\et (*gem surface*)]

Faulk•ner

fault, fault\ed, fault•ing

fault•find•ing

fault•i\ly

fault•less

fault•less\ly

fault\ly, fault•i\er, fault•i•est

faun (*satyr*) [*vs.* fawn (*young deer*)]

fau\na, *pl.* •nas, •nae

Faust or Faus•tus

Faus•ti\an

Fauve

Fauv•ism

faux pas, *pl.* faux pas

fa•vor, •vored, •vor•ing

fa•vor•a\ble

fa•vor•a•bly

fa•vor•ite

fa•vor•it•ism

fawn (*young deer*) [*vs.* faun (*satyr*)]

fawn, fawned, fawn•ing

fawn•ing\ly

fax, faxed, fax•ing

fay

faze (*to disconcert*), fazed, faz•ing [*vs.* phase (*aspect*)]

FBI (*Federal Bureau of Investigation*)

FCC (*Federal Communications Commission*)

FDA (*Food and Drug Administration*)

FDIC (*Federal Deposit Insurance Corporation*)

fe•al\ty

fear, feared, fear•ing

fear•ful

fear•ful\ly

fear•ful•ness

fear•less

fear•less\ly

fear•less•ness
fear•some
fea•si•bil•i\ty
fea•si\ble
feast, feast\ed, feast•ing
feat
feath\er, •ered, •er•ing
feath\er•bed•ding
feath•ered
feath\er•weight
feath•er\y
fea•ture, •tured, •tur•ing
fea•ture•less
fe•brile
Feb•ru•ar\y
fe•cal
fe•ces
feck•less
feck•less\ly
fe•cund
fe•cun•di\ty
fed
fe•da•yeen, pl.
fed•er\al
fed•er•al•ism
fed•er•al•ist
fed•er•al•ize, •ized, •iz•ing
Fed•er\al Re•serve note
fed•er•ate, •at\ed, •at•ing
fed•er•a•tion
fe•do\ra, pl. •ras
fee
fee•ble, •bler, •blest
fee\ble-•mind\ed
fee\ble-•mind\ed\ness
fee•ble•ness
fee•bly
feed, fed, feed•ing
feed•back
feed\er
feed•stuff
feel, felt, feel•ing
feel\er
feel•ing
feel•ing\ly
feet
feign, feigned, feign•ing
feint (to deceive), feint\ed,
feint•ing [vs. faint (to lose
consciousness)]
feist\y, •i\er, •i•est

feld•spar
fe•lic\i•tate, •tat\ed,
•tat•ing
fe•lic\i•ta•tion
fe•lic\i•ta•tor
fe•lic\i•tous
fe•lic\i•tous\ly
fe•lic•i\ty (happiness) [vs.
fa•cil•i\ty (ease)]
fe•line
fell, felled, fell•ing
fel•lah (Arabic peasant), pl.
fel•lahs, fel•la•hin,
fel•la•heen
fel•la•ti\o or fel•la•tion
fel•low (man or boy)
fel•low•man or fel•low
man, pl. •men or men
fel•low•ship
fel\on
fe•lo•ni•ous
fel•o\ny, pl. •nies
felt
fe•male
fem\i•nine
fem\i•nin•i\ty
fem\i•nism
fem\i•nist
femme fa•tale, pl. femmes
fa•tales
fem\o•ral
fe•mur, pl. fe•murs,
fem•o\ra
fen
fence, fenced, fenc•ing
fenc\er
fend, fend\ed, fend•ing
fend\er
fen•es•tra•tion
fen•nel
fe•ral
fer•ment (to change to
alcohol), •ment\ed,
•ment•ing [vs. fo•ment
(to instigate)]
fer•men•ta•tion
fer\mi
fer•mi\um
fern
fe•ro•cious
fe•ro•cious\ly

fe•roc•i\ty or
fe•ro•cious•ness
fer•ret, •ret\ed, •ret•ing
fer•ric
Fer•ris wheel
fer\ro•mag•net•ic
fer\ro•mag•ne•tism
fer•rous
fer•rule (metal ring) [vs.
fer•ule (rod)]
fer\ry, pl. •ries; •ried,
•ry•ing
fer\ry•boat
fer•tile
fer•til•i\ty
fer•ti•li•za•tion
fer•ti•lize, •lized, •liz•ing
fer•ti•liz\er
fer•ule (rod) [vs. fer•rule
(metal ring)]
fer•ven\cy
fer•vent
fer•vent\ly
fer•vid
fer•vid\ly
fer•vor
fes•tal
fes•ter, •tered, •ter•ing
fes•ti•val
fes•tive
fes•tive\ly
fes•tive•ness (festive
quality)
fes•tiv•i\ty (celebration), pl.
•ties
fes•toon, •tooned,
•toon•ing
fet\a
fe•tal or foe•tal
fetch, fetched, fetch•ing
fetch•ing\ly
fete or fête (celebration)
[vs. fate (destiny)]
fet\id
fet•ish
fet•ish•ism
fet•ish•ist
fet•lock
fet•ter, •tered, •ter•ing
fet•tle

fet•tuc•ci\ne *or*
fet•tuc•ci\ni

fe•tus *or* foe•tus, *pl.*
•tus\es

feud, feud\ed, feud•ing

feu•dal

feu•dal•ism

feu•dal•is•tic

fe•ver, •vered, •ver•ing

fe•ver•ish

fe•ver•ish\ly

few, few\er, few•est

fey

fez, *pl.* fez•zes

FHA (*Federal Housing
Administration*)

fi•an\cé (*engaged man*)

fi•an•cée (*engaged
woman*)

fi•as\co, *pl.* •cos, •coes

fi\at

fib, fibbed, fib•bing

fib•ber

fi•ber

fi\ber•board

fi\ber•fill

fi\ber•glass *or* fi•ber glass

fi\ber•op\tic

fi•ber op•tics *or*
fi\ber•op\tics

fi•bril

fi•bril•late, •lat\ed,
•lat•ing

fi•bril•la•tion

fi•brin

fi•brin\o•gen

fi•broid

fi•brous

fib•u•la, *pl.* •lae, •las

fib\u•lar

FICA *or* F.I.C.A. (*Federal
Insurance Contributions
Act*)

fiche

fick\le

fick•le•ness

fic•tion

fic•tion\al

fic•tion•al\i•za•tion

fic•tion•al•ize, •ized,
•iz•ing

fic•ti•tious (*imaginary*) [*vs.*
fac•tious (*contentious*) *and*
fac•ti•\tious (*artificial*)]

fic•ti•tious\ly

fic•tive

fid•dle, •dled, •dling

fid•dler

fid\dle•sticks

fi•del\i•ty

fidelity bond

fidg\et, •et\ed, •et•ing

fidg•et\y

fi•du•ci•ar\y, *pl.* •ar•ies

fie

fief

fief•dom

field, field\ed, field•ing

field\er

field test (*noun*)

field-•test (*verb*)

field ware•hous•ing

field•work *or* field work

field•work\er

fiend (*demon*) [*vs.* friend
(*comrade*)]

fiend•ish

fiend•ish\ly

fierce, fierc\er, fierc•est

fierce\ly

fierce•ness

fier\i•ness

fier\y, •i\er, •i•est

fi•es\ta

fife

FIFO (*first-in, first-out*)

fif•teen

fif•teenth

fifth

fifth\ly

fif•ti•eth

fif\ty, *pl.* •ties

fif\ty-•fif\ty *or* 50-\50

fight, fought, fight•ing

fight\er

fig•ment

fig•ur\a•tive

fig•ur\a•tive\ly

fig•ure, •ured, •ur•ing

fig•ure•head

fig•ur•ine

Fi\ji

Fi•ji\an

fil\a•ment

fil•bert

filch, filched, filch•ing

file (*folder; tool*) [*vs.* faille
(*ribbed fabric*)]

file, filed, fil•ing

file al•lo•ca•tion ta•ble
(*FAT*)

file lock•ing

file man•ag\er

file•name

filename ex•ten•sion

file serv\er

fi•let (*netting*) [*vs.* fil•let
(*boneless strip, as fish*)]

fi•let mi•gnon

fil•i\al

fil\i•bus•ter, •tered,
•ter•ing

fil\i•gree, •greed, •gree•ing

fil•ings, *pl.*

Fil\i•pi\no, *pl.* •nos

fill, filled, fill•ing

fill•a\ble

fill\er

fil•let (*boneless strip, as
fish; to debone*), fil•let\ed,
fil•let•ing [*vs.*
fi•let (*netting*)]

fill-•in

fill•ing

fil•lip

Fill•more

fil\ly, *pl.* •lies

film, filmed, film•ing

film\i•ness

film•strip

film\y, film•i\er, film•i•est

fil•ter (*strainer*) [*vs.*
phil•ter (*potion*)]

fil•ter, •tered, •ter•ing

fil•ter•a\ble

filth

filth\i•ness

filth\y, •i\er, •i•est

fil•tra\ble

fil•tra•tion

fin

fi•na•gle, •gled, •gling

fi•na•gler

fi•nal

fi•na\le (*last part*) [*vs.* fi•nal\ly (*at last*) and fine\ly (*delicately*)]

fi•nal•ist

fi•nal•i\ty

fi•na•li•za•tion

fi•na•lize, •lized, •liz•ing

fi•nal\ly (*at last*) [*vs.* fi•na\le (*last part*) and fine\ly (*delicately*)]

fi•nance, •nanced, •nanc•ing

finance com•pa\ny

fi•nan•cial

financial lease

fi•nan•cial\ly

fi•nan•cial state•ment

fin•an•cier

finch

find (*to locate*), found, find\ing [*vs.* fined (*penalized*)]

find•a\ble

find\er

find•er's fee

fin-•de-•siè\cle

find•ing

fine, fined, fin•ing; fin\er, fin•est

fined (*penalized*) [*vs.* find (*to locate*)]

fine\ly (*delicately*) [*vs.* fi•na\le (*last part*) and fi•nal\ly (*at last*)]

fine•ness (*thinness*) [*vs.* fi•nesse (*delicacy*)]

fin•er\y

fine•spun *or* fine-•spun

fi•nesse (*delicacy*) [*vs.* fine•ness (*thinness*)]

fi•nesse, •nessed, •ness•ing

fine-•tune, •tuned, •tun\ing

fin•ger, •gered, •ger•ing

fin\ger•board

fin•ger•ing

fin\ger•ling

fin\ger•nail

fin\ger•print, •print\ed, •print•ing

fin\ger•tip

fin•i\al

fin•ick\y

fin\is (*the end*)

fin•ish (*end; to end*), •ished, •ish•ing

fin•ished goods

fin•ish\er

fi•nite

fink

Fin•land

Finn

fin•nan had•die

finned

Finn•ish

fin\ny, •ni\er, •ni•est

F.I.O. (*free in and out*)

fiord

fir (*tree*) [*vs.* fur (*hairy animal skin*)]

fire, fired, fir•ing

fire•arm

fire•ball

fire•bomb, •bombed, •bomb•ing

fire•box

fire•brand

fire•break

fire•brick

fire•bug

fire•crack\er

fire•damp

fire•fight

fire•fight\er *or* fire fight\er

fire•fight•ing

fire•fly, *pl.* •flies

fire•house, *pl.* •hous\es

fire•less

fire•man, *pl.* •men

fire•place

fire•plug

fire•pow\er *or* fire pow\er

fire•proof, •proofed, •proof•ing

fire•side

fire•storm *or* fire storm

fire•trap

fire•wa\ter

fire•wood

fire•work

firm, firmed, firm•ing; firm\er, firm•est

fir•ma•ment

firm\ly

firm•ness

firm or•der

firm•ware

first

first aid (*noun*)

first-•aid (*adj.*)

first•born

first class (*noun*)

first-•class (*adj.*)

first•hand *or* first-•hand

first-•in, first-•out (*FIFO*)

first la\dy

first\ly

first-•night\er

first-•rate

first-•string

first-•string\er

firth

fis•cal (*financial*) [*vs.* phys\i•cal (*of the body*)]

fis•cal year

fish, *pl.* fish *or* fish\es; fished, fish•ing

fish•bowl *or* fish bowl

fish\er

fish•er•man, *pl.* •men

fish•er\y, *pl.* •er•ies

fish•hook

fish•i\ly

fish\i•ness

fish•ing

fish•wife, *pl.* •wives

fish\y, •i\er, •i•est

fis•sile

fis•sion, •sioned, •sion•ing

fis•sion•a\ble

fis•sure, •sured, •sur•ing

fist

fist•ful, *pl.* •fuls

fist\i•cuff

fis•tu\la, *pl.* •las, •lae

fit, fit•ted *or* fit, fit•ting; fit•ter, fit•test

fit•ful

fit•ful\ly

fit•ful•ness

fit\ly

fit•ness
fit•ter
fit•ting
fit•ting\ly
five
five-•and-•ten
fix, fixed, fix•ing
fix•at\ed
fix•a•tion
fix\a\tive
fixed
fixed as•set
fixed charge
fixed cost
fixed-•length field
fix•ed\ly
fixed pitch
fix\er
fix•ing
fix\i\ty
fix•ture
fizz, fizzed, fizz•ing
fiz•zle, •zled, •zling
fjord or fiord
FL (*Florida*)
flab
flab•ber•gast\ed
flab•bi•ness
flab\by, •bi\er, •bi•est
flac•cid
flack
flac\on
flag, flagged, flag•ging
flag•el•la•tion
flag•pole
fla•grant (*glaring*) [*vs.*
  fra•grant (*scented*)]
fla•gran\te de•lic\to
fla•grant\ly
flag•ship
flag•stone
flail, flailed, flail•ing
flair (*aptitude*) [*vs.* flare (*to*
  flame)]
flak
flake, flaked, flak•ing
flak\y, •i\er, •i•est
flam•bé, •béed, •bé•ing
flam•boy•ance
flam•boy•ant
flam•boy•ant\ly

flame, flamed, flam•ing
fla•men\co, *pl.* •cos
flame-•out
flame•throw\er
fla•min\go, *pl.* •gos, •goes
flam•ma•bil•i\ty
flam•ma\ble
Flan•ders
flange
flank, flanked, flank•ing
flan•nel
flan•nel\et or flan•nel•ette
flap, flapped, flap•ping
flap•jack
flap•per
flare (*to flame*), flared,
  flar•ing [*vs.* flair
  (*aptitude*)]
flare\up
flash, flashed, flash•ing
flash•back
flash•bulb or flash bulb
flash•card or flash card
flash•cube
flash\er
flash-•for\ward
flash•gun
flash\i•ly
flash\i•ness
flash•ing
flash•light
flash point or flash•point
flash\y, flash•i\er, flash•i•est
flask
flat, flat•ted, flat•ting;
  flat•ter, flat•test
flat•bed
flatbed scan•ner
flat•boat
flat•car
flat-•file da\ta•base
flat•fish, *pl.* •fish, •fish\es
flat•foot, *pl.* •feet, •foots
flat•foot\ed
flat•i\ron
flat\ly
flat•ness
flat-•out
flat-•screen dis•play
flat tech•nol\o\gy
  mon\i•tor

flat•ten, •tened, •ten•ing
flat•ter, •tered, •ter•ing
flat•ter\er
flat•ter•ing\ly
flat•ter\y
flat•tish
flat•top
flat\u•lence
flat\u•lent
flat•ware
Flau•bert
flaunt (*to display boldly*),
  flaunt\ed, flaunt•ing [*vs.*
  flout (*to scoff at*)]
flau•tist
fla•vor
fla•vored
fla•vor•ful
fla•vor•ing
fla•vor•less
flaw
flawed
flaw•less
flaw•less\ly
flax
flax\en
flay, flayed, flay•ing
flea (*small insect*) [*vs.* flee
  (*to run away*)]
flea•bag
flea-•bit\ten
fleck
fledg•ling
flee (*to run away*), fled,
  flee•ing [*vs.* flea (*small
  insect*)]
fleece, fleeced, fleec•ing
fleec\y, •i\er, •i•est
fleer, fleered, fleer•ing
fleer•ing\ly
fleet
fleet, fleet\er, fleet•est
fleet•ing
fleet•ing\ly
fleet\ly
fleet•ness
Flem•ing
Flem•ish
flesh, fleshed, flesh•ing
flesh•pots, *pl.*
flesh\y, •i\er, •i•est

fleur-•de-•lis, *pl.* •de-•lis

flew (*did fly*) [*vs.* flu
(*influenza*) and flue
(*chimney duct*)]

flex, flexed, flex•ing

flex•i•bil•i•ty

flex•i•ble

flex\i\ble-•rate mort•gage

flex•time *or* flex\i•time

flib•ber•ti•gib•bet

flick, flicked, flick•ing

flick\er, •ered, •er•ing

flied

fli\er *or* fly\er

flight

flight\i•ness

flight•ing

flight•less

flight\y, •i\er, •i•est

flim•flam

flim•si•ness

flim\sy, *pl.* •sies; •si\er,
•si•est

flinch, flinched, flinch•ing

fling, flung, fling•ing

flint

flint•lock

flint\y, •i\er, •i•est

flip, flipped, flip•ping;
flip\per, flip•pest

flip-•flop, •flopped,
•flop\ping

flip•pan\cy

flip•pant

flip•pant\ly

flip•per

flirt, flirt\ed, flirt•ing

flir•ta•tion

flir•ta•tious

flir•ta•tious\ly

flit, flit•ted, flit•ting

flit•ter

fliv•ver

float, float\ed, float•ing

float\er

float\ing-•point num•ber

float\ing-•point u\nit (*FPU*)

float\ing-•rate

flock, flocked, flock•ing

flocks (*groups*) [*vs.* phlox
(*the flower*)]

floe (*floating ice*) [*vs.* flow
(*to stream*)]

flog, flogged, flog•ging

flood, flood\ed, flood•ing

flood•gate

flood\light, •light\ed *or*
•lit, •light•ing

flood plain *or* flood•plain

floor, floored, floor•ing

floor•board

floor•ing

floor•walk\er

floo\zy *or* floo•zie, *pl.*
•zies

flop, flopped, flop•ping

flop•house, *pl.* •hous\es

flop\py, *pl.* •pies; •pi\er,
•pi•est

floppy disk

floppy drive

Flop•ti•cal disk (™)

flo\ra, *pl.* flo•ras, flo•rae

flo•ral

Flor•ence

Flor•en•tine

flo•res•cence (*bloom*) [*vs.*
fluo•res•cence (*light*)]

flo•ret

flor\id

Flor•i•da (*FL*)

Flor\i•dan *or* Flo•rid•i\an

flor\in

flo•rist

floss, flossed, floss•ing

floss\y, •i\er, •i•est

flo•ta•tion *or* floa•ta•tion

flo•til\la

flot•sam

flounce, flounced,
flounc•ing

floun•der (*the fish; to
struggle*), *pl.* •der *or*
•ders; •dered, •der•ing
[*vs.* foun•der (*to sink*)
and found\er (*one who
founds*)]

flour (*fine meal; to coat
with flour*), floured,
flour•ing [*vs.* flow\er
(*blossom*)]

flour•ish, •ished, •ish•ing

flour•ish•ing\ly

flour\y

flout (*to scoff at*), flout\ed,
flout•ing [*vs.* flaunt (*to
display boldly*)]

flow (*to stream*), flowed,
flow•ing [*vs.* floe (*floating
ice*)]

flow chart *or* flow•chart

flow\er (*blossom; to blossom*), •ered, •er\ing [*vs.*
flour (*fine meal*)]

flow•er•pot

flow•er\y, •er•i\er,
•er•i•est

flown

fl. oz. (*fluid ounce*)

flu (*influenza*) [*vs.* flew
(*did fly*) and flue (*chimney duct*)]

flub, flubbed, flub•bing

fluc•tu•ate, •at\ed, •at•ing

fluc•tu•a•tion

flue (*chimney duct*) [*vs.*
flew (*did fly*) and flu
(*influenza*)]

flu•en\cy

flu•ent

flu•ent\ly

fluff, fluffed, fluff•ing

fluff\i•ness

fluff\y, •i\er, •i•est

flu\id

flu•id\i\ty

flu•id\ly

flu\id ounce (*fl. oz.*)

fluke

fluk\y, •i\er, •i•est

flum•mox, •moxed,
•mox•ing

flung

flunk, flunked, flunk•ing

flun\ky *or* flun•key, *pl.*
•kies, •keys

fluo•resce, •resced,
•resc•ing

fluo•res•cence (*light*) [*vs.*
flo•res•cence (*bloom*)]

fluo•res•cent

fluor\i•date, •dat\ed,
•dat•ing

fluor\i•da•tion
fluor•ide
fluor•ine
fluor\o•car•bon
fluor\o•scope, •scoped, •scop•ing
flur\ry, pl. •ries; •ried, •ry•ing
flush, flushed, flush•ing
flus•ter, •tered, •ter•ing
flute
flut\ed
flut•ing
flut•ist or flautist
flut•ter, •tered, •ter•ing
flut•ter\y
flux
fly (insect), pl. flies
fly (to move through the air with wings), flew, flown, fly•ing
fly (baseball hit high and catchable), pl. flies; flied, fly•ing
fly•blown
fly\by or fly-•by, pl. •bys
fly-•by-•night
fly•catch\er
fly\er
fly•leaf, pl. •leaves
fly•pa•per
fly•speck
fly•specked
fly•way
fly•weight
fly•wheel
FM (frequency modulation)
FNMA (Federal National Mortgage Association)
f-\num\ber
foal, foaled, foal•ing
foam, foamed, foam•ing
foam\y, •i\er, •i•est
fob or f.o.b. (free on board)
fob, fobbed, fob•bing
fo•cal
fo'c's'le (forecastle)
fo•cus, pl. •cus\es, \ci; •cused or •cussed, •cus•ing or •cus•sing
fod•der

foe
foe•tal
foe•tus, pl. •tus\es
fog, fogged, fog•ging
fog\gy (misty), •gi\er, •gi•est [vs. fo\gy or fo•gey (old-fashioned person)]
fog•horn
fo\gy or fo•gey (old-fashioned person), pl. •gies or •geys [vs. fog\gy (misty)]
fo•gy•ish
foi•ble
foil, foiled, foil•ing
foist, foist\ed, foist•ing
fold, fold\ed, fold•ing
fold•a\way
fold\er
fold•out or fold-•out
fo•li•age
fo•li•at\ed
fo•lic ac\id
fo•li\o, pl. •li\os
folk
folk•lore
folk•lor\ic
folk•lor•ist
folk•si•ness
folk\sy, •si\er, •si•est
folk•way
fol•li•cle
fol•low, •lowed, •low•ing
fol•low\er
fol•low•ing
fol\low-•up
fol\ly, pl. •lies
fo•ment (to instigate), •ment\ed, •ment•ing [vs. fer•ment (to change to alcohol)]
fond, \er, •est
fon•dant
fon•dle, •dled, •dling
fon•dling (caressing) [vs. found\ling (abandoned infant)]
fond\ly
fond•ness
fon•due
font

font card
font car•tridge
font fam•i\ly
food
food chain
food\ie
food poi•son•ing
food proc•es•sor
food•stuff
fool, fooled, fool•ing
fool•er\y, pl. •er•ies
fool•har•di•ness
fool•har\dy
fool•ish
fool•ish\ly
fool•ish•ness
fool•proof
foot, pl. feet
foot•age
foot-•and-•mouth disease
foot•ball
foot•board
foot•bridge
foot-•can\dle
foot\er
foot•fall
foot•hill
foot•hold
foot•ing
foot•less
foot•light
foot•lock\er
foot•loose
foot•man, pl. •men
foot•note, •not\ed, •not•ing
foot•path, pl. •paths
foot-•pound
foot•print
foot•rest
foot•sore
foot•step
foot•stool
foot•wear
foot•work
fop
fop•per\y
fop•pish
for (in favor of) [vs. fore (front) and four (number)]

for•age, •aged, •ag•ing

for•ag\er

for•as•much as

for\ay

for•bear (to abstain),
•bore, •borne, •bear•ing
[vs. fore•bear (ancestor)]

for•bear•ance

for•bid, •bade or •bad or
•bid, •bid•den, •bid•ding

for•bid•ding

for•bid•ding\ly

force, forced, forc•ing

force-•feed, •fed, •feed\ing

force•ful (powerful) [vs.
for•ci•ble (done by
force)]

force•ful\ly

force•ful•ness

for•ceps, pl. •ceps or
•ci•pes

for•ci•ble (done by force)
[vs. force•ful (powerful)]

for•ci•bly

ford, ford\ed, ford•ing

fore (front) [vs. for (in
favor of) and four (num-
ber)]

fore-•and-•aft

fore•arm

fore•armed

fore•bear (ancestor) [vs.
for•bear (to abstain)]

fore•bod•ing

fore•cast, •cast or
•cast\ed, •cast•ing

fore•cast\er

fore•cas•tle or fo'c's'le

fore•close, •closed,
•clos•ing

fore•clo•sure

fore•doom, •doomed,
•doom•ing

fore•fa•ther

fore•fin•ger

fore•foot, pl. •feet

fore•front

fore•go•ing

fore•gone

fore•ground

fore•hand

fore•head

fore•ign

foreign cor•po•ra•tion

for•eign\er

for•eign ex•change (FX)

for•eign•ness

fore•knowl•edge

fore•leg

fore•limb

fore•lock

fore•man, pl. •men

fore•per•son

fore•wom\an, pl. •wom\en

fore•mast

fore•most

fore•name

fore•noon

fo•ren•sic

fore•or•dain, •dained,
•dain•ing

fore•part

fore•play

fore•quar•ter

fore•run•ner

fore•sail

fore•see, •saw, •seen,
•see•ing

fore•see•a\ble

fore•shad\ow, •owed,
•ow•ing

fore•short\en, •ened,
•en•ing

fore•sight

fore•sight\ed

fore•sight•ed•ness

fore•skin

for•est, •est\ed, •est•ing

fore•stall, •stalled,
•stall•ing

for•est•a•tion

for•est\ed

for•est\er

for•est\ry

fore•taste, •tast\ed,
•tast•ing

fore•tell, •told, •tell•ing

fore•thought

for•ev\er

for•ev\er•more

fore•warn, •warned,
•warn•ing

fore•word (preface) [vs.
for•ward (to the front)]

for•feit, •feit\ed, •feit•ing

for•fei•ture

for•fend, •fend\ed,
•fend•ing

for•gath\er, •ered, •er•ing

for•gave

forge, forged, forg•ing

forg\er

for•ger\y, pl. •ger•ies

for•get, •got, •get•ting

for•get•ful

for•get•ful\ly

for•get•ful•ness

for\get-•me-•not

for\get•ta\ble

forg•ing

for•giv•a\ble

for•give, •gave, •giv\en,
•giv•ing

for•give•ness

for•giv•ing

for\go, •went, •gone,
•go•ing

fork, forked, fork•ing

fork•ful, pl. •fuls

fork•lift

for•lorn

for•lorn\ly

form, formed, form•ing

for•mal

form•al\de•hyde

for•mal•ism

for•mal•ist

for•mal•i\ty, pl. •ties

for•mal•ize, •ized, •iz•ing

for•mal\ly (ceremonially)
[vs. for•mer\ly
(previously)]

for•mat, •mat•ted,
•mat•ting

for•ma•tion

form\a•tive

form\er (one that forms)

for•mer (earlier)

for•mer\ly (previously) [vs.
for•mal\ly (ceremonially)]

form feed

form•fit•ting

for•mic

For•mi\ca (™)
for•mi•da\ble
for•mi•da•bly
form•less
form•less•ness
For•mo\sa
for•mu\la, pl. •las, •lae
for•mu•la\ic
for•mu•late, •lat\ed, •lat•ing
for•mu•la•tion
for•ni•cate, •cat\ed, •cat•ing
for•ni•ca•tion
for•ni•ca•tor
for•sake, •sook, •sak\en, •sak•ing
for•sooth
for•swear, •swore, •sworn, •swearing
for•syth\i\a, pl. •syth•i\as
fort (army post)
forte (specialty)
for\te (loud; loudly)
FORTH (programming language)
forth (onward) [vs. fourth (next after third)]
forth•com•ing
forth•right
forth•right•ness
forth•with
for•ti•eth
for•ti•fi•a\ble
for•ti•fi•ca•tion
for•ti\fy, •fied, •fy•ing
for•tis•si•mo
for•ti•tude
Fort Lau•der•dale
fort•night
fort•night\ly
FORTRAN (programming language)
for•tress
for•tu•i•tous (accidental)
for•tu•nate (lucky)
for•tu•nate\ly
for•tune
for\tune-•tell\er
for\tune-•tell\ing
Fort Wayne

for\ty, pl. •ties
for\ty-•five
for\ty-•nin\er
fo•rum
for•ward, •ward\ed, •ward•ing
for•ward (to the front) [vs. fore•word (preface)]
for•ward\er
for•ward•ness
for•went
fos•sil
fos•sil\i•za•tion
fos•sil•ize, •ized, •iz•ing
fos•ter, •tered, •ter•ing
fought
foul, fouled, foul•ing
foul (offensive), foul\er, foul•est [vs. fowl (poultry)]
fou•lard
foul\ly
foul•mouthed
foul•ness
foul-•up
found, found\ed, found•ing
foun•da•tion
foun•der (to sink), •dered, •der•ing [vs. floun•der (the fish; to struggle)]
found\er (one who founds) [vs. floun•der (the fish; to struggle)]
found•ling (abandoned infant) [vs. fon•dling (caressing)]
found\ry, pl. •ries
fount
foun•tain
foun•tain•head
four (number) [vs. for (in favor of) and fore (front)]
four-•flush\er
four-•flush\ing
four•fold
four-•in-•hand
four-•o"\clock
four•post\er
four•score
four•some
four•square

four•teen
four•teenth
fourth (next after third) [vs. forth (onward)]
fourth class (noun)
fourth-•class (adj.)
four-•wheel or four-•wheeled
fowl (poultry), pl. fowls or fowl [vs. foul (offensive)]
fowl•ing piece
fox, pl. fox\es or fox; foxed, fox•ing
fox•glove
fox•hole
fox•hound
fox trot (noun)
fox-•trot (verb), •trot\ted, •trot\ting
fox\y, fox•i\er, fox•i•est
foy\er
FPT (freight pass-through)
FPU (floating-point unit)
fra•cas
frac•tion
frac•tion\al
frac•tious
frac•tious•ness
frac•ture, •tured, •tur•ing
frag•ile
fra•gil•i\ty
frag•ment, •ment\ed, •ment•ing
frag•men•tar\y
frag•men•ta•tion
fra•grance
fra•grant (scented) [vs. fla•grant (glaring)]
frail, \er, •est
frail\ly
frail\ty, pl. •ties
frame, framed, fram•ing
fram\er
frame-•up
frame•work
franc (coin) [vs. frank (candid)]
France
fran•chise, •chised, •chis•ing

fran•chi•see, *pl.* •sees
fran•chis\er
Fran•cis•can
Fran•cis of As•si\si
fran•ci\um
Franck
Fran\co
frank (*candid*), frank\er, frank•est [*vs.* franc (*coin*)]
Frank•en•stein
Frank•fort
Frank•furt
frank•furt\er
frank•in•cense
Frank•ish
Frank•lin
frank\ly
frank•ness
fran•tic
fran•ti•cal\ly
frappe *or* frap•pé
fra•ter•nal
fra•ter•nal\ly
fra•ter•ni\ty, *pl.* •ties
frat•er•ni•za•tion
frat•er•nize, •nized, •niz•ing
frat•ri•cid\al
frat•ri•cide
Frau, *pl.* Frau\en *or* Fraus
fraud
fraud\u•lence
fraud\u•lent
fraud\u•lent\ly
fraught
Fräu\lein, *pl.* •leins *or* •leinyfreak
fray, frayed, fray•ing
fraz•zle, •zled, •zling
freak, freaked, freak•ing
freak•ish
freak-•out *or* freak•out
freak\y
freck\le, •led, •ling
freck•led
Fred•die Mac (*Federal Home Loan Mortgage Corporation*)
free, freed, free•ing; fre\er, fre\est

free•base *or* free-•base, •based, •bas•ing *or* •bas\ing
free•bie
free•board
free•boot\er
free•born
freed•man, *pl.* •men
freed•wom\an, *pl.* •wom\en
free•dom
free-•for-•all
free hand (*noun*)
free•hand (*adj.*)
free•hold
free•hold\er
free•lance *or* free-•lance, •lanced, •lanc•ing *or* •lanc\ing
free•load\er
free\ly
free•man, *pl.* •men
free mar•ket
Free•ma\son
Free•ma\son\ry
free•ness
free on board
free port
free•stand•ing
free•stone
free•think\er
free•think•ing
Free•town
free trade
free trad\er
free•ware
free•way
free•wheel•ing
free will (*noun*)
free•will (*adj.*)
freez\a\ble
freeze (*to harden into ice*), froze, fro•zen, freez•ing [*vs.* frieze (*decorative band*)]
freeze-•dry, •dried, •dry\ing
freez\er
freight, freight\ed, freight•ing
freight•age

freight\er
freight for•ward\er
Fre•mont
French
French fries (*noun*)
French-•fry (*verb*), •fried, •fry•ing
French Gui•an\a
French•man, *pl.* •men
French•wom\an, *pl.* •wom\en
fre•net\ic
fren\zy, *pl.* •zies
fren•zied
Fre\on (™)
fre•quen\cy, *pl.* •cies
fre•quent, •quent\ed, •quent•ing
fre•quent\ly
fres\co, *pl.* •coes, •cos; •coed, •co•ing
fresh, fresh\er, fresh•est
fresh\en, •ened, •en•ing
fresh•en\er
fresh\et
fresh\ly
fresh•man, *pl.* •men
fresh•ness
fresh•wa•ter *or* fresh-•wa\ter
Fres\no
fret, fret•ted, fret•ting
fret•ful
fret•ful\ly
fret•ful•ness
fret•work
Freud
fri\a\ble
fri\ar (*monk*) [*vs.* fry\er *or* fri\er (*chicken*)]
fric•as•see, •seed, •see•ing
fric•tion
fric•tion\al
frictional un•em•ploy•ment
fric•tion feed
Fri•day
fried
friend (*comrade*) [*vs.* fiend (*demon*)]
friend•less

friend•li•ness

friend\ly, pl. •lies; •li\er, •li•est

friend•ship

frieze (decorative band) [vs. freeze (to harden into ice)]

frig•ate

fright

fright\en, •ened, •en•ing

fright•en•ing\ly

fright•ful

fright•ful\ly

frig\id

fri•gid•i\ty

frill

frill\i•ness

frill\y, •i\er, •i•est

fringe

fringed

fring•ing

fringe ben\e•fit

frip•per\y, pl. •per•ies

Fris•bee (™)

frisk, frisked, frisk•ing

frisk•i\ly

frisk\i•ness

frisk\y, •i\er, •i•est

frit•ter, •tered, •ter•ing

fri•vol•i\ty

friv\o•lous

friv\o•lous\ly

frizz, frizzed, frizz•ing

friz•zle, •zled, •zling

frizz\y, •i\er, •i•est

fro

frock

frog

frog•man, pl. •men

frol\ic, •icked, •ick•ing

frol•ic•some

from

frond

front, front\ed, front•ing

front•age

fron•tal

front-•end load

fron•tier

fron•tiers•man, pl. •men

fron•tis•piece

front-•run\ner or front•run•ner

frost, frost\ed, frost•ing

frost•bite

frost•bit•ten

frost\i•ness

frost•ing

frost\y, •i\er, •i•est

froth, frothed, froth•ing

froth\y, •i\er, •i•est

frown, frowned, frown•ing

frown•ing\ly

frowz\y, frowz•i\er, frowz•i•est

froze

fro•zen

fruc•ti\fy, •fied, •fy•ing

fruc•tose

fru•gal

fru•gal•i\ty

fru•gal\ly

fruit, pl. fruits or fruit

fruit•cake

fruit\ed

fruit fly

fruit•ful

fruit•ful\ly

fruit•ful•ness

fruit\i•ness

fru•i•tion

fruit•less

fruit•less\ly

fruit•less•ness

fruit\y, fruit•i\er, fruit•i•est

frump

frump\y

frus•trate, •trat\ed, •trat•ing

frus•trat•ing\ly

frus•tra•tion

frus•tum, pl. •tums, \ta

fry (dish of fried food), pl. fries

fry (young of fish), pl. fry

fry (to cook with fat or oil over direct heat), fried, fry•ing

fry\er or fri\er (chicken) [vs. fri\ar (monk)]

FSLIC (Federal Savings and Loan Insurance Corporation)

FTC (Federal Trade Commission)

fuch•sia, •sias

fud\dy-•dud\dy, pl. •dud\dies

fudge, fudged, fudg•ing

fu\el, •eled or •elled, •el•ing or •el•ling

fu•gal

fu•gi•tive

fugue

Füh•rer

Fu\ji

ful•crum, pl. •crums or •cra

ful•fill or ful•fil, •filled, •fill•ing

ful•fill•ment

full, full\er, full•est

full-•back

full-•blood\ed

full-•blown

full-•bod\ied

full cost•ing

full-•du\plex mode

full em•ploy•ment

Ful•ler

full\er

full-•fledged

full-•height drive

full•ness

full-•scale

full-•screen ed\i•tor

full serv•ice a\gen\cy

full-•time

full-•tim\er

full war•ran\ty

ful\ly

ful•mi•nate, •nat\ed, •nat•ing

ful•mi•na•tion

ful•some

fum•ble, •bled, •bling

fum•bling\ly

fume, fumed, fum•ing

fu•mi•gant

fu•mi•gate, •gat\ed, •gat•ing

fu•mi•ga•tion

fun

func•tion, •tioned, •tion•ing

func•tion\al
func•tion•al•ism
func•tion•al•i•ty
func•tion•al\ly
func•tion•ar\y, *pl.* •ar•ies
func•tion key
fund, fund\ed, fund•ing
fun•da•men•tal
fun•da•men•tal•ism
fun•da•men•tal•ist
fun•da•men•tal\ly
fund•ing
fu•ner\al (*ceremony for the dead*)
fu•ner•ar\y
fu•ne•re•al (*mournful*)
fun•gal
fun•gi\ble goods
fun•gi•cide
fun•gous
fun•gus, *pl.* fun\gi, fun•gus•es
fu•nic\u•lar
funk\i•ness
funk\y, funk•i•er, funk•i•est
fun•nel, •neled or •nelled, •nel•ing or •nel•ling
fun•nies, *pl.*
fun•ni\ly
fun•ni•ness
fun•ning
fun\ny, •ni•er, •ni•est
fur (*hairy animal skin*) [vs. fir (*tree*)]

fur•bish, •bished, •bish•ing
fu•ri•ous
fu•ri•ous•ness
furl, furled, furl•ing
fur•long
fur•lough, •loughed, •lough•ing
fur•nace
fur•nish, •nished, •nish•ing
fur•ni•ture
fu•ror
furred
fur•ri\er
fur•ri•ness
fur•row, •rowed, •row•ing
fur\ry (*having fur*), fur•ri•er, fur•ri•est [vs. fu\ry (*rage*)]
fur•ther, •thered, •ther•ing
fur•ther (*to a greater extent*) [vs. far•ther (*to a greater distance*)]
fur•ther•ance
fur•ther•more
fur•ther•most
fur•thest
fur•tive
fur•tive\ly
fur•tive•ness
fu\ry (*rage*), *pl.* •ries [vs. fur\ry (*having fur*)]
furze

fuse, fused, fus•ing
fu•se•lage
fuse•less
fu•si\ble
fu•sil•lade, •lad\ed, •lad•ing
fu•sion
fuss, fussed, fuss•ing
fuss•budg\et
fuss•i\ly
fuss•i•ness
fuss\y, fuss•i•er, fuss•i•est
fus•tian
fus\ty
fu•tile
fu•tile\ly
fu•til•i\ty
fu•ton
fu•ture
future shock
fu•tures trad•ing
fu•tur•ism
fu•tur•ist
fu•tur•is•tic
fu•tu•ri\ty, *pl.* •ties
fu•tur•ol\o•gist
fu•tur•ol•o\gy
futz, futzed, futz•ing
fuzz, *pl.* fuzz, fuzz\es; fuzzed, fuzz•ing
fuzz•i\ly
fuzz•i•ness
fuzz\y, •i•er, •i•est
FX (*foreign exchange*)

G

GA (*Georgia*)
GAAP (*generally accepted accounting principles*)
gab, gabbed, gab•bing
gab•ar•dine
gab•bi•ness
gab•ble, •bled, •bling
gab\by, •bi\er, •bi•est
ga•ble
ga•bled
Ga•bon
Ga•bri\el
gad, gad•ded, gad•ding
gad•a\bout
gad•fly, *pl.* •flies

gadg\et
gadg•et\ry
gad\o•lin•i\um
Ga•bo•ro\ne
Gael\ic
gaff (*hook*), gaffed, gaff•ing
gaffe (*blunder*)
gaf•fer
gag, gagged, gag•ging
gage (*challenge*) [vs. gauge (*measure*) and gouge (*to scoop out*)]
gag•gle
gai•e\ty, *pl.* •ties
gai\ly

gain, gained, gain•ing
gain•ful
gain•ful\ly
gain•say, •said, •say•ing
gain•say\er
gait (*walk*) [vs. gate (*hinged barrier*)]
ga\la
ga•lac•tic
ga•lac•tose
Gal\a•had
gal•ax\y, *pl.* •ax•ies
gale
Gal\i•lee
Gal\i•le\o

gall (*audacity*) [*vs.* Gaul (*ancient France*)]
gal•lant
gal•lant\ly
gal•lant\ry, *pl.* •ries
gall•blad•der *or* gall blad•der
gal•le•on (*sailing ship*) [*vs.* gal•lon (*unit of measure*)]
gal•ler\y (*raised area*), *pl.* •ler•ies
gal•ley (*kitchen*), *pl.* •leys
Gal•lic
Gal•li•cism
gall•ing
gal•li\um
gal•li•vant, •vant\ed, •vant•ing
gal•lon (*unit of measure*) [*vs.* gal•le•on (*sailing ship*)]
gal•lop, •loped, •lop•ing
gal•lows, *pl.* •lows, •lows\es
gall•stone
ga•lore
ga•losh
gal•va•nize, •nized, •niz•ing
gal•va•nom\e•ter
Ga•ma
Gam•bi\a
Gam•bi\an
gam•bit
gam•ble (*to bet*), •bled, •bling [*vs.* gam•bol (*to frolic*)]
gam•bler
gam•bol (*to frolic*), •boled *or* •bolled, •bol•ing *or* •bol•ling [*vs.* gam•ble (*to bet*)]
gam•brel roof
game, gamed, gam•ing; gam\er, gam•est
game•cock
game•keep\er
game•ly
game•ness
games•man•ship
gam•ete

gam\in
gam•ine
gam\i•ness
gam\ma, *pl.* •mas
gam\ma glob\u•lin
gam\ut
gam\y *or* gam\ey, gam•i\er, gam•i•est
gan•der
Gan•dhi
Gan•dhi\an
gang, ganged, gang•ing
Gan•ges
gan•gling
gan•gli\on, *pl.* •gli\a, •gli•ons
gang•plank
gan•grene
gan•gre•nous
gang•ster
gang•way
gan•try, *pl.* •tries
Gantt chart
gap, gapped, gap•ping
gape, gaped, gap•ing
gar, *pl.* gar *or* gars
ga•rage, •raged, •rag•ing
garb, garbed, garb•ing
gar•bage
gar•ble, •bled, •bling
gar•çon
gar•den, •dened, •den•ing
gar•de•nia, *pl.* •nias
gar\den-•va\ri\e\ty
Gar•field
gar•fish, *pl.* •fish *or* •fish\es
gar•gan•tu\an
gar•gle, •gled, •gling
gar•goyle
Gar\i\bal\di
gar•ish
gar•ish\ly
gar•ish•ness
gar•land, •land\ed, •land•ing
gar•lic
gar•lick\y
gar•ment
gar•ner, •nered, •ner•ing
gar•net
gar•nish, •nished, •nish•ing

gar•nish\ee, •nish•eed, •nish•ee•ing
gar•ret
gar•ri•son, •soned, •son•ing
gar•rote, •rot\ed *or* •rot•ted, •rot•ing *or* •rot•ting
gar•ru•li\ty
gar•ru•lous•ness
gar•ru•lous
gar•ter, •tered, •ter•ing
Gar\y
gas, *pl.* gas\es; gassed, gas•sing, gas•ses (*does gas*)
gas cham•ber
gas\e•ous
gash, gashed, gash•ing
gas•ket (*sealing ring*) [*vs.* cas•ket (*coffin*)]
gas•light
gas\o•hol
gas\o•line
gasp, gasped, gasp•ing
gas-•plas\ma display
gas sta•tion
gas\sy, •si\er, •si•est
gas•tric
gas•tri•tis
gas•tro•in\tes•ti•nal
gas\tro•nom•ic
gas•tron•o\my
gas\tro•pod
gate (*hinged barrier*) [*vs.* gait (*walk*)]
gate-•crash\er
gate•fold
gate•post
gate•way
gath\er, •ered, •er•ing
gath•er\er
gath•er•ing
GATT (*General Agreement on Tariffs and Trade*)
gauche
gauche\ly
gauche•ness
gau•che•rie
gau•cho, *pl.* •chos
gaud•i\ly

gaud\i•ness
gaud\y, •i\er, •i•est
gauge (*measure*), gauged,
 gaug•ing [vs. gage
 (*challenge*) and gouge
 (*to scoop out*)]
Gau•guin
Gaul (*ancient France*) [vs.
 gall (*audacity*)]
gaunt, \er, •est
gaunt•let
gaunt•ness
gauze
gauz\y, •i\er, •i•est
gave
gav\el, •eled or •elled,
 •el•ing or •el•ling
ga•votte
G.A.W. (*guaranteed
 annual wage*)
gawk, gawked, gawk•ing
gawk•i\ly
gawk\i•ness
gawk\y, •i\er, •i•est
gay, \er, •est
gaze, gazed, gaz•ing
ga•ze\bo, pl. •bos or
 •boes
ga•zelle, pl. •zelles or
 •zelle
ga•zette
gaz•et•teer
GB (*gigabyte*)
Gb (*gigabit*)
gear, geared, gear•ing
gear•shift
gear•wheel or gear wheel
gee
geese
gee•zer
ge•fil\te fish
Gei•ger count\er
gei•sha, pl. •sha or •shas
gel (*colloid*) [vs. jell (*to
 congeal*)]
gel, gelled, gel•ling
gel\a•tin
ge•lat\i•nous
geld, geld\ed, geld•ing
gel\id
gem

gem\i•nate, •nat\ed,
 •nat•ing
gem\i•na•tion
Gem\i\ni, pl.
 Gem\i\no•rum
gem\o•log\i•cal
gem•ol\o•gist
gem•ol\o\gy or
 gem•mol\o\gy
gem•stone
gen•darme, pl. •darmes
gen•der
gene
ge\ne\a•log\i•cal or
 ge\ne\a•log\ic
ge\ne\al\o•gist
ge\ne\al\o\gy, pl. •gies
gen•er\a
gen•er•al
gen•er•al•is•si•mo, pl.
 •mos
gen•er•al•i\ty, pl. •ties
gen•er•al•i\za•tion
gen•er•al•ize, •ized, •iz•ing
gen•er\al part•ner
general part•ner•ship
gen•eral practi•tioner
gen•er•al•ship
gen•eral store
gen•er•ate, •at\ed, •at•ing
gen•er•a•tion
gen•er•a•tion\al
gen•er\a•tive
gen•er\a•tor
ge•ner\ic
ge•ner\ic prod•uct
gen•er•ous
gen•er•ous\ly
gen\e\sis, pl. •ses
gene splic•ing
ge•net\ic
ge•net\i•cal\ly
ge•net\ic code
genetic en•gi•neer•ing
ge•net\i•cist
ge•net•ics
Ge•ne\va
Gen•ghis Khan
gen•ial
ge•ni•al•i\ty
gen•ial\ly

ge•nie
gen\i•tal (*of genitalia*) [vs.
 gen•teel (*polite*) and
 gen•tile (*not Jewish*) and
 gen•tle (*kindly*)]
gen\i•ta•li\a or gen\i•tals
gen\i•tive
gen\i•to•u\ri\nar\y
gen•ius, pl. gen•ius\es
 (*exceptional intellects*),
 gen\i\i (*guardian spirits*)
 [vs. ge•nus (*subdivision*)]
gen•lock
Gen\o\a
gen\o•cide
ge•nome
ge•no•mic DNA
gen\o•type
gen\re, pl. •res
gent
gen•teel (*polite*) [vs.
 gen\i•tal (*of genitalia*) and
 gen•tle (*kindly*)]
gen•tian
gen•tile (*not Jewish*) [vs.
 gen\i•tal (*of genitalia*) and
 gen•tle (*kindly*)]
gen•til•i\ty
gen•tle, •tled, •tling
gen•tle (*kindly*), •tler, •tlest
gen•tle•folk or
 gen\tle•folks, pl.
gen\tle•man, pl. •men
gen\tle•man\ly
gen\tle•ness
gen•tle•wom\an, pl.
 •wom\en
gen•tly
gen•tri•fi•ca•tion
gen•tri\fy, •fied, •fy•ing
gen•try
gen\u•flect, •flect\ed,
 •flect•ing
gen\u•flec•tion
gen\u•ine
gen\u•ine\ly
gen\u•ine•ness
ge•nus (*subdivision*), pl
 gen\e\ra or ge•nus\es [vs.
 gen•ius (*exceptional
 intellect*)]

ge\o•cen•tric
ge•ode
ge\o•des\ic
ge•od•e\sy
ge\o•det\ic
ge•og•ra•pher
ge\o•graph\i•cal
ge\o•graph\i•cal\ly
ge•og•ra•phy
ge\o•log\i•cal
ge•ol\o•gist
ge•ol•o\gy
ge\o•mag•ne•tism
ge\o•met•ri•cal\ly
ge\o•met•ric
ge\o•met•ri•cal
ge•om\e•try
ge\o•phys\i•cal
ge\o•phys\i•cist
ge\o•phys•ics
ge\o•po•lit\i•cal
ge\o•pol\i•tics
George
Geor•gia (GA)
Geor•gian
ge\o•sta•tion•ar\y
ge\o•syn•cline
ge\o•ther•mal or
    ge\o•ther•mic
ge•ra•ni\um
ger•bil
ger•er•os•i\ty
ger\i•at•ric
ger\i•at•rics
germ
Ger•man (the language)
ger•mane (relevant)
Ger•man\ic
ger•ma•ni\um
Ger•ma\ny
ger•mi•cid\al
ger•mi•cide
ger•mi•nate, •nat\ed,
    •nat•ing
ger•mi•na•tion
ge•ron•to•log\i•cal
ger•on•tol\o•gist
ger•on•tol•o\gy
ger•ry•man•der, •dered,
    •der•ing
Gersh•win

ger•und
Ge•sta\po
ges•tate, •tat\ed, •tat•ing
ges•ta•tion
ges•ta•tion\al
ges•tic\u•late, •lat\ed,
    •lat•ing
ges•tic\u•la•tion
ges•tur\al
ges•ture (movement),
    •tured, •tur•ing [vs.
    jest\er (clown)]
ge•sund•heit
get, got, got or got•ten,
    get•ting
get•a\way
get-•to\geth•er
Get•tys•burg
get\up or get-•up
gew•gaw
gey•ser
Gha\na
Gha•na•ian or Gha•ni\an
ghast\ly (horrible), •li\er,
    •li•est
gher•kin
ghet\to, pl. •tos or •toes
ghost
ghost\ly (spectral)
ghost•writ\ten
ghost-writ\er or ghost
    writ\er
ghoul (demon) [vs. goal
    (aim)]
ghoul•ish
Gia•co•met\ti
gi•ant
gi•ant•ess
gib•ber, •bered, •ber•ing
gib•ber•ish
gib•bon
gibe (to taunt), gibed,
    gib•ing [vs. jibe (to agree)
    and jive (the music)]
gib•let
Gi•bral•tar
gid•di•ness
gid\dy, •di\er, •di•est
Gide
gift
gift\ed

gig (job) [vs. jig (dance)]
gig\a•bit (Gb)
gig\a•byte (GB)
gi•gan•tic
gig•gle, •gled, •gling
gig•gly
GIGO (garbage in, garbage
    out)
gig•o\lo, pl. •los
Gi•la mon•ster
gild (to coat with gold),
    gild•ed, gild•ing [vs. guild
    (organization)]
gill
gilt (gold) [vs. guilt
    (blame)]
gilt-•edged or gilt-•edge
gim•bals
gim•crack
gim•crack•er\y
gim•let
gim•mick, •micked,
    •mick•ing
gim•mick\ry
gim•mick\y
gimp
gimp\y, •i\er, •i•est
gin, ginned, gin•ning
gin•ger
ginger ale
gin\ger•bread
gin•ger\ly
gin•ger•snap
gin•ger\y
ging•ham
gin•gi•vi•tis
gink\go or ging\ko, pl.
    •goes or •koes
Gin•nie Mae (Government
    National Mortgage
    Association)
gin•seng
Gip\sy, pl. •sies
gi•raffe
gird, gird\ed or girt,
    gird•ing
gird\er
gir•dle, •dled, •dling
girl
girl Fri•day, pl. girl
    Fri•days

girl•friend
girl•hood
girl•ish
girl scout
girt
girth
gis\mo or giz\mo, pl. •mos
gist (essence) [vs. jest (joke)]
give, gave, giv\en, giv•ing
give-•and-•take
give•a\way
give•back
giv\en
giv\er
giz\mo, pl. •mos
giz•zard
gla•cial
gla•cial\ly
gla•cier (ice mass) [vs. gla•zier (glass installer)]
glad, glad•der, glad•dest
glad•den, •dened, •den•ing
glade
glad hand (noun)
glad-•hand (verb), •hand\ed, •hand\ing
glad\i•a•tor
glad\i•a•to•ri\al
glad\i•o•lus, pl. •lus, \li, •lus\es
glad\ly
glad•ness
glad•some
glam•or•ize or glam•our•ize, •ized, •iz•ing
glam•or•ous
glam•our or glam\or
glamour stock
glance, glanced, glanc•ing
gland
glan•du•lar
glans, pl. glan•des
glare, glared, glar•ing
glar•ing\ly
Glas•gow
glas•nost
glass, glassed, glass•ing
glass ceil•ing
glass\es

glass•ware
glass\y, •i\er, •i•est
glau•co\ma
glaze, glazed, glaz•ing
gla•zier (glass installer) [vs. gla•cier (ice mass)]
gleam, gleamed, gleam•ing
glean, gleaned, glean•ing
glee
glee•ful
glen
Glen•dale
glib
glib\ly
glib•ness
glide, glid\ed, glid•ing
glid\er
glim•mer, •mered, •mer•ing
glimpse, glimpsed, glimps•ing
glint, glint\ed, glint•ing
glis•san\do, pl. \di or •dos
glis•ten, •tened, •ten•ing
glitch
glit•ter, •tered, •ter•ing
glit•ter\y
glitz\y, •i\er, •i•est
gloam•ing
gloat, gloat\ed, gloat•ing
glob
glob\al
glob•al•ism
glob•al•ist
glob•al\ly
globe
globe•trot•ter
glob\u•lar
glob•ule
glob\u•lin
glock\en•spiel
gloom
gloom\y, •i\er, •i•est
glop
glop\py, •pi\er, •pi•est
glor\i•fi•ca•tion
glo•ri\fy, •fied, •fy•ing
glo•ri•ous
glo•ri•ous\ly
glo\ry, pl. •ries; •ried, •ry•ing

gloss, glossed, gloss•ing
glos•sa\ry, pl. •ries
glos\so•la•li\a
gloss\y, •i\er, •i•est
glot•tal
glot•tis, pl. glot•tis\es, glot•ti•des
glove
gloved
glow, glowed, glow•ing
glow\er, •ered, •er•ing
glow•ing
glow•worm
glu•cose
glue, glued, glu•ing
glue\y, •i\er, •i•est
glum, glum•mer, glum•mest
glum\ly
glum•ness
glut, glut•ted, glut•ting
glu•ten
glu•ten•ous (like gluten)
glu•ti•nous (sticky)
glut•ton•ous (greedy)
glut•ton•ous\ly
glut•ton\y
glyc•er\in or glyc•er•ine
glyc•er\ol
gly•co•gen
gnarled
gnash, gnashed, gnash•ing
gnat
gnaw, gnawed, gnaw•ing
gneiss
gnome
gnom•ish
GNP or G.N.P. (gross national product)
gnu (antelope), pl. gnus, gnu [vs. knew (did know) and new (recent)]
go, went, gone, go•ing, goes
goad, goad\ed, goad•ing
go-•a\head
goal (aim) [vs. ghoul (demon)]
goal\ie
goal•keep\er
goal•keep•ing

goat
goat\ee
goat•herd
goat•skin
gob
gob•ble, •bled, •bling
gob\ble•dy•gook or
 gob\ble•de•gook
gob•bler
go-•be\tween
Go\bi
gob•let
gob•lin
God
god•child, pl. •chil•dren
god•daugh•ter
god•dess
god•fa•ther
God•head
god•hood
Go•di\va
god•less
god•like
god•li•ness
god\ly, •li\er, •li•est
god•moth\er
god•par•ent
god•send
god•son
God•win Aus•ten
Goe•the
go•fer or go-•fer
go-•get\ter
go-•get\ting
gog•gle, •gled, •gling
go-•go
go\ings-•on
goi•ter
gold•brick
gold dig•ger
gold\en
golden hand•cuffs
golden hand•shake
golden par\a•chute
gold•en•rod
gold•finch
gold•fish, pl. •fish or
 •fish\es
gold re•serve
gold•smith
gold stand•ard

golf, golfed, golf•ing
golf\er
Go•li•ath
gol\ly
go•nad
gon•do\la, pl. •las
gon•do•lier
gone
gon\er
gong
go/•no-•go
gon•or•rhe\a
goo
goo•ber
good, bet•ter, best
good-•by or good\by, pl.
 •bys or •byes
good de•liv•er\y
good-•for-•noth\ing
Good Fri•day
good-•heart\ed or
 good•heart\ed
good-•heart\ed\ness
good•hu\mored
good\ies
good-•look\ing
good\ly
good-•na\tured
good-•na\tured\ly
good•ness
good•will or good will
good\y-•good\y, pl.
 •good\ies
goo\ey, goo•i\er, goo•i•est
goof, goofed, goof•ing
goof•ball
goof-•off (noun)
goof\y, •i\er, •i•est
gook
goon
goose, pl. geese (birds),
 goos\es (pokes, prods);
 goosed, goos•ing
goose-•ber\ry, pl. •ries
goose flesh or goose•flesh
GOP or G.O.P. ("Grand
 Old Party," Republican
 party)
go•pher
go pub•lic
Gor•ba•chev

gore, gored, gor•ing
gorge, gorged, gorg•ing
gor•geous
gor•geous\ly
go•ril\la (large ape), pl. •las
 [vs. guer•ril\la or
 gue•ril\la (irregular
 soldier)]
gor\i•ness
Gor\ki
gor\y, •i\er, •i•est
gosh
gos•ling
gos•pel
gos•sa\mer
gos•sip, •siped or •sipped,
 •sip•ing or •sip•ping
gos•sip\y
got
Goth
goth\ic
go\to, pl. go•tos
got•ten
Gou\da
gouge (to scoop out),
 gouged, goug•ing [vs.
 gage (challenge) and
 gauge (measure)]
goug\er
gou•lash
gourd
gour•mand (big eater)
gour•met (epicure)
gout
gout\y
gov•ern, •erned, •ern•ing
gov•ern•a\ble
gov•ern•ance
gov•ern•ess
gov•ern•ment
gov•ern•men•tal
gov•ern•ment bond
gov•er•nor
gov•er•nor•ship
gown
Go\ya
gppm (graphics pages per
 minute)
grab, grabbed, grab•bing
grab•ber
grace, graced, grac•ing

grace•ful
grace•ful\ly
grace•less
grace•less\ly
grace•less•ness
gra•cious
gra•cious\ly
gra•cious•ness
grack\le
grad
gra•da•tion
grade, grad\ed, grad•ing
gra•di•ent
grad•u•al
grad\u•al•ism
grad\u•al•ly
grad\u•ate, •at\ed, •at•ing
grad\u•a•tion
graf•fi\ti, sing. \to
graft, graft\ed, graft•ing
graft\er
gra•ham
grail
grain
grain\i•ness
grain\y, •i\er, •i•est
gram•mar
gram•mar•i\an
gram•mat\i•cal
gram•mat\i•cal•ly
gra•na\ry, pl. •ries
grand, pl. grands (pianos),
  grand (money); grand\er,
  grand•est
grand•child, pl. •chil•dren
grand•daugh•ter
grande dame, pl. grandes
  dames
gran•dee
gran•deur
grand•fa•ther
gran•dil\o•quence
gran•dil\o•quent
gran•di•ose
grand\ly
grand\ma, pl. •mas
grand mal
grand•moth\er
grand•ness
grand\pa
grand•son

grand•stand
grange
gran•ite
gran\ny or gran•nie, pl.
  •nies
gra•no\la
grant, grant\ed, grant•ing
gran•tee
gran•tor
grants•man•ship
gran\u•la•ation
gran\u•lar
gran\u•lar•i\ty
gran\u•late, •lat\ed,
  •lat•ing
gran•ule
grape
grape•fruit
grape•shot
grape•vine
graph, graphed, graph•ing
graph\ic
graph\i•cal us\er
  in\ter•face (GUI)
graph\i•cal\ly
graph•ics
graph\ics-•based
graph\ics tab•let
graph•ite
graph•ol\o•gist
graph•ol\o\gy
grap•nel
grap•ple, •pled, •pling
grasp, grasped, grasp•ing
grass
grass•hop•per
grass\y, •i\er, •i•est
grate (metal frame) [vs.
  great (large; important)]
grate, grat\ed, grat•ing
grate•ful
grate•ful\ly
grate•ful•ness
grat\er
grat\i•fi•ca•tion
grat•i\fy, •fied, •fy•ing
grat•ing
grat\is
grat\i•tude
gra•tu•i•tous
gra•tu•i\ty, pl. •ties

gra•va•men, pl. •vam•i\na
grave, grav\er, grav•est
grav\el
grav•el\ly
grave\ly
grave•stone
grave•yard
grav\id
grav\i•tate, •tat\ed,
  •tat•ing
grav\i•ta•tion
grav\i•ta•tion\al
grav•i\ty
gra•vure
gra\vy, pl. •vies
gray or grey, grayed or
  greyed, gray•ing or
  grey•ing; gray\er or
  grey\er, gray•est or
  grey•est
gray•beard
gray•ish
gray•mail
gray•mail\er
gray mar•ket
gray•ness
gray scal•ing
graze, grazed, graz•ing
grease (soft fat), greased,
  greas•ing [vs. Greece
  (the country)]
grease•paint or grease
  paint
greas\i•ness
greas\y, s•i\er, •i•est
great (large; important),
  great\er, great•est [vs.
  grate (metal frame)]
great•coat
great•heart\ed
great\ly
great•ness
grebe
Gre•cian
Greece (the country) [vs.
  grease (soft fat)]
greed
greed•i\ly
greed\i•ness
greed\y, •i\er, •i•est
Greek

greek•ing
Greek Or•tho•dox
  Church
green, greened, green•ing;
  green\er, green•est
green•back
green•belt
green•er\y
green•-eyed
green•gro•cer
green•horn
green•house, pl. •hous\es
greenhouse ef•fect
greenhouse gas
green•ish
Green•land
Green•land\er
green•mail
green•mail\er
green•ness
Greens•bo\ro
green•sward
Green•wich
greet, greet•ed, greet•ing
gre•gar\i•ous
Gre•go•ri•an cal•en•dar
grem•lin
Gre•na\da
gre•nade
Gre•na•di\an
gren\a•dier
gren\a•dine
grew
grey, greyed, grey•ing;
  grey\er, grey•est
grey•hound or
  gray•hound
grid
grid•dle
grid\dle•cake
grid•i\ron
grid•lock
grief
griev•ance
grievance com•mit•tee
grieve, grieved, griev•ing
griev•ous
griev•ous\ly
grif•fin or grif•fon
grill (to broil), grilled,
  grill•ing

grille (grating)
grim, grim•mer,
  grim•mest
grim•ace, •aced, •ac•ing
grime
grim\ly
Grimm
grim•ness
grim•y, •i\er, •i•est
grin, grinned, grin•ning
grind, ground, grind•ing
grind\er
grind•stone
grip (to grasp), gripped,
  grip•ping
gripe (to complain), griped,
  grip•ing
grippe (influenza)
gris\ly (gruesome) [vs.
  gris•tly (cartilaginous)
  and griz•zly (bear)]
grist
gris•tle
gris•tly (cartilaginous),
  •tli•er, •tli•est [vs. gris\ly
  (gruesome) and griz•zly
  (bear)]
grit, grit•ted, grit•ting
grits
grit\ty, •ti\er, •ti•est
griz•zled
griz•zly (bear), pl. •zlies
  [vs. gris\ly (gruesome)
  and gris•tly
  (cartilaginous)]
groan (moan), groaned,
  groan•ing [vs. grown
  (matured)]
groats
gro•cer
gro•cer\y, pl. •cer•ies
grog
grog•gi\ly
grog•gi•ness
grog\gy, •gi\er, •gi•est
groin
grom•met or grum•met
groom, groomed,
  groom•ing
groove (indentation) [vs.
  grove (orchard)]

groove, grooved,
  groov•ing
groov•i\est
groov\ly, •i\er, •i•est
grope, groped, grop•ing
gross, pl. gross or
  gross\es; grossed,
  gross•ing; gross\er,
  gross•est
gross\ly
gross mar•gin
gross na•tion\al prod•uct
  (GNP)
gross•ness
gross prof\it
gross sales
gro•tesque
gro•tesque\ly
grot\to, pl. •toes or •tos
grouch, grouched,
  grouch•ing
grouch\y, •i\er, •i•est
ground, ground\ed,
  ground•ing
ground•hog or ground
  hog
ground•less
ground•swell
group, grouped, group•ing
group dis•count
group\er, pl. \er or •ers
group\ie
group in•sur•ance
group ther•a\py
group•ware
grouse, pl. grouse or
  grous\es; groused,
  grous•ing
grout, grout\ed, grout•ing
grove (orchard) [vs.
  groove (indentation)]
grov\el, •eled or •elled,
  •el•ing or •el•ling
grow, grew, grown,
  grow•ing
grow\er
growl, growled, growl•ing
grown (matured) [vs.
  groan (moan)]
grown\up
growth

growth fund
growth stock
grub, grubbed, grub•bing
grub•bi•ness
grub\by, •bi\er, •bi•est
grub•stake
grudge, grudged, grudg•ing
grudg•ing\ly
gru\el
gru•el•ing
grue•some
grue•some•ly
grue•some•ness
gruff, \er, •est
gruff\ly
gruff•ness
grum•ble, •bled, •bling
grum•bler
grump\i•ness
grump\y, •i\er, •i•est
grun\gy, •gi\er, •gi•est
grun•ion
grunt, grunt\ed, grunt•ing
Gru•yère
gua•ca•mo\le
Gua•da•la•ja\ra
Guam
Guang•zhou or
  Kwang•chow
gua•nine
gua\no
gua•ra\ni, pl. \ni or •nis
guar•an•tee, •teed, •tee•ing
guaranteed an•nu\al wage
  (G.A.W.)
guar•an•tor
guar•an\ty, pl. •ties; •tied,
  •ty•ing
guard, guard\ed, guard•ing
guard•ed\ly
guard•house, pl. •hous\es
guard•i\an
guard•i\an•ship
Gua•te•ma\la
Gua•te•ma•lan
gua\va, pl. •vas
gu•ber•na•to•ri\al
Guern•sey, pl. •seys
guer•ril\la or gue•ril\la
  (irregular soldier), pl. •las

[vs. go•ril\la (large ape)]
guess, guessed (did guess),
  guess•ing
guest (visitor)
guf•faw, •fawed, •faw•ing
GUI (graphical user interface)
guid•ance
guide, guid\ed, guid•ing
guide•book
guid\ed mis•sile
guide•line
guild (organization) [vs.
  gild (to coat with gold)]
guile
guile•ful
guile•less
guil•lo•tine, •tined, •tin•ing
guilt (blame) [vs. gilt
  (gold)]
guilt•i\ly
guilt•less
guilt\y, •i\er, •i•est
guin\ea, pl. •eas
Guin\ea-•Bis\sau
Guin•e\an
guin\ea pig
guise
gui•tar
gui•tar•ist
gulch
gul•den, pl. •dens or •den
gulf
gull, gulled, gull•ing
gul•let
gul•li•bil•i\ty
gul•li\ble
gul\ly, pl. •lies
gulp, gulped, gulp•ing
gum, gummed, gum•ming
gum ar\a•bic
gum\bo, pl. •bos
gum•drop
gum\my, •mi\er, •mi•est
gump•tion
gum•shoe
gun, gunned, gun•ning
gun•boat
gun•cot•ton
gun•fight
gun•fire

gung-•ho
gunk
gun•man, pl. •men
gun•ner
gun•ner\y
gun•ny•sack
gun•point
gun•pow•der
gun•shot
gun-•shy
gun•smith
gun•wale or gun•nel
gup\py, pl. •pies
gur•gle, •gled, •gling
gur•ney, pl. •neys
gu\ru, pl. •rus
gush, gushed, gush•ing
gush\er
gush\y, •i\er, •i•est
gus•set
gus\sy, •sied, •sy•ing
gust, gust\ed, gust•ing
gus•ta•to\ry
gus\to
gust\y (windy), •i\er, •i•est
gut, gut•ted, gut•ting
gut•less
guts\y (courageous), •i\er,
  •i•est
gut•ter
gut\ter•snipe
gut•tur•al
guy, guyed, guy•ing
Guy•a\na
Guy•a•nese
guz•zle, •zled, •zling
guz•zler
gym
gym•na•si\um, pl. •si•ums
  or •si\a
gym•nast
gym•nas•tic
gym•nas•tics
gym•no•sperm
gy•ne•co•log\i•cal
gy•ne•col\o•gist
gy•ne•col•o\gy
gyp, gypped, gyp•ping
gyp•sum
Gyp\sy, pl. •sies
gyp•sy moth

gy•rate, •rat\ed, •rat•ing
gy•ra•tion

gyr•fal•con
gy\ro

gy\ro•com•pass
gy\ro•scope

H

ha or hah
ha•be\as cor•pus
hab\er•dash•er\y, pl.
  •er•ies
ha•bil\i•ments
hab\it
hab•it•a•bil•i\ty
hab•it•a•ble
hab•it•ant
hab\i•tat
hab\i•ta•tion
hab\it•form\ing
ha•bit•u\al
ha•bit•u•al\ly
ha•bit•u•ate, •at\ed, •at•ing
ha•bit•u•a•tion
ha•bit•u\é
ha•ci•en\da, pl. •das
hack, hacked, hack•ing
hack\er
hack\ie
hack•les
hack•ney, pl. •neys
hack•neyed
hack•saw or hack saw
had
had•dock, pl. •dock or •docks
Ha•des
had\n't
hadst
haf•ni\um
hag
hag•gard
hag•gard•ness
hag•gle, •gled, •gling
Hague, The
ha•ha
hai\ku, pl. \ku
hail (to greet; ice) [vs. hale
  (healthy)]
hail•stone
hail•storm
hair (tresses) [vs. hare
  (rabbit)]
hair•ball
hair•breadth or
  hairs•breadth

hair•brush
hair•cloth
hair•cut
hair\do, pl. •dos
hair•dress\er
hair•dress•ing
hair\i•ness
hair•less
hair•like
hair•line
hair•piece
hair•pin
hair•rais•ing
hairs•breadth
hair•split•ting
hair•spring
hair•style or hair style
hair•styl•ist
hair trig•ger (noun)
hair•trig•ger (adj.)
hair\y, •i\er, •i•est
Hai\ti
Hai•tian
hajj or hadj, pl. hajj\es or
  hadj\es
haj\ji or hadj\i, pl. haj•jis or
  hadj\is
hake, pl. hake or hakes
hal•cy\on
hale, haled, hal•ing
hale (healthy) [vs. hail
  (to greet; ice)]
half, pl. halves
half•and•half
half•back
half•baked
half•breed
half•caste
half•cocked
half•du\plex mode
half•heart\ed
half•heart•edly
half•heart•ed•ness
half•height drive
half•life or half life, pl.
  •lives or lives
half•mast

half•slip
half•time or half•time
half•tone
half•track or half•track
half•truth, pl. •truths
half•way
half•way house
half•wit
half•wit\ted
hal\i•but, pl. •but or •buts
Hal\i•fax
hal\i•to•sis
hall (room) [vs. haul (to
  drag)]
hal•le•lu•jah or
  hal•le•lu•iah
hall•mark
hal•low (to make holy),
  •lowed, •low\ing [vs.
  ha\lo (ring of light) and
  hol•low (empty)]
Hal•low•een or
  Hal•low•e'en
hal•lu•ci•nate, •nat\ed,
  •nat•ing
hal•lu•ci•na•tion
hal•lu•ci•na•to\ry
hal•lu•ci•no•gen
hal•lu•ci•no•gen\ic
hall•way
ha\lo (ring of light), pl. •los
  or •loes; •loed, \lo•ing
  [vs. hal•low (to make
  holy) and hol•low
  (empty)]
hal\o•gen
halt, halt\ed, halt•ing
hal•ter
halt•ing\ly
hal•vah
halve (to divide in two),
  halved, halv•ing [vs. have
  (to possess)]
halves
hal•yard
ham, hammed, ham•ming
Ham•burg

ham•burg\er
Ham•il•ton
ham•let
ham•mer, •mered, •mer•ing
ham\mer•head
ham\mer•lock or ham•mer lock
ham\mer•toe
ham•mock
ham\my
ham•per, •pered, •per•ing
ham•ster
ham•string, •strung, •string•ing
Han•cock
hand, hand\ed, hand•ing
hand•bag
hand•ball
hand•bar•row
hand•bill
hand•book
hand•car
hand•cart
hand•clasp
hand•craft, •craft\ed, •craft•ing
hand•cuff, •cuffed, •cuff•ing
Han•del
hand•ful, pl. •fuls
hand•gun
hand\i•cap, •capped, •cap•ping
hand\i•cap•per
hand\i•craft
hand•i\ly
hand\i•ness
hand\i•work
hand•ker•chief
han•dle, •dled, •dling
han\dle•bar
han•dler
hand•made (made by hand)
hand•maid (servant) or hand•maid\en
hand-•me-•down
hand•out
hand•pick, •picked, •pick•ing

hand•rail
hand•saw
hand•set
hand•shake
hands-•off
hand•some (attractive), •som\er, •som•est [vs. han•som (cab)]
hand•some\ly
hand•some•ness
hands-•on
hand•spring
hand•stand
hand-•to-•hand
hand-•to-•mouth
hand-•to-•mouth buy•ing
hand•work
hand•writ•ing
hand•writ•ten
hand\y, •i\er, •i•est
hand\y•man, pl. •men
hang, hung, hanged, hang•ing
hang\ar (airplane shed) [vs. hang\er (garment holder)]
hang•dog
hang\er (garment holder) [vs. hang\ar (airplane shed)]
hang\er-•on, pl. hang\ers-•on
hang glid•ing
hang•ing
hang•man, pl. •men
hang•nail
hang•out
hang•o\ver
hang-•up or hang\up
hank
han•ker, •kered, •ker•ing
han\ky or han•kie, pl. •kies
han\ky-•pan\ky
Han•ni•bal
Ha•noi
han•som (cab) [vs. hand•some (attractive)]
Ha•nuk•kah or Cha•nu•kah
hap•haz•ard
hap•haz•ard\ly

hap•less
hap•loid
hap\ly
hap•pen, •pened, •pen•ing
hap•pen•stance
hap•pi\ly
hap•pi•ness
hap\py, •pi\er, •pi•est
hap\py-•go-•luck\y
ha\ra-•ki\ri
ha•rangue, •rangued, •rangu•ing
Ha•ra\re
ha•rass, •rassed, •rass•ing
ha•rass•ment
Har•bin
har•bin•ger
har•bor, •bored, •bor•ing
hard, \er, •est
hard-•and-•fast
hard•back
hard•ball
hard-•bit\ten
hard-•boiled
hard•bound
hard card
hard-•cod\ed
hard cop\y (noun)
hard-•cop\y (adj.)
hard-•core
hard•cov\er
hard cur•ren\cy
hard disk
hard\en, •ened, •en•ing
hard•en\er
hard fonts
hard goods
hard hat or hard•hat (noun)
hard-•hat (adj.)
hard•head\ed or hard-•head\ed
hard•head•ed•ness
hard•heart\ed
hard•heart•ed•ness
har•di•hood
har•di\ly (robustly) [vs. hard\ly (scarcely)]
har•di•ness
Har•ding

hard-•line *or* hard•line

hard-•lin\er

hard\ly *(scarcely)* [*vs.* har•di\ly *(robustly)*]

hard•ness

hard-•nosed

hard•pan

hard re•turn

hard•scrab•ble

hard-•shell *or* hard-•shelled

hard•ship

hard•tack

hard•top

hard•ware

hardware in•ter•rupt

hardware plat•form

hard-•wired

hard•wood

har\dy, •di\er, •di•est

hare *(rabbit)*, *pl.* hares *or* hare [*vs.* hair *(tresses)*]

hare•brained *or* hair•brained

Ha\re Krish\na

hare•lip

har\em

hark, harked, hark•ing

hark\en *(hearken)*, •ened, •en•ing

Har•lem

Har•lem•ite

har•le•quin

har•lot

har•lot\ry

harm, harmed, harm•ing

harm•ful

harm•ful\ly

harm•less

harm•less\ly

har•mon\ic

har•mon•i\ca, *pl.* •cas

har•mon\i•cal\ly

har•mon•ics

har•mo•ni•ous

har•mo•ni•ous\ly

har•mo•ni•um

har•mo•ni•za•tion

har•mo•nize, •nized, •niz•ing

har•mo\ny, *pl.* •nies

har•ness, •nessed, •ness•ing

harp, harped, harp•ing

harp\er *(one who harps)*

Har•pers Fer\ry *(site of John Brown's raid)*

harp•ist

har•poon, •pooned, •poon•ing

harp•si•chord

harp•si•chord•ist

har\py, *pl.* •pies

har•ri•dan

har•ri\er

Har•ris•burg

Har•ri•son

har•row

har•row•ing

har\ry, •ried, •ry•ing

harsh

harsh\ly

harsh•ness

hart *(deer)*, *pl.* harts *or* hart [*vs.* heart *(the organ)*]

Hart•ford

har\um-•scar\um

har•vest, •vest•ed, •vest•ing

har•vest\er

has

has-•been

hash, hashed, hash•ing

hash•ish

Ha•sid, *pl.* Ha•sid\im

Ha•sid\ic

has\n't

hasp

has•sle, •sled, •sling

has•sock

hast

has\ta la vis\ta

haste

has•ten, •tened, •ten•ing

hast•i\ly

hast\y, •i\er, •i•est

hat

hat•ted

hatch, hatched, hatch•ing

hatch•back

hatch•er\y, *pl.* •er•ies

hatch\et, •et\ed, •et•ing

hatch•way

hate, hat\ed, hat•ing

hate•ful

hate•ful\ly

hate•ful•ness

hat\er

hath

hat•less

ha•tred

hat•ter

haugh•ti\ly

haugh•ti•ness

haugh•ty, •ti\er, •ti•est

haul *(to drag)*, hauled, haul•ing [*vs.* hall *(room)*]

haul•age

haunch *(hip)* [*vs.* hunch *(suspicion)*]

haunt, haunt\ed, haunt•ing

haunt•ing\ly

haute cou•ture

haute cui•sine

hau•teur

Ha•van\a

have, *pl.* haves

have *(to possess)*, had, hav•ing [*vs.* halve *(to divide in two)*]

ha•ven *(refuge)* [*vs.* heav\en *(abode of God)*]

have-•not

have\n't

hav•er•sack

hav\oc

Ha•wai\i *(HI)*

Ha•wai•ian

hawk, hawked, hawk•ing

hawk\er

hawk-•eyed

Haw•kins

hawk•ish

haw•ser

haw•thorn

Haw•thorne ef•fect

hay *(dried grass)* [*vs.* hey *(the exclamation)*]

Hay\dn

Hayes

hay fe•ver

hay•fork

hay•loft
hay•mak\er
hay•mow
hay•seed
hay•stack
Hay•ward
hay•wire
haz•ard, •ard\ed, •ard•ing
haz•ard•ous
haz•ard•ous\ly
haze, hazed, haz•ing
ha•zel
ha\zel•nut
ha•zi•ly
ha•zi•ness
ha\zy, •zi\er, •zi•est
H-\bomb (*hydrogen bomb*)
HDTV (*high-definition television*)
he, *pl.* they, hes; him, *pl.* them; his, *pl.* their; his, *pl.* theirs
head, head\ed, head•ing
head•ache
head•band
head•board
head crash
head•dress
head•first
head•gear
head•hunt\er
head•hunt•ing
head•ing
head•land
head•less
head•light
head•line, •lined, •lin•ing
head•lock
head•long
head•man, *pl.* •men
head•mas•ter
head•mis•tress
head-•on
head•phone
head•piece
head•quar•ters, *pl.* •ters
head•rest
head•room
head•set
heads•man *or* head•man, *pl.* •men

head•stall
head•stone
head•strong
head•wait\er
head•wa•ters
head•way
head•wind
head•word
head\y, •i\er, •i•est
heal (*to get well*), healed, heal•ing [*vs.* heel (*back of foot*) *and* he'll (*he will*)]
heal\er
health
health•ful
health•i\ly
health\y, •i\er, •i•est
heap, heaped, heap•ing
hear (*to listen*), heard, hear•ing [*vs.* here (*in this place*)]
heard (*did listen*) [*vs.* herd (*group of animals*)]
hear\er
hear•ing
hear•ing-•ear dog
hark\en *or* hark\en, •ened, •en•ing
hear•say
hearse
heart (*the organ*) [*vs.* hart (*deer*)]
heart•ache
heart at•tack
heart•beat
heart•break
heart•break•ing
heart•bro•ken
heart•burn
heart\en, •ened, •en•ing
heart•en•ing\ly
heart•felt
hearth
hearth•stone
heart•i\ly
heart\i•ness
heart•less
heart•less\ly
heart•less•ness
heart•rend•ing

heart•rend•ing\ly
heart•sick
heart•strings
heart•throb
heart-•to-•heart
heart•warm•ing
heart\y, *pl.* heart•ies; heart•i\er, heart•i•est
heat, heat\ed, heat•ing
heat•ed\ly
heat\er
heath
hea•then, *pl.* •thens *or* •then
heath\er
heat•stroke
heave, heaved *or* hove, heav•ing
heave-•ho, *pl.* •hos
heav\en (*abode of God*) [*vs.* ha•ven (*refuge*)]
heav•en\ly
heav•en•ward
heav•i\ly
heav\i•ness
heav\y, *pl.* heav•ies; heav•i\er, heav•i•est
heav\y-•du\ty
heav\y-•hand\ed
heav\y-•hand\ed\ly
heav\y-•hand\ed\ness
heav\y-•heart\ed
heav\y•set
heav\y•weight
He•bra•ic
He•brew
Heb•ri•des, the
heck
heck\le, •led, •ling
heck•ler
hec•tare
hec•tic
hec\to•gram
hec\to•li\ter
hec\to•me•ter
hec•tor, •tored, •tor•ing
he'd
hedge, hedged, hedg•ing
hedge fund
hedge•hog
hedge•row

he•don•ism
he•don•ist
he•don•is•tic
hee\bie-•jee\bies
heed, heed\ed, heed•ing
heed•ful
heed•less
heel (back of foot) [vs. heal (to get well) and he'll (he will)]
heel, heeled, heel•ing
heel•less
heft, heft\ed, heft•ing
heft\i•ness
heft\y, •i\er, •i•est
he•gem\o\ny, pl. •nies
he•gi\ra or he\ji\ra., pl. •ras
Hei•del•berg
heif\er
height
height\en, •ened, •en•ing
Heim•lich ma•neu•ver
hei•nous
heir (inheritor) [vs. air (atmosphere) and e'er (ever) and ere (before) and err (to do wrong)]
heir ap•par•ent, pl. heirs ap•par•ent
heir•ess
heir•loom
heir pre•sump•tive, pl. heirs pre•sump•tive
heist, heist\ed, heist•ing
held
Hel\en
Hel•e\na
hel\i•cal
hel\i•cal-•scan car•tridge
hel\i•cop•ter
hel\i\o•cen•tric
hel\i\o•graph
hel\i\o•trope
hel\i•port
he•li•um
he•lix, pl. hel\i•ces or he\lix\es
he'll (he will) [vs. heal (to get well) and heel (back of foot)]

hell
hell•bent
hell•cat
hel•le•bore
Hel•len•ic
Hel•len•ism
Hel•len•is•tic
hell•gram•mite
hell•hole
hel•lion
hell•ish
hell•ish\ly
hel\lo, pl. •los
helm
hel•met
hel•met•ed
helms•man, pl. •men
hel\ot
help, helped, help•ing
help\er
help•ful
help•ful\ly
help•ful•ness
help•ing
help•less
help•less\ly
help•less•ness
help•mate or help•meet
Hel•sin\ki
hel•ter-•skel\ter
hem, hemmed, hem•ming
he-•man, pl. •men
he\ma•tite
he\ma•tol\o•gist
he\ma•tol\o•gy
he\ma•to\ma, pl. •mas or •ma\ta
Hem•ing•way
hem\i•sphere
hem\i•spher•ic
hem•line
hem•lock
he\mo•glo•bin
he\mo•phil\i\a
he\mo•phil\i\ac
hem•or•rhage, •rhaged, •rhag•ing
hem•or•rhag\ic
hem•or•rhoid
he\mo•stat
hemp

hen
hence (from now) [vs. thence (from that place) and whence (from where)]
hence•forth
hench•man, pl. •men
hen\na, pl. •nas; •naed, •na•ing
hen•peck
hen•pecked
hen\ry, pl. •ries or •rys
hep
hep\a•rin
he•pat\ic
hep\a•ti•tis
her
He\ra
her•ald, •ald\ed, •ald•ing
he•ral•dic
her•ald\ry
herb
her•ba•ceous
herb\al
herb•al•ist
her•bi•cid\al
herb\i•cide
her•bi•vore
her•biv\o•rous
her•cu•le\an
Her•cu•les
herd (group of animals) [vs. heard (did listen)]
herd, herd\ed, herd•ing
here (in this place) [vs. hear (to listen)]
here•a\bout or here•a\bouts
here•af\ter
here\by
he•red\i•tar\y
he•red•i\ty
here•in
here•in•af\ter or here•in•be\low
her•e\sy, pl. •sies
her\e•tic
he•ret\i•cal
here\to or here•un\to
here\to•fore
here•up\on

here•with
her•it•a•ble
her•it•age
her•maph•ro•dite
her•maph•ro•dit\ic
Her•mes
her•met\i•cal\ly
her•mit
her•mit•age
her•ni\a, pl. •ni\as or •ni\ae
he\ro, pl. •roes (brave people), •ros (sandwiches)
He•rod\o•tus
he•ro•ic
he•ro•i•cal\ly
her•o\in (drug)
her\o•ine (admired woman)
her\o•ism
her\on
her•pes
her•pes zos•ter
her•pe•tol•o\gy
Herr, pl. Her•ren
her•ring, pl. •ring or •rings
her•ring•bone
hers
her•self
hertz, pl. hertz or hertz\es
he's
hes\i•tan\cy
hes\i•tant
hes\i•tant\ly
hes\i•tate, •tat\ed, •tat•ing
hes\i•tat•ing\ly
hes\i•ta•tion
het\er\o•dox
het\er\o•dox\y
het\er\o•ge\ne\i\ty
het\er\o•ge\ne\ous
heterogeneous net•work
het\er\o•sex•u\al
het\er\o•sex•u•al•i\ty
heu•ris•tic
hew (to chop), hewed, hewed or hewn, hew•ing [vs. hue (color) and Hugh (the name)]
hex, hexed, hex•ing
hex\a•gon
hex•ag\o•nal

hex•am\e•ter
hey (the exclamation) [vs. hay (dried grass)]
hey•day
hi
HI (Hawaii)
Hi•a•le\ah
hi•a•tus, pl. •tus\es or •tus
hi•ba•chi, pl. •chis
hi•ber•nate, •nat\ed, •nat•ing
hi•ber•na•tion
hi•bis•cus, pl. •cus\es
hic•cup or hic•cough, •cuped or •cupped or •coughed, •cup•ing or •cup•ping or •cough•ing
hick
hick\o•ry, pl. •ries
hid•den
hidden file
hidden re•serves
hidden tax
hide (to conceal), hid, hid•den, hid•ing
hide (to thrash), hid•ed, hid•ing
hide-•and-•seek
hide•a\way
hide•bound
hid\e•ous
hid\e•ous\ly
hide•out or hide-•out
hie, hied, hie•ing
hi\er•ar•chic or hi\er•ar•chi•cal
hierarchical file sys•tem
hi\er•ar•chi•cal\ly
hi\er•ar•chy, pl. •chies
hi\er\o•glyph\ic
hi-•fi, pl. •fis
hig\gle•dy-•pig\gle\dy
high, pl. highs; \er, •est
high•ball, •balled, •ball•ing
high•born
high•boy
high•brow
high•chair
high-•den\si\ty
high\er (taller) [vs. hire (to employ)]

high\er-•up
high•fa•lu•tin or high•fa•lu•ting
high fi•del\i\ty (noun)
high-•fi\del\i\ty (adj.)
high-•five, •fived, •fiv\ing
high-•flown
high fre•quen\cy (noun)
high-•fre\quen\cy (adj.)
high-•hand\ed
high-•hand\ed\ly
high-•hand\ed\ness
high-•hat, •hat\ted, •hat\ting
high jinks (frolics) [vs. jinx (bad luck)]
high•land
high-•lev\el
high-•lev\el lan•guage
high•light
high\ly
high mem•o\ry
high-•mind\ed
high-•mind\ed\ness
high•ness
high-•pres\sure, \sured, \sur\ing
high-•res\o\lu•tion
high-•rise or high•rise
high•road
high-•sound\ing
high-•spir\ited
high-•strung
high•tail
high-•tech
high-•ten\sion
high-•test
high-•toned
high•way
high•way•man, pl. •men
hi•jack, •jacked, •jack•ing
hi•jack\er
hike, hiked, hik•ing
hik\er
hi•lar•i•ous
hi•lar•i•ous\ly
hi•lar•i\ty
hill
hill•bil\ly, pl. •lies
hill•ock
hill•side

hill•top

hill\y, •i\er, •i•est

hilt

him (*objective case of "he"*) [vs. hymn (*song*)]

Him\a•la•yan

Him\a•la•yas

him•self

hind, *pl.* hinds *or* hind

hind\er (*in the rear*)

hin•der (*to prevent*), •dered, •der•ing

Hin\di

hind•most

hind•quar•ter

hin•drance

hind•sight

Hin\du, *pl.* •dus

Hin•du•ism

Hin•du•stan

Hin•du•sta\ni

hinge, hinged, hing•ing

hint, hint\ed, hint•ing

hin•ter•land

hip, hip•per, hip•pest

hip•bone

hip-•hop

hip•hug•ger

hip•ness

hip•pie, *pl.* •pies

hip\po

Hip•po•crat\ic oath

hip•po•drome

hip•po•pot\a•mus, *pl.* •mus\es *or* \mi

hip•ster

hire (*to employ*), hired, hir•ing [vs. high\er (*taller*)]

hire•ling

hi-•res

hir•ing hall

Hi•ro•shi\ma

hir•sute

hir•sute•ness

his

His•pan\ic

hiss, hissed, hiss•ing

his•to•gram

his•tol\o•gist

his•tol•o\gy

his•to•ri\an

his•tor\ic

his•tor\i•cal

historical cost

his•tor\i•cal\ly

his•to\ry, *pl.* •ries

his•tri•on\ic

his•tri•on\i•cal\ly

his•tri•on•ics

hit, hit, hit•ting

hit-•and-•run

hitch, hitched, hitch•ing

hitch•hike, •hiked, •hik•ing

hitch•hik\er

hith\er

hith•er\to

Hit•ler

hit-•or-•miss

hit•ter

HIV (*human immuno-deficiency virus*)

hive

hives

HMO (*health maintenance organization*)

hoa\gy *or* hoa•gie, *pl.* •gies

hoard (*to amass*), hoard\ed, hoard•ing [vs. horde (*crowd*)]

hoard\er

hoar•frost

hoar\i•ness

hoarse (*husky in tone*), hoars\er, hoars•est [vs. horse (*the animal*)]

hoarse•ly

hoarse•ness

hoar\y, hoar•i\er, hoar•i•est

hoax, hoaxed, hoax•ing

hoax\er

hob•ble, •bled, •bling

hob\by, *pl.* •bies

hob\by•horse

hob\by•ist

hob•gob•lin

hob•nailed

hob•nob, •nobbed, •nob•bing

ho\bo, *pl.* •bos *or* •boes

Ho Chi Minh

hock, hocked, hock•ing

hock\ey

hock•shop

ho\cus-•po\cus

hodge•podge

Hodg•kin's disease

hoe, hoed, hoe•ing

hoe•cake

hoe•down

hog, hogged, hog•ging

ho•gan

hog•gish

hogs•head

hog•tie, •tied, •ty•ing

hog•wash

hog-•wild

hoi pol•loi

hoist, hoist\ed, hoist•ing

hok\ey, hok•i\er, hok•i•est

ho•kum

hold, held, hold•ing

hold\er

holder in due course

hold•ing

holding com•pa\ny

hold•o\ver

hold\up

hole (*opening*) [vs. whole (*entire*)]

hole, holed, hol•ing

hol\ey (*full of holes*) [vs. ho\ly (*sacred*) *and* whol\ly (*entirely*)]

hol\i•day (*day of commem-oration*) [vs. ho\ly day (*religious feast day*)]

ho•li\er-•than-•thou

ho•li•ness

ho•lis•tic

Hol•land

hol•lan•daise sauce

Hol•land\er

hol•ler, •lered, •ler•ing

Hol•ler•ith code

hol•low, •lowed, •low•ing

hol•low (*empty*), •low\er, •low•est [vs. hal•low (*to make holy*) *and* ha\lo (*ring of light*)]

hol•low•ness

hol\ly, *pl.* •lies

hol\ly•hock
Hol\ly•wood
Holmes
hol•mi\um
hol\o•caust
Hol\o•cene
hol\o•gram
hol\o•graph
hol\o•graph\ic
ho•log\ra•phy
Hol•stein
hol•ster, •stered, •ster•ing
ho•ly (sacred), •li\er, •li•est
[vs. hol\ey (full of holes)
and whol\ly (entirely)]
holy day (religious feast
day) [vs. hol\i•day (day of
commemoration)]
Ho\ly Ghost
hom•age
hom•burg
home, homed, hom•ing
home•bod\y, pl. •bod•ies
home•com\ing
home•grown
home•land
home•less
home•like
home•li•ness
home\ly (unattractive),
•li\er, •li•est [vs. hom\ey
or hom\ly (cozy)]
home•made
home•mak\er
home-•mak\ing
home of•fice
ho\me\o•path\ic
ho\me\op\a•thy
ho\me\o•sta•sis
ho\me\o•stat\ic
Ho•mer
hom\er
Ho•mer\ic
home•room or
   home room
home shop•ping
home•sick
home•sick•ness
home•spun
home•stead
home•stretch

home•ward
home•work
hom\ey or hom\ly (cozy),
•i\er, •i•est [vs. home\ly
(unattractive)]
hom\i•cid\al
hom\i•cide
hom\i•let•ics
hom\i•ly (sermon), pl. •lies
[vs. hom\i\ny (hulled
corn)]
hom•ing pi•geon
hom\i\ny (hulled corn) [vs.
hom\i•ly (sermon)]
ho\mo•ge\ne\i\ty
ho•mo•ge\ne\ous (alike)
[vs. ho•mog\e•nous (of
common origin)]
ho•mog\e•nized
ho•mog\e•nous (of com-
mon origin) [vs.
ho\mo•ge\ne\ous (alike)]
hom\o•graph
ho•mol\o•gous
hom\o•nym
ho\mo•phile
ho\mo•pho•bi\a
hom\o•phone
Ho\mo sa•pi•ens
ho\mo•sex•u\al
ho\mo•sex•u•al\i•ty
hom\y, •i\er, •i•est
hon
hon•cho, pl. •chos
Hon•du•ran
Hon•du•ras
hone, honed, hon•ing
hon•est
hon•est\ly
hon•es\ty
hon\ey, pl. hon•eys
hon\ey•bee or hon\ey bee
hon\ey•comb
hon\ey•dew
hon•eyed or hon•ied
hon\ey•moon, •mooned,
•moon•ing
hon\ey•moon•er
hon\ey•suck\le
Hong Kong
Ho•ni

honk, honked, honk•ing
honk\y-•tonk
Hon\o•lu\lu
hon\or, •ored, •or•ing
hon•or•a\ble
hon•or•a•bly
hon\o•rar•i\um, pl.
•rar•i•ums or •rar\i\a
hon•or•ar\y
hon•or•if\ic
Hon•shu
hooch or hootch
hood
hood\ed
hood•lum
hoo•doo, pl. •doos,
•dooed, •doo•ing
hood•wink, •winked,
•wink•ing
hoo\ey
hoof, pl. hoofs or hooves
or hoof
hook, hooked, hook•ing
hook\ah, pl. hook•ahs
hook\er
hook\up
hook•worm
hook\y or hook\ey
hoo•li•gan
hoo•li•gan•ism
hoop (circular band) [vs.
whoop (loud shout)]
hoop\la
hoo•ray
hoose•gow
Hoo•sier
hoot, hoot\ed, hoot•ing
hoot•en•an\ny, pl. •nies
Hoo•ver
hop, hopped, hop•ping
hope, hoped, hop•ing
hope•ful
hope•ful\ly
hope•less
hope•less\ly
hope•less•ness
hop•head
Ho\pi, pl. •pis or \pi
hop•per
hop•sack•ing
hop•scotch

Hor•ace

horde (crowd) [vs. hoard (to amass)]

ho•ri•zon

hor•i•zon•tal

horizontal in•te•gra•tion

hor•i•zon•tal•ly

hor•i•zon•tal merg\er

horizontal scroll•ing

hor•mo•nal

hor•mone

horn

horned

hor•net

horn•less

horn•pipe

horn\y, •i\er, •i•est

hor•o•log\ic

ho•rol\o•gist

ho•rol•o•gy

hor•o•scope

hor•ren•dous

hor•ri•ble

hor•ri•bly

hor•rid

hor•rif\ic

hor•ri\fy, •fied, •fy•ing

hor•ri•fy•ing\ly

hor•ror

hors de com•bat

hors d'oeuvre, pl. hors d'oeuvre or hors d'oeuvres

horse (the animal), pl. hors\es or horse; horsed, hors•ing [vs. hoarse (husky in tone)]

horse•back

horse•flesh

horse fly or horse•fly

horse•hair

horse•hide

horse•laugh

horse•less

horse•man, pl. •men

horse•man•ship

horse•play

horse•pow\er

horse•rad•ish

horse•shoe

horse•whip, •whipped, •whip•ping

horse•wom\an, pl. •wom\en

hors\y, •i\er, •i•est

hor•ta•to•ry

hor•ti•cul•tur\al

hor•ti•cul•ture

ho•san\na, pl. •nas

hose, pl. hose (stockings), hos\es (tubes); hosed, hos•ing

ho•sier\y

hos•pice

hos•pi•ta\ble (receptive)

hos•pi•tal (medical institution)

hos•pi•tal•i\ty, pl. •ties

hos•pi•tal\i•za•tion

hos•pi•tal•ize, •ized, •iz•ing

host, host\ed, host•ing

hos•tage

host com•put\er

hos•tel (lodging place) [vs. hos•tile (antagonistic)]

host•ess, •essed, •ess•ing

hos•tile (antagonistic) [vs. hos•tel (lodging place)]

hostile take•o\ver

hos•til•i•ties

hos•til•i\ty

hot, hot•ter, hot•test

hot•bed

hot-•blood\ed

hot•box or hot box

hot cake or hot•cake

hot dog (noun)

hot-•dog or hot•dog (verb), •dogged, •dog\ging or •dog•ging

ho•tel

hot•foot, pl. •foots

hot•head

hot•head\ed

hot•head•ed•ness

hot•house

hot key

hot link

hot\ly

hot rod (noun)

hot-•rod (verb), •rod\ded, •rod\ding

hot rod•der

hot•shot

hot spot or hot•spot

hound, hound\ed, hound•ing

hound's-•tooth

hour (60 minutes) [vs. our (belonging to us)]

hour•glass

hou\ri, pl. •ris

hour\ly

house, pl. hous\es; housed, hous•ing

house•boat

house•boy

house•break, •broke, •bro•ken, •break•ing

house•break\er

house•coat

house•fa\ther

house•fly or house fly, pl. •flies or flies

house•ful, pl. •fuls

house•hold

house•hold\er

house•hus•band

house•keep\er

house•keep•ing

house•maid

house•man, pl. •men

house•moth\er

house•par•ent

house•plant

house•sit or house-•sit, •sat, •sit•ting or •sit\ting

house sit•ter or house-•sit\ter

house•top

house•wares

house•warm•ing

house•wife, pl. •wives

house•wife\ly

house•work

hous•ing

Hous•ton

hove

hov•el

hov\er, •ered, •er•ing

hov\er•craft, pl. •craft

how
how•be\it
how•dah
how-•do-•you-•do or
   how-•de-•do, pl. •dos
how•ev\er
how•itz\er
howl, howled, howl•ing
howl\er
how•so•ev\er
how-•to
hoy•den
hoy•den•ish
Hoyle
hua•ra•che, pl. •ches
hub
hub•bub
hub•cap
hu•bris
huck\le•ber\ry, pl. •ries
huck•ster
HUD (Department of
   Housing and Urban
   Development)
hud•dle, •dled, •dling
Hud•son
hue (color) [vs. hew (to
   chop) and Hugh (the
   name)]
huff, huffed, huff•ing
huff\y, •i\er, •i•est
hug, hugged, hug•ging
huge, hug•er, hug•est
huge\ly
huge•ness
hug\ger-•mug\ger
Hugh (the name) [vs.
   hew (to chop) and hue
   (color)]
Hu\go
Hu•gue•not
huh
hu\la, pl. •las
hulk
hulk•ing
hull
hul•la•ba•loo, pl. •loos
hum, hummed, hum•ming
hu•man (of people)
hu•mane (compassionate)
hu•mane\ly

hu•mane•ness
hu\man•ism
hu\man•ist
hu\man•is•tic
hu\man•i•tar•i•an
hu\man•i•ties
hu\man•i•tar\i•an•ism
hu\man•i•ties
hu\man•i•ty
hu\man•ize, •ized, •iz•ing
hu\man•kind
hu•man\ly
hu\man•oid
hu•man re•sourc\es
hu•man rights
hum•ble, •bled, •bling;
   •bler, •blest
hum•bly
hum•bug, •bugged,
   •bug•ging
hum•ding\er
hum•drum
hu•mer\al
hu•mer\us (arm bone), pl.
   •mer\i [vs. hu•mor•ous
   (funny)]
hu•mid
hu•mid\i•fi•ca•tion
hu•mid\i•fi\er
hu•mid•i\fy, •fied, •fy•ing
hu•mid•i\ty
hu•mi•dor
hu•mil\i•ate, •at\ed, •at•ing
hu•mil\i•at•ing\ly
hu•mil\i•a•tion
hu•mil•i\ty
hum•mer
hum•ming•bird
hum•mock
hu•mon•gous
hu•mor, •mored, •mor•ing
hu•mor•ist
hu•mor•less
hu•mor•ous (funny) [vs.
   hu•mer\us (arm bone)]
hu•mor•ous\ly
hump, humped, hump•ing
hump•back
hump•backed
humph
hu•mus

Hun
hunch (suspicion) [vs.
   haunch (hip)]
hunch, hunched,
   hunch•ing
hunch•back
hunch•backed
hun•dred, pl. •dreds or
   •dred
hun•dred•fold
hun•dredth
hun•dred•weight, pl.
   •weights or •weight
hung
Hun•gar•i\an
Hun•ga\ry
hun•ger, •gered, •ger•ing
hun•gri\ly
hun•gry, •gri\er, •gri•est
hunk
hun•ker, •kered, •ker•ing
hunk\y-•do\ry
hunt, hunt\ed, hunt•ing
hunt\er
hunt•ress
hunts•man, pl. •men
Hunts•ville
hur•dle (barrier) [vs.
   hur•tle (to rush)]
hur•dle, •dled, •dling
hur•dler
hur\dy-•gur\dy, pl.
   •gur\dies
hurl, hurled, hurl•ing
hurl\er
hurl\y-•burl\y
Hu•ron, pl. •rons or •ron
hur•rah or hur•ray, •rahed
   or •rayed, •rah•ing or
   •ray•ing
hur•ri•cane
hur•ried\ly
hur\ry, pl. •ries; •ried,
   •ry•ing
hurt, hurt, hurt•ing
hurt•ful
hur•tle (to rush), •tled,
   •tling [vs. hur•dle
   (barrier)]
hus•band, •band\ed,
   •band•ing

hus•band\ry
hush, hushed, hush•ing
hush-•hush
husk, husked, husk•ing
husk•i\ly
husk\i•ness
husk\y, pl. husk•ies;
  husk•i\er, husk•i\est
hus•sar
hus\sy, pl. •sies
hus•tings
hus•tle, •tled, •tling
hus•tler
hut
hutch
hutz\pa or hutz•pah
huz•zah, pl. •zahs; •zahed,
  •zah•ing,
hy•a•cinth
hy•brid
hy•dra, pl. •dras or •drae
hy•dran•gea, pl. •geas
hy•drant
hy•drau•lic
hy•drau•lics
hy•dro, pl. •dros
hy\dro•car•bon
hy\dro•ceph\a•lus or
  hy•dro•ceph•a\ly
hy\dro•chlo•ric ac\id
hy\dro•cor•ti•sone
hy\dro•e•lec•tric
hy\dro•e•lec•tric•i\ty
hy\dro•foil
hy\dro•gen
hy\dro•gen•a•tion
hy\dro•gen bomb
hy\dro•pho•bi\a
hy\dro•phone
hy\dro•plane
hy\dro•pon\ic

hy\dro•pon•ics
hy\dro•stat\ic
hy\dro•stat\ics
hy•drous
hy•drox•ide
hy•e\na, pl. •nas
hy•giene
hy•gi\en\ic
hy•gi\en\i•cal\ly
hy•gien•ist
hy•men
hy•me•ne\al
hymn (song) [vs. him
  (objective case of "he")]
hymn
hym•nal
hype
hy•per
hy•per•ac•tive
hy•per•ac•tiv•i\ty
hy•per•bar\ic
hy\per•bo•la (curve), pl.
  •las
hy•per•bo•le
  (exaggeration)
hy\per•bol\ic or
  hy\per•bol\i•cal
hy\per•crit\i•cal
hy•per•crit\i•cal\ly
hy•per•in•fla•tion
hy•per•me\di\a
hy•per•sen•si•tive
hy\per•sen•si•tive•ness or
  hy\per•sen•si•tiv•i\ty
hy•per•son\ic
hy•per•ten•sion
hy•per•ten•sive
hy•per•text
hy•per•thy•roid
hy•per•thy•roid•ism
hy•per•troph\ic

hy•per•tro•phy
hy\per•ven•ti•late, •lat\ed,
  •lat•ing
hy\per•ven•ti•la•tion
hy•phen
hy•phen•ate, •at\ed,
  •at•ing
hy•phen•a•tion
hyp•no•sis, pl. •ses
hyp•not\ic
hyp•not\i•cal\ly
hyp•no•tism
hyp•no•tist
hyp•no•tiz•a\ble
hyp•no•tize, •tized,
  •tiz•ing
hy\po, pl. •pos
hy\po•al\ler•gen\ic
hy\po•chon•dri\a
hy\po•chon•dri\ac
hy•poc•ri\sy, pl. •sies
hyp\o•crite
hyp\o•crit\i•cal
hyp\o•crit\i•cal\ly
hy•po•der•mic
hy\po•gly•ce•mi\a
hy\po•gly•ce•mic
hy•pot\e•nuse
hy•poth\e•ca•tion
hy•po•ther•mi\a
hy•poth\e•sis, pl. •ses
hy•poth\e•size, •sized,
  •siz•ing
hy•po•thet\i•cal
hy•po•thet\i•cal\ly
hy•po•thy•roid
hy•po•thy•roid•ism
hys•ter•ec•to\my, pl. •mies
hys•te•ri\a
hys•ter\i•cal
hys•ter•ics

I

I (me), pl. we, I's; me, pl.
  us; my, pl. our; mine, pl.
  ours [vs. aye (yes) and
  eye (organ of sight)]
IA (Iowa)
i\amb
i\am•bic
I-\beam point\er

I\be•ri\a
I\be•ri\an
i•bex (mountain goat), pl.
  i•bex\es or ib\i•ces or
  i•bex
i•bis (wading bird), pl.
  i•bis\es or i•bis
Ib•sen

i•bu•pro•fen
ICC (Interstate Commerce
  Commission)
ice, iced, ic•ing
ice•berg
ice•box
ice•break\er
ice•cap

ice cream
iced
Ice•land
Ice•lan•dic
ice•man, pl. •men
ice skate (noun)
ice-•skate (verb), •skat\ed,
 •skat\ing
ich•thy•ol\o\gy
i\ci•cle
i\ci\ly
i\ci•ness
ic•ing
ick\y, •i\er, •i•est
i\con
i\con\ic
i\co•nic•i\ty
i\con\o•clasm
i\con\o•clast
i\con\o•clas•tic
ic•tus, pl. •tus\es or •tus
ICU (intensive care unit)
i\cy, i\ci\er, i\ci•est
ID (Idaho)
ID (identification), pl. IDs
 or ID's
I'd (I would)
id
I\da•ho (ID)
I\da•ho\an
i\de\a
i\de\al (perfect) [vs. i\dle
 (inactive) and i\dol
 (object of worship) and
 i\dyll (pastoral poem)]
i\de\al•ism
i\de\al•ist
i\de\al•is•tic
i\de\al\i•za•tion
i\de\al•ize, •ized, •iz•ing
i\de•al\ly
i\dée fixe, pl. i\dée fixes
i\den•ti•cal
i\den•ti•cal\ly
i\den•ti•fi•a\ble
i\den•ti•fi•ca•tion
i\den•ti•fied goods
i\den•ti\fy, •fied, •fy•ing
i\den•ti\ty, pl. •ties
id\e\o•gram
i\de\o•log\i\cal

i\de\ol\o\gy, pl. \gies
ides
id\i•o\cy, pl. •cies
id•i\om
id\i\o•mat\ic
id\i\o•mat\i•cal\ly
id\i\o•path\ic
id\i\o•syn•cra\sy, pl. •sies
id\i\o•syn•crat\ic
id•i\ot
id\i•ot\ic
id\i•ot\i•cal\ly
i\dle (inactive; to be idle),
 i\dler, i\dlest; i\dled,
 i\dling [vs. i\de\al
 (perfect) and i\dol (object
 of worship) and i\dyll
 (pastoral poem)]
i\dle•ness
i\dler
i\dly
i\dol (object of worship)
 [vs. i\de\al (perfect) and
 i\dle (inactive) and i\dyll
 (pastoral poem)]
i\dol\a•ter
i\dol\a•trous
i\dol\a•try
i\dol•ize, •ized, •iz•ing
i\dyll (pastoral poem) [vs.
 i\de\al (perfect) and i\dle
 (inactive) and i\dol
 (object of worship)]
i\dyl•lic
i.e. (that is) [vs. e.g. (for
 example)]
IEEE (Institute of Electrical
 and Electronics Engineers)
if
if\fy, •fi\er, •fi•est
ig•loo, pl. •loos
ig•ne•ous
ig•nite, •nit\ed, •nit•ing
ig•ni•tion
ig•no•bil•i\ty
ig•no•ble
ig•no•bly
ig•no•min\i•ous
ig•no•min\i•ous\ly
ig•no•min\y
ig•no•ra•mus, pl. •mus\es

ig•no•rance
ig•no•rant
ig•no•rant\ly
ig•nore, •nored,
 •nor•ing
i\gua\na, pl. •nas
IL (Illinois)
il\e\i•tis
il\e\um (intestine), pl.
 \e•ums
Il\i\ad
il\i\um (hip bone), pl. \i\a
ilk
I'll (I will) [vs. aisle (passage) and isle (island)]
ill (sick), worse, worst
ill-•ad\vised
ill-•ad\vis\ed\ly
ill-•bred
il•le•gal
il•le•gal•i\ty
il•le•gal\ly
il•leg•i•bil•i\ty
il•leg•i•ble (hard to read)
 [vs. el\i•gi•ble (qualified)]
il•leg•i•bly
il•le•git\i•ma\cy
il•le•git\i•mate
il•le•git\i•mate\ly
ill-•fat\ed
ill-•got\ten
ill-•hu\mor
ill-•hu\mored
il•lib•er\al
il•lic•it (illegal) [vs. e\lic•it
 (to bring forth)]
il•lic•it\ly
il•lic•it•ness
il•lim•it•a\ble
il•lim•it•a•bly
Il•li•nois (IL)
il•lit•er\a\cy
il•lit•er•ate
ill-•man\nered
ill-•na\tured
ill-•na\tured\ly
ill-•na\tured\ness
ill•ness
il•log\i•cal
il•log\i•cal\ly
ill-•starred

ill-•treat, •treat\ed, •treat\ing

ill-•treat\ment

il•lu•mi•nate, •nat\ed, •nat\ing

il•lu•mi•nat•ing\ly

il•lu•mi•na•tion

il•lu•mine, •mined, •min•ing

ill-•use, •used, •us\ing

il•lu•sion (*false idea*) [*vs.* al•lu•sion (*reference*)]

il•lu•sive (*deceptive*) [*vs.* al•lu•sive (*suggestive*) and e•lu•sive (*evasive*)]

il•lu•so\ry

il•lus•trate, •trat\ed, •trat•ing

il•lus•tra•tion

il•lus•tra•tive

il•lus•tra•tive\ly

il•lus•tra•tor

il•lus•tri•ous

il•lus•tri•ous\ly

il•lus•tri•ous•ness

ill will (*noun*)

ill-•willed (*adj.*)

I'm (*I am*)

im•age, •aged, •ag•ing

im•age\ry

i\mag\i•na•ble

im•ag\i•nar\y

im•ag\i•na•tion

im•ag\i•na•tive

im•ag\i•na•tive\ly

im•ag•ine, •ined, •in•ing, •ines (*forms a mental image*)

i\ma•go, *pl.* •goes or •gi•nes (*adult insects*)

i\mam

im•bal•ance

im•be•cile

im•be•cil\ic

im•bed, •bed\ded, •bed•ding

im•bibe, •bibed, •bib•ing

im•bro•glio, *pl.* •glios

im•bue, •bued, •bu•ing

IMF or I.M.F. (*International Monetary Fund*)

im\i•tate, •tat\ed, •tat•ing

im\i•ta•tion

im\i•ta•tive

im\i•ta•tor

im•mac\u•late

im•mac\u•late\ly

im•ma•nence

im•ma•nent (*inherent*) [*vs.* em\i•nent (*renowned*) and im•mi•nent (*impending*)]

im•ma•te•ri\al

im•ma•ture

im•ma•ture\ly

im•ma•tur•i\ty

im•meas•ur•a\ble

im•meas•ur•a\bly

im•me•di•a\cy

im•me•di•ate

im•me•di•ate\ly

im•me•mo•ri\al

im•mense

im•mense\ly

im•men•si\ty

im•merse, •mersed, •mers•ing

im•mers•i\ble

im•mer•sion

im•mi•grant

im•mi•grate (*to come to a new country*), •grat\ed, •grat•ing [*vs.* em\i•grate (*to leave one's country*)]

im•mi•nence

im•mi•nent (*impending*) [*vs.* em\i•nent (*renowned*) and im•ma•nent (*inherent*)]

im•mi•nent\ly

im•mo•bile

im•mo•bil•i\ty

im•mo•bi•li•za•tion

im•mo•bi•lize, •lized, •liz•ing

im•mod•er•ate

im•mod•er•ate\ly

im•mod•est

im•mod•est\ly

im•mod•es\ty

im•mo•late, •lat\ed, •lat•ing

im•mo•la•tion

im•mor\al (*licentious*) [*vs.* a\mor\al (*without moral standards*) and im•mor•tal (*everlasting*)]

im•mo•ral•i\ty, *pl.* •ties

im•mor•al\ly

im•mor•tal (*everlasting*)

im•mor•tal•i\ty

im•mor•tal•ize, •ized, •iz•ing

im•mor•tal\ly

im•mov•a•bil•i\ty

im•mov•a\ble or im•move•a\ble

im•mune

im•mu•ni\ty

im•mu•ni•za•tion

im•mu•nize, •nized, •niz•ing

im•mu•no•log\i•cal

im•mu•nol\o\gy

im\mu\no•sup•pres•sive

im•mure, •mured, •mur•ing

im•mu•ta•bil•i\ty

im•mu•ta\ble

im•mu•ta\bly

imp

im•pact, •pact\ed, •pact•ing

impact print\er

im•pair, •paired, •pair•ing

im•pair•ment

im•pal\a, *pl.* •pal\as or •pal\a

im•pale, •paled, •pal•ing

im•pale•ment

im•pal•pa\ble

im•pal•pa\bly

im•pan\el, •eled or •elled, •el•ing or •el•ling

im•part, •part\ed, •part•ing

im•par•tial

im•par•ti•al•i\ty

im•par•tial\ly

im•pass•a\ble (*not passable*) [*vs.* im•pass•i\ble (*incapable of suffering*) and im•pos•si\ble (*not possible*)]

im•passe
im•pas•si\ble (*incapable of suffering*)
im•pas•sioned
im•pas•sioned\ly
im•pas•sive
im•pas•sive\ly
im•pas•siv•i\ty
im•pas\to
im•pa•tience (*lack of patience*)
im•pa•tiens (*the plant*), *pl.* •tiens
im•pa•tient
im•pa•tient\ly
im•peach, •peached, •peach•ing
im•peach•a\ble
im•peach•ment
im•pec•ca\ble
im•pec•ca•bly
im•pe•cu•ni•ous
im•pe•cu•ni•ous•ness
im•ped•ance
im•pede, •ped\ed, •ped•ing
im•ped\i•ment
im•ped\i•men\ta, *pl.*
im•pel, •pelled, •pel•ling
im•pend, •pend\ed, •pend•ing
im•pen\e•tra•bil•i\ty
im•pen\e•tra•ble
im•pen\e•tra•bly
im•pen\i•tence
im•pen\i•tent
im•per\a•tive
im•per\a•tive\ly
im•per•cep•ti•ble
im•per•cep•ti•bly
im•per•cep•tive
im•per•fect
im•per•fec•tion
im•per•fect\ly
im•per•fect•ness
im•per•fo•rate
im•pe•ri\al
im•pe•ri•al•ist
im•pe•ri•al•is•tic
im•per\il, •iled or •illed, •il•ing or •il•ling

im•per\il•ment
im•pe•ri•ous
im•pe•ri•ous\ly
im•pe•ri•ous•ness
im•per•ish•a\ble
im•per•ma•nence
im•per•ma•nent
im•per•ma•nent\ly
im•per•me•a•bil•i\ty
im•per•me•a\ble
im•per•son\al
im•per•son\al\ly
im•per•son•ate, •at\ed, •at•ing
im•per•son•a•tion
im•per•son\a•tor
im•per•ti•nence
im•per•ti•nent
im•per•ti•nent\ly
im•per•turb•a•bil•i\ty
im•per•turb•a•ble
im•per•turb•a•bly
im•per•vi•ous
im•per•vi•ous\ly
im•pe•ti\go
im•pet\u•os•i\ty
im•pet\u•ous
im•pet\u•ous\ly
im•pe•tus
im•pi•e\ty
im•pinge, •pinged, •ping•ing
im•pinge•ment
im•pi•ous
im•pi•ous\ly
imp•ish
imp•ish\ly
imp•ish•ness
im•plac•a•bil•i\ty
im•plac•a•ble
im•plac•a•bly
im•plant, •plant\ed, •plant•ing
im•plau•si•bil•i\ty
im•plau•si•ble
im•plau•si•bly
im•ple•ment, •ment\ed, •ment•ing
im•ple•men•ta•tion
im•pli•cate, •cat\ed, •cat•ing

im•pli•ca•tion
im•plic\lt
implicit cost
im•plic•it\ly
im•plied war•ran\ty
im•plode, •plod\ed, •plod•ing
im•plore, •plored, •plor•ing
im•plor•ing\ly
im•plo•sion
im•ply, •plied, •ply•ing
im•po•lite
im•po•lite\ly
im•pol\i•tic
im•pon•der•a\ble
im•port, •port\ed, •port•ing
im•por•tance
im•por•tant
im•por•tant\ly
im•por•ta•tion
im•port\er
im•port quo\ta
im•por•tu•nate
im•por•tu•nate\ly
im•por•tune, •tuned, •tun•ing
im•por•tun•i\ty
im•pose, •posed, •pos•ing
im•pos•ing\ly
im•po•si•tion
im•pos•si•bil•i\ty
im•pos•si•ble (*not possible*) [*vs.* im•pass•a•ble (*not passable*) and im•pass•i•ble (*incapable of suffering*)]
im•pos•si•bly
im•post
im•pos•tor or im•post\er (*pretender*)
im•pos•ture (*fraud*)
im•po•tence
im•po•tent
im•po•tent\ly
im•pound, •pound\ed, •pound•ing
im•pov•er•ish, •ished, •ish•ing
im•pov•er•ish•ment

im•prac•ti•ca\ble (*not feasible*)
im•prac•ti•cal (*not useful*)
im•prac•ti•cal•i\ty
im•pre•ca•tion
im•pre•cise
im•pre•ci•sion *or* im•pre•cise•ness
im•preg•na•bil•i\ty
im•preg•na•ble
im•preg•nate, •nat•ed, •nat•ing
im•preg•na•tion
im•pre•sa•ri\o, *pl.* •ri\os
im•press, •pressed, •press•ing
im•pres•sion
im•pres•sion•a\ble
im•pres•sion•ism
im•pres•sion•ist
im•pres•sive
im•pres•sive\ly
im•pres•sive•ness
im•press•ment
im•prest fund
im•pri•ma•tur
im•print, •print\ed, •print•ing
im•pris\on, •oned, •on•ing
im•pris•on•ment
im•prob•a•bil•i\ty
im•prob•a•ble
im•prob•a•bly
im•promp\tu, *pl.* •tus
im•prop\er
im•prop•er\ly
im•pro•pri•e\ty, *pl.* •ties
im•prove, •proved, •prov•ing
im•prove•ment
im•prov\i•dence
im•prov\i•dent
im•prov\i•dent\ly
im•prov\i•sa•tion
im•prov\i•sa•tion\al
im•pro•vise, •vised, •vis•ing
im•pru•dence
im•pru•dent
im•pu•dence
im•pu•dent

im•pu•dent\ly
im•pugn, •pugned, •pugn•ing
im•pulse
im•pul•sion
im•pulse i\tem
im•pul•sive
im•pul•sive\ly
im•pul•sive•ness
im•pu•ni\ty
im•pure
im•pure\ly
im•pure•ness
im•pu•ri\ty
im•put•a\ble
im•pu•ta•tion
im•pute, •put\ed, •put•ing
im•put\ed in•ter•est
in (*within*) [*vs.* inn (*hotel*)]
IN (*Indiana*)
in•a•bil•i\ty
in ab•sen•tia
in•ac•ti•vate, •vat\ed, •vat•ing
in•ad\e•qua•cy
in•ad\e•quate
in•ad\e•quate\ly
in•ad•vert•ence
in•ad•vert•ent
in•ad•vert•ent\ly
in•al•ien•a\ble
in•am\o•ra•ta, *pl.* •tas
in•ane (*lacking sense*) [*vs.* in•sane (*mad*)]
in•ane\ly
in•an\i•mate
in•an•i\ty
in•apt (*not fitting*) [*vs.* in•ept (*incompetent*)]
in•ar•tic\u•late
in•ar•tic\u•late\ly
in•ar•tic\u•late•ness
in•as•much as
in•at•ten•tion
in•at•ten•tive
in•au•gu•ral
in•au•gu•rate, •rat\ed, •rat•ing
in•au•gu•ra•tion
in•board
in•born

in•bound
in•bred
Inc. (*incorporated*)
In\ca
in•cal•cu•la\ble
in•cal•cu•la•bly
In•can
in•can•des•cence
in•can•des•cent
in•can•ta•tion
in•ca•pa•bil•i\ty
in•ca•pa\ble
in•ca•pa•bly
in•ca•pac\i•tate, •tat\ed, •tat•ing
in•car•cer•ate, •at\ed, •at•ing
in•car•cer•a•tion
in•car•nate
in•car•na•tion
in•cen•di•ar\y, *pl.* •ar•ies
in•cense
in•censed
in•cen•tive
in•cep•tion
in•cer•ti•tude
in•ces•sant
in•ces•sant\ly
in•cest
in•ces•tu•ous
inch, inched, inch•ing
in•cho•ate
inch•worm
in•ci•dence
in•ci•dent
in•ci•den•tal
in•ci•den•tal\ly
in•cin•er•ate, •at\ed, •at•ing
in•cin•er•a•tion
in•cin•er\a•tor
in•cip\i•ent\ly
in•cise, •cised, •cis•ing
in•ci•sion
in•ci•sive
in•ci•sive\ly
in•ci•sor
in•cite (*to stir up*), •cit\ed, •cit•ing [*vs.* in•sight (*understanding*)]
in•cite•ment

in•ci•vil•i•ty
in•clem•ent
in•cli•na•tion
in•cline, •clined, •clin•ing
in•clude, •clud\ed,
•clud•ing
in•clu•sion
in•clu•sive
in•clu•sive•ly
in•clu•sive•ness
in•cog•ni\to
in•co•her•ence
in•co•her•ent
in•co•her•ent•ly
in•com•bus•ti\ble
in•come
income fund
income state•ment
income tax
in•com•men•su•rate
in•com•mu•ni•ca\do
in•com•pa•ra•ble
in•com•pat•i•bil•i•ty
in•com•pat•i•ble
in•com•pat•i•bly
in•com•pe•tence
in•com•pe•tent
in•com•pe•tent•ly
in•com•plete
in•com•plete•ly
in•com•plete•ness
in•com•pre•hen•si\ble
in•con•gru•i•ty
in•con•gru•ous
in•con•gru•ous•ly
in•con•se•quen•tial
in•con•se•quen•tial•ly
in•con•sid•er•a\ble
in•con•sid•er•ate
in•con•sid•er•ate•ly
in•con•sid•er•ate•ness
in•con•sol•a•ble
in•con•spic\u•ous
in•con•spic\u•ous•ly
in•con•spic\u•ous•ness
in•con•stan\cy
in•con•stant
in•con•stant•ly
in•con•test•a•ble
in•con•test•a•bly
in•con•ti•nence

in•con•ti•nent
in•con•tro•vert•i\ble
in•con•ven•ience, •ienced,
•ienc•ing
in•con•ven•ient
in•con•ven•ient•ly
in•cor•po•rate, •rat\ed,
•rat•ing
in•cor•po•ra•tion
in•cor•po\re\al
in•cor•rect
in•cor•rect•ly
in•cor•ri•gi\ble
in•cor•ri•gi•bly
in•cor•rupt•i\ble
in•crease, •creased,
•creas•ing
in•creas•ing•ly
in•cred•i•ble (*unbelievable*)
in•cred•i•bly
in•cre•du•li\ty
in•cred\u•lous (*skeptical*)
in•cre•ment
in•cre•men•tal back\up
incremental cost
incremental rev\e•nue
in•crim\i•nate, •nat\ed,
•nat•ing
in•crim\i•na•tion
in•crim\i•na•to\ry
in•crust *or* encrust,
•crust\ed, •crust•ing
in•crus•ta•tion
in•cu•bate, •bat\ed,
•bat•ing
in•cu•ba•tion
in•cu•ba•tor
in•cu•bus, *pl.* \bi *or*
•bus\es
in•cul•cate, •cat\ed,
•cat•ing
in•cul•ca•tion
in•cul•pate, •pat\ed,
•pat•ing
in•cum•ben\cy
in•cum•bent
in•cu•nab•u•la
in•cur, •curred, •cur•ring
in•cur•a•ble
in•cur•a•bly
in•cu•ri•ous

in•cur•sion
in•debt\ed
in•de•cen\cy
in•de•cent
in•de•cent•ly
in•de•ci•pher•a\ble
in•de•ci•sion
in•de•ci•sive
in•de•ci•sive•ly
in•de•ci•sive•ness
in•dec\o\rous
in•deed
in•de•fat•i•ga\ble
in•de•fat•i•ga•bly
in•de•fen•si•ble
in•de•fen•si•bly
in•de•fin•a•ble
in•def\i•nite
in•def\i•nite•ly
in•del•i•ble
in•del•i•bly
in•del\i•ca\cy
in•del\i•cate
in•del\i•cate•ly
in•dem•ni•fi•ca•tion
in•dem•ni•fy, •fied, •fy•ing
in•dem•ni•ty, *pl.* •ties
in•dent, •dent\ed,
•dent•ing
in•den•ta•tion
in•den•ture, •tured,
•tur•ing
in•de•pend•ence
in•de•pend•ent
independent au•di•tor
independent con•trac•tor
in•de•pend•ent•ly
in-•depth
in•de•scrib•a•ble
in•de•scrib•a•bly
in•de•struct•i•bil•i•ty
in•de•struct•i•ble
in•de•ter•mi•na\cy
in•de•ter•mi•nate
in•dex, *pl.* •dex\es *or*
•di•ces
index ar•bi•trage
in•dex•a•tion
in•dex\er
In•di\a
In•di\an

In•di•an\a (IN)
In•di•an\an or
  In•di•an•i\an
In•di•an•ap\o•lis
in•di•cate, •cat\ed,
  •cat\ing
in•dic\a•tive
in•di•ca•tor
in•dict (to accuse),
  •dict\ed, •dict•ing [vs.
  in•dite (to compose)]
in•dict\a•ble
in•dict•ment
in•dif•fer•ence
in•dif•fer•ent
in•dif•fer•ent\ly
in•dig\e•nous (native to)
in•di•gent (poor)
in•di•gest•i\ble
in•di•ges•tion
in•dig•nant
in•dig•nant\ly
in•dig•na•tion
in•dig•ni\ty, pl. •ties
in•di\go
in•di•rect
in•di•rect\ly
in•di•rect•ness
in•di•rect tax
in•dis•creet
in•dis•creet\ly
in•dis•cre•tion
in•dis•crim\i•nate
in•dis•pen•sa\ble
in•dis•posed
in•dis•po•si•tion
in•dis•put•a\ble
in•dis•put•a•bly
in•dis•sol\u•ble
in•dis•tinct
in•dis•tinct\ly
in•dite (to compose),
  •dit\ed, •dit•ing [vs.
  in•dict (to accuse)]
in•di•vid•u\al
in•di•vid•u•al•ism
in•di•vid•u•al•ist
in•di•vid•u•al•i\ty
in•di•vid•u•al\ly
in•di•vid•u•al re•tire•ment
ac•count (IRA)

in•di•vid\u•a•tion
in•di•vis•i•bil•i\ty
in•di•vis•i\ble
in•di•vis•i•bly
In\do•chi\na
In\do•chi•nese, pl. •nese
in•doc•tri•nate, •nat\ed,
  •nat•ing
in•doc•tri•na•tion
In\do-Eu\ro\pe\an
in•do•lence
in•do•lent
in•dom\i•ta\ble
in•dom\i•ta•bly
In\do•ne•sia
In\do•ne•sian
in•door
in•doors
in•du•bi•ta\ble
in•du•bi•ta•bly
in•duce, •duced, •duc•ing
in•duce•ment
in•duct, •duct\ed,
  •duct•ing
in•duct•ance
in•duc•tee
in•duc•tion
in•duc•tive
in•dulge, •dulged,
  •dulg•ing
in•dul•gence, •genced,
  •genc•ing
in•dul•gent
in•dus•tri•al (of industry)
  [vs. in•dus•tri•ous
  (diligent)]
industrial es•pi•o•nage
industrial goods
in•dus•tri•al•ism
in•dus•tri•al•ist
in•dus•tri•al\i•za•tion
in•dus•tri•al•ize, •ized,
  •iz•ing
in\dus\tri\al-•strength
in•dus•tri•ous (diligent)
  [vs. in•dus•tri•al (of
  industry)]
in•dus•tri•ous\ly
in•dus•tri•ous•ness
in•dus•try, pl. •tries
in•e•bri•at\ed

in•e•bri•a•tion
in•ed\i•bil•i\ty
in•ed\i\ble
in•ed\u•ca\ble
in•ef•fa\ble
in•ef•fa•bly
in•ef•fec•tive
in•ef•fec•tu•al
in•ef•fi•ca•cy (lack of
  power)
in•ef•fi•cien\cy (wasteful-
  ness)
in•ef•fi•cient
in•ef•fi•cient\ly
in•e\las•tic de•mand
inelastic sup•ply
in•el•e•gant
in•el\i•gi•bil•i\ty
in•el\i•gi\ble
in\e•luc•ta\ble
in•ept (incompetent) [vs.
  in•apt (not fitting)]
in•ept\i•tude
in•ept\ly
in•ept•ness
in\e•qual•i\ty, pl. •ties
in•ert
in•er•tia
in•er•tial
in•ert\ly
in•es•cap•a\ble
in•es•cap•a•bly
in•es•ti•ma\ble
in•es•ti•ma•bly
in•ev\i•ta•bil•i\ty
in•ev\i•ta\ble
in•ev\i•ta•bly
in•ex•act
in•ex•act\ly
in•ex•cus•a\ble
in•ex•cus•a•bly
in•ex•haust•i\ble
in•ex•haust•i•bly
in•ex•o\o•ra\ble
in•ex\o•ra•bly
in•ex•pe•ri•enced
in•ex•pert
in•ex•pi•a\ble
in•ex•pli•ca\ble
in•ex•pli•ca•bly
in•ex•press•i\ble

in•ex•tin•guish•a\ble
in ex•tre•mis
in•ex•tri•ca\ble
in•fal•li•bil•i\ty
in•fal•li•ble
in•fal•li•bly
in•fa•mous
in•fa\my, *pl.* •mies
in•fan\cy, *pl.* •cies
in•fant
in•fan•ti•cide
in•fan•tile
in•fant in•dus•try
in•fan•try
in•fan•try•man, *pl.* •men
in•fat•u•ate, •at\ed, •at•ing
in•fat•u•a•tion
in•fect, •fect\ed, •fect•ing
in•fec•tion
in•fec•tious
in•fec•tious\ly
in•fec•tious•ness
in•fe•lic\i•tous
in•fe•lic•i\ty
in•fer, •ferred, •fer•ring
in•fer•ence
in•fer•en•tial
in•fe•ri•or
in•fe•ri•or•i\ty
in•fer•nal
in•fer\no, *pl.* •nos
in•fer•tile
in•fer•til•i\ty
in•fest, •fest\ed, •fest•ing
in•fes•ta•tion
in•fi•del
in•fi•del•i\ty, *pl.* •ties
in•field
in•field\er
in•fight•ing
in•fil•trate, •trat\ed,
  •trat•ing
in•fil•tra•tion
in•fil•tra•tor
in•fi•nite
in•fi•nite\ly
in•fin•i•tes•i•mal
in•fin•i•tes•i•mal\ly
in•fin•i•tive (*verb form*)
in•fin•i\ty (*boundlessness*)
in•firm

in•fir•ma\ry, *pl.* •ries
in•fir•mi\ty, *pl.* •ties
in•flame, •flamed,
  •flam•ing
in•flam•ma•bil•i\ty
in•flam•ma\ble
in•flam•ma•tion
in•flam•ma•to\ry
in•flat•a\ble
in•flate, •flat\ed, •flat•ing
in•fla•tion
in•fla•tion•ar\y
inflationary spi•ral
in•flect, •flect\ed, •flect•ing
in•flec•tion (*voice tone*)
in•flex•i•bil•i\ty
in•flex•i\ble
in•flex•i•bly
in•flict, •flict\ed, •flict•ing
in•flic•tion (*something
  imposed*)
in-•flight *or* in•flight
in•flow
in•flu•ence, •enced,
  •enc•ing
in•flu•en•tial
in•flu•en\za
in•flux
in\fo
in•fold, •fold\ed, •fold•ing
in\fo•mer•cial
in•form, •formed,
  •form•ing
in•for•mal
in•for•mal•i\ty
in•for•mal\ly
in•form•ant
in•for•ma•tion
in•form\a•tive
in•form\er
in\fo•tain•ment
in•fra
in•frac•tion
in\fra•red *or* in\fra-•red
in\fra•son•ic
in\fra•struc•ture
in•fre•quen\cy
in•fre•quent
in•fre•quent\ly
in•fringe, •fringed,
  •fring•ing

in•fringe•ment
in•fu•ri•ate, •at\ed, •at•ing
in•fu•ri•at•ing\ly
in•fuse, •fused, •fus•ing
in•fu•sion
in•gen•ious (*inventive*)
in•gen•ious\ly
in•gé•nue *or* in•ge•nue
in•ge•nu•i\ty
in•gen•u•ous (*artless*)
In•gen•u•ous\ly
in•gen•u•ous•ness
in•gest, •gest\ed,
  •gest•ing
in•ges•tion
in•glo•ri•ous
in•glo•ri•ous\ly
in•got
in•grained
in•grate
in•gra•ti•ate, •at\ed,
  •at•ing
in•gra•ti•a•tion
in•grat\i•tude
in•gre•di•ent
in•gress
in•grown
in•gui•nal
in•hab\it, •it\ed, •it•ing
in•hab•it•a\ble
in•hab•it•ant
in•hal•ant
in•ha•la•tor
in•hale, •haled, •hal•ing
in•hal\er
in•here, •hered, •her•ing
in•her•ent
in•her•ent\ly
in•her\it, •it\ed, •it•ing
in•her•it•ance
inheritance tax
in•hib\it, •it\ed, •it•ing
in•hi•bi•tion
in•hib\i•tor
in-•house
in•hu•man
in•hu•mane
in•hu•mane\ly
in•hu•man•i\ty
in•im\i•cal
in•im\i•ta\ble

in•iq•ui•tous

in•iq•ui\ty, pl. •ties

in\i•tial, •tialed or •tialled, •tial•ling or •tial•ling

in\i•tial\ly

in\i•tial mark\up

in\i•ti•ate, •at•ed, •at•ing

in\i•ti•a•tion

in\i•ti•a•tive

in•ject, •ject•ed, •ject•ing

in•jec•tion

in•jec•tor

in•junc•tion

in•jure, •jured, •jur•ing

in•ju•ri•ous

in•ju\ry, pl. •ju•ries

in•jus•tice

ink, inked, ink•ing

ink•blot

ink\i•ness

ink-•jet print\er

ink•ling

ink\y, •i\er, •i•est

in•laid

in•land

in-•law

in•lay, •laid, •lay•ing

in•let

in•mate

in me•mo•ri\am

in•most

inn (hotel) [vs. in (within)]

in•nards

in•nate

in•nate\ly

in•nate•ness

in•ner

in\ner-•di•rect\ed

in•ner•most

in•ner•sole

in•ner•spring

in•ner•vate (to invigorate), •vat\ed, •vat•ing [vs. en•er•vate (to weaken)]

in•ner•va•tion

in•ning

inn•keep\er

in•no•cent

in•no•cent\ly

in•noc\u•ous

in•noc\u•ous\ly

in•no•vate, •vat\ed, •vat•ing

in•no•va•tion

in•nu•en\do, pl. •dos or •does

in•nu•mer•a\ble

in•nu•mer•ate

in•oc\u•late, •lat\ed, •lat•ing

in•oc\u•la•tion

in•of•fen•sive

in•of•fen•sive\ly

in•op•er•a\ble

in•op•er\a•tive

in•op•por•tune

in•or•di•nate

in•or•di•nate\ly

in•or•gan\ic

in•pa\tient

in•put, •put•ted or •put, •put•ting

input de•vice

in\put/•out\put

in•quest

in•qui•e•tude

in•quire or en•quire, •quired, •quir•ing

in•quir\er

in•quir•ing\ly

in•quir\y or en•quiry, pl. •quir•ies

in•qui•si•tion

in•quis\i•tive

in•quis\i•tive•ness

in•quis\i•tor

in-•res\i\dence

in•road

in•sane (mad) [vs. in•ane (lacking sense)]

in•sane\ly

in•san\i•ty

in•sa•tia•bil•i\ty

in•sa•tia\ble

in•sa•tia\bly

in•scribe, •scribed, •scrib•ing

in•scrip•tion

in•scru•ta•bil•i\ty

in•scru•ta\ble

in•seam

in•sect

in•sec•ti•cide

in•sec•ti•vore

in•sec•tiv\o•rous

in•se•cure

in•se•cure\ly

in•se•cu•ri\ty, pl. •ties

in•sem\i•nate, •nat\ed, •nat•ing

in•sem\i•na•tion

in•sen•sate

in•sen•si•bil•i\ty

in•sen•si\ble

in•sen•si\bly

in•sen•si•tive

in•sen•si•tive\ly

in•sen•si•tiv•i\ty

in•sen•ti•ence

in•sen•ti•ent

in•sep\a•ra\ble

in•sert (to put in), •sert\ed, •sert•ing

in•ser•tion

in•sert mode

in•set (something set in)

in•set, •set, •set•ting

in•shore

in•side

in•sid\er

insider trad•ing

in•sid\i•ous

in•sight (understanding) [vs. in•cite (to stir up)]

in•sig•ni\a, pl. •ni\a or •ni\as

in•sin•cere

in•sin•cere\ly

in•sin•cer•i\ty

in•sin\u•ate, •at\ed, •at•ing

in•sin\u•a•tion

in•sip•id

in•sist, •sist\ed, •sist•ing

in•sist•ence

in•sist•ent

in si\tu

in•so•far

in•sole

in•so•lence

in•so•lent

in•so•lent\ly

in•sol\u•bil•i\ty
in•sol\u•ble
in•sol•ven\cy
in•sol•vent
in•som•ni\a
in•som•ni\ac
in•so•much as
in•sou•ci•ance
in•sou•ci•ant
in•spect, •spect\ed,
    •spect•ing
in•spec•tion
in•spec•tor
in•spi•ra•tion
in•spi•ra•tion\al
in•spire, •spired, •spir•ing
in•sta•bil•i\ty
in•stall, •stalled, •stall•ing
in•stal•la•tion
in•stall•ment
installment plan
installment pur•chase
installment sale
in•stance
in•stant
in•stan•ta•ne•ous
in•stan•ta•ne•ous\ly
in•stant\ly
in•stead
in•step
in•sti•gate, •gat\ed,
    •gat•ing
in•sti•ga•tion
in•sti•ga•tor
in•still, •stilled, •still•ing
in•stinct
in•stinc•tive
in•sti•tute, •tut\ed,
    •tut•ing
in•sti•tu•tion
in•sti•tu•tion\al
in•sti•tu•tion•al\i•za•tion
in•sti•tu•tion•al•ize, •ized,
    •iz•ing
in•struct, •struct\ed,
    •struct•ing
in•struc•tion
in•struc•tion\al
in•struc•tive
in•struc•tor
in•stru•ment

in•stru•men•tal
in•stru•men•tal•ist
in•stru•men•ta•tion
in•sub•or•di•nate
in•sub•or•di•na•tion
in•sub•stan•tial
in•suf•fer•a•ble
in•suf•fer•a•bly
in•suf•fi•cient
in•suf•fi•cient\ly
in•su•lar
in•su•lar•i\ty
in•su•late, •lat\ed, •lat•ing
in•su•la•tion
in•su•la•tor
in•su•lin
in•sult, •sult\ed, •sult•ing
in•su•per•a\ble
in•sup•port•a\ble
in•sur•a\ble
insurable risk
in•sur•ance (*protection*)
    [*vs.* as•sur•ance
    (*confidence*)]
in•sure, •sured, •sur•ing
in•sur\er
in•sur•gence
in•sur•gent
in•sur•mount•a\ble
in•sur•rec•tion
in•sur•rec•tion•ist
in•tact
in•tagl\io, *pl.* •tagl•ios *or*
    •ta•gli
in•take
in•tan•gi\ble
intangible as•set
in•te•ger
in•te•gral
in•te•grate, •grat\ed,
    •grat•ing
integrated ar•chi•tec•ture
integrated cir•cuit
integrated soft•ware
in•te•gra•tion
in•teg•ri\ty
in•teg\u•ment
in•tel•lect
in•tel•lec•tu\al
in•tel•lec•tu•al•ize, •ized,
    •iz•ing

in•tel•lec•tu•al\ly
in•tel•li•gence
in•tel•li•gent
in•tel•li•gent\ly
in•tel•li•gent•si\a
in•tel•li•gent ter•mi•nal
in•tel•li•gi•bil•i\ty
in•tel•li•gi\ble
in•tel•li•gi•bly
in•tem•per•ance
in•tem•per•ate
in•tend, •tend\ed,
    •tend•ing
in•tend\ed
in•tense (*extreme*) [*vs.*
    in•tents (*purposes*)]
in•tense\ly
in•ten•si•fi•ca•tion
in•ten•si•fi\er
in•ten•si•fy, •fied, •fy•ing
in•ten•si•ty, *pl.* •ties
in•ten•sive
in•tent, *pl.* in•tents
    (*purposes*) [*vs.* in•tense
    (*extreme*)]
in•ten•tion
in•ten•tion\al
in•ten•tion•al\ly
in•tent\ly
in•tent•ness
in•ter, •terred, •ter•ring
in\ter- (*between; among*)
    [*vs.* in\tra- (*within*)]
in\ter•act, •act\ed,
    •act•ing
in\ter•ac•tion
in\ter•ac•tive
interactive pro•gram
in\ter•breed, •bred,
    •breed•ing
in\ter•cede, •ced\ed,
    •ced•ing
in\ter•cept, •cept\ed,
    •cept•ing
in•ter•cep•tion
in•ter•cep•tor
in•ter•ces•sion
in\ter•change, •changed,
    •chang•ing
in\ter•change•a\ble
in\ter•col•le•giate

in•ter•com
in•ter•con•nect, •nect\ed, •nect\ing
in•ter•con•ti•nen•tal
in•ter•cos•tal
in•ter•course
in•ter•cul•tur\al
in\ter•de•nom\i•na\tion\al
in\ter•de•part•men•tal
in\ter•de•pend•ence
in\ter•de•pend•ent
in\ter•dict, •dict\ed, •dict\ing
in\ter•dic•tion
in\ter•dis•ci•pli•nar\y
in•ter•est
in•ter•est\ed
in•ter•est•ing
in\ter•face, •faced, •fac•ing
in\ter•faith
in\ter•fere, •fered, •fer•ing
in•ter•fer•ence
in•ter•fer\on
in•ter\im
in•te•ri\or
in\ter•ject, •ject\ed, •ject•ing
in\ter•jec•tion
in\ter•lace, •laced, •lac•ing
in\ter•lard, •lard\ed, •lard•ing
in\ter•leave fac•tor
in\ter•leu•kin
in\ter•lock, •locked, •lock•ing
in\ter•loc\u•to\ry
in\ter•lope, •loped, •lop•ing
in\ter•lop\er
in\ter•lude
in\ter•mar•riage
in\ter•mar\ry, •ried, •ry•ing
in\ter•me\di•ar\y, pl. •ar•ies
in\ter•me\di•ate
in•ter•ment (burial) [vs. in•tern•ment (confinement)]
in\ter•mez\zo, pl. •mez•zos or •mez\zi

in•ter•mi•na\ble
in•ter•mi•na•bly
in\ter•min•gle, •gled, •gling
in•ter•mis•sion
in•ter•mit•tent
in•ter•mix, •mixed, •mix•ing
in•tern, •terned, •tern•ing
in•ter•nal
internal au•dit
internal au•di•tor
in\ter\nal-•com\bus•tion en•gine
in•ter•nal com•mand
internal fonts
in•ter•nal•ize, •ized, •iz•ing
in•ter•nal\ly
in•ter•nal mo•dem
internal rev\e•nue
in•ter•na•tion\al
in•ter•na•tion•al\ly
in•ter•ne\cine
in•tern\ee
in\ter•net
in•tern•ist
in•tern•ment (confinement) [vs. in•ter•ment (burial)]
in•tern•ship
in•ter•of\fice
in\ter•pel•la•tion (questioning) [vs. in\ter•po•la•tion (insertion)]
in•ter•per•son\al
in•ter•plan\e•tar\y
in\ter•play
in•ter•po•late, •lat\ed, •lat•ing
in\ter•po•la•tion (insertion) [vs. in\ter•pel•la•tion (questioning)]
in\ter•pose, •posed, •pos•ing
in\ter•po•si•tion
in•ter•pret
in•ter•pre•ta•tion

in•ter•pret\er
in\ter•ra\cial
in•ter•re•lat\ed
in•ter•ro•gate, •gat\ed, •gat•ing
in•ter•ro•ga•tion
in•ter•ro•ga•tor
in•ter•rog\a•to\ry, pl. •to•ries
in•ter•rupt (noun)
in•ter•rupt (verb), •rupt\ed, •rupt•ing
in•ter•rup•tion
in•ter•scho•las•tic
in•ter•sect, •sect\ed, •sect•ing
in•ter•sec•tion
in•ter•ses•sion
in•ter•sperse, •spersed, •spers•ing
in\ter•state (between states) [vs. in•tes•tate (without a will) and in\tra•state (within a state)]
in•ter•stel•lar
in•ter•stice, pl. •stic\es
in•ter•twine, •twined, •twin•ing
in•ter•ur•ban
in•ter•val
in•ter•vene, •vened, •ven•ing
in•ter•view, •viewed, •view•ing
in•ter•view\er
in•ter•vo•cal\ic
in•ter•weave, •wove or •weaved, •weaved or •wo•ven, •weav•ing
in•tes•ta•cy
in•tes•tate (without a will) [vs. in\ter\state (between states) and in\tra•state (within a state)]
in•tes•ti•nal
in•tes•tine
in•ti•fa\da
in•ti•mate, •mat\ed, •mat•ing
in•ti•mate\ly

in•ti•ma•tion
in•tim\i•date, •dat\ed,
• dat•ing
in•tim\i•da•tion
in\to
in•tol•er•a•ble
in•tol•er•a•bly
in•tol•er•ance
in•tol•er•ant
in•to•na•tion
in•tone, •toned, •ton•ing
in to\to
in•tox\i•cant
in•tox\i•cate, •cat\ed,
• cat•ing
in•tox\i•ca•tion
in\tra- (within) [vs. in\ter-
(between; among)]
in•trac•ta•bil•i\ty
in•trac•ta\ble
in\tra•mu•ral
in•tran•si•gence
in•tran•si•gent or
in•tran•si•geant
in•tran•si•tive
in•tran•si•tive\ly
in\tra•pre•neur
in\tra•state (within a state)
[vs. in\ter•state (between
states) and in•tes•tate
(without a will)]
in\tra•u\ter\ine
in\tra•ve\nous
in\tra•ve\nous\ly
in•trep\id
in•trep\id\ly
in•trigue, •trigued,
• tri•guing
in•tri•guer
in•tri•guing\ly
in•trin•sic
in•trin•si•cal\ly
in\tro•duce, •duced,
• duc•ing
in\tro•duc•tion
in\tro•duc•to\ry
in•tro\it
in\tro•spec•tion
in\tro•spec•tive
in\tro•vert, •vert\ed,
• vert•ing

in•trude, •trud\ed,
• trud•ing
in•trud\er
in•tru•sion
in•tru•sive
in•tu\it, •it\ed, •it•ing
in•tu•i•tion
in•tu•i•tive
In•u\it or In•nu\it, pl. •its
or \it
in•un•date, •dat\ed,
• dat•ing
in•un•da•tion
in•ure, •ured, •ur•ing
in•vade, •vad\ed, •vad•ing
in•vad\er
in•val\id (not valid)
in•va•lid (sick person),
• lid\ed, •lid•ing
in•val\i•date, •dat\ed,
• dat•ing
in•val\i•da•tion
in•val\u•a\ble
in•var\i•a\ble
in•var\i•a\bly
in•va•sion
in•vec•tive
in•veigh, •veighed,
• veigh•ing
in•vei•gle, •gled, •gling
in•vent, •vent\ed,
• vent•ing
in•ven•tion
in•ven•tive
in•ven•tive•ness
in•ven•tor
in•ven•to\ry, pl. •to•ries;
• to•ried, •to•ry•ing
In•ver•ness
in•verse
in•verse\ly
in•ver•sion
in•vert, •vert\ed, •vert•ing
in•ver•te•brate
in•vert\ed tree
in•vest, •vest\ed, •vest•ing
in•ves•ti•gate, •gat\ed,
• gat•ing
in•ves•ti•ga•tion
in•ves•ti•ga•tor
in•ves•ti•ture

in•vest•ment
investment bank
investment com•pa\ny
in•ves•tor
in•vet•er•ate
in•vid\i•ous
in•vid\i•ous\ly
in•vig•or•ate, •at\ed,
• at•ing
in•vin•ci•bil•i\ty
in•vin•ci\ble
in•vi•o•la•bil•i\ty
in•vi•o•la\ble
in•vi•o•late
in•vis•i•bil•i\ty
in•vis•i\ble
invisible hand
in•vis•i•bly
in•vi•ta•tion
in•vi•ta•tion\al
in•vite, •vit\ed, •vit•ing
in•vi•tee
in•vit•ing
in vi•tro
in•vo•ca•tion
in•voice, •voiced, •voic•ing
in•voke, •voked, •vok•ing
in•vol•un•tar•i\ly
in•vol•un•tar\y
in•vo•lu•tion
in•volve, •volved,
• volv•ing
in•volve•ment
in•vul•ner\a•bil•i\ty
in•vul•ner\a•ble
in•ward or in•wards
in•ward\ly
I/O (input/output)
i\o•dide
i\o•dine
i\o•dize, •dized, •diz•ing
i\on
I\on\ic (of classical Greek
architecture)
i\on\ic (of ions)
i\on•i•za•tion
i\on•ize, •ized, •iz•ing
i\on•iz\er
i\on\o•sphere
I\on\o•spher\ic
i\o\ta, pl. •tas

IOU or I.O.U., pl. IOUs or
  IOU's or I.O.U.'s
I\o\wa (IA)
I\o•wan
ip\e•cac
ip\so fac\to
IRA or I.R.A. (individual
  retirement account)
I\ran
I\ra•ni\an
I\raq
I\ra\qi
i\ras•ci•bil•i\ty
i\ras•ci\ble (easily angered)
  [vs. e\ras•a\ble (removable)]
i\rate
i\rate\ly
Ire•land
ir\i•des•cence
ir\i•des•cent
i\rid•i\um
i\ris, pl. i\ris\es or (parts of
  eye) i\ri•des or (plants)
  i\ris
I\rish
I\rish•man, pl. •men
I\rish•wom\an, pl.
  •wom\en
irk, irked, irk•ing
irk•some
i\ron, i\roned, i\ron•ing
i\ron•clad
i\ron•ic
i\ron\i•cal\ly
i\ron•ing
i\ron•ware
i\ron•work
i\ro\ny, pl. •nies
Ir\o•quoi\an
Ir\o•quois, pl. •quois
ir•ra•di•ate, •at\ed, •at•ing
ir•ra•di•a•tion
ir•ra•tion•al
ir•ra•tion•al\ly
ir•re•cov•er•a\ble
ir•re•deem•a\ble
ir•ref•u\ta\ble
ir•reg\u•lar
ir•reg\u•lar•i\ty
ir•rel\e•vance

ir•rel\e•vant (not
  pertinent) [vs.
ir•rev•er•ent (lacking
  respect)]
ir•re•li•gious
ir•re•me•di•a\ble
ir•re•me•di•a\bly
ir•rep\a•ra\ble
ir•re•place•a\ble
ir•re•press•i\ble
ir•re•proach•a\ble
ir•re•sist•i\ble
ir•re•sist•i\bly
ir•res•o•lute
ir•res•o•lu•tion
ir•re•spec•tive
ir•re•spon•si•bil•i\ty
ir•re•spon•si•ble
ir•re•spon•si•bly
ir•re•triev•a\ble
ir•rev•er•ence
ir•rev•er•ent (lacking
  respect) [vs. ir•rel\e•vant
  (not pertinent)]
ir•re•vers•i\ble
ir•rev\o•ca\ble
ir•rev\o•ca\bly
ir•ri•ga\ble
ir•ri•gate, •gat\ed, •gat•ing
ir•ri•ga•tion
ir•ri•ta•bil•i\ty
ir•ri•ta\ble
ir•ri•ta\bly
ir•ri•tate, •tat\ed,
  •tat•ing
ir•ri•ta•tion
ir•rupt, \ed, •ing
IRS (Internal Revenue
  Service)
is
I\saac
I\sa•iah
ISDN (integrated services
  digital network)
i\sin•glass
I\sis
Is•lam
Is•lam•a\bad
Is•lam•ic
is•land
is•land\er

isle (island) [vs. aisle (passage) and I'll (I will)]
is•let (small island) [vs.
  eye•let (small hole)]
isn't (is not)
i\so•late, •lat\ed, •lat•ing
i\so•la•tion
i\so•la•tion•ism
i\so•la•tion•ist
i\so•mer
i\so•met•ric
i\sos•ce•les
i\so•tope
Is•ra•el
Is•rae\li, pl. •lis or \li
Is•ra•el•ite
is•su•ance
is•sue, •sued, •su•ing
Is•tan•bul
isth•mus, pl. •mus\es or \mi
it, pl. they; it, pl. them; its,
  pl. theirs; its; theirs
I\tal•ian
I\tal•ic
i\tal\i•ci•za•tion
i\tal\i•cize, •cized, •ciz•ing
i\tal•ics
It•a\ly
itch, itched, itch•ing
itch\y, •i\er,
  •i•est
-ite
i\tem
i\tem\i•za•tion
i\tem•ize, •ized, •iz•ing
itemized de•duc•tions
itemized state•ment
it•er•ate, •at\ed, •at•ing
it•er•a•tion
i\tin•er•ant
i\tin•er•ar\y, pl. •ar•ies
it'll (it will)
its (belonging to it)
it's (it is)
it•self
it\ty-•bit\ty or it\sy-•bit\sy
IUD (intrauterine device)
I've
i\vo\ry, pl. •ries
i\vy
I\wo Ji\ma

J

jab, jabbed, jab•bing
jab•ber, •bered, •ber•ing
ja•bot
jack, jacked, jack•ing
jack\al
jack\a•napes
jack•ass
jack•boot
jack•daw
jack\et, •et\ed, •et•ing
jack•ham•mer
jack-•in-•the-•box or jack-•in-•a-•box, pl. •box\es
jack-•in-•the-•pul\pit, pl. •pul\pits
jack•knife, pl. •knives; •knifed, •knif•ing
jack-•of-•all-•trades, pl. jacks-•of-•all-•trades
jack-•o'-•lan\tern
jack•pot
jack rab•bit
jack•screw
Jack•son
Jack•son•ville
jack•straw
Ja•cob
Jac•quard loom
Ja•cuz\zi (™)
jade
jad\ed
jag, jagged (jerked, jogged), jag•ging
jag•ged (raggedly notched)
jag•ged\ly
jag•gies
jag•uar
jai a\lai
jail, jailed, jail•ing
jail•bird
jail•break
jail\er
Ja•kar\ta or Dja•kar\ta
ja•la•pe\ño or ja•la•pe\no, pl. •ños or •nos
ja•lop\y, pl. •lop•ies
jal•ou•sie (louvered shutter) [vs. jeal•ous\y (envy)]

jam (to squeeze; fruit preserve), jammed, jam•ming [vs. jamb (vertical sidepiece)]
Ja•mai\ca
Ja•mai•can
jamb (vertical sidepiece) [vs. jam (to squeeze; fruit preserve)]
jam•bo•ree (merry gathering) [vs. ju•bi•lee (anniversary celebration)]
James•town
jam-•packed
jam ses•sion
Jane Doe
Jan\et (woman's name)
Ja•net (French psychologist)
jan•gle, •gled, •gling
jan\i•tor
jan\i•to•ri\al
Jan\u•ar\y
Ja•pan
ja•pan, •panned, •pan•ning
Jap\a•nese, pl. •nese
jar, jarred, jar•ring
jar•di•niere
jar•gon
jar•ring\ly
jas•mine or jes•sa•mine
jas•per
ja\to or JATO (jet-assisted takeoff), pl. ja•tos or JATOs
jaun•dice
jaun•diced
jaunt
jaun•ti\ly
jaun•ti•ness
jaun\ty, •ti\er, •ti•est
Ja\va
Jav\a•nese
jave•lin
jaw, jawed, jaw•ing
jaw•bone, •boned, •bon•ing
jaw•break\er
jawed
jaw•less

jay
Jay•cee
jay•walk, •walked, •walk•ing
jay•walk\er
jazz, jazzed, jazz•ing
jazz\y, •i\er, •i•est
JCS or J.C.S. (Joint Chiefs of Staff)
jeal•ous (envious) [vs. zeal•ous (enthusiastic)]
jeal•ous\ly
jeal•ous\y (envy), pl. •ous•ies [vs. jal•ou•sie (louvered shutter)]
jeans
Jeep (™)
jeer, jeered, jeer•ing
jeer•ing\ly
Jef•fer•son
Jef•fer•so•ni\an
Je•ho•vah
Je•ho•vah's Wit•ness\es
je•june (insipid)
je•ju•num (part of intestine)
jell (to congeal), jelled, jell•ing [vs. gel (colloid)]
Jell-\O (™)
jel\ly, pl. •lies
jel\ly•bean
jel\ly•fish, pl. •fish or •fish\es
jel\ly•like
jel\ly roll
jen\ny, pl. •nies
jeop•ard•ize, •ized, •iz•ing
jeop•ard\y
jer\e•mi\ad
Jer\e•mi\ah
jerk, jerked, jerk•ing
jer•kin
jerk•wa•ter
jerk\y (spasmodic), •i\er, •i•est
jer\ky (jerked meat)
jer\ry-•built
jer•sey, pl. •seys
Je•ru•sa•lem

jest (*joke; to jest*), jest\ed,
  jest\ing [*vs. gist
  (essence)*]
jest\er (*clown*) [*vs.
  ges•ture (movement)*]
jest•ing•ly
Jes•u\it
Jes\u•it\i•cal
Je•sus
jet, jet•ted, jet•ting
jet lag or jet•lag
jet•lin\er
jet-•pro\pelled
jet•sam (*cargo thrown
  overboard*) [*vs. jet•ti•son
  (to discard)*]
jet set
jet-•set\ter
jet stream
jet•ti•son (*to discard*),
  •soned, •son•ing [*vs.
  jet•sam (cargo thrown
  overboard)*]
jet\ty, pl. •ties
Jew
jew\el
jew•eled or jew•elled
jew•el\er
jew•el•like
jew•el\ry
Jew•ish
Jew•ish•ness
Jew\ry (*Jewish people*) [*vs.
  ju\ry (verdict-rendering
  group)*]
Jez\e•bel
jib
jibe (*to agree*), jibed,
  jib•ing [*vs. gibe (to taunt)
  and jive (the music)*]
jif\fy or jiff, pl. jif•fies or
  jiffs
jig (*dance*), jigged, jig•ging
  [*vs. gig (job)*]
jig•ger, •gered, •ger•ing
jig•gle (*move jerkily*), •gled,
  •gling [*vs. jin•gle (ringing
  sound)*]
jig•gly, •gli\er, •gli•est
jig•saw
ji•had

jilt, jilt\ed, jilt•ing
Jim Crow (*noun*)
Jim-•Crow (*adj.*)
jim-•dan\dy
jim\my, pl. •mies; •mied,
  •my•ing
jim\son•weed
jin•gle (*ringing sound*) [*vs.
  jig•gle (move jerkily)*]
jin•gle, •gled, •gling
jin•gly, •gli\er, •gli•est
jin\go
jin•go•ism
jin•go•ist
jin•go•is•tic
jinn or jin\ni, pl. jinns or
  jinn; jin•nis or jin\ni
jinx (*bad luck*) [*vs. high
  jinks (frolics)*]
j.i.t. (*just-in-time
  manufacturing*)
jit•ney, pl. •neys
jit•ter, •tered, •ter•ing
jit•ter•bug
jit•ters
jit•ter\y
jive (*the music*), jived,
  jiv•ing [*vs. gibe (to taunt)
  and jibe (to agree)*]
job, jobbed, job•bing
job ac•tion
job a\nal\y•sis
job•ber
job bid•ding
job•hold\er
job•less
job•less•ness
job lot
job shop
jock
jock\ey, pl. •eys; •eyed,
  •ey•ing
jock•strap
jo•cose (*playful*) [*vs.
  joc•und (cheerful)*]
joc\u•lar
joc\u•lar•i\ty
joc•und (*cheerful*) [*vs.
  jo•cose (playful)*]
jodh•pur
jog, jogged, jog•ging

jog•ger
jog•gle, •gled, •gling
Jo•han•nes•burg
john
John Doe
John•son
joie de vi•vre
join, joined, join•ing
join\er
join field
joint
joint con•tract
joint\ly
joint-•stock com•pa\ny
joint ten•an\cy
joint ten•ant
joint ven•ture
joist
joke, joked, jok•ing
jok\er
jok•ing\ly
jol•li\ty
jol\ly, pl. •lies; •lied, •ly•ing;
  •li\er, •li•est
jolt, jolt\ed, jolt•ing
Jo•nah
Jones
jon•quil
Jon•son
Jor•dan
Jor•da•ni\an
Jo•seph
josh (*to tease*), joshed,
  josh•ing [*vs. joss stick
  (incense)*]
josh•ing\ly
Josh\u\a
joss stick (*incense*) [*vs.
  josh (to tease)*]
jos•tle, •tled, •tling
jot, jot•ted, jot•ting
joule
jounce, jounced, jounc•ing
jour•nal
jour•nal•ese
jour•nal•ism
jour•nal•ist
jour•nal•is•tic
jour•nal vouch\er
jour•ney, pl. •neys; •neyed,
  •ney•ing

jour•ney•man, pl. •men
joust (medieval combat) [vs. just (equitable)]
joust, joust\ed, joust•ing
jo•vi\al
jo•vi•al•i\ty
jo•vi•al\ly
jowl
jowled
jowl\y, •i\er, •i•est
joy
Joyce
Joyc•e\an
joy•ful
joy•ful\ly
joy•ful•ness
joy•less
joy•ous
joy•ous\ly
joy•ous•ness
joy•ride, •rode, •rid•den, •rid•ing
joy•rid\er
joy•stick
JP or J.P. (justice of the peace)
Jr. (junior)
ju•bi•lant
ju•bi•lant\ly
ju•bi•la•tion
ju•bi•lee (anniversary celebration) [vs. jam•bo•ree (merry gathering)]
Ju•da\ic
Ju•da•ism
Ju•das
Ju\de\o-•Chris\tian or Ju\dae\o-•Chris\tian
judge, judged, judg•ing
judge•ship
judg•ment
judg•men•tal
ju•di•ca•ture
ju•di•cial (of courts) [vs. ju•di•cious (prudent)]

ju•di•cial\ly
ju•di•ci•ar\y, pl. •ar•ies
ju•di•cious (prudent) [vs. ju•di•cial (of courts)]
ju•di•cious\ly
ju•di•cious•ness
ju\do
jug
Jug•ger•naut
jug•gle, •gled, •gling
jug•gler (tosser and catch-er of balls)
jug\u•lar (vein in neck)
juice, juiced, juic•ing
juice\less
juic\er
juic•i\ly
juic\i•ness
juic\y, •i\er, •i•est
ju•jit\su
ju•jube
juke•box
ju•lep
ju•li•enne
Ju\ly
jum•ble, •bled, •bling
jum\bo, pl. •bos
jumbo cer•ti•fi\i•cate
jump, jumped, jump•ing
jump\er
jump\i•ness
jump•ing-•off place
jump-•start, •start\ed, •start\ing
jump•suit
jump\y, •i\er, •i•est
junc•tion (meeting point)
junc•ture (critical point of time)
June
Ju•neau
jun•gle
jun•ior (Jr.)
ju•ni•per
junk, junked, junk•ing

junk bond
Jun•ker (Prussian aristocrat)
junk\er (worn-out car)
jun•ket, •ket\ed, •ket•ing
jun•ke•teer or jun•ket\er
junk\ie, pl. junk•ies
junk mail
junk\y, •i\er, •i•est
Ju\no
jun\ta, pl. •tas
Ju•pi•ter
Ju•ras•sic
ju•rid\i•cal
ju•ris•dic•tion
ju•ris•dic•tion\al strike
ju•ris•pru•dence
ju•rist
ju•ror
ju\ry (verdict-rendering group), pl. •ries [vs. Jew\ry (Jewish people)]
ju\ry-•rigged
just (equitable) [vs. joust (medieval combat)]
jus•tice
justice of the peace (JP)
jus•ti•fi•a•ble
jus•ti•fi•a•bly
jus•ti•fi•ca•tion
jus•ti\fy, •fied, •fy•ing
just-•in-•time man\u•fac•tur•ing (j.i.t.)
just\ly
just•ness
jut, jut•ted, jut•ting
jute
ju•ve•nile
ju•venile delin•quency
ju•venile delin•quent
jux•ta•pose, •posed, •pos•ing
jux•ta•po•si•tion
JV or J.V. (joint venture)

K

ka•bob
ka•bu\ki
Ka•bul
kad•dish, pl. kad•di•shim

kaf\fee•klatsch or kaf•fee klatsch
kai•ser
kale

ka•lei•do•scope
ka•lei•do•scop\ic
ka•mi•ka\ze, pl. •zes
Kam•pa\la

Kam•pu•che\a
Kam•pu•che\an
kan•ban
kan•ga•roo, pl. •roos or
•roo
Kan•san
Kan•sas (KS)
Kant
Kant•i\an
ka•o•lin
ka•pok
kap\pa, pl. •pas
ka•put
Ka•ra•chi
Kar\a•kul or car\a•cul
kar\at (gold weight) [vs.
car\at (gem weight) and
car\et (insert mark) and
car•rot (the vegetable)]
ka•ra\te
Kar\en (woman's name)
Ka•ren (member of
Burmese people)
kar\ma
kar•mic (of fate) [vs.
com\ic (funny)]
kart•ing
ka•sha
Kat•man\du or
Kath•man\du
ka\ty•did
kay\ak, •aked, •ak•ing
kay\o, pl. kay\os; kay•oed,
kay\o•ing
ka•zoo, pl. •zoos
KB (kilobyte)
Kb (kilobit)
Keats
ke•bab or ka•bob
keel, keeled, keel•ing
keen, keened, keen•ing;
keen\er, keen•est
keen\ly
keen•ness
keep, kept, keep•ing
keep\er
keep•ing
keep•sake
keg
kelp
Kelt (Celt)

Kelt\ic
kel•vin
ken, kenned or kent,
ken•ning
Ken•ne\dy
ken•nel, •neled or •nelled,
•nel•ing or •nel•ling
Ken•tuck•i\an
Ken•tuck\y (KY)
Ken\ya
Ken•yan
Ke•ogh ac•count
Keogh plan
kept
ker\a•tin
ker•chief
Ker•mit
ker•nel (seed) [vs.
colo•nel (military officer)]
ker\o•sene or ker\o•sine
kes•trel
ketch
ketch\up or cat•sup
ket•tle
ket\tle•drum
key (lock opener), pl. keys;
keyed, key•ing [vs. cay
(island) and quay
(wharf)]
key•board, •board\ed,
•board•ing
key•hole
key-•man in•sur•ance
Keynes•i\an
key•note
key•not\er
key•pad
key•punch, •punched,
•punch•ing
key•punch\er
key•stone
KGB or K.G.B. (Soviet
secret police)
khak\i, pl. khak\is
khan
Khar•kov
Khar•toum
kib•butz (Israeli community
settlement), pl. •but•zim
kib•itz (to meddle), •itzed,
•itz•ing

kib•itz\er
ki•bosh
kick, kicked, kick•ing
kick•back
kick\er
kick-•off or kick-•off
kick•stand
kick\y, kick•i\er,
kick•i•est
kid, kid•ded, kid•ding
kid•der
kid•die or kid\dy, pl. •dies
kid•nap, •napped or
•naped, •nap•ping or
•nap•ing
kid•nap•per or •nap\er
kid•ney, pl. •neys
kiel•ba\sa, pl. •sas or \sy
Ki\ev
Ki•ga\li
kill (to slay), killed, kill•ing
[vs. kiln (oven) and kin
(relatives)]
kill\er
kill•ing
kill-•joy or kill•joy
kiln (oven) [vs. kill (to slay)
and kin (relatives)]
ki\lo, pl. •los
kil\o•bit (Kb)
kil\o•byte (KB)
kil\o•flop
kil\o•gram
kil\o•hertz, pl. •hertz or
•hertz\es
kil\o•me\ter
kil\o•ton
kil\o•watt
kilt
kilt\ed
kil•ter
ki•mo\no, pl. •nos
kin (relatives) [vs. kill (to
slay) and kiln (oven)]
kind, kind\er, kind•est
kin\der•gar•ten
kind•heart\ed
kind•heart\ed\ly
kind•heart\ed•ness
kin•dle (to begin burning),
•dled, •dling

kin•dling (*material for starting* fire)

kind\ly (*benevolent*), •li\er, •li•est

kind•ness

kin•dred

kin\e•scope

kin•es\the•sia

kin•es\thet\ic

ki•net\ic

kin•folk *or* kin•folks, *pl.*

king

king•dom

king•fish\er

king\ly

king•pin

king•ship

king-•size *or* king-•sized

Kings•ton

Kings•town

kink, kinked, kink•ing

kin•ka•jou, *pl.* •jous

kink\y, •i\er, •i•est

Kin•sha\sa

kin•ship

kins•man, *pl.* •men

kins•wom\an, *pl.* •wom\en

ki•osk

kip•per

Ki•ri•ba\ti

kis•met

kiss

kiss•a\ble

kiss-•and-•tell

kiss\er

kit

kitch\en

kitch\en•ette

kite, kit\ed, kit•ing

kith

kitsch

kitsch\y

kit•ten

kit•ten•ish

kit\ty, *pl.* •ties

kit\ty-•cor\nered *or* kit\ty-•cor\ner

ki\wi, *pl.* •wis

KKK *or* K.K.K. (*Ku Klux Klan*)

klep\to•ma•ni\a

klep\to•ma•ni\ac

klieg light

kludge, kludged, kludg•ing

klutz

klutz\i•ness

klutz\y, •i\er, •i•est

knack (*aptitude*) [*vs.* knock (*to strike*)]

knack•wurst *or* knock•wurst

knap•sack

knave (*rogue*) [*vs.* nave (*church area*)]

knav•er\y

knav•ish

knead (*to work dough*), knead\ed, knead•ing [*vs.* need (*to require*)]

knee, kneed, knee•ing

knee•cap, •capped, •cap•ping

knee-•deep

kneel, knelt *or* kneeled, kneel•ing

knew (*did know*) [*vs.* gnu (*antelope*) *and* new (*recent*)]

knick•ers

knick•knack

knife, *pl.* knives; knifed, knif•ing

knight (*noble; to confer knighthood upon*), knight\ed, knight•ing [*vs.* night (*darkness*)]

knight-•er\rant, *pl.* knights-•er\rant

knight•hood

knight•li•ness

knight\ly

knish

knit (*to join*), knit•ted *or* knit, knit•ting [*vs.* nit (*insect egg*)]

knit•ter

knit•wear

knob

knock (*to strike*), knocked, knock•ing [*vs.* knack (*aptitude*)]

knock•down

knock\er

knock-•knee

knock-•kneed

knock•out

knock•wurst

knoll

knot (*tied cluster*), knot•ted, knot•ting [*vs.* not (*no*)]

knot•hole

knot\ty, •ti\er, •ti•est

know (*to understand*), knew, known, know•ing [*vs.* no (*negative*)]

know•a\ble

know-•how

know•ing

know•ing\ly

know-•it-•all

knowl•edge

knowl•edge\a\ble *or* knowl•edg\a\ble

knows (*understands*) [*vs.* noes (*negatives*) *and* nose (*organ of smell*)]

Knox•ville

knuck\le, •led, •ling

knuck\le•head

knuck\le•head\edy

knurl, knurled, knurl•ing

KO (*knockout*), *pl.* KOs *or* KO's; KO'd, KO\'ing

ko•a\la, *pl.* •las

kohl (*black powder*) [*vs.* coal (*the mineral*)]

kohl•ra\bi, *pl.* \bies

ko\la (*nut*), *pl.* •las [*vs.* co\la (*soft drink*) *and* COLA (*cost of living adjustment*)]

kook

kook\y (*eccentric*), •i\er, •i•est [*vs.* cook\ie (*flat cake*)]

ko•peck *or* ko•pek

Ko•ran (*Islamic text*)

Ko•re\an (*language of Korea*)

ko•sher, •shered, •sher•ing

kow•tow, •towed,
•tow•ing

Krem•lin

Krem•lin•ol•o\gy

Krish\na

kró\na (*Icelandic coin*), *pl.*
•nur

kro\na (*Swedish coin*), *pl.*
•nor

kro\ne (*former Austrian
coin*), *pl.* •nen

kro\ne (*Danish or
Norwegian coin*), *pl.* •ner

kryp•ton

KS (*Kansas*)

Kua\la Lum•pur

ku•dos

kud\zu, *pl.* •zus

Ku Klux\er

Ku Klux Klan (*KKK*)

kum•quat

kung fu

Kurd (*member of Asian people*) [*vs.* curd (*cheese*)]

Ku•wait

Ku•wai\ti

kvetch, kvetched,
kvetch•ing

kwa•cha, *pl.* •chas

Kwang•chow

KY (*Kentucky*)

Kyo\to

Kyu•shu

L

LA (*Louisiana*)

lab

la•bel, •beled or •belled,
•bel•ing or •bel•ling

la•bi\al

la•bile

la•bi\um, *pl.* •bi\a

la•bor, •bored, •bor•ing

lab\o•ra•to\ry (*scientific
workshop*), *pl.* •ries [*vs.*
lav\a•to\ry (*washroom*)]

la•bored

la\bor-•in\ten\sive

la•bo•ri•ous

la•bo•ri•ous\ly

la•bor re•la•tions

la\bor-sav•ing or la\bor-
•sav\ing

Lab•ra•dor

lab\y•rinth

lab\y•rin•thine

lac (*resin*) [*vs.* lack (*deficiency*)]

lace (*netlike fabric*), laced,
lac•ing [*vs.* laze (*to loaf*)]

lac•er•ate, •at\ed, •at•ing

lac•er•a•tion

lach•ry\mal (*of tears*)

lach•ry•mose (*mournful*)

lack (*deficiency*), lacked,
lack•ing [*vs.* lac (*resin*)]

lack\a•dai•si•cal

lack\ey, *pl.* •eys

lack•lus•ter

la•con\ic

la•con\i•cal\ly

lac•quer, •quered,
•quer•ing

lac•ri•mal

la•crosse

lac•tate, •tat\ed,
•tat•ing

lac•ta•tion

lac•tic

lac•tic ac\id

lac•tose

la•cu\na, *pl.* •nae or •nas

lad

lad•der

lad•die

lad\en

la-•di-•da or la-•de-•da

lad•ing

la•dle, •dled, •dling

la\dy, *pl.* •dies

la\dy•bug

la\dy•fin•ger

la\dy-•in-•wait\ing, *pl.*
la\dies-•in-•wait\ing

la\dy•like

la\dy•love

la\dy•ship

la\dy's-•slip\per or la\dy-
•slip\per

La•fa•yette

lag, lagged, lag•ging

la•ger

lag•gard

lag•gard\ly

lag•ging in•di•ca•tor

la•gniappe

la•goon

La•gos

La•hore

laid

laid-•back

lain (*past participle of "lie"*)
[*vs.* lane (*path*)]

lair (*den*) [*vs.* lay\er
(*stratum*)]

lais•sez faire or lais•ser
faire

la•i\ty

lake

lal\ly•gag or lol\ly•gag,
•gagged, •gag•ging

lam (*to thrash*), lammed,
lam•ming [*vs.* lamb
(*young sheep*)]

la\ma (*monk*), *pl.* •mas [*vs.*
lla\ma (*the animal*)]

la•ma•ser\ly, *pl.* •ser•ies

lamb (*young sheep*) [*vs.*
lam (*to thrash*)]

lam•baste or lam•bast,
•bast\ed, •bast•ing

lamb\da, *pl.* •das

lam•bent

lam•bent\ly

lamb•kin

lame (*disabled*), lam\er,
lam•est

la\mé (*the fabric*)

lame•brain

lame-brained

lame\ly

lame•ness

la•ment, •ment\ed,
•ment•ing

la•ment•a\ble

lam•en•ta•tion

lam•i\na, *pl.* •nae or
•nas

lam\i•nar

lam\i•nate, •nat\ed, •nat•ing

lam\i•na•tion

lamp

lamp•black

lam•poon, •pooned, •poon•ing

lamp•post

lam•prey, pl. •preys

LAN (local area network)

lance, lanced, lanc•ing

Lan•ce\lot

lanc\er

lan•cet

land, land\ed, land•ing

land•fall

land•fill

land•ing

land•locked

land•lord

land•lub•ber

land•mark, •marked, •mark•ing

land•mass

land of•fice

land-•of\fice busi•ness

land•scape, •scaped, •scap•ing

landscape o\ri•en•ta•tion

land•scap\er

land•slide

lane (path) [vs. lain (past participle of "lie")]

lan•guage

lan•guid

lan•guish, •guished, •guish•ing

lan•guor

lan•guor•ous

lank, lank\er, lank•est

lank\i•ness

lank\y, •i\er, •i•est

lan\o•lin

Lan•sing

lan•tern

lan\tern-•jawed

lan•tha•num

lan•yard

La\os

La\o•tian

lap, lapped, lap•ping

La Paz

lap belt

lap dog

la•pel

lap\i•dar\y, pl. •dar•ies

lap\in

lap\is laz•u\li

Lap•land

Lapp

lapse (to subside; error), lapsed, laps•ing [vs. e\lapse (to pass)]

lap•top

laptop com•put•er

lap•wing

lar•board

lar•ce•nous

lar•ce\ny, pl. •nies

larch

lard, lard\ed, lard•ing

lard\er (one that lards)

lar•der (pantry)

lar\es and pe•na•tes, pl.

large, larg\er, larg•est

large-•foot\print com•put•er

large\ly

large•ness

lar•gess or lar•gesse

lar\go, pl. •gos

lar•i\at

lark

lark•spur

lar\va (young insect), pl. •vae [vs. la\va (molten rock)]

lar•val

la•ryn•ge\al

lar\yn•gi•tis

lar•ynx, pl. la•ryn•ges or lar•ynx\es

la•sa•gna

las•civ\i•ous

la•ser

laser disc

laser print\er

lash, lashed, lash•ing

lass

las•sie

las•si•tude

las\so, pl. •sos or •soes; •soed, \so•ing

last, last\ed, last•ing

last-•in, first-•out (LIFO)

last•ing\ly

last\ly

latch, latched, latch•ing

latch•key, pl. •keys

late, lat\er (afterward), lat•est [vs. lat•ter (second of two)]

late•com\er

late\ly

la•ten\cy

late•ness

la•tent

lat•er\al

lat•er•al\ly

la•tex

lath (strip of wood), pl. laths

lathe (machine)

lath\er, •ered, •er•ing

lath•er\y

Lat\in

La•ti\na, pl. •nas

Lat\in A\mer\i•ca

Lat\in A\mer\i•can (noun)

Lat\in-•A\mer\i\can (adj.)

La•ti\no, pl. •nos

lat\i•tude

lat\i•tu•di•nar•i\an

la•trine

lat•ter (second of two) [vs. lat\er (afterward)]

Lat\ter-•day Saint

lat•tice

lat•ticed

lat•tice•work

Lat•vi\a

Lat•vi\an

laud (to praise), laud\ed, laud•ing [vs. cum lau\de (with honor) and lord (noble)]

laud•a\ble

laud•a\bly

lau•da•num

laud\a•to\ry

laugh, laughed, laugh•ing

laugh•a\ble

laugh•a\bly

laugh•ing\ly

laugh•ing•stock

laugh•ter

launch, launched,
launch•ing

launch\er

laun•der, •dered,
•der•ing

laun•der•ette or
laun•drette

laun•dress

Laun•dro•mat (™)

laun•dry, pl. •dries

laun\dry•man, pl. •men

laun\dry•wom\an, pl.
•wom\en

lau•re•ate

lau•rel

la•va (molten rock) [vs.
lar\va (young insect)]

lav\a•liere or lav\a•lier

lav\a•to\ry (washroom), pl.
•ries [vs. lab\o•ra•to\ry
(scientific workshop)]

lav•en•der

lav•ish, •ished, •ish•ing

lav•ish\ly

law

law•-a\bid\ing

law•break\er

law•break•ing

law•ful

law•ful\ly

law•giv\er

law•less

law•less•ness

law•mak\er

law•man, pl. •men

lawn

law•ren•ci\um

law•suit

law•yer

lax, lax\er, lax•est

lax\a•tive

lax•i\ty

lax\ly

lax•ness

lay (to set down; secular),
laid, lay•ing [vs. lei
(wreath) and lie (to speak
falsely; to recline) and lye
(alkaline solution)]

lay•a\way plan

lay\er (stratum), •ered,
•er•ing [vs. lair (den)]

lay•ette

lay•man, pl. •men

lay•off

lay•out

lay•o\ver

Laz\a•rus

laze (to loaf), lazed, laz•ing
[vs. lace (netlike fabric)]

la•zi\ly

la•zi•ness

la\zy, •zi\er, •zi•est

la\zy•bones

la\zy Su•san or la\zy
su•san

LBO (leveraged buyout)

LCD (liquid crystal dis-
play), pl. LCDs or LCD's

L-\do\pa

lb., pl. lbs, lb

lea (meadow) [vs. lee
(shelter)]

leach (to filter), leached,
leach•ing [vs. leech
(bloodsucking insect; to
cling to and drain)]

lead (soft metal), [vs. led
(guided)]

lead (to guide), led,
lead•ing

lead\ed (made with lead)

lead\en (heavy)

lead\er (guide) [vs. lied\er
(art songs)]

lead•er•less

lead•er•ship

lead•ing

leading in•di•ca•tor

leaf (unit of foliage; to turn
pages), pl. leaves; leafed,
leaf\ing, leafs [vs. lief
(gladly)]

leaf•hop•per

leaf•less

leaf•let, •let\ed or •let•ted,
•let\ing or •let•ting

leaf•stalk

leaf\y, •i\er, •i•est

league, leagued, lea•guing

leak (where liquid escapes;
to leak), leaked, leak•ing
[vs. leek (the vegetable)]

leak•age

leak\y, •i\er, •i•est

lean (to incline; thin),
leaned, lean•ing; lean\er,
lean•est [vs. lien (claim)]

lean•ness

lean•-to, pl. •tos

leap, leaped or leapt,
leap•ing

leap•frog, •frogged,
•frog•ging

learn, learned
(ascertained) or learnt,
learn•ing

learn\ed (erudite)

learn\er

learn•ing

learn\ing- •dis\a\bled

learn mode

lease, leased, leas•ing

lease•back

lease•hold

lease•hold\er

leash, leashed,
leash•ing

least (smallest) [vs. lest
(unless)]

leath\er

leath•er•neck

leath•er\y

leave, left, leav•ing

leav\en, •ened, •en•ing

leav•en•ing

leave-•tak\ing

leav•ings

Leb\a•nese, pl. •nese

Leb\a•non

lech\er (lewd person) [vs.
lec•ture (discourse)]

lech•er•ous

lech•er•ous\ly

lech•er\y

lec\i•thin

lec•tern

lec•ture (discourse),
•tured, •tur•ing [vs.
lech\er (lewd person)]

lec•tur\er

LED (*light-emitting diode*),
  pl. LEDs or LED's
led (*guided*) [vs. lead (*soft metal*)]
ledge
ledg\er
lee (*shelter*) [vs. lea (*meadow*)]
leech (*bloodsucking insect; to cling to and drain*),
  leeched, leech•ing [vs. leach (*to filter*)]
leek (*the vegetable*) [vs. leak (*where liquid escapes; to let liquid escape*)]
leer, leered, leer•ing
leer\y, •i\er, •i•est
lees
lee•ward
lee•way
left
left-•hand
left-•hand\ed
left•ism
left•ist
left•o•ver
left wing (*noun*)
left-•wing (*adj.*)
left-•wing\er
left\y, *pl.* left•ies
leg, legged, leg•ging
leg•a\cy, *pl.* •cies
le•gal
le•gal•ese
le•gal in•stru•ment
le•gal•ism
le•gal•is•tic
le•gal•i•ty
le•gal\i•za•tion
le•gal•ize, •ized, •iz•ing
le•gal\ly
le•gal ten•der
leg•ate
leg\a•tee
le•ga•tion
le•ga\to
leg•end
leg•end•ar\y
leg\er•de•main
leg•ged

leg•gings
leg\gy, •gi\er, •gi•est
Leg•horn
leg•i•bil•i•ty
leg•i\ble
leg•i•bly
le•gion (*multitude*) [vs. le•sion (*wound*)]
le•gion•ar\y, *pl.* •ar•ies
le•gion•naire
le•gion•naires' dis•ease
leg•is•late, •lat\ed, •lat•ing
leg•is•la•tion
leg•is•la•tive
leg•is•la•tor
leg•is•la•ture
le•git
le•git\i•ma\cy
le•git\i•mate•ly
le•git\i•mize, •mized, •miz•ing
leg•less
leg•man, *pl.* •men
leg•room
leg•ume
le•gu•mi•nous
leg•work
lei (*wreath*), *pl.* leis [vs. lay (*to set down; secular*) and lie (*to speak falsely; to recline*) and lye (*alkaline solution*)]
Leip•zig
lei•sure
lei•sure\ly
leit•mo\tif
lem•ming
lem\on
lem•on•ade
lem\on law
lem•on\y
le•mur
lend, lent, lend•ing
lend\er
lend-•lease
lends (*gives temporary use of*) [vs. lens (*eyepiece*)]
length
length\en, •ened, •en•ing
length•wise or
  length•ways

length\y, •i\er, •i•est
le•ni•en\cy
le•ni•ent
le•ni•ent\ly
Le•nin
Le•nin•grad
Le•nin•ism
Le•nin•ist
lens (*eyepiece*), *pl.* lens\es [vs. lends (*gives temporary use of*)]
Lent (*religious fast*)
lent (*did lend*)
Lent\en
len•til (*the legume*) [vs. lin•tel (*beam*)]
Le\o
le•one (*monetary unit of Sierra Leone*)
le•o\nine
leop•ard
le•o\tard
lep\er
lep•re•chaun
lep•ro\sy
lep•rous
les•bi\an
les•bi•an•ism
lese ma•jes\ty or lèse ma•jes\ty
le•sion (*wound*) [vs. le•gion (*multitude*)]
Le•so•tho
less
les•see
less•en (*to decrease*), •ened, •en•ing [vs. les•son (*instruction*)]
less•er (*smaller*) [vs. les•sor (*one who gives a lease*)]
les•son (*instruction*) [vs. less•en (*to decrease*)]
les•sor (*one who gives a lease*) [vs. less\er (*smaller*)]
lest (*unless*) [vs. least (*smallest*)]
let, let, let•ting
let•down
le•thal

le•thal\ly
le•thar•gic
le•thar•gi•cal\ly
leth•ar\gy
let's (let us)
lets (permits)
let•ter, •tered, •ter•ing
letter bomb
letter car•rier
let\ter•head
let•ter•ing
let\ter of cred\it
let\ter-•per•fect
let\ter•press
let\ter-•qual\i\ty
let•tuce
let•up
leu•ke•mi\a
leu•ke•mic
leu•ko•cyte or leu•co•cyte
lev\ee (embankment) [vs.
lev\y (tax)]
lev\el, •eled or •elled,
•el•ing or •el•ling
lev\el•er
lev\el•head\ed
lev\el•head•ed•ness
lev•el•ly
lev•el•ness
lev\er, •ered, •er•ing
lev•er•age, •aged, •ag•ing
leveraged buy•out (LBO)
le•vi•a•than
Le•vi's
lev\i•tate (to rise), •tat\ed,
•tat•ing
lev\i•ta•tion
lev\i•ty (gaiety)
lev\y (tax), pl. lev•ies;
lev•ied, lev\y•ing [vs.
lev\ee (embankment)]
lewd, \er, •est
lewd\ly
lewd•ness
lex\i•cal
lex\i•cog•ra•pher
lex\i•co•graph\ic
lex\i•cog•ra•phy
lex\i•con
LF (line feed)
li•a•bil•i\ty, pl. •ties

liability in•sur•ance
li•a\ble (responsible) [vs.
li•bel (defamation)]
li•ai•son
li\ar (one who tells
untruths) [vs. lyre (small
harp)]
lib
li•ba•tion
li•bel (defamation), •beled
or •belled, •bel•ing or
•bel•ling [vs. li•a\ble
(responsible)]
li•bel•ous
lib•er•al
lib•er•al•ism
lib•er•al•i\ty
lib•er•al•i\za•tion
lib•er•al•ize, •ized, •iz•ing
lib•er•al•ly
lib•er•ate, •at\ed, •at•ing
lib•er•a•tion
lib•er•a\tor
Li•be•ri\a
Li•be•ri•an
lib•er•tar•i•an
lib•er•tine
lib•er•ty, pl. •ties
li•bid\i•nous
li•bi•do, pl. •dos
Li•bra, pl. •bras
li•brar•i•an
li•brar\y, pl. •brar•ies
li•bret•tist
li•bret•to, pl. •bret•tos or
•bret\ti
Li•bre•ville
Lib\y\a
Lib•y\an
lice
li•cense, •censed,
•cens•ing
li•cen•see
li•cen•ti•ate
li•cen•tious
li•cen•tious\ly
li•cen•tious•ness
li•chee
li•chen (fungus) [vs. lik\en
(to compare)]
lic\it

lick, licked, lick•ing
lick\e\ty-•split
lick•ing
lic\o•rice
lid
lie (to recline), lay, lain,
ly•ing
lie (to speak falsely), lied,
ly•ing [vs. lay (to set
down; secular) and lei
(wreath) and lye (alkaline
solution)]
Liech•ten•stein
lied, pl. lied\er (art songs)
[vs. lead\er (guide)]
lie de•tec•tor
lief (gladly) [vs. leaf (unit of
foliage; to turn pages)]
Li•ège
liege
lien (claim) [vs. lean (to
incline; thin)]
lieu (stead) [vs. loo (toilet)]
lieu•ten•ant
lieutenant colo•nel
life, pl. lives
life•blood
life•boat
life•guard
life in•sur•ance
life•less
life•like
life•line
life•long
lif\er
life•sav\er
life•sav\ing
life-•size or life-•sized
life style or life-•style
life•time
life•work
LIFO (last in, first out)
lift, \ed, •ing
lift•off or lift-•off
lig\a•ment
lig\a•ture, •tured,
•tur•ing
light, light\ed or lit,
light•ing; light\er, light•est
light bar

light•e\mit\ting di•ode (LED)

light\en, light•ened, light•en•ing (making lighter) [vs. light•ning (electrical discharge in sky)]

light•en\er

light\er

light•face

light-•fin\gered

light-•foot\ed

light•head\ed

light•heart\ed

light•heart•ed\ly

light•heart•ed•ness

light•house, pl. •hous\es

light•ing

light\ly

light-•mind\ed

light•ness

light•ning (electrical dis-charge in sky) [vs. light•en•ing (making lighter)]

light pen

light•weight

light-•year

lig•ne•ous

lik•a•bil•i\ty

lik•a\ble or like•a\ble

like, liked, lik•ing

like•li•hood

like\ly, •li\er, •li•est

like-•mind\ed

like-•mind\ed\ness

lik\en (to compare), •ened, •en•ing [vs. li•chen (fun-gus)]

like•ness

like•wise

lik•ing

li•lac

Lil•li•pu•tian

Li•long\we

lilt, lilt\ed, lilt•ing

lil\y, pl. lil•ies

lil\y-•liv\ered

li•ma bean

limb (appendage) [vs. limn (to draw)]

lim•ber, •bered, •ber•ing

lim•ber•ness

limb•less

lim\bo, pl. •bos

Lim•burg\er

lime

lime•ade

lime•light

lim•er•ick

lime•stone

lim\it, •it\ed, •it•ing

lim\i•ta•tion

lim•it\ed

limited li•a•bil•i\ty com•pa\ny

limited part•ner

limited part•ner•ship

limited war•ran\ty

lim•it\er

lim•it•less

limn (to draw), limned, limn•ing [vs. limb (appendage)]

lim\o, pl. lim\os

lim•ou•sine

limp, limped, limp•ing; limp\er, limp•est

lim•pet (marine animal)

lim•pid (clear)

lim•pid•i\ty

limp\ly

limp•ness

lin•age (number of lines) [vs. lin\e\age (ancestry)]

linch•pin

Lin•coln

lin•den

line, lined, lin•ing

lin\e\age (ancestry) [vs. lin•age (number of lines)]

lin\e\al (of direct descent) [vs. lin\e\ar (of lines)]

lin\e\a•ment (feature) [vs. lin\i•ment (salve)]

lin\e\ar (of lines) [vs. lin\e\al (of direct descent)]

lin\e\ar•i\ty

line•back\er

line ed\i•tor

line feed (LF)

line•man (football player; telephone repairman), pl. •men [vs. lines•man (sports official)]

lin\en

line of cred\it

line print\er

line printer ter•mi•nal

lin\er

lines•man (sports official), pl. •men [vs. line•man (football player; telephone repairman)]

line\up

lin•ger, •gered, •ger•ing

lin•ge•rie

lin•ger•ing

lin•ger•ing\ly

lin\go, pl. •goes

lin•gua fran\ca, pl. lin•gua fran•cas

lin•gual

lin•gui\ne or lin•gui\ni

lin•guist

lin•guis•tic

lin•guis•tics

lin\i•ment (salve) [vs. lin\e\a•ment (feature)]

lin•ing

link, linked, link•ing

link•age

link-•ed\it, •ed\it\ed, •ed\it\ing

link ed\i•tor

link\er

links (golf course) [vs. lynx (the animal)]

link\up

lin•net

li•no•le\um

Lin\o•type (™)

lin•seed oil

lint

lin•tel (beam) [vs. len•til (the legume)]

lint\y, •i\er, •i•est

li\on

li\on•heart•ed

li•on•ize, •ized, •iz•ing

lip, lipped, lip•ping

lip\id
lip\o•suc•tion
lip•read, •read, •read•ing
lip•read\er
lip•read•ing
lip•stick
lip-•sync or lip-•synch,
  •synced or •synched,
  •sync\ing or •synch\ing
liq\ue•fac•tion
liq\ue•fi•a\ble
liq\ue•fi\er
liq\ue•fy, •fied, •fy•ing
li•queur (alcoholic beverage that is a cordial) [vs.
  liq•uor (any alcoholic
  beverage)]
liq•uid
liq•ui•date, •dat\ed,
  •dat\ing
liq•ui•da•tion
liquidation val\ue
liq•ui•da•tor
liq•uid crys•tal dis•play
  (LCD)
li•quid•i\ty
liq•uor (any alcoholic beverage) [vs. li•queur (alcoholic beverage that is a
  cordial)]
li\ra, pl. li\ras or li\re
Lis•bon
lisle
LISP (programming
  language)
lisp, lisped, lisp•ing
lis•some or lis•som
list, list\ed, list•ing
list bro•ker
listed stock
lis•ten, •tened, •ten•ing
lis•ten\er
list•ing
list•less
list•less\ly
list•less•ness
list price
Liszt
lit•a\ny, pl. •nies
li•tchi or li•chee, pl. •tchis
  or •chees

li•ter (liquid measure) [vs.
  lit•ter (strewn objects)]
lit•er•a\cy
lit•er•al (exact) [vs.
  lit•to•ral (of a shore)]
lit•er•al\ly
lit•er•al•ness
lit•er•ar\y
lit•er•ate (educated)
lit\e•ra\ti (well-educated
  people)
lit•er•a•ture (written
  works) [vs. lit•té•ra•teur
  or lit•te•ra•teur (writer)]
lithe, lith\er, lith•est
lithe•some
lith•i\um
lith\o•graph, •graphed,
  •graph•ing
li•thog•ra•pher
lith\o•graph\ic
li•thog•ra•phy
lith\o•sphere
Lith\u•a•ni\a
Lith\u•a•ni\an
lit\i•gant
lit\i•gate, •gat\ed, •gat•ing
lit\i•ga•tion
lit\i•ga•tor
li•ti•gious
li•ti•gious•ness
lit•mus
lit•ter (strewn objects),
  •tered, •ter•ing [vs. li•ter
  (liquid measure)]
lit•té•ra•teur or
  lit•te•ra•teur (writer) [vs.
  lit•er•a•ture (written
  works)]
lit\ter•bug
lit•ter\er
little, less or less\er, least
lit•tle, lit•tler, lit•tlest
lit\tle•neck
lit•to•ral (of a shore) [vs.
  lit•er•al (exact)]
li•tur•gi•cal
lit•ur•gist
lit•ur\gy, pl. •gies
liv•a•bil•i\ty
liv•a\ble or live•a\ble

live, lived, liv•ing
lived (did live) [vs. liv\id
  (enraged; flushed; ashen)]
live•li•hood
live•li•ness
live•long
live\ly, •li\er, •li•est
liv•en, •ened, •en•ing
liv\er
liv•er•ied
liv•er•ish
Liv•er•pool
Liv•er•pud•li\an
liv•er•wort
liv•er•wurst
liv•er•ly, pl. •er•ies
lives
live•stock
liv\id (enraged; flushed;
  ashen) [vs. lived (did live)]
liv•id\ly
liv•ing
liv•ing will
liz•ard
lla•ma (the animal), pl.
  •mas [vs. la•ma (monk)]
lo (behold!) [vs. low (to
  moo; not high)]
load (burden), \ed, •ing [vs.
  lode (mineral deposit)]
load\er
load fund
loaf, pl. loaves; loafed,
  loaf•ing
loaf\er
Loaf\er (™)
loam
loan (to lend), loaned,
  loan•ing [vs. lone (solitary)]
loan\er
loan shark
loan•shark•ing
loan•word
loath (reluctant)
loathe (to hate), loathed,
  loath•ing
loath•some
loath•some•ness
loaves
lob, lobbed, lob•bing

lo•bar

lob\by, pl. •bies; •bied, •by•ing

lob\by•ist

lobe

lo•bot•o•my, pl. •mies

lob•ster, pl. •ster or •sters

lo•cal (confined)

local ar\e\a net•work (LAN)

lo•cale (place)

lo•cal•i•ty, pl. •ties

lo•cal\i•za•tion

lo•cal•ize, •ized, •iz•ing

lo•cal\ly

lo•cat•a\ble

lo•cate, •cat\ed, •cat•ing

lo•cat\er

lo•ca•tion

loch (lake)

lock (fastener; to fasten),
locked, lock•ing

lock\er

lock\et

lock•jaw

lock•out

locks (fasteners) [vs. lox
(cured salmon)]

lock•smith

lock•step

lock\up

lo\co

lo•co•mo•tion

lo•co•mo•tive

lo•co•mo•tor

lo\co•weed

lo•cus (locality), pl. \ci

lo•cust (the insect)

lo•cu•tion

lode (mineral deposit) [vs.
load (burden)]

lo•den

lode•star

lode•stone

lodge (cabin; to stick),
lodged, lodg•ing [vs. loge
(theater section)]

lodg\er

lo\ess (loamy deposit) [vs.
loose (to release; unat-
tached) and lose (to mis-
place) and loss (some-
thing lost)]

loft, loft\ed, loft•ing

loft•i\ly

loft\i•ness

loft\y, •i\er, •i•est

log, logged, log•ging

lo\gan•ber\ry, pl. •ries

log\a•rithm

log\a•rith•mic

loge (theater section) [vs.
lodge (cabin; to stick)]

log•ger

log\ger•head

log•ic

log\i•cal

logical da\ta struc•ture

log\i•cal\ly

lo•gi•cian

log in or log on

lo•gi•ness

lo•gis•tics

log•jam

lo\go, pl. •gos

LOGO (programming
language)

log off or log out

log\o•type

log•roll•ing

lo\gy, •gi\er, •gi•est

loin

loin•cloth, pl. •cloths

loi•ter, •tered, •ter•ing

loi•ter\er

loll, lolled,

loll•ing

lol•li•pop

Lo\mé

Lon•don

lone (solitary) [vs. loan (to
lend)]

lone•li•ness

lone•ly, •li\er, •li•est

lon\er

lone•some

lone•some•ness

long, longed, long•ing;
long\er, long•est

long•boat

long dis•tance (noun)

long-•dis\tance (adj.)

long-•drawn-•out

lon•gev\i•ty

long•hair

long•hand

long•ing

long•ing\ly

lon•gi•tude

lon•gi•tu•di•nal

long-•lived

long-•play\ing

long-•range

long•shore•man, pl. •men

long•stand•ing

long-•suf\fer\ing

long-•term

long-•term as•set

long•time

long-•wind\ed

long•word

loo (toilet) [vs. lieu (stead)]

look, looked, look•ing

look-•and-•feel

look\er

look\er-•on, pl. look\ers-
•on

look•ing glass

look•out

look-•see

loom, loomed, loom•ing

loon

loon\y, pl. loon•ies

loop (closed circuit; to
make a closed circuit),
looped, loop•ing [vs.
loupe (small magnifier)]

loop•hole

loop\y, •i\er, •i•est

loose (to release; unat-
tached), loosed, loos•ing;
loos\er, loos•est [vs.
lo\ess (loamy deposit)
and lose (to misplace)
and loss (something lost)]

loose-•leaf

loose\ly

loos\en, •ened, •en•ing

loose•ness

loot (booty; to pillage),
loot\ed, loot•ing [vs. lute
(stringed instrument)]

loot\er

lop (to cut off), lopped,
lop•ping

lope (*to run slowly*), loped, lop•ing

lop•sid\ed

lop•sid•ed\ly

lop•sid•ed•ness

lo•qua•cious

lo•qua•cious•ness

lo•quac•i\ty

lo•ran

lord (*noble*), lord\ed, lord•ing [*vs.* laud (*to praise*) *and* cum lau\de (*with honor*)]

lord\ly, •li\er, •li•est

lord•ship

lore

lo-•res (*low-resolution*)

lor•gnette

lorn

lor\ry, *pl.* •ries

Los An•ge•les

lose (*to misplace*), lost, los•ing [*vs.* lo\ess (*loamy deposit*) *and* loose (*to release; unattached*) *and* loss (*something lost*)]

los\er

loss (*something lost*) [*vs.* lo\ess (*loamy deposit*) *and* loose (*to release; unattached*) *and* lose (*to misplace*)]

loss lead\er

loss ra•tio

lost

lot

Lo•thar\i\o, *pl.* •thar\i•os

lo•tion

lot•ter\y, *pl.* •ter•ies

lot\to

lo•tus, *pl.* •tus\es

loud, \er, •est

loud\ly

loud•mouth, *pl.* •mouths

loud•mouthed

loud•ness

loud•speak\er

Lou\is

Lou•i•si•an\a (*LA*)

Lou\is•ville

lounge, lounged, loung•ing

loupe (*small magnifier*) [*vs.* loop (*closed circuit; to make a closed circuit*)]

louse, *pl.* lice (*insects*), lous\es (*lowlifes*); loused, lous•ing

lous•i\ly

lous\i•ness

lous\y, •i\er, •i•est

lout

lou•ver *or* lou•vre

lou•vered

lov•a\ble *or* love•a\ble

love, loved, lov•ing

love•bird

love•less

love•li•ness

love•lorn

love\ly, *pl.* •lies; •li\er, •li•est

love•mak•ing

lov\er

love•sick

lov•ing

lov•ing\ly

low (*to moo; not high*), lowed, low•ing; low\er, low•est [*vs.* lo (*behold!*)]

low•brow

low-•cal (*low-calorie*)

low•down

low\er, •ered, •er•ing

low•er•case

low\er class (*noun*)

low\er-•class (*adj.*)

low-•key *or* low-•keyed

low•land

low-•lev\el for•mat

low-•lev\el lan•guage

low•life, *pl.* •lifes

low•li•ness

low\ly, •li\er, •li•est

low-•mind•ed

low•ness

low-•res\o\lu•tion

low-•rise

low-•spir\it\ed

lox (*cured salmon*) [*vs.* locks (*fasteners*)]

loy\al

loy•al•ist

loy•al\ly

loy•al\ty

loz•enge

LSD (*hallucinogenic drug, lysergic acid diethylamide*)

LSI (*large-scale integration*)

Ltd. *or* ltd. (*limited*)

Lu•an\da

lu\au, *pl.* •aus

Lub•bock

lube, lubed, lub•ing

lu•bri•cant

lu•bri•cate, •cat\ed, •cat•ing

lu•bri•ca•tion

lu•bri•ca•tor

lu•bri•cious

lu•bric•i\ty

lu•cid

lu•cid•i\ty

lu•cid\ly

Lu•ci•fer

Lu•cite (™)

luck, lucked, luck•ing

luck•i\ly

luck•less

luck\y, •i\er, •i•est

lu•cra•tive

lu•cra•tive\ly

lu•cra•tive•ness

lu•cre

lu•cu•brate, •brat\ed, •brat•ing

lu•cu•bra•tion

Lud•dite

lu•di•crous

lu•di•crous\ly

lu•di•crous•ness

luff, luffed, luff•ing

lug, lugged, lug•ging

lug•ga\ble com•put\er

lug•gage

lu•gu•bri•ous

lu•gu•bri•ous\ly

lu•gu•bri•ous•ness

Luke

luke•warm

luke•warm\ly

luke•warm•ness

lull, lulled, lull•ing

lull•a\by, *pl.* •bies

lum•ba\go
lum•bar (of the loins)
lum•ber (cut timber; to cut timber), •bered, •ber•ing
lum•ber•jack
lum•ber•man
lum•ber•yard
lu•mi•nar\y, pl. •nar•ies
lu•mi•nes•cence
lu•mi•nes•cent
lu•mi•nos•i\ty
lu•mi•nous
lu•mi•nous\ly
lum•mox
lump, lumped, lump•ing
lump\i•ness
lump\y, •i\er, •i•est
lu•na\cy
lu•nar
lu•na•tic
lunch, lunched, lunch•ing
lunch•box com•put\er
lunch•eon
lunch•eon•ette
lunch•room
lung
lunge, lunged, lung•ing
lunk•head
lu•pine
lu•pus
lurch, lurched, lurch•ing
lure, lured, lur•ing
lu•rid

lu•rid\ly
lu•rid•ness
lurk, lurked, lurk•ing
Lu•sa\ka
lus•cious
lus•cious•ness
lush, \er, •est
lush•ness
lust, lust\ed, lust•ing
lus•ter
lus•ter•less
lust•ful
lust\i\ly
lust\i•ness
lus•trous
lust\y, •i\er, •i•est
lute (stringed instrument) [vs. loot (booty; to pil-lage)]
lu•te•ti\um
Lu•ther
Lu•ther\an
Lu•ther•an•ism
Lux•em•bourg
lux\u•ri•ance
lux\u•ri•ant (abundant) [vs. lux\u•ri•ous (sumptu-ous)]
lux\u•ri•ant\ly
lux\u•ri•ate, •at\ed, •at•ing
lux\u•ri•ous (sumptuous) [vs. lux\u•ri•ant (abun-dant)]

lux\u•ri•ous\ly
lux\u•ri•ous•ness
lux•u\ry, pl. •ries
ly•ce\um
lye (alkaline solution) [vs. lay (to set down; secular) and lei (wreath) and lie (to speak falsely; to recline)]
ly•ing
ly\ing-•in, pl. ly\ings-•in, ly\ing-•ins
Lyme dis•ease
lymph
lym•phat\ic
lymph node
lym•phoid
lym•pho\ma, pl. •mas, •ma\ta
lynch, lynched, lynch•ing
lynch\er
lynx (the animal), pl. lynx\es or lynx [vs. links (golf course)]
Ly•ons
lyre (small harp) [vs. li\ar (one who tells untruths)]
lyr\ic
lyr\i•cal\ly
lyr\i•cism
lyr\i•cist
ly•ser•gic ac\id di•eth\yl•am\ide (LSD)

M

MA (Massachusetts)
M.A. (Master of Arts)
ma, pl. mas
ma'am
ma•ca•bre
mac•ad\am
mac•ad•am•ize, •iz\ed, •iz•ing
Ma•cao
ma•caque
mac\a•ro\ni
mac\a•roon
ma•caw
mace (clublike weapon)
Mace (™), (chemical spray) Maced, Mac•ing

Mac\e\do•ni\a
Mac\e\do•ni\an
mac•er•ate, •at\ed, •at•ing
mac•er•a•tion
mach or Mach
ma•chet\e, pl. •chet\es
Mach\i•a•vel•li\an
mach\i•na•tion
ma•chine, •chined, •chin•ing
ma\chine-•de\pend•ent
ma\chine-•in\de\pend•ent
ma•chine gun
machine lan•guage
ma\chine-•read\a•ble
ma•chin•er\y

ma•chin•ist
ma•chis\mo
ma•cho, pl. •chos
Mac•in•tosh (™)
mack•er\el, pl. \el or •els
mack\i•naw
mack•in•tosh (raincoat) [vs. Mc•In•tosh (the apple) and Mac•in•tosh (the computer)]
mac•ra•mé
mac\ro, pl. •ros
mac\ro•bi•ot\ic
mac\ro•bi•ot•ics
mac\ro•cosm
mac\ro•ec\o\nom•ics

ma•cron
mad, mad•der, mad•dest
Mad\a•gas•car
mad\am, pl. mad•ams
mad•ame (Mme.), pl. mes•dames
mad•cap
mad•den, •dened, •den•ing
made (produced) [vs. maid (servant)]
Ma•dei\ra
mad\e•moi•selle (Mlle.), pl. mad\e•moi•selles or mes•de•moi•selles
made-•to-•or\der
made-•up
mad•house, pl. •hous\es
Mad\i•son
mad\ly
mad•man, pl. •men
mad•ness
Ma•don\na
Ma•dras (city)
mad•ras (fabric)
Ma•drid
mad•ri•gal
mad•wom\an, pl. •wom\en
mael•strom
maes•tro, pl. maes•tros
Ma•fi\a
ma•fi•o\so, pl. \si or •sos
mag\a•zine
Ma•gel\lan
ma•gen\ta
mag•got
Ma\gi (pl. of Magus)
mag\ic
mag\i•cal
mag\i•cal•ly
ma•gi•cian
mag•is•trate
mag\ma (mineral mixture)
mag\na (great)
Mag\na Car\ta or Char\ta
mag•na•nim•i\ty
mag•nan\i•mous
mag•nan\i•mous\ly
mag•nate (influential person)
mag•ne•sia
mag•ne•si\um

mag•net (metal that attracts iron)
mag•net\ic
mag•net\i•cal\ly
mag•net\ic bub•ble
magnetic disk
magnetic drum
magnetic res\o•nance im•ag•ing (MRI)
mag•net•ism
mag•net•ize, •ized, •iz•ing
mag•ne\to, pl. •tos
mag•ne•tom\e•ter
mag•ni•fi•ca\tion
mag•nif\i•cence
mag•nif\i•cent
mag•nif\i•cent\ly
mag•ni•fi\er
mag•ni•fy, •fied, •fy•ing
mag•ni•tude
mag•no\lia, pl. •lias
mag•num
mag•num o\pus
mag•pie
Ma•gus, pl. \gi
Mag•yar
ma•ha•ra•jah, pl. •jahs
ma•ha•ra•nee, pl. •nees
ma•ha•ri•shi, pl. •shis
ma•hat\ma, pl. •mas
Ma•hi•can, pl. •cans or •can
mah-•jongg or mah•jong
ma•hog•a\ny
maid (servant) [vs. made (produced)]
maid\en
maid\en•head
maid\en•hood
maid•en\ly
maid•serv•ant
mail (letters; to mail), mailed, mail•ing [vs. male (masculine)]
mail•box
mail\er
mail•lot
mail•man, pl. •men
mail merge
mail or•der (noun)
mail-•or\der (adj.)

maim, maimed, maim•ing
main
Maine (ME)
Main\er
main•frame
main•land
main line (noun)
main•line (verb), •lined, •lin•ing
main\ly
main•mast
main mem\o\ry
main•sail
main•spring
main•stay
main•stream
main•tain, •tained, •tain•ing
main•tain•a\ble
main•te•nance
maî•tre or maî•tre d, pl. maî•tre or maî•tre d's
maî•tre d'hô•tel, pl. maî•tres d'hô•tel
maize (corn) [vs. maze (labyrinth)]
ma•jes•tic
ma•jes•ti•cal\ly
maj•es\ty, pl. •ties
ma•jol\i•ca
ma•jor, •jored, •jor•ing
ma\jor-•do\mo, pl. \mos
ma•jor•ette
ma•jor•i\ty, pl. •ties
ma•jor med\i•cal
make, made, mak•ing
make-•be\lieve
make-•do, pl. •dos
mak\er
make•shift
make\up or make-•up
make-•work
mak•ing
mal\a•chite
mal•ad•just\ed
mal•ad•just•ment
mal•a•droit
mal•a•dy, pl. •dies
Mal\a•gas\y Re•pub•lic
ma•laise
mal•a•mute or mal\e\mute

mal•a\prop•ism
ma•lar•i\a
ma•lar•i\al
ma•lar•key
mal\a•thi\on
Ma•la\wi, pl. •wis or \wi
Ma•la•wi\an
Ma•lay
Ma•lay•sia
Ma•lay•sian
mal•con•tent
Mal•dives
male (masculine) [vs. mail (letters)]
mal\e•dic•tion
mal\e•fac•tion
mal\e•fac•tor
ma•lef\ic
ma•lef\i•cence
ma•lef\i•cent
male•ness
ma•lev\o•lence
ma•lev\o•lent
ma•lev\o•lent•ly
mal•fea•sance
mal•for•ma•tion
mal•formed
mal•func•tion, •tioned, •tion•ing
Ma\li
mal•ice
ma•li•cious
ma•li•cious•ly
ma•lign, •ligned, •lign•ing
ma•lig•nan•cy
ma•lig•nant
ma•lin•ger, •gered, •ger•ing
ma•lin•ger•er
mall (shopping center) [vs. maul (to handle roughly)]
mal•lard, pl. •lards or •lard
mal•le•a•bil•i\ty
mal•le•a•ble
mal•let
mal•le•us, pl. mal•le•i
mal•low
mal•nour•ished
mal•nu•tri•tion
mal•oc•clu•sion
mal•o\dor•ous

mal•prac•tice
malt
Mal\ta
malt\ed milk
Mal•thu•sian
malt•ose
mal•treat, •treat\ed, •treat\ing
mal•treat•ment
ma\ma or mam\ma, pl. •mas
mam\bo, pl. •bos; •boed, \bo•ing
mam•mal
mam•ma•li\an
mam•ma\ry
mam•mo•gram
mam•mog•ra•phy
mam•mon
mam•mon•ism
mam•moth
man, pl. men; manned, man•ning
man\a•cle, •cled, •cling
man•age, •aged, •ag•ing
man•age•a•ble
man•age•ment
management con•sult•ant
management in•for•ma•tion sys•tem (MIS)
man•ag\er
man\a•ge•ri\al
ma•ña\na, pl. •nas
man\a•tee, pl. •tees
Man•ches•ter
Man•chu, pl. •chus or •chu
Man•chu•ri\a
Man•chu•ri\an
man•da•rin
man•date, •dat\ed, •dat•ing
man•da•to\ry
man•di•ble
man•dib\u•lar
man•do•lin
man•drake
man•drel or man•dril (machine tool)
man•drill (monkey)
mane

man-•eat\er
man-•eat\ing
ma•nège or ma•nege (horsemanship) [vs. mé•nage (household)]
ma•neu•ver
ma•neu•ver•a\ble
man Fri•day, pl. men Fri•day or Fri•days
man•ful
man•ful\ly
man•ga•nese
mange
man•ger
man•gi•ness
man•gle, •gled, •gling
man•go, pl. •goes or •gos
man•grove
man•gy, •gi\er, •gi•est
man•han•dle, •dled, •dling
Man•hat•tan
man•hole
man•hood
man-•hour
man•hunt
ma•ni\a, pl. •ni\as
ma•ni\ac
ma•ni•a•cal
man\ic
man\ic-•de•pres\sive
man\i•cure, •cured, •cur•ing
man\i•cur•ist
man\i•fest, •fest\ed, •fest•ing
man\i•fes•ta•tion
man\i•fest\ly
man\i•fes•to, pl. •tos or •toes
man\i•fold
man\i•kin or man•ni•kin
Ma•nil\a
man\i\oc
ma•nip\u•la•ble
ma•nip\u•late, •lat\ed, •lat•ing
ma•nip\u•la•tion
ma•nip\u•la•tive
ma•nip\u•la•tor
Man\i•to•ba
man•kind

man•li•ness
man\ly, •li\er, •li•est
man-•made
Mann
man\na
manned
man•ne•quin or man\i•kin
man•ner (way) [vs. man\or (estate)]
man•nered
man•ner•ism
man•ner\ly
man•nish
ma•noeu•vre, •vred, •vring
man-•of-•war, pl. men-•of- •war
man\or (estate) [vs. man•ner (way)]
ma•no•ri\al
man•pow\er
man•qué
man•sard roof
manse
man•serv•ant, pl. men•serv•ants
man•sion
man-•sized or man-•size
man•slaugh•ter
man•sue•tude
man•ta, pl. •tas
man•tel (fireplace frame)
man•til\la, pl. •las
man•tis, pl. •tis\es or •tes
man•tle (cloak)
man•tra, pl. •tras
man•u\al
man\u•al\ly
man\u•fac•ture, •tured, •tur•ing
man\u•fac•tur\er
man\u•fac•tur•ing
manufacturing cost
manufacturing o\ver•head
man\u•mis•sion
man\u•mit, •mit•ted, •mit•ting
ma•nure, •nured, •nur•ing
man\u•script
Manx
man\y, more, most

Mao•ism
Mao•ist
Ma•o\ri, pl. •ris or \ri
Mao Ze•dong or Mao Tse-•tung
map, mapped, map•ping
map file
ma•ple
mar, marred, mar•ring
mar\a•bou, pl. •bous
ma•rac\a, pl. •rac\as
mar\a•schi\no
mar\a•thon
mar\a•thon\er
ma•raud
ma•raud\er
mar•ble, •bled, •bling
mar•ble•ize, •ized, •iz•ing
mar•cel, •celled, •cel•ling
march, marched, march•ing
march\er
mar•chion•ess
Mar\di Gras
mare (female horse) [vs. may\or (city official)]
ma\re (dark lunar plain), pl. ma•ri\a
mare's-•nest
mar•ga•rine
mar•gin, •gined, •gin•ing
mar•gin\al
mar•gi•na•li\a
mar•gin call
margin rate
mar•gue•rite
ma•ri•a•chi, pl. •chis
Ma•rie An•toi•nette
mar\i•gold
ma•ri•jua\na
ma•rim\ba, pl. •bas
ma•ri•na, pl. •nas
mar\i•nade (seasoned liquid)
mar\i•nate (to steep in marinade), •nat\ed, •nat•ing
ma•rine
mar\i•ner
mar\i•on•ette

mar\i•tal (of marriage) [vs. mar•shal (police officer) and mar•tial (warlike)]
mar\i•tal\ly
mar\i•time
mar•jo•ram
mark (visible impression; to mark), marked, mark•ing [vs. marque (product model)]
mark•down
marked
mark•ed\ly
mark\er
mar•ket, •ket\ed, •ket•ing
mar•ket•a\ble
mar•ket e\con\o\my
mar•ket•er
mar•ket•ing
mar•ket•place
mar•ket price
market re•search
market share
market val\ue
mark•ka, pl. •kaa
Mar•kov chain
mark price
marks•man, pl. •men
marks•man•ship
mark\up
mar•lin, pl. •lin or •lins
mar•line•spike
mar•ma•lade
mar•mo•set
mar•mot
ma•roon
marque (product model) [vs. mark (visible impression)]
mar•quee (theater sign)
mar•quess (British noble-man)
mar•quis (European noble-man), pl. •quis\es or •quis
mar•quise (European noblewoman), pl. •quis\es
mar•riage (wedding) [vs. mi•rage (illusion)]
mar•riage•a\ble
mar•row
mar\ry, •ried, •ry•ing

Mars
Mar•seilles
marsh
mar•shal (*police officer*) [vs. mar\i•tal (*of marriage*) and mar•tial (*warlike*)]
mar•shal, •shaled or •shalled, •shal•ing or •shal•ling
marsh•mal•low
marsh\y, •i\er, •i•est
mar•su•pi\al
mart
mar•ten (*the animal*), pl. •tens or •ten [vs. mar•tin (*the bird*)]
mar•tial (*warlike*) [vs. mar\i•tal (*of marriage*) and mar•shal (*police officer*)]
Mar•tian
mar•tin (*the bird*) [vs. mar•ten (*the animal*)]
mar•ti•net
mar•tin•gale
mar•ti\ni, pl. •nis
mar•tyr, •tyred, •tyr•ing
mar•tyr•dom
mar•vel, •veled or •velled, •vel•ing or •vel•ling
mar•vel•ous
mar•vel•ous\ly
Marx•i\an
Marx•ism
Marx•ist
Mar\y
Mar\y•land (*MD*)
mar•zi•pan
mas•car\a, •car•aed, •car\a•ing
mas•cot
mas•cu•line
mas•cu•lin•i\ty
ma•ser
mash, mashed, mash•ing
mask (*face covering*), masked, mask•ing [vs. masque (*elaborate play*)]
mas•och•ism
mas•och•ist
mas•och•is•tic

mas•och•is•ti•cal\ly
ma•son
Ma•son\ic
ma•son\ry
masque (*elaborate play*) [vs. mask (*face covering*)]
mas•quer•ade, •ad\ed, •ad\ing
mas•quer•ad\er
mass, massed, mass•ing
massed (*assembled*) [vs. mast (*upright pole*)]
Mas•sa•chu•setts (*MA*)
mas•sa•cre, •cred, •cring
mas•sage, •saged, •sag•ing
mas•seur
mas•seuse
mas•sive
mas•sive\ly
mas•sive•ness
mass mar•ket•ing
mass me•di\a
mass-•pro•duce, \duced, \duc\ing
mass pro•duc•tion
mass stor•age
mast (*upright pole*) [vs. massed (*assembled*)]
mas•tec•to•my, pl. •mies
mas•ter, •tered, •ter•ing
mas\ter•ful
mas\ter•ful\ly
mas•ter\ly
mas\ter•mind, •mind\ed, •mind•ing
mas\ter•piece
mas\ter•stroke
mas\ter•work
mas\ter\y
mast•head
mas•ti•cate, •cat\ed, •cat•ing
mas•ti•ca•tion
mas•tiff
mas•to•don
mas•toid
mas•tur•bate, •bat\ed, •bat•ing
mas•tur•ba•tion
mat (*pad*) [vs. matte (*dull*)]
mat\a•dor

match, matched, match•ing
match•book
match•less
match•mak\er
ma\té or ma\te (*beverage*), pl. •tés or •tes
mate (*to marry; spouse*), mat\ed, mat•ing
ma•te\ri\al (*substance*) [vs. ma•té•ri•el (*equipment*)]
ma•te\ri•al•ism
ma•te\ri•a•list
ma•te\ri•al•is•tic
ma•te\ri•al•i•za•tion
ma•te\ri•al•ize, •ized, •iz•ing
ma•te\ri•al\ly
ma•te\ri•als han•dling
ma•té•ri•el (*equipment*) [vs. ma•te\ri•al (*substance*)]
ma•ter•nal
ma•ter•nal\ly
ma•ter•ni\ty
math
math co•proc•es•sor
math\e•mat\i•cal
math\e•mat\i•cal\ly
math\e•ma•ti•cian
math\e•mat•ics
mat\i•née or mat\i•nee
ma\tri•arch
ma\tri•ar•chal
ma\tri•ar•chy
mat•ri•cid\al
mat•ri•cide
ma•tric\u•late, •lat\ed, •lat•ing
ma•tric\u•la•tion
mat\ri•mo•ni\al
mat\ri•mo•ny, pl. •nies
ma•trix, pl. ma•tri•ces or ma•trix\es
ma•tron
ma•tron\ly
matte (*dull*) [vs. mat (*pad*)]
mat•ted (*padded*)
mat•ted or matt\ed (*having a dull surface*)
mat•ter, •tered, •ter•ing

mat\ter-•of-•fact
mat\ter-•of-•fact\ly
Mat•thew
mat•ting (*pad; material for pads*)
mat•ting or matt•ing (*dull surface; finishing with a dull surface*)
mat•tress
mat\u•ra•tion
ma•ture, •tured, •tur•ing
ma•ture\ly
ma•tu•ri\ty
maturity yield
mat\zo or mat•zoh, *pl.* •zos or •zot, •zohs or •zoth
maud•lin
maul (*to handle roughly*), mauled, maul•ing [*vs.* mall (*shopping center*)]
Mau•pas•sant
Mau•ri•ta•ni\a
Mau•ri•ta•ni\an
Mau•ri•tian
Mau•ri•tius
mau•so•le\um, *pl.* •le•ums or •le\a
mauve
ma•ven or ma•vin
mav•er•ick
maw
mawk•ish
mawk•ish\ly
max\i, *pl.* max\is
max•il\la, *pl.* •il•lae
max•il•lar\y
max\im
max\i•mal
max\i•mal\ly
max\i•mize, •mized, •miz•ing
max\i•mum, *pl.* •mums or \ma
may, might
Ma\ya, *pl.* •yas or \ya
May\an
may•be, *pl.* •bes
may•flow\er
may•fly, *pl.* •flies
may•hem

may\o
may•on•naise
may\or (*city official*) [*vs.* mare (*female horse*) and ma\re (*dark lunar plain*)]
may•or\al
may•or•al\ty
May•pole
maze (*labyrinth*) [*vs.* maize (*corn*)]
ma•zur\ka, *pl.* •kas
Mb (*megabit*)
MB (*megabyte*)
MBA or M.B.A. (*Master of Business Administration*)
Mc\Coy
Mc•In•tosh (*the apple*) [*vs.* mack•in•tosh (*raincoat*) and Mac•in•tosh (*the computer*)]
Mc\Kin•ley
MD (*Maryland*)
MD (*Doctor of Medicine*)
mdse. (*merchandise*)
ME (*Maine*)
me
mead
mead\ow
mead\ow•lark
mea•ger
mea•ger\ly
meal
meal•time
meal\y, •i\er, •i•est
meal\y-•mouthed or meal\y•mouthed
mean (*midway point*) [*vs.* me•di\an (*middle number*)]
mean (*to intend; unkind*), meant, mean•ing; mean\er, mean•est [*vs.* mien (*demeanor*)],
me•an•der, •dered, •der•ing
mean•ing
mean•ing•ful
mean•ing•less
mean\ly
mean•ness
meant

mean•time
mea•sles
mea•sly, •sli\er, •sli•est
meas•ur•a\ble
meas•ur•a•bly
meas•ure, •ured, •ur•ing
meas•ure•less
meas•ure•ment
meat (*flesh food*) [*vs.* meet (*to encounter*) and mete (*to allot*)]
meat•ball
meat\y, •i\er, •i•est
Mec\ca
me•chan\ic
me•chan\i•cal
mechanical mouse
me•chan\i•cal\ly
me•chan•ics
mech•an•ism
mech\a•nis•tic
mech\a•ni•za•tion
mech\a•nize, •nized, •niz\ing
med•al (*metal disk*) [*vs.* med•dle (*to interfere*) and met\al (*element*) and met•tle (*fortitude*)]
med•al•ist
me•dal•lion
med•dle (*to interfere*), •dled, •dling
med•dler
med\dle•some
me•di\a
me•di\al
me•di\an (*middle number*) [*vs.* mean (*midway point*)]
me•di•ate, •at\ed, •at•ing
me•di•a•tion
me•di•a•tor
med\ic
med\i•ca\ble
Med\i•caid
med\i•cal
med\i•cal\ly
me•dic\a•ment
Med\i•care
med\i•cate, •cat\ed, •cat•ing
med\i•ca•tion

me•dic\i•nal
me•di•e\val or
me•di•ae•val
me•di•e•val•ist
me•di•o•cre
me•di•oc•ri\ty
med\i•tate, •tat\ed,
•tat•ing
med\i•ta•tion
med\i•ta•tive
Med\i•ter•ra•ne\an
me•di\um, pl. •di\a or
•di•ums
me\di\um-•res\o\lu\tion
med•ley, pl. •leys
me•dul\la ob•long\a\ta, pl.
me•dul\la ob•long\a•tas
meek, \er, •est
meek\ly
meek•ness
meer•schaum
meet (to encounter), met,
meet•ing [vs. meat (flesh
food) and mete (to allot)]
meg\a•bit (Mb)
meg\a•byte (MB)
meg\a•cy•cle
meg\a•flop (MFLOP)
meg\a•hertz, pl. •hertz or
•hertz\es
meg\a•hit
meg\a\lo•ma•ni\a
meg\a\lo•ma•ni\ac
meg\a•lop\o•lis
meg\a•phone
meg\a•ton
mei•o•sis
mel•an•chol\y
Mel\a•ne•sia
Mel\a•ne•sian
mé•lange, pl. •langes
mel\a•nin
mel\a•nism
mel\a•no\ma, pl. •mas or
•ma\ta
Mel\ba toast
Mel•bourne
meld, meld\ed, meld•ing
me•lee or mê•lée
mel•lif•lu•ous
mel•lif•lu•ous\ly

mel•low, •lowed, •low•ing;
•low\er, •low•est
me\lod\ic
me•lod\i•cal\ly
me•lo•di•ous
me•lo•di•ous\ly
me•lo•di•ous•ness
mel\o•dra•ma, pl. •mas
mel\o•dra•mat\ic
mel•o\dy, pl. •dies
mel•on
melt, melt\ed, melt•ing
melt•down
Mel•ville
mem•ber
mem\ber•ship
mem•brane
mem•bra•nous
me•men\to, pl. •tos or
•toes
mem\o, pl. mem\os
mem•oir
mem\o•ra•bil\i\a
mem\o•ra•ble
mem\o•ra•bly
mem\o•ran•dum, pl.
•dums or \da
me•mo•ri\al
mem\o•ri•za•tion
mem\o•rize, •rized,
•riz•ing
mem\o\ry, pl. •ries
memory dump
mem\o\ry-•res\i\dent
Mem•phis
men
men•ace, •aced, •ac•ing
men•ac•ing\ly
mé•nage or me•nage
(household) [vs. ma•nège
(horsemanship)]
me•nag•er\ie
mend, mend\ed, mend•ing
men•da•cious
men•da•cious\ly
men•dac•i\ty
Men•del
men•de•le•vi\um
Men•dels•sohn
men•di•cant
men•folk or men•folks

me•ni\al
men•in•git•is
Men•non•ite
men\o•pau•sal
men\o•pause
me•nor\ah
men•ses
men•stru\al
men•stru•ate, •at\ed,
•at•ing
men•stru•a•tion
men•su•ra•ble
men•su•ra•tion
mens•wear
men•tal
men•tal•ist
men•tal•i\ty
men•tal\ly
men•thol
men•tho•lat•ed
men•tion, •tioned,
•tion•ing
men•tor
men\u, pl. men\us
menu bar
men•u-•driv\en
me\ow
mer•can•tile
mer•ce•nar\y, pl. •nar•ies
mer•cer\i•za•tion
mer•cer•ize, •ized, •iz•ing
mer•chan•dise, •dised,
•dis•ing
merchandise mart
mer•chan•dis\er
mer•chan•dis•ing
mer•chant
merchant bank
mer•chant•man, pl. •men
mer•ci•ful
mer•ci•ful\ly
mer•ci•less
mer•ci•less\ly
mer•cu•ri\al
mer•cu\ry
mer'•cy, pl. •cies
mere, mer•est
mere\ly
mer\e\tri•cious (tawdry)
[vs. mer\i•to•ri•ous
(praiseworthy)]

mer•gan•ser, pl. •sers or •ser

merge, merged, merg•ing

merg\ee

merg\er

me•rid•i\an

me•ringue

mer\it, •it\ed, •it•ing

mer\i•to•ri•ous (*praise-worthy*) [vs. mer\e\tri•cious (*tawdry*)]

mer\it rat•ing

Mer•lin

mer•maid

mer•man, pl. •men

mer•ri\ly

mer•ri•ment

mer\ry, mer•ri\er, mer•ri•est

mer•ry-•go-•round

mer\ry•mak\er

mer\ry•mak\ing

me\sa, pl. •sas

mé•sal•li•ance, pl. •li•anc\es

mes•cal

mes•ca•line

mes•dames (*Mmes.*)

mes•de•moi•selles (*Mlles.*)

mesh, meshed, mesh•ing

mes•mer•ism

mes•mer•ize, •ized, •iz•ing

Mes\o•po•ta•mi\a

Mes\o•po•ta•mi\an

mes\o•sphere

Mes\o•zo\ic

mes•quite

mess, messed, mess•ing

mes•sage

mes•sei•gneurs

mes•sen•ger

Mes•si\ah

Mes•si•an\ic

mes•sieurs (*MM.*)

mess•i\ly

mess\i•ness

Messrs. (pl. of "*Mr.*")

mess\y, •i\er, •i•est

mes•ti\zo, pl. •zos or •zoes

met

met\a•bol\ic

me•tab\o•lism

me•tab\o•lize, •lized, •liz•ing

met\a•car•pal

met\a•car•pus, pl. \pi

met\al (*element*) [vs. med\al (*metal disk*) and med•dle (*to interfere*) and met•tle (*fortitude*)]

me•tal•lic

me•tal•li•cal\ly

met•al•lur•gist

met•al•lur\gy

met\a•mor•phic

met\a•mor•phism

met\a•mor•phose, •phosed, •phos•ing, •phos\es

met\a•mor•pho•sis, pl. •ses

met\a•phor

met\a•phor\i•cal

met\a•phor\i•cal\ly

met\a•phys\i•cal

met\a•phys•ics

me•tas•ta•sis (*spread of malignant cells*), pl. •ses [vs. me•tath\e•sis (*transposition*)]

me•tas•ta•size, •sized, •siz•ing

met\a•stat\ic

met\a•tar•sal

met\a•tar•sus, pl. \si

me•tath\e•sis (*transposition*), pl. •ses [vs. me•tas•ta•sis (*spread of malignant cells*)]

mete (*to allot*), met\ed, met•ing [vs. meat (*flesh food*) and meet (*to encounter*)]

me•te\or

me•te•or\ic

me•te•or•ite

me•te•or•oid

me•te•or\o•log\i•cal

me•te•or•ol\o•gist

me•te•or•ol\o\gy

me•ter, •tered, •ter•ing

me\ter-•kil\o\gram-•sec\ond

meth\a•done

meth•ane

meth\a•nol

me•thinks, me•thought

meth\od

me•thod\i•cal

me•thod\i•cal\ly

Meth•od•ist

meth•od\o•log\i•cal

Me•thu•se•lah

meth\yl

me•tic\u•lous

me•tic\u•lous\ly

me•tic\u•lous•ness

mé•tier or me•tier

me•tre

met•ric

met•ri•ca•tion

met•ri•cize, •cized, •ciz•ing

met•rics

met•ric sys•tem

met\ro•nome

me•trop\o•lis, pl. •lis\es

met\ro•pol\i•tan

met•tle (*fortitude*) [vs. med\al (*metal disk*) and med•dle (*to interfere*) and met\al (*element*)]

met•tle•some

mew, mewed, mew•ing

mewl, mewled, mewl•ing

Mex\i•can

Mex\i•co

mez•za•nine

mez\zo-•so\pran\o, pl. \pran\os

mfg. (*manufacturing*)

MFLOP (*mega floating-point operations per second*)

MFM (*modified frequency modulation*)

mfr. (*manufacturer*), pl. mfrs.

mgr or Mgr (*manager*)

MHz (*megahertz*)

MI (*Michigan*)

MIA (missing in action)
Mi·am·i
mi·as·ma, pl. ·mas
mi\ca
mice
Mi·chel·an·ge·lo
Mich\i·gan (MI)
Mich\i·gan·der or
  Mich\i·gan·ite
mi·cro, pl. ·cros
mi·crobe
mi·cro·bi·ol·o·gist
mi·cro·bi·ol\o·gy
mi·cro·chip
mi·cro·com·put\er
mi·cro·cosm
mi·cro·ec\o\nom·ics
mi·cro·fiche
mi·cro·film
mi·cro·flop\py, pl. ·pies
mi·cro·groove
mi·cro·jus·ti·fi·ca·tion
mi·crom\e·ter
mi·cron, pl. ·crons
Mi·cro·ne·sia
Mi·cro·ne·sian
mi·cro·or\gan·ism
mi·cro·phone
mi·cro·proc·es·sor
mi·cro·scope
mi·cro·scop·ic
mi·cro·scop\i·cal\ly
mi·cros·co\py
mi·cro·spac·ing
mi·cro·sur·ger\y
mi·cro·wav·a·ble
mi\cro·wave, ·waved,
  ·wav·ing
mid
mid·air
Mi·das
mid·day
mid·den
mid·dle
mid\dle-·aged
Mid·dle A\mer\i·can
  (noun)
Mid\dle-·A\mer\i·can
  (adj.)
mid\dle·brow
mid·dle class (noun)

mid\dle-·class (adj.)
Mid·dle East
mid\dle·man, pl. ·men
mid·dle man·age·ment
middle man·ag\er
mid\dle-·of-·the-·road
mid·dle·weight
Mid·dle West
mid·dling
mid\dy (blouse), pl. ·dies
  [vs. mid\i (skirt) and
  MIDI (musical instrument
  digital interface)], pl. ·dies
Mid·east
Mid·east·ern
midge
midg\et
mid\i (skirt), pl. mid\is [vs.
  mid\dy (blouse)]
MIDI (musical instrument
  digital interface)
mid·land
mid·night
mid·point
mid·riff
mid·ship·man, pl. ·men
midst
mid·stream
mid·sum·mer
mid·term
mid·town
mid·way
mid·week
Mid·west
Mid·west·ern
Mid·west·ern\er
mid·wife, pl. ·wives
mid·wife·ry
mid·win·ter
mid·year
mien (demeanor) [vs.
  mean (to intend; unkind)]
miff
miffed
might (power) [vs. mite
  (small thing)]
might·i\ly
might\i·ness
might\y, might·i\er,
  might·i·est
mi·gnon·ette

mi·graine
mi·grant
mi·grate, ·grat\ed,
  ·grat·ing
mi·gra·tion
mi·gra·to\ry
mi·ka·do, pl. ·dos
mike, miked, mik·ing
mil (unit of length) [vs. mill
  (factory)]
mi·la\dy, pl. ·dies
Mi·lan
mild, \er, ·est
mil·dew, ·dewed,
  ·dew·ing
mild·ly
mild·ness
mile
mile·age or mil·age
mile·post
mil\er
mile·stone
mi·lieu, pl. mi·lieus or
  mi·lieux
mil\i·tan\cy
mil\i·tant
mil\i·tant\ly
mil\i·ta·rism
mil\i·ta·rist
mil\i·ta·ris·tic
mil\i·tar\y
mil\i·tate (to have an
  effect), ·tat\ed, ·tat·ing
  [vs. mit\i·gate (to make
  less severe)]
mi·li·tia
mi·li·tia·man, pl. ·men
milk, milked, milk·ing
milk\i·ness
milk·maid
milk·man, pl. ·men
milk shake or milk·shake
milk·sop
milk\y, ·i\er, ·i·est
mill (factory; to grind),
  milled, mill·ing [vs. mil
  (unit of length)]
mill·age
mil·le·nar\y (a thousand)
  [vs. mil·li·ner\y (women's
  hats)]

mil•len•ni\al

mil•len•ni\um, *pl.* •ni•ums
  or •ni\a

Mil•ler (*last name*)

mill\er (*one who mills*)

mil•let

mill\li•gram

mil\li•li•ter

mill\li•me•ter

mil•li•ner

mil•li•ner\y (*women's hats*)
  [*vs.* mil•le•nar\y (*a thousand*)]

mil•lion, *pl.* •lions or •lion

mil•lion•aire

mil•lionth

mil\li•pede

mill•race

mill•stone

mill•stream

mill•wright

milque•toast

milt

Mil•ton

Mil•wau•kee

mime, mimed, mim•ing

mim\e\o•graph, •graphed,
  •graph•ing

mi•me•sis

mi•met•ic

mim\ic, •icked, •ick•ing

mim•ic\ry, *pl.* •ries

mi•mo\sa, *pl.* •sas

min\a•ret

min\a•to\ry

mince (*to chop fine*),
  minced, minc•ing [*vs.*
  mints (*candies*)]

mince•meat

mind, mind\ed, mind•ing

mind-•blow\ing

mind•ful

mind•less

mine, mined, min•ing

min\er (*mine worker*) [*vs.*
  mi•nor (*lesser*)]

min•er•al

min•er•al\o•gist

min•er•al\o•gy

Mi•ner\va

min\e\stro\ne

mine•sweep\er

min•gle, •gled, •gling

min\i, *pl.* min\is

min\i•a•ture

min\i•a•tur•ist

min\i•a•tur\i•za•tion

min\i•a•tur•ize, •ized,
  •iz•ing

min\i•bike

min\i•bus

min\i•com•put\er

min\im

min\i•mal

minimal re•cal•cu•la•tion

min\i•mal•ism

min\i•mal•ist

min\i•mal\ly

min\i•max

min\i•mi•za•tion

min\i•mize, •mized,
  •miz•ing

min\i•mum, *pl.* •mums or
  \ma

minimum wage

min•ion

min\i•se•ries, *pl.* •ries

min\i•skirt

min•is•ter, •tered, •ter•ing

min•is•te\ri•al

min•is•trant

min•is•tra•tion

min•is•try, *pl.* •tries

mink, *pl.* minks or mink

Min•ne•ap\o•lis

min\ne•sing\er

Min•ne•so\ta (*MN*)

Min•ne•so•tan

min•now, *pl.* •nows or
  •now

Mi•no\an

mi•nor (*lesser*) [*vs.* min\er
  (*mine worker*)]

mi•nor•i\ty, *pl.* •ties

minority in•ter•est

min•strel

min•strel show

min•strel\sy

mints (*candies*) [*vs.* mince
  (*to chop fine*)]

mint, mint\ed, mint•ing

mint ju•lep

mint\y, •i\er, •i•est

min\u•end

min•u\et

mi•nus

mi•nus•cule

mi•nus sign

mi•nute (*to note down; 60
  seconds*), •ut\ed, •ut•ing

mi•nute (*very small*),
  •nut•est

mi•nute\ly

Min•ute•man, *pl.* •men

mi•nute•ness

mi•nute steak

mi•nu•ti\a, *pl.* •ti\ae

minx

Mi\o•cene

MIPS (*million instructions
  per second*)

mir\a•cle

mi•rac\u•lous

mi•rac\u•lous\ly

mi•rage (*illusion*) [*vs.*
  mar•riage (*wedding*)]

mire

mir•ror, •rored, •ror•ing

mirth

mirth•ful

MIS (*management informa-
  tion system*)

mis•ad•ven•ture

mis•al•li•ance

mis•an•thrope

mis•an•throp\ic

mis•an•thro\py

mis•ap•pre•hend,
  •hend\ed, •hend•ing

mis•ap•pre•hen•sion

mis•ap•pro•pri•ate, •at\ed,
  •at•ing

mis•ap•pro•pri•a•tion

mis•be•got•ten

mis•be•have, •haved,
  •hav•ing

mis•be•hav•ior

misc. (*miscellaneous*)

mis•call, •called, •call•ing

mis•car•riage

mis•car\ry, •ried, •ry•ing

mis•cast, •cast, •cast•ing

mis•ceg\e\e•na•tion

mis•cel•la•ne•ous

mis•cel•la\ny, *pl.* •nies

mis•chance

mis•chief

mis•chie•vous

mis•chie•vous\ly

mis•con•ceive, •ceived, •ceiv•ing

mis•con•cep•tion

mis•con•duct, •duct\ed, •duct•ing

mis•con•strue, •strued, •stru•ing

mis•count, •count\ed, •count•ing

mis•cre•ant

mis•cue

mis•deed

mis•de•mean\or

mis•di•rect, •rect\ed, •rect•ing

mise-•en-•scène, *pl.* •scènes

mi•ser

mis•er•a•ble

mis•er•a•bly

mi•ser•li•ness

mi•ser\ly

mis•er\y, *pl.* •er•ies

mis•fea•sance

mis•fire, •fired, •fir•ing

mis•fit

mis•for•tune

mis•giv•ing

mis•guide, •guid\ed, •guid•ing

mis•han•dle, •dled, •dling

mis•hap

mish•mash

mis•in•form, •formed, •form•ing

mis•in•for•ma•tion

mis•in•ter•pret, •pret\ed, •pret•ing

mis•in•ter•pre•ta•tion

mis•judge, •judged, •judg•ing

mis•judg•ment

mis•lay, •laid, •lay•ing

mis•lead, •led, •lead•ing

mis•man•age, •aged, •ag•ing

mis•man•age•ment

mis•match, •matched, •match•ing

mis•no•mer

mi•sog\a•mist

mi•sog•a\my (*hostility to marriage*)

mi•sog\y•nist

mi•sog•y\ny (*hostility to women*)

mis•place, •placed, •plac•ing

mis•play, •played, •play•ing

mis•print, •print\ed, •print•ing

mis•pri•sion

mis•pro•nounce, •nounced, •nounc•ing

mis•pro•nun•ci•a•tion

mis•quote, •quot\ed, •quot•ing

mis•read, •read, •read•ing

mis•rep•re•sent, •sent\ed, •sent•ing

mis•rep•re•sen•ta•tion

mis•rule

miss, *pl.* miss\es; missed, miss•ing

mis•sal (*prayer book*) [vs. mis•sile (*weapon*) and mis•sive (*letter*)]

missed (*failed*) [vs. mist (*haze*)]

mis•shap\en

mis•sile (*weapon*) [vs. mis•sal (*prayer book*) and mis•sive (*letter*)]

mis•sile\ry

miss•ing

mis•sion

mis•sion•ar\y, *pl.* •ar•ies

Mis•sis•sip\pi (*MS*)

Mis•sis•sip•pi\an

mis•sive (*letter*) [vs. mis•sal (*prayer book*) and mis•sile (*weapon*)]

Mis•sour\i (*MO*)

Mis•sour•i\an

mis•spell, •spelled, •spell•ing

mis•spell•ing

mis•spend, •spent, •spend•ing

mis•state, •stat\ed, •stat•ing

mis•state•ment

mis•step

mist (*haze; to become misty*), mist\ed, mist•ing [vs. missed (*failed*)]

mis•take, •took, •tak\en, •tak•ing

mis•tak•en\ly

mis•ter

mist\i•ness

mis•tle•toe

mis•treat, •treat\ed, •treat•ing

mis•treat•ment

mis•tress

mis•tri\al

mis•trust, •trust\ed, •trust•ing

mis•trust•ful

mist\y, •i\er, •i•est

mis•un•der•stand, •stood, •stand•ing

mis•un•der•stand•ing

mis•use, •used, •us•ing

mite (*small thing*) [vs. might (*power*)]

mit\i•gate (*to make less severe*), •gat\ed, •gat•ing [vs. mil\i•tate (*to have an effect*)]

mit\i•ga•tion

mi•to•sis

mitt

mit•ten

mix, mixed, mix•ing

mixed cost

mixed e\con•o\my

mixed-•up

mix\er

mix•ture

mix-•up

Mlle. (*mademoiselle*), *pl.* Mlles.

MM. (*messieurs*)

Mme. (*madame*), pl.
  Mmes.
MN (*Minnesota*)
mne•mon\ic (*aiding the
  memory*) [*vs.*
  pneu•mon\ic (*of the
  lungs*)]
MO (*Missouri*)
moan, moaned, moan•ing
moat (*trench*) [*vs.* mote
  (*speck*)]
mob, mobbed, mob•bing
mo•bile
mo•bil•i\ty
mo•bi•li•za•tion
mo•bi•lize, •lized, •liz•ing
mob•ster
moc•ca•sin
mo•cha
mock, mocked, mock•ing
mock•er\y
mock•ing•bird
mock•ing\ly
mock-•up or mock\up
mod
mod\al (*of a mode*) [*vs.*
  mod\el (*example*)]
mo•dal•i\ty
mode (*manner*) [*vs.*
  mowed (*cut down*)]
mod\el (*example*); •eled or
  •elled, •el•ing or •el•ling
  [*vs.* mod\al (*of a mode*)]
mo•dem (*modulator-
  demodulator*)
mod•er•ate, •at\ed, •at•ing
mod•er•ate\ly
mod•er•a•tion
mod•er\a•tor
mod•ern
mod•ern•ism
mod•ern•ist
mod•ern•is•tic
mo•der•ni\ty
mod•ern\i•za•tion
mod•ern•ize, •ized, •iz•ing
mod•ern•ness
mod•est
mod•est\ly
mod•es\ty
mod\i•cum

mod\i•fi•ca•tion
mod\i•fi•er
mod•i\fy, •fied, •fy•ing
mod•ish
mod•ish\ly
mod•ish•ness
mo•diste
mod\u•lar
modular ar•chi•tec•ture
mod\u•late, •lat\ed,
  •lat•ing
mod\u•la•tion
mod\u•la•tor
mod\u•la\tor-
  •de\mod\u\la\tor
  (*modem*)
mod•ule
mo•dus op\e•ran\di
mo•gul
mo•hair
Mo•ham•med
Mo•ham•med\an
Mo•ham•med•an•ism
Mo•hawk, *pl.* •hawks or
  •hawk
Mo•he•gan, *pl.* •gans or
  •gan
Mo•hi•can, *pl.* •cans or
  •can
moi•e\ty, *pl.* •ties
moi\ré, *pl.* •rés
moist, \er, •est
mois•ten, •tened, •ten•ing
moist•en\er
moist\ly
moist•ness
mois•ture
mois•tur•ize, •ized, •iz•ing
mois•tur•iz\er
mo•lar
mo•las•ses
mold, mold\ed, mold•ing
mold\er, •ered, •er•ing
mold•ing
mold\y, •i\er, •i•est
mole
mo•lec\u•lar
mol\e\cule
mole•hill
mole•skin
mo•lest, •lest\ed, •lest•ing

mo•les•ta•tion
mo•lest\er
Mo•lière
moll
mol•li•fi•ca•tion
mol•li•fi\er
mol•li\fy, •fied, •fy•ing
mol•lusk or mol•lusc
mol•ly•cod•dle, •dled,
  •dling
molt, molt\ed, molt•ing
mol•ten
mo•lyb•de•num
mom
mom-•and-•pop store
mo•ment
mo•men•tar•i\ly
mo•men•tar\y
mo•men•tous
mo•men•tous•ness
mo•men•tum, *pl.* \ta or
  •tums
mom\my or mom•mie, *pl.*
  •mies
Mon•a\co
mon•arch
mo•nar•chi•cal or
  mo•nar•chic
mon•ar•chism
mon•ar•chist
mon•ar•chist\ic
mon•ar•chy, *pl.* •chies
mon•as•ter\y, *pl.* •ter•ies
mo•nas•tic
mo•nas•ti•cism
mon•au•ral
Mon•day
mon\e•tar•i\ly
mon\e•ta•rism
mon\e•ta•rist
mon\e•tar\y
mon•ey
mon•eys or mon•ies
mon•ey•bags
mon\ey-•chang\er
mon•eyed
mon\ey•lend\er
mon\ey•mak\er
mon\ey•mak•ing
mon\ey mar•ket
money of ac•count

money or•der
Mon•gol
Mon•go•li\a
Mon•go•li\an
mon•gol•ism
Mon•gol•oid
mon•goose, pl. •goos\es
mon•grel
mon•ied
mon\i•ker or mon\ick\er
mon\i•tor, •tored,
•tor•ing
monk
mon•key, pl. •keys; •keyed,
•key•ing
mon\key•shines
mon•key wrench
mon\o
mon\o•chro•mat•ic
mon\o•chro•mat\i•cal\ly
mon\o•chrome
monochrome mon\i•tor
mon\o•cle
mon\o•cled
mon\o•clo•nal
mon\o•cot\y•le•don•ous
mo•nog\a•mous
mo•nog\a•mous\ly
mo•nog\a•my
mon\o•gram, •grammed,
•gram•ming
mon\o•graph
mon\o•lin•gual
mon\o•lith
mon\o•lith\ic
mon\o•log•ist or
mon\o•logu•ist
mon\o•logue or
mon\o•log
mon\o•ma•ni\a, pl. •ni\as
mon\o•ma•ni\ac
mon\o•mer
mon\o•nu•cle•o•sis
mon\o•phon\ic
mo•nop\o•list
mo•nop\o•lis•tic
mo•nop\o•lize, •lized,
•liz•ing
mo•nop\o\ly, pl. •lies
mo•nop•so\ny, pl. •nies
mon\o•rail

mon\o•so•di\um
glu•ta•mate (MSG)
mon\o•spac•ing
mon\o•syl•lab\ic
mon\o•syl•la•ble
mon\o•the•ism
mon\o•the•ist
mon\o•the•is•tic
mon\o•tone
mo•not\o•nous
mo•not\o•nous\ly
mo•not\o•nous•ness
mo•not•o\ny
mon•ox•ide
Mon•roe
mon•sei•gneur, pl.
mes•sei•gneurs
mon•sieur, pl. mes•sieurs
mon•si•gnor, pl.
mon•si•gnors or
mon•si•gno\ri
mon•soon
mon•ster
mon•stros•i\ty
mon•strous
mon•tage, pl. •tag\es
Mon•tan\a (MT)
Mon•tan\an
Mon•te Car\lo
Mon•tes•so\ri meth\od
Mon•te•vi•de\o
Mont•gom•er\y
month
month\ly, pl. •lies
Mont•pel•ier
Mont•re\al
mon•u•ment
mon•u•men•tal
mon•u•men•tal\ly
moo, pl. moos; mooed,
moo•ing
mooch, mooched,
mooch•ing
mood
mood•i\ly
mood\i•ness
mood\y, •i\er, •i•est
moon
moon•beam
moon•light
moon•light•ing

moon•lit
moon•scape
moon•shine
moon•shot or moon shot
moon•stone
moon•struck
moon•walk
moor, moored, moor•ing
Moor•ish
moose (the animal), pl.
moose [vs. mouse (the
rodent) and mousse
(whipped dessert)]
moot (debatable) [vs.
mute (silent)]
mop, mopped, mop•ping
mope, moped (brooded),
mop•ing
mo•ped (motorized bicycle
with pedals)
mop•pet
mo•raine
mor\al (ethical)
mo•rale (mood)
mor•al•ist
mor•al•is•tic
mor•al•is•ti•cal\ly
mo•ral•i\ty, pl. •ties
mor•al•ize, •ized, •iz•ing
mor•al\ly
mo•rass
mor\a•to•ri\um, pl.
•to•ri\a or •to•ri•ums
mo•ray, pl. •rays
mor•bid
mor•bid•i\ty
mor•bid\ly
more
mo•rel
more•o\ver
mo•res
morgue
mor\i•bund
Mor•mon
Mor•mon•ism
morn (morning) [vs.
mourn (to grieve)]
morn•ing (early part of day)
[vs. mourn•ing (grieving)]
morn•ing glo\ry or
morn•ing–glo\ry

Mo•roc•can
Mo•roc\co
mo•ron
mo•ron\ic
mo•ron\i•cal\ly
mo•rose
mo•rose\ly
mo•rose•ness
mor•pheme
mor•phe•mic
mor•phine
mor•pho•log\i•cal
mor•phol•o\gy
mor•row
Morse code
mor•sel
mor•tal•i\ty, pl. •ties
mor•tal\ly
mor•tar, •tared, •tar•ing
mor\tar•board
mort•gage, •gaged,
•gag•ing
mortgage bond
mort•ga•gee
mort•ga•gor or
mort•gag\er
mor•ti•cian
mor•ti•fi•ca•tion
mor•ti\fy, •fied, •fy•ing
mor•tise
mor•tu•ar\y, pl. •ar•ies
mo•sa\ic (inlaid stone)
Mo•sa\ic (of Moses)
Mos•cow
Mo•ses
mo•sey, •seyed, •sey•ing
Mos•lem, pl. •lems, •lem
mosque
mos•qui\to, pl. •toes or
•tos
moss
moss•back
moss\y, •i\er, •i•est
most
most\ly
mote (speck) [vs. moat
(trench)]
mo•tel
mo•tet
moth, pl. moths

moth•ball, •balled,
•ball•ing
moth\er, •ered, •er•ing
moth•er•board
moth•er•hood
moth\er-•in-•law, pl.
moth\ers-•in-•law
moth\er•land
moth\er•less
moth\er•li•ness
moth•er\ly
moth\er-of-•pearl
mo•tif (theme) [vs.
mo•tive (purpose)]
mo•tile
mo•til•i\ty
mo•tion, •tioned, •tion•ing
mo•tion•less
mo•tion pic•ture
mo•ti•vate, •vat•ed,
•vat•ing
mo•ti•va•tion
mo•ti•va•tion\al
mo•tive (purpose) [vs.
mo•tif (theme)]
mot•ley
mo\to•cross
mo•tor, •tored, •tor•ing
mo\tor•bike
mo\tor•boat
mo\tor•cade
mo\tor•car
mo\tor•cy•cle, •cled,
•cling
mo\tor•cy•clist
mo•tor•ist
mo\tor•man, pl. •men
mot•tle, •tled, •tling
mot\to, pl. •toes or •tos
moue, pl. moues
mound
mount, mount\ed,
mount•ing
moun•tain
moun•tain•eer
moun•tain•ous
Moun•tain stand•ard time
(MST)
moun•tain•top
moun•te•bank
Moun•tie, pl. •ties

mount•ing
mourn (to grieve),
mourned, mourn•ing [vs.
morn (morning)]
mourn\er
mourn•ful
mourn•ful\ly
mourn•ing (grieving) [vs.
morn•ing (early part of
day)]
mouse (the rodent), pl.
mice [vs. moose (the
animal) and mousse
(whipped dessert)]
mouse point\er
mouse•pad
mous\er
mouse•trap
mous\i•ness
mousse (whipped dessert)
[vs. moose (the animal)
and mouse (the rodent)]
mous•tache
mous\y, •i\er, •i•est
mouth, pl. mouths;
mouthed, mouth•ing
mouth•ful, pl. •fuls
mouth•part
mouth•piece
mouth•wash
mouth-•wa\ter\ing
mou•ton (sheepskin fur)
[vs. mut•ton (meat from
sheep)]
mov•a\ble or
move•a\ble
movable rul\er
move, moved, mov•ing
move•ment
mov\er
mov\ie
mov•ing
mov\ing-•bar men\u
mow, mowed (cut down),
mowed or mown,
mow•ing [vs. mode
(manner)]
Mo•zam•bique
Mo•zart
Mo•zar•te\an
moz•za•rel\la

mpg or m.p.g. (*miles per gallon*)

mph or m.p.h. (*miles per hour*)

Mr., *pl.* Messrs.

MRI (*magnetic resonance imaging*)

Mrs., *pl.* Mmes.

MS (*Mississippi*)

Ms., *pl.* Mses.

MSG (*monosodium glutamate*)

MSI (*Marketing Science Institute*)

MST or M.S.T. (*Mountain standard time*)

MT (*Montana*)

MTBF (*mean time between failures*)

mtg. (*mortgage*)

mu

much, more, most

mu•ci•lage

mu•ci•lag\i•nous

muck

muck•r ak\er

mu•cous (*of mucus*)

mu•cus (*body substance*)

mud

mud•di•ness

mud•dle, •dled, •dling

mud\dle•head\ed

mud\dy, •died, •dy•ing; •di\er, •di•est

mud•sling•ing

muen•ster

mu•ez•zin

muff, muffed, muff•ing

muf•fin

muf•fle

muf•fler

muf\ti, *pl.* •tis

mug, mugged, mug•ging

mug•ger

mug•gi•ness

mug\gy, •gi\er, •gi•est

mug•wump

Mu•ham•mad

Mu•ham•mad\an

Mu•ham•mad•an•ism

muk•luk

mu•lat\to, *pl.* •toes

mul•ber\ry, *pl.* •ries

mulch

mule

mul•ish

mull, mulled, mull•ing

mul•lah, *pl.* •lahs

mul•lein

mul•let, *pl.* •let or •lets

mul•li•gan stew

mul•li•ga•taw\ny

mul\ti•dis•ci•pli\nar\y

mul\ti•far\i•ous

mul\ti•far\i•ous•ly

mul\ti•far\i•ous•ness

mul\ti•form

mul\ti•fre•quen\cy

mon\i•tor

mul\ti•func•tion

pe•riph•er\al

mul\ti•me•di\a

mul\ti•na\tion\al

mul•ti•ple

mul\ti\ple-•choice

mul\ti•ple scle•ro•sis

mul\ti•plex, •plexed, •plex•ing

mul\ti•pli•cand

mul\ti•pli•ca•tion

mul\ti•plic\i•ty, *pl.* •ties

mul\ti•pli\er

multiplier ef•fect

mul•ti•ply, •plied, •ply•ing

mul•ti•ply

mul\ti•proc•ess\ing

mul\ti•scan•ning

mon\i•tor

mul\ti•stage

mul\ti•task•ing

mul•ti•tude

mul•ti•tu•di•nous

mul\ti•us\er

mul\ti•vi•ta•min

mum

mum•ble, •bled, •bling

mum•bler

mum\ble•ty•peg

mum\bo jum\bo

mum•mi•fi•ca•tion

mum•mi\fy, •fied, •fy•ing

mum\my, *pl.* •mies; •mied, •my•ing

mumps

munch, munched, munch•ing

mun•dane

Mu•nich

mu•nic\i•pal

municipal bond

mu•nic\i•pal•i\ty, *pl.* •ties

mu•nif\i•cence

mu•nif\i•cent

mu•nif\i•cent\ly

mu•ral

mu•ral•ist

mur•der, •dered, •der•ing

mur•der\er

mur•der•ess

mur•der•ous

mur•der•ous\ly

murk

murk•i\ly

murk\i•ness

murk\y, •i\er, •i•est

mur•mur, •mured, •mur•ing

mus•ca•tel

mus•cle (*body tissue*), •cled, •cling [vs. mus•sel (*shellfish*)]

mus\cle•bound

mus•cu•lar

mus•cu•lar dys•tro•phy

mus•cu•lar•i\ty

mus•cu•la•ture

muse, mused, mus•ing

mu•sette

mu•se\um

mush, mushed, mush•ing

mush\i•ness

mush•room, •roomed, •room•ing

mush\y, •i\er, •i•est

mu•sic

mu•si•cal (*of music*)

mu•si•cale (*musical gathering*)

mu•si•cal•i\ty

mu•si•cal\ly

mu•si•cian

mu•si•cian•ship

mu•si•col\o•gist

mu•si•col•o\gy

musk
mus•kel•lunge, *pl.* •lung\es or •lunge
mus•ket
mus•ket•eer
musk\i•ness
musk•mel\on
musk\ox or musk ox, *pl.* •ox\en
musk•rat, *pl.* •rats or •rat
Mus•lim (*adherent of the religion*), *pl.* •lims or •lim
mus•lin (*cotton fabric*)
muss, mussed, muss•ing
mus•sel (*shellfish*) [vs. mus•cle (*body tissue*)]
Mus•so•li\ni
muss
muss\y, •i\er, •i•est
must
mus•tache or mous•tache
mus•tached
mus•tang
mus•tard (*pungent condiment*)
mus•ter, •tered (*gathered*), •ter•ing
mus•ti•ness
must\n't

mus\ty, •i\er, •i•est
mu•ta•bil•i\ty
mu•ta\ble
mu•tant
mu•tate, •tat\ed, •tat•ing
mu•ta•tion
mute (*silent*), mut\er, mut\est; mut\ed, mut•ing [vs. moot (*debatable*)]
mute\ly
mute•ness
mu•ti•late, •lat\ed, •lat•ing
mu•ti•la•tion
mu•ti•neer
mu•ti•nous
mu•ti\ny, *pl.* •nies; •nied, •ny•ing
mutt
mut•ter, •tered, •ter•ing
mut•ton (*meat from sheep*) [vs. mou•ton (*sheepskin fur*)]
mu•tu\al
mutual fund
mu•tu•al\ly
muu•muu, *pl.* •muus
muz•zle, •zled, •zling
my
My•an•mar

my•as•the•ni\a
my•as•then\ic
my•col\o•gist
my•col•o\gy
my•e\li•tis
My\lar (™)
my\na or my•nah, *pl.* •nas or •nahs
my•o•pi\a
my•op\ic
myr•i\ad
myrrh
myr•tle
my•self
mys•te•ri•ous
mys•te•ri•ous\ly
mys•ter\y, *pl.* •ter•ies
mys•tic
mys•ti•cal
mys•ti•cal\ly
mys•ti•cism
mys•ti•fi•ca•tion
mys•ti\fy, •fied, •fy•ing
mys•tique
myth
myth\i•cal
myth\o•log\i•cal
my•thol\o•gist
my•thol\o\gy, *pl.* •gies

N

NA or N.A. (*not applicable*)
nab, nabbed, nab•bing
na•bob
na•cre•ous
na•dir
nag, nagged, nag•ging
Na•hua\tl
nai\ad, *pl.* •ads or •a•des
nail, nailed, nail•ing
Nai•ro\bi
na•ive or na•ïve
na•ive\ly
na•ive\té or na•ïve\té
na•ked
na•ked\ly
na•ked•ness
nam\by-•pam\by, *pl.* \bies
name, named, nam•ing
name•a\ble

name brand
name\less
name\ly
name•plate
name•sake
Na•mib•i\a
Na•mib•i\an
nan•keen
Nan•king
nan\ny, *pl.* •nies
nan\o•sec•ond
nap, napped, nap•ping
na•palm, •palmed, •palm•ing
nape
naph•tha
naph•tha•lene or naph•tha•line
nap•kin
Na•ples

na•po•le•on
Na•po•le•on•ic
narc or nark
nar•cis•sism
nar•cis•sist (*self-centered person*)
nar•cis•sis•tic
nar•cis•sus (*the flower*), *pl.* •cis•sus or •cis•sus\es or •cis\si
nar•co•sis
nar•cot\ic
nar\es, *pl.* nar\is
nar•rate, •rat\ed, •rat•ing
nar•ra•tion
nar•ra•tive
nar•ra•tor
nar•row, •rowed, •row•ing; •row\er, •row•est

nar•row•ly

nar\row-•mind\ed

nar\row-•mind\ed\ness

nar•whal

nar\y

NASA (*National Aeronautics and Space Administration*)

na•sal

na•sal•i\ty

na•sal\i•za•tion

na•sal•ize, •ized, •iz•ing

na•sal\ly

nas•cence

nas•cent

NASDAQ (*National Association of Securities Dealers Automated Quotations*)

Nash•ville

nas•ti\ly

nas•ti•ness

nas•tur•tium, *pl.* •tiums

nas\ty, *pl.* •ties; •ti\er, •ti•est

na•tal

na•tes, *pl.*

na•tion

na•tion\al

national bank

national brand

national debt

na•tion•al•ism

na•tion•al•ist

na•tion•al•is•tic

na•tion•al•i\ty, *pl.* •ties

na•tion•al\i•za•tion

na•tion•al•ize, •ized, •iz•ing

na•tion•al\ly

na•tion•hood

na•tion•wide

na•tive

Na•tive A\mer\i•can

na•tiv•ism

na•tiv•i\ty, *pl.* •ties

nat\ty, •ti\er, •ti•est

nat\u•ral

nat\u•ral•ism

nat\u•ral•ist

nat\u•ral•is•tic

nat\u•ral\i•za•tion

nat\u•ral•ize, •ized, •iz•ing

nat\u•ral\ly

nat\u•ral se•lec•tion

na•ture

Nau•ga•hyde (™)

naught *or* nought [*vs.* nou•gat (*candy*)]

naugh•t\ly

naugh•ti•ness

naugh\ty, •ti\er, •ti•est

nau•se\a

nau•se•ate, •at\ed, •at•ing

nau•se•at•ing\ly

nau•seous

nau•ti•cal

nau•ti•cal\ly

nau•ti•lus, *pl.* nau•ti•lus\es *or* nau•ti\li

Nav•a\jo *or* Nav•a\ho, *pl.* •jos *or* •joes *or* \jo; •hos *or* •hoes *or* \ho

na•val (*of a ship*)

nave (*church area*) [*vs.* knave (*rogue*)]

na•vel (*umbilicus*)

na•vel or•ange

nav\i•ga•bil•i\ty

nav\i•ga\ble

nav\i•gate, •gat\ed, •gat•ing

nav\i•ga•tion

nav\i•ga•tor

na\vy, *pl.* •vies

nay (*no*) [*vs.* neigh (*whinny*) *and* nee (*born*)]

nay•say\er

Naz\a•reth

Na\zi, *pl.* •zis

Na•zism

N-\bomb (*neutron bomb*)

NBS *or* N.B.S. (*National Bureau of Standards*)

NC (*North Carolina*)

n/c *or* NC (*no charge*)

NC-•17 (*motion-picture rating*)

ND (*North Dakota*)

NE (*Nebraska*)

Ne•an•der•thal

neap

Ne•a•pol\i•tan

near, neared, near•ing; near\er, near•est

near\by

near-•let\ter qual•i\ty

near\ly

near mon\ey

near•ness

near•sight\ed

near•sight•ed•ness

neat, \er, •est

neath *or* 'neath

neat\ly

neat•ness

Ne•bras\ka (*NE*)

Ne•bras•kan

neb•u\la, *pl.* •lae *or* •las

neb\u•lar

neb\u•lous

nec•es•sar•i\ly

nec•es•sar\y

ne•ces•si•tate, •tat\ed, •tat•ing

ne•ces•si\ty, *pl.* •ties

neck, necked, neck•ing

neck•er•chief

neck•lace

neck•line

neck•tie

ne•crol•o\o\gy, *pl.* •gies

nec\ro•man•cer

nec\ro•man•cy

ne•crop\o•lis, *pl.* •lis\es

ne•cro•sis

ne•crot\ic

nec•tar

nec•tar•ine

nee *or* née (*born*) [*vs.* nay (*no*) *and* neigh (*whinny*)]

need (*to require*), need\ed, need•ing, needs *or* need [*vs.* knead (*to work dough*)]

need•ful

need\i•ness

nee•dle, •dled, •dling

nee\dle•point

need•less

need•less\ly

need•less•ness

nee•dle trades

nee\dle•work

need\n't
needs
need\y, •i\er, •i•est
ne'er
ne'er-•do-well
ne•far\i•ous
ne•gate, •gat\ed, •gat•ing
ne•ga•tion
neg\a•tive
negative float
negative in•come
negative income tax
neg\a•tive\ly
neg\a•tive•ness
neg\a•tive op•tion
neg\a•tiv•ism
neg\a•tiv•i\ty
ne•glect, •glect\ed,
   •glect•ing
ne•glect\ful
ne•glect\ful\ly
neg•li•gee or neg•li•gée, pl.
   •gees or •gées
neg•li•gence
neg•li•gent (careless)
neg•li•gent\ly
neg•li•gi\ble (unimportant)
ne•go•ti•a•bil•i\ty
ne•go•ti•a•ble
negotiable bond
negotiable in•stru•ment
ne•go•ti•ate, •at\ed,
   •at•ing
ne•go•ti•a•tion
ne•go•ti•a•tor
Neg•ri•tude
Ne•gro, pl. •groes
Ne•groid
Neh\ru
neigh (whinny) [vs. nay
   (no) and nee (born)]
neigh•bor
neigh•bor•hood
neigh•bor•ing
neigh•bor•li•ness
neigh•bor\ly
nei•ther (not either) [vs.
   neth\er (lower)]
nel•son
nem\a•tode
nem\e•sis, pl. •ses

ne\o•clas•si•cal
ne\o•clas•si•cism
ne\o•co•lo•ni•al
ne\o•co•lo•ni•al•ism
ne\o•dym•i\um
Ne\o•lith\ic
ne•ol\o•gism
ne\on
ne\o•na•tal
ne\o•nate
ne\o•phyte
ne\o•plasm
ne\o•plas•tic
ne\o•prene
Ne•pal
Nep\a•lese
ne•pen•the
neph\ew
ne•phrit•ic
ne•phri•tis
ne plus ul•tra
nep\o•tism
nep\o•tist
Nep•tune
nep•tu•ni•um
nerd\y, •i\er, •i•est
Ne\ro
nerve, nerved, nerv•ing
nerve cell
nerve•less
nerv•ous
nerv•ous\ly
nerv•ous•ness
nerv\y, •i\er, •i•est
nest, nest\ed, nest•ing
nest\er
nes•tle, nes•tled, nes•tling
   (pressing affectionately)
nest•ling (young bird)
net, net•ted, net•ting
net earn•ings
neth\er (lower) [vs.
   nei•ther (not either)]
Neth\er•lands
neth\er•most
neth\er world or
   neth\er•world
net in•come
net prof\it
net sales

net•ting
net•tle
net•tle•some
net•work, •worked,
   •work•ing
net•work\er
net•work•ing
net•work in\ter•face card
network serv\er
net worth
neu•ral
neu•ral•gia
neu•ral•gic
neu•ral net•work
neur•as•the•ni\a
neur•as•then\ic
neu•ri•tis
neu\ro•log\i•cal
neu•rol\o•gist
neu•rol\o•gy
neu•ron
neu•ron\al
neu\ro•sis, pl. •ses
neu\ro•sur•geon
neu\ro•sur•ger\y
neu•rot\ic
neu•rot•ic•al\ly
neu•rot\i•cism
neu\ro•trans•mit•ter
neu•ter (asexual), •tered,
   •ter•ing
neu•tral (not taking sides)
neu•tral•ism
neu•tral•ist
neu•tral•i\ty
neu•tral\i•za•tion
neu•tral•ize, •ized, •iz•ing
neu•tral\ly
neu•tri\no, pl. •nos
neu•tron
Ne•vad\a (NV)
Ne•vad\an
nev\er
nev\er•more
nev\er-•nev\er land
nev\er•the•less
ne•vus, pl. \vi
new (recent), \er, •est [vs.
   gnu (antelope) and knew
   (did know)]
New•ark

New Bed•ford
new•born, *pl.* •born *or*
  •borns
New Bruns•wick
new•com•er
new\el
New Eng•land
New Eng•land•er
new•fan•gled
new-•fash\ioned
New•found•land
New Hamp•shire (*NH*)
New Hamp•shir•ite
New Jer•sey (*NJ*)
New Jer•sey•ite
new•ly
new•ly•wed
New Mex•ico (*NM*)
new•ness
New Or•le\ans
New•port News
news
news•boy
news•cast
news•cast•er
news•deal•er
news•let•ter
news•man, *pl.* •men
news•pa•per
news•pa•per•man, *pl.*
  •men
news•pa\per•wom\an, *pl.*
  •wom\en
new•speak
news•print
news•reel
news•stand
news•wor•thi•ness
news•wor•thy
news\y, news•i\er,
  news•i•est
newt
New Tes•ta•ment
new•ton
New•to•ni\an
New York (*NY*)
New York\er
New York Stock
  Ex•change (*NYSE*)
New Zea•land
New Zea•land\er

next
next-•door
nex\us, *pl.* nex\us
Nez Percé, *pl.* Nez
  Per•cés *or* Nez Percé
NF (*no funds*)
NH (*New Hampshire*)
ni•a•cin
Ni•ag\a\ra Falls
nib
nib•ble, •bled, •bling
nibs (*his or her nibs*)
Nic\a•ra•gua
Nic\a•ra•guan
nice, nic\er, nic•est
nice\ly
nice•ness
ni•ce\ty, *pl.* \ties
niche (*recess*)
nick (*dent; to dent*),
  dent\ed, dent•ing
nick\el, •eled *or* •elled,
  •el•ing *or* •el•ling
nick\el•o\de\on
nick\el•er, •ered, •er•ing
nick•name, •named,
  •nam•ing
nic\o•tine
nic\o•tin\ic ac\id
niece
Nie•tzsche
nif\ty, •ti\er, •ti•est
Ni•ger
Ni•ge•ri\a
Ni•ge•ri\an
nig•gard\ly
nig•gling
nigh
night (*darkness*)] [*vs.*
  knight (*noble*)]
night•cap
night•clothes
night•club, •clubbed,
  •club•bing
night•fall
night•gown
night•hawk
night\ie, *pl.* •ies
night\ly
night•mare

night•mar•ish
night•shade
night•shirt
night•spot
night•time
night•walk\er
ni•hil•ism
ni•hil•ist
ni•hil•is•tic
nil
Nile
nim•ble
nim•ble•ness
nim•bly
nim•bus, *pl.* \bi *or* •bus\es
Nim•rod
nin•com•poop
nine
nine•pins
nine•teen
nine•teenth
nine•ti•eth
nine\ty, *pl.* •ties
nin\ny, *pl.* •nies
ninth
ni•o•bi\um
nip, nipped, nip•ping
nip•per
nip•ple
Nip•pon
Nip•pon•ese
nip\py, •pi\er, •pi•est
nir•va\na
Ni•sei, *pl.* •sei
ni\si
nit (*insect egg*) [*vs.* knit (*to
  join*)]
ni•ter
nit•pick *or* nit-•pick,
  •picked, •pick•ing *or*
  •pick\ing
nit•pick\er
ni•trate
ni•tric ac\id
ni•trite
ni\tro•gen
ni•trog\e\nous
ni•tro•glyc•er\in
ni•trous ox•ide
nit\ty-•grit\ty
nit•wit

nix, nixed, nix•ing
Nix\on
NJ (*New Jersey*)
NLRB (*National Labor Relations Board*)
NM (*New Mexico*)
No
no (*negative*) [*vs.* know (*to understand*)]
no, *pl.* noes *or* nos
No\ah
No•bel•ist
No•bel•i\um
No•bel prize
no•bil•i\ty
no•ble, •bler, •blest
no\ble•man, *pl.* •men
no\ble•ness
no•blesse o\blige
no\ble•wom\an, *pl.* •wom\en
no•bly
no•bod\y, *pl.* •bod•ies
noc•tur•nal
noc•turne
nod, nod•ded, nod•ding
nod\al
node
nod\u•lar
nod•ule
No\el
no-•fault
no-•fault in•sur•ance
no-•frills serv•ice
no-•good
noise, noised, nois•ing
noise•less
noise•less\ly
noise•mak•er
nois•i\ly
nois\i•ness
noi•some (*obnoxious*)
nois\y (*loud*), •i\er, •i•est
nol\le pros\e\qui
no\lo con•ten•de\re
no-•load fund
no•mad
no•mad\ic
nom de plume, *pl.* noms de plume
no•men•cla•ture

nom\i•nal
nominal cap\i•tal
nominal val\ue
nominal wag\es
nom\i•nal\ly
nom\i•nate, •nat\ed, •nat•ing
nom\i•na•tion
nom\i•na•tive
nom\i•nee
non•age
non\a•ge•nar•i\an
non•a•ligned
non•a•lign•ment
non•ap•pear•ance
nonce
non•cha•lance
non•cha•lant
non•cha•lant\ly
non•com
non•com•bat•ant
non•com•mis•sioned of•fi•cer
non•com•mit•tal
non•com•mit•tal\ly
non com•pos men•tis
non•con•duc•tor
non•con•form•ist
non•con•form•i\ty
non•con•trib\u•to\ry
non•co•op\er\a•tion *or* non\co-•op\er\a\tion
non•cu•mu•la•tive
non•cur•rent
non•dair\y
non•de•duc•ti\ble
non•de•script
none (*not one*) [*vs.* nun (*woman in religious order*)]
non•en•ti\ty, *pl.* •ties
none•such
none•the•less
non•e\vent
non•fat
non•fic•tion
non•im•pact print\er
non•in•ter•ac•tive pro•gram
non•in•ter•laced mon\i•tor

non•in•ter•ven•tion
non•met\al
no-•no, *pl.* •nos *or* •no's
non•ob•jec•tive
no-•non\sense
non•op•er\a•tive
non•pa•reil
non•par•ti•san
non•per•son
non•plus, •plussed *or* •plused, •plus•sing *or* •plus•ing
non•prof\it
non•pro•lif•er•a•tion
non•re•cur•ring charge
non•res\i•dent
non•re•stric•tive
non•sched•uled
non•sec•tar•i\an
non•sense
non•sen•si•cal
non•sen•si•cal\ly
non se•qui•tur
non•sex•ist
non•skid
non•stand•ard
non•stick
non•stop
non•sup•port
non•tax•a\ble
non trop\po
non-\U (*not upper-class*)
non•un•ion
non•vi\o•lence
non•vi\o•lent
non•vol\a•tile mem\o\ry
noo•dle
nook
noon
no one
noose
nope
nor
Nor•dic
norm
nor•mal
nor•mal•ize, •ized, •iz•ing
nor•mal\ly
Nor•man
Nor•man\dy
nor•ma•tive

norm•ing
Norse
Norse•man, pl. •men
north
North A\mer\i\ca
North Car\o•li\na (NC)
North Car\o•lin•i\an
North Da•ko\ta (ND)
North Da•ko•tan
north•east
north•east\er
north•east•ern
north•er\ly
north•ern
north•ern\er
north•ern•most
north•ward
north•west
north•west•er\ly
north•west•ern
Nor•way
Nor•we•gian
nos. or Nos. (numbers)
nose (organ of smell),
  nosed, nos•ing [vs.
  knows (understands) and
  noes (negatives)]
nose•bleed
nose•dive, •dived, •div•ing
nose•gay
nosh
no-•show
nos•i\ly
nos\i•ness
nos•tal•gia
nos•tal•gic
nos•tal•gi•cal\ly
nos•tril
nos•trum
nos\y or nos\ey, nos•i\er,
  nos•i•est
not (no) [vs. knot (tied
  cluster)]
no\ta be\ne
no•ta\ble
no•ta•bly
no•ta•ri•za•tion
no•ta•rize, •rized, •riz•ing
no•ta\ry, pl. •ries
no•ta•tion
notch

note, not\ed, not•ing
note•book
notebook com•put\er
not\ed
note•pap\er
note•pa•per
notes re•ceiv•a\ble
note•wor•thy
noth•ing
noth•ing•ness
no•tice, •ticed, •tic•ing
no•tice•a\ble
no•tice•a•bly
no•ti•fi•ca•tion
no•ti\fy, •fied, •fy•ing
no•tion
no•tion\al
no•to•ri•e\ty
no•to•ri•ous
no•to•ri•ous\ly
no-•trump
not•with•stand•ing
nou•gat (the candy)
nought (nothing)
noun
nour•ish, •ished, •ish•ing
nour•ish•ment
nou•veau riche, pl.
  nou•veaux riches
nou•velle cui•sine
no\va, pl. •vas or •vae
No\va Sco•tia
No\va Sco•tian
no•va•tion
nov\el
nov•el•ette
nov•el•ist
nov•el\i•za•tion
nov•el•ize, •ized, •iz•ing
no•vel\la, pl. •vel•las
nov•el\ty, pl. •ties
No•vem•ber
no•ve\na
nov•ice
no•vi•ti•ate
No•vo•caine (™)
now
NOW ac•count (nego-
  tiable order of withdrawal
  account)
now•a•days

no•where
no-•win
no•wise
nox•ious
noz•zle (spout) [vs.
  nuz•zle (to snuggle)]
NSF (not sufficient funds)
NSFnet (National Science
  Foundation network)
nth
nt. wt. (net weight)
nu•ance
nub•bin
nub\by, •bi\er, •bi•est
nu•bile
nu•cle\ar
nu•cle\ar re•ac•tor
nu•cle•ate, •at\ed, •at•ing
nu•cle•a•tion
nu•cle\ic ac\id
nu•cle•o•lar
nu•cle•o•lus, pl. \li
nu•cle•on
nu•cle•us, pl. •cle\i or
  •cle•us\es
nude, nud\er, nud•est
nudge, nudged, nudg•ing
nud•ism
nud•ist
nu•di\ty
nu•ga•to\ry
nug•get
nui•sance
nuisance tax
nuke, nuked, nuk•ing
null
null char•ac•ter
nul•li•fi•ca•tion
nul•li\fy, •fied, •fy•ing
nul•li\ty
null-•mo\dem ca•ble
numb, numbed, numb•ing
numb\er (more incapable
  of sensation), numb•est
num•ber (figure; to count)
num•ber crunch•ing
num•bered ac•count
num\ber•less
numb\ly
numb•ness
nu•mer\a\cy

nu•mer•al
nu•mer•a•tor
nu•mer•ic key•pad
numeric mode
nu•mer\i•cal or nu•mer\ic
nu•mer\i•cal\ly
nu•mer•ol\o•gist
nu•mer•ol\o•gy
nu•mer•ous
nu•mis•mat•ics
nu•mis•ma•tist
num•skull or numb•skull
nun (woman in religious order) [vs. none (not one)]
nun•ci\o, pl. •ci\os •ci\os
nun•ner\y, pl. •ner•ies
nup•tial
nurse, nursed, nurs•ing
nurse•maid

nurs•er\y, pl. •er•ies
nurs•er\y•man, pl. •men
nurs•ling or nurse•ling
nur•ture, •tured, •tur•ing
nut
nut•crack\er
nut•hatch
nut•meat
nut•meg
nut•pick
nu•tri\a
nu•tri•ent
nu•tri•ment
nu•tri•tion
nu•tri•tion\al
nu•tri•tion•al\ly
nu•tri•tion•ist
nu•tri•tious
nu•tri•tious\ly
nu•tri•tious•ness

nu•tri•tive
nuts
nut•shell
nut•ti\ly
nut•ti•ness
nut\ty, •ti\er, •ti•est
nuz•zle (to snuggle), •zled, •zling [vs. noz•zle (spout)]
NV (Nevada)
NY (New York)
NYC or N.Y.C. (New York City)
nyb•ble
ny•lon
nymph
nym\pho•ma\ni\a
nym\pho•ma\ni\ac
NYSE (New York Stock Exchange)

oaf
oaf•ish
oak
oak\en
oa•kum
oar (long paddle) [vs. o'er (over) and or (otherwise) and ore (mineral)]
oar•lock
oars•man, pl. •men
o\a\sis, pl. \ses
OAS (Organization of American States)
OASI (Old Age and Survivors Insurance)
oat
oath, pl. oaths
oat•meal
ob•bli•ga\to, pl. •tos or \ti
ob•du•ra\cy
ob•du•rate
ob•du•rate•ness
o\be•di•ence
o\be•di•ent
o\bei•sance
o\bei•sant
ob\e•lisk
o\bese
o\be•si\ty

o\bey, o\beyed, o\bey•ing
ob•fus•cate, •cat\ed, •cat•ing
ob•fus•ca•tion
ob•fus•ca•to\ry
o\bi, pl. o\bis, o\bi
o\bit
ob\i•ter dic•tum, pl. ob\i•ter dic\ta
o\bit\u•ar\y, pl. •ar•ies
ob•ject, •ject\ed, •ject•ing
object code
ob•jec•tion
ob•jec•tion•a\ble
ob•jec•tive
ob•jec•tiv•i\ty
ob•jec•tor
ob\ject-o\ri\en•ted
ob•jet d'art, pl. ob•jets d'art
ob•late
ob•li•gate, •gat\ed, •gat•ing
ob•li•ga•tion
o\blig\a•to\ry
o\blige, o\bliged, o\blig•ing
ob•li•gee
ob•li•gor
o\blique

o\bliq•ui\ty
o\blique•ness
ob•lit•er•ate, •at\ed, •at•ing
ob•lit•er•a•tion
ob•liv•i\on
ob•liv\i•ous
ob•liv\i•ous•ness
ob•long
ob•lo•quy, pl. •quies
o\boe
o\bo•ist
ob•scene
ob•scen•i\ty
ob•scu•rant•ism
ob•scu•rant•ist
ob•scure, •scured, •scur•ing
ob•scure\ly
ob•scur•i\ty
ob•se•qui•ous
ob•serv•ance
ob•serv•ant
ob•ser•va•tion
ob•serv\a•to\ry, pl. •ries
ob•serve, •served, •serv•ing
ob•serv\er

ob•sess, •sessed, •sess•ing
ob•ses•sion
ob•sess•ive
ob•sess•ive\ly
ob•sid•i\an
ob•so•les•cence
ob•so•les•cent
ob•so•lete
ob•sta•cle
ob•stet•ri•cal or
  ob•stet•ric
ob•stet•tri•cian
ob•stet•rics
ob•sti•na•cy
ob•sti•nate
ob•strep•er•ous
ob•struct, •struct\ed,
  •struct•ing
ob•struc•tion
ob•struc•tion•ism
ob•struc•tion•ist
ob•struc•tive
ob•struc•tive•ness
ob•tain, •tained, •tain•ing
ob•tain•a•ble
ob•trude, •trud\ed,
  •trud•ing
ob•tru•sion
ob•tru•sive
ob•tru•sive•ness
ob•tuse
ob•verse
ob•vi•ate, •at\ed, •at•ing
ob•vi•a•tion
ob•vi•ous
oc\a•ri\na, pl. •nas
oc•ca•sion, •sioned,
  •sion•ing
oc•ca•sion•al
Oc•ci•dent
oc•ci•den•tal
oc•clude, •clud\ed,
  •clud•ing
oc•clu•sion
oc•clu•sive
oc•cult
oc•cult•ism
oc•cu•pan•cy
oc•cu•pant
oc•cu•pa•tion
oc•cu•pa•tion\al

oc•cu•py, •pied, •py•ing
oc•cur, •curred, •cur•ring
oc•cur•rence
o\cean
o\cea•naut
o\cean•go\ing or o\cean-
  •go\ing
o\ce•an\ic
o\cea•nog•ra•pher
o\cea•no•graph\ic
o\cea•nog•ra•phy
oc\e•lot
o\cher or o\chre
o'\clock
OCR (optical character
  recognition)
oc•ta•gon
oc•tag\o•nal
oc•tane
oc•tave
oc•ta\vo, pl. •vos
oc•tet
Oc•to•ber
oc\to•ge•nar•i\an
oc\to•pus, pl. •pus\es or
  \pi
oc•to•roon
oc\u•lar
oc\u•list
OD (overdose)
o\da•lisque
odd, \er, •est
odd•ball
odd-•e\ven pric•ing
odd foot\er
odd•i\ty, pl. •ties
odd•ment
odds
odds-•on
ode (poem) [vs. owed (did
  owe)]
O\din
o\di•ous
o\di•um
o\dom\e•ter
o\dor
o\dor•if•er•ous
o\dor•ous
O\dys•se\us
Od•ys•sey, pl. •seys
oed\i•pal

Oed\i•pus
OEM (original equipment
  manufacturer)
oe•nol\o•gist
oe•nol•o\gy or e\nol\o\gy
oe•no•phile
o'er (over) [vs. oar (long
  paddle) and or (other-
  wise) and ore (mineral)]
oeu•vre, pl. oeu•vres
of (belonging to)
off (away from)
of•fal (garbage) [vs. awful
  (very bad)]
off•beat
off-•col\or
of•fend, •fend\ed,
  •fend•ing
of•fense or of•fence
of•fen•sive
of•fer, •fered, •fer•ing
of•fer•ing
of•fer•to\ry, pl. •ries
off•hand
off•hand•ed\ly
off•hand•ed•ness
off-•hour
of•fice
office au\to•ma•tion
of•fice•hold\er
office park
of•fi•cer
of•fi•cial (authorized) [vs.
  of•fi•cious (meddle-
  some)]
of•fi•cial•dom
of•fi•cial\ly
of•fi•ci•ant
of•fi•ci•ate, •at\ed, •at•ing
of•fi•cious (meddlesome)
  [vs. of•fi•cial (authorized)]
off•ing
off•ish
off-•key
off-•lim\its
off-•line or off•line
off-•load or off•load
off•print
off-•put\ting
off-•sea\son
off•set, •set, •set•ting

off•shoot
off•shore
off•side
off•spring, pl. •spring
off•stage
off-•the-•cuff
off-•the-•rec\ord
off-•the-•shelf
off-•the-•wall
off•track
off-•white
oft
of•ten
o\gle, o\gled, o\gling
o\gre
OH (Ohio)
oh (exclamation of
surprise), pl. oh's or ohs;
ohed, oh•ing [vs. owe (to
be indebted)]
O\hi\o (OH)
ohm
o\ho
oil, oiled, oil•ing
oil•cloth
oil\i•ness
oil•skin
oil\y, •i\er, •i•est
oink, oinked, oink•ing
oint•ment
O\jib\wa or O\jib•way, pl.
•was or \wa; •ways or
•way
OK (Oklahoma)
OK or O.K., pl. OKs or
OK's or O.K.'s; OK'd or
O.K.'ed, OK"\ing or
O.K.'\ing
o\kay, pl. o\kays; o\kayed,
o\kay•ing
o\key-•doke or o\key-
•do\key
O\ki•na\wa
O\ki•na•wan
O\kla•ho\ma (OK)
O\kla•ho•man
o\kra, pl. o\kras
old, old\er or eld•er,
old•est or eld•est
old\en
old-•fash\ioned

old\ie
old-•line
Old Tes•ta•ment
old-•time
old-•tim\er
Ol•du•vai Gorge
Old World (noun)
old-•world (adj.)
o\lé, pl. o\lés
o\le•ag\i•nous
o\le•an•der
o\le•o•mar•ga•rine
ol•fac\to•ry
ol\i•garch
ol\i•gar•chic
ol\i•gar•chy, pl. •chies
Ol\i•go•cene
ol\i•gop\o\ly, pl. •lies
ol•ive
O\lym•pi\a
O\lym•pic
O\lym•pus
Om
O\man
O\ma\ni
OMB or O.M.B. (Office of
Management and Budget)
om•buds•man, pl. •men
o\me•ga, pl. •gas
o\me\ga-\3 fat\ty ac\id
om•e•let or om•e•lette
o\men
om\i•nous
o\mis•sion
o\mit, o\mit•ted,
o\mit•ting
om•ni•bus, pl. •bus\es
om•nip\o•tence
om•nip\o•tent
om•ni•pres•ence
om•ni•pres•ent
om•nis•cience
om•nis•cient
om\ni•um-•gath\er\um, pl.
\ums
om•ni•vore
om•niv\o•rous
on
o\nan•ism
on-•board mem\o\ry
on-•board mo•dem

once
once-•o\ver
on•co•gene
on•co•log\i•cal
on•col\o•gist
on•col\o•gy
on•com•ing
one (single) [vs. won (did
win)]
one-•di\men\sion\al
O\nei\da, pl. •das or \da
O'\Neill
one-•lin\er
one•ness
one-•on-•one
on•er•ous
one•self or one's self
one-•shot
one-•sid\ed
one-•sid\ed\ness
one-•time or one•time
one-•track
one-•up\man\ship
one-•way
on•go•ing
on•ion
on\ion•skin
on-•line or on•line
on-•line serv•ice
on•look\er
on•look•ing
on\ly
on\o•mat\o•poe\ia
on\o•mat\o•poe\ic or
on\o•mat\o•po•et\ic
On•on•da\ga, pl. •gas or
\ga
on•rush
on•rush•ing
on•set
on•slaught
on spec
On•tar\i\o
on-•the-•job train•ing
on\to
on•to•ge•net\ic or
on•to•gen\ic
on•tog•e\ny or
on•to•gen\e•sis
on•to•log\i•cal or
on•to•log\ic

on•tol•o\gy
o\nus, *pl.* o\nus\es
on•ward *or* on•wards
on\yx
oo•dles
OOP (*object-oriented programming*)
OOPL (*object-oriented programming language*)
ooze, oozed, ooz•ing
o\pac•i\ty
o\pal
o\pal•es•cence
o\pal•es•cent
o\paque
OPEC (*Organization of Petroleum Exporting Countries*)
Op-•Ed (*newspaper page*)
o\pen
o\pen-•and-•shut
o\pen-•date la•bel•ing
o\pen dis•play
o\pen-•end
o\pen-•end\ed
o\pen\er
o\pen-•faced
o\pen•hand\ed
o\pen-•heart\ed
o\pen-•hearth
o\pen-•heart sur•ger\y
o\pen•ing
o\pen mar•ket
o\pen-•mind\ed
o\pen•work
op•er\a (*music drama*), *pl.* •er\as
o\per\a (*plural of "opus"*)
op•er•a\ble
op•er•ate, •at\ed, •at•ing
op•er•at\ic
op•er•at•ing
en•vi•ron•ment
operating ex•pens\es
operating in•come
operating sys•tem
op•er•a•tion
op•er•a•tion\al
op•er•a•tive
op•er•a•tor
op•er•et\ta, *pl.* •tas

oph•thal•mol\o•gist
oph•thal•mol\o\gy
o\pi•ate
o\pine, o\pined, o\pin•ing
o\pin•ion
o\pin•ion•at\ed
o\pi\um
o\pos•sum, *pl.* •sums *or* •sum
op•po•nent
op•por•tune
op•por•tun•ism
op•por•tun•ist
op•por•tun•is•tic
op•por•tu•ni\ty, *pl.* •ties
op•pose, •posed, •pos•ing
op•po•site (*facing*) [*vs.* ap•po•site (*suitable*)]
op•po•si•tion (*resistance*) [*vs.* apposition (*placing together*)]
op•press, •pressed, •press•ing
op•pres•sion
op•pres•sive
op•pres•sor
op•pro•bri•ous
op•pro•bri\um
opt, opt\ed, opt•ing
op•tic
op•ti•cal
optical disc
op•ti•cal\ly
op•ti•cal mouse
optical scan•ner
optical scan•ning
op•ti•cian
op•tics
op•ti•mal
op•ti•mism
op•ti•mist
op•ti•mis•tic
op•ti•mum, *pl.* \ma *or* •mums
op•tion
op•tion\al
op\to•me•chan\i•cal mouse
op•tom\e•trist
op•tom\e•try
op\u•lence

op\u•lent
o\pus, *pl.* o\pus\es *or* o\pe\ra
or (*otherwise*) [*vs.* oar (*long paddle*) *and* o'er (*over*) *and* ore (*mineral*)]
OR (*Oregon*)
or\a•cle (*shrine*) [*vs.* auri-cle (*outer ear*)]
o\rac\u•lar
o\ral (*spoken*) [*vs.* au•ral (*of hearing*)]
or•ange
or•ange•ade
o\rang•u\tan *or* o\rang•u\tang *or* o\rang•ou•tang
o\rate, •rat\ed, •rat•ing
o\ra•tion
or\a•tor
or\a•tor\i•cal
or\a•to•ri\o, *pl.* •ri\os
or\a•to\ry
orb
or•bit, •bit\ed, •bit•ing
or•bit\al
or•chard
or•ches•tra, *pl.* •tras
or•ches•tral
or•ches•trate, •trat\ed, •trat•ing
or•ches•tra•tion
or•ches•tra•tor
or•chid
or•dain, •dained, •dain•ing
or•dain•ment
or•deal
or•der, •dered, •der•ing
order cy•cle
or•der•li•ness
or•der\ly, *pl.* •lies
or•di•nal
or•di•nance (*law*) [*vs.* ord•nance (*military weapons*)]
or•di•nar•i\ly
or•di•nar•i•ness
or•di•nar\y
ordinary in•come
or•di•nate
or•di•na•tion

ord•nance (*military weapons*) [*vs.* or•di•nance (*law*)]

Or•do•vi•cian

or•dure

ore (*mineral*) [*vs.* o'er (*over*) and or (*otherwise*)]

o\reg•a\no

Or\e\gon (*OR*)

O\res•tes

or•gan

or•gan\dy or or•gan•die, *pl.* •dies

or•gan•elle

or•gan•ic

or•gan\i•cal\ly

or•gan•ism

or•gan•ist

or•gan\i•za•tion

or•gan\i•za•tion\al

or•gan•ize, •ized, •iz•ing

or•gan•ized

or•gan\iz\er

or•gan\za

or•gasm, •gasmed, •gasm•ing

or•gas•mic

or•gas•tic

or•gi•as•tic

or\gy, *pl.* •gies

o\ri•el

o\ri•ent, •ent\ed, •ent•ing

o\ri•en•tal

o\ri•en•ta•tion

or\i•fice

or\i•fi•cial

o\ri•ga•mi

or\i•gin

o\rig\i•nal

o\rig\i•nal•i\ty

o\rig\i•nal\ly

o\rig\i•nate, •nat\ed, •nat•ing

o\rig\i•na•tion

o\rig\i•na•tor

o\ri•ole

O\ri•on

Or•lon (™)

or•mo\lu

or•na•ment, •ment\ed, •ment•ing

or•na•men•tal

or•na•men•ta•tion

or•nate

or•nate\ly

or•nate•ness

or•ner\i•ness

or•ner\y

or•ni•thol\o\gy

o\ro•tund

o\ro•tun•di\ty

or•phan, •phaned, •phan•ing

or•phan•age

Or•phe\us

or•ris

or•tho•don•tal

or•tho•don•tic

or•tho•don•tics

or•tho•don•tist

or•tho•dox

or•tho•dox\y

or•tho•graph\ic

or•thog•ra•phy

or•tho•pe•dic

or•tho•pe•dics

or•tho•pe•dist

Or•well

Or•well•i\an

os (*bone*), *pl.* os\sa

os (*mouth*), *pl.* o\ra

O\sage, *pl.* O\sag\es or O\sage

O\sa\ka

os•cil•late (*to go back and forth*), •lat\ed, •lat•ing

os•cu•late (*to kiss*), •lat\ed, •lat•ing

OSHA (*Occupational Safety and Health Administration*)

o\sier

Os\lo

os•mi•um

os•mo•sis

os•mot\ic

os•prey, *pl.* •preys

os•se•ous

os•si•fi•ca•tion

os•si\fy, •fied, •fy•ing

os•ten•si•ble

ostensible part•ner

os•ten•ta•tion

os•ten•ta•tious

os\te\o•path

os•te•op\a•thy

os\te\o•po•ro•sis

os•tra•cism

os•tra•cize, •cized, •ciz•ing

os•trich

OTC (*over-the-counter*)

oth\er

oth\er•wise

oth\er•world\ly

o\ti•ose

o\to•lar•yn•gol\o•gist

o\to•lar•yn•gol•o\gy

Ot•ta\wa, *pl.* •was or \wa

ot•ter, *pl.* •ters or •ter

ot•to•man, *pl.* •mans

Oua•ga•dou•gou

ou•bli•ette

ouch

ought (*should*) [*vs.* aught (*zero*)]

Oui\ja (™)

ounce

our (*belonging to us*) [*vs.* hour (*60 minutes*)]

ours

our•selves

oust, oust\ed, oust•ing

oust\er

out

out•age

out-•and-•out

out•back

out•bal•ance, •anced, •anc•ing

out•board

out•bound

out•break

out•build•ing

out•burst

out•cast

out•class, •classed, •class•ing

out•come

out•crop, •cropped, •crop•ping

out•cry, *pl.* •cries

out•dat\ed

out•dis•tance, •tanced, •tanc•ing
out•do, •did, •done, •do•ing
out•door
out•doors
out\er
out\er•most
out\er•wear
out•field
out•field\er
out•fit, •fit•ted, •fit•ting
out•fit•ter
out•flank, •flanked, •flank•ing
out•flow
out•fox, •foxed, •fox•ing
out\go, pl. •goes; •went, •gone, •go•ing
out•grow, •grew, •grown, •grow•ing
out•growth
out•house, pl. •hous\es
out•ing
out•land•ish
out•last, •last\ed, •last•ing
out•law, •lawed, •law•ing
out•lay
out•let
out•line, •lined, •lin•ing
outline font
out•live, •lived, •liv•ing
out•look
out•ly•ing
out•ma•neu•ver, •vered, •ver•ing
out•mod\ed
out•num•ber
out-•of-•bod\y
out-•of-•date
out-•of-•doors
out-•of-•the-•way
out•pa•tient or out-•pa\tient
out•place•ment
out•post
out•pour•ing
out•put, •put\ted or •put, •put•ting
output de•vice
out•rage, •raged, •rag•ing

out•ra•geous
out•rank, •ranked, •rank•ing
ou•tré
out•reach, •reached, •reach•ing
out•rig•ger
out•right
out•run, •ran, •run, •run•ning
out•sell, •sold, •sell•ing
out•set
out•shine, •shone, •shin•ing
out•side
out•sid\er
out•size
out•skirt
out•smart, •smart\ed, •smart•ing
out•source, •sourced, •sourc•ing
out•spo•ken
out•spread, •spread, •spread•ing
out•stand•ing
out•stretch, •stretched, •stretch•ing
out•strip, •stripped, •strip•ping
out•take
out•vote, •vot\ed, •vot•ing
out•ward
out•weigh, •weighed, •weigh•ing
out•wit, •wit•ted, •wit•ting
out•work, •worked, •work•ing
ou\zo
o\va
o\val
O\val Of•fice
o\va\ry, pl. •ries
o\vate
o\va•tion
ov\en
o\ver
o\ver•a\chieve, \chieved, \chiev•ing

o\ver•a\chiev\er
o\ver•act, •act\ed, •act•ing
o\ver•age
o\ver•all
o\ver•arm
o\ver•awe, •awed, •aw•ing
o\ver•bal•ance, •anced, •anc•ing
o\ver•bear•ing
o\ver•bite
o\ver•blown
o\ver•board
o\ver•bought
o\ver•cast
o\ver•charge, •charged, •charg•ing
o\ver•coat
o\ver•come, •came, •come, •com•ing
o\ver\do (to overindulge), •did, •done, •do•ing [vs. o\ver•due (late)]
o\ver•dose (OD)
o\ver•draft
o\ver•draw, •drew, •drawn, •draw•ing
o\ver•drive
o\ver•due (late) [vs. o\ver\do (to overindulge)]
o\ver•flight
o\ver•flow, •flowed, •flow•ing
overflow er•ror
o\ver•fly, •flew, •flown, •fly•ing
o\ver•grow, •grew, •grown, •grow•ing
o\ver•grown
o\ver•growth
o\ver•hand
o\ver•hang, •hung, •hang•ing
o\ver•haul, •hauled, •haul•ing
o\ver•head
overhead scan•ner
o\ver•hear, •heard, •hear•ing
o\ver•joyed

o\ver•kill
o\ver•laid win•dows
o\ver•land
o\ver•lap, •lapped,
•lap•ping
o\ver•lay
o\ver•look, •looked,
•look•ing
o\ver•lord, •lord\ed,
•lord•ing
o\ver\ly
o\ver•much
o\ver•night
o\ver•pass
o\ver•play, •played,
•play•ing
o\ver•pow\er, •ered,
•er•ing
o\ver•qual\i•fied
o\ver•reach, •reached,
•reach•ing
o\ver•ride, •rode,
•rid•den, •rid•ing
o\ver•rule, •ruled, •rul•ing
o\ver•run, •ran, •run,
•run•ning
o\ver•seas or o\ver•sea
o\ver•see, •saw, •seen,
•see•ing
o\ver•se\er
o\ver•sexed
o\ver•shad\ow, •owed,
•ow•ing
o\ver•shoe
o\ver•shoot, •shot,
•shoot•ing

o\ver•sight
o\ver•size or o\ver•sized
o\ver•sleep, •slept,
•sleep•ing
o\ver•state, •stat\ed,
•stat•ing
o\ver•stay, •stayed,
•stay•ing
o\ver•step, •stepped,
•step•ping
o\ver•strike mode
o\ver•stuffed
o\ver•sub•scribe,
•scribed, •scrib•ing
o\vert
o\ver•take, •took, •tak\en,
•tak•ing
o\ver-the-•count\er
(OTC)
o\ver•throw, •threw,
•thrown, •throw•ing
o\ver•time
o\vert\ly
o\ver•tone
o\ver•ture
o\ver•turn, •turned,
•turn•ing
o\ver•view
o\ver•ween•ing
o\ver•whelm, •whelmed,
•whelm•ing
o\ver•write, •wrote,
•writ•ten, •writ•ing
o\ver•wrought
Ov\id
o\vi•duct

o\vip\a•rous
o\void
ov\u•lar
ov\u•late, •lat\ed, •lat•ing
ov\u•la•tion
ov•ule
o\vum, pl. o\va
ow (expression of pain)
owe (to be indebted),
owed, ow•ing [vs. oh
(exclamation of surprise)]
owed (did owe) [vs. ode
(poem)]
owl
owl•ish
own, owned, own•ing
own\er
own•er•ship
ox, pl. ox\en or ox\es
ox•blood
ox•bow
ox•ford
ox\i•dant
ox\i•da•tion
ox•ide
ox\i•dize, •dized, •diz•ing
ox\i•diz\er
ox\y•a\cet\y•lene
ox\y•gen
ox\y•gen•ate, •at\ed,
•at•ing
ox\y•gen•a•tion
ox\y•mo•ron
oys•ter
o\zone
o\zone lay\er

P

PA (Pennsylvania)
pa
pab\u•lum
PAC (political action committee), pl. PACs or
PAC's
pace (step; to step), paced,
pac•ing
pa\ce (with due respect)
pace•mak\er
pac\er
pace•set•ter
pach\y•derm

pach\y•san•dra, pl. •dras
pa•cif\ic
pac\i•fi•ca•tion
Pa•cif\ic O\cean
Pacific time (PT)
pac\i•fi\er
pac\i•fism
pac\i•fist
pac•i\fy, •fied, •fy•ing
pack, packed, pack•ing
pack•age, •aged, •ag•ing
packed (bundled) [vs. pact
(agreement)]

packed file
pack\er
pack\et
pack\et-•switched
pack•horse
pack•ing
pack•sad•dle
Pac-•Man de•fense
pact (agreement) [vs.
packed (bundled)]
pad, pad•ded, pad•ding
pad char•ac•ter
pad•dle, •dled, •dling

pad•dock
pad\dy (*rice field*), pl. •dies [vs. pat\ty (*flat mass*)]
pad•lock, •locked, •lock•ing
pa•dre, pl. •dres
pae\an
pa•gan
pa•gan•ism
page, paged, pag•ing
pag•eant
pag•eant\ry
page de•scrip•tion lan•guage
paged vir•tu\al mem\o\ry
page-•mode mem\o\ry
page print\er
page-•white dis•play
pag\i•na•tion
pa•go\da, pl. •das
paid (*pd.*)
paid-•in cap\i•tal
paid-•in sur•plus
pail (*bucket*) [vs. pale (*lacking color*)]
pail•ful, pl. •fuls
pain (*suffering*), pained, pain•ing [vs. pane (*window section*)]
Paine
pain•ful
pain•ful\ly
pain•kill\er
pain•kill•ing
pain•less
pain•less\ly
pains•tak•ing
pains•tak•ing\ly
paint, paint\ed, paint•ing
paint•brush
paint\er
paint•ing
paint pro•gram
pair (*two*), pl. pairs or pair [vs. pare (*to trim*) and pear (*the fruit*)]
pais•ley, pl. •leys
pa•ja•mas
Pa•ki•stan
Pa•ki•sta\ni
pal, palled, pal•ling

pal•ace
pal\a•din
pal•an•quin
pal•at•a\ble
pal\a•tal
pal•ate (*roof of mouth*) [vs. pal•let (*bed*) and pal•ette (*paint tablet*)]
pa•la•tial
Pa•lat\i•nate
pal\a•tine
pa•lav\er
pale (*lacking color*), paled, pal•ing; pal\er, pal•est [vs. pail (*bucket*)]
pale•face
pale•ness
Pa•le\o•cene
pa•le•on•tol\o•gist
pa•le•on•tol•o\gy
Pa•le\o•zo\ic
Pal•es•tine
Pal•es•tin•i\an
pal•ette (*paint tablet*) [vs. pal•ate (*roof of mouth*) and pal•let (*bed*)]
pal•frey, pl. •freys
pal\i•mo\ny
pal•imp•sest
pal•in•drome
pal•ing
pal\i•sade
pall (*gloomy effect*), palled, pall•ing [vs. Paul (*the name*)]
pal•la•di\um, pl. •di\a
pall•bear\er
pal•let (*bed*) [vs. pal•ate (*roof of mouth*) and pal•ette (*paint tablet*)]
pal•li•ate, •at\ed, •at•ing
pal•li•a•tion
pal•li•a•tive
pal•lid
pal•ling (*associating as pals*)
pall•ing (*becoming tiresome*)
pal•lor
palm (*part of hand; the tree*), palmed, palm•ing [vs. psalm (*hymn*)]

pal•mate or pal•mat\ed
Pal•mer (*last name*)
palm\er (*pilgrim*)
pal•met\to, pl. •tos or •toes
palm•ist
palm•is•try
palm•top
palmtop com•put\er
palm\y, •i\er, •i•est
pal\o•mi\no, pl. •nos
pal•pa\ble
pal•pa\bly
pal•pate (*to examine by touch*), •pat\ed, •pat•ing
pal•pa•tion
pal•pi•tate (*to throb*), •tat\ed, •tat•ing
pal•pi•ta•tion
pal•sied
pal\sy, pl. •sies
pal•tri•ness
pal•try (*trifling*) [vs. poul•try (*fowl*)]
pam•pas
pam•per, •pered, •per•ing
pam•phlet
pam•phlet•eer
Pam•yat
pan, panned, pan•ning
pan\a•ce\a, pl. •ce\as
pa•nache
Pan•a\ma, pl. •mas
Pan•a\ma Ca•nal
Pan\a•ma•ni\an
Pan-•A\mer\i\can
pan•cake
pan•chro•mat\ic
pan•cre\as
pan•cre•at\ic
pan\da, pl. •das
pan•dem\ic
pan•de•mo•ni\um, pl. •ums
pan•der, •dered, •der•ing
P&L (*profit and loss*)
Pan•do\ra
pane (*window section*) [vs. pain (*suffering*)]
pan\e\gyr\ic

pan\el, •eled or •elled,
•el•ing or •el•ling
pan•el•ist
pang
pan•han•dle, •dled, •dling
pan•han•dler
pan\ic, •icked, •ick•ing
pan•ick\y
pan•nier or pan•ier
pan\o•ply, pl. •plies
pan\o•ram\a, pl. •ram•as
pan\o•ram•ic
pan\sy, pl. •sies
pant, pant\ed, pant•ing
pan•ta•loon
pan•the•ism
pan•the•ist
pan•the•is•tic
pan•the•is•ti•cal
pan•the•on
pan•ther, pl. •thers or
•ther
pant•ies
pan•to•mime, •mimed,
•mim•ing
pan•to•mim\ic
pan•to•mim•ist
pan•to•then\ic ac\id
pan•try, pl. •tries
pants
pant•suit or pants suit
pant\y•hose
pant\y•waist
pap
Pap test
pa\pa, pl. •pas
pa•pa\cy, pl. •cies
pa•pal
pa•pa\ya, pl. •yas
pa•per, •pered, •per•ing
pa•per•back
pa\per•board
pa\per•boy
pa•per clip
pa\per•hang\er
pa\per•hang•ing
pa•per prof\it
pa\per-•white dis•play
pa\per•weight
pa\per•work
pa\pier-•mâ\ché

pa•poose
pap•ri\ka
Pap\ua New Guin\ea
pa•py•rus, pl. •py\ri or
•py•rus\es
par, parred, par•ring
par\a•ble
pa•rab\o•la, pl. •las
par\a•chute, •chut\ed,
•chut•ing
pa•rade, •rad\ed, •rad•ing
pa•rad\er
par\a•digm
par\a•dise
par\a•di•si•a•cal
par\a•di•si•a•cal\ly
par\a•di•si•a•cal\ly
par\a•dox
par\a•dox\i•cal
par\a•dox\i•cal\ly
par•af•fin
par\a•gon
par\a•graph, •graphed,
•graph•ing
Par\a•guay
Par\a•guay\an
par\a•keet
par\a•le•gal
par•al•lax
par•al•lel, •leled, •lel•ing
parallel in•ter•face
par•al•lel\o•gram
parallel port
parallel print\er
parallel proc•ess•ing
pa•ral\y•sis, pl. •ses
par\a•lyze, •lyzed, •lyz•ing
par\a•lyz•ing\ly
Par\a•mar•i\bo
par\a•me•ci\um, pl. •ci\a
par\a•med\i•cal
pa•ram\e•ter (math vari-
able; limit) [vs.
pe•rim\e•ter (boundary)]
par\a•met•ric or
par\a•met•ri•cal
par\a•mil\i•tar\y
par\a•mount
par\a•mour
par\a•noi\a

par\a•pet
par\a•pher•na•lia
par\a•phrase, •phrased,
•phras•ing
par\a•ple•gi\a
par\a•ple•gic
par\a•pro•fes•sion\al
par\a•psy•chol\o•gist
par\a•psy•chol\o\gy
par\a•site
par\a•sol
par\a•sym•pa•thet\ic
par\a•thi\on
par\a•thy•roid
par\a•troop
par•bake, •baked, •bak•ing
par•boil, •boiled, •boil•ing
par•cel, •celed or •celled,
•cel•ing or •cel•ling
par•cel post
parch, parched, parch•ing
parch•ment
par•don, •doned,
•don•ing
par•don•a\ble
par•don•a•bly
pare (to trim), pared,
par•ing [vs. pair (two)
and pear (the fruit)]
par\e\gor\ic
par•ent, •ent\ed, •ent•ing
par•ent•age
par•ent•ing
paren•tal
par•ent di•rec•to\ry
pa•ren•the•sis, pl. •ses
par•ent•hood
par•ent•ing
pa•re•sis
pa•ret\ic
pa•re\ve or par\ve
par ex•cel•lence
par•fait
pa•ri\ah
pa•ri•e•tal
par\i-•mu•tu\el or
par\i•mu•tu\el
Par\is
par•ish (church district)
[vs. per•ish (to die)]
pa•rish•ion\er

par•i\ty, *pl.* •ties
parity check
parity check•ing
park, parked, park•ing
par\ka, *pl.* •kas
park•ing me•ter
Par•kin•son's disease
park•way
par•lance
par•lay (*to bet*)
par•ley (*conference*), *pl.*
•leys; •leyed, •ley•ing
par•lia•ment
par•lia•men•tar•i\an
par•lor
Par•me•san
par•mi•gia\na
pa•ro•chi•al
par•o\dy, *pl.* •dies; •died,
•dy•ing
pa•role, •roled, •rol•ing
par•ox•ysm
par•quet, •queted,
•quet•ing
par•que•try
par•ri•cld\al
par•ri•cide
par•rot, •rot\ed, •rot•ing
par\ry, *pl.* •ries; •ried,
•ry•ing
parse, parsed, pars•ing
par•si•mo\ny
pars•ley
pars•nip
par•son
par•son•age
part, part\ed, part•ing
par•take, •took, •tak\en,
•tak•ing
par•terre
par•the•no•gen\e•sis
par•the•no•ge\net•ic
Par•the•non
par•tial
par•tial\ly
par•tic\i•pate, •pat\ed,
•pat•ing
par•tic\i•pa•tive
par•tic\i•pa•to\ry
par•ti•ci•ple
par•ti•cle

par\ti•col\ored *or* par\ty-
•col\ored
par•tic\u•lar
par•tic\u•lar\i•za•tion
par•tic\u•lar•ize, •ized,
•iz•ing
par•tic\u•late
part•ing
par•ti•san
par•ti•san•ship
par•ti•tion, •tioned,
•tion•ing
part\ly
part•ner, •nered, •ner•ing
par•tridge, *pl.* •tridg\es *or*
•tridge
part-•song
part-•time
part-•tim\er
par•tu•ri•tion
part•way
par\ty, *pl.* •ties; •tied,
•ty•ing
par val\ue
par•ve\nu, *pl.* •nus
Pas\a•de\na
pas•cal
Pas•cal (*programming
language*)
pas•chal
pa•sha, *pl.* •shas
pass, passed,
pass•ing
pass•a\ble (*acceptable*) [*vs.*
pass•i\ble (*capable of
emotion*)]
pass•a\bly
pas•sage, •saged, •sag•ing
pas•sage•way
pass•book
pas\sé
passed (*did pass*) [*vs.* past
(*former time*)]
pas•sel
pas•sen•ger
pass•er\by *or* pass•er-•by,
pl. pass•ers\by *or*
pass\ers-•by
pass•i\ble (*capable of
emotion*) [*vs.* pass•a\ble
(*acceptable*)]

pas•sim
pass•ing
pas•sion
pas•sion•ate
pas•sion•ate\ly
pas•sive
passive in•come
pas•sive\ly
pas•sive smok•ing
pass•key, *pl.* •keys
Pass•o\ver
pass•port
pass-•through
pass•word
past (*former time*) [*vs.*
passed (*did pass*)]
pas\ta, *pl.* •tas
paste, past\ed, past•ing
paste•board
pas•tel
pas•tern
Pas•teur
pas•teur\i•za•tion
pas•teur•ize, •ized, •iz•ing
pas•teur•iz\er
pas•tiche
pas•time
past\i•ness
pas•tor
pas•to•ral (*rustic*)
pas•to•rale (*musical composition*)
pas•tra\mi
pas•try, *pl.* •tries
pas•tur•age
pas•ture, •tured, •tur•ing
past\y, *pl.* past•ies
pat, pat\ted, pat•ting
patch, patched, patch•ing
patch•a\ble
patch\er
patch\i•ness
patch•work
patch\y, •i\er, •i•est
pate (*top of head*)
pâte (*pottery paste*)
pâ\té (*meat paste*), *pl.* •tés
pa•tel\la, *pl.* •tel•las *or*
•tel•lae
pa•tel•lar
pat•ent, •ent\ed, •ent•ing

pat•ent\ly
pa\ter•fa•mil•i•as
pa•ter•nal
pa•ter•nal•ism
pa•ter•nal•is•tic
pa•ter•nal\ly
pa•ter•ni•ty
pa\ter•nos•ter
Pat•er•son
path, *pl.* paths
pa•thet\ic
pa•thet\i•cal\ly
path•find\er
path•name
path\o•gen
pa•thol\o•gist
pa•thol•o\gy, *pl.* •gies
pa•thos (*tender quality*)
[*vs.* ba•thos (*anticlimax*)]
path•way
pa•tience (*forbearance*)
pa•tient, *pl.* •tients (*doc-tor's clients*)
pa•tient\ly
pat\i•na, *pl.* •ti•nas
pat\i\o, *pl.* •i\os
pat•ness
pat•ois, *pl.* pat•ois
pa•tri•arch
pa•tri•ar•chal
pa•tri•cian
pat•ri•cide
pat•ri•mo\ny, *pl.* •nies
pa•tri\ot
pa•tris•tic *or*
  pa•tris•ti•cal
pa•tris•ti•cal\ly
pa•trol, •trolled, •trol•ing
pa•trol•man, *pl.* •men
pa•tron
pa•tron•age
pa•tron•ize, •ized, •iz•ing
pat•ro•nym\ic
pat\sy, *pl.* •sies
pat•ter, •tered, •ter•ing
pat•tern, •terned,
  •tern•ing
pat•terned
pat\ty (*flat mass*), *pl.* •ties
[*vs.* pad\dy (*rice field*)]
pau•ci\ty

Paul (*the name*) [*vs.* pall
  (*gloomy effect*)]
Paul Bun•yan
Pau•line (*first name*)
Paul•ine (*of the apostle
  Paul*)
paunch
pau•per
pause (*delay*), paused,
  paus•ing [*vs.* paws
  (*animal feet*)]
pave, paved, pav•ing
pave•ment
pa•vil•ion
pav•ing
Pav•lov
Pav•lov•i\an
paw, pawed, paw•ing
pawn, pawned, pawn•ing
pawn•bro•ker
pawn•bro•king
pawn•shop
paw•paw
paws (*animal feet*) [*vs.*
  pause (*delay*)]
pay, paid, pay•ing
pay•back
pay\ee
pay\er
pay•load
pay•mas•ter
pay•ment (*pmt.*)
pay•off
pay•o\la
pay•out
pay•roll
payroll tax
PBS (*Public Broadcasting
  System*)
PBX (*telephone*)
PC (*personal computer*), *pl.*
  PCs *or* PC's
PC (*politically correct*)
pd. (*paid*)
p/e (*price-earnings ratio*)
pea, *pl.* peas
peace (*freedom from war*)
  [*vs.* piece (*portion*)]
peace•mak\er
peace•mak•ing
peace•time

peach
pea•cock, *pl.* •cocks *or*
  •cock
peak (*pointed top*) [*vs.*
  peek (*to look*) *and* pique
  (*to irritate*)]
peaked (*pointed*) [*vs.*
  peeked (*looked*) *and*
  piqued (*aroused*)]
peak\ed (*pale and thin*)
peak•ed•ness
peal (*to resound*), pealed,
  peal•ing [*vs.* peel (*to
  strip*)]
pea•nut
pear (*the fruit*) [*vs.* pair
  (*two*) *and* pare (*to trim*)]
pearl (*the gem*) [*vs.* purl
  (*knitting stitch*)]
Pearl Har•bor
peas•ant
peat
peat\y, peat•i\er, peat•i•est
peb•ble
peb•bled
pe•can
pec•ca•dil\lo, *pl.* •loes *or*
  •los
pec•ca\ry, *pl.* •ries *or* \ry
peck, pecked, peck•ing
pec•tin
pec•tin•ous
pec•to•ral
pec\u•late, •lat\ed, •lat•ing
pec\u•la•tion
pe•cu•liar
pe•cu•liar\ly
pe•cu•ni•ar\y
ped\a•gogue
ped\a•go\gy
ped\al (*foot lever; to propel
  with a pedal*), •aled *or*
  •alled, •al•ing *or* •al•ling
  [*vs.* ped•dle (*to sell*)]
ped•ant
pe•dan•tic
ped•dle (*to sell*), •dled,
  •dling
ped•er•as\ty
ped•es•tal
pe•des•tri\an

pe•di•at•ric

pe•di•a•tri•cian

pe•di•at•rics

ped\i•cab

ped\i•cure

ped\i•cur•ist

ped\i•gree

ped\i•ment

pe•dom\e•ter

peek (to look), peeked,
peek•ing [vs. peak
(pointed top) and pique
(to irritate)]

peel (to strip), peeled,
peel•ing [vs. peal (to
resound)]

peep, peeped, peep•ing

peep•hole

peer (equal; to look),
peered, peer•ing [vs.
pier (dock)]

peer•less

peer-•to-•peer

peeve

peeved

pee•vish

pee•vish\ly

pee•vish•ness

pee•wee

peg, pegged, peg•ging

Peg\a•sus

peg\legged

peign•oir

pe•jo•ra•tive

Pe•king

Pe•king•ese or Pe•kin•ese,
pl. •ese

pe•koe

pel\i•can

pel•la•gra

pel•let

pell-•mell or pell•mell

pel•lu•cid

pel•lu•cid\ly

pelt, pelt\ed, pelt•ing

pel•vic

pel•vis, pl. •vis\es
or •ves

pem•mi•can

pen, penned, pen•ning

pe•nal

pe•nal\i•za•tion

pe•nal•ize, •ized, •iz•ing

pen•al\ty, pl. •ties

pen•ance (punishment)
[vs. pen•nants (flags)]

pence

pen•chant

pen•cil, •ciled or •cilled,
•cil•ing or •cil•ling

pend•ant

pend•ent

pend•ing

pen•du•lous

pen•du•lum

pen\e•trate, •trat\ed,
•trat•ing

pen\e•trat•ing

pen\e•trat•ing\ly

pen\e•tra•tion

penetration pric•ing

pen•guin

pen\i•cil•lin

pe•nile

pen•in•su\la, pl. •las

pen•in•su•lar

pe•nis, pl. •nis\es or •nes

pen\i•tent

pen\i•ten•tia\ry, pl. •ries

pen\i•tent\ly

pen•knife, pl. •knives

pen•light

pen•man, pl. •men

pen•man•ship

Penn

pen name

pen•nant, pl. •nants (flags)
[vs. pen•ance
(punishment)]

pen•ni•less

Penn•syl•va•nia (PA)

pen\ny, pl. pen•nies (U.S.),
pence (Britain)

pen\ny-•pinch\ing

pen•sion

pension plan

pen•sive

pen•sive\ly

pent

pen\ta•cle

pen\ta•gon

pen•tag\o•nal

pen•tam\e•ter

Pen\ta•teuch

pen•tath•lon

Pen\te•cost

pent•house, pl. •hous\es

pent-•up

pe•nu•che

pe•nul•ti•mate

pe•num•bra, pl. •brae or
•bras

pe•nu•ri•ous

pe•nu•ri•ous•ness

pen•u\ry

pe\on

pe•o\ny, pl. •nies

peo•ple, pl. •ples; •pled,
•pling

pep, pepped, pep•ping

pep•per, •pered, •per•ing

pep\per•corn

pep•per\i•ness

pep\per•mint

pep\per•o\ni, pl. •nis

pep•per\y

pep•sin

pep•tic

per•ad•ven•ture

per•am•bu•la•tor

per an•num

per•cale

per cap•i\ta

per•ceiv•a\ble

per•ceive, •ceived,
•ceiv•ing

per•cent or per cent

per•cent•age

per•cen•tile

per•cep•ti\ble

per•cep•ti\bly

per•cep•tion

per•cep•tive

per•cep•tive\ly

per•cep•tive•ness

per•cep•tiv•i\ty

per•cep•tu•al

per•cep•tu•al\ly

perch, pl. perch or
perch\es; perched,
perch•ing

per•chance

per•cip•i•ent

per•co•late, •lat\ed, •lat•ing

per•co•la•tor

per•cus•sion

per•cus•sion•ist

per di\em

per•di•tion

per\e•gri•na•tion

per•emp•to•ri\ly

per•emp•to•ri•ness

per•emp•to\ry

per•en•ni•al

per•en•ni•al\ly

pe•re•stroi\ka

per•fect (*faultless*) [*vs.* pre•fect (*magistrate*)]

per•fect, •fect\ed, •fect•ing

per•fect•i\bil•i\ty

per•fect•i\ble

per•fec•tion

per•fec•tion•ism

per•fec•tion•ist

per•fect•ness

per•fi\dy, *pl.* •dies

per•fo•rate, •rat\ed, •rat•ing

per•force

per•form, •formed, •form•ing

per•for•mance

performance rat•ing

per•form\er

per•fume, •fumed, •fum•ing

per•fum•er\y, *pl.* •er•ies

per•func•to•ri\ly

per•func•to•ri•ness

per•func•to\ry

per•haps

per\i•car•di\um, *pl.* •di\a

Per\i•cles

per\i•gee

per\i•he•li\on, *pl.* •he•li\a

per\il, •iled *or* •illed, •il•ing *or* •il•ling

pe•rim\e•ter (*boundary*) [*vs.* pa•ram\e•ter (*math variable; limit*)]

per\i•ne\al

per\i•ne\um, *pl.* •ne\a

pe•ri\od

pe•ri•od\ic (*recurring at intervals*)

per•i\od\ic acid (*chemical*)

pe•ri•od\ic ex•pense

pe•ri•od\ic in•ven•to\ry

pe•ri•od\i•cal

pe•ri•od\i•cal\ly

per\i•o•don•tal

per\i•pa•tet\ic

pe•riph•er\al

peripheral de•vice

pe•riph•er•al\ly

pe•riph•er\y, *pl.* •er•ies

per\i•scope

per•ish (*to die*), •ished, •ish•ing [*vs.* par•ish (*church district*)]

per•ish•a•bil•i\ty

per•ish•a\ble

per\i•stal•sis, *pl.* •ses

per\i•stal•tic

per\i•to•ne\al

per\i•to•ne\um, *pl.* •to•ne•ums *or* •to•ne\a

per\i•to•ni•tis

per\i•wig

per•jure, •jured, •jur•ing

per•jur\er

per•ju\ry, *pl.* •ries

perk (*perquisite*)

perk (*to become cheerful; to percolate*), perked, perk•ing

per\ma•frost

per•ma•nent

per•ma•nent\ly

per•me•a\ble

per•me•ate, •at\ed, •at•ing

Per•mi\an

per•mis•si\ble

per•mis•sion

per•mis•sive

per•mis•sive\ly

per•mis•sive•ness

per•mit, •mit•ted, •mit•ting

per•mu•ta•tion

per•ni•cious

per•ni•cious\ly

per•ni•cious•ness

per\o•ra•tion

per•ox•ide, •id\ed, •id•ing

per•pen•dic\u•lar

per•pen•dic\u•lar•i\ty

per•pen•dic\u•lar\ly

per•pe•trate, •trat\ed, •trat•ing

per•pe•tra•tion

per•pe•tra•tor

per•pet\u\al

perpetual in•ven•to\ry

per•pet\u•al\ly

per•pet\u•ate, •at\ed, •at•ing

per•pet\u•a•tion

per•pe•tu•i\ty

per•plex, •plexed, •plex•ing

per•qui•site (*benefit*) [*vs.* pre•req•ui•site (*precondition*)]

per se

per•se•cute (*to harass*), •cut\ed, •cut•ing [*vs.* pros\e\cute (*to begin legal proceedings*)]

per•se•cu•tor

per•se•vere, •vered, •ver•ing

per-•share

Per•sia

Per•sian

Persian Gulf

per•si•flage

per•sim•mon

per•sist, •sist\ed, •sist•ing

per•snick•et\y

per•son

per•son•a\ble

per•son•age

per•son\al (*private*) [*vs.* per•son•nel (*employees*)]

personal com•put\er (*PC*)

per•son•al•i\ty, *pl.* •ties

per•son•al•ize, •ized, •iz•ing

per•son\al prop•er\ty

per•so\na non gra\ta

per•son\i•fy, •fied, •fy•ing

per•son•nel (*employees*) [*vs.* per•son\al (*private*)]

per•spec•tive (*view*) [*vs.* pro•spec•tive (*potential*)]

per•spi•ca•cious
per•spi•ca•cious\ly
per•spi•cac\i•ty
per•spic\u•ous
per•spic\u•ous\ly
per•spic\u•ous•ness
per•spi•ra•tion
per•spire, •spired,
•spir•ing
per•suade, •suad\ed,
•suad•ing
per•sua•sion
PERT chart (program eval-
uation and review tech-
nique chart)
pert (jaunty)
per•tain, •tained, •tain•ing
per•ti•na•cious
per•ti•na•cious\ly
per•ti•nac\i\ty
per•ti•nence
per•ti•nent
per•ti•nent\ly
pert\ly
pert•ness
per•turb, •turbed,
•turb•ing
per•turb•a\ble
Pe\ru
pe•ruse, •rused, •rus•ing
per•vade, •vad\ed,
•vad•ing
per•va•sive
per•verse
per•verse\ly
per•ver•sion
per•ver•si\ty, pl. •ties
per•vert, vert\ed,
•vert•ing
per•vert•i\ble
pe•se\ta, pl. •tas
pesk•i\ly
pesk\i•ness
pes\ky, •ki\er, •ki•est
pe\so, pl. •sos
pes•si•mism
pes•si•mist
pes•si•mis•tic
pes•si•mis•ti•cal\ly
pest
pes•ter, •tered, •ter•ing

pes•ti•cid\al
pes•ti•cide
pes•tif•er•ous
pes•ti•lence
pes•ti•lent
pes•tle
pet, pet•ted, pet•ting
PET (positron emission
tomography)
pet\al
pet•aled or pet•alled
pe•tard
pe•ter, •tered, •ter•ing
pet\i•ole
pe•tit bour•geois (mem-
ber of lower middle class)
pe•tit (lesser) [vs. pet\ty
(insignificant)]
pe•tite (diminutive)
pet\it four (small tea
cake), pl. pet•its fours
pe•ti•tion, •tioned,
•tion•ing
pe•ti•tion\er
pet•rel (the bird) [vs.
pet•rol (gasoline)]
pet•ri\fy, •fied, •fy•ing
pet\ro•chem\i•cal
pet\ro•dol•lars
pet•rol (gasoline) [vs.
pet•rel (the bird)]
pet\ro•la•tum
pe\tro•le\um
pet\ro•log\ic or
pet\ro•log\i•cal
pet\ro•log\i•cal\ly
pe•trol\o•gist
pe•trol\o\gy
pet•ti•coat
pet•ti•fog•ger
pet•ti•fog•ging
pet•ti\ly
pet•ti•ness
pet\ty (insignificant), •ti\er,
•ti•est [vs. pe•tit (lesser)
and pe•tite (diminutive)]
petty cash
pet\u•lance
pet\u•lant
pet\u•lant\ly
pe•tu•nia, pl. •nias

pew
pe•wee
pew•ter
pe•yo\te
PG (motion-picture rating)
PG-•13 (motion-picture
rating)
phag\o•cyte
phag\o•cyt\ic
pha•lan•ger
pha•lanx, pl. pha•lanx\es
or pha•lan•ges
phal•lus, pl. phal\li or
phal•lus\es
phan•tasm
phan•tas•ma•go•ri\a, pl.
•ri\as
phan•tas•mal
phan•tas•mic
phan•tas•mi•cal
phan•ta\sy (fantasy), pl.
•sies; •sied, •sy•ing
phan•tom
phan•tom•like
phantom stock
Phar•aoh
Phar\i•see
phar•ma•ceu•ti•cal
phar•ma•cist
phar•ma•co•log\i•cal or
phar•ma•co•log\ic
phar•ma•col\o•gist
phar•ma•col\o\gy
phar•ma•co•poe\ia or
phar•ma•co•pe\ia, pl. •ias
phar•ma•cy, pl. •cies
phar•yn•gi•tis
phar•ynx, pl. pha•ryn•ges
or phar•ynx\es
phase (aspect; to phase),
phased, phas•ing [vs. faze
(to disconcert)]
phase•out or phase-•out
Ph.D. (Doctor of Philosophy)
pheas•ant
phe\no•bar•bi•tal
phe•nol
phe•no•lic
phe•nom\e•non, pl. \na or
•nons
phe•no•type

phe•no•typ\ic or
  phe•no•typ\i•cal
pher\o•mo•nal
pher\o•mone
phi
phi\al
Phil\a•del•phi•a
phi•lan•der, •dered,
  •der•ing
phi•lan•der\er
phi•lan•thro\py, pl. •pies
phil\a•tel\ic
phil\a•tel\i•cal\ly
phi•lat\e•list
phi•lat\e•ly
phil•har•mon\ic
phi•lip•pic
Phil•ip•pines
phil•is•tine
phil\o•den•dron, pl.
  •drons or •dra
phi•lol\o•gy
phi•los\o•pher
phil\o•soph\i•cal
phi•los\o•phize, •phized,
  •phiz•ing
phi•los\o•phy, pl. •phies
phil•ter (potion) [vs. fil•ter
  (strainer)]
phle•bi•tis
phle•bot\o•my, pl. •mies
phlegm
phleg•mat\ic
phleg•mat\i•cal\ly
phlox (the flower), pl. phlox
  or phlox\es [vs. flocks (groups)]
Phnom Penh
pho•bi\a, pl. •bi\as
pho•bic
phoe\be, pl. •bes
Phoe•ni•cia
phoe•nix
phone, phoned, phon•ing
pho•neme
phone phreak
pho•net•ics
phon•ics
pho•ni•ness
pho•no•graph
pho•no•log\i•cal or
  pho•no•log\ic

pho•nol\o•gist
pho•nol\o•gy, pl. •gies
pho\ny, pl. •nies; •nied,
  •ny•ing; •ni\er, •ni•est
phoo\ey
phos•phate
phos•phor
phos•pho•res•cence
phos•pho•res•cent
phos•phor\ic ac\id
phos•pho•rus
pho\to•cell
pho\to•cop\y, pl. •cop\ies;
  •cop•ied, •cop\y•ing
pho\to•e•lec•tric
pho\to•en•grav\er
pho\to•gen\ic
pho\to•graph, •graphed,
  •graph•ing
pho\to•graph•a\ble
pho•tog•ra•phy
pho\to•jour\nal•ism
pho\to•jour\nal•ist
pho\to•me•chan\i•cal
pho•tom\e•ter
pho\to•mi\cro•graph
pho\to•mi\crog•ra•phy
pho\to•mur\al
pho\to•mu•ral•ist
pho•ton
pho•ton\ic
pho\to•sen•si•tive
pho\to•sen•si•ti•za•tion
pho\to•sen•si•tize, •tized,
  •tiz•ing
pho\to•syn•the•sis
pho\to•syn•thet\ic
pho\to•syn•thet\i•cal\ly
phrase, phrased, phras•ing
phra•se•ol\o\gy
phreak
phre•nol\o•gy
phy•lac•ter\y, pl. •ter•ies
phy•log\e•nist
phy•log•e\ny
phy•lum, pl. \la
phys•ic (medicine) [vs.
  phy•sique (body structure)
  and psy•chic (mental)]
phys\i•cal (of the body) [vs.
  fis•cal (financial)]

physical data structure
physical in•ven•to\ry
phys\i•cal\ly
phys\i•cal mem\o•ry
phy•si•cian
phys\i•cist
phys•ics
phys\i•og•no•my, pl.
  •mies
phys\i•ol\o•gy
phys\i\o•ther\a•pist
phys\i\o•ther•a\py
phy•sique (body structure)
  [vs. phys•ic (medicine)
  and psy•chic (mental)]
pi (Greek letter) [vs. pie
  (pastry)]
pi\a•nis•si•mo, pl. •mos
pi•an•ist
pi•an\o (musical
  instrument), pl. •an\os
pi•a\no (soft; softly)
pi\an\o•forte
pi•as•ter or pi•as•tre
pi•az\za, pl. pi•az•zas or
  piaz\ze
pic, pl. pix or pics
pi\a•ca, pl. •cas
pic\a•resque (roguish) [vs.
  pic•tur•esque (quaint)]
Pi•cas\so
pic\a•yune
pic•co•lo, pl. •los
pick, picked, pick•ing
pick\ax or pick•axe, pl.
  •ax\es
pick•er\el, pl. \el or •els
pick\et, •et\ed, •et•ing
pick•et•er
pick\le, •led, •ling
pick•pock\et
pick\up
pick\y, •i\er, •i•est
pic•nic, •nicked, •nick•ing
pic•nick\er
pi\co•sec•ond
pic•to•ri\al
pic•ture (image), •tured,
  •tur•ing [vs. pitch\er
  (container; baseball
  player)]

pic·tur·esque *(quaint)* [*vs.*
  pic\a·resque *(roguish)*]
pic·tur·esque\ly
pic·tur·esque·ness
pid·dling
pidg\in *(jargon)* [*vs.*
  pi·geon *(the bird)*]
pie *(pastry)* [*vs.* pi *(Greek*
  letter)]
pie·bald
piece *(portion)*, pieced,
  piec·ing [*vs.* peace
  (freedom from war)]
pièce de ré·sis·tance, *pl.*
  pièces de ré·sis·tance
piece·meal
piece·work
piece·work\er
pied
pied-à-·terre, *pl.* pieds-
  ·à-·terre
pie-·eyed
pier *(dock)* [*vs.* peer
  (equal; to look)]
pierce, pierced, pierc·ing
Pierre
pi·e\ty, *pl.* ·ties
pif·fle
pig, pigged, pig·ging
pi·geon *(the bird)* [*vs.*
  pidg\in *(jargon)*]
pi·geon·hole, ·holed,
  ·hol·ing
pi\geon-·toed
pig·gish
pig·gish·ness
pig\gy or pig·gie, *pl.* ·gies;
  ·gi\er, ·gi·est
pig\gy·back
pig\gy·back, ·backed,
  ·back·ing
pig·head\ed
pig·head·ed·ness
pig·ment, ·ment\ed,
  ·ment\ing
pig·men·ta·tion
pig·ment\ed
pig·pen
pig·skin
pig·tail
pike, *pl.* pike *or* pikes

pik\er
pi·laf
pi·las·ter
pi·las·tered
Pi·late
pil·chard
pile, piled, pil·ing
piles
pile\up
pil·fer, ·fered, ·fer·ing
pil·fer·age
pil·grim
pil·grim·age
pill
pil·lage, ·laged, ·lag·ing
pil·lar
pil·lared
pill·box
pil·lion
pil·lo\ry, *pl.* ·ries; ·ried,
  ·ry\ing
pil·low, ·lowed, ·low·ing
pil\low·case
pi·lot, ·lot\ed, ·lot·ing
pi·lot·house, *pl.*
  ·hous\es
PIM *(personal information
  manager)*
pi·men\to, *pl.* ·tos
pimp, pimped, pimp·ing
pim·per·nel
pim·ple
PIN *(personal identification
  number)*
pin, pinned, pin·ning
pin\a·fore
pi·ña\ta, *pl.* ·tas
pin·ball machine
pince-·nez, *pl.* pince-·nez
pin·cers
pinch, pinched, pinch·ing
pinch-·hit, ·hit, ·hit\ting
pin·cush·ion
pine, pined, pin·ing
pin·e\al gland
pine·ap\ple
pin feed
ping
Ping-·Pong (™)
pin·head
pin·hole

pin·ion *(gear; wing)* [*vs.*
  pi·ñon *(pine nut)* and
  pin·yin *(Chinese transliteration system)*]
pink, \er, ·est
pink·eye
pink\ie *or* pink\y, *pl.*
  pink·ies
pink·ing shears
pin·na·cle
pi·noch\le
pi·ñon *(pine nut)*, *pl.*
  pi·ñons *or* pi·ño·nes [*vs.*
  pin·ion *(gear; wing)* and
  pin·yin *(Chinese transliteration system)*]
pin·point, ·point\ed,
  ·point\ing
pin·prick
pin·set·ter
pin·striped
pint
pin\to, *pl.* ·tos
pin\up
pin·wheel
pin·yin *(Chinese transliteration system)* [*vs.* pin·ion
  (gear; wing) and pi·ñon
  (pine nut)]
pi·o·neer, ·neered,
  ·neer\ing
pi·ous
pi·ous\ly
pi·ous·ness
pip
pipe, piped, pip·ing
pipe·line
pip·pin
pip·squeak
pi·quan\cy
pi·quant
pique *(to irritate)*, piqued,
  piqu·ing [*vs.* peak *(pointed top)* and peek *(to
  look)*]
pi·qué *(the fabric)*
piqued *(aroused)* [*vs.*
  peaked *(pointed)* and
  peeked *(looked)*]
pi·ra\cy, *pl.* ·cies
pi·ra·nha, *pl.* ·nhas *or* ·nha

pi•rate, •rat\ed, •rat•ing
pi•rat\i•cal
pir•ou•ette, •et•ted,
 •et•ting
pis•ca•to\ry or
 pis•ca•to•ri\al
Pis•ces
pis•mire
pis•tach\i\o, pl. •chi\os
pis•til (flower part)
pis•tol (handgun)
pis\tol-•whip, •whipped,
 •whip\ping
pis•ton
pit, pit•ted, pit•ting
pi\ta, pl. •tas
pit•a•pat
pitch, pitched, pitch•ing
pitch-•black
pitch•blende
pitch-•dark
pitch\er (container; baseball player) [vs. pic•ture
 (image)]
pitch•fork
pitch•man, pl. •men
pit\e•ous
pit\e•ous•ly
pit\e•ous•ness
pit•fall
pith
pith\y, •i\er, •i•est
pit\i•a•ble
pit\i•ful
pit\i•ful\ly
pit\i•less
pit\i•less•ly
pit\i•less•ness
pi•ton
pit•tance
pit\ter-•pat\ter, \tered,
 \ter\ing
Pitts•burgh
pi•tu•i•tar\y, pl. •tar•ies
pit\y, pl. pit•ies; pit•ied,
 pit\y•ing
pit\y•ing\ly
piv\ot, •ot\ed,
 •ot•ing
pix, pl. of pic
pix\el

pix\ie or pix\y, pl. pix•ies
pi•zazz or piz•zazz
piz\za, pl. •zas
piz•ze•ri\a, pl. •ri\as
piz•zi•ca\to, pl. \ti
pl. (plural)
P/L or P&L (profit and loss)
PL/1 (programming lan-
 guage)
plac\ard
pla•cate, •cat\ed, •cat•ing
place, placed, plac•ing
pla•ce\bo, pl. \bos or
 \boes
place•ment
pla•cen\ta, pl. •tas or •tae
pla•cen•tal
plac\id
pla•cid•i\ty or plac•id•ness
plac•id\ly
plack\et
pla•gia•rize, •rized, •riz•ing
plague (epidemic disease;
 to torment), plagued,
 pla•guing [vs. plaque
 (inscribed tablet)]
plaid
plain (clear), \er, •est [vs.
 plane (airplane; tool)]
plain•clothes•man or
 plain•clothes man, pl.
 •men or men
plain\ly
plain•ness
plains•man, pl. •men
plain•song
plaint
plain•tiff (one who sues)
plain•tive (mournful)
plain•tive\ly
plain va•nil\la
plait (braid; to braid),
 plait\ed, plait•ing [vs. plat
 (map) and plate (dish)
 and pleat (crease)]
plan, planned, plan•ning
pla•nar
plane (airplane; tool; to use
 a plane), planed, plan•ing
 [vs. plain (clear)]
plan\et

plan\e\tar•i\um, pl.
 \tar\i•ums or \tar\i\a
plan\e\tes\i•mal
plank
plank•ton
plan•ner
plant, plant\ed, plant•ing
plant•a•ble
plan•tar (of the sole of the
 foot)
plan•tain
plan•ta•tion
plant\er (one who plants)
plaque (inscribed tablet)
 [vs. plague (epidemic
 disease)]
plas\ma
plasma dis•play
plas•ter, •tered, •ter•ing
plas\ter•board
plas\ter•er
plas•tic
plas•tic sur•ger\y
plat (map), plat•ted,
 plat•ting [vs. plait (braid)
 and pleat (crease)]
plate (dish), plat\ed,
 plat•ing
pla•teau, pl. •teaus or
 •teaux; •teaued,
 •teau•ing
plate-•tec\ton\ic
plat•form
plat\i•num
plat\i•tude
Pla\to
Pla•ton\ic
pla•toon
plat•ter
plat\y, pl. plat\y or plat\ys
 or plat•ies
plat\y•pus, pl. •pus\es or
 \pi
plau•dit
plau•si•bil•i\ty
plau•si\ble
plau•si•bly
play, played, play•ing
play•act, •act\ed, •act•ing
play•back
play•bill

play•boy
play\er
play•ful
play•ful\ly
play•ful•ness
play•go\er
play•ground
play•house, *pl.* •hous\es
play•mate
play-•off
play•pen
play•thing
play•wright
pla\za, *pl.* •zas
plea, *pl.* pleas
plead, plead\ed *or* pled,
   plead•ing
plead•a\ble
plead\er
pleas•ant
pleas•ant\ly
pleas•ant•ness
pleas•ant\ry, *pl.* •ries
please, pleased, pleas•ing
pleas•ing\ly
pleas•ur•a\ble
pleas•ur•a•bly
pleas•ure
pleat (*crease*), pleat\ed,
   pleat•ing [*vs.* plait (*braid*)
   and plat (*map*) and plate
   (*dish*)]
ple•be\ian
pleb\i•scite
plec•trum, *pl.* •tra, •trums
pled
pledge, pledged, pledg•ing
Pleis•to•cene
ple•na\ry
plen\i•po•ten•ti•ar\y, *pl.*
   •ar•ies
plen\i•tude
plen•te•ous
plen•te•ous•ness
plen•te•ous•ness
plen•ti•ful
plen•ti•ful\ly
plen\ty
pleu•ri\sy
Plex\i•glas (™)
plex\us, *pl.* •us\es *or* \us

pli•a•bil\i\ty
pli•a\ble
pli•an\cy
pli•ant
pli\ers
plight, plight\ed, plight•ing
plod, plod•ded, plod•ding
plod•der
plod•ding\ly
plop, plopped, plop•ping
plot, plot•ted, plot•ting
plov\er
plow, plowed, plow•ing
plow•a\ble
plow\er
plow•share
ploy
pluck, plucked, pluck•ing
pluck•i\ly
pluck\i•ness
pluck\y, •i\er, •i•est
plug, plugged, plug•ging
plug-•com\pat\i\ble
plum (*the fruit*)
plum•age
plum•aged
plumb (*perpendicular*)
plumb (*to measure, as*
   depth), plumbed,
   plumb•ing
plumb\er
plumb•ing
plume
plum•met, •met\ed,
   •met•ing
plump, plumped,
   plump•ing; plump\er,
   plump•est
plump•ness
plun•der, •dered, •der•ing
plun•der•a\ble
plun•der•er
plunge, plunged, plung•ing
plung\er
plunk, plunked, plunk•ing
plunk\er
plu•per•fect
plu•ral
plu•ral•ism
plu•ral•ist
plu•ral•is•tic

plu•ral•is•ti•cal\ly
plu•ral•i\ty, *pl.* •ties
plu•ral\i•za•tion
plu•ral•ize, •ized, •iz•ing
plus
plush, \er, •est
plush\ly
Plu•tarch
Plu\to
plu•toc\ra•cy, *pl.* •cies
plu•ton
plu•to•ni\um
ply, *pl.* plies; plied, ply•ing
Plym•outh
ply•wood
PMS (*premenstrual syn-*
   drome)
pmt. (*payment*)
pneu•mat\ic
pneu•mo•nia
pneu•mon\ic (*of the lungs*)
   [*vs.* mne•mon\ic (*aiding*
   the memory)]
poach, poached,
   poach•ing
pock\et, •et\ed, •et•ing
poc\ket•book
pock\et•knife, *pl.* •knives
pock•marked
pod
po•di•a•try
po•di\um, *pl.* •di•ums *or*
   •di\a
Poe
po\em
po•e\sy, *pl.* •sies
po\et
po•et\ic
po\et lau•re•ate, *pl.*
   po•ets lau•re•ate
po•et\ry
po•grom
poi
poign•an\cy
poign•ant
poign•ant\ly
poin•ci•an\a, *pl.* •an\as
poin•set•ti\a, *pl.* •ti\as
point
point-•and-•click
point-•blank

point\er
poin•til•lism
poin•til•list
point•less
point•less•ly
point•less•ness
point of pur•chase (*noun*)
point-•of-•pur\chase (*adj.*)
poise, poised, pois•ing
poised
poi•son, •soned, •son•ing
poi•son\er
poi•son pill
poke, poked, pok•ing
pok\er (*card game*) [*vs.* pol\ka (*lively dance*)]
pok•i\ly
pok\i•ness
pok\y, •i\er, •i•est
pol
Po•land
po•lar
Po•lar\is
po•lar•i\ty, *pl.* •ties
po•lar\i•za•tion
po•lar•ize, •ized, •iz•ing
Po•lar•oid (™)
pole (*long rod; to use a pole*), poled, pol•ing [*vs.* poll (*survey*)]
pole•cat, *pl.* •cats or •cat
po•lem•ic
po•lem•ics
pole•star
pole vault (*noun*)
pole-•vault (*verb*), •vault\ed, •vault•ing
pole-•vault\er
po•lice, •liced, •lic•ing
po•lice•man, *pl.* •men
pol\i•cy, *pl.* •cies
pol\i•cy•hold\er
po•li\o•my\e\li•tis
Po•lish (*of Poland*)
pol•ish (*to make glossy*), •ished, •ish•ing
Po•lit•bu\ro
po•lite, •lit\er, •lit•est
po•lite•ly
po•lite•ness
pol\i•tesse

po•li•tic
po•lit\i•cal
po•lit\i•cal•ly
po•li•ti•cian
po•lit\i•cize, •cized, •ciz•ing
po•lit\i\co, *pl.* •cos
pol\i•tics
Polk
pol\ka (*lively dance*), *pl.* •kas; •kaed, •ka•ing [*vs.* pok\er (*card game*)]
poll (*survey*), polled, poll•ing [*vs.* pole (*long rod; to use a pole*)]
pol•len
pol•li•nate, •nat\ed, •nat•ing
pol•li•na•tion
pol•li•wog or pol•ly•wog
poll•ster
pol•lute, •lut\ed, •lut•ing
pol•lut\er
po•lo
pol\o•naise
po•lo•ni•um
pol•ter•geist
pol\y•clin\ic
pol\y•es•ter
pol\y•eth•yl•ene
po•lyg\a•mist
po•lyg•a•my
pol\y•glot
pol\y•glot•ism
pol\y•gon
po•lyg\o•nal
pol\y•graph, •graphed, •graph•ing
pol\y•he•dral
pol\y•he•dron, *pl.* •drons, •dra
pol\y•math
pol\y•mer
pol\y•mer•ase chain re•ac•tion
Pol\y•ne•sia
pol\y•no•mi\al
pol\yp
po•lyph\o\ny
pol\y•sty•rene
pol\y•syl•lab\ic

pol\y•syl•la•ble
pol\y•tech•nic
pol\y•the•ism
pol\y•the•ist
pol\y•the•is•tic
pol\y•the•is•ti•cal
pol\y•un•sat\u•rat\ed
pol\y•vi•nyl
po•made
pome•gran•ate
pom•mel (*knob*), •meled or •melled, •mel•ing or •mel•ling [*vs.* pum•mel (*to beat*)]
pomp
pom•pa•dour
pom•pa\no, *pl.* \no, •nos
pom•pom or pom-•pom
pomp•ous
pomp•ous\ly
pon•cho, *pl.* •chos
pond
pon•der, •dered, •der•ing
pon•der\o\sa pine
pon•der•ous
pon•der•ous\ly
pone
pon•gee
pon•iard
pon•tiff
pon•tif\i\i•cate, •cat\ed, •cat•ing
pon•toon
po\ny, *pl.* •nies; •nied, •ny•ing
po\ny•tail
Pon\zi scheme
pooch
poo•dle
pooh
pooh-•pooh, •poohed, •pooh\ing
pool, pooled, pool•ing
poop, pooped, poop•ing
poor (*impoverished*), \er, •est [*vs.* pore (*tiny opening; to read*) and pour (*to send flowing*)]
poor•house, *pl.* •hous\es
pop, popped, pop•ping
pop•corn

pope
pop•gun
pop•in•jay
pop•lar (*the tree*) [vs.
    pop\u•lar (*well-liked*)]
pop•lin
pop•o\ver
pop\py, *pl.* •pies
pop\py•cock
pop\u•lace (*common peo-
    ple*) [vs. pop\u•lous
    (*thickly populated*)]
pop\u•lar (*well-liked*) [vs.
    pop•lar (*the tree*)]
pop\u•lar\i•za•tion
pop\u•lar•ize, •ized, •iz•ing
pop\u•lar•ly
pop•u•late, •lat•ed, •lat•ing
pop•u•la•tion
pop•u•lism
pop•u•list
pop\u•lous (*thickly popu-
    lated*) [vs. pop\u•lace
    (*common people*)]
pop-•up u\til•i\ty
pop-•up win•dow
por•ce•lain
porch
por•cine
por•cu•pine
pore (*tiny opening; to
    read*), pored, por•ing [vs.
    poor (*impoverished*) and
    pour (*to send flowing*)]
por\gy, *pl.* \gy or •gies
pork
porn or por\no
por\no•graph\ic
por•nog•ra•phy
po•rous
po•rous•ness
por•phy•rit•ic
por•phy\ry
por•poise, *pl.* •poise or
    •pois\es
por•ridge
por•rin•ger
port, port\ed, port•ing
port•a\ble
portable com•put\er
por•tage, •taged, •tag•ing

por•tal
Port-•au-•Prince
port•cul•lis
por•tend, •tend\ed,
    •tend•ing
por•tent
por•ten•tous
por•ten•tous\ly
por•ter
por\ter•house
port•fo•li\o, *pl.* •li\os
port•hole
por•ti•co, *pl.* •coes or •cos
por•ti•coed
por•tiere or por•tière
por•tiered
por•tion, •tioned,
    •tion•ing
Port•land
port•li•ness
port\ly, •li\er, •li•est
port•man•teau, *pl.* •teaus
    or •teaux
Port Mores\by
Port-•of-•Spain
Por\to No\vo
por•trait
por•trait•ist
por•trait o\ri•en•ta•tion
por•trai•ture
por•tray, •trayed,
    •tray•ing
Por•tu•gal
Por•tu•guese, *pl.* •guese
pose, posed, pos•ing
Po•sei•don
pos\er (*puzzling problem*)
po•seur (*affected person*)
posh
pos\it, •it\ed, •it•ing
po•si•tion, •tioned,
    •tion•ing
po•si•tion•al
pos\i•tive
pos\i•tive•ness
pos\i•tron
pos\e
pos•sess, •sessed,
    •sess•ing
pos•ses•sion
pos•ses•sive

pos•ses•sive\ly
pos•ses•sive•ness
pos•ses•sor
pos•si\ble
pos•sum, *pl.* •sums or
    •sum
post, post\ed, post•ing
post•age
post\al
post•card or post card
post•date, •dat\ed,
    •dat•ing
post\er
pos•te•ri\or
pos•te•ri•or\i\ty
pos•te•ri•or\ly
pos•ter•i\ty
pos•tern
post•fem\i•nism
post•fem\i•nist
post•grad\u•ate
post•haste
post•hu•mous
post•hu•mous\ly
post•hyp•not\ic
pos•til•ion
pos•til•ioned
post•in•dus•tri•al
post•lude
post•man, *pl.* •men
post•mark, •marked,
    •mark•ing
post•mas•ter
post•mod•ern
post•mod•ern•ism
post•mod•ern•ist
post•mor•tem
post•na•sal
post of•fice (*noun*)
post-•of\fice (*adj.*)
post•op•er\a•tive
post•op•er\a•tive\ly
post•paid
post•par•tum
post•pone, •poned,
    •pon•ing
post•pone•ment
post•pran•di\al
post•proc•es•sor
post•script
post•struc•tur•al•ism

pos•tu•late, •lat\ed,
 •lat\ing
pos•tu•la•tion
pos•tur•al
pos•ture, •tured, •tur•ing
post•war
po\sy, *pl.* •sies
pot, pot•ted, pot•ting
po•ta•bil•i\ty
po•ta•ble
pot•ash
po•tas•si\um
po•ta\to, *pl.* •toes
pot•bel•lied
pot•bel\ly, *pl.* •lies
pot•boil\er
po•tent
po•ten•tate
po•ten•tial
po•ten•tial\ly
pot•herb
pot•hold\er
pot•hole
pot•hook
po•tion
pot•latch
pot•luck
Po•to•mac
pot•pie
pot•pour\ri, *pl.* •ris
pot•sherd
pot•shot
pot•tage
pot•ted
pot•ter
pot•ter\y
pouch
poul•tice
poul•try (*fowl*) [*vs.* pal•try
 (*trifling*)]
pounce, pounced,
 pounc•ing
pound, *pl.* pounds or
 pound; pound\ed,
 pound•ing
pour (*to send flowing*),
 poured, pour•ing [*vs.*
 pore (*tiny opening; to*
 read) *and* poor
 (*impoverished*)]
pout, pout\ed, pout•ing

pov•er\ty
pov•er\ty-•strick\en
pow•der, •dered, •der•ing
pow\er, •ered, •er•ing
pow\er•bro•ker or
 pow\er bro•ker
pow•er•ful
pow•er•ful\ly
pow\er•house, *pl.*
 •hous\es
pow•er•less
pow\er us\er
pow•wow
pox
pp. (*pages*)
PR (*Puerto Rico*)
prac•ti•ca\ble (*feasible*)
prac•ti•cal (*useful*)
prac•ti•cal•i\ty
prac•ti•cal\ly
prac•tice, •ticed, •tic•ing
prac•ti•tion\er
Prae•to•ri\an Guard
prag•mat\ic
prag•mat\i•cal\ly
prag•ma•tism
prag•ma•tist
Prague
Prai\a
prai•rie
praise, praised, prais•ing
praise•wor•thi\ly
praise•wor•thi•ness
praise•wor•thy
pra•line
prance, pranced,
 pranc•ing
prank
pra\se\o•dym•i\um
prate, prat\ed, prat•ing
prat•fall
prat•tle, •tled, •tling
prawn
pray (*to entreat*), prayed,
 pray•ing [*vs.* prey
 (*victim*)]
prayer (*worshipful petition*)
pray\er (*one who prays*)
preach, preached,
 preach•ing
pre•am•ble

pre•ar•range, •ranged,
 •rang•ing
pre•ar•range•ment
Pre•cam•bri\an or Pre-
 •Cam\bri\an
pre•can•cer•ous
pre•car\i•ous
pre•car\i•ous\ly
pre•cau•tion
pre•cau•tion•ar\y
pre•cede (*to go before*),
 •ced\ed, •ced•ing [*vs.*
 pro•ceed (*to continue*)]
prec\e•dence (*priority*)
prec\e•dent, *pl.* •dents
 (*examples*)
pre•ced•ing
pre•cept
pre•cep•tor
pre•cinct
pre•ci•os•i\ty,
 pl. •ties
pre•cious
pre•cious•ness
prec\i•pice
pre•cip\i•tant
pre•cip\i•tate, •tat\ed,
 •tat•ing
pre•cip\i•tate\ly
pre•cip\i•ta•tion
pre•cip\i•tous
pré•cis (*summary*), *pl.* •cis
pre•cise (*exact*)
pre•cise\ly
pre•ci•sion
pre•clude, •clud\ed,
 •clud•ing
pre•co•cious
pre•coc•i\ty
pre-•Co\lum\bi\an
pre•cog•ni•tion
pre•cog•ni•tive
pre•con•ceived
pre•con•cep•tion
pre•con•di•tion, •tioned,
 •tion•ing
pre•cur•sor
pre•cur•so\ry
pre•date, •dat\ed, •dat•ing
pre•da•tion
pred\a•tor

pred\a•to\ry
pre•de•cease, •ceased, •ceas•ing
pred\e•ces•sor
pre•des•ti•na•tion
pre•des•tine, •tined, •tin•ing
pre•de•ter•mi•na•tion
pre•de•ter•mine, •mined, •min•ing
pre•dic\a•ment
pred\i•cate
pre•dict, •dict\ed, •dict•ing
pre•dict•a•ble
pre•dic•tion (*prophecy*)
pre•di•gest, •gest\ed, •gest•ing
pre•di•lec•tion (*preference*)
pre•dis•pose, •posed, •pos•ing
pre•dis•po•si•tion
pre•dom\i•nance
pre•dom\i•nant
pre•dom\i•nant\ly
pre•dom\i•nate, •nat\ed, •nat•ing
pre•em\i•nence
pre•em\i•nent *or* pre-em\i•nent
pre•em\i•nent\ly
pre•empt *or* pre-•empt, •empt\ed, •empt\ing *or* •empt\ing
pre•emp•tion
pre•emp•tive
preemptive right
preen, preened, preen•ing
pre•fab
pre•fab•ri•cat\ed
pre•fab•ri•ca•tion
pref•ace, •aced, •ac•ing
pref\a•to\ry
pre•fect (*magistrate*) [vs. per•fect (*faultless*)]
pre•fec•ture
pre•fer, •ferred, •fer•ring
pref•er•a•bly
pref•er•a•ble
pref•er•ence
pref•er•en•tial

pre•fer•ment
pre•ferred stock
pre•fig•ure, •ured, •ur•ing
pre•fix
preg•nan\cy
preg•nant
pre•hen•sile
pre•his•tor\ic
pre•judge, •judged, •judg•ing
pre•judg•ment
prej\u•dice, •diced, •dic•ing
prej\u•di•cial
prel•a\cy
prel•ate
pre•lim\i•nar\y, *pl.* •nar•ies
pre•lit•er•ate
prel•ude
pre•mar\i•tal
pre•ma•ture
pre•ma•ture\ly
pre•med\i•tate, •tat\ed, •tat•ing
pre•med\i•ta•tion
pre•mier (*leading; prime minister*)
pre•miere (*first performance; to give a premiere*), •miered, •mier•ing
prem•ise
pre•mi\um
pre•mo•ni•tion
pre•mon\i•to\ry
pre•na•tal
pre•na•tal\ly
pre•oc•cu•pa•tion
pre•oc•cu\py, •pied, •py•ing
pre•op•er•a•tive
pre•or•dain, •dained, •dain•ing
prep, prepped, prep•ping
pre•pack•age, •aged, •ag•ing
pre•paid
prepaid ex•pense
prep\a•ra•tion
pre•par\a•to\ry
pre•pare, •pared, •par•ing

pre•par\ed•ness
pre•pay, •paid, •pay•ing
pre•pay•ment
pre•pon•der•ance
pre•pon•der•ant
prep\o•si•tion (*grammatical form*) [vs. prop\o•si•tion (*offer*)]
prep\o•si•tion\al
pre•pos•sess, •sessed, •sess•ing
pre•pos•sess•ing
pre•pos•ter•ous
prep\py *or* prep•pie, *pl.* •pies
prep school
pre•puce
pre•quel
pre•re•cord, •cord\ed, •cord•ing
pre•req•ui•site (*precondition*) [vs. per•qui•site (*benefit*)]
pre•re•tail•ing
pre•rog\a•tive
pres•age, •aged, •ag•ing
pres•by•o•pi\a
pres•by•te•ri•an
pre•school
pre•school\er
pre•science
pre•scient
pre•scribe (*to order*), •scribed, •scrib•ing [vs. pro•scribe (*to prohibit*)]
pre•scrip•tion
pre•scrip•tive
pres•ence (*being at a place*)
pres•ent (*gift; here*)
pre•sent (*to give*), •sent\ed, •sent•ing
pres•ent•a•ble
pres•en•ta•tion
presentation graph•ics
pres\ent-•day
pre•sen•ti•ment
pres•ent\ly
pres•er•va•tion
pres•er•va•tion•ist
pre•serv\a•tive

pre•serve, •served,
•serv•ing
pre•serv•er
pre•set, •set, •set•ting
pre•side, •sid•ed, •sid•ing
pres\i•den•cy
pres\i•dent
pres\i•den•tial
pre•sid\i•um, pl. •sid\i•ums
or •sid\i•a
press, pressed, press•ing
press\er
press•ing
press•man, pl. •men
pres•sure, •sured, •sur•ing
pres•sur•ize, •ized, •iz•ing
pres\ti•dig\i•ta•tion
pres•tige
pres•tig•ious
pres•to, pl. •tos
pre•sum•a•ble
pre•sum•a•bly
pre•sume, •sumed,
•sum•ing
pre•sump•tion
pre•sump•tive
pre•sump•tu•ous
pre•sup•pose, •posed,
•pos•ing
pre•sup•po•si•tion
pre•teen
pre•tend, •tend\ed,
•tend•ing
pre•tend\er
pre•tense
pre•ten•sion
pre•ten•tious
pre•ten•tious\ly
pre•ten•tious•ness
pre•test
pret•er\it or pret•er•ite
pre•ter•nat\u•ral
pre•test, •test\ed,
•test•ing
pre•text
Pre•to•ri\a
pret•ti\fy, •fied, •fy•ing
pret•ti\ly
pret•ti•ness
pret\ty, pl. •ties; •tied,
•ty•ing; •ti\er, •ti•est

pret•zel
pre•vail, •vailed, •vail•ing
prev\a•lence
prev\a•lent
pre•var\i•cate, •cat\ed,
•cat•ing
pre•var\i•ca•tion
pre•var\i•ca•tor
pre•vent, •vent\ed,
•vent•ing
pre•vent•a•ble or
pre•vent•i•ble
pre•ven•tion
pre•ven•tive or
pre•vent\a•tive
preventive main•te•nance
pre•view, •viewed,
•view•ing
pre•vi•ous
pre•vi•ous\ly
pre•war
prex\y, pl. prex•ies
prey (victim; to victimize),
preyed, prey•ing [vs.
pray (to entreat)]
pri•ap\ic
price, priced, pric•ing
price con•trol
price-•earn\ings ra•ti\o
(p/e)
price e\las•tic•i\ty
price in•dex
price lead\er
price•less
price war
prick, pricked,
prick•ing
prick\le, •led, •ling
prick\ly, •li\er, •li•est
pride, prid\ed, prid•ing
prie-•dieu, pl. •dieus or
•dieux
priest
priest•ess
priest•hood
priest\ly, •li\er, •li•est
prig
prig•gish
prim, prim•mer,
prim•mest
pri•ma\cy

pri\ma don\na, pl. pri\ma
don\nas
pri\ma fa•ci\e
pri•mal
pri•ma•ri\ly
pri•ma\ry, pl. •ries
primary li•a•bil•i\ty
primary of•fer•ing
pri•mate
prime, primed, prim•ing
prim\er
prime rate
pri•me•val or pri•mae•val
prim\i•tive
prim\ly
prim•ness
pri•mo•gen\i•tor
pri•mo•gen\i•ture
pri•mor•di\al
primp, primped, primp•ing
prim•rose
prince
prince\ly, •li\er, •li•est
prin•cess
prin•ci•pal (foremost)
prin•ci•pal•i\ty, pl. •ties
prin•ci•pal\ly
prin•ci•ple (fundamental
law)
prin•ci•pled
print, print\ed, print•ing
print•a\ble
print\ed cir•cuit
printed circuit board
print\er
print•ing
print•out
print qual•i\ty mode
print serv\er
print spool\er
print spool•ing
print•wheel
pri\or
pri•or•ess
pri•or\i•tize, •tized,
•tiz•ing
pri•or•i\ty, pl. •ties
pri•o\ry, pl. •ries
prism
pris•mat\ic
pris\on

pris•on\er
pris•si\ly
pris\si•ness
pris\sy, •si\er, •si•est
pris•tine
prith\ee
pri•va\cy, pl. •cies
pri•vate
pri•va•teer
pri•vate en•ter•prise
private la•bel
pri•vate\ly
pri•vate sec•tor
pri•va•tion
priv\et
priv\i•lege
priv\i•leged
priv\y, pl. priv•ies
prize, prized, priz•ing
prize•fight or prize fight
prize•fight\er
pro, pl. pros
prob•a•bil•i\ty, pl. •ties
prob•a\ble
prob•a•bly
pro•bate, •bat\ed, •bat•ing
pro•ba•tion
pro•ba•tion•ar\y
pro•ba•tion\er
probe, probed, prob•ing
pro•bi\ty
prob•lem
prob•lem•at\ic or
  prob•lem•at\i•cal
pro•bos•cis, pl. •bos•cis\es
  or •bos•ci•des
pro•caine
pro•ce•dur\al
pro•ce•dure
pro•ceed (to continue),
  •ceed\ed, •ceed•ing [vs.
  pre•cede (to go before)]
proc•ess, pl. •ess\es;
  •essed, •ess•ing
process cost•ing
pro•ces•sion
pro•ces•sion\al
proc•ess num•ber
proc•es•sor
pro-•choice or pro•choice
pro-•choic\er

pro•claim, •claimed,
  •claim•ing
proc•la•ma•tion
pro•cliv•i\ty, pl. •ties
pro•cras•ti•nate, •nat\ed,
  •nat•ing
pro•cras•ti•na•tion
pro•cras•ti•na•tor
pro•cre•ate, •at\ed, •at•ing
pro•cre•a•tion
pro•cre•a•tive
Pro•crus•te\an
Pro•crus•tes
proc•tol\o•gist
proc•tol•o\gy
proc•tor, •tored, •tor•ing
pro•cur•a\ble
proc•u•ra•tor
pro•cure, •cured, •cur•ing
pro•cure•ment
pro•cur\er
prod, prod•ded, prod•ding
prod\i•gal
prod\i•gal•i\ty
pro•di•gious
pro•di•gious\ly
prod\i•gy (genius), pl. •gies
  [vs. pro•té\gé (one
  guided by another)]
prod•uce (vegetables)
pro•duce (to make),
  •duced, •duc•ing
pro•duc\er
producer goods
prod•uct
product cost
product
  di•ver\si•fi•ca•tion
pro•duc•tion
production budg\et
production con•trol
pro•duc•tive
pro•duc•tive\ly
pro•duc•tive•ness
pro•duc•tiv•i\ty
prod•uct li•a•bil•i\ty
product mix
prod•uct-•o\ri\ent\ed
prof
Prof. (professor)
prof\a•na•tion

pro•fane, •faned, •fan•ing
pro•fane\ly
pro•fan•i\ty, pl. •ties
pro•fess, •fessed, •fess•ing
pro•fes•sion
pro•fes•sion\al
pro•fes•sion•al•ism
pro•fes•sion•al\ly
pro•fes•sor
pro•fes•so•ri\al
prof•fer, •fered, •fer•ing
pro•fi•cien\cy
pro•fi•cient
pro•fi•cient\ly
pro•file, •filed, •fil•ing
prof\it (gain), •it\ed, •it•ing
  [vs. proph\et (person
  who speaks for God)]
prof•it•a•bil•i\ty
prof•it•a\ble
prof•it•a•bly
prof•it-•and-•loss (P/L)
prof•it cen•ter
prof•it•eer, •eered,
  •eer•ing
prof\it•less
profit shar•ing
prof•li•ga\cy
prof•li•gate
pro for\ma
pro forma in•voice
pro•found
pro•found\ly
pro•fun•di\ty
pro•fuse
pro•fuse\ly
pro•fu•sion
pro•gen\i•tor
prog•e\ny, pl. \ny or •nies
pro•ges•ter•one
prog•na•thous or
  prog•nath\ic
prog•no•sis, pl. •ses
prog•nos•ti•cate, •cat\ed,
  •cat•ing
prog•nos•ti•ca•tion
prog•nos•ti•ca•tor
pro•gram, •grammed or
  •gramed, •gram•ming or
  •gram•ing
pro•gram•ma\ble

pro•gram•mat\ic
pro•grammed
  in•struc•tion
pro•gram•mer
pro•gram•ming lan•guage
pro•gram trad•ing
prog•ress (*development*)
pro•gress (*to develop*),
  pro•gressed,
  pro•gress•ing
pro•gres•sion
pro•gres•sive
pro•gres•sive\ly
pro•hib\it, •it\ed, •it•ing
pro•hi•bi•tion
pro•hi•bi•tion•ist
pro•hib\i•tive
pro•hib\i•to\ry
proj•ect (*something
  planned*)
pro•ject (*to protrude*),
  pro•ject\ed, pro•ject•ing
pro•jec•tile
pro•jec•tion
pro•jec•tion•ist
pro•jec•tor
pro•le•gom\e•non, *pl.* \na
pro•le•tar•i\an
pro•le•tar•i\at
pro-•life
pro-•lif\er
pro•lif•er•ate, •at\ed,
  •at•ing
pro•lif•er•a•tion
pro•lif\ic
pro•lif\i•cal\ly
pro•lix
pro•lix•i\ty
PROLOG (*programming
  language*)
pro•logue *or* pro•log
pro•long, •longed,
  •long•ing
pro•lon•ga•tion
prom
PROM (*programmable
  read-only memory*)
prom\e•nade, •nad\ed,
  •nad•ing
Pro•me•the\us
prom\i•nence

prom\i•nent
prom\i•nent\ly
prom•is•cu•i\ty
pro•mis•cu•ous
pro•mis•cu•ous\ly
prom•ise, •ised, •is•ing
prom•is•so\ry note
prom•on•to\ry, *pl.* •ries
pro•mote, •mot\ed,
  •mot•ing
pro•mot\er
pro•mo•tion
pro•mo•tion\al
prompt, prompt\ed,
  prompt•ing; prompt\er,
  prompt•est
prompt\er
prompt\ly
prompt•ness
prom•ul•gate, •gat\ed,
  •gat•ing
prom•ul•ga•tion
prone
prong
pronged
prong•horn, *pl.* •horns *or*
  •horn
pro•nom\i•nal
pro•noun
pro•nounce, •nounced,
  •nounc•ing
pro•nounce•a\ble
pro•nounced
pro•nounce•ment
pron\to
pro•nun•ci•a•tion
proof, proofed, proof•ing
proof•read, •read,
  •read•ing
proof•read\er
prop, propped, prop•ping
prop\a•gan\da
prop\a•gan•dist
prop\a•gan•dize, •dized,
  •diz•ing
prop\a•gate, •gat\ed,
  •gat•ing
prop\a•ga•tion
pro•pane
pro•pel, •pelled, •pel•ling
pro•pel•lant

pro•pel•ler
pro•pen•si\ty, *pl.* •ties
prop\er
prop•er\ly
prop•er•tied
prop•er•ty, *pl.* •ties
proph•e\cy (*prediction*), *pl.*
  •cies
proph•e\sy (*to foretell*),
  •sied, •sy•ing
proph\et (*person who
  speaks for God; one who
  foretells*) [*vs.* prof\it
  (*gain*)]
pro•phet\ic
pro•phy•lac•tic
pro•phy•lax\is, *pl.* •lax\es
pro•pin•qui\ty
pro•pi•ti•ate, •at\ed,
  •at•ing
pro•pi•ti•a•tion
pro•pi•ti•a•to\ry
pro•pi•tious
pro•po•nent
pro•por•tion
pro•por•tion\al
proportional pitch
pro•por•tion•ate
pro•pos\al
pro•pose, •posed,
  •pos•ing
prop\o•si•tion (*offer*) [*vs.*
  prep\o•si•tion (*grammatical form*)]
pro•pound, •pound\ed,
  •pound•ing
pro•pri•e•tar\y
pro•pri•e\tor
pro•pri•e\tor•ship
pro•pri•e\ty, *pl.* •ties
pro•pul•sion
pro•rate, •rat\ed, •rat•ing
pro•sa\ic
pro•sce•ni\um, *pl.* •ni•ums
  or •ni\a
pro•sciut\to
pro•scribe (*to prohibit*),
  •scribed, •scrib•ing [*vs.*
  pre•scribe (*to order*)]
pro•scrip•tion
prose

pros\e\cute (*to begin legal proceedings*), \cut\ed, \cut\ing [*vs.* per•se•cute (*to harass*)]

pros\e\cu•tion

pros\e\cu•tor

pros\e\lyt•ism

pros\e\lyt•ize, •ized, •iz•ing

pros\e\lyt•iz\er

pros•o\dy

pros•pect, •pect\ed, •pect•ing

pro•spec•tive (*potential*) [*vs.* per•spec•tive (*view*)]

pros•pec•tor

pros•pec•tus, *pl.* •tus\es

pros•per, •pered, •per•ing

pros•per•i\ty

pros•per•ous

pros•tate (*male gland*) [*vs.* pros•trate (*lying flat*)]

pros•the•sis, *pl.* •ses

pros•thet\ic

pros•ti•tute, •tut\ed, •tut•ing

pros•ti•tu•tion

pros•trate (*lying flat*) [*vs.* pros•tate (*male gland*)]

pros•tra•tion

pros\y, •i\er, •i•est

prot•ac•tin•i\um

pro•tag\o•nist

pro•te\an (*changeable*) [*vs.* pro•tein (*food source*)]

pro•tect, •tect\ed, •tect•ing

pro•tec•tion

pro•tec•tion•ism

pro•tec•tion•ist

pro•tec•tive

pro•tec•tive\ly

pro•tec•tive•ness

pro•tec•tor

pro•tec•tor•ate

pro•té\gé (*one guided by another*), *pl.* •gés [*vs.* prod\i\gy (*genius*)]

pro•té•gée (*a woman or girl guided by another*), *pl.* •gées

pro•tein (*food source*) [*vs.* pro•te\an (*changeable*)]

pro tem•po\re

pro•test, •test\ed, •test•ing

Prot•es•tant

Prot•es•tant•ism

prot•es•ta•tion

pro•to•col

pro•ton

pro\to•plasm

pro\to•type, •typed, •typ•ing

pro•to•zo\an, *pl.* •zo•ans or •zo\a

pro•tract, •tract\ed, •tract•ing

pro•trac•tion

pro•trac•tor

pro•trude, •trud\ed, •trud•ing

pro•tru•sion

pro•tu•ber•ance

pro•tu•ber•ant

proud, \er, •est

proud\ly

prov•a•bil•i\ty

prov•a\ble

prove, proved, prov\en, prov•ing

prov\e•nance

Pro•ven•çal

prov•en•der

prov•erb

pro•ver•bi\al

pro•vide, •vid\ed, •vid•ing

prov\i•dence

prov\i•dent

prov\i•den•tial

prov\i•den•tial\ly

prov\i•dent\ly

pro•vid\er

prov•ince

pro•vin•cial

pro•vin•cial•ism

pro•vi•sion

pro•vi•sion, •sioned, •sion•ing

pro•vi•sion\al

pro•vi•sion•al\ly

pro•vi\so, *pl.* •sos or •soes

prov\o•ca•tion

pro•voc\a•tive

pro•voc\a•tive\ly

pro•voke, •voked, •vok•ing

pro•vo•lo\ne

pro•vost

prow

prow•ess

prowl, prowled, prowl•ing

prowl\er

prox•im•i\ty

prox\y, *pl.* prox•ies

proxy fight

prude

pru•dence

pru•dent

pru•den•tial

pru•dent\ly

prud•er\y

prud•ish

prune, pruned, prun•ing

pru•ri•ence

pru•ri•ent

Prus•sia

Prus•sian

pry, pried, pry•ing

psalm (*hymn*) [*vs.* palm (*part of hand; the tree*)]

psalm•ist

pseu\do, *pl.* •dos

pseu\do•code

pseu\do•nym

pshaw

psi

psit•ta•co•sis

pso•ri•a•sis

psst or pst

psych, psyched, psych•ing

psy•che

psych\e•del\ic

psy•chi•at•ric

psy•chi•a•trist

psy•chi•a•try

psy•chic (*mental*) [*vs.* phys\ic (*medicine*) and phy•sique (*body structure*)]

psy•cho, *pl.* •chos

psy\cho•a•nal\y•sis

psy\cho•an\a•lyst
psy\cho•an\a•lyze, •lyzed, •lyz•ing
psy\cho•dra\ma
psy\cho•gen\ic
psy\cho•log\i•cal
psy\chol\o•gist
psy\chol•o\gy
psy\cho•neu•ro•sis, pl. •ses
psy\cho•path
psy\cho•path\ic
psy\cho•sex•u\al
psy\cho•sis, pl. •ses
psy\cho•so•mat\ic
psy\cho•ther\a•pist
psy\cho•ther•a\py, pl. •pies
psy\chot\ic
psy\cho•tron\ic
PT or P.T. (Pacific time)
ptar•mi•gan, pl. •gans or •gan
pter\o•dac•tyl
Ptol•e\my
pto•maine
pub
pu•ber\ty
pu•bes•cence
pu•bes•cent
pu•bic (of the lower abdomen)
pub•lic (of the community)
pub•li•ca•tion
pub•lic cor•po•ra•tion
public do•main soft•ware
pub•li•cist
pub•lic•i\ty
pub•li•cize, •cized, •ciz•ing
pub•lic•ly
pub•lic sale
pub•lic sec•tor
pub\lic-•serv\ice
pub\lic-•spir\it•ed
pub•lic u\til\i\ty
pub•lish, •lished, •lish•ing
pub•lish\er
Puc•ci\ni
puce
puck

puck\er, •ered, •er•ing
pud•ding
pud•dle, •dled, •dling
pudg\y, •i\er, •i•est
pueb\lo, pl. •los
pu•er•ile
pu•er•il•i\ty
pu•er•per\al
Puer\to Ri•can
Puer\to Ri\co (PR)
puff, puffed, puff•ing
puff•ball
puf•fin
puff\i•ness
puff\y, •i\er, •i•est
pug
pu•gi•lism
pu•gi•list
pu•gi•lis•tic
pug•na•cious
pug•na•cious•ly
pug•nac•i\ty
pug-•nosed
pu•is•sance
pu•is•sance
puke, puked, puk•ing
puk\ka
pul•chri•tude
pul•ing (whimpering)
pull, pulled, pull•ing (drawing toward oneself)
pull•back
pull-•down men\u
pul•let
pul•ley, pl. •leys
Pull•man (™), pl. •mans
pull•out
pull•o\ver
pull-•up or pull\up
pul•mo•nar\y
pulp, pulped, pulp•ing
pul•pit
pulp\y, •i\er, •i•est
pul•sar
pul•sate, •sat\ed, •sat•ing
pul•sa•tion
pulse, pulsed, puls•ing
pul•ver•i•za•tion
pul•ver•ize, •ized, •iz•ing
pu\ma, pl. •mas
pum•ice

pum•mel (to beat), •meled or •melled, •mel•ing or •mel•ling [vs. pom•mel (knob)]
pump, pumped, pump•ing
pump\er
pum•per•nick\el
pump•kin
pump prim•ing
pun, punned, pun•ning
punch, punched, punch•ing
punch card
punch-•drunk
punch\y, •i\er, •i•est
punc•til\i•ous
punc•til\i•ous\ly
punc•til\i•ous•ness
punc•tu\al
punc•tu•al•i\ty
punc•tu•al\ly
punc•tu•ate, •at\ed, •at•ing
punc•tu•a•tion
punc•ture, •tured, •tur•ing
pun•dit
pun•dit\ry
pun•gen•cy
pun•gent
pun•gent\ly
pu•ni•ness
pun•ish, •ished, •ish•ing
pun•ish•a\ble
pun•ish•ment
pu•ni•tive
punk
punk rock
punk rock\er
pun•ster
punt, punt\ed, punt•ing
punt\er
pu\ny, •ni\er, •ni•est
pup
pu\pa, pl. •pae or •pas
pu•pal (of a pupa)
pu•pil (student)
pup•pet
pup•pet•eer
pup•pet\ry
pup\py, pl. •pies
pur•blind

pur•chas•a\ble
pur•chase, •chased, •chas•ing
purchase or•der
pur•chas\er
pur•chas•ing a\gent
pure, pur\er, pur•est
pure•bred
pu•rée or pu•ree, •réed or •reed, •rée•ing or •ree•ing
pure\ly
pur•ga•tive
pur•ga•to\ry
purge, purged, purg•ing
pu•ri•fi•ca•tion
pu•ri•fi\er
pu•ri\fy, •fied, •fy•ing
Pu•rim
pu•rine
pur•ism
pur•ist
pu•ri•tan
pur\i•tan\i•cal
pur\i•tan•ism
pu•ri\ty
purl (knitting stitch; to purl), purled, purl•ing [vs. pearl (the gem)]
pur•lieu, pl. •lieus
pur•loin, •loined, •loin•ing
pur•ple, •pled, •pling; •pler, •plest
pur•plish
pur•port, •port\ed, •port•ing
pur•port\ed
pur•port•ed\ly
pur•pose
pur•pose•ful
pur•pose•less
purr, purred, purr•ing
purse, pursed, purs•ing
purs\er
pur•su•a\ble

pur•su•ance
pur•su•ant
pur•sue, •sued, •su•ing
pur•su\er
pur•suit
pu•ru•lence
pu•ru•lent
pur•vey, •veyed, •vey•ing
pur•vey\or
pur•view
pus (body fluid in sores) [vs. puss (cat)]
push, pushed, push•ing
push but•ton (noun)
push-•but\ton (adj.)
push\er
push\i•ness
push mon\ey
push•o\ver
push-•up
push\y, •i\er, •i•est
pu•sil•la•nim•i\ty
pu•sil•lan•i•mous
pus•like
puss (cat) [vs. pus (body fluid in sores)]
puss•like
puss\y (cat), puss•ies
pus\sy (puslike), •si\er, •si•est
puss\y•foot, •foot\ed, •foot•ing
pus•tule
put (to place), put, put•ting [vs. putt (golf stroke)]
pu•ta•tive
put-•call ra•tio
put-•down or put•down
put-•on
put op•tion
pu•tre•fac•tion
pu•tre\fy, •fied, •fy•ing
pu•tres•cence

pu•tres•cent
pu•trid
putsch
putt (golf stroke), putt\ed, putt•ing [vs. put (to place)]
put•ter (one who puts)
putt\er (club for hitting golf stroke)
put•ter (to occupy oneself casually)
put•ter\er
put•ting (placing)
putt•ing (hitting the golf stroke)
put•tre•fac•tion
put\ty, •tied, •ty•ing
puz•zle, •zled, •zling
puz\zle•ment
puz•zler
pyg\my, pl. •mies
py•jam\as
py•lon
py•lor\ic
py•lo•rus, pl. •lo\ri
Pyong•yang
py•or•rhe\a or py•or•rhoe\a
pyr\a•mid, •mid\ed, •mid•ing
py•ram\i•dal
pyramid sell•ing
pyre
Pyr\e\nees
py•re\thrin
Py•rex (™)
py•rim\i•dine
py•rite or py•rites
py\ro•ma•ni\ac
py\ro•tech•nics
Pyr•rhic vic•to\ry
Py•thag\o•ras
Py•thag\o•re\an
py•thon

Q

Qa•tar
Qa•tar\i
Q.E.D. (which was to be demonstrated)
QIC (quarter-inch cartridge)

qt. (quart), pl. qt., qts.
qua
quack, quacked, quack•ing
quack•er\y

quad
quad den•si\ty
quad•ran•gle
quad•ran•gu•lar
quad•rant

quad\ra•phon\ic or
  quad•ri•phon\ic
quad•rat\ic
quad•ren•ni\al
quad•ren•ni\um, pl.
  •ni•ums, •ni\a
quad•ri•ceps, pl. •ceps\es,
  •ceps
quad\ri•lat•er\al
quad\ri•lat•er•al\ly
quad•rille
quad•ril•lion, pl. •lions or
  •lion
quad•ri•ple•gi\a
quad•ri•ple•gic
quad•ru•ped
quad•ru•pe•dal
quad•ru•ple, •pled, •pling
quad•ru•plet
quad•ru•pli•cate
quaff (to drink), quaffed,
  quaff•ing [vs. coif (hair
  style)]
quag•mire
qua•hog or qua-•haug
quail (to shrink with fear),
  quailed, quail•ing
quail (the bird), pl. quails
  or quail
quaint, \er, •est
quaint\ly
quaint•ness
quake, quaked, quak•ing
Quak\er
Quak•er•ism
quak\y, •i\er, •i•est
qual\i•fi•ca•tion
qual\i•fied
qual\i•fy, •fied, •fy•ing
qual\i•ta•tive
qual\i•ta•tive\ly
qual•i•ty, pl. •ties
quality as•sur•ance
quality cir•cle
quality time
qualm
quan•da\ry, pl. •ries
quant
quan•ti•fy, •fied, •fy•ing
quan•ti•ta•tive
quan•ti•ty, pl. •ties

quan•tum, pl. \ta
quar•an•tine, •tined,
  •tin•ing
quark
quar•rel, •reled or •relled,
  •rel•ing or •rel•ling
quar•rel•some
quar•ry, pl. •ries; •ried,
  •ry•ing
quart
quar•ter, •tered, •ter•ing
quar\ter•back
quar\ter-•inch car•tridge
  (QIC)
quar•ter\ly, pl. •lies
quar\ter•mas•ter
quar•tet
quar•to, pl. •tos
quarts (32-ounce units)
quartz (mineral)
qua•sar
quash (to subdue),
  quashed, quash•ing [vs.
  squash (to crush; the
  vegetable)]
qua\si
Quat\er•nar\y
quat•rain
qua•ver, •vered, •ver•ing
qua•ver\er
qua•ver•ing\ly
quay (wharf) [vs. cay
  (island) and key (lock
  opener)]
Quayle
quea•si•ness
quea\sy, •si\er, •si•est
Que•bec
queen
queen\ly, •li\er, •li•est
Queens
queen-•size or queen-
  •sized
queer, \er, •est
quell, quelled, quell•ing
quench, quenched,
  quench•ing
quench\er
quench•less
quer\u•lous
quer\u•lous\ly

que\ry, pl. •ries; •ried,
  •ry•ing
query by ex•am•ple
query lan•guage
quest, quest\ed,
  quest•ing
ques•tion, •tioned,
  •tion•ing
ques•tion•a\ble
ques•tion mark
ques•tion•naire
queue (line; sequence),
  queued, queu•ing [vs.
  cue (signal)]
quib•ble, •bled, •bling
quib•bler
quiche
quick, \er, •est
quick\en, •ened, •en•ing
quick-•freeze, •froze,
  •fro\zen, •freez\ing
quick\ie
quick•lime
quick•ness
quick•sand
quick•sil•ver
quick-•tem\pered
quick-•wit\ted
quid pro quo, pl. quid pro
  quos or quids pro quo
qui•es•cence
qui•es•cent
qui\et (still), •et\ed,
  •et•ing; •et\er, •et\est [vs.
  quite (very) and quit (to
  leave)]
qui•et\ly
qui•e•tude
qui•e•tus, pl. •tus\es
quill
quilt, quilt\ed, quilt•ing
quilt\ed
quilt\er
quince
qui•nine
quint
quin•tes•sence
quin•tes•sen•tial
quin•tet
quin•til•lion, pl. •lions or
  •lion

quin•tu•ple, •pled, •pling

quin•tu•plet

quip, quipped, quip•ping

quip•ster

quire (24 sheets) [vs. choir (chorus)]

quirk

quirk\i•ness

quirk\y, •i\er, •i•est

quirt

quis•ling

quit (to leave), quit or quit•ted, quit•ting [vs. qui\et (still) and quite (very)]

quit•claim

quite (very)

Qui'to

quits

quit•tance

quit•ter

quiv\er, •ered, •er•ing

quiv•er\y

quix•ot\ic

quiz, pl. quiz•zes; quizzed, quiz•zing

quiz•zi•cal

quiz•zi•cal\ly

quoit

quon•dam

Quon•set hut (™)

quo•rum

quo\ta (allotment)

quo•ta•tion

quotation mark

quote (saying; to repeat another's words), quot\ed, quot•ing

quoth

quo•tid•i\an

quo•tient

q.v. (which see)

QWERTY (standard typewriter or computer keyboard)

R

Ra or Re

Ra•bat

rab•bet (a notch in timber) [vs. rab•bit (the animal)]

rab•bi, pl. •bis (clergy) [vs. ra•bies (disease)]

rab•bin•ate

rab•bin\i•cal

rab•bit (the animal), pl. •bits or •bit [vs. rab•bet (a notch in timber)]

rab•ble

rab\ble-•rous\er

rab\ble-•rous\ing

Rab\e•lais

Rab\e•lai•si\an

rab\id

ra•bies (disease) [vs. rab•bis (clergy)]

rac•coon, pl. •coons or •coon

race, raced, rac•ing

race•horse

ra•ceme

rac\er

race•track

race•way

ra•chit\ic

ra•chi•tis

ra•cial

ra•cial•ism

ra•cial•ist

ra•cial\ly

rac•i\ly

rac\i•ness

rac•ism

rac•ist

rack, racked, rack•ing

rack\et

rack•et•eer, •eered, •eer•ing

rack•ing\ly

rack job•ber

rac•on•teur

rac•quet•ball

rac\y, •i\er, •i•est

rad

ra•dar

ra\dar•scope

ra•di•al

ra•di•ance

ra•di•ant

ra•di•ant\ly

ra•di•ate, •at\ed, •at•ing

ra•di•a•tion

ra•di•a•tor

rad\i•cal

rad\i•cal•ism

rad\i•cal\i•za•tion

rad\i•cal•ize, •ized, •iz•ing

rad\i•cal\ly

ra•dic•chi\o

ra•di\i

ra•di\o, pl. •di\os; •di•oed, •di•o•ing

ra\di\o•ac•tive

ra\di\o•ac•tive\ly

ra\di\o•ac•tiv•i\ty

ra\di\o•gram

ra\di\o•i\so\tope

ra\di\o•i\so•top\ic

ra•di•ol•o•gist

ra•di•ol•o\gy

ra•di•om\e•ter

ra\di•o•met•ric

ra•di•om\e•try

ra\di\o•scop•ic or ra\di\o•scop\i•cal

ra•di•os\co\py

ra\di\o•tel\e•graph, •graphed, •graph•ing

ra\di\o•tel\e•graph\ic

ra\di\o•te•leg•ra•phy

ra\di\o•tel\e•phone, •phoned, •phon•ing

ra•di\o tel\e•scope

ra\di\o•ther\a•pist

ra\di\o•ther\a\py

rad•ish

ra•di•um

ra•di•us, pl. •di\i or •di•us\es

ra•don

RAF or R.A.F. (Royal Air Force)

raf•fi\a

raff•ish

raff•ish\ly

raff•ish•ness

raf•fle, •fled, •fling

raft

raf•ter

rag, ragged (*did tease*),
rag•ging [*vs.* rag•ged
(*tattered*)]
ra•ga, *pl.* •gas
rag\a•muf•fin
rag•bag
rage, raged, rag•ing
rag•ged (*tattered*) [*vs.*
ragged (*did tease*)]
rag•ged\ness
rag•ged\y
rag•ing\ly
rag•lan sleeve
ra•gout
rag•tag *and* bob•tail
rag•time
rag•weed
rah
raid, raid\ed, raid•ing
raid\er
rail, railed, rail•ing
rail•ler\y
rail•road, •road\ed,
•road•ing
rail•way
rai•ment
rain (*shower; to rain*),
rained, rain•ing [*vs.* reign
(*sovereignty*) *and* rein
(*strap of harness*)]
rain•bow
rain check *or* rain•check
rain•coat
rain•drop
rain•fall
rain for•est
Rain•ier (*the mountain*)
rain•i•er (*more rainy*)
rain•mak\er
rain•storm
rain•wa•ter
rain\y, •i\er, •i•est
raise (*to lift*), raised,
rais•ing [*vs.* rays (*light
beams*) *and* raze (*to tear
down*)]
rai•sin
rai•son d'ê\tre, *pl.*
rai•sons d'ê\tre
ra•jah, *pl.* •jahs
rake, raked, rak•ing

rake-•off
rak•ish
rak•ish\ly
rak•ish•ness
Ra•leigh
ral\ly, *pl.* •lies; •lied,
•ly•ing
RAM (*random-access
memory*)
ram, rammed, ram•ming
ram•ble, •bled, •bling
ram•bler
ram•bunc•tious
ram•bunc•tious•ness
RAM cache
RAM disk
ram\e•kin
ram\i•fi•ca•tion
ram\i•fy, •fied, •fy•ing
ram•jet
ramp
ram•page, •paged, •pag•ing
ramp•ant
ramp•ant\ly
ram•part
RAM-•res\i\dent
ram•rod
ram•shack\le
ran
ranch, ranched, ranch•ing
ranch\er, *pl.* •ers
ranch house
ranch•man, *pl.* •men
ran•cid
ran•cor
ran•cor•ous
rand, *pl.* rand
R&D (*research and devel-
opment*)
ran•dom
ran•dom-•ac\cess
mem\o\ry (*RAM*)
ran•dom\i•za•tion
ran•dom•ize, •ized, •iz•ing
ran•dom•iz\er
ran•dom•ly
rand\y, •i\er, •i•est
rang
range, ranged, rang•ing
rang\er
rang\y, •i\er, •i•est

rank, ranked, rank•ing;
rank\er, rank•est
rank *and* file
ran•kle, •kled, •kling
ran•sack, •sacked,
•sack•ing
ran•som, •somed,
•som•ing
rant, rant\ed, rant•ing
rap (*to strike*), rapped,
rap•ping [*vs.* wrap (*to
enclose*)]
ra•pa•cious
ra•pac•i\ty
rape, raped, rap•ing
Raph\a\el
rap\id
ra•pid•i\ty
rap•id\ly
rap•ids
ra•pi\er
rap•ine
rap•ist
rapped (*struck*) [*vs.* rapt
(*engrossed*) *and* wrapped
(*enclosed*)]
rap•per
rap•port
rap•proche•ment
rap•scal•lion
rapt (*engrossed*) [*vs.*
rapped (*struck*) *and*
wrapped (*enclosed*)]
rapt\ly
rapt•ness
rap•ture
rap•tur•ous
ra\ra a\vis, *pl.* ra•rae a\ves
rare, rar\er, rar•est
rare•bit
rar\e\fac•tion
rar\e\fy, \fied, \fy•ing
rare\ly
rar•ing
rar•i\ty
ras•cal
ras•cal\ly
rash, \er, •est
rash\ly
rash•ness
rasp, rasped, rasp•ing

rasp•ber\ry, *pl.* •ries

rasp\y, •i\er, •i•est

ras•ter graph•ics

rat, rat•ted, rat•ting

ratch\et, •et\ed, •et•ing

rate, rat\ed, rat•ing

rate cut•ting

rath\er

raths•kel•ler

rat\i•fi•ca•tion

rat\i\fy, •fied, •fy•ing

rat•ing

ra•tio, *pl.* •tios

ra•ti•oc\i•nate, •nat\ed, •nat•ing

ra•ti•oc\i•na•tion

ra•tion, •tioned, •tion•ing

ra•tion\al (*reasonable*)

ra•tion•ale (*logical basis*)

ra•tion•al•ism

ra•tion•al•ist

ra•tion•al•is•tic

ra•tion•al\i•ty

ra•tion•al\i•za•tion

ra•tion•al•ize, •ized, •iz•ing

ra•tion•al\ly

rat•like

rat•tan

rat•tle, •tled, •tling

rat\tle•brained

rat•tler

rat\tle•snake

rat\tle•trap

rat•tling

rat•trap

rat\ty, •ti\er, •ti•est

rau•cous

rau•cous\ly

rau•cous•ness

raun•chi•ness

raun•chy, •chi\er, •chi•est

rav•age, •aged, •ag•ing

rave, raved, rav•ing

Ra•vel (*composer*)

rav\el (*to disentangle; to entangle*), •eled *or* •elled, •el•ing *or* •el•ling

ra•ven (*the bird*)

rav\en (*to prowl for food*), •ened, •en•ing

rav•en•ous

rav•en•ous\ly

ra•vine

rav•ing

ra•vi•o\li

rav•ish, •ished, •ish•ing

rav•ish\er

rav•ish•ing

rav•ish•ment

raw, \er, •est

raw•boned

raw•hide

raw•ness

ray

ray\on

rays (*light beams*) [*vs.* raise (*to lift*) and raze (*to tear down*)]

raze *or* rase (*to tear down*), razed *or* rased, raz•ing *or* ras•ing

ra•zor

razz, razzed, razz•ing

raz\zle-•daz\zle

rcpt. (*receipt*)

re (*with reference to*)

reach, reached, reach•ing

re•act, •act\ed, •act•ing

re•ac•tance

re•ac•tant

re•ac•tion

read, read (*did read*), read•ing [*vs.* red (*the color*)]

read•a•bil\i\ty

read•a\ble

read\er

read•er•ship

read•ing

read-•me file

read-•on\ly

read-only mem\o\ry (ROM)

read•out *or* read-•out

read/•write head

read\y, read•ied, read\y•ing; read•i\er, read•i•est

read\y•made *or* ready-•made

Rea•gan

re•a\gent

re\al (*true*) [*vs.* reel (*spool; to sway*)]

real ac•count

real es•tate

real in•come

re•al•ism

re•al•i\ty (*real thing*), *pl.* •ties [*vs.* re•al\ty (*property*)]

re•al•iz•a\ble

realizable val\ue

re•al•ize (*to understand*), •ized, •iz•ing [*vs.* re•lies (*depends on*)]

re•al\ly

realm

re\al•po•li•tik

re\al prop•er\ty

re\al-•time clock

re\al-•time sys•tem

Re\al•tor (™)

re•al\ty (*property*) [*vs.* re•al•i\ty (*real thing*)]

ream, reamed, ream•ing

ream\er

reap, reaped, reap•ing

reap\er

rear, reared, rear•ing

rear•most

rear•ward

rea•son, •soned, •son•ing

rea•son•a\ble

rea•son•a\ble•ness

rea•son•a\bly

re•as•sur•ance

re•as•sure, •sured, •sur•ing

re•as•sur•ing\ly

re•bate, •bat\ed, •bat•ing

re•bat\er

reb\el (*one who revolts*)

re•bel (*to revolt*), •belled, •bel•ling

re•bel•lion

re•bel•lious

re•bel•lious\ly

re•bel•lious•ness

re•birth

re•boot, •boot\ed, •boot•ing

re•bound (*to spring back*),
•bound\ed, •bound•ing
[vs. re•dound (*to result*)]
re•buff, •buffed, •buff•ing
re•buke, •buked, •buk•ing
re•buk•ing\ly
re•bus, *pl.* •bus\es
re•but, •but•ted, •but•ting
re•but•tal
rec. (*receipt; record*)
re•cal•ci•trance
re•cal•ci•trant
re•call, •called, •call•ing
re•cant, •cant\ed,
•cant•ing
re•can•ta•tion
re•cap, •capped, •cap•ping
re•ca•pit\u•late, •lated,
•lat•ing
re•ca•pit\u•la•tion
re•cap•ture, •tured,
•tur•ing
recd. or rec'd. (*received*)
re•cede, •ced\ed, •ced•ing
re•ceipt
re•ceiv•a\ble
re•ceive, •ceived,
•ceiv•ing
re•ceiv\er
re•ceiv\er•ship
re•ceiv•ing a\pron
re•cent
re•cent\ly
re•cep•ta•cle
re•cep•tion
re•cep•tion•ist
re•cep•tive
re•cep•tor
re•cess, •cessed, •cess•ing
re•ces•sion
re•ces•sive
re•cher•ché
re•cid\i•vism
re•cid\i•vist
rec\i\pe, *pl.* •pes
re•cip\i•ent
re•cip•ro•cal
re•cip•ro•cate, •cat\ed,
•cat•ing
re•cip•ro•ca•tion
rec\i•proc\i\ty

re•cit\al
rec\i•ta•tion
rec\i•ta•tive
re•cite, •cit\ed, •cit•ing
reck•less
reck•less\ly
reck•less•ness
reck\on, •oned, •on•ing
re•claim, •claimed,
•claim•ing
rec•la•ma•tion
re•cline, •clined, •clin•ing
re•clin\er
rec•luse
re•clu•sive
rec•og•ni•tion
rec•og•niz•a\ble
re•cog•ni•zance
rec•og•nize, •nized,
•niz•ing
re•coil, •coiled, •coil•ing
rec•ol•lect, •lect\ed,
•lect•ing
rec•ol•lec•tion
re•com•bi•nant
rec•om•mend, •mend\ed,
•mend•ing
rec•om•men•da•tion
rec•om•pense, •pensed,
•pens•ing
rec•on•cil•a\ble
rec•on•cile, •ciled, •cil•ing
rec•on•cil\i•a•tion
rec•on•dite
re•con•nais•sance
re•con•noi•ter, •tered,
•ter•ing
re•con•sid\er, •ered,
•er•ing
re•con•sid•er•a•tion
re•con•sti•tute, •tut\ed,
•tut•ing
re•con•struct, •struct\ed,
•struct•ing
re•con•struc•tion
rec•ord (*noun*)
re•cord (*verb*), •cord\ed,
•cord•ing
re•cord•a\ble
re•cord\er
re•cord•ing

re-•count (*to count again*),
•count\ed, •count•ing
re•count (*to narrate*),
•count\ed, •count•ing
re•coup, •couped,
•coup•ing
re•course
re-•cov\er (*to cover
again*), \ered, \er\ing
re•cov\er (*to regain*),
•ered, •er•ing
re•cov•er•a\ble
re•cov•er\y
re-•cre•ate (*to create
anew*), •at\ed, •at\ing
rec•re•ate (*to amuse oneself*), •at\ed, •at•ing
rec•re•a•tion
rec•re•a•tion\al
re•crim\i•nate, •nat\ed,
•nat•ing
re•crim\i•na•tion
re•cru•des•cence
re•cruit, •cruit\ed,
•cruit•ing
re•cruit\er
re•cruit•ment
rec•tal
rec•tal\ly
rec•tan•gle
rec•ti•fi•a\ble
rec•ti•fi•ca•tion
rec•ti•fi\er
rec•ti•fy, •fied, •fy•ing
rec•ti•lin\e\ar
rec•ti•tude
rec\to, *pl.* •tos
rec•tor
rec•to\ry, *pl.* •ries
rec•tum, *pl.* •tums or •ta
re•cum•ben\cy
re•cum•bent
re•cu•per•ate, •at\ed,
•at•ing
re•cu•per•a•tion
re•cu•per•a•tive
re•cur, •curred, •cur•ring
re•cur•rence
re•cur•rent
re•cur•rent\ly
re•cy•cla\ble

re•cy•cle, •cled, •cling

red (*the color*), red•der, red•dest [*vs.* read (*did read*)]

red-•blood\ed

red•cap

red car•pet (*noun*)

red-•car\pet (*adj.*)

red•coat

red•den, •dened, •den•ing

red•dish

re•deem, •deemed, •deem•ing

re•deem•a\ble

re•deem•er

re•demp•tion

redemption price

re•demp•tive

red-•hand\ed

red•head

red•head\ed

red-•hot

re•dis•count, •count\ed, •count•ing

re•dis•trict, •trict\ed, •trict•ing

red-•let\ter

red-•light dis•trict

red•line, •lined, •lin•ing

red•lined text

red•neck *or* red-•neck

red•ness

red\o•lence

red\o•lent

re•doubt

re•doubt•a\ble

re•dound (*to result*), •dound\ed, •dound•ing [*vs.* re-•bound (*to spring back*)]

re•dress, •dressed, •dress•ing

red•skin

re•duce, •duced, •duc•ing

re•duc•tion

re•duc•tive

re•dun•dan\cy

re•dun•dant

re•dux

red•wood

reed

reed\i•ness

reed\y, •i\er, •i•est

reef

reef\er

reek (*to smell strongly*), reeked, reek•ing [*vs.* wreak (*to inflict*) *and* wreck (*to destroy*)]

reel (*spool; to sway*), reeled, reel•ing [*vs.* re\al (*true*)]

re•en•try, *pl.* •tries

re•face, •faced, •fac•ing

re•fec•to\ry, *pl.* •ries

re•fer, •ferred, •fer•ring

ref•er\ee (*arbitrator*), •eed, •ee•ing [*vs.* rev•er\ie (*musing*)]

ref•er•ence

ref•er•en•dum, *pl.* •dums *or* \da

ref•er•ent

re•fer•ral

re•fill, •filled, •fill•ing

re•fill•a\ble

re•fine, •fined, •fin•ing

re•fine•ment

re•fin•er\y, *pl.* •er•ies

re•flag, •flagged, •flag•ging

re•fla•tion

re•flect, •flect\ed, •flect•ing

re•flec•tion

re•flec•tive

re•flec•tive\ly

re•flec•tor

re•flex

re•flex•ive

re•flex•ive\ly

re•for•est, •est\ed, •est•ing

re•for•est•a•tion

re-•form (*to form again*), •formed, •form\ing

re•form (*to end wrong conduct*), •formed, •form•ing

ref•or•ma•tion

re•form\a•to\ry, *pl.* •ries

re•form\er

re•fract, •fract\ed, •fract•ing

re•frac•tion

re•frac•tive

re•frac•to\ry

re•frain, •frained, •frain•ing

re•fresh, •freshed, •fresh•ing

re•fresh\er

re•fresh•ing

re•fresh•ment

re•fresh rate

re•frig•er•ant

re•frig•er•ate, •at\ed, •at•ing

re•frig•er•a•tion

re•frig•er\a•tor

ref•uge, •uged, •ug•ing

ref\u•gee

re•ful•gence

re•ful•gent

re•fund, •fund\ed, •fund•ing

re•fund•a\ble

re•fur•bish, •bished, •bish•ing

re•fur•bish•ment

re•fus\al

refusal to deal

ref•use (*garbage*)

re•fuse (*say no*), •fused, •fus•ing

re•fut•a\ble

ref\u•ta•tion

re•fute, •fut\ed, •fut•ing

re•gal (*royal*)

re•gale (*to entertain*), •galed, •gal•ing

re•ga•li\a

re•gal\ly

re•gard, •gard\ed, •gard•ing

re•gard•ing

re•gard•less

re•gat\ta, *pl.* •tas

re•gen\cy, *pl.* •cies

re•gen•er•a\cy

re•gen•er•ate, •at\ed, •at•ing

re•gen•er•a•tion

re•gen•er\a•tive

re•gent

reg•gae
reg•i•cide
re•gime *or* ré•gime
reg•i•men
reg•i•ment, •ment\ed,
•ment•ing
reg•i•men•tal
reg•i•men•ta•tion
Re•gi\na
re•gion
re•gion\al
re•gion•al•ism
re•gion•al•ly
reg•is•ter (*to enroll*),
•tered, •ter•ing
reg•is•trant
reg•is•trar (*record keeper*)
reg•is•tra•tion
reg•is•try, *pl.* •tries
reg•nant
re•gress, •gressed,
•gress•ing
re•gres•sion
re•gres•sive
re•gret, •gret•ted,
•gret•ting
re•gret•ful
re•gret•ta•ble
re•group, •grouped,
•group•ing
reg•u•lar
reg•u•lar•i\ty
reg•u•lar•ize, •ized, •iz•ing
reg•u•lar•ly
reg•u•late, •lat\ed, •lat•ing
reg•u•la•tion
reg•u•la•tive
reg•u•la•tor
reg•u•la•to\ry
re•gur•gi•tate, •tat\ed,
•tat•ing
re•gur•gi•ta•tion
re•hab, •habbed,
•hab•bing
re•ha•bil\i•tate, •tat\ed,
•tat•ing
re•ha•bil\i•ta•tion
re•ha•bil\i•ta•tive
re•hash, •hashed,
•hash•ing
re•hears\al

re•hearse, •hearsed,
•hears•ing
Reich
reign (*sovereignty; to rule*),
reigned, reign•ing [*vs.*
rain (*shower*) *and* rein
(*strap of harness*)]
re•im•burse, •bursed,
•burs•ing
re•im•burse•ment
rein (*strap of harness; to
use a rein*), reined,
rein•ing
re•in\car•nate
re•in\car•na•tion
rein•deer, *pl.* •deer *or*
•deers
re•in\force *or* re•en•force,
\forced *or* •forced,
\forc•ing *or* •forc•ing
re•in\force•ment
re•in\state, •stat\ed,
•stat•ing
re•in\state•ment
re•in\sure, \sured, \sur•ing
re•in\vest•ment
reinvestment rate
REIT (*real-estate investment trust*)
re•it•er•ate, •at\ed, •at•ing
re•it•er•a•tion
re•ject, •ject\ed, •ject•ing
re•jec•tion
re•joice, •joiced, •joic•ing
re•join, •joined, •join•ing
re•join•der
re•ju•ve•nate, •nat\ed,
•nat•ing
re•ju•ve•na•tion
re•lapse, lapsed, •laps•ing
re•late, •lat\ed, •lat•ing
re•la•tion
re•la•tion\al da\ta•base
re•la•tion•ship
rel\a•tive
rel\a•tive•ly
rel\a•tiv•i\ty
re•lax, •laxed, •lax•ing
re•lax•ant
re•lax•a•tion
re•lay, •layed, •lay•ing

re•lease, •leased, •leas•ing
rel\e•gate, •gat\ed, •gat•ing
rel\e•ga•tion
re•lent, •lent\ed, •lent•ing
re•lent•less
re•lent•less\ly
re•lent•less•ness
rel\e•vance
rel\e•vant
re•li•a•bil•i\ty
re•li•a\ble
re•li•a\bly
re•li•ance
re•li•ant
rel\ic
re•lief
re•lies (*depends on*) [*vs.*
re•al•ize (*to understand*)]
re•lieve, •lieved, •liev•ing
re•li•gion
re•li•gious, *pl.* •gious
re•li•gious\ly
re•lin•quish, •quished,
•quish•ing
re•lin•quish•ment
rel\i•quar\y, *pl.* •quar•ies
rel•ish, •ished, •ish•ing
re•live, •lived, •liv•ing
re•lo•cate, •cat\ed,
•cat•ing
re•lo•ca•tion
re•luc•tance
re•luc•tant
re•luc•tant\ly
re\ly, •lied, •ly•ing
rem (*radiation measure*)
REM (*rapid eye movement*)
re•main, •mained,
•main•ing
re•main•der, •dered,
•der•ing
re•mand, •mand\ed,
•mand•ing
re•mark, •marked,
•mark•ing
re•mark•a\ble
re•mark•a\bly
Rem•brandt
re•me•di\al
re•me•di•al\ly
remedial main•te•nance

rem\e\dy, *pl.* •dies; •died,
•dy•ing

re•mem•ber, •bered,
•ber•ing

re•mem•brance

re•mind, •mind\ed,
•mind•ing

re•mind\er

rem\i•nisce, •nisced,
•nisc•ing

rem\i•nis•cence

rem\i•nis•cent

re•miss

re•mis•sion

re•miss•ness

re•mit, •mit•ted, •mit•ting

re•mit•tance

rem•nant

re•mod•el, •eled *or* •elled,
•el•ing *or* •el•ling

re•mon•strance

re•mon•strate, •strat\ed,
•strat•ing

re•morse

re•morse•ful

re•morse•less

re•mote, •mot\er,
•mot•est

re•mote con•trol (*noun*)

re\mote-•con\trol (*adj.*)

re•mote•ly

re•mote•ness

re•mov•a\ble

removable car•tridge

re•mov\al

re•move, •moved,
•mov•ing

rè•mu•ner•ate, •at\ed,
•at•ing

re•mu•ner•a•tion

re•mu•ner\a•tive

Ren•ais•sance

re•nal

rend, rent, rend•ing

ren•der (*to provide; to represent*), •dered, •der•ing

rend\er (*one who tears*)

ren•dez•vous, *pl.* •vous;
•voused, •vous•ing

ren•di•tion

ren\e•gade

re•nege, •neged, •neg•ing

re•new, •newed, •new•ing

re•new•a\ble

re•new\al

ren•net

ren•nin

Re\no

Re•noir

re•nounce, •nounced,
•nounc•ing

re•nounce•ment

ren\o•vate, •vat\ed,
•vat•ing

ren\o•va•tion

ren\o•va•tor

re•nown

rent, rent\ed, rent•ing

rent\al

rent\er

re•nun•ci•a•tion

re•or•der point

rep

re•pair

re•pair, •paired, •pair•ing

re•pair•man, *pl.* •men

rep\a•ra\ble *or*
re•pair•a\ble

rep\a•ra•tion

rep•ar•tee

re•past

re•pa•tri•ate, •at\ed,
•at•ing

re•pa•tri•a•tion

re•pay, •paid, •pay•ing

re•pay•ment

re•peal, •pealed, •peal•ing

re•peat, •peat\ed,
•peat•ing

re•peat•ed\ly

re•peat•er

re•pel, •pelled, •pel•ling

re•pel•lent *or* re•pel•lant

re•pent, •pent\ed,
•pent•ing

re•pent•ance

re•pent•ant

re•per•cus•sion

rep•er•toire

rep•er•to\ry, *pl.* •ries

rep\e•ti•tion

rep\e•ti•tious

re•pet\i•tive

re•pine, •pined, •pin•ing

re•place, •placed, •plac•ing

re•place•a\ble

re•place•ment

replacement cost

re•play, •played, •play•ing

re•plen•ish, •ished,
•ish•ing

re•plen•ish•ment

re•plete

re•ple•tion

rep•li\ca, *pl.* •cas

rep•li•cate, •cat\ed,
•cat•ing

rep•li•ca•tion

re•ply, *pl.* •plied, •ply•ing,
•plies

re\po

re•port, •port\ed,
•port•ing

re•port•age

re•port•ed\ly

re•port\er

re•port writ\er

re•pose, •posed, •pos•ing

re•pose•ful

re•pos\i•tor\y, *pl.* •tor•ies

re•pos•sess, •sessed,
•sess•ing

re•pos•ses•sion

rep•re•hen•si\ble

rep•re•hen•si\bly

rep•re•sent, •sent\ed,
•sent•ing

rep•re•sen•ta•tion

rep•re•sen•ta•tion\al

rep•re•sent\a•tive

re•press, •pressed,
•press•ing

re•pres•sion

re•pres•sive

re•prieve, •prieved,
•priev•ing

rep•ri•mand, •mand\ed,
•mand•ing

re•pris\al

re•prise, •prised, •pris•ing

re•proach, •proached,
•proach•ing

re•proach•ful

re•proach•ful\ly
rep•ro•bate
re•pro•duce, •duced, •duc•ing
re•pro•duc•i•ble
re•pro•duc•tion
reproduction cost
re•pro•duc•tive
re•proof
re•prove, •proved, •prov•ing
re•prov•ing\ly
rep•tile
rep•til\i\an
re•pub•lic
re•pub•li•can
re•pub•li•can•ism
Re•pub•li•can Par\ty
re•pu•di•ate, •at\ed, •at•ing
re•pu•di•a•tion
re•pug•nance
re•pug•nant
re•pulse, •pulsed, •puls•ing
re•pul•sion
re•pul•sive
re•pul•sive\ly
re•pul•sive•ness
re•pur•chase a\gree•ment
rep\u•ta•bil•i\ty
rep\u•ta•ble
rep\u•ta•tion
re•pute
re•put\ed
re•put•ed\ly
re•quest, •quest\ed, •quest•ing
req\ui\em
re•quire, •quired, •quir•ing
re•quire•ment
req•ui•site
req•ui•si•tion, •tioned, •tion•ing
re•quit\al
re•quite, •quit\ed, •quit•ing
re•run, •ran, •run, •running
re•sale
re•scind, •scind\ed, •scind•ing

re•scis•sion
res•cue, •cued, •cu•ing
res•cu\er
re•search, •searched, •search•ing
re•search\er
re•sec•tion
re•sem•blance
re•sem•ble, •bled, •bling
re•sent, •sent\ed, •sent•ing
re•sent•ful
re•sent•ful\ly
re•sent•ment
res•er•pine
res•er•va•tion
re•serve, •served, •serv•ing
reserve bank
reserved word
reserve re•quire•ment
res•erv•ist
res•er•voir
re•set but•ton
re•side, •sid\ed, •sid•ing
res\i•dence (home) [vs. res\i•dents (those who reside)]
res\i•den\cy, pl. •cies
res\i•dent
resident buy\er
resident fonts
res\i•den•tial
re•sid\u\al
residual in•come
residual val\ue
res\i•due
re•sign, •signed, •sign•ing
res•ig•na•tion
re•signed
re•sign•ed\ly
re•sil•ience
re•sil•ient
res\in
re•sist, •sist\ed, •sist•ing
re•sist•ance
re•sist•ant
re•sist\er (one who resists)
re•sis•tor (electrical device)
re•size, •sized, •siz•ing

re•sole, •soled, •sol•ing
res\o•lute
res\o•lute\ly
res\o•lu•tion
re•solv•a\ble
re•solve, •solved, •solv•ing
res\o•nance
res\o•nant
res\o•nate, •nat\ed, •nat•ing
res\o•na•tor
re•sort, •sort\ed, •sort•ing
re•sound, •sound\ed, •sound•ing
re•sound•ing\ly
re•source
re•source•ful
re•source•ful•ness
re•spect, •spect\ed, •spect•ing
re•spect•a•bil•i\ty
re•spect•a•ble
re•spect•a•bly
re•spect•ful
re•spect•ful\ly (with defer-ence)
re•spect•ing
re•spec•tive
re•spec•tive\ly (sequentially)
res•pi•ra•tion
res•pi•ra•tor
res•pi•ra•to\ry
re•spire, •spired, •spir•ing
res•pite
re•splend•ent
re•splend•ent\ly
re•spond, •spond\ed, •spond•ing
re•spond•ent
re•sponse
re•spon•si•bil•i\ty, pl. •ties
re•spon•si•ble
re•spon•si•bly
re•spon•sive
re•spon•sive\ly
re•spon•sive•ness
rest (repose), rest\ed, rest•ing [vs. wrest (to pull away)]

res•tau•rant
res•tau•ra•teur, *pl.* •teurs
rest•ful
rest•ful\ly
res•ti•tu•tion
res•tive
res•tive\ly
rest•less
rest•less\ly
rest•less•ness
res•to•ra•tion
re•stor\a•tive
re•store, •stored,
    •stor•ing
re•strain, •strained,
    •strain•ing
re•straint
restraint of trade
re•strict, •strict\ed,
    •strict•ing
restricted stock
re•stric•tion
re•stric•tive
re•sult, •sult\ed, •sult•ing
re•sult•ant
ré•su\mé *or* re•su\me
    (*summary of past jobs*)
re•sume (*to continue*),
    •sumed, •sum•ing
re•sump•tion
re•sur•gence
re•sur•gent
res•ur•rect, •rect\ed,
    •rect•ing
res•ur•rec•tion
re•sus•ci•tate, •tat\ed,
    •tat•ing
re•sus•ci•ta•tion
re•sus•ci•ta•tor
re•tail, •tailed, •tail•ing
re•tail\er
re•tail•ing
re•tail sales
re•tain, •tained, •tain•ing
re•tained earn•ings
re•tain\er
re•take, •took, •tak\en,
    •tak•ing
re•tal\i•ate, •at\ed,
    •at•ing
re•tal\i•a•tion

re•tal\i•a•tive *or*
    re•tal\i•a•to\ry
re•tard, •tard\ed, •tard•ing
re•tard•ant
re•tar•da•tion
re•tard\ed
retch (*to vomit*), retched,
    retch•ing [*vs.* wretch
    (*unfortunate person*)]
re•ten•tion
re•ten•tive
re•ten•tive•ness
ret\i•cence
ret\i•cent
ret\i\na, *pl.* \i•nas *or* \i•nae
ret\i•nue
re•tire, •tired,
    •tir•ing
re•tire•ment
re•tir•ing
re•tool, •tooled, •tool•ing
re•tort, •tort\ed, •tort•ing
re•touch, •touched,
    •touch•ing
re•trace, •traced, •trac•ing
re•tract, •tract\ed,
    •tract•ing
re•tract•a\ble *or*
    re•tract•i\ble
re•trac•tion
re•tread
re•treat
re•trench
re•tread (*to put a new
    tread on*), •tread\ed,
    •tread•ing
re-tread (*to walk again*),
    •trod, •trod\den *or*
    •trod, •tread\ing
re•treat, •treat\ed,
    •treat•ing
re•trench, •trenched,
    •trench•ing
re•trench•ment
ret•ri•bu•tion
re•trib\u•tive
re•triev\al
re•trieve, •trieved,
    •triev•ing
re•triev\er
ret\ro

ret\ro•ac\tive
retroactive pay
ret\ro•ac\tive\ly
ret\ro•fit, •fit•ted, •fit,
    •fit•ting
ret\ro•grade
ret\ro•gress, •gressed,
    •gress•ing
ret\ro•gres•sion
ret\ro•gress•ive
ret\ro•rock\et
ret\ro•spect
ret\ro•spec•tive
ret\ro•spec•tive\ly
re•turn, •turned, •turn•ing
re•turn•a\ble
re•turn•ee
re•turn key
Reu•ben sand•wich
Ré•u\nion
re•un•ion
re-•up, •upped, •up\ping
rev, revved, rev•ving
re•vamp, •vamped,
    •vamp•ing
re•veal, •vealed, •veal•ing
rev•eil\le (*bugle call*),
rev\el, •eled *or* •elled,
    •el•ing *or* •el•ling
rev\e•la•tion
rev•el•er *or* rev•el•ler
rev•el\ry (*merrymaking*)
re•venge, •venged,
    •veng•ing
re•venge•ful
rev\e•nue
revenue bond
re•ver•ber•ate, •at\ed,
    •at•ing
re•ver•ber•a•tion
re•vere, •vered, •ver•ing
rev•er•ence
rev•er•end (*minister*)
rev•er•ent (*respectful*)
rev•er•en•tial
rev•er•ent•ly
rev•er•ie (*musing*) [*vs.*
    ref•er•ee (*arbitrator*)]
re•ver•sal
re•verse, •versed,
    •vers•ing

reverse split
reverse vid\e\o
re•vers•i\ble
re•ver•sion
re•vert, •vert\ed, •vert•ing
re•vet•ment
re•view (*critique*), •viewed, •view•ing [vs. re•vue (*theatrical entertainment*)]
re•view\er
re•vile, •viled, •vil•ing
re•vile•ment
re•vise, •vised, •vis•ing
re•vi•sion
re•vi•sion•ism
re•vi•sion•ist
re•vi•tal\i•za•tion
re•vi•tal•ize, •ized, •iz•ing
re•viv•al
re•viv•al•ist
re•vive, •vived, •viv•ing
re•viv\i•fi•ca•tion
re•viv\i\fy, •fied, •fy•ing
rev\o•ca•ble or re•vok•a•ble
rev\o•ca•tion
re•voke, •voked, •vok•ing
re•volt, •volt\ed, •volt•ing
rev\o•lu•tion
rev\o•lu•tion•ar\y, pl. •ies
rev\o•lu•tion•ize, •ized, •iz•ing
re•volve, •volved, •volv•ing
re•volv\er
re•volv•ing cred\it
revolving fund
revolving loan
re•vue (*theatrical entertainment*) [vs. re•view (*critique*)]
re•vul•sion
re•ward (*recompense*), •ward\ed, •ward•ing
re•word (*to change wording*), •word\ed, •word•ing
re•write, •wrote, •writ•ten, •writ•ing
Rey•kja•vik

RFD or R.F.D. (*rural free delivery*)
RGB mon\i•tor (*red, green, blue monitor*)
rhap•sod\ic or rhap•sod\i•cal
rhap•so•dize, •dized, •diz•ing
rhap•so\dy, pl. •dies
rhe\a, pl. rhe\as
rhe\o•stat
rhe•sus mon•key
rhet\o•ric
rhe•tor\i•cal
rhe•tor\i•cal•ly
rheu•mat\ic
rheu•ma•tism
rheu•ma•toid
rheum\y (*ill with a cold*), •i\er, •i•est [vs. room\y (*spacious*)]
Rh factor (*antigens in blood*)
Rhine
rhine•stone
rhi•ni•tis
rhi•no, pl. •nos or \no
rhi•noc•er\os, pl. •os\es or \os
rhi•zome
rho (*Greek letter*) [vs. roe (*fish eggs*) and row (*to propel with oars*)]
Rhode Is•land (*RI*)
Rho•de•sia
Rho•de•sian
rho•do•den•dron
rhom•boid
rhom•bus, pl. •bus\es or \bi
Rhone or Rhône
rhu•barb
rhyme (*verse*), rhymed, rhym•ing
rhym\er
rhythm (*beat*)
rhyth•mic or rhyth•mi•cal
rhyth•mi•cal\ly
RI (*Rhode Island*)
ri\al

rib, ribbed, rib•bing
rib•ald
rib•ald\ry
rib•bon, •boned, •bon•ing
ri\bo•fla•vin
ri\bo•nu\cle\ic ac\id
rice
rich, \er, •est
Rich•ards
rich\es, pl.
rich\ly
Rich•mond
rich•ness
Rich•ter scale
rick•ets
rick•et\y, •et•i\er, •et•i•est
rick•rack or ric•rac
rick•shaw
ric\o•chet, •cheted or •chet•ted, •chet•ing or •chet•ting
ri•cot\ta
rid, rid, rid•ding
rid•dance
rid•den
rid•dle, •dled, •dling
ride, rode, rid•den, rid•ing
rid\er
rid•er•less
rid•er•ship
ridge
ridged
ridge•pole
ridg\y, •i\er, •i•est
rid\i•cule, •culed, •cul•ing
ri•dic\u•lous
ri•dic\u•lous\ly
ri•dic\u•lous•ness
riel
rife
riff
rif•fle (*to shuffle*), •fled, •fling [vs. ri•fle (*firearm*)]
riff•raff
ri•fle (*firearm*), •fled, •fling [vs. rif•fle (*to shuffle*)]
ri•fle•man, pl. •men
rift
rig, rigged, rig•ging
rig\a•ma•role (*rigmarole*)
rig•ging

right (*correct; to make right*), \er, •est; \ed, •ing [*vs.* rite (*ceremony*) and wright (*worker*) and write (*to put words on paper*)]
right•eous
right•eous•ly
right•eous•ness
right•ful
right•ful•ly
right hand (*noun*)
right-•hand (*adj.*)
right-•hand\ed
right-•hand\ed\ness
right•ist
right\ly
right-•mind\ed
right•ness
right of way or right-•of-•way, *pl.* rights of way or right of ways or rights-•of-•way, right-•of-•ways
rights on
right-•to-•life
right-•to-•llf\er
right-•to-•work
right wing (*noun*)
right-•wing (*adj.*)
right-•wing\er
rig\id
ri•gid•i\ty or rig•id•ness
rig•id\ly
rig•ma•role or rig\a•ma•role
rig\or
rig\or mor•tis
rig•or•ous
rig•or•ous\ly
rile, riled, ril•ing
rill
rim, rimmed, rim•ming
rime
rind
ring (*to sound, as a bell*), rang, rung, ring•ing [*vs.* wring (*to twist*)]
ring (*to encircle*), ringed, ring•ing [*vs.* wring (*to twist*)]
ring\er
ring•lead\er

ring•let
ring•mas•ter
ring•side
ring to•pol\o\gy
ring•worm
rink
rink\y-•dink
rinse, rinsed, rins•ing
Ri\o de Ja•nei\ro
Ri\o Gran\de
ri\ot, •ot\ed, •ot•ing
ri•ot\er
ri•ot•ous
RIP (*rest in peace*)
rip, ripped, rip•ping
ripe, rip\er, rip•est
rip\en, •ened, •en•ing
ripe•ness
rip•off or rip-•off
ri•poste, •post\ed, •post•ing
rip•per
rip•ple, •pled, •pling
rip•ple ef•fect
rip\ple-•through ef•fect
rip-•roar\ing
rip•saw
rip•tide
RISC (*reduced instruction set computer*)
rise, rose, ris\en, ris•ing
ris\er
ris•i•bil•i\ty
ris•i•ble
ris•ing
risk, risked, risk•ing
risk ar•bi•trage
risk cap\i•tal
risk man•age•ment
risk\y (*hazardous*), •i\er, •i•est
ris•qué (*not quite proper*)
rite (*ceremony*) [*vs.* right (*correct*) and wright (*worker*) and write (*to put words on paper*)]
rit\u\al
rit\u\al•ism
rit\u\al•is•tic
rit\u\al\ly
ritz\y, •i\er, •i•est

ri•val, •valed or •valled, •val•ing or •val•ling
ri•val\ry
riv\en
riv\er
riv•er•side
riv\et, •et\ed or •et•ted, •et•ing or •et•ting
riv•et\er
Riv\i•er\a
riv\u•let
Ri•yadh
ri•yal or ri\al
RLL (*run length limited*)
RNA (*transmitter of genetic information*)
roach, *pl.* roach\es or roach
road (*street*) [*vs.* rode (*did ride*) and rowed (*did row*)]
road•bed
road•block
road•run•ner
road show or road•show
road•side
road•ster
road•way
road•work
roam, roamed, roam•ing
roan
roar, roared, roar•ing
roast, roast\ed, roast•ing
roast\er
rob, robbed, rob•bing
rob•ber
rob•ber\y, *pl.* •ber•ies
robe, robed, rob•ing
rob\in
ro•bot
ro•bot\ic
ro•bot•ics
ro•bust
ro•bust\ly
ro•bust•ness
Roch•es•ter
rock, rocked, rock•ing
rock and roll
rock\er
rock\et, •et\ed, •et•ing
rock•et\ry
rock-•ribbed

rock\ly, •i\er, •i•est

ro•co\co

rod

rode (did ride) [vs. road (street) and rowed (did row)]

ro•dent

ro•de\o, pl. •de\os

Ro•din

roe (fish eggs) [vs. rho (Greek letter) and row (to propel with oars)]

Roent•gen or Rönt•gen

rogue (scoundrel) [vs. rouge (red cosmetic)]

ro•guer\y

ro•guish

roil (to induce turbulence), roiled, roil•ing [vs. roy\al (of a sovereign)]

roist\er, •ered, •er•ing

roist•er\er

role or rôle (actor's part)

role-•play\ing

roll (bread; to turn over), rolled, roll•ing

roll•back

roll\er

roll\er skate (noun)

roll\er-•skate (verb), •skat\ed, •skat\ing

rol•lick•ing

roll•o\ver

rollover mort•gage

ro\ly-•po\ly

ROM (read-only memory)

ro•maine

Ro•man

ro•man à clef, pl. ro•mans à clef

Ro•man Cath\o•lic

ro•mance, •manced, •manc•ing

Ro•man•esque

Ro•ma•ni\a or Ru•ma•ni\a

Ro•ma•ni\an

ro•man•tic

ro•man•ti•cal\ly

ro•man•ti•cism

ro•man•ti•cize, •cized, •ciz•ing

Rom\a\ny

Rome

Ro•me\o, pl. •me\os

romp, romped, romp•ing

romp\er

Rom\u•lus

ron•deau (poem)

ron\do (musical form)

roof, pl. roofs; roofed, roof•ing

roof\er

roof•less

roof•top

rook, rooked, rook•ing

rook•er\y, pl. •er•ies

rook\ie

room, roomed, room•ing

room\er (lodger) [vs. ru•mor (hearsay)]

room•ette

room•ful

room\li•ness

room•mate

room\y (spacious), •i\er, •i•est [vs. rheum\y (ill with a cold)]

Roo•se•velt

roost, roost\ed, roost•ing

roost\er

root (plant part), root\ed, root•ing [vs. rout (to defeat) and route (course of travel)]

root di•rec•to\ry

root\er

root•less

root•stock

rope, roped, rop•ing

Roque•fort

Ror•schach test

ro•sa\ry, pl. •ries

rose (the flower; did rise) [vs. rows (lines)]

ro\sé (pink wine)

ro•se\ate

Ro•seau

rose•bud

rose•bush

rose-•col\ored

rose•mar\y, pl. •mar•ies

ro•sette

rose•wood

Rosh Ha•sha•nah

ros\in

ros\li•ness

ros•ter

ros•trum, pl. •trums or •tra

ros\ly, •i\er, •i•est

rot, rot•ted, rot•ting

ro•ta\ry, pl. •ries

ro•tate, •tat\ed, •tat•ing

ro•ta•tion

rote (repetition) [vs. wrote (did write)]

rot•gut

ro•tis•ser\ie

ro•tor

ro\to•till\er

rot•ten, \er, •est

rot•ten•ness

Rot•ter•dam

ro•tund

ro•tun\da, pl. •das

ro•tun•di\ty

rou•é, pl. rou\és

rouge (red cosmetic), rouged, roug•ing [vs. rogue (scoundrel)]

rough (coarse; to make rough), rough\er, rough•est; roughed, rough•ing [vs. ruff (collar)]

rough•age

rough-•and-•read\y

rough-•and-•tum\ble

rough\en

rough-•hewn

rough•house,, •housed, •hous•ing

rough\ly

rough•neck

rough•ness

rough•shod

rou•lette

Rou•ma•ni\a (Romania)

Rou•ma•ni\an

round, round\ed, round\ing; round\er, round•est

round•a\bout

round lot

round\ly

round•ness

round-•shoul\dered

round ta•ble (*noun*)

round-•ta\ble (*adj.*)

round-•the-•clock

round trip (*noun*)

round-•trip (*adj.*)

round\up

round•worm

rouse (*to awaken*), roused, rous•ing [vs. rows (*quarrels*)]

Rous•seau

roust•a\bout

rout (*to defeat*), rout\ed, rout•ing [vs. root (*plant part*)]

route (*course of travel*), rout\ed, rout•ing

route sheet

rou•tine

rou•tine\ly

rove, roved, rov•ing

rov\er

row (*to propel with oars*), rowed, row•ing [vs. rho (*Greek letter*) and roe (*fish eggs*)]

row•boat

row•di•ness

row\dy, *pl.* •dies; •di\er, •di•est

row•dy•ism

rowed (*did row*) [vs. road (*street*) and rode (*did ride*)]

row\el, •eled, •el•ing, •elled, •el•ling

row\er

rows (*lines*) [vs. rose (*the flower; did rise*)]

rows (*quarrels*) [vs. rouse (*to awaken*)]

roy\al (*of a sovereign*) [vs. roil (*to induce turbulence*)]

roy•al•ist

roy•al\ly

roy•al\ty, *pl.* •ties

RSVP (*please respond to this invitation*)

rub, rubbed, rub•bing

ru•ba\to, *pl.* •tos or \ti

rub•ber

rub•ber•ize, •ized, •iz•ing

rub\ber•neck, •necked, •neck•ing

rub•ber stamp (*noun*)

rub\ber-•stamp (*verb*)

rub•ber\y

rub•bish

rub•ble (*broken stone*)

rub•down

rube

ru•bel\la

Ru•bens

Ru•bik's Cube

ru•ble or rou•ble (*monetary unit*)

ru•bric

ru\by, *pl.* •bies

ruck•sack

ruck\us

rud•der

rud•der•less

rud•di•ness

rud\dy, •di\er, •di•est

rude, rud\er, rud•est

rude\ly

rude•ness

ru•di•ment

ru•di•men•ta\ry

rue, rued, ru•ing

rue•ful

rue•ful\ly

ruff (*collar*) [vs. rough (*coarse*)]

ruf•fi\an

ruf•fle, •fled, •fling

rug

Rug\by

rug•ged

rug•ged\ly

rug•ged•ness

Ruhr

ru\in (*destruction*), •ined, •in\ing [vs. rune (*alphabetic character*)]

ru•in•a•tion

ru•in•ous

rule, ruled, rul•ing

rul\er

ruler line

rul•ing

rum

Ru•ma•ni\a (Romania)

rum\ba, *pl.* •bas; •baed, \ba•ing

rum•ble, •bled, •bling

ru•mi•nant

ru•mi•nate, •nat\ed, •nat•ing

ru•mi•na•tion

ru•mi•na•tive

rum•mage, •maged, •mag•ing

rum\my

ru•mor (*hearsay*), •mored, •mor•ing [vs. room\er (*lodger*)]

rump

rum•ple, •pled, •pling

rum•pus

run, ran, run, run•ning

run•a\bout

run•a\round

run•a\way

run-down

rune (*alphabetic character*) [vs. ru\in (*destruction*)]

rung (*did ring; crosspiece*) [vs. wrung (*did wring*)]

run\ic

run-•in

run•ner

run\ner-•up, *pl.* run\ners-•up

run\ny, •ni\er, •ni•est

run•off

run-•of-•the-•mill

run-•on

runt

run-•through

run•time

runtime er•ror

runtime ver•sion

runtish

runt\y, •i\er, •i•est

run•way

ru•pee

ru•pi\ah, *pl.* \ah or •ahs

rup•ture, •tured, •tur•ing

ru•ral
ruse
rush
rusk
rus•set
Rus•sia
Rus•sian
rust, rust\ed, rust•ing
rus•tic

rus•ti•ca•tion
rust\i•ness
rus•tle, •tled, •tling
rustler
rust\y, •i\er, •i•est
rut, rut•ted, rut•ting
ru•ta•ba\ga, pl. •gas
Ruth
ruth•less

ruth•less•ly
ruth•less•ness
Rwan\da
Rwan•dan
Rx (prescription)
ry\a rug
rye (the grain) [vs. wry
 (lopsided)]
Ryu•kyu Is•lands

S

Sab•bath
sab•bat\i•cal
sa•ber
sa•ber•like
Sa•bin vac•cine
sa•ble, pl. •bles or •ble
sab\o•tage, •taged,
 •tag•ing
sab\o•teur
sa•bra, pl. •bras
SAC (Strategic Air
 Command)
sac (pouch, as of animal)
 [vs. sack (bag)]
sac•cha•rin (sugar substitute)
sac•cha•rine (excessively
 sweet)
sac•er•do•tal
sa•chet (small scented
 bag) [vs. sa•shay (to
 walk)]
sack (bag) [vs. sac (pouch,
 as of animal)]
sack•cloth
sack•ful, pl. •fuls
sac•ra•ment
sac•ra•men•tal
Sac•ra•men\to
sa•cred
sa•cred•ness
sac•ri•fice, •ficed, •fic•ing
sac•ri•fi•cial
sac•ri•lege
sac•ri•le•gious
sac•ri•le•gious•ly
sac•ris•tan
sac•ris\ty, pl. •ties
sac\ro•il\i\ac
sac•ro•sanct

sac•ro•sanct•ness
sac•rum, pl. sac\ra
sad, sad•der, sad•dest
sad•den, •dened, •den•ing
sad•dle, •dled, •dling
sad\dle•bag
Sad•du•cee
sa•dism
sa•dist
sa•dis•tic
sa•dis•ti•cal\ly
sad\ly
sad•ness
sa\do•mas\o•chism
sa\do•mas\o•chist
sa\do•mas\o•chis•tic
sa•fa\ri, pl. •ris
safe, saf\er, saf•est
safe-•con\duct
safe-•de•pos\it
safe•guard, •guard\ed,
 •guard•ing
safe•keep•ing
safe\ly
safe•ness
safe•ty, pl. •ties
safety stock
saf•flow\er
saf•fron
sag, sagged, sag•ging
sa\ga, pl. •gas
sa•ga•cious
sa•gac•i\ty
sage, sag\er, sag•est
sage•brush
sag\gy, •gi\er, •gi•est
Sag•it•tar\i\us
Sa•har\a
sa•hib
said

ruth•less•ly

Sai•gon
sail (to travel by boat),
 sailed, sail•ing [vs. sale
 (act of selling)]
sail•boat
sail•cloth
sail•fish, pl. •fish or •fish\es
sail\or
saint
saint\ed
saint•hood
saint•li•ness
saint•ly
sake (benefit; purpose)
sa•ke or sa•ké (Japanese
 fermented rice beverage)
sa•laam (bow; to bow),
 •laamed, •laam•ing [vs.
 sa•la•mi (sausage)]
sal•a•ble or sale•a\ble
sa•la•cious
sa•la•cious\ly
sa•la•cious•ness
sal\ad
sa•la•man•der
sa•la•mi (sausage), pl. •mis
 [vs. sa•laam (bow)]
sal\a•ried
sal\a\ry, pl. •ries
sale (act of selling) [vs. sail
 (to travel by boat)]
sale•a\ble
sale and lease•back
Sa•lem
sales a\gent
sales check
sales•clerk
sales com•mis•sion
sales•man, pl. •men
sales•man•ship

sales•per•son
sales pro•mo•tion
sales quo\ta
sales rep•re•sent•a\tive
sales•room
sales slip
sales tax
sales•wom\an, *pl.*
  •wom\en
sal\i•cyl\ic ac\id
sa•li•ence
sa•li•ent
sa•li•ent\ly
sa•line
sa•lin•i\ty
Salis•bur\y steak
sa•li\va
sal\i•var\y
sal\i•vate, •vat•ed, •vat•ing
sal\i•va•tion
Salk vaccine
sal•low, \er, •est
sal•low•ness
sal\ly, *pl.* •lies; •lied, •ly•ing
salm\on, *pl.* •ons or \on
sal•mo•nel\la
sa•lon (*reception room*)
sa•loon (*barroom*)
sal\sa
salt, salt\ed, salt•ing
salt•cel•lar
salt\ed
sal•tine
salt\i•ness
salt•pe•ter or salt•pe•tre
salt•shak\er
salt•wa•ter
salt\y, •i\er, •i•est
sa•lu•bri•ous
sal\u•tar\y
sal\u•ta•tion
sa•lute, •lut\ed, •lut•ing
Sal•va•dor
Sal•va•do•ran or
  Sal•va•do•ri\an
sal•vage (*to save*), •vaged,
  •vag•ing [*vs.* sel•vage
  (*fabric edge*)]
sal•vage•a\ble
sal•va•tion
sal\ve (*hail!*)

salve (*ointment; to soothe,
  to salvage*), salved,
  salv\ing
sal•ver (*tray*)
salv\er (*one who soothes
  or salvages*)
sal\vo, *pl.* •vos or •voes
sa•mar•i\um
sam\ba, *pl.* •bas; •baed,
  •ba•ing
same
same•ness
sam•iz•dat
Sa•mo\a
Sa•mo\an
sam\o•var
sam•pan
sam•ple, •pled, •pling
sam•pler
Sam•son
Sam\u•el
sam\u•rai, *pl.* •rai
Sa•n'a or Sa•naa
San An•to•ni\o
san\a•to•ri\um, *pl.*
  •to•ri•ums or •to•ri\a
sanc•ti•fi•ca•tion
sanc•ti\fy, •fied, •fy•ing
sanc•ti•mo•ni•ous
sanc•ti•mo•ni•ous\ly
sanc•tion, •tioned,
  •tion•ing
sanc•ti\ty
sanc•tu•ar\y, *pl.* •ar•ies
sanc•tum, *pl.* •tums or \ta
sand, sand\ed, sand•ing
san•dal
san•daled
san\dal•wood
sand•bag, •bagged,
  •bag•ging
sand•bank
sand•blast, •blast\ed,
  •blast•ing
sand•box
sand\er, *pl.* sand•ers (*those
  who sand*)
San•ders (*last name*)
sand•hog
San Di•e\go
sand\i•ness

S&L (*savings-and-loan*)
sand•lot
sand•man, *pl.* •men
sand•pa•per, •pered,
  •per•ing
sand•pi•per
sand•stone
sand•storm
sand•wich, •wiched,
  •wich•ing
sand\y, •i\er, •i•est
sane, san\er, san•est
sane\ly
San Fran•cis•can
San Fran•cis\co
sang
sang-•froid
san•gri\a or san•gri\a
san•gui•nar\y
san•guine
san\i•tar\i\um, *pl.*
  •tar\i•ums or •tar\i\a
san\i•tar\y
san\i•ta•tion
san\i•tize, •tized, •tiz•ing
san\i•tized
san•i\ty
sank
sans
San Sal•va•dor
San•skrit
sans ser\if
San\ta Claus
Santa Fe
San•te•ri\a or San•te•ri\a
San•ti•a\go
San\to Do•min\go
Sao Pau\lo
Sao To\mé *and* Prín•ci\pe
  or Sao To\me *and*
  Prin•ci\pe
sap, sapped, sap•ping
sa•pi•ence
sa•pi•ent
sap•less
sap•ling
sap•phire
sap•pi•ness
sap\py, •pi\er, •pi•est
sap\ro•phyte
sap\ro•phyt\ic

sap•suck•er

Sar\a•cen

Sar\ah

sa•ran

sar•casm

sar•cas•tic

sar•cas•ti•cal\ly

sar•co\ma, *pl.* •mas *or*
•ma\ta

sar•coph\a•gus, *pl.* \gi *or*
•gus\es

sar•dine, *pl.* •dine *or*
•dines

Sar•din\i\a

sar•don\ic

sar•don\i•cal\ly

sa\ri, *pl.* •ris

sa•rong

sar\sa•pa•ril\la

sar•to•ri\al

sar•to•ri\al\ly

SASE (*self-addressed
stamped envelope*)

sash

sa•shay (*to walk*), •shayed,
•shay•ing [*vs.* sa•chet
(*small scented bag*)]

Sas•katch\e•wan

sass, sassed, sass•ing

sas\sa•fras

sas\sy, •si\er, •si•est

SAT (™)

sat

Sa•tan

sa•tan\ic

satch\el

sate, sat\ed, sat•ing

sa•teen

sat•el•lite

sa•ti•ate, •at\ed, •at•ing

sa•ti•a•tion

sa•ti•e\ty

sat\in

sat\in•wood

sat•ire (*irony*) [*vs.* sa•tyr
(*woodland deity*)]

sa•tir\i•cal

sat\i•rist (*humorous writer*)
[*vs.* si•tar•ist (*musician*)]

sat\i•rize, •rized, •riz•ing

sat•is•fac•tion

sat•is•fac•to•ri\ly

sat•is•fac•to\ry

sat•is\fy, •fied, •fy•ing

sa•to\ri

sa•trap

sat\u•ra•ble

sat\u•rate, •rat\ed, •rat•ing

sat\u•ra•tion

Sat•ur•day

Sat\ur•day–•night spe•cial

Sat•urn

sat•ur•nine

sa•tyr (*woodland deity*) [*vs.*
sat•ire (*irony*)]

sa•ty•ri•a•sis

sa•tyr\ic

sauce, sauced, sauc•ing

sauce•pan

sau•cer

sau•ci\ly

sau•ci•ness

sau\cy, •ci\er, •ci•est

Sau\di A\ra•bi\a

sau\er•kraut

Saul

sau\na, *pl.* •nas

saun•ter, •tered, •ter•ing

sau•ri\an

sau•sage

sau•té, •téed, •té•ing

Sau•ternes

sav•a\ble *or* save•a\ble

sav•age, •aged, •ag•ing

sav•age\ly

sav•age\ry

sa•van\na *or* sa•van\nah,
pl. •nas *or* •nahs

Sa•van•nah

sa•vant, *pl.* sa•vants

save, saved, sav•ing

sav\er (*one who saves*) [*vs.*
sa•vor (*to taste with relish*)]

sav\ings ac•count

sav\ings–•and–•loan (*S&L*)

sav\ings bank

savings bond

sav•ior *or* sav•iour

sa•voir–•faire

sa•vor (*to taste with relish*), •vored, •vor•ing [*vs.*
sav\er (*one who saves*)]

sa•vor\y

sav\vy, •vi\er, •vi•est

saw, sawed, saw•ing

saw•bones, *pl.* •bones

saw•buck

saw•dust

saw•horse

saw•mill

saw–•toothed

saw•yer

sax

Sax\on

sax\o•phone

sax\o•phon•ist

say, said, say•ing

say–•so, *pl.* say–•sos

SBA (*Small Business
Administration*)

SC (*South Carolina*)

scab

scab•bard

scab•by, •bi\er, •bi•est

sca•bies

scab•rous

scads

scaf•fold

scal•a\ble font

scal\a•wag

scald, scald\ed, scald•ing

scale, scaled, scal•ing

scal•lion

scal•lop, •loped, •lop•ing

scalp, scalped, scalp•ing

scal•pel

scalp\er

scal\y, •i\er, •i•est

scam, scammed,
scam•ming

scamp, scamped,
scamp•ing

scamp\er, •ered, •er•ing

scam\pi, *pl.* \pi

scan, scanned, scan•ning

scan•dal

scan•dal•ize, •ized, •iz•ing

scan\dal•mon•ger

scan•dal•ous

scan•dal•ous\ly

Scan•di•na•vi\a

Scan•di•na•vi\an

Scan•lon plan

scan•ner
scan•sion
scant
scant•ies
scant\i\ly
scant\i•ness
scant\ly
scant•ness
scant\y, •i\er, •i•est
scape•goat
scape•grace
scap\u\la, pl. •las or •lae
scar, scarred, scar•ring
scar\ab
scarce, scarc\er, scarc•est
scarce\ly
scar•ci\ty
scare, scared, scar•ing
scare•crow
scarf, pl. scarfs or scarves
scar\i•fi•ca•tion
scar\i\fy, •fied, •fy•ing
scar\i•ness
scar•let
scar\y, r•i\er, r•i•est
scat, scat•ted, scat•ting
scath•ing
scath•ing\ly
scat\o•log\i•cal
sca•tol\o\gy
scat•ter, •tered, •ter•ing
scat\ter•brain
scat\ter•brained
scav•enge, •enged,
  •eng•ing
scav•en•ger
sce•nar\i\o, pl. •nar\i\os
sce•nar•ist
scene (place of action) [vs.
  seen (viewed)]
scen•er\y
sce•nic
sce•ni•cal\ly
scent (odor) [vs. cent (penny) and sent (did send)]
scent\ed
scents (odors) [vs. cents
  (pennies) and sense
  (faculty)]
scep•ter

scep•tered
scep•tic
sched•ule, •uled, •ul•ing
sche•mat\ic
scheme, schemed,
  schem•ing
schem\er
scher\zo, pl. scher•zos or
  scher\zi
Schick test
schil•ling
schism
schis•mat\ic
schist
schiz•oid
schiz\o•phre•ni\a
schiz\o•phren\ic
schle•miel
schlep, schlepped,
  schlep•ping
schlock
schmaltz or schmalz
schmaltz\y, •i\er, •i•est
Schmidt
schnapps
schnau•zer
schnook
schol\ar
schol•ar\ly
scho•las•tic
scho•las•ti•cal\ly
school, schooled,
  school•ing
school•boy
school•girl
school•house, pl.
  •hous\es
school•marm
school•mas•ter
school•mate
school•room
school•teach\er
school•teach•ing
school•work
school•yard
schoon\er
Schu•bert
schuss, schussed,
  schuss•ing
schwa, pl. schwas

sci•at\ic
sci•at\i\ca
sci•ence
science fic•tion
sci•en•tif\ic
sci•en•tif\i•cal\ly
sci•en•tist
sci-•fi (science fiction)
scim\i•tar
scin•til\la, pl. •las
scin•til•late, •lat\ed,
  •lat\ing
scin•til•la•tion
sci\on
scis•sor, •sored, •sor•ing
scis•sors
scle•ro•sis, pl. •ses
scle•rot\ic
scoff, scoffed, scoff•ing
scoff•law
scold, scold\ed, scold•ing
sco•li•o•sis
sconce
scone
scoop, scooped,
  scoop•ing
scoot, scoot\ed,
  scoot•ing
scoot\er
scope, scoped, scop•ing
scor•bu•tic
scorch, scorched,
  scorch•ing
score, pl. scores or score;
  scored, scor•ing
score•board
score•less
scor\er
scorn, scorned, scorn•ing
scorn•ful
scorn•ful\ly
Scor•pi\o, pl. •pi\os
scor•pi\on
scotch (to put an end to),
  scotched, scotch•ing
Scotch•man, pl. •men
Scotch tape (™)
scot-•free
Scot•land
Scots
Scots•man, pl. •men

Scots•wom\an, pl. •wom\en

Scot•tie

Scot•tish (of Scotland)

scoun•drel

scour, scoured, scour•ing

scourge, scourged, scourg•ing

scout, scout\ed, scout•ing

scout•mas•ter

scow

scowl, scowled, scowl•ing

scrab•ble, •bled, •bling

Scrab•ble (™)

scrab•bler

scrag•gly, •gli\er, •gli•est

scram, scrammed, scram•ming

scram•ble, •bled, •bling

scram•bler

scrap, scrapped, scrap•ping

scrap•book

scrape, scraped, scrap•ing

scrap\er

scrap heap or scrap•heap

scrap•per

scrap•ple

scrap\py, •pi\er, •pi•est

scratch, scratched, scratch•ing

scratch\i•ness

scratch\y, •i\er, •i•est

scrawl, scrawled, scrawl•ing

scrawl\y, •i\er, •i•est

scrawn\i•ness

scream, screamed, scream•ing

scream\er

screech

screech\y, •i\er, •i•est

screen

screen an\i•ma•tor

screen blank\er

screen cap•ture

screen dump

screen flick\er

screen•play

screen sav\er

screen•writ\er

screw, screwed, screw•ing

screw•ball

screw•driv\er

screw\y, •i\er, •i•est

scrib•ble, •bled, •bling

scrib•bler

scribe

scrim

scrim•mage, •maged, •mag•ing

scrimp, scrimped, scrimp•ing

scrim•shaw

scrip (currency; certificate)

script (handwriting)

script lan•guage

scrip•tur\al

scrip•ture

script•writ\er

scrive•ner

scrod

scrof\u•la

scrof\u•lous

scroll, scrolled, scroll•ing

Scrooge

scro•tal

scro•tum, pl. \ta or •tums

scrounge, scrounged, scroung•ing

scroung\er

scroung\y, •i\er, •i•est

scrub

scrub, scrubbed, scrub•bing

scrub•ber

scrub\by, •bi\er, •bi•est

scruff

scruff\y, •i\er, •i•est

scrump•tious

scrunch, scrunched, scrunch•ing

scru•ple, •pled, •pling

scru•pu•los•i\ty

scru•pu•lous

scru•pu•lous\ly

scru•ti•nize, •nized, •niz•ing

scru•ti\ny, pl. •nies

SCSI port (small computer systems interface port)

scu\ba, pl. •bas; •baed, •ba•ing

scud, scud•ded, scud•ding

scuff, scuffed, scuff•ing

scuf•fle, •fled, •fling

scull (oar) [vs. skull (skeleton of head)]

scul•ler\y, pl. •ler•ies

scul•lion

sculpt, sculpt\ed, sculpt•ing

sculp•tor (artist)

sculp•tur\al

sculp•ture (three-dimensional art)

scum

scum\my, •mi\er, •mi•est

scup•per

scur•ril•i\ty

scur•ril•ous

scur•ril•ous\ly

scur\ry, •ried, •ry•ing

scur\vy

scutch•eon

scut•tle, •tled, •tling

scut\tle•butt

scuzz\y, •i\er, •i•est

scythe, scythed, scyth•ing

SD (South Dakota)

SDR (special drawing rights)

sea (ocean) [vs. see (to perceive)]

sea•bed

sea•board

sea•coast

sea•far\er

sea•far•ing

sea•food

sea•go•ing

sea horse or sea•horse

seal, pl. seals or seal; sealed, seal•ing

seal•ant

seal\er

seal•ing (closing tightly) [vs. ceil•ing (top of room)]

seal•skin

seam (stitched juncture) [vs. seem (to appear)]

sea•man (*sailor*), pl. •men
  [vs. se•men (*male repro-*
  ductive fluid)]
sea•man•ship
seamed
seam•less
seam•stress
seam\y, •i\er, •i•est
sé•ance
sea•plane
sea•port
sear (*to burn*), seared,
  sear•ing [vs. seer
  (*prophet*) and sere
  (*withered*)]
search, searched,
  search•ing
search-•and-•re\place
search•light
sea•scape
sea•shell or sea shell
sea•shore
sea•sick
sea•sick•ness
sea•side
sea•son (*time of year; to*
  give flavor to), •soned,
  •son•ing
sea•son•a•ble (*timely*)
sea•son\al (*of the season*)
sea•son\al•ly
sea•son\al
  un•em•ploy•ment
sea•son•ing
seat, seat\ed, seat•ing
seat belt
Se•at\tle
sea•ward
sea•way
sea•weed
sea•wor•thy
se•ba•ceous
seb•or•rhe\a
SEC or S.E.C. (*Securities*
  and Exchange Commission)
se•cant
se•cede, •ced\ed, •ced•ing
se•ces•sion
se•ces•sion•ist
se•clud\ed
se•clu•sion

sec•ond, •ond\ed,
  •ond•ing
sec•ond•ar\i\ly
sec•ond•ar\y, pl. •ar•ies
secondary mar•ket
secondary of•fer•ing
secondary stor•age
sec•ond class (*noun*)
sec\ond-•class (*adj.*)
sec\ond-•guess, •guessed,
  •guess\ing
sec•ond hand (*noun*)
sec\ond•hand (*adj.*)
sec•ond\ly
sec\ond-•rate
sec\ond-•sto\ry man
sec\ond-•string\er
se•cre\cy
se•cret
sec•re•tar•i\al
sec•re•tar\i\at
sec•re•tar\y, pl. •tar•ies
se•crete, •cret\ed,
  •cret•ing
se•cre•tion
se•cre•tive
se•cret\ly
sect
sec•tar\i\an
sec•tion, •tioned, •tion•ing
sec•tion\al
sec•tion•al•ism
sec•tor
sec\u•lar
sec\u•lar•ism
sec\u•lar•ist
sec\u•lar\i\za•tion
sec\u•lar•ize, •ized,
  •iz•ing
se•cure, •cured, •cur•ing
se•cured loan
se•cure\ly
se•cu•ri\ty, pl. •ties
security an\a•lyst
secy or sec'y (*secretary*)
se•dan
se•date, •dat\ed, •dat•ing
se•date\ly
se•da•tion
sed\a•tive
sed•en•tar\y

Se•der, pl. Se•ders or
  Se•da•rim
sedge
sed\i•ment
sed\i•men•ta\ry
sed\i•men•ta•tion
se•di•tion
se•di•tious
se•duce, •duced, •duc•ing
se•duc\er
se•duc•tion
se•duc•tive
sed\u•lous
see (*to perceive*), saw,
  seen, see•ing [vs. sea
  (*ocean*)]
seed (*plant ovule*), pl.
  seeds or seed [vs. cede
  (*to give up*)]
seed, pl. seeds or seed;
  seed\ed, seed•ing
seed\i•ness
seed•less
seed•ling
seed mon\ey
seed\y, •i\er, •i•est
see•ing
seek, sought, seek•ing
seek\er
seek time
seem (*to appear*), seemed,
  seem•ing [vs. seam
  (*stitched juncture*)]
seem•ing\ly
seem•li•ness
seem\ly, •li\er, •li•est
seen (*viewed*) [vs. scene
  (*place of action*)]
seep, seeped, seep•ing
seep•age
se\er (*one who sees*)
seer (*prophet*) [vs. sear (*to*
  burn) and sere (*withered*)]
seer•suck\er
see•saw, •sawed, •saw•ing
seethe, seethed, seeth•ing
see-•through
seg•ment, •ment\ed,
  •ment•ing
seg•ment\ed vir•tu\al
  mem\o\ry

seg•men•ta•tion

seg•re•gate, •gat\ed, •gat•ing

seg•re•ga•tion

seg•re•ga•tion•ist

se•gue, •gued, •gue•ing

sei•gnior

seine

seis•mic

seis•mo•graph

seis•mog•ra•pher

seis•mo•graph\ic

seis•mog•ra•phy

seis•mo•log\ic

seis•mo•log\i•cal

seis•mol•ogy

seize, seized, seiz•ing

sei•zure

sel•dom

se•lect, •lect\ed, •lect•ing

se•lec•tion

se•lec•tive

se•lect•man, *pl.* •men

se•lec•tor

sel•e•nite

se•le•ni\um

sel•e•nog•ra•pher

sel•e•nog•ra•phy

self, *pl.* selves

self-•ad\dressed

self-•as\sur\ance

self-•cen\tered

self-•con\fi\dence

self-•con\fi\dent

self-•con\scious

self-•con\scious\ly

self-•con\scious\ness

self-•con\tained

self-•con\trol

self-•con\trolled

self-•de\fense

self-•de\ni\al

self-•de\struct,. •de\struct\ed, •de\struct\ing

self-•de\struc\tion

self-•de\struc\tive

self-•de\ter\mi\na\tion

self-•es\teem

self-•ev\i\dent

self-•ex\plan\a\to\ry

self-•ex\pres\sion

self-•ful\fill\ing

self-•gov\ern\ing

self-•gov\ern\ment

self-•im\age

self-•im\por\tance

self-•im\por\tant

self-•in\sur\ance

self-•in\sure, \sured, \sur\ing

self-•in\ter\est

self•ish

self•ish\ly

self•ish•ness

self•less

self•less\ly

self•less•ness

self-•liq\ui\dat\ing

self-•made

self-•pos\ses\sion

self-•pro\pelled *or* self- •pro\pel\ling

self-•reg\u\lat\ing

self-•re\li\ance

self-•re\li\ant

self-•re\spect

self-•re\straint

self-•right\eous

self-•right\eous\ly

self-•right\eous\ness

self-•sac\ri\fice

self-•sac\ri\fic\ing

self•same

self-•seek\ing

self-•serv\ice

self-•serv\ing

self-•start\er

self-•start\ing

self-•styled

self-•suf\fi\cien\cy

self-•suf\fi\cient

self-•taught

self-•wind\ing

sell (*to offer for money*), sold, sell•ing [vs. cell (*small compartment*)]

sell\er (*one who sells*) [vs. cel•lar (*basement*)]

sell\ers' mar•ket

sell•ing point

sell-•off

sell•out

sell-•through

selt•zer

sel•vage (*fabric edge*) [vs. sal•vage (*to save*)]

selves

se•man•tic

semantic er•ror

se•man•ti•cist

se•man•tics

sem\a•phore, •phored, •phor•ing

sem•blance

se•men (*male reproductive fluid*) [vs. sea•man (*sailor*)]

se•mes•ter

sem\i, *pl.* \is

sem\i•an\nu\al

sem\i•au\to•mat\ic

sem\i•cir•cle

sem\i•cir•cu•lar

sem\i•co•lon

sem\i•con•duc•tor

sem\i•fi•nal

sem\i•fi•nal•ist

sem\i•month\ly, *pl.* •lies

sem\i•nal

sem\i•nar

sem\i•nar•i\an

sem\i•nar\y, *pl.* •nar•ies

Sem\i•nole, *pl.* •noles *or* •nole

se•mi•ot•ics

sem\i•per•me•a\ble

sem\i•pre•cious

sem\i•pri•vate

sem\i•pro•fes•sion\al

sem\i•skilled

Sem•ite

Se•mit\ic

sem\i•tone

sem\i•trail\er

sem\i•trop\i•cal

sem\i•var•i•a\ble cost

sem\i•vow•el

sem\i•week\ly, *pl.* •lies

sen•ate

sen\a•tor

sen\a•to•ri\al

send, sent, send•ing

send\er

send-•off
Sen\e\ca, *pl.* •cas *or* \ca
Sen\e•gal
Sen\e•ga\lese, *pl.* •lese
se•nes•cence
se•nes•cent
se•nile
se•nil•i\ty
sen•ior
sen•ior•i\ty, *pl.* •ties
sen\na
se•ñor, *pl.* se•ñors *or*
    se•ño•res
se•ño\ra, *pl.* •ras
se•ño•ri\ta, *pl.* •tas
sen•sa•tion
sen•sa•tion\al
sen•sa•tion•al•ism
sen•sa•tion•al•is•tic
sense (*faculty; to sense*),
sense, sensed, sens•ing
    [*vs.* cents (*pennies*) and
    scents (*odors*)]
sense•less
sens\es (*faculties*) [*vs.*
    cen•sus (*population
    count*)]
sen•si•bil•i\ty, *pl.* •ties
sen•si\ble
sen•si\bly
sen•si•tive
sen•si•tiv•i\ty
sen•si•ti•za•tion
sen•si•tize, •tized, •tiz•ing
sen•sor
sen•so\ry
sen•su\al
sen•su•al•i\ty
sen•su•al•ly
sen•su•ous
sen•su•ous•ly
sen•su•ous•ness
sent (*did send*) [*vs.* cent
    (*penny*) and scent (*odor*)]
sen•te•men•tal•ist
sen•tence, •tenced,
    •tenc•ing
sen•ten•tious
sen•tient
sen•ti•ment
sen•ti•men•tal

sen•ti•men•tal•i\ty
sen•ti•men•tal•ize, •ized,
    •iz•ing
sen•ti•men•tal\ly
sen•ti•nel
sen•try, *pl.* •tries
Seoul
se•pal
sep\a•ra\ble
sep\a•rate, •rat\ed,
    •rat\ing
sep\a•rate•ly
sep\a•ra•tion
sep\a•ra•tism
sep\a•ra•tist
sep\a•ra•tor
se•pi\a
sep•sis
Sep•tem•ber
sep•tet
sep•tic
sep•ti•ce•mi\a
sep•tu•a•ge•nar\i\an
Sep•tu•a•gint
sep•tum, *pl.* \ta
sep•ul•cher
se•pul•chral
se•quel
se•quence, •quenced,
    •quenc•ing
se•quen•tial
sequential ac•cess
se•ques•ter, •tered,
    •ter•ing
se•ques•tra•tion
se•quin
se•quined
se•quoi\a, *pl.* •quoi\as
se\ra
se•ra•glio, *pl.* •glios
se•ra\pe, *pl.* •pes
ser•aph, *pl.* •aphs *or*
    \a•phim
se•raph•ic
Serb
Ser•bi\a
Ser•bi\an
Ser\bo-•Cro\a\tian
sere (*withered*) [*vs.* sear
    (*to burn*) and seer
    (*prophet*)]

ser\e•nade, •nad\ed,
    •nad•ing
ser•en•dip•i•tous
ser•en•dip•i\ty
se•rene
se•rene\ly
se•ren•i\ty
serf (*peasant*) [*vs.* surf
    (*waves*)]
serf•dom
serge (*cloth*) [*vs.* surge
    (*swelling movement*)]
ser•geant
se•ri\al (*story in install-
    ments; of a sequence*) [*vs.*
    ce•re•al (*grain*)]
serial bond
serial in\ter•face
se•ri•al\i•za•tion
se•ri•al•ize, •ized, •iz•ing
se•ri\al mouse
serial print\er
se•ries (*related group*), *pl.*
    •ries
ser\if
se•ri•ous (*important*)
se•ri•ous\ly
se•ri•ous•ness
ser•mon
ser•mon•ize, •ized, •iz•ing
se•rol\o•gist
se•rol\o\gy
se•rous
ser•pent
ser•pen•tine
ser•rat\ed
ser•ra•tion
ser•ried
se•rum, *pl.* se•rums *or*
    se\ra
serv•ant
serve, served, serv•ing
serv\er
serv\er-•based
Ser•vice (*the poet*)
serv•ice (*help; to repair*),
    •iced, •ic•ing
serv•ice•a\ble
serv•ice busi•ness
service cen•ter
service charge

serv•ice•man, *pl.* •men
ser•vi•ette
ser•vile
ser•vil•i\ty
serv•ing
ser•vi•tor
ser•vi•tude
ser\vo, *pl.* •vos
ser\vo•mech•an•ism
ser\vo•mo•tor
ses\a•me
ses\qui•cen•ten•ni•al
ses•sion (*meeting*) [*vs.* ces•sion (*yielding*)]
set, set, set•ting
set•back
set•tee
set•ter
set•ting
set•tle, •tled, •tling
set•tle•ment
set•tler
set-•to, *pl.* •tos
set\up
sev\en
sev•en•teen
sev•en•teenth
sev\en\teen-•year lo•cust
sev•enth
sev•en•ti•eth
sev•en\ty, *pl.* •ties
sev\er, •ered, •er•ing
sev•er\al
sev•er•al\ly
sev•er•ance
severance pay
severance tax
se•vere
se•vere\ly
se•vere•ness
se•ver•i\ty
Se•ville
sew (*to stitch*), sewed, sewn *or* sewed, sew•ing [*vs.* so (*thus*) and sow (*to plant*)]
sew•age *or* sew•er•age
sew\er
sex
sex\a•ge•nar\i\an
sex•i\ly

sex\i•ness
sex•ism
sex•ist
sex•less
sex•pot
sex•tant
sex•tet *or* sex•tette
sex•ton
sex•tu•ple, •pled, •pling
sex\u\al
sex\u•al•i\ty
sex\u•al\ly
sex\y, •i\er, •i•est
Sey•chelles
SF *or* s-\f (*science fiction*)
sh
shab•bi\ly
shab•bi•ness
shab\by, •bi\er, •bi•est
shack, shacked, shack•ing
shack\le, •led, •ling
shad, *pl.* shad *or* shads
shade, shad\ed, shad•ing
shad\i•ness
shad\ow, •owed, •ow•ing
shad\ow•box, •boxed, •box•ing
shad\ow price
shad•ow\y, •i\er, •i•est
shad\y, •i\er, •i•est
shaft
shag, shagged, shag•ging
shag•gi•ness
shag\gy, •gi\er, •gi•est
shah
shake, shook, shak\en, shak•ing
shake•down
shak\er
Shake•speare
Shake•spear•e\an *or* Shake•spear•i\an
shake-•up
shak\y, •i\er, •i•est
shale
shall
shal•lot
shal•low, •low\er, •low•est
shalt

sham, shammed, sham•ming
sha•man
sham•ble, •bled, •bling
sham•bles
shame, shamed, sham•ing
shame•faced
shame•ful
shame•ful\ly
shame•less
sham•poo, •pooed, •poo•ing
sham•rock
shang•hai, •haied, •hai•ing
Shan\gri-•la
shan't (*shall not*)
Shan•tung
shan\ty (*hut*), *pl.* •ties [*vs.* chan•tey (*sailor's song*)]
shape, shaped, shap•ing
shape•less
shape•less•ness
shape\ly, •li\er, •li•est
shard *or* sherd
share, shared, shar•ing
share•crop•per
share•hold\er
share•ware
shark
shark•skin
sharp, sharp\er, sharp•est
sharp\en, •ened, •en•ing
sharp•en•er
sharp-•eyed
sharp\ly
sharp•ness
sharp•shoot\er
sharp•shoot•ing
sharp-•tongued
shat•ter, •tered, •ter•ing
shat\ter•proof
shave, shaved, shaved *or* shav\en, shav•ing
shav\er
Shaw
shawl
Shaw•nee, *pl.* •nees *or* •nee
s/he
she, *pl.* they, shes
sheaf, *pl.* sheaves

shear (*to clip*), sheared, sheared *or* shorn, shear•ing [*vs.* sheer (*transparent*)]

sheath (*a case*)

sheathe (*to encase*), sheathed, sheath•ing

she•bang

she'd

shed, shed, shed•ding

sheen

sheep, *pl.* sheep

sheep•dog *or* sheep dog

sheep•fold

sheep•ish

sheep•ish\ly

sheep•ish•ness

sheep•skin

sheer (*transparent*), \er, •est [*vs.* shear (*to clip*)]

sheer•ness

sheet

sheet-•fed scan•ner

sheet feed\er

sheet•ing

sheik *or* sheikh (*Arab chief*) [*vs.* chic (*stylish*) and chick (*baby chicken*)]

sheik•dom *or* sheikh•dom

shek\el

shelf, *pl.* shelves

she'll (*she will*)

shell, shelled, shell•ing

shel•lac *or* shel•lack, •lacked, •lack•ing

Shel•ley

shell•fish, *pl.* •fish *or* •fish\es

shell-•shocked

shel•ter, •tered, •ter•ing

shelve, shelved, shelv•ing

she•nan\i•gans

shep•herd, •herd\ed, •herd•ing

sher•bet

sher•iff

Sher\pa, *pl.* •pas

sher\ry, *pl.* •ries

she's (*she is*)

shib•bo•leth

shied

shield, shield\ed, shield•ing

shift, shift\ed, shift•ing

shift-•click

shift click•ing

shift•i\ly

shift\i•ness

shift•less

shift•less•ness

shift\y, •i\er, •i•est

shill, shilled, shill•ing (*posing as a customer*)

shil•le•lagh

shil•ling (*old British coin*)

shil\ly-•shal\ly, •shal\lied, •shal\ly\ing

shim•mer, •mered, •mer•ing

shim•mer\y

shin, shinned, shin•ning

shin•bone

shin•dig

shine, shone *or* shined, shin•ing

shin\er

shin•gle, •gled, •gling

shin•gles

shin\i•ness

shin\ny, •nied, •ny•ing

Shin\to

Shin\to•ist

shin\y, •i\er, •i•est

ship, shipped, ship•ping

ship•board

ship•build\er

ship•build•ing

ship•mate

ship•ment

ship•per

ship•ping

ship•shape

ship•wreck, •wrecked, •wreck•ing

ship•yard

shire

shirk, shirked, shirk•ing

shirk\er

shirred eggs

shirt•ing

shirt•tail

shirt•waist

shish ke•bab

shiv

Shi\va *or* Si\va

shiv\er, •ered, •er•ing

shiv•er\y

shlep *or* shlepp, shlepped, shlep•ping

shoal

shoat

shock, shocked, shock•ing

shock\er

shock•ing

shock•proof

shod

shod•di\ly

shod•di•ness

shod\dy, •di\er, •di•est

shoe (*foot covering*), *pl.* shoes; shod *or* shoed, shoe•ing [*vs.* shoo (*to send away*)]

shoe•horn

shoe•lace

shoe•less

shoe•mak\er

shoe•shine

shoe•string

shoe•tree

sho•gun

sho•gun•ate

shone (*did shine*) [*vs.* shown (*did show*)]

shoo (*to send away*) [*vs.* shoe (*foot covering*)]

shoo-•in

shook

shoot (*to fire a gun*), shot, shoot•ing [*vs.* chute (*inclined channel*)]

shoot\er

shoot•out

shop, shopped, shop•ping

shop•keep\er

shop•lift, •lift\ed, •lift•ing

shop•lift\er

shoppe

shop•per

shop•ping cen•ter

shop•talk

shop•worn

shore, shored, shor•ing

shore•bird

shore•line

shorn

short, \er, •est

short•age

short•bread

short•cake

short•change, •changed, •chang•ing

short cir•cuit (*noun*)

short-•cir\cuit (*verb*), •cir\cuit\ed, •cir\cuit\ing

short•com•ing

short•cut

short\en, •ened, •en•ing

short•hand

short-•hand\ed

Short•horn

short-•lived

short\ly

short•ness

short or•der (*noun*)

short-•or\der (*adj.*)

short-•range

short sale

short sell•ing

short shrift

short•sight\ed

short•sight\ed\ly

short•sight•ed•ness

short•stop

short-•tem\pered

short term (*noun*)

short-•term (*adj.*)

short-•term debt

short ton

short-•waist\ed

short•wave

short-•wind\ed

short•word

Sho•sho\ne or Sho•sho\ni, *pl.* •nes or •nis, \ne or \ni

shot, *pl.* shots or shot

shot•gun, •gunned, •gun•ning

shot-•put\ter

should

shoul•der, •dered, •der•ing

should\n't

shout, shout\ed, shout•ing

shove, shoved, shov•ing

shov\el, •eled or •elled, •el•ing or •el•ling

shov•el•ful, *pl.* •fuls

show, showed, shown, show•ing

show•boat

show•case, •cased, •cas•ing

show•down

show\er, •ered, •er•ing

show•i\ly

show\i•ness

show•ing

show•man, *pl.* •men

show•man•ship

shown (*did show*) [*vs.* shone (*did shine*)]

show-•off

show•piece

show•place

show•room

show\y, •i\er, •i•est

shpt. (*shipment*)

shrank

shrap•nel

shred, shred•ded, shred, shred•ding

shred•der

Shreve•port

shrew

shrewd, \er, •est

shrewd\ly

shrewd•ness

shrew•ish

shriek, shrieked, shriek•ing

shrike

shrill, \er, •est

shrill•ness

shril\ly

shrimp, *pl.* shrimps or shrimp

shrine

shrink, shrank or shrunk, shrunk or shrunk\en, shrink•ing

shrink•a\ble

shrink•age

shrink-•wrap, •wrapped, •wrap\ping

shrive, shrove or shrived,

shriv\en or shrived, shriv•ing

shriv\el, •eled or •elled, •el•ing or •el•ling

shroud, shroud\ed, shroud•ing

shrove

shrub

shrub•ber\y

shrub\by, •bi\er, •bi•est

shrug, shrugged, shrug•ging

shrunk

shrunk\en

shuck

shud•der (*to tremble*)

shtg. (*shortage*)

shuck, shucked, shuck•ing

shud•der (*to tremble*); •dered, •der•ing [(*vs. shut•ter (window cover)*)]

shuf•fle, •fled, •fling

shuf\fle•board

shun, shunned, shun•ning

shunt, shunt\ed, shunt•ing

shush, shushed, shush•ing

shut, shut, shut•ting

shut•down

shut•eye

shut-•in

shut•out

shut•ter (*window cover*), •tered, •ter•ing [*vs. shud•der (to tremble)*]

shut\ter•bug

shut•tle, •tled, •tling

shut\tle•cock

shy, *pl.* shies; shied, shy•ing; shy\er or shi\er, shy•est or shi•est

Shy•lock

shy\ly

shy•ness

shy•ster

Si\am

Si•a•mese, *pl.* •mese

Si•be•ri\a

Si•be•ri\an

sib\i•lance

sib\i•lant

sib•ling

sib\yl

sic (so)

Si•cil•ian

Sic\i\ly

sick (ill), \er, •est

sick•bed

sick\en, •ened, •en•ing

sick\le

sick\ly, •ll\er, •li•est

sick•ness

sick•out

sick•room

side (edge), sid\ed, sid•ing [vs. sighed (did sigh)]

side arm (noun)

side•arm (adj.)

side•bar

side•board

side•burns

side•car

side•kick

side•light

side•line, •lined, •lin•ing

side•long

side•man pl •men

si•de\re\al

side•sad•dle

side•show

side•split•ting

side•step, •stepped, •step•ping

side•stroke, •stroked, •strok•ing

side•swipe, •swiped, •swip•ing

side•track, •tracked, •track•ing

side•walk

side•wall

side•ways

sid•ing

si•dle, •dled, •dling

siege

si•en\na

si•er\ra, pl. •ras

Si•er\ra Le•o\ne

si•es\ta, pl. •tas

sieve

sift, sift\ed, sift•ing

SIG (special interest group)

sigh, sighed, sigh•ing

sighed (did sigh) [vs. side (edge)]

sighs (audible exhalations) [vs. size (dimensions)]

sight (vision) [vs. cite (to refer to) and site (location)]

sight draft

sight\ed

sight•less

sight-•read, •read, •read\ing

sight•see•ing

sight•se\er

sig\ma, pl. •mas

sign (indication) [vs. sine (angle ratio)]

sign (to use sign language), signed, sign•ing

sig•nal, •naled or •nalled, •nal•ing or •nal•ling

sig•nal\ly

sig•na•to\ry, pl. •ries

sig•na•ture

signature loan

sign•board

sign\er

sig•net (small seal) [vs. cyg•net (young swan)]

sig•nif\i•cance

sig•nif\i•cant

sig•nif\i•cant\ly

sig•ni•fi•ca•tion

sig•ni\fy, •fied, •fy•ing

si•gnor, pl. •gnors

si•gno\ra, pl. •ras

si•gno•ri\na, pl. •nas

sign•post

Sikh

si•lage

si•lence, •lenced, •lenc•ing

si•lenc\er

si•lent

si•lent\ly

si•lent part\ner

sil•hou•ette, •et•ted, •et•ting

sil\i\ca

sil\i•cate

sil\i•con (chemical element in sand and computer chips)

sil\i•cone (fluid polymer)

Sil\i•con Val•ley

sil\i•co•sis

silk

silk\en

silk•screen, •screened, •screen•ing

silk•worm

silk\y, •i\er, •i•est

sill

sil•li•ness

sil\ly, pl. •lies; •li\er, •li•est

si\lo, pl. •los

silt, silt\ed, silt•ing

silt\y

Si•lu•ri\an

sil•ver, •vered, •ver•ing

sil\ver•fish, pl. •fish or •fish\es

sil\ver•smith

sil\ver-•tongued

sil\ver•ware

sil•ver\y

sim\i\an

sim\i•lar

sim\i•lar•i\ty

sim\i•lar\ly

sim\i\le

si•mil\i•tude

SIMM (single in-line memory module)

sim•mer, •mered, •mer•ing

si•mo\ny

sim•pa•ti\co

sim•per, •pered, •per•ing

sim•ple (plain), [vs. sim•plis•tic (oversimpli-fied)]

sim•ple, •pler, •plest

simple in•ter•est

sim•ple•mind\ed or sim\ple-•mind\ed

sim•ple•ness

sim•ple•ton

sim•plic•i\ty

sim•pli•fi•ca•tion

sim•pli\fy, •fied, •fy•ing

sim•plis•tic (oversimplified) [vs. sim•ple (plain)]

sim•ply

sim\u•late, •lat\ed, •lat•ing

sim\u•la•tion

sim\u•la•tor

si•mul•cast, •cast, •cast\ed, •cast•ing

si•mul•ta•ne•ous

si•mul•ta•ne•ous\ly

sin, sinned, sin•ning

Si•nai

since

sin•cere

sin•cere\ly

sin•cer•i\ty

sine (angle ratio) [vs. sign (indication)]

si•ne•cure

si\ne di\e

si\ne qua non

sin\ew

sin•ew\y

sin•ful

sing, sang, sung, sing•ing (vocalizing) [vs. singe•ing (scorching)]

sing•a\ble

sing-•a\long

Sin•ga•pore

singe, singed, singe•ing (scorching) [vs. sing•ing (vocalizing)]

sing\er

sin•gle, •gled, •gling

sin\gle-•breast\ed

sin\gle-•den\si\ty

sin\gle-•en\try

sin\gle-•hand\ed

sin\gle-•hand\ed\ly

sin\gle-•lens re•flex cam•era

sin\gle-•mind\ed

sin\gle-•mind\ed\ly

sin\gle-•pre\ci\sion

sin\gle-•sid\ed

sin\gle•ton

sin\gle-•track

sin•gly

sing•song

sin•gu•lar

sin•gu•lar•i\ty

sin•gu•lar•ly

Sin•ha•lese, pl. •lese

sin•is•ter

sink, sank or sunk, sunk or sunk•en, sink•ing

sink•a\ble

sink\er

sink•hole

sink•ing fund

sin•ner

sin tax

sin\u•ous

si•nus, pl. •nus\es

si•nus\i•tis

Sioux, pl. Sioux

sip, sipped, sip•ping

si•phon

sir

sire, sired, sir•ing

si•ren

sir•loin

si•roc\co, pl. •cos

sis

si•sal

sis•si•fied

sis\sy, pl. •sies

sis•ter

sis•ter•hood

sis\ter-•in-•law, pl. sis\ters-•in-•law

sis•ter\ly

Sis\y•phus

sit, sat, sit•ting

si•tar

si•tar•ist (musician) [vs. sat\i•rist (humorous writer)]

sit•com

sit-•down

site (location), sit\ed, sit•ing [vs. cite (to refer to) and sight (vision)]

sit-•in

sit•ter

sit•ting

sit\u•at\ed

sit\u•a•tion

sit-•up

six

six-•pack

six•pence, pl. •pence or •penc\es

six-•shoot\er

six•teen

six•teenth

sixth

six•ti•eth

six\ty, pl. •ties

siz•a\ble or size•a\ble

size (dimensions) [vs. sighs (audible exhalations)]

siz•zle, •zled, •zling

skate (the fish), pl. skates or skate

skate (ice skate or roller skate; to skate) skat\ed, skat•ing

skate•board

skat\er

ske•dad•dle

skeet

skein

skel\e•tal

skel\e•ton

skep•tic or scep•tic

skep•ti•cal or scep•ti•cal

skep•ti•cal\ly

skep•ti•cism or scep•ti•cism

sketch, sketched, sketch•ing

sketch\y, •i\er, •i•est

skew, skewed, skew•ing

skew\er, •ered, •er•ing

ski, pl. skis or ski; skied, ski•ing

skid, skid•ded, skid•ding

ski\er

skiff

skilled

skil•let

skill•ful

skill•ful\ly

skim, skim, skimmed, skim•ming

skimp, skimped, skimp•ing

skimp\i•ness

skimp\y, •i\er, •i•est

skin, skinned, skin•ning

skin-deep

skin div\er

skin div•ing

skin flick

skin•flint
skin•ni•ness
skin\ny, •ni\er, •ni•est
skin\ny-•dip, •dipped,
 •dip\ping
skin•tight
skip, skipped, skip•ping
skip loss
skip•per
skir•mish, •mished,
 •mish•ing
skirt, skirt\ed, skirt•ing
skit
skit•ter, •tered, •ter•ing
skit•tish
skoal
skul•dug•ger\y or
 skull•dug•gery, pl.
 •ger•ies
skulk, skulked, skulk•ing
skull (skeleton of head) [vs.
 scull (oar)]
skull•cap
skunk, pl. skunks or skunk
sky, pl. skies; skied or
 skyed, sky•ing
sky•cap
sky•div•ing or sky div•ing
sky-•high
sky•jack, •jacked, •jack•ing
sky•jack\er
sky•lark, •larked, •lark•ing
sky•light
sky•line or sky line
sky mar•shal
sky•rock\et, •et\ed, •et•ing
sky•scrap\er
sky•ward
sky•writ\er
sky•writ•ing
slab
slack, slacked, slack•ing;
 slack\er, slack•est
slack\en, •ened, •en•ing
slack\er
slack•ness
slacks
slag
slain
slake, slaked, slak•ing
sla•lom

slam, slammed, slam•ming
slam-•bang
slam•mer
slan•der, •dered, •der•ing
slan•der\er
slan•der•ous
slang
slang\y, •i\er, •i•est
slant, slant\ed, slant•ing
slant•wise
slap, slapped, slap•ping
slap•dash
slap•hap\py
slap•stick
slash, slashed, slash•ing
slash-•and-•burn
slash\er
slat
slat•ted
slate, slat\ed, slat•ing
slate PC
slath\er, •ered, •er•ing
slat•tern\ly
slaugh•ter, •tered, •ter•ing
slaugh•ter•house, pl.
 •hous\es
Slav
slave, slaved, slav•ing
slav\er, •ered, •er•ing
slav•er\y
Slav\ic
slav\ish
slav•ish\ly
slaw
slay (to kill), slew, slain,
 slay•ing [vs. sleigh (sled)]
slay\er
sleaze
slea•zi•ness
slea\zy, •zi\er, •zi•est
sled
sledge, sledged, sledg•ing
sledge•ham•mer
sleek, \er, •est
sleek•ness
sleep, slept, sleep•ing
sleep\er
sleep•i\ly
sleep\i•ness
sleep•less
sleep•less•ness

sleep•walk, •walked,
 •walk•ing
sleep•walk\er
sleep•wear
sleep\y, •i\er, •i•est
sleet
sleet\y, •i\er, •i•est
sleeve
sleeve•less
sleigh (sled) [vs. slay (to
 kill)]
sleight of hand
slen•der, •der\er, •der•est
slen•der•ize, •ized, •iz•ing
slen•der•ness
slept
sleuth
slew (large quantity; killed)
 [vs. slue (to turn)]
slice, sliced, slic•ing
slic\er
slick, \er, •est
slick\ly
slick•ness
slide, slid, slid•ing
slid\er
slight, \er, •est
slight\ly
slight•ness
slim, slimmed, slim•ming;
 slim•mer, slim•mest
slime
slim\i•ness
slim•ness
slim\y, •i\er, •i•est
sling, slung, sling•ing
sling•shot
slink, slunk, slink•ing
slink\y, •i\er, •i•est
slip, slipped, slip•ping
slip•case
slip•cov\er
slip•knot or slip knot
slip•page
slip•per
slip•per\y
slip•shod
slip-•up
slit, slit, slit•ting
slith\er, •ered, •er•ing
sliv\er

slob

slob•ber, •bered, •ber•ing

sloe (*a fruit*) [vs. slow (*not fast*)]

sloe-•eyed

slog, slogged, slog•ging

slo•gan

sloop

slop, slopped, slop•ping

slope, sloped, slop•ing

slop•pi•ness

slop\py, •pi\er, •pi•est

slosh, sloshed, slosh•ing

slot

sloth

sloth•ful

slot•ted

slouch, slouched, slouch•ing

slough, sloughed, slough•ing

Slo•vak

slov•en\ly

slow (*not fast; to slow*), \er, •est; slowed, slow•ing [vs. sloe (*a fruit*)]

slow•down

slow\ly

slow mo•tion (*noun*)

slow-•mo\tion (*adj.*)

slow•ness

slow•poke

slow-•wit\ted

slow-•wit\ted\ly

sludge

slue (*to turn*), slued, slu•ing [vs. slew (*large quantity; killed*)]

slug, slugged, slug•ging

slug•gard

slug•ger

slug•gish

slug•gish•ness

sluice, sluiced, sluic•ing

slum, slummed, slum•ming

slum•ber, •bered, •ber•ing

slum•lord

slump, slumped, slump•ing

slung

slunk

slur, slurred, slur•ring

slurp, slurped, slurp•ing

slush, slushed, slush•ing

slush\y, •i\er, •i•est

slut

sly, sly\er or sli\er, sly•est or sli•est

sly\ly

sly•ness

smack, smacked, smack•ing

smack\ers

small, \er, •est

small busi•ness

small-•foot\print com•put\er

small•ish

small-•mind\ed

small•ness

small•pox

small-•scale

small-•time

smart, \er, •est

smart al\eck or al\ec (*noun*)

smart-•al\eck (*adj.*)

smart-•al\eck\y

smart\en, •ened, •en•ing

smart\ly

smart•ness

smart ter•mi•nal

smash, smashed, smash•ing

smash•ing

smash-•up

smat•ter•ing

smear, smeared, smear•ing

smell, smelled or smelt, smell•ing

smell\y, •i\er, •i•est

smelt, *pl.* smelt or smelts; smelt\ed, smelt•ing

smelt\er

smid•gen or smid•gin

smile, smiled, smil•ing

smil•ing\ly

smirk, smirked, smirk•ing

smite, smote, smit•ten, smit•ing

smith

smith•er•eens

smith\y, *pl.* smith•ies

smock

smog

smog\gy, •gi\er, •gi•est

smoke, smoked, smok•ing

smoke•less

smok\er

smoke•stack

smok\i•ness

smok\y, •i\er, •i•est

smol•der or smoul•der, •dered, •der•ing

smooch, smooched, smooch•ing

smooth, \er, •est; smoothed, smooth•ing

smooth\ly

smooth•ness

smor•gas•bord or smör•gås•bord

smote

smoth\er, •ered, •er•ing

smudge, smudged, smudg•ing

smudg\y, •i\er, •i•est

smug, smug•ger, smug•gest

smug•gle, •gled, •gling

smug•gler

smug\ly

smug•ness

smut

smut•ti•ness

smut\ty, •ti\er, •ti•est

snack, snacked, snack•ing

snag, snagged, snag•ging

snail

snake, snaked, snak•ing

snake•like

snak\y, •i\er, •i•est

snap, snapped, snap•ping

snap•drag\on

snap•per

snap•pish

snap\py, •pi\er, •pi•est

snap•shot

snare, snared, snar•ing

snarl, snarled, snarl•ing

snarl•ing\ly

snatch, snatched, snatch•ing

sneak, sneaked or snuck, sneak•ing
sneak\er
sneak\y, •i\er, •i•est
sneer, sneered, sneer•ing
sneeze, sneezed, sneez•ing
sneeze•guard
snick\er, •ered, •er•ing
snide
sniff, sniffed, sniff•ing
sniff\er ad
snif•fle, •fled, •fling
snif•ter
snig•ger, •gered, •ger•ing
snip, snipped, snip•ping
snipe, pl. snipes or snipe; sniped, snip•ing
snip\er
snip•pet
snip\py, •pi\er, •pi•est
snit
snitch, snitched, snitch•ing
sniv\el, •eled or •elled, •el•ing or •el•ling
snob
snob•ber\y
snob•bish
snob•bish•ness
snood
snoop, snooped, snoop•ing
snoop\y, •i\er, •i•est
snoot\i•ness
snoot\y, •i\er, •i•est
snooze, snoozed, snooz•ing
snore, snored, snor•ing
snor•kel, •keled, •kel•ing
snor•kel\er
snort, snort\ed, snort•ing
snot
snot\ty, •ti\er, •ti•est
snout
snow, snowed, snow•ing
snow•ball, •balled, •ball•ing
Snow•belt or Snow Belt
snow•bound
snow•drift
snow•drop

snow•fall
snow•flake
snow•man, pl. •men
snow•mo•bile, •biled, •bil•ing
snow•plow, •plowed, •plow•ing
snow•shoe
snow•storm
snow•suit
snow\y, •i\er, •i•est
snub, snubbed, snub•bing
snub-•nosed
snuck
snuff, snuffed, snuff•ing
snuff•box
snuf•fle, •fled, •fling
snug, snug•ger, snug•gest
snug•gle, •gled, •gling
snug\ly
so (thus) [vs. sew (to stitch) and sow (to plant)]
so-•and-•so, pl. so-•and- •sos
soak, soaked, soak•ing
soap, soaped, soap•ing
soap•box or soap box
soap\i•ness
soap op•er\a
soap•stone
soap•suds
soap\y, •i\er, •i•est
soar (to fly upward), soared, soar•ing [vs. sore (painful)]
soared (did soar) [vs. sward (turf) and sword (weapon with blade)]
sob, sobbed, sob•bing
sob•bing\ly
so•ber, •bered, •ber•ing; •ber\er, •ber•est
so•ber\ly
so•bri•e\ty
so•bri•quet
so-•called
soc•cer
so•cia•bil•i\ty
so•cia\ble
so•cia\bly
so•cial

so•cial•ism
so•cial•ist
so•cial•is•tic
so•cial•ite
so•cial\i•za•tion
so•cial•ize, •ized, •iz•ing
so•cial\ly
so•cial se•cu•ri\ty
so•ci•e•tal
so•ci•e\ty, pl. •ties
so\ci\o•ec\o•nom•ic
so\ci\o•log\i•cal
so•ci•ol\o•gist
so•ci•ol\o\gy
so\ci\o•path
sock, pl. socks; socked, sock•ing
sock\et
Soc•ra•tes
So•crat\ic
sod
so\da, pl. •das
sod•den
so•di\um
sodium pen\to•thal
sod•om\y
so\fa, pl. •fas
so\fa bed or so\fa•bed
So•fi\a
soft, \er, •est
soft•ball
soft-•boiled
soft cop\y
soft-•core
soft-•cov\er
soft cur•ren\cy
soft\en, •ened, •en•ing
soft•en\er
soft fonts
soft goods
soft-•heart\ed
soft\ly
soft•ness
soft ped\al (noun)
soft-•ped\al (verb), \aled or \alled, \al\ing or \al\ling
soft re•turn
soft-•sec\tored
soft soap (noun)
soft-•soap (verb), •soaped, •soap\ing

soft•ware

software in•ter•rupt

software pi•ra•cy

software plat•form

soft•wood

soft\y or soft\ie, *pl.* •ties

sog•gi•ness

sog\gy, •gi\er, •gi•est

soi•gné or soi•gnée

soil, soiled, soil•ing

soi•ree or soi•rée

so•journ, •journed, •journ•ing

sol•ace, •aced, •ac•ing

so•lar

so•lar\i\um, *pl.* •lar\i•ums or •lar\i\a

sold

sol•der (*fusible alloy*), •dered, •der•ing

sol•der\er

sol•dier (*military person; to be a soldier*), •diered, •dier•ing

sol•dier\ly

sole (*only; the fish*), *pl.* sole or soles [*vs.* soul (*spirit*)]

sol\e\cism

sole\ly

sol•emn

so•lem•ni\ty

sol•em•nize, •nized, •niz•ing

sol•emn\ly

so•le•noid

sole pro•pri•e\tor•ship

so•lic\it, •it\ed, •it•ing

so•lic\i•ta•tion

so•lic\i•tor

so•lic\i•tous

so•lic\i•tude

sol\id

sol\i•dar\i\ty, *pl.* •ties

so•lid\i•fi•ca•tion

so•lid\i\fy, •fied, •fy•ing

so•lid•i\ty

sol•id\ly

sol•id•-state

so•lil\o•quize, •quized, •quiz•ing

so•lil\o•quy, *pl.* •quies

sol•ip•sism

sol\i•taire

sol\i•tar\y, *pl.* •tar•ies

sol\i•tude

so\lo, *pl.* •los or \li, •loed, •lo•ing

so•lo•ist

Sol\o•mon

so long

sol•stice

sol•u•bil•i\ty

sol•u\ble

sol•ute

so•lu•tion

solve, solved, solv•ing

sol•ven\cy

sol•vent

solv\er

So•ma•li\a

So•ma•li\an

so•mat\ic

som•ber

som•ber\ly

som•bre\ro, *pl.* •ros

some (*certain*) [*vs.* sum (*total*)]

some•bod\y, *pl.* •bod•ies

some•day

some•how

some•one

some•place

som•er•sault, •sault\ed, •sault•ing

some•thing

some•time

some•times

some•what

some•where

som•nam•bu•lism

som•nam•bu•list

som•no•lence

som•no•lent

son (*male child*) [*vs.* sun (*star*)]

so•nar

so•na\ta, *pl.* •tas

song

song•bird

song•fest

song•ster

son\ic

son-•in-•law, *pl.* sons-•in-•law

son•net

son\ny

so•nor•i\ty

so•no•rous

soon, \er, •est

soot

sooth (*truth*)

soothe (*to calm*), soothed, sooth•ing

sooth•ing

sooth•ing\ly

sooth•say\er

sooth•say•ing

soot\y, •i\er, •i•est

SOP (*standard operating procedure*)

sop, sopped, sop•ping

soph•ism

soph•ist

so•phis•ti•cate

so•phis•ti•cat\ed

so•phis•ti•ca•tion

soph•ist\ry, *pl.* •ries

Soph\o•cle\an

Soph\o•cles

soph\o•more

soph\o•mor\ic

sop\o•rif\ic

sop•ping

sop\py, •pi\er, •pi•est

so•pran\o, *pl.* •pran\os

sor•bet

sor•cer\er

sor•cer•ess

sor•cer\y

sor•did

sor•did•ness

sore (*painful*), sor\er, sor•est [*vs.* soar (*to fly upward*)]

sore•head

sore\ly

sore•ness

sor•ghum

so•ror•i\ty, *pl.* •ties

sor•rel

sor•ri\ly

sor•row, •rowed, •row•ing

sor•row•ful

sor•row•ful\ly

sor\ry, •ri\er, •ri•est

sort, sort\ed, sort•ing

sort\er

sor•tie, •tied, •tie•ing

SOS (signal for help), pl.
  SOSs or SOS's

so-•so or so so

sot\to vo\ce

sou•brette

souf•flé

sought

soul (spirit) [vs. sole (only;
  the fish)]

soul•ful

soul•ful\ly

soul•ful•ness

soul•less

sound, \ed, •ing; \er, •est

sound•less

sound\ly

sound•ness

sound•proof, •proofed,
  •proof•ing

sound•track or sound
  track

soup, souped, soup•ing

soup•çon

soup\y, •i\er, •i•est

sour, soured, sour•ing;
  sour\er, sour•est

source, sourced,
  sourc•ing

source code

source di•rec•to\ry

sour•dough

sour\ly

sour•ness

sour•puss

souse

soused

south

South Car\o•li\na (SC)

South Da•ko\ta (SD)

south•east

South•east A\sia

south•east•ern

south•east•ward

south•ern

south•ern\er

south•paw

south•ward

south•west

south•west•er\ly

south•west•ern

sou•ve•nir

sov•er•eign

sov•er•eign\ty, pl. •ties

So•vi\et

sow (to plant), sowed,
  sown or sowed, sow•ing
  [vs. sew (to stitch) and
  so (thus)]

So•we\to

sox

soy

soy•bean

spa, pl. spas

space, spaced, spac•ing

space buy\er

space•craft, pl. •crafts or
  •craft

spaced-•out

space•flight

space•man, pl. •men

space•port

space•ship

space shut•tle

space sta•tion

space•suit

space•walk

spac\ey or spac\y,
  spac•i\er, spac•i•est

spa•cious

spa•cious\ly

spa•cious•ness

spack\le, •led, •ling

spade, spad\ed, spad•ing

spade•ful, pl. •fuls

spade•work

spa•ghet\ti

Spain

spake

span, spanned, span•ning

span•dex

span•gle

span•gled

Span•iard

span•iel

Span•ish

Span•ish A\mer\i•can
  (noun)

Span\ish-•A\mer\i\can
  (adj.)

spank, spanked, spank•ing

span•ner

spar, sparred, spar•ring

spare, spared, spar•ing

spare•ribs

spar•ing

spar•ing\ly

spark, sparked, spark•ing

spar•kle, •kled, •kling

spar•kler

spar•row

sparse

sparse\ly

sparse•ness or spar•si\ty

Spar\ta

Spar•tan

spasm

spas•mod\ic

spas•mod\i•cal\ly

spas•tic

spat

spate

spa•tial

spat•ter, •tered, •ter•ing

spat\u\la, pl. •las

spav•ined

spawn, spawned,
  spawn•ing

spay, spayed, spay•ing

speak, spoke, spo•ken,
  speak•ing

speak•eas\y, pl. •eas•ies

speak\er

speak\er-•de\pend•ent

spear (the weapon; to
  spear), speared,
  spear•ing [vs. sphere
  (ball)]

spear•head, •head\ed,
  •head•ing

spear•mint

spec, spec'd or specked or
  specced, spec'•ing or
  speck•ing or spec•cing

spe•cial

special char•ac•ter

special draw•ing rights
  (SDR)

spe•cial•ist

spe•cial\i•za•tion
spe•cial•ize, •ized, •iz•ing
spe•cial jour•nal
spe•cial\ly
spe•cial\ty, pl. •ties
spe•cie (coined money)
  [vs. spe•cies (class)]
spe•cies, pl. •cies
spe•cif\ic
spe•cif\i•cal\ly
spec\i•fi•ca•tion
spec\i•fic•i\ty
spec•cif\ic lien
spec\i\fy, •fied, •fy•ing
spec\i•men
spe•cious
spe•cious\ly
speck, specked, speck•ing
speck\le, •led, •ling
specs
spec•ta•cle
spec•tac\u•lar
spec•tac\u•lar\ly
spec•ta•tor
spec•ter
spec•tral
spec\tro•scope
spec\tro•scop\ic
spec•tros\co•py
spec•trum, pl. •tra or
  •trums
spec\u•late, •lat•ed,
  •lat•ing
spec\u•la•tion
spec\u•la•tive
spec\u•la•tor
speech
speech•less
speed, sped or speed\ed,
  speed•ing
speed•boat
speed\er
speed•i\ly
speed•om\e•ter
speed•ster
speed\up
speed•way
speed\y, •i\er, •i•est
spe•le•ol\o•gist
spe•le•ol\o\gy
spell, spelled, spell•ing

spell•bind\er
spell•bind•ing
spell•bound
spell check\er
spell\er
spell•ing
spe•lunk\er
spend, spent, spend•ing
spend•a\ble
spend\er
spend•thrift
spent
sperm, pl. sperm or
  sperms
sper•mat\o•zo\on, pl. •zo\a
sper•mi\cide
spew, spewed, spew•ing
sphere (ball) [vs. spear
  (the weapon)]
sphere
spher\i•cal
sphe•roid
sphinc•ter
sphinx, pl. sphinx\es or
  sphin•ges
spice, spiced, spic•ing
spic\i•ness
spick-•and-•span
spic\y, •i\er, •i•est
spi•der
spiel
spiff\y, •i\er, •i•est
spig\ot
spike, spiked, spik•ing
spik\y, •i\er, •i•est
spill, spilled or spilt,
  spill•ing
spill•age
spill•way
spin, spun, spin•ning
spi\na bif\i\da
spin•ach
spi•nal
spin•dle
spin•dly, •dli\er, •dli•est
spine
spine•less
spin\et
spin•na•ker
spin•ner
spin-•off or spin•off

spin•ster
spin•ster•hood
spin\y, •i\er, •i•est
spi•ra•cle
spi•ral, •raled or •ralled,
  •ral•ing or •ral•ling
spire
spir\it, •it\ed, •it•ing
spir•it•less
spir•it\u\al
spir•it\u•al•ism
spir•it\u•al•ist
spir•it\u•al•is•tic
spir•it\u•al•i\ty
spir•it\u•al\ly
spir•it\u•ous
spi•ro•chete
spit (eject saliva), spit or
  spat, spit•ting
spit (impale on a spit),
  spit•ted, spit•ting
spit•ball
spite
spite•ful
spit•fire
spit•tle
spit•toon
splash, splashed,
  splash•ing
splash•down
splash\y, •i\er, •i•est
splat
splat•ter, •tered, •ter•ing
splay, splayed, splay•ing
splay•foot\ed
spleen
splen•did
splen•did\ly
splen•dor
sple•net\ic
splice, spliced, splic•ing
splint, splint\ed, splint•ing
splint\er (one who splints)
splin•ter (sharp piece of
  wood; to break into
  pieces), •tered, •ter•ing
splin•ter\y
split, split, split•ting
split-•lev\el
splotch, splotched,
  splotch•ing

splotch\y, •i\er, •i•est
splurge, splurged,
   splurg•ing
splut•ter, •tered, •ter•ing
spoil, spoiled or spoilt,
   spoil•ing
spoil•age
spoil\er
spoil•sport
Spo•kane
spoke
spo•ken
spokes•man, pl. •men
spokes•wom\an, pl.
   •wom\en
spo•li•a•tion
sponge, sponged,
   spong•ing
spong\er
spong\y, •i\er, •i•est
spon•sor, •sored, •sor•ing
spon•sor•ship
spon•ta•ne•i\ty
spon•ta•ne•ous
spon•ta•ne•ous\ly
spoof, spoofed, spoof•ing
spook, spooked,
   spook•ing
spook\y, •i\er, •i•est
spool, spooled, spool•ing
spool\er
spool•ing
spoon, spooned,
   spoon•ing
spoon•bill
spoon\er•ism
spoon-•feed, •fed,
   •feed\ing
spoon•ful, pl. •fuls
spoor (animal trail)
spo•rad\ic
spo•rad\i•cal\ly
spore (seed)
sport
sport•ing
spor•tive
sports•cast
sports•cast\er
sports•cast•ing
sports•man, pl. •men
sports•man•like

sports•man•ship
sport\y, •i\er, •i•est
spot, spot•ted, spot•ting
spot check (noun)
spot-•check (verb),
   •checked, •check\ing
spot•less
spot•light, •light\ed or •lit,
   •light•ing
spot mar•ket
spot•ted
spot•ter
spot•ti•ness
spot trad•ing
spot\ty, •ti\er, •ti•est
spous\al
spouse
spout, spout\ed, spout•ing
sprain, sprained,
   sprain•ing
sprang
sprat, pl. sprats or sprat
sprawl, sprawled,
   sprawl•ing
spray, sprayed, spray•ing
spread, spread, spread•ing
spread-•ea\gle, •gled, \gling
spread•sheet
spree
sprig
spright•li•ness
spright\ly, •li\er, •li•est
spring, sprang or sprung,
   sprung, spring•ing
spring•board
Spring•field
spring•time
spring\y, •i\er, •i•est
sprin•kle, •kled, •kling
sprin•kler
sprin•kling
sprint, sprint\ed,
   sprint•ing
sprint\er
sprite
spritz, spritzed, spritz•ing
sprock\et
sprout, sprout\ed,
   sprout•ing
spruce, spruced, spruc•ing
sprung

spry, spry\er or spri\er,
   spry•est or spri•est
spud
spume
spu•mo\ni or spu•mo\ne
spun
spunk
spunk\y, •i\er, •i•est
spur, spurred, spur•ring
spurge
spu•ri•ous
spu•ri•ous\ly
spu•ri•ous•ness
spurn, spurned, spurn•ing
spurt, spurt\ed, spurt•ing
sput•nik
sput•ter, •tered, •ter•ing
spu•tum, pl. \ta
spy, pl. spies; spied, spy•ing
spy•glass
squab, pl. squabs or squab
squab•ble, •bled, •bling
squad
squad•ron
squal\id
squall, squalled, squall•ing
squal\or
squa•mous or squa•mose
squan•der, •dered,
   •der•ing
square, squared,
   squar•ing; squar\er,
   squar•est
square dance (noun)
square-•dance (verb),
   •danced, •danc\ing
square\ly
square•ness
square-•rigged
squash (to crush; the vegetable), squashed,
   squash•ing; pl. squash\es
   or squash [vs. quash (to
   subdue)]
squash\y, •i\er, •i•est
squat, squat•ted,
   squat•ting
squat•ter
squaw
squawk, squawked,
   squawk•ing

squeak, squeaked,
 squeak•ing
squeak\ly, •i\er, •i•est
squeal, squealed,
 squeal•ing
squeal\er
squeam•ish
squeam•ish•ness
squee•gee, •geed,
 •gee•ing
squeez•a\ble
squeeze, squeezed,
 squeez•ing
squelch, squelched,
 squelch•ing
squib
squid, pl. squid or squids
squig•gle
squint, squint\ed,
 squint•ing
squire, squired, squir•ing
squirm, squirmed,
 squirm•ing
squir•rel, pl. •rels or •rel;
 •reled or •relled, •rel•ing
 or •rel•ling
squirt, squirt\ed,
 squirt•ing
squish, squished,
 squish•ing
SRAM (static random
 access memory)
Sri Lan\ka
Sri Lan•kan
SSI (Supplemental Security
 Income)
SST (supersonic transport)
St. (street)
stab, stabbed, stab•bing
sta•bil•i\ty
sta•bi•li•za•tion
sta•bi•lize, •lized, •liz•ing
sta•bi•liz\er
sta•ble, •bled, •bling; •bler,
 •blest
stac•ca\to, pl. •tos or •ti
stack, stacked, stack•ing
sta•di•um, pl. •di•ums or
 •di\a
staff (stick), pl. staffs or
 staves

staff (group of employees;
 to employ), pl. staffs;
 staffed, staff•ing [vs.
 staph (staphylococcus)]
staff\er
staff•ing
stag
stage, staged, stag•ing
stage•coach
stage•craft
stage•hand
stage•struck or stage-
 •struck
stag•fla•tion
stag•ger, •gered, •ger•ing
stag•nant
stag•nate, •nat\ed,
 •nat•ing
stag•na•tion
staid (sedate) [vs. stayed
 (remained)]
staid\ly
stain, stained, stain•ing
stain•less
stair (step) [vs. stare (to
 gaze)]
stair•case
stair•way
stair•well or stair well
stake (post; to wager),
 staked, stak•ing [vs.
 steak (cut of meat)]
stake•out
sta•lac•tite (deposit hang-
 ing from cave ceiling)
sta•lag•mite (deposit on
 cave floor)
stale, stal\er, stal•est
stale•mate, •mat\ed,
 •mat•ing
stale•ness
Sta•lin
stalk (plant stem; to
 pursue), stalked, stalk•ing
 [vs. stork (the bird)]
stall, stalled, stall•ing
stal•lion
stal•wart
sta•men, pl. sta•mens or
 stam\i\na
stam\i\na

stam•mer, •mered,
 •mer•ing
stam•mer\er
stam•mer•ing\ly
stamp, stamped,
 stamp•ing
stam•pede, stam•pede,
 •ped\ed, •ped•ing
stance
stanch or staunch (to stop
 a flow), stanched or
 staunched, stanch•ing or
 staunch•ing [vs. staunch
 (steadfast)]
stan•chion
stand, stood, stand•ing
stand•ard
stand\ard-•bear\er
stand•ard cost sys•tem
stand•ard\i•za•tion
stand•ard•ize, •ized,
 •iz•ing
stand•ard of liv•ing
stand\by, pl. •bys
standby costs
stand\ee
stand-•in
stand•ing
stand•off or stand-•off
stand•off•ish or stand-
 •off\ish
stand•out or stand-•out
stand•pipe
stand•point
stand•still
stand-•up or stand\up
stank
stan\za, pl. •zas
staph (staphylococcus) [vs.
 staff (group of employees;
 to employ)]
staph\y\lo•coc•cus, pl.
 •coc\ci
sta•ple, •pled, •pling
sta•pler
star, starred, star•ring
star•board
starch, starched,
 starch•ing
starch\y, •i\er, •i•est
star•dom

stare (to gaze), stared,
star•ing [vs. stair (step)]
star•fish, pl. •fish or
•fish\es
star•gaz\er
star•gaz•ing
stark, \er, •est
stark•ness
star•less
star•let
star•light
star•ling
star•lit
star\ry, •ri\er, •ri•est
star\ry-•eyed
start, start\ed, start•ing
start bit
start\er
star•tle, •tled, •tling
star to•pol\o\gy
start-•up
start-•up time
star•va•tion
starve, starved, starv•ing
starve•ling
stash, stashed, stash•ing
state, stat\ed, stat•ing
state bank
state•craft
state•hood
state•house, pl. •hous\es
state•less
state•less•ness
state•li•ness
state\ly, •li\er, •li•est
state•ment
Stat\en Is\land
state of the art (noun)
state-•of-•the-•art (adj.)
state•room
states•man, pl. •men
states•man•like
states•man•ship
stat\ic
static RAM (SRAM)
static var•i•a\ble
sta•tion, •tioned,
•tion•ing
sta•tion•ar\y (fixed in
place)

sta•tion•er\y (writing
materials)
sta•tis•tic
sta•tis•ti•cal
stat\i•sti•cian
sta•tis•tics
stat\u•ar\y
stat•ue (sculpture) [vs.
stat•ure (height) and
stat•ute (law)]
stat\u•esque
stat\u•ette
stat•ure (height) [vs.
stat\ue (sculpture) and
stat•ute (law)]
sta•tus
sta•tus quo
stat•ute (law) [vs. stat\ue
(sculpture) and stat•ure
(height)]
stat\u•to\ry
statutory tax rate
staunch or stanch (stead-
fast), \er, •est [vs. stanch
(to stop a flow)]
staunch\ly
stave, staved or stove,
stav•ing
stay
stayed (remained) [vs.
staid (sedate)]
stead
stead•fast
stead•fast\ly
stead•i\ly
stead\y, pl. stead•ies;
stead•ied, stead\y•ing;
stead•i\er, stead•i•est
steak (cut of meat) [vs.
stake (post; to wager)]
steal (to rob), stole,
sto•len [vs. steel (refined
iron)]
stealth
stealth•i\ly
stealth\y, •i\er, •i•est
steam, steamed, steam•ing
steam•boat
steam\er
steam•fit•ter or steam
fit•ter

steam•roll\er, •ered,
•er•ing
steam•ship
steam\y, •i\er, •i•est
steed
steel (refined iron) [vs.
steal (to rob)]
steel\y, •i\er, •i•est
steep, steeped, steep•ing;
steep\er, steep•est
stee\ple
stee\ple•chase
stee\ple•jack
steep\ly
steep•ness
steer (the animal), pl.
steers or steer
steer (to guide), steered,
steer•ing
steer•age
steg\o•saur
stein
stel•lar
stem, stemmed,
stem•ming
stem•ware
stench
sten•cil, •ciled or •cilled,
•cil•ing or •cil•ling
sten\o, pl. sten\os
ste•nog•ra•pher
sten\o•graph\ic
ste•nog•ra•phy
sten•to•ri•an
step (a gait; to step),
stepped, step•ping [vs.
steppe (a plain)]
step•broth\er
step•child, pl. •child•ren
step•daugh•ter
step-•down
step•fa•ther
step•lad•der
step•moth\er
step•par•ent
steppe (a plain) [vs. step
(a gait; to step)]
stepped cost
step•ping•stone or
step•ping stone
step•sis•ter

step•son
step-•up
ster\e\o, pl. ster\e\os
ster\e\o•phon\ic
ster\e\o•scope
ster\e\o•type, •typed,
•typ•ing
ster\e\o•typ\ic
ster•ile
ste•ril•i\ty
ster\i•li•za•tion
ster\i•lize, •lized, •liz•ing
ster\i•liz\er
ster•ling
stern, \er, •est
stern\ly
stern•ness
ster•num, pl. \na or
•nums
ste•roid
ster•to•rous
stet, stet•ted, stet•ting
steth\o•scope
ste•ve•dore
stew, stewed, stew•ing
stew•ard
stew•ard•ess
stew•ard•ship
stick, stuck, stick•ing
stick\er
sticker price
sticker shock
stick\i•ness
stick-•in-•the-•mud
stick\le•back
stick•ler
stick•pin
stick\up
stick\y, •i\er, •i•est
stiff, stiffed, stiff•ing;
stiff\er, stiff•est
stiff-•arm, •armed,
•arm\ing
stiff\en, •ened, •en•ing
stiff•en\er
stiff\ly
stiff-•necked
stiff•ness
sti•fle, •fled, •fling
stig\ma, pl. stig•ma\ta or
stig•mas

stig•ma•tize, •tized,
•tiz\ing
stile (set of steps) [vs.
style (mode; fashion)]
sti•let\to, pl. •tos or •toes
still, stilled, still•ing; still\er,
still•est
still•birth
still•born
still life (noun), pl. still lifes
still-•life (adj.)
still•ness
stilt
stilt\ed
Stil•ton
stim\u•lant
stim\u•late, •lat\ed,
•lat•ing
stim\u•la•tion
stim\u•lus, pl. \li
sting, stung, sting•ing
sting\er
stin•gi\ly
stin•gi•ness
sting•ray
stin\gy, •gi\er, •gi•est
stink, stank or stunk,
stunk, stink•ing
stink\er
stint (period of time)
sti•pend
stip•ple, •pled, •pling
stip\u•late, •lat\ed, •lat•ing
stip\u•la•tion
stir, stirred, stir•ring
stir-•cra\zy
stir-•fry, •fried, •fry\ing
stir•rer
stir•ring
stir•rup
stitch, stitched, stitch•ing
stoat
stock, stocked, stock•ing
stock•ade
stock•brok\er
stock cer•tif\i•cate
stock com•pa\ny
stock div\i•dend
stock ex•change
stock•hold\er
Stock•holm

stock\i•ness
stock\i•nette
stock•ing
stock•job•ber
stock mar•ket
stock op•tion
stock•pile, •piled, •pil•ing
stock quo•ta•tion
stock reg•is•tra•tion
stock split
stock-•still
stock ta•ble
stock\y, •i\er, •i•est
stodg\i•ness
stodg\y, •i\er, •i•est
sto\gy or sto•gie, pl. •gies
sto\ic
sto•i•cal
sto•i•cal\ly
sto•i•cism
stoke, stoked, stok•ing
stok\er
stole
sto•len (robbed)
stol\id
stol•id\ly
stol•len (sweet bread)
stom•ach
stom\ach•ache
stom•ach\er
stomp, stomped,
stomp•ing
stone, pl. stones or stone;
stoned, ston•ing
stone•wall, •walled,
•wall•ing
ston\i•ness
ston\y, •i\er, •i•est
stood
stooge
stool
stoop (to bend); stooped,
stoop•ing [vs. stoup
(basin)]
stop, stopped, stop•ping
stop bit
stop•cock
stop•gap
stop•light
stop or•der

stop•o\ver
stop•page
stop pay•ment
stop•per
stop•watch
stor•age
storage de•vice
store, stored, stor•ing
store•front
store•house, pl. •hous\es
store•keep\er
store•room
sto•ried
stork (the bird), pl. storks
  or stork [vs. stalk (plant
  stem; to pursue)]
storm, stormed,
  storm•ing
storm•i\ly
storm\y, •i\er, •i•est
sto\ry, pl. •ries
sto\ry•board
sto\ry•book
sto\ry•tell\er
sto\ry•tell\ing
stoup (basin) [vs. stoop
  (to bend)]
stout, •er, •est
stout-•heart\ed
stout\ly
stout•ness
stove
stove•pipe
stow, stowed, stow•ing
stow•age
stow•a\way
St. Pe•ters•burg
stra•bis•mus
strad•dle, •dled, •dling
strafe, strafed, straf•ing
strag•gle, •gled, •gling
strag•gler
strag•gly, •gli\er, •gli•est
straight (direct), \er, •est
  [vs. strait (narrow waterway)]
straight-•arm, •armed,
  •arm\ing
straight•a\way
straight•edge
straight\en (direct), •ened, •en•ing

straight-•faced
  straight•for•ward
straight•ness
strain, strained, strain•ing
strain\er
strait (narrow waterway)
  [vs. straight (direct)]
strait•Jack\et
strait-•laced
strand, strand\ed,
  strand•ing
strange, strang\er (odder),
  strang•est
strange\ly
strange•ness
stran•ger (newcomer)
stran•gle, •gled, •gling
stran•gle•hold
stran•gler
stran•gu•la•tion
strap, strapped, strap•ping
strap•less
stra\ta
strat\a•gem
stra•te•gic
stra•te•gi•cal\ly
strat\e•gist
strat\e•gy, pl. •gies
strat\i•fi•ca•tion
strat\i•fy, •fied, •fy•ing
strat\o•sphere
stra•tum, pl. stra\ta or
  stra•tums
Strauss
Stra•vin•sky
straw
straw•ber\ry, pl. •ries
stray, strayed, stray•ing
streak, streaked, streak•ing
streak\er
streak\y, •i\er, •i•est
stream, streamed,
  stream•ing
stream\er
stream•line, •lined, •lin•ing
street
street•car
street name
street-•smart
street•walk\er
street•wise

strength
strength\en
stren\u•ous
stren\u•ous\ly
stren\u•ous•ness
strep
strep\to•coc•cus, pl.
  •coc\ci
strep\to•my•cin
stress, stressed, stress•ing
stressed-•out
stress•ful
stretch, stretched,
  stretch•ing
stretch•a\ble
stretch\er
stretch\y, •i\er, •i•est
strew, strewed, strewn or
  strewed, strew•ing
stri•at\ed
strick\en
strict, \er, •est
strict\ly
strict•ness
stric•ture
stride, strode, strid•den,
  strid•ing
stri•dent
stri•dent\ly
strife
strike, struck, struck (hit)
  or strick\en (afflicted),
  strik•ing
strike fund
strike•out
strik\er
strik•ing price
string, strung, string•ing
strin•gen•cy
strin•gent
strin•gent\ly
string\er
string\y, •i\er, •i•est
strip, stripped, strip•ping
stripe
striped
strip•ling
strip-•min\ing
strip•per
strip-•search, •searched,
  •search\ing

strip•tease
strip•teas\er
strive, strove or strived,
   striv\en or strived,
   striv•ing
strobe
stro\bo•scope
strode
stroke, stroked, strok•ing
stroll, strolled, stroll•ing
stroll\er
strong, strong\er,
   strong•est
strong-•arm, •armed,
   •arm\ing
strong•box
strong•hold
strong\ly
strong•man, pl. •men
strong-•mind\ed
stron•ti\um
strop, stropped,
   strop•ping
strove
struck
struc•tur\al
structure, •tured, •tur•ing
structured
   pro•gram•ming
stru•del
strug•gle, •gled, •gling
strum, strummed,
   strum•ming
strum•pet
strung
strut, strut•ted, strut•ting
strych•nine
stub, stubbed, stub•bing
stub•ble
stub•born
stub•born•ness
stub\by, •bi\er, •bi•est
stuc\co, pl. •coes or •cos;
   •coed, •co•ing
stuck
stuck-•up
stud, stud•ded, stud•ding
stud•book
stu•dent
stud•ied
stu•di\o, pl. •di\os

stu•di•ous
stud\y, pl. stud•ies;
   stud•ied, stud\y•ing
stuff, stuffed, stuff•ing
stuff\i•ness
stuff•ing
stuff\y, •i\er, •i•est
stul•ti•fi•ca•tion
stul•ti\fy, •fied, •fy•ing
stum•ble, •bled, •bling
stump, stumped,
   stump•ing
stun, stunned, stun•ning
stung
stunk
stun•ning
stun•ning•ly
stunt, stunt•ed, stunt•ing
stu•pe•fac•tion
stu•pe\fy, •fied, •fy•ing
stu•pen•dous
stu•pid, \er, •est
stu•pid•i\ty
stu•por
stur•di\ly
stur•di•ness
stur\dy, •di\er, •di•est
stur•geon, pl. •geon or
   •geons
stut•ter, •tered, •ter•ing
stut•ter\er
St. Vin•cent and the
   Gren\a•dines
sty, pl. sties
Styg•i\an
style (mode; fashion),
   styled, styl•ing [vs. stile
   (set of steps)]
styl•ish
styl•ist
sty•lis•tic
sty•lis•ti•cal\ly
styl•ize, •ized, •iz•ing
sty•lus, pl. \li or •lus\es
sty•mie, pl. •mies; •mied,
   •mie•ing
styp•tic
sty•rene
Sty\ro•foam (™)
Styx
sua•sion

suave
suave\ly
sub, subbed, sub•bing
sub-a\tom\ic
sub•com•mit•tee
sub•com•pact
sub•con•scious
sub•con•scious\ly
sub•con•ti•nent
sub•con•tract, •tract\ed,
   •tract•ing
sub•con•trac•tor
sub•cul•ture
sub•cu•ta•ne•ous
sub•deb
sub•di•rec•to\ry, pl. •ries
sub•di•vide, •vid\ed,
   •vid•ing
sub•di•vi•sion
sub•due, •dued, •du•ing
sub•head
sub•ject, •ject\ed, •ject•ing
sub•jec•tion
sub•jec•tive
sub•jec•tiv•i\ty
sub•ju•gate, •gat\ed,
   •gat•ing
sub•ju•ga•tion
sub•junc•tive
sub•lease, •leased,
   •leas•ing
sub•let, •let, •let•ting
sub•li•cense, •censed,
   •cens•ing
sub•li•cen•see
sub•li•cen•sor
sub•li•mate, •mat\ed,
   •mat•ing
sub•li•ma•tion
sub•lime, •limed, •lim•ing
sub•lim\i•nal
sub•lim•i\ty
sub•ma•chine gun
sub•mar•gin\al
sub•ma•rine
sub•merge, •merged,
   •merg•ing
sub•mer•gence
sub•merse, •mersed,
   •mers•ing
sub•mers•i\ble

sub•mer•sion
sub•mi\cro•scop\ic
sub•mis•sion
sub•mis•sive
sub•mit, •mit•ted,
•mit•ting
sub•nor•mal
sub•or•bit\al
sub•or•di•nate, •nat\ed,
•nat•ing
sub•or•di•na•tion
sub•orn, •orned, •orn•ing
sub•or•na•tion
sub•plot
sub•poe\na or sub•pe\na,
pl. •nas; •naed, •na•ing
sub ro\sa
sub•rou•tine
sub•scribe, •scribed,
•scrib•ing
sub•scrib\er
sub•script
sub•scrip•tion
sub•se•quent
sub•se•quent\ly
sub•ser•vi•ence
sub•ser•vi•ent
sub•set
sub•side, •sid\ed, •sid•ing
sub•sid•ence
sub•sid\i•ar\y, pl. •ar•ies
subsidiary ac•count
sub•si•dize, •dized,
•diz•ing
sub•si\dy, pl. •dies
sub•sist, •sist\ed, •sist•ing
sub•sist•ence
sub•soil
sub•son\ic
sub•stance
sub•stand•ard
sub•stan•tial
sub•stan•tial\ly
sub•stan•ti•ate, •at\ed,
•at•ing
sub•stan•ti•a•tion
sub•stan•tive
sub•sta•tion
sub•sti•tute, •tut\ed,
•tut•ing
sub•sti•tu•tion

sub•stra•tum, pl. •stra\ta
or •stra•tums
sub•struc•ture
sub•sume, •sumed,
•sum•ing
sub•teen
sub•ter•fuge
sub•ter•ra•ne\an
sub•ti•tle, •tled, •tling
sub•tle, •tler, •tlest
sub•tle\ty
sub•to•tal, •taled or
•talled, •tal•ing or
•tal•ling
sub•tract, •tract\ed,
•tract•ing
sub•trac•tion
sub•tra•hend
sub•trop\i•cal
sub•urb
sub•ur•ban
sub•ur•ban•ite
sub•ur•bi\a
sub•ven•tion
sub•ver•sion
sub•ver•sive
sub•vert, •vert\ed,
•vert•ing
sub•way
suc•ceed, •ceed\ed,
•ceed•ing
suc•cess
suc•cess•ful
suc•cess•ful\ly
suc•ces•sion
suc•ces•sive
suc•ces•sive\ly
suc•ces•sor
suc•cinct
suc•cinct\ly
suc•cinct•ness
suc•cor (to help), •cored,
•cor•ing [vs. suck\er
(gullible person)]
suc•co•tash
suc•cu•lence
suc•cu•len\cy
suc•cu•lent
suc•cumb, •cumbed,
•cumb•ing
such

such and such
such•like
suck, sucked, suck•ing
suck\er (gullible person; to
make a sucker of), •ered,
•er•ing [vs. suc•cor (to
help)]
suck\le, •led, •ling
su•crose
suc•tion, •tioned,
•tion•ing
Su•dan
Su•da•nese
sud•den
sud•den\ly
sud•den•ness
suds
suds\y, •i\er, •i•est
sue, sued, su•ing
suede or suède
su\et
Su\ez Ca•nal
suf•fer, •fered, •fer•ing
suf•fer•ance
suf•fer\er
suf•fer•ing
suf•fice, •ficed, •fic•ing
suf•fi•cien\cy
suf•fi•cient
suf•fi•cient\ly
suf•fix
suf•fo•cate, •cat\ed,
•cat•ing
suf•fo•ca•tion
suf•frage
suf•fra•gette
suf•fra•gist
suf•fuse, •fused, •fus•ing
suf•fu•sion
sug\ar, •ared, •ar•ing
sug\ar•cane or sug\ar cane
sug\ar•coat, •coat\ed,
•coat•ing
sug\ar•less
sug\ar•plum
sug\ar\y
sug•gest, •gest\ed,
•gest•ing
sug•gest\i•bil•i\ty
sug•gest\i\ble
sug•ges•tion

sug•ges•tive

sug•ges•tive\ly

su\i•cid\al

su\i•cide

su\i ge•ne\ris

suit (set of clothes; to adapt), \ed, •ing [vs. suite (series of rooms) and sweet (sugary)]

suit•a•bil•i\ty

suit•a•ble

suit•a•bly

suit•case

suite (series of rooms) [vs. suit (set of clothes; to adapt) and sweet (sugary)]

suit•ing

suit•or

su•ki•ya\ki

Suk•koth or Suk•kot

sul\fa (the drug)

sul•fate

sul•fide

sul•fur (the chemical element)

sul•fu•ric

sulk, sulked, sulk•ing

sulk•i\ly

sulk\i•ness

sulk\y, pl. sulk•ies; sulk•i\er, sulk•i•est

sul•len

sul•len\ly

sul•len•ness

sul\ly, •lied, •ly•ing

sul•phur

sul•tan

sul•tan•ate

sul•try, •tri\er, •tri•est

sum (total) [vs. some (certain)]

sum, summed, sum•ming

su•mac

Su•ma•tra

sum•mar•i\ly

sum•ma•rize, •rized, •riz•ing

sum•ma\ry (synopsis), pl. •ries

sum•ma•tion

sum•mer, •mered, •mer•ing

sum•mer•house, pl. •hous\es

sum\mer•time

sum•mer\y (like summer)

sum•mit

sum•mon, •moned, •mon•ing

sum•mons, pl. •mons\es

su\mo

sump•tu•ous

sun (star) [vs. son (male child)]

sun•bath, pl. •baths

sun•bathe, •bathed, •bath•ing

sun•bath\er

sun•beam

Sun•belt or Sun Belt

sun•bon•net

sun•burn, •burned or •burnt, •burn•ing

sun•burst

sun•dae (ice cream with toppings)

Sun•day (day of the week)

sun•der, •dered, •der•ing

sun•di\al

sun•down

sun•dries

sun•dry

sun•flow\er

sung

sun•glass\es

sunk

sunk cost

sunk\en

sun•lamp

sun•light

sun•lit

sun\ny, •ni\er, •ni•est

sun•rise

sunrise in•dus•try

sun•roof, pl. •roofs

sun•screen or sun screen

sun•set

sunset in•dus•try

sun•shine

sun•spot

sun•stroke

sun•tan, •tanned, •tan•ning

sun•up

Sun Yat-•sen

sup, supped, sup•ping

su•per

su\per•a•bun•dance

su\per•a•bun•dant

su\per•an•nu•at\ed

su•perb

su•perb\ly

su\per•car\go, pl. •goes or •gos

su\per•charge, •charged, •charg•ing

su\per•charg\er

su\per•cil\i•ous

su\per•com•put\er

su\per•con•duc•tiv•i\ty

su\per•con•duc•tor

su\per•e•go, pl. \gos

su\per•er\o•ga•tion

su\per•e\rog\a•to\ry

su\per•fi•cial

su\per•fi•ci•al•i\ty

su\per•fi•cial\ly

su\per•flu•i\ty

su•per•flu•ous

su\per•he•ro, pl. •roes

su\per•high•way

su\per•hu•man

su\per•im•pose, •posed, •pos•ing

su\per•in•tend, •tend\ed, •tend•ing

su\per•in•ten•dence

su\per•in•ten•den\cy

su\per•in•tend•ent

su•pe•ri\or

su•pe•ri•or•i\ty

su\per•la•tive

su\per•la•tive\ly

su\per•man, pl. •men

su\per•mar•ket

su\per•nal

su\per•nat\u•ral

su\per•no\va, pl. •vas or •vae

su\per•nu•mer•ar\y, pl. •ar•ies

su\per•pow\er

su\per•script
su\per•scrip•tion
su\per•sede, •sed\ed,
•sed\ing
su\per•son\ic
su\per•star
su\per•sti•tion
su\per•sti•tious
su\per•struc•ture
su\per•tank\er
su\per•vene, •vened,
•ven•ing
su\per•ven•tion
su\per•vise, •vised, •vis•ing
su\per•vi•sion
su\per•vi•sor
su\per•vi•so\ry
su•pine
sup•per
sup•plant, •plant\ed,
•plant•ing
sup•ple, •pler, •plest
sup•ple•ment, •ment\ed,
•ment•ing
sup•ple•men•ta\ry
sup•pli•ant
sup•pli•cant
sup•pli•cate, •cat\ed,
•cat•ing
sup•pli•ca•tion
sup•pli\er
sup•ply (quantity on hand;
to furnish), pl. •plies;
•plied, •ply•ing
sup•ply (in a supple way)
sup\ply-•side
sup•port, •port\ed,
•port•ing
sup•port\er
sup•port•ive
sup•pose, •posed,
•pos•ing
sup•pos•ed\ly
sup•po•si•tion
sup•pos\i\to\ry, pl. •ries
sup•press, •pressed,
•press•ing
sup•pres•sant
sup•pres•sion
sup•pu•ra•tion
su\pra•na•tion\al

su•prem\a•cist
su•prem\a\cy
su•preme
Supreme Be•ing
Supreme Court
su•preme\ly
sur•cease
sur•charge, •charged,
•charg•ing
sure, sur\er, sur•est
sure•fire
sure•foot\ed
sure•ly
sure•ness
sur\e\ty, pl. \ties
surety bond
surf (waves; to ride a surf-
board), surfed, surf•ing
[vs. serf (peasant)]
sur•face, •faced, •fac•ing
surf•board
sur•feit
sur•feit\ed
surf\er
surf•ing
surge (swelling movement;
to swell), surged, surg•ing
[vs. serge (cloth)]
sur•geon
sur•ger\y
sur•gi•cal
sur•gi•cal\ly
Su•ri•na\me or Su•ri•nam
Su•ri•na•mese
sur•li•ness
sur\ly, •li\er, •li•est
sur•mise, •mised, •mis•ing
sur•mount, •mount\ed,
•mount•ing
sur•name
sur•named
sur•pass, •passed,
•pass•ing
sur•plice (vestment)
sur•plus (excess)
surplus val\ue
sur•prise, •prised,
•pris•ing
sur•pris•ing\ly
sur•re\al
sur•re•al•ism

sur•re•al•ist
sur•re•al•is•tic
sur•ren•der, •dered,
•der•ing
sur•rep•ti•tious
sur•ro•gate
sur•round, •round\ed,
•round•ing
sur•tax, •taxed, •tax•ing
sur•veil•lance
sur•vey, pl. •veys; •veyed,
•vey•ing
sur•vey\or
sur•viv\al
sur•viv•al•ist
sur•vive, •vived, •viv•ing
sur•vi•vor
sus•cep•ti•bil•i\ty
sus•cep•ti•ble
sus•pect, •pect\ed,
•pect•ing
sus•pend, •pend\ed,
•pend•ing
sus•pend\ers
sus•pense
suspense ac•count
sus•pense•ful
sus•pen•sion
sus•pi•cion
sus•pi•cious
sus•pi•cious\ly
sus•tain, •tained, •tain•ing
sus•te•nance
su•ture, •tured, •tur•ing
Su\va
svelte
swab or swob, swabbed or
swobbed, swab•bing or
swob•bing
swad•dle, •dled, •dling
swag
swag•ger, •gered, •ger•ing
Swa•hi•li
swain
swal•low, •lowed, •low•ing
swal\low•tail
swam
swa\mi, pl. •mis
swamp, swamped,
swamp•ing
swamp\y, •i\er, •i•est

swan

swank, swanked,
 swank•ing; swank\er,
 swank•est

swank\y, •i\er, •i•est

swans•down

swap, swapped, swap•ping

swapping in

swapping out

sward (*turf*) [*vs.* soared
 (*did soar*) and sword
 (*weapon with blade*)]

swarm, swarmed,
 swarm•ing

swarth\y, •i\er, •i•est

swash•buck•ler

swas•ti•ka, *pl.* •kas

swat, swat•ted, swat•ting

swatch

swath (*strip*)

swathe (*to wrap*),
 swathed, swath•ing

swat•ter

sway, swayed, sway•ing

sway•back *or*
 sway•backed

Swa\zi•land

swear, swore, sworn,
 swear•ing

swear•word

sweat, sweat *or* sweat\ed,
 sweat•ing

sweat eq•ui\ty

sweat\er

sweat•pants *or* sweat
 pants

sweat•shirt

sweat•shop

sweat\y, •i\er, •i•est

Swede

Swe•den

Swed•ish

sweep, swept, sweep•ing

sweep\er

sweep•ing\ly

sweeps

sweep•stakes

sweet (*sugary*), \er, •est
 [*vs.* suit (*set of clothes; to
 adapt*) and suite (*series
 of rooms*)]

sweet•bread

sweet•bri\er *or*
 sweet•bri\ar

sweet\en, •ened, •en•ing

sweet•en\er

sweet•heart

sweetheart con•tract

sweet•ish

sweet\ly

sweet•meat

sweet•ness

sweet-•talk, •talked,
 •talk\ing

swell, swelled, swol•len *or*
 swelled, swell•ing

swell•head\ed

swel•ter, •tered, •ter•ing

swept

swept•back

swerve, swerved,
 swerv•ing

swift, \er, •est

swift\ly

swift•ness

swig, swigged, swig•ging

swill, swilled, swill•ing

swim, swam, swum,
 swim•ming

swim•mer

swim•suit

swin•dle, •dled, •dling

swin•dler

swine, *pl.* swine

swing, swung, swing•ing

swing\er

swing loan

swipe, swiped, swip•ing

swirl, swirled, swirl•ing

swish, swished, swish•ing

Swiss, *pl.* Swiss

switch, switched,
 switch•ing

switch•blade

switch•board

switch\er

switch-•hit, •hit, •hit\ting

switch-•hit\ter

Switz\er•land

swiv\el, •eled *or* •elled,
 •el•ing *or* •el•ling

swiz•zle stick

swob, swobbed,
 swob•bing

swol•len

swoon, swooned,
 swoon•ing

swoop, swooped,
 swoop•ing

sword (*weapon with
 blade*) [*vs.* soared (*did
 soar*) and sward (*turf*)]

sword•fish, *pl.* •fish\es *or*
 •fish

sword•play

swords•man, *pl.* •men

swore

sworn

swum

swung

Syb\a•rite

Syb\a•rit\ic

syc\a•more

syc\o•phan\cy

syc\o•phant

syc\o•phan•tic

Syd•ney

syl•lab\ic

syl•lab\i•ca•tion *or*
 syl•lab\i•fi•ca•tion

syl•lab\i\fy, •fied, •fy•ing

syl•la•ble

syl•la•bus, *pl.* •bus\es *or*
 \bi

syl•lo•gism

syl•lo•gis•tic

sylph

syl•van

sym•bi•o•sis, *pl.* •ses

sym•bi•ot\ic

sym•bol (*sign*) [*vs.* cym•bal
 (*percussion instrument*)]

sym•bol\ic

sym•bol\i•cal\ly

sym•bol•ism

sym•bol•ize, •ized, •iz•ing

sym•met•ri•cal

sym•met•ri•cal\ly

sym•me•try, *pl.* •tries

sym•pa•thet\ic

sym•pa•thet\i•cal\ly

sym•pa•thize, •thized,
 •thiz•ing

sym•pa•thiz•er
sym•pa•thy, *pl.* •thies
sym•phon•ic
sym•pho\ny, *pl.*
•nies
sym•po•si•um, *pl.*
•si•ums *or* •si\a
symp•tom
symp•to•mat•ic
syn\a•gogue
syn•apse
sync *or* synch, synced
 or synched, sync•ing
 or synch•ing
syn•chro•ni•za•tion
syn•chro•nize, •nized,
 •niz•ing
syn•chro•nous
syn•co•pate, •pat\ed,
 •pat•ing
syn•co•pa•tion
syn•co\pe

syn•di•cate, •cat\ed, •cat•ing
syn•di•ca•tion
syn•di•ca•tor
syn•drome
syn•er•gism
syn•er•gis•tic
syn•fu\el
syn\od
syn\o•nym
syn•on\y•mous
syn•op•sis, *pl.* •ses
syn•tac•tic *or*
 syn•tac•ti•cal
syn•tax
syntax er•ror
syn•the•sis, *pl.* •ses
syn•the•size, •sized,
 •siz•ing
syn•the•siz\er
syn•thet\ic
syn•thet\i•cal\ly
syn•thet\ic fu\el

syph\i•lis
syph\i•lit\ic
Syr\a•cuse
Syr\i\a
Syr•i\an
sy•ringe
syr\up
syr•up\y
sys\op
sys•tem
sys•tem•at\ic
sys•tem•at\i•cal\ly
sys•tem\a•tize, •tized,
 •tiz•ing
sys•tem call
sys•tem\ic
sys•tem\i•cal\ly
sys•tems a\nal\y•sis
systems an\a•lyst
systems soft•ware
sys•to\le
sys•tol\ic

---

tab, tabbed, tab•bing
tab\by, *pl.* •bies
tab char•ac•ter
tab•er•nac\le
ta•ble, •bled, •bling
tab•leau (*picturesque
 grouping*), *pl.* tab•leaux *or*
 tab•leaus [*vs.* tab•loid
 (*newspaper*)]
ta\ble•cloth, *pl.* •cloths
ta•ble d'hôte, *pl.* ta•bles
 d'hôte
ta\ble-•hop, •hopped,
 •hop\ping
ta\ble-•hop\per
ta\ble•land
ta\ble•spoon
ta\ble•spoon•ful, *pl.* •fuls
tab•let
ta\ble•ware
tab•loid (*newspaper*) [*vs.*
 tab•leau (*picturesque
 grouping*)]
ta•boo, *pl.* •boos
tab\u•lar
tab\u•late, •lat\ed, •lat•ing
tab\u•la•tion

tab\u•la•tor
T-\ac\count (*the bookkeeping account*)
ta•cet (*musical direction*)
 [*vs.* tacit (*implied*)]
ta•chom\e•ter
tach\y•car•di\a
tac\it (*implied*)
tac•it\ly
tac•it•ness
tac\i•turn
tac\i•tur•ni\ty
tack, tacked, tack•ing
tacked (*nailed*) [*vs.* tact
 (*diplomacy*)]
tack\i•ness
tack\le, •led, •ling
tack•ler
tacks (*nails*) [*vs.* tax
 (*money paid to govern-
 ment; to impose a tax*)]
tack\y, •i\er, •i•est
ta\co, *pl.* •cos
Ta•co\ma
tact (*diplomacy*) [*vs.*
 tacked (*nailed*)]
tact•ful

tact•ful\ly
tac•ti•cal
tac•ti•cal\ly
tac•ti•cian
tac•tics
tac•tile
tact•less
tact•less\ly
tad
tad•pole
taf•fe\ta, *pl.* •tas
taf\fy, *pl.* •fies
Taft
tag, tagged, tag•ging
Ta•ga•log, *pl.* •logs *or* •log
Ta•hi\ti
Ta•hi•tian
t'ai chi ch'uan *or* tai chi
 chuan
tail (*rear part; to follow*),
 tailed, tail•ing [*vs.* tale
 (*story*)]
tail coat *or* tail•coat
tail•gate, •gat\ed, •gat•ing
tail•gat\er
tail•less
tail•light

tai•lor, •lored, •lor•ing
tail•pipe
tail•spin
taint, taint\ed, taint•ing
Tai•pei
Tai•wan
Tai•wan•ese, *pl.* •ese
take, took, tak\en, tak•ing
take•a\ble
take•off
take•out
take•o\ver
tak\er
tak•ing
talc
tal•cum pow•der
tale (*story*) [vs. tail (*rear part; to follow*)]
tale•bear\er
tal•ent
tal•ent\ed
tal•is•man, *pl.* •mans
talk, talked, talk•ing
talk\a•tive
talk\a•tive•ness
talk\er
talk\ing-•to, *pl.* •tos
tall, \er, •est
Tal•la•has•see
tal•low
tal\ly, *pl.* •lies; •lied, •ly•ing
tal•ly\ho, *pl.* •hos
Tal•mud
Tal•mud\ic
tal\on
tam
tam•a\ble *or* tame•a\ble
ta•ma\le, *pl.* •les
tam\a•rind
tam•bou•rine
tame, tamed, tam•ing; tam\er, tam•est
tame•a\ble
tame\ly
tame•ness
tam\er
Tam\il
tam-•o'-•shan\ter
tamp, tamped, tamp•ing
Tam\pa
tam•per, •pered, •per•ing

tam•pon
tan, tanned, tan•ning; tan•ner, tan•nest
tan\a•ger
tan•dem
T'ang *or* Tang
tangtan•ge\lo, *pl.* •los
tan•gent
tan•gen•tial
tan•ge•rine
tan•gi•bil•i\ty
tan•gi\ble
tangible as•set
tan•gi\bly
tan•gle, •gled, •gling
tan•go, *pl.* •gos; •goed, •go•ing
tank
tan•kard
tank\er
tank•ful, *pl.* •fuls
tan•ner\y, *pl.* •ner•ies
tan•nin
tan\sy, *pl.* •sies
tan•ta•lize, •lized, •liz•ing
tan•ta•liz\er
tan•ta•liz•ing\ly
tan•ta•lum
tan•ta•mount
tan•trum
Tan•za•ni\a
Tan•za•ni\an
Tao•ism
Tao•ist
tap, tapped, tap•ping
tap dance
tap-•danc\er
tape, taped, tap•ing
tap\er (*one who tapes*)
ta•per (*candle; to become thinner at one end*), •pered, •per•ing
tap•es•try, *pl.* •tries
tape•worm
tap\i•o\ca
ta•pir (*the animal*), *pl.* •pirs *or* •pir
tap•per
tap•root
taps
tar, tarred, tar•ring

tar•an•tel\la (*the dance*), *pl.* •las
ta•ran•tu\la (*the spider*), *pl.* •las
tar•di\ly
tar•di•ness
tar\dy, •di\er, •di•est
tare (*weight*) [vs. tear (*rip; to rip*)]
tar•get, •get\ed, •get•ing
tar•iff
tar•nish, •nished, •nish•ing
ta\ro (*edible tuber*), *pl.* •ros
ta•rot cards (*cards for fortune telling*)
tar•pau•lin
tar•pon, *pl.* •pons *or* •pon
tar•ra•gon
tar\ry, •ried, •ry•ing
tar•sal
tar•sus, *pl.* \si
tart, tart\ed, tart•ing; tart\er, tart•est
tar•tan
tar•tar
tar•tar\ic ac\id
tart\ly
tart•ness
task
task•mas•ter
task switch•ing
Tas•ma•ni\a
Tas•ma•ni\an
tas•sel
tas•seled *or* tas•selled
taste, tast\ed, tast•ing
taste•ful
taste•ful\ly
taste•less
taste•less\ly
tast\er
tast\i•ness
tast\ly, •i\er, •i•est
tat, tat•ted, tat•ting
ta•ta\mi, *pl.* \mi *or* •mis
tat•ter
tat•tered
tat\ter•de•mal•ion
tat•ter•sall
tat•ting
tat•tle, •tled, •tling

tat•tler

tat\tle•tale

tat•too, pl. •toos; •tooed, •too•ing

tat•too•ist

tau

taught (did teach) [vs. taut (tense)]

taunt (to mock), taunt\ed, taunt•ing

taunt•ing\ly

taupe

Tau•rus

taut (tense), \er, •est [vs. taught (did teach) and taunt (to mock)]

taut\ly

taut•ness

tau\to•log•ic or tau•tol\o•gous

tau•tol\o\gy, pl. •gies

tav•ern

taw•dri•ness

taw•dry, •dri\er, •dri•est

taw•ni•ness

taw\ny, •ni\er, •ni•est

tax (money paid to government; to impose a tax), taxed, tax•ing [vs. tacks (nails)]

tax•a\ble

tax-•de\ferred

tax\er

tax-•ex\empt

tax ex•emp•tion

tax-•free

tax\i, pl. tax\is; tax•ied, tax\i•ing

tax\i•cab

tax\i•der•mist

tax\i•der\my

tax lien

tax\o•nom\ic

tax•on\o\my

tax•pay\er

tax•pay•ing

tax rate

tax re•turn

tax shel\ter

tax-•shel\tered

tax shield

Tay•lor

T-\bill (treasury bill)

T-\bond (treasury bond)

T-\bone steak

tbs. or tbsp. (tablespoon)

T cell (thymus-derived cell)

Tchai•kov•sky

tea (beverage) [vs. tee (golf peg)]

teach, taught, teach•ing

teach\er

tea•cup

teak

tea•ket\tle

teal, pl. teals or teal

team (group; to join together), teamed, team•ing [vs. teem (to swarm)]

team•mate

team•ster

team•work

tea•pot

tear (rip; to rip), tore, torn, tear•ing [vs. tare (weight)]

tear (drop of fluid from eye; to weep), teared, tear•ing [vs. tier (row)]

tear•drop

tear gas (noun)

tear-•gas (verb), •gassed, •gas\sing

tear•jerk\er

tear-•off men\u

teas (beverages)

tease (to provoke), teased, teas•ing

tea•sel

teas•ing\ly

tea•spoon

tea•spoon•ful, pl. •fuls

teat

tech\ie

tech•ne•ti\um

tech•ni•cal

tech•ni•cal•i\ty, pl. •ties

tech•ni•cal\ly

tech•ni•cian

Tech•ni•col\or (™)

tech•nics (study of a mechanical art)

tech•nique, pl. •niques (skilled methods)

tech•noc•ra\cy, pl. •cies

tech•no•log\i•cal

tech•no•log\i•cal\ly

tech•nol\o•gist

tech•nol\o\gy, pl. •gies

tec•ton•ics

ted\dy bear

te•di•ous

te•di•ous\ly

te•di\um

tee (golf peg; to strike a golf ball from a tee), teed, tee•ing [vs. tea (beverage)]

teem (to swarm), teemed, teem•ing [vs. team (group; to join together)]

teen

teen•age or teen•aged

teen•ag\er

teen\y•bop•per

tee•pee (tepee)

tee shirt (T-shirt)

tee•ter, •tered, •ter•ing

teeth (plural of tooth)

teethe (to grow teeth), teethed, teeth•ing

tee•to•tal\er

Tef•lon (™)

Te•gu•ci•gal\pa

Te•he•ran or Teh•ran

tek•tite

Tel A\viv

tel\e•cast, •cast or •cast\ed, •cast•ing

tel\e•cast\er

tel\e•com•mu•ni•ca•tions

tel\e•com•mut•ing

tel\e•con•fer•ence, •enced, •enc•ing

tel\e•cop\y, •cop•ied, •cop\y•ing

tel\e•gen\ic

tel\e•gram

tel\e•graph, •graphed, •graph•ing

te•leg•ra•pher or te•leg•ra•phist

te•leg•ra•phy
tel•e•ki•ne•sis
tel•e•mar•ket•er
tel•e•mar•ket•ing
te•lem\e\ter, •tered,
•ter•ing
tel\e•met•ric
te•lem\e•try
tel\e\o•log\i•cal
ar•gu•ment
tel\e•ol\o\gy
tel\e•path\ic
tel\e•path\i•cal\ly
te•lep\a•thy
tel\e•phone, •phoned,
•phon•ing
tel\e•phon\ic
te•leph\o\ny
tel\e•pho\to
tel\e•play
tel\e•por•ta•tion
tel\e•scope, •scoped,
•scop•ing
tel\e•scop\ic
tel\e•thon
Tel\e•type (™)
tel•e•van•ge•lism
tel•e•van•ge•list
tel\e•vise, •vised, •vis•ing
tel\e•vi•sion (TV)
tel\ex, •exed, •ex•ing
tell, told, tell•ing
tell\er
Tel•ler
tell•ing\ly
tell•tale
tel•lu•ri\um
tel\ly, pl. •lies
Tel•star (™)
te•mer\i\ty
temp
tem•per, •pered, •per•ing
tem•per\a (painting tech-
nique) [vs. tem•pu\ra
(Japanese food)]
tem•per\a•ment
tem•per\a•men•tal
tem•per•ance
tem•per•ate
tem•per•ate\ly
tem•per•ate•ness

tem•per\a•ture
tem•pest
tem•pes•tu•ous
tem•pes•tu•ous\ly
tem•pes•tu•ous•ness
tem•plate
tem•ple
tem\po, pl. •pos or \pi
tem•po•ral
tem•po•rar\i\ly
tem•po•rar\y, pl. •rar•ies
tem•po•rize, •rized,
•riz•ing
tempt, \ed, •ing
temp•ta•tion
tempt•ing\ly
tem•pu\ra (Japanese food)
[vs. tem•per\a (painting
technique)]
ten
ten\a\ble
te•na•cious
te•na•cious\ly
ten•an\cy, pl. •cies
ten•ant (occupant; to
dwell), •ant\ed, •ant•ing
[vs. ten\et (belief)]
tend, tend\ed, tend•ing
ten•den\cy, pl. •cies
ten•den•tious
tend\er (one who tends;
auxiliary ship)
ten•der (to bid; soft),
•dered, •der•ing; •der\er,
•der•est
ten•der\er
ten\der•foot, pl. •foots or
•feet
ten\der-•heart\ed
ten•der•ize, •ized, •iz•ing
ten•der•iz\er
ten•der•loin
ten•der\ly
ten•der•ness
ten•der of•fer
ten•di•ni•tis
ten•don (cord connecting
muscle and bone) [vs.
ten\on (projection
inserted into mortise)]
ten•dril

ten\e•brous
ten\e•ment
ten\et (belief) [vs. ten•ant
(occupant; to dwell)]
ten•fold
Ten•nes•se\an
Ten•nes•see (TN)
ten•nis
Ten•ny•son
ten\on (projection inserted
into mortise) [vs. ten•don
(cord connecting muscle
and bone)]
ten\or (male singer; pur-
port) [vs. ten•ure (term)]
ten•pins
tense, tensed, tens•ing;
tens\er, tens•est
tense\ly
tense•ness
ten•sile
ten•sion, •sioned,
•sion•ing
tent
ten•ta•cle
ten•ta•cled
ten•tac\u•lar
ten•ta•tive
ten•ta•tive\ly
ten•ta•tive•ness
ten•ter•hook
tenth
ten\u•ous
ten\u•ous\ly
ten\u•ous•ness
ten•ure (term) [vs. ten\or
(male singer; purport)]
te•pee or tee•pee
tep\id
te•qui\la
ter\a•bit (Tb)
ter\a•byte (TB)
ter•bi\um
ter•cen•ten•ar\y, pl.
•ar•ies
ter\i•ya\ki
term, termed, term•ing
ter•ma•gant
term bond
ter•mi•na•ble
ter•mi•nal

terminal em\u•la•tion

ter•mi•nal\ly

ter•mi•nate, •nat\ed, •nat•ing

ter•mi•na•tor

ter•mi•no•log\i•cal

ter•mi•nol\o\gy, pl. •gies

term in•sur•ance

ter•mi•nus, pl. \ni or •nus\es

ter•mite

tern (the bird) [vs. turn (to rotate)]

ter•na\ry

terp•si•cho•re\an

ter•race, •raced, •rac•ing

ter•ra cot\ta, pl. ter\ra cot•tas

ter\ra fir\ma

ter•rain

ter\ra in•cog•ni\ta

ter•ra•pin

ter•rar\l\um, pl. •rar\l•ums or •rar\i\a

ter•raz\zo

ter•res•tri\al

ter•res•tri•al\ly

ter•ri\ble

ter•ri\bly

ter•ri\er

ter•rif\ic

ter•rif\i•cal\ly

ter•ri\fy, •fied, •fy•ing

ter•ri•fy•ing\ly

ter•ri•to•ri\al

ter•ri•to•ry, pl. •ries

ter•ror

ter•ror•ism

ter•ror•ist

ter•ror•ize, •ized, •iz•ing

ter\ry, pl. •ries

terse

terse\ly

terse•ness

ter•ti•ar\y

test, test\ed, test•ing

tes•ta•ment

tes•tate

tes•ta•tor

tes•tes

tes•ti•cle

tes•tic\u•lar

tes•ti\fy, •fied, •fy•ing

tes•ti•mo•ni\al

tes•ti•mo\ny

tes•ti•ness

tes•tis, pl. •tes

tes•tos•ter•one

tes\ty, •ti\er, •ti•est

tet\a•nal

tet\a•nus

tête-•à-•tête, pl. tête-•à- •têtes

teth\er, •ered, •er•ing

tet\ra, pl. •ras

tet\ra•cy•cline

tet\ra•gram

tet\ra•he•dral

tet\ra•he•dron, pl. •drons or •dra

te•tram\e•ter

Teu•ton

Teu•ton\ic

tev\a•tron

Tex\an

Tex\as (TX)

text

text•book

text ed\i•tor

text file

tex•tile

tex•tu\al

tex•tur\al

tex•ture, •tured, •tur•ing

Thai, pl. Thais

Thai•land

thal\a•mus, pl. \mi

tha•lid\o•mide

thal•li\um

Thames

than (compared to) [vs. then (at that time)]

than\a•tol•o\gy

thane

thank, thanked, thank•ing

thank•ful

thank•ful\ly

thank•ful•ness

thank•less

thank•less\ly

thanks•giv•ing

that, pl. those

thatch, thatched, thatch•ing

Thatch\er

that's (that is)

thaw, thawed, thaw•ing

the

the\a•ter or thea•tre

the•at•ri•cal

the•at•ri•cal•i\ty

the•at•ri•cal\ly

thee

thee•ing and thou•ing

theft

their (belonging to them) [vs. there (at that place) and they're (they are)]

theirs

the•ism

the•ist

the•is\tic

them

the•mat\ic

the•mat\i•cal\ly

theme

them•selves

then (at that time) [vs. than (compared to)]

thence (from that place) [vs. hence (from now) and whence (from where)]

thence•forth

the•oc•ra\cy, pl. •cies

the•o•crat\ic

the•o•lo•gian

the•o•log\i•cal

the•ol\o\gy, pl. •gies

the•o•rem

the•o•ret\i•cal

the•o•ret\i•cal\ly

the•o•re•ti•cian

the•o•rist

the•o•rize, •rized, •riz•ing

the•o\ry, pl. •ries

the•os\o•phy

ther\a•peu•tic

ther\a•peu•tics

ther\a•pist

ther\a•py, pl. •pies

there (at that place) [vs. their (belonging to them) and they're (they are)]

there•a\bout *or*
  there•a\bouts
there•af\ter
there\at
there\by
there•for (*in exchange*)
there•fore (*consequently*)
there\in
there\of
there\on
there\to *or* there•un\to
there•to•fore
there•up\on
there•with
ther•mal
thermal print\er
ther\mo•dy•nam•ics
ther•mom\e•ter
ther\mo•nu\cle\ar
ther\mo•plas•tic
ther•mos
ther\mo•stat
the•sau•rus, *pl.*
  •sau•rus\es *or* •sau\ri
these
The•se\us
the•sis, *pl.* •ses
Thes•pi\an
the\ta
they, them, their, theirs
they're (*they are*) [*vs.*
  their (*belonging to them*)
  and there (*at that place*)]
thi•a•mine *or* thi•a•min
thick, •er, •est
thick\en, •ened, •en•ing
thick•en\er
thick\et
thick•head\ed
thick\ly
thick•ness
thick•set
thick-•skinned
thief, *pl.* thieves
thiev•er\y
thiev•ing
thigh
thigh•bone
thim•ble
thim•ble•ful, *pl.* •fuls
Thim•phu *or* Thim\bu

thin, thinned, thin•ning;
  thin•ner, thin•nest
thine
thing
thing\a•ma•bob
think, thought, think•ing
think\er
think tank
thin\ly
thin•ner
thin•ness
thin-•skinned
third
third-•class
third de•gree (*noun*)
third-de•gree (*adj.*)
third mar•ket
third-•rate
Third World
thirst, thirst\ed, thirst•ing
thirst•i\ly
thirst\y, •i\er, •i•est
thir•teen
thir•teenth
thir•ti•eth
thir\ty, *pl.* •ties
this, *pl.* these
this•tle
this\tle•down
thith\er
thong (*leather strip*) [*vs.*
  tong (*tongs, a two-armed*
  implement) *and* tongue
  (*organ in mouth*)]
Thor
tho•rac\ic
tho•rax, *pl.* tho•rax\es *or*
  tho•ra•ces
Tho•reau
tho•ri\um
thorn
thorn\y, •i\er, •i•est
thor•ough (*complete*) [*vs.*
  threw (*did throw*) *and*
  through (*by means of*)]
thor•ough•bred
thor•ough•fare
thor•ough•go•ing
thor•ough\ly
thor•ough•ness
those

thou, thee, thy, thine
though
thought
thought•ful
thought•ful\ly
thought•ful•ness
thought•less
thought•less\ly
thought•less•ness
thou•ing
thou•sand, *pl.* •sands *or*
  •sand
thou•sandth
thrall
thrash (*to strike*), thrashed,
  thrash•ing [*vs.* thresh (*to*
  beat out grain)]
thread, thread\ed,
  thread•ing
thread•bare
threat
threat\en, •ened, •en•ing
three
three-•di\men\sion\al
386 com•put\er
three•fold
three•score
three•some
thren\o\dy, *pl.* •dies
thresh (*to beat out grain*),
  threshed, thresh•ing [*vs.*
  thrash (*to strike*)]
thresh\er
thresh•old
threw (*did throw*) [*vs.*
  thor•ough (*complete*)
  and through (*by means*
  of)]
thrice
thrift
thrift•i\ly
thrift•less
thrifts
thrift•shop
thrift\y, •i\er, •i•est
thrill, thrilled, thrill•ing
thrill\er
thrive, thrived, thriv•ing
throat
throat•i\ly
throat\y, •i\er, •i•est

throb, throbbed, throb•bing

throes (*pangs*) [*vs.* throws (*does hurl*)]

throm•bo•sis

throm•bus, *pl.* \bi

throne (*royal chair*) [*vs.* thrown (*hurled*)]

throng, thronged, throng•ing

throt•tle, •tled, •tling

through (*by means of*) [*vs.* thor•ough (*complete*) and threw (*did throw*)]

through•out

through•put

through•way (*thruway*)

throw, threw, thrown (*hurled*), throw•ing [*vs.* throne (*royal chair*)]

throw•a\way

throw•back

throw\er

throws (*does hurl*) [*vs.* throes (*pangs*)]

thru (*through*)

thrum, thrummed, thrum•ming

thrush

thrust, thrust, thrust•ing

thru•way or through•way

thud, thud•ded, thud•ding

thug

thu•li\um

thumb, thumbed, thumb•ing

thumb•nail

thumb•screw

thumb•tack, •tacked, •tack•ing

thump, thumped, thump•ing

thun•der, •dered, •der•ing

thun\der•bolt

thun\der•clap

thun\der•cloud

thun•der•head

thun•der•ous

thun\der•show\er

thun\der•storm

thun\der•struck

Thurs•day

thus

thwack, thwacked, thwack•ing

thwart, thwart\ed, thwart•ing

thy

thyme (*the herb*) [*vs.* time (*duration; to measure time*)]

thy•mus, *pl.* •mus\es or \mi

thy•roid

thy•roid•ec•to\my

thy•rox\in

thy•self

ti•ar\a, *pl.* •ar\as

Ti•ber

Ti•bet

Ti•bet\an

tib\i\a, *pl.* tib\i\ae or tib•i\as

tic (*muscle spasm*)

tick (*the arachnid*)

tick (*click; did click*), ticked, tick•ing

tick\er tape

tick\et, •et\ed, •et•ing

tick•ing

tick\le, •led, •ling

tick•ler

tickler file

tick•lish

tick•lish•ness

tick-•tack-•toe or tic-•tac-•toe

tid\al

tid•bit

tid\dly•winks

tide (*rise and fall of ocean; to carry*), tid\ed, tid•ing [*vs.* tied (*fastened*)]

tide•land

tide•wa•ter

ti•di\ly

ti•di•ness

ti•dings

ti\dy, •died, •dy•ing; •di\er, •di•est

tie, tied (*fastened*), ty•ing [*vs.* tide (*rise and fall of ocean; to carry*)]

tie-•dye, •dyed, •dye\ing

tie-•in

tier (*row*) [*vs.* tear (*drop of fluid from eye; to weep*)]

tiered

tie rod

tie-•up

tiff

TIFF (*tagged image file format*)

Tif•fa\ny glass

ti•ger, *pl.* •gers or •ger

tight, \er, •est

tight\en, •ened, •en•ing

tight-•fist\ed or tight•fist\ed

tight-•lipped

tight\ly

tight•ness

tight•rope

tights

tight•wad

ti•gress (*female tiger*)

Ti•gris (*river*)

tike (*tyke*)

til\de, *pl.* •des

tile, tiled, til•ing

tiled win•dows

till (*until*)

till (*to plow*), tilled, till•ing

till•age

till\er (*one who tills*)

til•ler (*rudder part*)

tilt, tilt\ed, tilt•ing

tim•bale, *pl.* •bales

tim•ber (*wood*)

tim•bered

tim\ber•line

tim•bre (*sound quality*)

time (*duration; to measure time*), timed, tim•ing [*vs.* thyme (*the herb*)]

time-•and-•mo\tion

time•card

time de•pos\it

time draft

time-•hon\ored

time•keep\er

time•less

time loan

time\ly, •li\er, •li•est

time-•out or time•out, pl. •outs

time•piece

tim\er

time-•shar\ing

time•ta•ble

time•worn

tim\id

ti•mid•i\ty

tim•id\ly

tim•ing

tim•or•ous

tim•or•ous•ness

Tim\o•thy

tim•pa\ni or tym•pa\ni

tim•pa•nist

tin, tinned, tin•ning

tinc•ture

tin•der

tin\der•box

tine

tin•foil

tinge, tinged, tinge•ing or ting•ing

tin•gle, •gled, •gling

tin•gly, •gli\er, •gli•est

ti•ni•ness

tin•ker, •kered, •ker•ing

tin•ker•er

tin•kle, •kled, •kling

tin•ni\ly

tin•ni•ness

tin•ni•tus

tin\ny, •ni\er, •ni•est

tin par\a•chute

tin plate or tin•plate

tin•sel

tint, tint\ed, tint•ing

tin•tin•nab•u•la•tion

tin•type

ti\ny, •ni\er, •ni•est

tip, tipped, tip•ping

tip•off

tip•per

tip•ple, •pled, •pling

tip•pler

tip•si\ly

tip•si•ness

tip•ster

tip\sy, •si\er, •si•est

tip•toe, •toed, •toe•ing

tip•top

ti•rade

Ti•ra\në or Ti•ra\na

tire, tired, tir•ing

tire•less

tire•less\ly

tire•some

tire•some\ly

'tis (it is)

tis•sue

tit

ti•tan

ti•tan•ic

ti•ta•ni\um

tithe, tithed, tith•ing

Ti•tian

tit•il•late, •lat\ed, •lat•ing

tit•il•la•tion

ti•tle, •tled, •tling

title bar

title search

tit•mouse, pl. •mice

tit•ter, •tered, •ter•ing

tit•tle

tit\u•lar

tiz\zy, pl. •zies

TM (trademark)

TN (Tennessee)

T-\note (treasury note)

TNT (the explosive)

to (toward) [vs. too (also; excessive) and two (the number)]

toad

toad•stool

toad\y, pl. toad•ies, toad•ied, toad\y•ing

toast, toast\ed, toast•ing

toast\er

toast•mas•ter

toast\y, toast•i\er, toast•i•est

to•bac\co, pl. •cos or •coes

to•bac•co•less

to•bac•co•nist

to•bog•gan, •ganed, •gan•ing

toc•sin (alarm bell) [vs. tox\in (poison)]

to•day

tod\dle, •dled, •dling

tod•dler

tod\dy, pl. •dies

to-•do, pl. •dos

toe (foot digit; to touch with the toes), toed, toe•ing [vs. tow (to pull)]

toe•hold or toe-•hold

toe•nail

tof•fee

to\fu

to\ga, pl. •gas

to•gaed

to•geth\er

to•geth•er•ness

tog•gle key

To\go

To\go•lese

togs

toil (labor; to toil), toiled, toil•ing

toile (transparent fabric)

toil\er

toi•let (bathroom fixture)

toi•let\ry, pl. •ries

toi•lette (grooming)

toil•some

toke, toked, tok•ing

to•ken, •kened, •ken•ing

to•ken•ism

to\ken-•ring net•work

To•ky\o

To•ky\o•ite

told

tole (metalware) [vs. toll (fee; to sound)]

To•le\do

tol•er•a•ble

tol•er•a•bly

tol•er•ance

tol•er•ant

tol•er•ant\ly

tol•er•ate, •at\ed, •at•ing

tol•er•a•tion

toll (fee; to sound), tolled, toll•ing [vs. tole (metalware)]

toll•booth, pl. •booths

toll•gate
Tol•stoy or Tol•stoi
tol\u•ene
tom
tom\a•hawk
to•ma\to, pl. •toes
tomb (grave) [vs. tome (book)]
tom•boy
tom•boy•ish
tomb•stone
tom•cat, •cat•ted, •cat•ting
Tom Col•lins
tome (book) [vs. tomb (grave)]
tom•fool•er\y
Tom\my gun
to•mog•ra•phy
to•mor•row
tom-•tom
ton
ton\al
to•nal•i\ty, pl. •ties
tone, toned, ton•ing
tone arm or tone•arm
tone-•deaf
tone•less
ton\er
tong (tongs, a two-armed implement) [vs. thong (leather strip) and tongue (organ in mouth)]
Ton\ga
tongs
tongue (organ in mouth; to play tones), tongued, tongu•ing
tongue-•lash\ing
tongue-•tied
ton\ic
to•night
ton•nage
ton•sil
ton•sil•lec•to\my, pl. •mies
ton•sil•li•tis
ton•so•ri\al
ton•sure
ton•sured
ton\y, •i\er, •i•est
To\ny, pl. To•nys

too (also; excessive) [vs. to (toward) and two (the number)]
took
tool (implement; to shape with a tool), tooled, tool•ing [vs. tulle (net fabric)]
toot, toot\ed, toot•ing
tooth, pl. teeth
tooth•ache
tooth•brush
toothed
tooth•less
tooth•paste
tooth•pick
tooth•some
tooth\y, •i\er, •i•est
top, topped, top•ping
to•paz
top•coat
top-•down pro•gram•ming
To•pe\ka
top flight (noun)
top-•flight (adj.)
top-•heav\y
to•pi•ar\y
top\ic
top\i•cal
top•knot
top•less
top-•lev\el
top man•age•ment
top•mast
top•most
top•notch or top-•notch
top\o•graph\ic or top\o•graph\i•cal
to•pog•ra•phy (surface features), pl. •phies [vs. ty•pog•ra•phy (printing)]
top\o•log\ic
to•pol\o\gy
top•ping
top•ple, •pled, •pling
TOPS (transparent operating system)
top•sail
top-•se\cret
top•side

top•soil
top\sy-•tur\vy
toque
To•rah, pl. •rahs
torch, torched, torch•ing
torch•bear\er
torch•light
tore
tor\e\a•dor
tor•ment, •ment\ed, •ment•ing
tor•men•tor
torn
tor•na\do, pl. •does or •dos
To•ron\to
To•ron•to•ni\an
tor•pe\do, pl. •does; •doed, \do•ing
tor•pid
tor•por
torque
tor•rent
tor•ren•tial
tor•rid
tor•rid•i\ty
tor•sion
tor\so, pl. •sos or \si
tort (wrongful act)
torte (rich cake), pl. tortes
tor•tel•li\ni
tor•til\la, pl. •las
tor•toise
tor•toise•shell or tortoise shell
tor•tu•ous (twisting) [vs. tor•tur•ous (painful)]
tor•tu•ous\ly
tor•ture, •tured, •tur•ing
tor•tur\er
tor•tur•ous (painful) [vs. tor•tu•ous (twisting)]
To\ry, pl. •ries
toss, tossed, toss•ing
toss\up
tot, tot•ted, tot•ting
to•tal, •taled or •talled, •tal•ing or •tal•ling
to•tal\i•tar\i\an
to•tal\i•tar\i\an•ism
to•tal•i\ty

to•tal\i•za•tor
to•tal\ly
tote, tot\ed, tot•ing
to•tem
tot•ter, •tered, •ter•ing
tou•can
touch, touched, touch•ing
touch•a\ble
touch and go (noun)
touch-•and-•go (adj.)
touch•down
tou•ché
touched
touch\i•ly
touch\i•ness
touch•ing
touch•ing\ly
touch•screen
touch•stone
touch tab•let
touch\y, •i\er, •i•est
tough, toughed, tough•ing; tough\er, tough•est
tough•en, •ened, •en•ing
tough\ly
tough-mind\ed
tough•ness
tou•pee
tour, toured, tour•ing
tour de force, pl. tours de force
Tou•rette's syn•drome
tour•ism
tour•ist
tour•is\ta
tour•ma•line
tour•na•ment
tour•ni•quet
tou•sle, •sled, •sling
tout, tout\ed, tout•ing
tow (to pull), towed, tow•ing [vs. toe (foot digit)]
tow•age
to•ward or to•wards
tow\el, •eled or •elled, •el•ing or •el•ling
tow\er, •ered, •er•ing
tower con•fig\u•ra•tion
tow-•head\ed

tow•hee
town
town house or town•house
town•ship
towns•peo•ple
tow•path, pl. •paths
tox\e•mi\a
tox\ic
tox•ic•i\ty
tox\i•col\o•gist
tox\i•col\o•gy
tox\ic shock syn•drome
tox\in (poison) [vs. toc•sin (alarm bell)]
toy, toyed, toy•ing
TPI (tracks per inch)
trace, traced, trac•ing
trace\a\ble
trac\er
trac\er\y, •er•ies
tra•che\a, pl. •che\ae or •che\as
tra•che\al
tra•che•ot\o\my, pl. •mies
tra•cho\ma
trac•ing
track (parallel rails; path; to pursue a trail), tracked, track•ing [vs. tract (region; pamphlet)]
track•a\ble
track•ball
track\er
track•less
track light•ing
tract (region; pamphlet) [vs. track (parallel rails; path; to pursue a trail)]
trac•ta\ble
trac•tion
trac•tor
tractor feed
tractor-trail\er
trade, trad\ed, trad•ing
trade ac•cept•ance
trade as•so•ci•a•tion
trade bal•ance
trade def\i•cit
trade dis•count
trade-•in

trade•mark, •marked, •mark•ing
trade name
trade-•off or trade•off
trad\er
trades•man, pl. •men
trade sur•plus
trades•wom\an, pl. •wom\en
trade un•ion
tra•di•tion
tra•di•tion•al
tra•di•tion•al\ly
tra•duce, •duced, •duc•ing
traf•fic, •ficked, •fick•ing
traf•fick\er
traf•fic man•ag\er
tra•ge•di\an
trag\e•dy, pl. •dies
trag\ic
trag\i•cal\ly
trag\i•com\e\dy, pl. •dies
trag\i•com\ic
trail (path; to drag), trailed, trail•ing [vs. tri\al (judicial proceeding)]
trail•blaz\er
trail\er
train, trained, train•ing
train\ee
train\er
train•ing
traipse, traipsed, traips•ing
trait
trai•tor
trai•tor•ous
tra•jec•to\ry, pl. •ries
tram
tram•mel, •meled or •melled, •mel•ing or •mel•ling
tramp, tramped, tramp•ing
tram•ple, •pled, •pling
tram•po•line
tram•way
trance
tran•quil
tran•quil•i\ty

tran•quil•ize *or*
  tran•quil•lize, •ized *or*
  •lized, •iz•ing *or* •liz•ing
tran•quil•iz•er *or*
  tran•quil•liz•er
tran•quil•li\ty
tran•quil\ly
trans•act, •act\ed, •act\ing
trans•ac•tion
transaction cost
transaction proc•ess•ing
trans•at•lan•tic
trans•ceiv•er
tran•scend, •scend\ed,
  •scend•ing
tran•scend•ence
tran•scend•ent
tran•scen•den•tal
tran•scen•den•tal•ism
tran•con•ti•nen•tal
tran•scribe, •scribed,
  •scrib•ing
tran•script
tran•scrip•tion
trans•duc\er
tran•sept
trans•fer, •ferred, •fer•ring
trans•fer•a\ble
trans•fer\al *or*
  trans•fer•ral
trans•fer price
trans•fig\u•ra•tion
trans•fig•ure, •ured,
  •ur•ing
trans•fix, •fixed, fix•ing
trans•form, •formed,
  •form•ing
trans•for•ma•tion
trans•form\er
trans•fuse, •fused,
  •fus•ing
trans•fu•sion
trans•gress, •gressed,
  •gress•ing
trans•gres•sion
trans•gres•sor
tran•sient
tran•sis•tor
tran•sit, •sit\ed, •sit•ing
tran•si•tion
tran•si•tion\al

tran•si•tive
tran•si•to\ry
trans•late, •lat\ed, •lat•ing
trans•la•tion
trans•la•tor
trans•lit•er•ate, •at\ed,
  •at•ing
trans•lit•er•a•tion
trans•lu•cence
trans•lu•cent
trans•mi•gra•tion
trans•mis•si\ble
trans•mis•sion
trans•mit, •mit•ted,
  •mit•ting
trans•mit•tal
trans•mit•ter
trans•mog•ri\fy, •fied,
  •fy•ing
trans•mut•a\ble
trans•mu•ta•tion
trans•mute, •mut\ed,
  •mut•ing
trans•na•tion\al
trans•o\ce\an\ic
tran•som
trans•pa•cif\ic
trans•par•en\cy
trans•par•ent
trans•par•ent\ly
tran•spire, •spired,
  •spir•ing
trans•plant, •plant\ed,
  •plant•ing
trans•plan•ta•tion
tran•spon•der
trans•port, •port\ed,
  •port•ing
trans•port•a\ble
  com•put\er
trans•por•ta•tion
trans•pose, •posed,
  •pos•ing
trans•po•si•tion
trans•sex\u\al
trans•ship *or* tran•ship,
  •shipped, •ship•ping
tran•ship•ment
tran•sub•stan•ti•a•tion
trans•verse
trans•verse\ly

trans•ves•tism
trans•ves•tite
trap, trapped, trap•ping
trap•door
tra•peze
trap\e•zoid
trap\e•zoi•dal
trap•per
trap•pings
trap•shoot\er
trap•shoot•ing
trash, trashed, trash•ing
trash\y, •i\er, •i•est
trau\ma, *pl.* •mas *or*
  •ma\ta
trau•mat\ic
trau•ma•tize, •tized,
  •tiz•ing
tra•vail *(toil)*
trav•el *(to journey)*, •eled
  or •elled, •el•ing *or*
  •el•ling
trav•el\er *or* trav•el•ler
trav•el\er's check
trav•el•ing sales•man
trav\e•logue *or* trav\e•log
tra•verse, •versed,
  •vers•ing
trav•es\ty, *pl.* •ties; •tied,
  •ty•ing
trawl\er
tray
treach•er•ous
treach•er•ous\ly
treach•er\y, *pl.* •er•ies
trea•cle
tread, trod, trod•den *or*
  trod, tread•ing
trea•dle
tread•mill
trea•son
trea•son•a\ble
treas•ure, •ured, •ur•ing
treas•ur\er
treas\ure-•trove
treas•ur\y, *pl.* •ur•ies
treasury bill
treasury bond
treasury note
treasury stock
treat, treat\ed, treat•ing

trea•ties (*formal agreements*)

trea•tise (*written exposition*)

treat•ment

trea\ty, *pl.* •ties

tre•ble, •bled, •bling

tree, treed, tree•ing

tree•less

tre•foil

trek, trekked, trek•king

trel•lis

trem•ble, •bled, •bling

tre•men•dous

tre•men•dous•ly

trem\o•lo, *pl.* •los

trem\or

trem\u•lous

trem\u•lous•ly

trench

trench•ant

trench\er•man, *pl.* •men

trend

trend\i•ness

trend\y, •i\er, •i•est

Tren•ton

Tren•to•ni\an

trep\i•da•tion

tres•pass, •passed, •pass•ing

tres•pass\er

tress

tres•tle

trey

tri\ad

tri•ad\ic

tri•age

tri\al (*judicial proceeding*) [*vs.* trail (*path; to drag*)]

trial bal•ance

tri•an•gle

tri•an•gu•lar

tri•an•gu•late, •lat\ed, •lat•ing

tri•an•gu•la•tion

Tri•as•sic

trib\al

tribe

trib\u•la•tion

tri•bu•nal

trib•une

trib\u•tar\y, *pl.* •tar•ies

trib•ute

trice

tri•cen•ten•ni\al

tri•ceps, *pl.* •ceps\es or •ceps

tri•cer\a•tops

trich\i•no•sis or trich\i•ni•a•sis

tri•chot•o\my

trick, tricked, trick•ing

trick\er•y

trick\i•ly

trick\i•ness

trick\le, •led, •ling

trick\le-•down the•o\ry

trick•ster

trick\y, •i\er, •i•est

tri•col\or

tri•cy•cle

tri•dent

tried

tried-and-true

tri•en•ni\al

tri•en•ni•al\ly

Tri•este

tri•fect\a, *pl.* •fect\as

tri•fle, •fled, •fling

tri•fo•cal

trig•ger, •gered, •ger•ing

tri•glyc•er•ide

trig\o•no•met•ric

trig\o•nom\e•try

tri•lat•er\al

tri•lin•gual

trill, trilled, trill•ing

tril•lion, *pl.* •lions or •lion

tril•lionth

tril•li\um

tril\o\gy, *pl.* •gies

trim, trimmed, trim•ming; trim•mer, trim•mest

tri•mes•ter

trim\ly

trim•mer

trim•mings

trim•ness

tri•month\ly

trine

Trin\i•dad *and* To•ba\go

trin•i\ty, *pl.* •ties

Trin•i\ty

trin•ket

tri\o, *pl.* tri\os

trip, tripped, trip•ping

tri•par•tite

tripe

tri•ple, •pled, •pling

trip•ham\mer

trip•let

tri\ple-•tax-•free

tri•ple witch•ing hour

tri•plex

trip•li•cate

trip\ly

tri•pod

Trip\o\li

trip•per

trip•tych

tri•sect, •sect\ed, •sect•ing

tri•syl•lab\ic

tri•syl•la•ble

trite, trit\er, trit•est

trite•ness

trit\i•um

tri•umph, •umphed, •umph•ing

tri•um•phant

tri•um•phant\ly

tri•um•vi•rate

triv\et

triv\i\a

triv\i•al

triv\i•al•i\ty

triv\i•al•ize, •ized, •iz•ing

tro•cha\ic (*of a trochee*)

troche (*losenge*)

tro•chee (*poetic meter*)

trod

trod•den

trog•lo•dyte

troi\ka, *pl.* •kas

Tro•jan

troll, trolled, troll•ing

trol•ley *pl.* •leys

trol•lop

Trol•lope

trom•bone

troop (*company of soldiers; to flock together*), trooped, troop•ing [*vs.* troupe (*company of actors*)] troop\er (*police officer*) [vs. troup\er (*actor*)]

trope

tro•phy, *pl.* •phies

trop\ic

trop\i•cal

tro•pism

trop\o•sphere

trot, trot•ted, trot•ting

troth

trot•ter

trou•ba•dour

trou•ble, •bled, •bling

trou\ble•mak\er

trou\ble•shoot\er

trou\ble•some

trough

trounce, trounced, trounc•ing

troupe (*company of actors*) [vs. troop (*company of soldiers*)]

troup\er (*actor*) [vs. troop\er (*police officer*)]

trou•sers

trous•seau, *pl.* •seaux or •seaus

trout, *pl.* trout or trouts

trow\el

troy

tru•an\cy

tru•ant

truce

truck, trucked, truck•ing

truck•age

truck\er

truck\le

truck•load

truc\u•lence

truc\u•lent

trudge, trudged, trudg•ing

true, trued, tru•ing or true•ing; tru\er, tru•est

true-•blue

truf•fle

tru•ism (*cliché*) [vs. truth (*fact*)]

tru\ly

Tru•man

trump, trumped, trump•ing

trump•er\y

trum•pet, •pet\ed, •pet•ing

trum•pet\er

trun•cate, •cat\ed, •cat•ing

trun•ca•tion

trun•cheon

trun•dle bed

trunk

truss, trussed, truss•ing

trust, trust\ed, trust•ing

trust•bust\er

trust com•pa•ny

trust deed

trust\ee (*administrator*) [vs. trust\y (*reliable; trusted convict*)]

trust\ee•ship

trust•ful

trust•ful\ly

trust fund

trust ter•ritory

trust•wor•thi•ness

trust•wor•thy

trust\y (*reliable; trusted convict*), *pl.* trust•ies; trust•i\er, trust•i•est [vs. trust\ee (*administrator*)]

truth (*fact*), *pl.* truths [vs. tru•ism (*cliché*)]

truth•ful

truth•ful\ly

truth•ful•ness

try, *pl.* tries; tried, try•ing

try•out

tryst

tsar (*czar*)

tset\se

T-\shirt or tee shirt

tsp. (*teaspoon*)

T square

TSR (*terminate-and-stay-resident software program*), *pl.* TSRs or TSR's

tsu•na\mi, *pl.* •mis

TTL mon\i•tor (*transistor-transistor logic monitor*)

tub

tu\ba (*musical instrument*), *pl.* •bas [vs. tu•ber (*underground stem*)]

tub\by, •bi\er, •bi•est

tube

tube•less

tu•ber (*underground stem*)

tu•ber•cu•lar

tu•ber•cu•lo•sis

tube•rose

tu•ber•ous

tub•ing

tu•bu•lar

tu•bule

tuck, tucked, tuck•ing

Tuck\er

tuck•ered

Tuc•son

Tues•day

tuft

tuft\ed

tug, tugged, tug•ging

tug•boat

tu•i•tion

tu•la•re•mi\a

tu•lip

tulle (*net fabric*) [vs. tool (*implement*)]

Tul\sa

tum•ble, •bled, •bling

tum•ble-•down

tum•bler

tum\ble•weed

tu•mes•cent

tum\my, *pl.* •mies

tu•mor

tu•mor•ous

tu•mult

tu•mul•tu•ous

tu\na, *pl.* \na or •nas

tun•dra, *pl.* •dras

tune, tuned, tun•ing

tune•ful

tune•less

tune•less\ly

tun\er

tune-•up

tung•sten

tu•nic

tun•ing fork

Tu•nis

Tu•ni•sia

Tu•ni•sian

tun•nel, •neled or •nelled, •nel•ing or •nel•ling

tur•ban (*headdress*)

tur•bid

tur•bine (*motor*)

tur\bo•fan

tur\bo•jet

tur\bo•prop

tur•bot, *pl.* •bot or •bots

tur•bu•lence

tur•bu•lent

tur•bu•lent\ly

tu•reen

turf, *pl.* turfs

tur•gid

tur•gid•i\ty

tur•gid\ly

Tu•rin

Turk

tur•key, *pl.* •keys or •key

Turk•ish

tur•mer\ic

tur•moil

turn (*to rotate*), turned, turn•ing [*vs.* tern (*the bird*)]

turn•a\bout

turn•a\round

turn•coat

Tur•ner (*last name*)

turn\er (*one that turns*)

turn•ing point

tur•nip

turn•key, *pl.* •keys

turnkey sys•tem

turn•off

turn•out

turn•o\ver

turn•pike

turn•stile

turn•ta\ble

tur•pen•tine

tur•pi•tude

tur•quoise

tur•ret

tur•tle, *pl.* •tles or •tle

tur\tle•dove

tur\tle•neck

tusk

tusked

tus•sle, •sled, •sling

Tut•ankh\a•men

tu•te•lage

tu•tor, •tored, •tor•ing

tu•to•ri\al

tut\ti-•frut\ti

tu•tu, *pl.* •tus

tux (*tuxedo*)

tux\e\do, *pl.* •dos

TV (*television*)

TVA (*Tennessee Valley Authority*)

twad•dle

twain

twang, twanged, twang•ing

'twas (*it was*)

tweak, tweaked, tweak•ing

tweed

tweed\y, •i\er, •i•est

'tween (*between*)

tweet, tweet•ed, tweet•ing

tweet\er

tweez•ers

twelfth

twelve

Twelve-•Step

twelve-•tone

twen•ti•eth

twen\ty, *pl.* •ties

twen•ty-•one

twen\ty-•twen\ty or 20-•20

twerp

twice

twid•dle, •dled, •dling

twig

twi•light

twill

twin

twine, twined, twin•ing

twinge

twi-•night

twi-•night\er

twin•kle, •kled, •kling

twin-•size or twin-•sized

twirl, twirled, twirl•ing

twist, twist\ed, twist•ing

twist\ed-•pair ca•ble

twist\er

twit, twit•ted, twit•ting

twitch, twitched, twitch•ing

twit•ter, •tered, •ter•ing

twit•ter\y

'twixt (*betwixt*)

two (*the number*), *pl.* twos [*vs.* to (*toward*) and too (*also; excessive*)]

two-•bit

two-•by-•four

286 com•put\er

two-•faced

two•fer

two-•fist\ed

two•fold

two-•ply

two•some

two-•tier

two-•time, •timed, •tim\ing

two-•tim\er

two-•way

TWX (*Teletypewriter Exchange*)

TX (*Texas*)

ty•coon

ty•ing

tyke or tike

Ty•ler

tym•pa\ni (*timpani*)

tym•pan\ic mem•brane

tym•pa•nist

tym•pa•num, *pl.* •nums or \na

type, typed, typ•ing

type•cast, •cast, •cast•ing

type•script

type•set, •set, •set•ting

type•set•ter

type•writ\er

ty•phoid

ty•phoon

ty•phus

typ\i•cal

typ\i•cal\ly

typ\i\fy, •fied, •fy•ing

typ•ist

ty\po•graph\ic or ty\po•graph\i•cal

typographical er•ror

ty\po•graph\i•cal\ly
ty•pog•ra•phy (*printing*)
[*vs.* to•pog•ra•phy (*surface features*)]
ty•pol•o\gy

ty•ran•ni•cal
ty•ran•ni•cal\ly
tyr•an•nize, •nized, •niz•ing
ty•ran•no•saur

tyr•an\ny, *pl.* •nies
ty•rant
ty\ro, *pl.* •ros
Ty•rol *or* Ti•rol
Ty•ro•le\an

U

u\biq•ui\ty
U-\boat (*German submarine*)
UCC (*Uniform Commercial Code*)
ud•der (*milk gland*) [*vs.* ut•ter (*to speak*)]
UFO (*unidentified flying object*), *pl.* UFOs *or* UFO's
U\gan\da
U\gan•dan
ugh
ug\li (*citrus fruit*), *pl.* ug•lis *or* ug•lies
ug•li•ness
ug\ly (*unattractive*), •li\er, •li\est
uh
UHF (*ultrahigh frequency*)
U.K. *or* UK (*United Kingdom*)
u\kase
U\kraine
U\krain•i\an
u\ku•le\le, *pl.* •les
U\lan Ba•tor
ul•cer
ul•cer•ate, •at\ed, •at•ing
ul•cer•a•tion
ul\na, *pl.* •nae *or* •nas
Ul•ster
ul•te•ri\or
ul•ti•mate
ultimate con•sum\er
ul•ti•mate\ly
ul•ti•ma•tum, *pl.* •tums *or* \ta
ul•tra, *pl.* •tras
ul\tra•con•serv\a•tive
ul\tra•high
ultrahigh fre•quen\cy (*UHF*)
ul\tra•ma•rine

ul\tra•mod•ern
ul\tra•son\ic
ul\tra•sound
ul\tra•vi\o•let
ul\u•late, •lat\ed, •lat•ing
ul\u•la•tion
U\lys•ses
um•bel
um•ber
um•bil\i•cal
um•bil\i•cus, *pl.* •bil\i\ci
um•bra, *pl.* •bras *or* •brae
um•brage
um•brel\la, *pl.* •las
umbrella pol\i\cy
um•laut
ump
um•pire (*referee; to referee*), •pir\ed, •pir•ing [*vs.* em•pire (*domain*)]
ump•teen
ump•teenth
UN *or* U.N. (*United Nations*)
un•a\ble (*not able*) [*vs.* en•a\ble (*to give power*)]
un•a\bridged
un•ac•com•pa•nied
un•ac•count•a\ble
un•ac•count•a\bly
un•ac•cus•tomed
un•af•fect\ed
un-•A\mer\i\can
u\na•nim•i\ty
u\nan\i•mous
u\nan\i•mous\ly
un•armed
un•as•sail•a\ble
un•as•sum•ing
un•at•tached
un•a\vail•ing
un•a\vail•ing\ly
un•a\void•a\ble
un•a\void•a\bly

un•a•ware
un•a•wares
un•bal•anced
un•bar, •barred, •bar•ring
un•bear•a\ble
un•bear•a\bly
un•beat\en
un•be•com•ing
un•be•known *or* un•be•knownst
un•be•lief
un•be•liev•a\ble
un•be•liev•a\bly
un•be•liev•er
un•bend, •bent, •bend•ing
un•bend•ing
un•bi\ased
un•bid•den
un•bind, •bound, •bind•ing
un•blessed *or* un•blest
un•blush•ing
un•blush•ing\ly
un•bolt, •bolt\ed, •bolt•ing
un•born
un•bos\om, •omed, •om•ing
un•bound\ed
un•bowed
un•bri•dled
un•bro•ken
un•bur•den, •dened, •den•ing
un•but•ton, •toned, •ton•ing
un\called-•for
un•can\ny
un•cap, •capped, •cap•ping
un•ceas•ing
un•ceas•ing\ly
un•cer\e•mo•ni•ous
un•cer\e•mo•ni•ous\ly
un•cer•tain
un•cer•tain\ty
un•char\i•ta•ble

un•char\i•ta•bly
un•chart\ed
un•chris•tian
un•ci\al
un•cir•cum•cised
un•civ\il
un•civ\i•lized
un•clad
un•clasp, •clasped,
•clasp•ing
un•cle
un•clean, \er, •est
un•clean\ly
un•clean•ness
un•cloak, •cloaked,
•cloak•ing
un•clog, •clogged,
•clog•ging
un•clothed
un•com•fort•a•ble
un•com•fort•a•bly
un•com•mit•ted
un•com•mon
un•com•mu•ni•ca•tive
un•com•pro•mis•ing
un•con•cern
un•con•cerned
un•con•di•tion\al
un•con•di•tion•al\ly
un•con•scion•a•ble
un•con•scion•a•bly
un•con•scious
un•con•sti•tu•tion\al
un•con•ven•tion\al
un•cork, •corked,
•cork•ing
un•count\ed
un•cou•ple, •pled, •pling
un•couth
un•cov\er, •ered, •er•ing
un•cross, •crossed,
•cross•ing
unc•tion
unc•tu•ous
unc•tu•ous•ness
un•cut
un•daunt\ed
un•de•cid\ed
un•de•lete, •let\ed,
•let•ing
un•de•mon•stra•tive

un•de•ni•a•ble
un•de•ni•a•bly
un•der
un\der•a•chieve,
•a\chieved, \a•chiev•ing
un\der•a•chiev\er
un\der•act, •act\ed,
•act•ing
un\der•age
un\der•arm
un\der•bel\ly, pl. •lies
un\der•bid, •bid, •bid•ding
un\der•brush
un\der•cap\i•tal•ized
un\der•car•riage
un\der•charge, •charged,
•charg•ing
un\der•class•man, pl.
•men
un\der•clothes or
un•der•cloth•ing
un\der•coat
un\der•cov\er
un\der•cur•rent
un\der•cut, •cut, •cut•ting
un\der•de•vel•oped
un\der•dog
un\der•done
un\der•em•ployed
un\der•em•ploy•ment
un\der•es•ti•mate,
•mat\ed, •mat•ing
un\der•es•ti•ma•tion
un\der•ex•pose, •posed,
•pos•ing
un\der•ex•po•sure
un\der•flow
un\der•foot
un\der•gar•ment
un\der•go, •went, •gone,
•go•ing
un\der•grad\u•ate
un\der•ground
un\der•growth
un\der•hand
un\der•hand\ed
un\der•hand•ed\ly
un\der•in•sure, •sured,
•sur•ing
un\der•lie, •lay, •lain,
•ly•ing

un\der•line, •lined, •lin•ing
un\der•ling
un\der•ly•ing
un•der•mine, •mined,
•min•ing
un\der•most
un\der•neath
un\der•nour•ished
un\der•pants
un\der•pass
un\der•pay, •paid, •pay•ing
un\der•pin•ning
un\der•play, •played,
•play•ing
un\der•price, •priced,
•pric•ing
un\der•priv\i•leged
un\der•pro•duce, •duced,
•duc•ing
un\der•pro•duc•tion
un\der•rate, •rat\ed,
•rat•ing
un\der•score, •scored,
•scor•ing
un\der•sea
un\der•seas
un\der sec•re•tar\y or
un\der•sec•re•tar\y
un\der•sell, •sold, •sell•ing
un\der•sexed
un\der•shirt
un\der•shorts
un\der•shot
un\der•side
un\der•signed
un\der•sized
un\der•skirt
un\der•slung
un\der•staffed
un\der•stand, •stood,
•stand•ing
un\der•stand•a•ble
un\der•stand•a•bly
un\der•stand•ing
un\der•state, •stat\ed,
•stat•ing
un\der•state•ment
un\der•stood
un\der•stud\y, pl. •stud•ies
un\der•take, •took,
•tak\en, •tak•ing

un\der•tak\er
un\der•tak•ing
un\der-•the-•count\er
un\der•things, *pl.*
un\der•tone
un\der•tow
un\der•val\u•a•tion
un\der•val\ue, •ued, \u•ing
un\der•wa•ter
un\der•wear
un\der•weight
un\der•world
un\der•write, •wrote,
•writ•ten, \writ •ing
un\der•writ\er
un•de•sir•a\ble
un•dies, *pl.*
un\do (*to reverse*), •did,
•done, •do•ing [*vs.*
en•due (*to provide*) *and*
un•due (*excessive*)]

undo com•mand

un•doubt\ed
un•doubt\ed\ly
un•dress, •dressed,
•dress•ing
un•due (*excessive*) [*vs.*
en•due (*to provide*) *and*
un\do (*to reverse*)]
un•du•lant
un•du•late, •lat\ed, •lat•ing
un•du•la•tion
un•du\ly
un•dy•ing
un•earned

unearned in•cre•ment

un•earth, •earthed,
•earth•ing
un•earth\ly
un•eas•i\ly
un•eas\i•ness
un•eas\y, •eas•i•er,
•eas•i•est
un•em•ploy•a\ble
un•em•ployed
un•em•ploy•ment

unemployment ben\e•fit
unemployment
in•sur•ance

un•e\qual
un•e\qualed

un•e\qual\ly
un•e\quiv\o•cal
un•err•ing
UNESCO (*United Nations
Educational, Scientific, and
Cultural Organization*)
un•e\ven
un•e\ven\ly
un•e\vent•ful
un•ex•am•pled
un•ex•cep•tion•a\ble
un•ex•cep•tion•a\bly
un•ex•cep•tion•al
un•ex•pect\ed
un•ex•pect\ed\ly
un•fail•ing
un•fail•ing\ly
un•fair
un•fair\ly
un•faith•ful
un•faith•ful\ly
un•fa•mil•iar
un•fas•ten, •tened,
•ten•ing
un•fa•vor•a\ble
un•feel•ing
un•feel•ing\ly
un•feigned
un•fit, •fit•ted, •fit•ting
un•flap•pa\ble
un•fledged
un•flinch•ing
un•fold (*to lay open*),
•fold\ed, •fold•ing [*vs.*
en•fold (*to wrap*)]
un•for•get•ta\ble
un•formed
un•for•tu•nate
un•for•tu•nate\ly
un•found\ed
un•friend•li•ness
un•friend\ly, •li\er, •li•est
un•frock, •frocked,
•frock•ing
un•furl, •furled, •furl•ing
un•gain\ly
un•god•li•ness
un•god\ly
un•gov•ern•a\ble
un•gra•cious
un•grate•ful

un•guard\ed
un•guent
un•gu•late
un•hand, •hand\ed,
•hand•ing
un•hap•pi\ly
un•hap•pi•ness
un•hap\py, •pi\er, •pi•est
un•har•ness, •nessed,
•ness•ing
un•health\y, •health•i\er,
•health•i•est
un•heard
un•heard-•of
un•hinge, •hinged,
•hing•ing
un•ho\ly, •li\er, •li•est
un•hook, •hooked,
•hook•ing
un•horse, •horsed,
•hors•ing
u\ni•cam•er\al
UNICEF (*United Nations
International Children's
Emergency Fund, now
"United Nations Children's
Fund"*)
u\ni•corn
u\ni•cy•cle, •cled, •cling
u\ni•fi•ca•tion
u\ni•form, •formed,
•form•ing
Uniform Com•mer•cial
Code (*UCC*)
u\ni•form•i\ty
u\ni•form\ly
u\ni\fy, •fied, •fy•ing
u\ni•lat•er\al
un•im•peach•a\ble
un•in•hib•it\ed
un•in•sur•a\ble risk
un•in•tel•li•gent
un•in•ten•tion\al
un•in•ter•est\ed
un•ion
un•ion•ism
un•ion•ize, •ized, •iz•ing
u\nique
u\nique\ly
u\ni•sex
u\ni•son

u\nit
U\ni•tar•i\an
u\nite, u\nit\ed, u\nit•ing
U\nit\ed King•dom (*UK*)
United Na•tions (*UN*)
United States (*US*)
United States
  Em•ploy•ment Serv•ice
  (*USES*)
United States Trade•mark
  As•so•ci•a•tion (*USTA*)
u\nit•ize, •ized, •iz•ing
u\nit trust
u\ni\ty, *pl.* •ties
u\ni•va•lent
u\ni•ver•sal
u\ni•ver•sal•ist
u\ni•ver•sal•i\ty
u\ni•ver•sal\ly
U\ni•ver•sal Prod•uct
  Code (*UPC*)
u\ni•verse
u\ni•ver•si\ty, *pl.* •ties
UNIX (*the operating
  system*)
un•just
un•just\ly
un•kempt
un•kind, •er, •est
un•kind\ly
un•kind•ness
un•know•ing
un•known
un•lace, •laced, •lac•ing
un•law•ful
un•law•ful\ly
un•law•ful•ness
un•learn, un•learned (*for-
  got knowledge of*),
  un•learn•ing
un•learn\ed (*uneducated*)
un•leash, •leashed,
  •leash•ing
un•less
un•let•tered
un•like
un•like•li•hood
un•like\ly, •li\er, •li•est
un•lim•ber, •bered,
  •ber•ing
un•lim•it\ed

un•load, •load\ed,
  •load•ing
un•lock, •locked, •lock•ing
un•looked-•for
un•loose, •loosed,
  •loos•ing
un•luck•i\ly
un•luck\i•ness
un•luck\y, •luck•i\er,
  •luck•i•est
un•make, •made, •mak•ing
un•man, •manned,
  •man•ning
un•man\ly, •li\er, •li•est
un•manned
un•man•ner\ly
un•mask, •masked,
  •mask•ing
un•mean•ing
un•men•tion•a\ble
un•mer•ci•ful
un•mind•ful
un•mis•tak•a\ble
un•mis•tak•a\bly
un•mit\i•gat\ed
un•nat\u•ral
un•nat\u•ral\ly
un•nec•es•sar\i\ly
un•nec•es•sar\y
un•nerve, •nerved,
  •nerv•ing
un•num•bered
un•oc•cu•pied
un•or•gan•ized
un•pack, •packed,
  •pack•ing
un•par•al•leled
un•per•son
un•pin, •pinned, •pin•ning
un•pleas•ant
un•pleas•ant\ly
un•pleas•ant•ness
un•plug, •plugged,
  •plug•ging
un•plumbed
un•pop\u•lar
un•pop\u•lar•i\ty
un•prec•e•dent\ed
un•pre•dict•a\ble
un•prin•ci•pled
un•print•a\ble

un•pro•fes•sion\al
un•prof•it•a\ble
un•qual\i•fied
un•ques•tion•a\ble
un•quote, •quot\ed,
  •quot•ing
un•rav\el, •eled *or* •elled,
  •el•ing *or* •el•ling
un•read
un•re\al
un•rea•son•a\ble
un•rea•son•a\ble•ness
un•rea•son•a\bly
un•rea•son•ing
un•re•con•struct\ed
un•re•gen•er•ate
un•re•lent•ing
un•re•mit•ting
un•re•served
un•rest
un•ripe
un•ri•valed
un•roll (*to display*),
  •rolled, •roll•ing [*vs.*
  en•roll (*to enlist*)]
un•ruf•fled
un•ru•li•ness
un•ru\ly, •li\er, •li•est
un•sad•dle, •dled, •dling
un•sat\u•rat\ed
un•sa•vor\y
un•scathed
un•schooled
un•sci•en•tif\ic
un•scram•ble, •bled, •bling
un•screw, •screwed,
  •screw•ing
un•scru•pu•lous
un•seal, •sealed, •seal•ing
un•sealed
un•sea•son•a\ble
un•seat, •seat\ed, •seat•ing
un•se•cured loan
un•seem\ly, •li\er, •li•est
un•self•ish
un•set•tle, •tled, •tling
un•shack\le, •led, •ling
un•sheathe, •sheathed,
  •sheath•ing
un•sight\ly
un•skilled

un•skill•ful
un•snap, •snapped, •snap•ping
un•snarl, •snarled, •snarl•ing
un•so•phis•ti•cat•ed
un•sound, \er, •est
un•spar•ing
un•speak•a•ble
un•speak•a•bly
un•sta\ble
un•sta\bly
un•stead•i\ly
un•stead\i•ness
un•stead\y
un•stop, •stopped, •stop•ping
un•strung
un•stuck
un•stud•ied
un•sub•stan•tial
un•sung
un•tan•gle, •gled, •gling
un•taught
un•tax•a\ble
un•taxed
un•think•a•ble
un•think•ing
un•ti\dy, •di\er, •di•est
un•tie, •tied, •ty•ing
un•til
un•time\ly
un\to
un•told
un•touch•a\ble
un•to\ward
un•true, •tru\er, •tru•est
un•truth, pl. •truths
un•truth•ful•ness
un•tu•tored
un•used
un•u•su\al
un•u•su•al\ly
un•ut•ter•a\ble
un•ut•ter•a•bly
un•var•nished
un•veil, •veiled, •veil•ing
un•voiced
un•want\ed (not wanted) [vs. un•wont\ed (rare)]
un•war\y

un•well
un•whole•some
un•whole•some•ness
un•wield\y
un•will•ing
un•will•ing\ly
un•wind, •wound, •wind•ing
un•wise, •wis\er, •wis•est
un•wit•ting
un•wont\ed (rare) [vs. un•want\ed (not wanted)]
un•wor•thi•ness
un•wor•thy
un•wrap (to uncover), •wrapped, •wrap•ping [vs. en•wrap (to wrap around)]
un•writ•ten
un•zip, •zipped, •zip•ping
up, upped, up•ping
up-•and-•com\ing
up•beat
up•braid, •braid\ed, •braid•ing
up•bring•ing
UPC (Universal Product Code)
up•chuck, •chucked, •chuck•ing
up•com•ing
up•coun•try
up•date, •dat\ed, •dat•ing
up•draft
up•end, •end\ed, •end•ing
up-•front
up•grade, •grad\ed, •grad•ing
up•heav\al
up•hill
up•hold, •held, •hold•ing
up•hol•ster, •stered, •ster•ing
up•hol•ster\er
up•hol•ster\y
up•keep
up•land
up•lift, •lift\ed, •lift•ing
up•load, •load\ed, •load•ing

up•mar•ket
up\on
up•per
up\per•class•man, pl. •men
up\per•cut, •cut, •cut•ting
up•per man•age•ment
up\per•most
Up•per Vol\ta
up•pish
up•pi\ty
up•raise, •raised, •rais•ing
up•rear, •reared, •rear•ing
up•right, •right\ed, •right•ing
up•ris•ing
up•roar
up•roar\i•ous
up•root, •root\ed, •root•ing
UPS ('™, United Parcel Service)
UPS (uninterruptible power supply)
up•scale
up•set, •set, •set•ting
upset price
up•shot
up•side
up•side down (adv.)
up\side-•down (adj.)
up•si•lon
up•stage, •staged, •stag•ing
up•stairs
up•stand•ing
up•start
up•state
up•stream
up•stroke
up•surge, •surged, •surg•ing
up•swing, •swung, •swing•ing
up•take
up•tick
up•tight
up-•to-•date
up•town

up•turn, •turned,
 •turn•ing
up•ward or up•wards
up\ward-•com\pat\i\ble
up•ward\ly
u\ra•cil
U\ral Moun•tains, *pl.*
u\ran\ic
u\ra•ni•um
U\ra•nus
urb
ur•ban (*of a city*)
ur•bane (*sophisticated*)
ur•ban•i•ty
ur•ban\i•za•tion
ur•ban•ize, •ized, •iz•ing
ur•chin
Ur\du
u\re\a
u\re•mi\a
u\re•mic
u\re•ter
u\re•thane
u\re•thra, *pl.* •thrae or
 •thras
u\re•thral
urge, urged, urg•ing
ur•gen\cy
ur•gent
ur•gent\ly
u\ric
u\ri•nal
u\ri•nal\y•sis, *pl.* •ses
u\ri•nar\y
u\ri•nate, •nat\ed,
 •nat•ing
u\rine

urn (*vase*) [*vs.* earn (*to gain*)]
u\ro•gen\i•tal
u\rol\o•gist
u\rol\o•gy
Ur\sa Ma•jor
Ursa Mi•nor
ur•sine
ur•ti•car\i\a
U\ru•guay
U\ru•guay\an
U.S. or US (*United States*)
us
USA or U.S.A. (*United
 States of America*)
us•a•bil•i•ty
us\a•ble or use\a•ble
us•age
use, used, us•ing
use•ful
use•ful\ly
use•ful•ness
use•less
use•less\ly
use•less•ness
us\er
us\er-•de\fined
us\er-•friend\ly
us\er group
user in\ter•face
us\er•name
USES (*United States
 Employment Service*)
use tax
ush\er, •ered, •er•ing
ush•er•ette
USTA (*United States
 Trademark Association*)

u\su\al
u\su•al\ly
u\sur\er
u\sur\i•ous
u\surp, u\surped,
 u\surp•ing
u\sur•pa•tion
u\surp\er
u\su\ry,
UT (*Utah*)
U\tah (*UT*)
U\tah\an
u\ten•sil
u\ter•ine
u\ter\us, *pl.* u\ter\i or
 u\ter•us\es
u\til\i•tar\i\an
u\til•i\ty, *pl.* •ties
utility pro•gram
u\ti•li\za•tion
u\ti•lize, •lized, •liz•ing
ut•most
U\to•pi\a, *pl.* •pi\as
U\to•pi\an
u\to•pi\an
ut•ter (*absolute*)
ut•ter (*to speak*), •tered,
 •ter•ing [*vs.* ud•der (*milk
 gland*)]
ut•ter•ance
ut•ter\ly
ut•ter•most
U-\turn
u\vu\la, *pl.* •las or •lae
u\vu•lar
ux\o•ri•ous
U\zi, *pl.* U\zis

V

VA (*Virginia*)
va•can\cy, *pl.* •cies
va•cant
va•cate, •cat\ed, •cat•ing
va•ca•tion, •tioned,
 •tion•ing
va•ca•tion\er
vac•ci•nate, •nat\ed,
 •nat•ing
vac•ci•na•tion
vac•cine
vac•il•late, •lat\ed, •lat•ing

vac•il•la•tion
va•cu•i\ty
vac\u•ous
vac\u•ous\ly
vac\u•um, *pl.* \u•ums or
 \u\a; \u•umed, \u•um•ing
vacuum clean\er
vac\u•um-•packed
va\de me•cum, *pl.* va\de
 me•cums
Va•duz
vag\a•bond

va•gar\y, *pl.* •gar•ies
va•gi\na, *pl.* •nas or •nae
vag\i•nal
va•gran\cy
va•grant
vague, va•guer, va•guest
vague\ly
vague•ness
vain (*conceited; futile*), \er,
 •est [*vs.* vane (*blade*) and
 vein (*blood vessel*)]
vain•glo•ri•ous

vain•glo\ry

vain\ly

val•ance (*short drape*) [vs. va•lence (*chemical combining power*)]

vale (*valley*) [vs. veil (*something that conceals*)]

val\e\dic•to•ri\an

val\e\dic•to\ry, *pl.* •ries

va•lence (*chemical combining power*) [vs. val•ance (*short drape*)]

Va•len•ci\a

Va•len•ci•ennes

val•en•tine

val•et, •et•ed, •et•ing

Val•hal\la

val•iance

val•iant

val•iant\ly

val\id

val\i•date, •dat•ed, •dat•ing

val\i•da•tion

va•lid•i•ty

val•id\ly

va•lise

Val•i\um (™)

Val•kyr\ie

Val•let\ta

val•ley, *pl.* •leys

val\or

val•or•ous

val•or•ous\ly

val\u•a\ble

val\u•a•tion

val•ue, •ued, \u•ing

val•ue-•add\ed tax (*VAT*)

val•ue-•less

valve

va•moose, •moosed, •moos•ing

vamp, vamped, vamp•ing

vam•pire

van

va•na•di\um

Van Al•len belt

Van Bu•ren

Van•cou•ver

van•dal

van•dal•ism

van•dal•ize, •ized, •iz•ing

Vandyke beard

vane (*blade*) [vs. vain (*conceited; futile*) and vein (*blood vessel*)]

van Gogh

van•guard

va•nil\la

van•ish, •ished, •ish•ing

van•i\ty, *pl.* •ties

van•quish, •quished, •quish•ing

van•tage

Va•nu•a•tu

Va•nu•a•tu\an

vap\id

va•pid•i\ty or vap•id•ness

va•por

va•por\i•za•tion

va•por•ize, •ized, •iz•ing

va•por•ous

va\por•ware

va•que\ro, *pl.* •ros

var\i\a•bil•i\ty

var\i•a\ble

var\i\a•ble-•length field

var\i•a\ble life

var\i\a•ble-•rate

var\i•a•bly

var\i•ance

var\i•ant

var\i•a•tion

var\i•col•ored

var\i•cose

var\i•e•gat\ed

var•ied

var\i•e•gate, •gat\ed, •gat•ing

va•ri•e•tal

va•ri•e\ty, *pl.* •ties

variety store

var\i•ous

var\i•ous\ly

var•let

var•mint

var•nish, •nished, •nish•ing

var•si\ty, *pl.* •ties

var\y (*to alter*), var•ied, var\y•ing [vs. ver\y (*extremely*)]

vas•cu•lar

vase

va•sec•to\my, *pl.* •mies

Vas\e\line (™)

vas\o•mo•tor

vas•sal (*feudal tenant*) [vs. ves•sel (*ship; container*)]

vas•sal•age

vast, \er, •est

vast\ly

vast•ness

VAT (*value added tax*)

vat

Vat\i•can

Vatican Cit\y

vaude•ville

vaude•vil•lian

vault, vault\ed, vault•ing

vault\er

vaunt, vaunt\ed, vaunt•ing

VCR (*videocassette recorder*)

VD (*venereal disease*)

V-\Day (*Victory Day*)

VDT (*video display terminal*)

veal

vec•tor, •tored, •tor•ing

vector graph•ics

vec•to•ri\al

Ve\da, *pl.* •das

Ve•dan\ta

Ve•dan•tic

Ve•dic

veep

veer, veered, veer•ing

veg\e•ta•ble

veg\e•tar\i\an

veg\e•tar\i•an•ism

veg\e•tate, •tat\ed, •tat•ing

veg\e•ta•tion

veg\e•ta•tive

ve•he•mence

ve•he•ment

ve•he•ment\ly

ve•hi•cle

ve•hic\u•lar

veil (*something that conceals; to veil*), veiled, veil•ing [vs. vale (*valley*)]

vein (*blood vessel*), veined, vein•ing [vs. vain (*conceited; futile*) and vane (*blade*)]

ve•lar
Vel•cro (™)
veld *or* veldt
vel•lum
ve•loc•i\ty, *pl.* •ties
ve•lour *or* ve•lours
ve•lum, *pl.* \la
vel•vet
vel•vet•een
vel•vet\y
ve•nal (*mercenary*) [vs. ve•ni\al (*forgivable*)]
ve•nal•i\ty
vend, vend\ed, vend•ing
vend\ee
ven•det\ta, *pl.* •tas
ven•dor
ve•neer
ven•er•a•ble
ven•er•ate, •at\ed, •at•ing
ven•er•a•tion
ve•ne•re•al
venereal dis•ease
Ve•ne•tian
ve•ne•tian blind
Ven\e•zue•la
Ven\e•zue•lan
venge•ance
venge•ful
venge•ful\ly
ve•ni\al (*forgivable*) [vs. ve•nal (*mercenary*)]
Ven•ice
ve•ni\re•man, *pl.* •men
ven\i•son
ven\om
ven•om•ous
ve•nous
vent, vent\ed, vent•ing
ven•ti•late, •lat\ed, •lat•ing
ven•ti•la•tion
ven•ti•la•tor
ven•tral
ven•tri•cle
ven•tric\u•lar
ven•tril\o•quism
ven•tril\o•quist
ven•ture, •tured, •tur•ing
venture cap\i•tal
venture cap\i•tal•ist
ven•ture•some

ven\ue
Ve•nus, *pl.* •us\es
Ve•nu•si\an
ve•ra•cious (*truthful*) [vs. vo•ra•cious (*greedy*)]
ve•rac•i\ty, *pl.* •ties
ve•ran\da *or* ve•ran\dah, *pl.* •das *or* •dahs
verb
ver•bal
ver•bal\i•za•tion
ver•bal•ize, •ized, •iz•ing
ver•bal\ly
ver•ba•tim
ver•be\na, *pl.* •nas
ver•bi•age
ver•bose
ver•bos•i\ty
ver•bo•ten
ver•dant
Ver\di
ver•dict
ver•di•gris
ver•dure
verge, verged, verg•ing
verg\er
ver•i•est
ver\i•fi•a•ble
ver\i•fi•ca•tion
ver\i•fy, •fied, •fy•ing
ver\i\ly
ver\i•si•mil\i•tude
ver\i•ta\ble
ver\i•ta•bly
vé•ri•té (*cinéma vérité*)
ver•i\ty (*truth*), *pl.* •ties
ver•meil
ver•mi•cel\li
ver•mic\u•lite
ver•mi•form
ver•mil•ion
ver•min, *pl.* ver•min
ver•min•ous
Ver•mont (*VT*)
Ver•mont\er
ver•mouth
ver•nac\u•lar
ver•nal
Ver•nier
ver•ni\er
ve•ron\i\ca, *pl.* •cas

Ver•sailles
ver•sa•tile
ver•sa•til•i\ty
verse
versed
ver•si•cle
ver•si•fi•ca•tion
ver•si•fi\er
ver•si\fy, •fied, •fy•ing
ver•sion
ver\so, *pl.* •sos
ver•sus
ver•te•bra, *pl.* •brae *or* •bras
ver•te•bral
ver•te•brate
ver•tex, *pl.* •tex\es *or* •ti•ces
ver•ti•cal
vertical in•te•gra•tion
vertical jus•ti•fi•ca•tion
ver•ti•cal\ly
ver•ti•cal merg\er
vertical scroll•ing
ver•tig\i•nous
ver•ti\go, *pl.* ver•ti•goes *or* ver•tig\i•nes
verve
ver\ly (*extremely*) [vs. var\ly (*to alter*)]
very high fre•quen\cy (*VHF*)
very low fre•quen\cy (*VLF*)
ves\i•cle
ve•sic\u•lar
ves•per
Ves•puc\ci
ves•sel (*ship; container*) [vs. vas•sal (*feudal tenant*)]
vest, vest\ed, vest•ing
Ves\ta
ves•tal
vest\ed
vested in•ter•est
ves•ti•bule
ves•tige
ves•tig•i\al
vest•ing
vest•ment

vest-•pock\et

ves•try, *pl.* •tries

Ve•su•vi\an

Ve•su•vi\us

vet (*animal doctor*)

vet (*to appraise*), vet•ted, vet•ting

vetch

vet•er\an

vet•er\i•nar\i\an

vet•er\i•nar\y, *pl.* •nar•ies

ve\to, *pl.* •toes; •toed, \to•ing

vex, vexed, vex•ing

vex•a•tion

vex\a•tious

VGA (*video graphics array*)

VHF (*very high frequency*)

vi\a

vi•a•bil•i\ty

vi•a\ble

vi•a•duct

vi\al (*bottle*) [vs. vile (*very bad*) and vi\ol (*string instrument*)]

vi•and

vibes, *pl.*

vi\bra•harp

vi•bran\cy

vi•brant

vi•brant\ly

vi\bra•phone

vi\bra•phon•ist

vi•brate, •brat\ed, •brat•ing

vi•bra•tion

vi•bra\to, *pl.* •tos

vi•bra•tor

vi•bur•num

vic\ar

vic•ar•age

vi•car\i•ous

vi•car\i•ous\ly

vice (*evil practice*) [vs. vise (*clamp*)]

vice-•ad\mi\ral

vice-•ad\mi\ral\ty

vice•ge\rent

vice pres\i•dent *or* vice-•pres\i\dent

vice•roy

vi\ce ver\sa

vi•chys•soise

vi•cin•i\ty, *pl.* •ties

vi•cious

vi•cious cir•cle

vi•cious\ly

vi•cious•ness

vi•cis•si•tude

vic•tim

vic•tim\i•za•tion

vic•tim•ize, •ized, •iz•ing

vic•tor

Vic•to•ri\a

Vic•to•ri\an

Vic•to•ri•an•ism

vic•to•ri•ous

vic•to\ry, *pl.* •ries

vict•ual, •ualed *or* •ualled, •ual•ing *or* •ual•ling

vi•cu\na *or* vi•cu\ña, *pl.* •nas *or* •ñas

vi\de

vid\e\o, *pl.* vid\e\os

video a\dapt\er

vid\e\o•cas•sette

videocassette re•cord\er (*VCR*)

vid\e\o•disc

vid\e\o dis•play ter•mi•nal (*VDT*)

video game

video mode

video stand•ard

vid\e\o•tape, •taped, •tap•ing

vid\e\o•tex *or* vid\e\o•text

vie, vied, vy•ing

Vi•en\na

Vi•en•nese, *pl.* •nese

Vien•tiane

Vi\et•nam *or* Vi\et Nam

Vi\et•nam•ese

view, viewed, view•ing

view\er

view•find\er

view•point

vig\il

vig\i•lance

vig\i•lant

vig\i•lan•te, *pl.* •tes

vig\i•lan•tism

vi•gnette

vig\or

vig•or•ous

Vi•king

Vi\la

vile (*very bad*), vil\er, vil•est [vs. vi\al (*bottle*) and vi\ol (*string instrument*)]

vile•ness

vil\i•ti•ca•tion

vil\i\fy, •fied, •fy•ing

vil\la, *pl.* •las

vil•lage

vil•lag\er

vil•lain (*scoundrel*)

vil•lain•ous

vil•lain\y, *pl.* •lain•ies

vil•lein (*serf*)

vil•lein•age

vim

vin, *pl.* vins

vin•ai•grette

Vin\ci

vin•di•cate, •cat\ed, •cat•ing

vin•di•ca•tion

vin•di•ca•tive (*justifying*)

vin•dic•tive (*vengeful*)

vin•dic•tive\ly

vin•dic•tive•ness

vine

vin\e\gar

vin\e\gar\y

vine•yard

vi\no

vi•nous

vin•tage

vint•ner

vi•nyl

vi\ol (*string instrument*) [vs. vi\al (*bottle*) and vile (*very bad*)]

vi•o\la (*string instrument; the flower*), *pl.* •las [vs. voi•là (*behold!*)]

vi•o•late, •lat\ed, •lat•ing

vi•o•la•tion (*transgression*) [vs. vo•li•tion (*act of willing*)]

vi•o•lence

vi•o•lent
vi•o•lent\ly
vi•o•let
vi•o•lin
vi•o•lin•ist
vi•ol•ist
vi\o\lon•cel•list
vi\o\lon•cel\lo, *pl.* •los
VIP or V.I.P. (*very important person*)
vi•per
vi•per•ous
vi•ra\go, *pl.* •goes or •gos
vi•ral
vir\e\o, *pl.* vir•e\os
Vir•gil
vir•gin
vir•gin\al
Vir•gin\ia (*VA*)
vir•gin•ian
vir•gin•i\ty
Vir•gin Mar\y
Vir\go
vir•gule
vir•ile
vi•ril•i\ty
vi•rol\o•gist
vi•rol\o•gy
vir•tu\al
virtual disk
vir•tu•al\ly
vir•tu\al mem\o\ry
virtual re•al\i\ty
vir•tue
vir•tu•os•i\ty (*skill*)
vir•tu•o\so, *pl.* •sos or \si
vir•tu•ous
vir•tu•ous\ly
vir•tu•ous•ness (*virtue*)
vir\u•lence
vir\u•lent
vi•rus, *pl.* •rus\es
vi\sa, *pl.* •sas, •saed, •sa•ing
vis•age
vis-à-vis, *pl.* •vis
vis•cer\a, *pl.* vis•cus
vis•cer\al
vis•cid
vis•cose
vis•cos•i\ty, *pl.* •ties
vis•count

vis•count•ess
vis•cous
vise (*clamp*) [*vs.* vice (*evil practice*)]
Vish\nu
vis•i•bil•i\ty
vis•i•ble
vis•i•bly
vi•sion
vi•sion•ar\y, *pl.* •ar•ies
vis\it, •it\ed, •it•ing
vis•it•ant
vis•it•a•tion
vis\i•tor
vi•sor or vi•zor, •sored or •zored, •sor•ing or •zor•ing
vis\ta, *pl.* •tas
vis\u\al
vis\u•al\i•za•tion
vis\u•al•ize, •ized, •iz•ing
vis\u•al\ly
vi•tal
vi•tal•i\ty
vi•tal•ize, •ized, •iz•ing
vi•tal\ly
vi•tals
vi•ta•min
vi•ti•ate, •at\ed, •at•ing
vit\i•cul•ture
vit•re•ous
vit•ri\ol
vi•tu•per•a•tion
vi•tu•per\a•tive
vi•va
vi•va•ce
vi•va•cious
vi•va•cious\ly
vi•vac•i\ty
viv•id
viv•id\ly
viv•id•ness
viv\i•fy, •fied, •fy•ing
viv\i•sec•tion
vix\en
vix•en•ish
viz.
vi•zier
VLF or vlf (*very low frequency*)

VLSI (*very large-scale integration*)
V-\necked
vo•ca\ble
vo•cab\u•lar\y, *pl.* •lar•ies
vo•cal
vo•cal\ic
vo•cal•ist
vo•cal\i•za•tion
vo•cal•ize, •ized, •iz•ing
vo•cal\ly
vo•ca•tion (*career*) [*vs.* av\o•ca•tion (*hobby*)]
vo•ca•tion\al
voc\a•tive
vo•cif•er•ate, •at\ed, •at•ing
vo•cif•er•a•tion
vo•cif•er•ous
vo•cif•er•ous\ly
vod\ka
vogue
vogu•ish
voice, voiced, voic•ing
voice/•da\ta switch
voice•less
voice mail
voice-•o\ver
voice•print
voice rec•og•ni•tion
void, void\ed, void•ing
void•a\ble
voi•là or voi•la (*behold!*) [*vs.* vi•o\la (*string instrument; the flower*)]
voile
vol. (*volume*)
vol\a•tile
volatile mem\o\ry
volatile stock
vol\a•til•i\ty
vol•can\ic
vol•can•ism
vol•ca\no, *pl.* •noes or •nos
vole
Vol\ga
vo•li•tion (*act of willing*) [*vs.* vi•o•la•tion (*transgression*)]
vo•li•tion\al

vol•ley, pl. •leys; •leyed, •ley•ing
vol\ley•ball
volt
volt•age
vol•ta•ic
Vol•taire
volt•me\ter
vol\u•bil•i•ty
vol\u•ble
vol\u•bly
vol•ume
volume la•bel
vol\u•met•ric
vo•lu•mi•nous
vo•lu•mi•nous\ly
vol•un•tar\i\ly
vol•un•ta•rism
vol•un•tar\y
vol•un•teer, •teered, •teer•ing
vo•lup•tu•ar\y, pl. •ar•ies
vo•lup•tu•ous
vo•lup•tu•ous•ness
vom\it, •it\ed, •it•ing

voo•doo, pl. •doos; •dooed, •doo•ing
voo•doo•ism
vo•ra•cious (greedy) [vs. ve•ra•cious (truthful)]
vo•ra•cious\ly
vo•rac•i\ty
vor•tex, pl. •tex\es, •ti•ces
vo•ta\ry, pl. •ries
vote, vot\ed, vot•ing
vot\er
vo•tive
vouch, vouched, vouch•ing
vouch\er, •ered, •er•ing
vouch•safe, •safed, •saf•ing
vow, vowed, vow•ing
vow\el
vox po•pu\li
voy•age, •aged, •ag•ing
voy•ag\er
vo•ya•geur, pl. •geurs
vo•yeur
vo•yeur•ism

voy•eur•is•tic
VRAM (video RAM)
vs. (versus)
VT (Vermont)
Vul•can
vul•can\i•za•tion
vul•can•ize, •ized, •iz•ing
vul•gar
vul•gar\i\an
vul•gar•ism
vul•gar•i\ty, pl. •ties
vul•gar\i•za•tion
vul•gar•ize, •ized, •iz•ing
vul•gar\ly
Vul•gate
vul•ner•a•bil•i\ty
vul•ner•a•ble
vul•ner•a•bly
vul•pine
vul•ture
vul•tur•ine
vul•va, pl. •vae or •vas
vul•val or vul•var
vul•vi•form
vy•ing

W

WA (Washington)
wab•ble, •bled, •bling
Wac (Women's Army Corps member)
wack•i\ly
wack\i•ness
wack\y, •i\er, •i•est
wad, wad•ded, wad•ding
wad•dle, •dled, •dling
wade (to walk through resistant material), wad\ed, wad•ing [vs. weighed (did weigh)]
wad\ers
Waf (Women in the Air Force)
wa•fer
wa•fer•like
waf•fle, •fled, •fling
waft, waft\ed, waft•ing
wag, wagged, wag•ging
wage, waged, wag•ing
wage con•trol
wage•less

wa•ger, •gered, •ger•ing
wa•ger\er
wag•er\y
wag•gish
wag•gish\ly
wag•gish•ness
wag•gle, •gled, •gling
wag•gle dance
Wag•ner
wag\on
wa•hi•ne, pl. \ne
wa•hoo, pl. •hoos or •hoo
waif
wail (to cry), wailed, wail•ing [vs. wale (ridge) and whale (the mammal)]
wail•ing\ly
wain•scot•ing
wain•wright
waist (narrowest part of torso) [vs. waste (to squander)]
waist•band
waist•coat

waist•line
wait (to stay), wait\ed, wait•ing [vs. weight (heaviness; to add weight to)]
wait\er
wait•ress
wait state
waive (to forgo), waived, waiv•ing [vs. wave (surging movement)]
waiv\er (relinquishment) [vs. wa•ver (to vacillate)]
wake, waked or woke, waked or wok\en, wak•ing
wake•ful
wake•ful•ness
wak\en, •ened, •en•ing
Wal•dorf sal\ad
wale (ridge), waled, wal•ing [vs. wail (to cry) and whale (the mammal)]
Wales

walk, walked, walk•ing
walk•a\way
walk\ie-•talk\ie or walk\y-
•talk\y, pl. •talk\ies
walk-•in
walk-•on
walk•out or walk\out
walk•o\ver
walk-•up
walk•way
wall, walled, wall•ing
wal•la\by, pl. •bies or \by
wall•board
wal•let
wall•eye, pl. •eyes or •eye
wall•flow\er
wall-•like
Wal•loon
wal•lop, •loped, •lop•ing
wal•lop•ing
wal•low, •lowed, •low•ing
wall•pa•per, •pered,
•per•ing
Wall Street
wal•nut
wal•rus, pl. •rus\es or •rus
waltz, waltzed, waltz•ing
waltz•like
wam•pum
wan
WAN (wide-area network)
wand
wan•der (to roam),
•dered, •der•ing [vs.
won•der (to speculate)]
wan•der\er
wan•der•lust
wand•like
wane, waned, wan•ing
wan•gle, •gled, •gling
wan\na\be or wan\na\bee,
pl. •bes or •bees
wan•ness
want (to desire), want\ed,
want•ing [vs. wont
(habit) and won't (will
not)]
want ad
wan•ton (unjustifiable) [vs.
won ton or won\ton
(Chinese dumpling)]

wan•ton\ly
wan•ton•ness
wap\i\ti, pl. •tis or \ti
war (armed conflict; to fight
a war), warred, war•ring
[vs. wore (did wear)]
war•ble, •bled, •bling
war•bler
war bond
war•bon•net or war
bon•net
ward (division; to avert),
ward\ed, ward•ing [vs.
warred (fought)]
war•den
ward\er
ward•robe
ward•room
ware (merchandise) [vs.
wear (have on the body)
and where (at what
place)]
ware•house, pl. •hous\es;
•housed, •hous•ing
warehouse re•ceipt
wares
war•fare
war•fa•rin
war•head
war-•horse
war•i\ly
war\i•ness
war•like
war•lock
war•lord
warm, warmed, warm•ing;
warm\er, warm•est
warm-•blood\ed or
warm•blood\ed
warm-•blood\ed\ness
warm boot
warmed-•o\ver
warm\er
warm-•heart\ed or
warm•heart\ed
warm-•heart\ed\ly
warm-•heart\ed\ness
warm\ly
warm•ness
war•mon•ger
war•mon•ger•ing

warmth
warm\up or warm-•up
warn, warned, warn•ing
War•ner (last name)
warn\er (one who warns)
warn•ing
warn•ing\ly
warp, warped, warp•ing
war•path
war•plane
warp speed
war•rant, •rant\ed,
•rant•ing
war•rant•less
war•ran•tor
war•ran\ty, pl. •ties; •tied,
•ty•ing
warranty deed
warred (fought) [vs. ward
(division)]
war•ren
war•ri\or
War•saw
war•ship
wart
wart•hog
war•time
war\y, war•i\er, war•i•est
was
wash, washed, wash•ing
wash•a•bil•i\ty
wash•a\ble
wash-•and-•wear
wash•board
wash•bowl
wash•cloth, pl. •cloths
washed-•out
washed-•up
wash\er
wash\er•wom\an, pl.
•wom\en
wash\i•ness
wash•ing
wash•ing ma•chine
Wash•ing•ton (WA)
wash•out
wash•room
wash•stand
wash•tub
wash•wom\an, pl.
•wom\en

was\n't *(was not)*

WASP or Wasp *(white Anglo-Saxon Protestant)*

wasp *(insect)*

wasp•ish

wasp-•waist\ed

was•sail

Was•ser•mann test

wast *(archaic "was")*

wast•age

waste *(to squander)*, wast\ed, wast•ing [*vs. waist (narrowest part of torso)*]

waste•bas•ket

waste•ful

waste•ful\ly

waste•ful•ness

waste•land

waste•pa•per

wast•rel

watch, watched, watch•ing

watch•band

watch•dog, •dogged, •dog•ging

watch\er

watch•ful

watch•ful\ly

watch•ful•ness

watch•mak\er

watch•mak•ing

watch•man, *pl.* •men

watch•tow\er

watch•word

wa•ter, •tered, •ter•ing

wa\ter•bed

wa\ter•borne

Wa\ter•bur\y

wa\ter•col\or

wa\ter•col\or•ist

wa\ter-•cool, •cooled, •cool\ing

wa\ter•course

wa\ter•craft

wa\ter•cress

wa•tered stock

wa\ter•fall

wa\ter•fowl, *pl.* •fowls or •fowl

wa\ter•front

Wa\ter•gate

wa\ter\i•ness

wa\ter•less

wa•ter line *or* wa\ter•line

wa\ter•logged

Wa•ter•loo

wa\ter•mark

wa\ter•marked

wa\ter•mel\on

wa•ter pow\er *or* wa\ter•pow\er

wa\ter•proof, •proofed, •proof•ing

wa\ter-•re\pel\lent

wa\ter-•re\sist\ant

wa\ter•shed

wa\ter•side

wa\ter-•ski, •skied, •ski\ing

wa\ter-•ski\er

wa\ter•spout

wa•ter ta•ble *or* wa\ter•ta\ble

wa\ter•tight

wa\ter•way

wa\ter•wheel *or* wa•ter wheel

wa\ter•works, *pl.* •works

wa•ter\y

WATS *(Wide Area Tele-communications Service)*

watt

watt•age

wat•tle

wat•tled

wave *(surging movement)*, waved, wav•ing [*vs. waive (to forgo)*]

wave•length *or* wave length

wave•like

wa•ver *(to vacillate)*, •vered, •ver•ing [*vs. wai•ver (relinquishment)*]

wav\er *(one who waves)*

wa•ver\er

wa•ver•ing\ly

wav\i•ness

wav\y, •i\er, •i•est

wax, waxed, wax•ing

wax\en

wax\i•ness

wax•like

wax pa•per

wax•wing

wax•works

wax\y, •i\er, •i•est

way *(manner)* [*vs. weigh (to measure heaviness) and whey (part of milk)*]

way•bill

way•far\er

way•lay, •laid, •lay•ing

way-•out

way•side

way•ward

way•ward\ly

way•ward•ness

way•worn

we *(plural of "I")*, us, our, ours [*vs. wee (tiny)*]

weak *(not strong)*, \er, •est [*vs. week (seven successive days)*]

weak\en, •ened, •en•ing

weak•fish, *pl.* •fish *or* •fish\es

weak-•kneed

weak•ling

weak\ly *(sickly)* [*vs. week\ly (once a week; a weekly publication)*]

weak•ness

weal *(well-being)* [*vs. we'll (we will) and wheal (swelling) and wheel (disk on axis; to wheel)*]

wealth

wealth\y, •i\er, •i•est

wean, weaned, wean•ing

weap\on

weap•oned

weap•on•less

weap•on\ry

wear *(have on the body)*, wore, worn, wear•ing [*vs. ware (merchandise) and where (at what place)*]

wear\er

wea•ri\ly

wea•ri•ness

wea•ri•some

wea•ry, •ried, •ry•ing;
•ri\er, •ri•est

wea•ry•ing\ly

wea•sel, pl. •sels or •sel;
•seled, •sel•ing

wea•sel\ly (adj.)

wea•sel word

wea\sel-•word\ed

weath\er (atmospheric
condition; to endure),
•ered, •er•ing [vs.
wheth\er (if)]

weath\er-•beat\en

weath\er•board

weath\er-•bound

weath\er•cock

weath\er•glass

weath•er•ing

weath\er•ize, •ized,
•iz•ing

weath\er•proof, •proofed,
•proof•ing

weath\er-•strip or
weath\er strip (noun)

weath\er-•strip (verb),
•stripped, •strip\ping

weath\er vane or
weath\er•vane

weath\er-•wise

weath\er•worn

weave, wove or weaved,
wo•ven or wove,
weav•ing

Wea•ver (last name)

weav\er (one who weaves)

web

webbed

web•bing

web•foot, pl. •feet

web-•foot\ed

web•like

Web•ster

we'd (we would)

wed, wed•ded or wed,
wed•ding

wedge, wedged, wedg•ing

wedge•like

wed•lock

Wednes•day

wee (tiny) [vs. we (plural
of "I")]

weed, weed\ed, weed•ing

weed\i•ness

weed•less

weed•like

weed\y, •i\er, •i•est

week (seven successive
days) [vs. weak (not
strong)]

week•day

week•end, •end\ed,
•end•ing

week\ly (once a week; a
weekly publication), pl.
•lies [vs. weak\ly (sickly)]

wee•nie or wie•nie

wee\ny

weep, wept, weep•ing

weep\i•ness

weep•ing

weep\y, •i\er, •i•est

wee•vil

weft

weigh (to measure heavi-
ness), weighed, weigh•ing
[vs. way (manner) and
whey (part of milk)]

weighed (did weigh) [vs.
wade (to walk through
resistant material)]

weight (heaviness; to add
weight to), weight\ed,
weight•ing [vs. wait (to
stay)]

weight•i\ly

weight\i•ness

weight•less

weight•less\ly

weight•less•ness

weight•lift\er

weight•lift•ing

weight\y, •i\er, •i•est

weir

weird, •er, •est

weird\ly

weird•ness

weird\o, pl. weird\os

welch, welched,
welch•ing

welch\er

wel•come, •comed,
•com•ing

weld, weld\ed, weld•ing

weld\er

wel•fare

wel•fare state

wel•kin

we'll (we will) [vs. weal
(well-being) and wheal
(swelling) and wheel (disk
on axis; to wheel)]

well, welled, well•ing;
bet•ter, best

well-•ad\vised

well-•ap\point\ed

well-•bal\anced

well-•be\ing

well•born

well-•bred

well-•de\fined

well-•dis\posed

well-•done

well-•fa\vored

well-•fed

well-•fixed

well-•found\ed

well-•groomed

well-•ground\ed

well•head

well-•heeled

well-•in\formed

Wel•ling•ton

well-•in\ten\tioned

well-•knit

well-•known

well-•man\nered

well-•mean\ing

well•ness

well-•nigh

well-•off

well-•or\dered

well-•read

well-•round\ed

well-•spo\ken

well•spring

well-•thought-•of

well-•timed

well-•to-•do

well-•turned

well-•wish\er

well-•wish\ing

well-•worn

Welsh

welsh *or* welch, welshed *or* welched, welsh•ing *or* welch•ing
Welsh cor\gi
welsh\er
Welsh rab•bit
welt
wel•ter, •tered, •ter•ing
wel\ter•weight
wen
wench
wend, wend\ed, wend•ing
went
wept
we're
were\n't
were•wolf, *pl.* •wolves
wert
Wes•ley
west
West Bank
west•er•li•ness
west•er\ly, *pl.* •lies
west•ern
West•ern\er
west•ern\i•za•tion
west•ern•ize, •ized, •iz•ing
West Virgin\ia (*WV*)
west•ward
wet (*to moisten; moistened*), wet•ted, wet•ting; wet•ter, wet•test [*vs.* whet (*to sharpen*)]
wet•ness
wet nurse (*noun*)
wet-•nurse (*verb*), •nursed, •nurs\ing
we've
whack, whacked, whack•ing
whack\y, whack•i\er, whack•i•est
whale (*to thrash*), whaled, whal•ing
whale (*the mammal*), *pl.* whales *or* whale [*vs.* wail (*to cry*) *and* wale (*ridge*)]
whale•boat
whale•bone
whale•like

whal\er
wham, whammed, wham•ming
wham\my, *pl.* •mies
wharf, *pl.* wharves *or* wharfs
wharf•age
what
what•ev\er
what-•if a\nal\y•sis
what•not
what•so•ev\er
wheal (*swelling*) [*vs.* weal (*well-being*) *and* we'll (*we will*) *and* wheel (*disk on axis; to wheel*)]
wheat
whee•dle, •dled, •dling
whee•dler
whee•dling\ly
wheel (*disk on axis; to wheel*), wheeled, wheel•ing [*vs.* weal (*well-being*) *and* we'll (*we will*) *and* wheal (*swelling*)]
wheel•bar•row
wheel•base
wheel•chair
wheel\er-•deal\er
wheel•wright
wheeze, wheezed, wheez•ing
wheez\y, •i\er, •i•est
whelk
whelp
when
whence [*vs.* hence (*from now*) *and* thence (*from that place*)]
when•ev\er
where (*at what place*) [*vs.* ware (*merchandise*) *and* wear (*have on the body*)]
where•a•bouts
where\as, *pl.* where•as\es
where\at
where\by
where•fore
where•from
where\in
where\of

where\on
where•so•ev\er
where\to
where•up\on
wher•ev\er
where•with
where•with\al
wher\ry, *pl.* •ries
whet (*to sharpen*), whet•ted, whet•ting [*vs.* wet (*to moisten; moistened*)]
wheth\er (*if*) [*vs.* weath\er (*atmospheric condition; to endure*)]
whet•stone
whew
whey (*part of milk*) [*vs.* way (*manner*) *and* weigh (*to measure heaviness*)]
which (*what one*) [*vs.* witch (*sorceress*)]
which•ev\er
which•so•ev\er
whiff, whiffed, whiff•ing
Whig
Whig•gish
while (*interval; to spend, as time*) [*vs.* wile (*trick*)]
while, whiled, whil•ing
whiles
whi•lom
whilst
whim
whim•per, •pered, •per•ing
whim•per\er
whim•per•ing\ly
whim•si•cal
whim•si•cal•i\ty
whim•si•cal\ly
whim\sy *or* whim•sey, *pl.* •sies *or* •seys
whine (*complaining sound; to whine*), whined, whin•ing [*vs.* wine (*fermented beverage*)]
whin\er
whin•ing\ly
whin\ny, *pl.* •nies; •nied, •ny•ing

whip, whipped, whip•ping

whip•cord

whip•lash

whip•like

whip\per•snap•per

whip•pet

whip•ple•tree

whip•poor•will or whip-
•poor-•will

whip•saw, •sawed,
•saw•ing

whir or whirr, whirred,
whir•ring

whirl, whirled, whirl•ing

whirl\i•gig

whirl•pool

whirl•wind

whirl\y•bird

whisk, whisked, whisk•ing

whisk broom

whisk\er

whisk•ered

whisk•er\y

whis•key or whis\ky, pl.
•keys or •kies

whis•per, •pered, •per•ing

whis•per\y

whist

whis•tle, •tled, •tling

whis•tle•a\ble

whis•tle stop (noun)

whis\tle-•stop (verb),
•stopped, •stop\ping

whit (bit) [vs. wit (cleverness)]

white, whit\er, whit•est

white•cap

white-•col\lar

white•fish, pl. •fish or
•fish\es

white•head

White•horse

white knight

whit\en, •ened, •en•ing

white-•shoe

white•space

white•wall

white•wash, •washed,
•wash•ing

whith\er (where) [vs.
with\er (to shrivel)]

whith\er•so•ev\er

whit•ish

whit•ish•ness

whit•low

Whit•man

Whit•ney

Whit•sun•day

whit•tle, •tled, •tling

whit•tler

whiz or whizz, whizzed,
whiz•zing

WHO (World Health
Organization)

who

whoa

who•dun\it

who•ev\er

whole (entire) [vs. hole
(opening)]

whole•heart\ed

whole•heart•ed\ly

whole•heart•ed•ness

whole•ness

whole•sale, •saled, •sal•ing

whole•sal\er

whole•some

whole•some•ness

whole wheat (noun)

whole-•wheat (adj.)

who'll

whol\ly (entirely) [vs.
hol\ey (full of holes) and
ho\ly (sacred)]

whom

whom•ev\er

whom\so

whom•so•ev\er

whoop (loud shout; to
whoop), whooped,
whoop•ing [vs. hoop
(circular band)]

whoop•ing cough

whoosh, whooshed,
whoosh•ing

whop•per

whop•ping

who're

whore (prostitute; to be a
whore), whored,
whor•ing [vs. hoar
(frost)]

whorl

who's (who is)

whose (belonging to
whom)

whose•so•ev\er

whos•ev\er

who\so

who•so•ev\er

WI (Wisconsin)

Wich\i\ta

wick

wick, wicked (drew off by
capillary action), wick•ing

wick\ed (evil)

wick•ed\ly

wick\er

wick•er•work

wick\et

wide, wid\er, wid\est

wide-•ar\e\a net•work
(WAN)

wide-•a\wake

wide-•a\wake\ness

wide-•eyed

wide•mouthed

wid\en, •ened, •en•ing

wide•ness

wide•spread

widg•eon, pl. •eons or
•eon

wid\ow, •owed, •ow•ing

wid•ow\er

width

wield, wield\ed,
wield•ing

wield•a\ble

wield\er

wie•ner

Wie•ner

wife, pl. wives

wife•dom

wife•less

wig, wigged, wig•ging

wig•gle, •gled, •gling

wig•gle room

wig•less

wig•let

wig•like

wig•wag, •wagged,
•wag•ging

wig•wam

wild, wild\ed, wild•ing;
wild\er, wild•est
wild•cat, pl. •cats or •cat;
•cat•ted, •cat•ting
wil•de•beest, pl. •beests
or •beest
wil•der•ness
wild-eyed
wild•fire
wild•fowl
wild-goose chase
wild•ing
wild\ly
wild•ness
wile (trick) [vs. while
(interval; to spend, as
time)]
wiles
wil\i•ness
will, would or willed,
willed, will•ing
will•ful or wil•ful
will•ful\ly
will•ful•ness
Wil•liam
wil•lies
will•ing
will•ing\ly
will•ing•ness
will-less
will-o'-the-wisp
wil•low
wil•low\y
will•pow\er or will
pow\er
wil\ly-nil\ly
Wil•son
wilt, wilt\ed, wilt•ing
Wil•ton
wil\y, •i\er, •i•est
wimp
wimp\y, •i\er, •i•est
win, won, win•ning
wince, winced, winc•ing
winch, winched, winch•ing
Win•ches•ter drive
wind (moving air; to make
short of breath), wind\ed,
wind•ing
wind (to meander),
wound, wind•ing

wind•age
wind•bag
wind•break
wind-bro\ken
wind•burn
wind•burned
wind•chill fac•tor
wind\ed
wind•fall
wind•flow\er
Wind•hoek
wind•i\ly
wind\i•ness
wind•ing
wind•jam•mer
wind•lass
wind•mill
win•dow
win•dow•ing
win\dow•less
win\dow•pane
win\dow-shop, •shopped,
•shop\ping
win•dow-shop\per
win•dow•sill
wind•pipe
wind•shield
Wind•sor
wind•storm
wind•surf, •surfed,
•surf•ing
wind•surf\er
wind-swept
wind\up
wind•ward
wind\y, •i\er, •i•est
wine (fermented beverage;
to supply with wine),
wined, win•ing [vs.
whine (complaining
sound; to whine)]
win•er\y, pl. •er•ies
wing, winged, wing•ing
wing•like
wing•spread
wink, winked, wink•ing
win•kle, •kled, •kling
win•na\ble
win•ner
win•ning
win•ning\ly

Win•ni•peg
win•now, •nowed,
•now•ing
win•now\er
win\o, pl. win\os
win•some
win•ter, •tered, •ter•ing
win•ter•green
win\ter•ize, •ized, •iz•ing
win\ter•kill, •killed,
•kill•ing
win\ter•time
win•tri•ness
win•try, •tri\er, •tri•est
win-win
win\y, •i\er, •i•est
wipe, wiped, wip•ing
wire, wired, wir•ing
wire•less
wire•like
Wire•pho\to (™), pl. •tos
wire•pull\er
wire•pull\ing
wire•tap, •tapped,
•tap•ping
wire•tap•per
wir\y, •i\er, •i•est
Wis•con•sin (WI)
Wis•con•sin•ite
wis•dom
wis•dom tooth
Wise
wise
wise, wised, wis•ing;
wis\er, wis•est
wise•a\cre
wise•crack, •cracked,
•crack•ing
wise\ly
wish, wished, wish•ing
wish•bone
wish•ful
wish\y-wash\y
wisp
wis•te•ri\a or wis•tar\i•a,
pl. •te•ri\as or •tar•i\as
wist•ful
wist•ful\ly
wist•ful•ness
wit (cleverness) [vs. whit
(bit)]

witch (*sorceress*) [vs. which (*what one*)]

witch•er\y

witch hunt or witch-•hunt

witch-•hunt\ing

witch•ing

witch•like

witch\y, •i\er, •i•est

with\al

with•draw, •drew, •drawn, •draw•ing

with•draw\al

with•drawn

with\er (*to shrivel*), •ered, •er•ing [vs. whith\er (*where*)]

with•er•ing\ly

with•ers

with•hold, •held, •hold•ing

with•hold•ing tax

with\in

with•out

with•stand, •stood, •stand•ing

wit•less

wit•ness, •nessed, •ness•ing

wit•ti•cism

wit•ti\ly

wit•ti•ness

wit•ting

wit•ting\ly

wit\ty, •ti\er, •ti•est

wive, wived, wiv•ing

wives

wiz•ard

wiz•ard\ry

wiz•ened

wob•ble, •bled, •bling

wob•bly, •bli\er, •bli•est

woe

woe•be•gone

woe•ful

woe•ful\ly

woe•ful•ness

wok

woke

wok\en

wolf, *pl.* wolves; wolfed, wolf•ing

wolf•hound

wolf•like

wolfs•bane

wol•ver•ine

wom\an, *pl.* wom\en

wom\an•hood

wom\an•ish

wom\an•ish•ness

wom\an•ize, •ized, •iz•ing

wom\an•kind

wom\an•less

wom\an•like

wom\an•li•ness

wom\an\ly

wom\an-•suf\fra\gist

womb

wom•bat

wombed

wom\en

wom\en•folk or wom\en•folks

wom\en's lib•er•a•tion

won (*did win*) [vs. one (*single*)]

won (*Korean monetary unit*), *pl.* won

won•der (*to speculate*), •dered, •der•ing [vs. wan•der (*to roam*)]

won•der•ful

won•der•ful\ly

won•der•land

won•der•ment

won•drous

won•drous\ly

wont (*habit*) [vs. want (*to desire*) and won't (*will not*)]

won't (*will not*)

wont\ed

won ton or won•ton (*Chinese dumpling*) [vs. wan•ton (*unjustifiable*)]

woo, wooed, woo•ing

wood (*lumber*) [vs. would (*might*)]

wood•bine

wood•block

wood•carv\er

wood•carv•ing

wood•chuck

wood•cock, *pl.* •cocks or •cock

wood•craft

wood•crafts•man, *pl.* •men

wood•cut

wood•cut•ter

wood•cut•ting

wood\ed

wood\en

wood•en\ly

wood•en•ness

wood\en•ware

wood•li•ness

wood•land

wood•man, *pl.* •men

wood•peck\er

wood•pile

wood•ruff

wood•shed, •shed•ded, •shed•ding

woods•man, *pl.* •men

woods\y, •i\er, •i•est

wood•wind

wood•work

wood•work•ing

wood\y, •i\er, •i•est

wood\y or wood\ie, *pl.* wood•ies

woo\er

woof, woofed, woof•ing

woof\er

wool

wool\en

wool•gath\er, •ered, •er•ing

wool•gath•er•ing

wool•lies or wool•ies

wool•li•ness

wool\ly

wooz\y, •i\er, •i•est

Worces•ter

word, word\ed, word•ing

word•age

word•book

word•ing

word•play

word proc•ess•ing

word proc•es•sor

Words•worth

wore (*did wear*) [vs. war (*armed conflict*)]

work, worked or wrought, working

work•a\ble

work\a•day

work\a•hol\ic

work\a•hol•ism

work•bench

work•book

work•day

work\er

work•ers' com•pen•sa•tion

work force

work•horse

work•house, *pl.* •hous\es

work•ing as•set

working cap\i•tal

working di•rec•to\ry

work•ing•man, *pl.* •men

work load or work•load

work•man, *pl.* •men

work•man•like or work•man\ly

work•man•ship

work•men's com•pen•sa•tion

work•out

work•place

work•room

work rules

work•shop

work•sta•tion

work•ta•ble

work\up

work•week

world

world•beat\er or world-•beat\er

world•li•ness

world•ly, •li\er, •li•est

world•ly-•wise

World War I

World War II

world•wide or world-•wide

WORM (*write-once, read-many optical disc*)

worm, wormed, worm•ing

worm gear or worm•gear

worm•like

worm•wood

worn

worn-•out

wor•ri\er

wor•ri•ment

wor•ri•some

wor•ri•some•ly

wor•ri•some•ness

wor\ry, *pl.* •ries; •ried, •ry•ing

wor•ry•ing\ly

wor\ry•wart

worse

wors\en, •ened, •en•ing

wor•ship, •shiped or shipped, •ship•ing or •ship•ping

wor•ship\er

wor•ship•ful

worst (*most bad*), worst\ed, worst•ing [vs. wurst (*sausage*)]

worst\ed (*defeated*)

wor•sted (*fabric*)

wort

worth

wor•thi\ly

wor•thi•ness

worth•less

worth•less•ly

worth•less•ness

worth•while

worth•while•ness

wor•thy, *pl.* •thies; •thi\er, •thi•est

would (*might*) [vs. wood (*lumber*)]

would-•be

would\n't (*would not*)

wouldst

wound, wound\ed, wound•ing

wound•ing•ly

wove

wo•ven

wow, wowed, wow•ing

WP (*word processing*)

wrack, wracked, wrack•ing

wraith

wraith•like

wran•gle, •gled, •gling

wrap (*to enclose*), wrapped, wrap•ping [vs. rap (*to strike*)]

wrap•a\round or wrap-•a\round

wrapped (*enclosed*) [vs. rapped (*struck*) and rapt (*engrossed*)]

wrap•per

wrap•ping

wrap-•up

wrath

wreak (*to inflict*), wreaked, wreak•ing [vs. reek (*to smell strongly*) and wreck (*to destroy*)]

wreath, *pl.* wreaths

wreathe, wreathed, wreath•ing

wreath•like

wreck (*to destroy*), wrecked, wreck•ing [vs. reek (*to smell strongly*) and wreak (*to inflict*)]

wreck•age

wreck\er

wren

wrench, wrenched, wrench•ing

wrench•ing\ly

wrest (*to pull away*), wrest\ed, wrest•ing [vs. rest (*repose*)]

wres•tle, •tled, •tling

wres•tler

wres•tling

wretch (*unfortunate person*) [vs. retch (*to vomit*)]

wretch\ed

wretch•ed\ly

wretch•ed•ness

wrig•gle, •gled, •gling

wright (*worker*) [vs. right (*correct*) and rite (*ceremony*) and write (*to put words on paper*)]

wring (*to twist*), wrung,
wring•ing [*vs.* ring
(*encircle; to sound*)]

wring\er

wrin•kle, •kled, •kling

wrin•kly, •kli\er, •kli•est

wrist

wrist•band

wrist•watch *or* wrist watch

writ

write (*to put words on
paper*), wrote, writ•ten,
writ•ing [*vs.* right (*correct*) and rite (*ceremony*)
and wright (*worker*)]

write-•down

write-•in

write-•off

write-•pro\tect, \tect\ed,
\tect\ing

writ\er

write-•up

writhe, writhed,
writh•ing

writh•ing\ly

writ•ing

writ•ten

wrong, wronged,
wrong•ing

wrong•do\er

wrong•ful

wrong•ful\ly

wrong•head\ed *or* wrong-
•head\ed

wrong•head•ed\ly

wrong•head•ed•ness

wrong\ly

wrong•ness

wrote (*did write*) [*vs.* rote
(*repetition*)]

wroth

wrought

wrought i\ron (*noun*)

wrought-•i\ron (*adj.*)

wrought-•up

wrung (*did wring*) [*vs.*
rung (*did ring; crosspiece*)]

wry (*lopsided*) [*vs.* rye
(*the grain*)]

wry\ly

wry•neck

wry•ness

wurst (*sausage*) [*vs.* worst
(*most bad*)]

VV (West Virginia)

WY (Wyoming)

Wy•o•ming (WY)

Wy•o•ming•ite

WYSIWYG (*what you see
is what you get*)

X

X chro•mo•some

XD (*without dividend, "ex
dividend"*)

xe•non

xen\o•pho•bi\a

xen\o•pho•bic

xe\ro•graph\ic

xe•rog•ra•phy

Xe•rox (™)

xi

x in (*without interest, "ex
interest"*)

X\mas

X\mo\dem

x-\ra\di\a\tion

x-\ray *or* X-\ray, \rayed,
\ray\ing

xy•lem

xy\lo•phone

xy\lo•phon•ist

Y

yacht

yacht•ing

yachts•man, *pl.* •men

Ya•hoo, *pl.* •hoos

Yah•weh

yak

yak *or* yack, yakked *or*
yacked, yak•king *or*
yack•ing

y'all (*you all*) [*vs.* yawl (*sailboat*) and yowl (*loud cry*)]

yam

yam•mer, •mered,
•mer•ing

yang

Yan•gon

Yang•tze

yank, yanked, yank•ing

Yan•kee

yap, yapped, yap•ping

yard

yard•age

yard•arm

yard•man, *pl.* •men

yard•stick

yar•mul\ke, *pl.* •kes

yarn, yarned, yarn•ing

yar•row

yaw, yawed, yaw•ing

yawl (*sailboat*) [*vs.* y'all
(*you all*) and yowl (*loud
cry*)]

yawn, yawned, yawn•ing

yaws

Y chro•mo•some

y\clept

ye

yea

yeah

year

year•book

year•ling

year\ly, *pl.* •lies

yearn, yearned, yearn•ing

year-•round

yeast

yeast\y, •i\er, •i•est

yegg

yell, yelled, yell•ing

yel•low, •lowed, •low•ing;
•low\er, •low•est

yel•low fe•ver

yel•low•ish

yelp, yelped, yelp•ing

Yel•tsin

Yem\en

yen (*craving*), *pl.* yens

yen (*Japanese monetary unit*), *pl.* yen
yeo•man, *pl.* •men
yeo•man\ry
yes, yes\es; yessed, yes•sing
ye•shi\va, *pl.* •vas
yes-•man, *pl.* •men
yes\ter•day
yes\ter•year
yet
yew (*tree*) [*vs.* ewe (*female sheep*) and you (*person addressed*)]
Yid•dish
yield, yield\ed, yield•ing
yin *and* yang
yip, yipped, yip•ping
yip•pie
Y\mo\dem
yo•del, •deled *or* •delled, •del•ing *or* •del•ling
yo\ga
yo\gi, *pl.* •gis
yo•gurt *or* yo•ghurt
yoke (*frame for joining animals; to join*), *pl.* yokes *or* yoke; yoked, yok•ing

yo•kel
Yo•ko•ha\ma
yolk (*part of egg*)
yolked
yolk\y
Yom Kip•pur
yon
yon•der
Yon•kers
yoo-•hoo, •hooed, •hoo\ing
yore (*time past*) [*vs.* your (*belonging to you*) and you're (*you are*)]
you (*person addressed*), you, your, yours [*vs.* ewe (*female sheep*) and yew (*tree*)]
you'll (*you will*) [*vs.* Yule (*Christmas*)]
young, young\er, young\est
young•ish
young•ster
Youngs•town
your (*belonging to you*) [*vs.* yore (*time past*) and you're (*you are*)]

you're (*you are*)
yours
your•self, *pl.* •selves
yours tru\ly
youth, *pl.* youths *or* youth
youth•ful
youth•ful\ly
youth•ful•ness
yowl (*loud cry; to yowl*), yowled, yowl•ing [*vs.* y'all (*you all*) and yawl (*sailboat*)]
yo-•yo, *pl.* •yos
yo-•yo stock
yt•ter•bi\um
yt•tri\um
yuc\ca, *pl.* •cas
yuck\y, •i\er, •i•est
Yu•go•sla•vi\a
Yu•go•sla•vi\an
Yu•kon
Yule (*Christmas*) [*vs.* you'll (*you will*)]
yule•tide
yum\my, •mi\er, •mi•est
yup *or* yep
yup•pie, *pl.* •pies

Z

zai•ba•tsu, *pl.* •tsu
Za•ire *or* Za•ïre
Zam•bi\a
za•ni•ness
za\ny, *pl.* •nies; •ni\er, •ni•est
Zan•zi•bar
zap, zapped, zap•ping
zeal
zeal\ot
zeal•ous (*enthusiastic*) [*vs.* jeal•ous (*envious*)]
zeal•ous\ly
ze•bra, *pl.* •bras, •bra
ZEG (*zero economic growth*)
Zeit•geist
Zen
ze•nith
zeph\yr
zep•pe•lin

ze\ro, *pl.* •ros, •roes; •roed, •ro•ing
ze\ro-•based
ze\ro-•cou\pon
ze\ro pop\u•la•tion growth
ze\ro-•sum
ze\ro wait state
zest
zest•ful
zest\y, •i\er, •i•est
ze\ta, *pl.* •tas
Zeus
zig•zag, •zagged, •zag•ging
zilch
zil•lion, *pl.* •lions, •lion
Zim•bab\we
Zim•bab•we\an
zinc
zing\er
zing\y, •i\er, •i•est

zin•ni\a, *pl.* •ni\as
Zi\on
Zi•on•ism
Zi•on•ist
zip, zipped, zip•ping
ZIP code (™, *Zone Improvement Program code for mail*)
zip•per, •pered, •per•ing
zip\py, •pi\er, •pi•est
zir•con
zir•co•ni\um
zit
zith\er
Z\mo\dem
zo•di\ac
zo•di•a•cal
zom•bie
zon\al
zone, zoned, zon•ing
zoned-•bit re•cord•ing

zone pric•ing
zonked
zoo, *pl.* zoos
zo•o\log\i•cal
zo•ol\o\gist
zo•ol\o\gy
zoom, zoomed, zoom•ing

zoom box
zoom lens
zo•o\phyte
zo•o\phyt\ic
Zo•ro•as•ter
Zo•ro•as•tri•an•ism
zuc•chi\ni, *pl.* \ni, •nis

Zu\lu, *pl.* •lus, \lu
Zu\ni *or* Zu\ñi, *pl.* •nis *or*
•ñis, \ni *or* \ñi
Zu•rich
zwie•back
zy•gote
zy•mur\gy

Guide for Writers

PUNCTUATION

There is a considerable amount of variation in punctuation practices. At one extreme are writers who use as little punctuation as possible. At the other extreme are writers who use too much punctuation in an effort to make their meaning clear. The principles presented here represent a middle road. As in all writing, consistency of style is essential.

The punctuation system is presented in six charts. Since punctuation marks are frequently used in more than one way, some marks appear on more than one chart. Readers who are interested in the various uses of a particular mark can scan the left column of each chart to locate relevant sections.

1. Sentence-level punctuation

Guidelines	Examples
Ordinarily an independent clause is made into a sentence by beginning it with a capital letter and ending it with a period.	Some of us still support the mayor. Others think he should retire. There's only one solution. We must reduce next year's budget.
Independent clauses may be combined into one sentence by using the words *and, but, yet, or, nor, for,* and *so.* The first clause is usually followed by a comma.	The forecast promised beautiful weather, but it rained every day. Take six cooking apples and put them into a flameproof dish.
The writer can indicate that independent clauses are closely connected by joining them with a semicolon.	Some of us still support the mayor; others think he should retire. There was silence in the room; even the children were still.
When one independent clause is followed by another that explains or exemplifies it, they can be separated by a colon. The second clause may or may not begin with a capital letter.	There's only one solution: we must reduce next year's budget. The conference addresses a basic question: How can we take the steps needed to protect the environment?
Sentences that ask a question should be followed by a question mark.	Are they still planning to move to Houston? What is the population of Norway?
Sentences that express strong feeling may be followed by an exclamation mark.	Watch out! That's a stupid thing to say!

Guidelines	Examples
• **?** • **!** End-of-sentence punctuation is sometimes used after groups of words that are not independent clauses. This is especially common in advertising and other writing that seeks to reflect the rhythms of speech.	Somerset Estates has all the features you've been looking for. Like state-of-the-art facilities. A friendly atmosphere. And a very reasonable price. Sound interesting? Phone today!

2. Separating Elements in Clauses

When one of the elements in a clause is compounded, that is, when there are two or more subjects, predicates, objects, and so forth, punctuation is necessary.

Guidelines	Examples
When two elements are compounded, they are usually joined together with a word such as *and* or *or* without any punctuation. Occasionally more than two elements are joined in this way.	Haiti and the Dominican Republic share the island of Hispaniola. Tuition may be paid by check or charged to a major credit card. I'm taking history and English and biology this semester.
, Compounds that contain more than two elements are called series. Commas are used to separate items in a series, with a word such as *and* or *or* usually occurring between the last two items.	England, Scotland, and Wales share the island of Great Britain. Environmentally conscious businesses use recycled paper, photocopy on both sides of a sheet, and use ceramic cups. We frequently hear references to government of the people, by the people, for the people.
; When the items in a series are very long or have internal punctuation, separation by commas can be confusing, and semicolons may be used instead.	Next year, they plan to open stores in Pittsburgh, Pennsylvania; Cincinnati, Ohio; and Baltimore, Maryland. Students were selected on the basis of grades; tests of vocabulary, memory, and reading; and teacher recommendations.

Note: Some writers omit the final comma when punctuating a series, and newspapers and magazines often follow this practice. Book publishers and educators, however, usually follow the practice recommended above.

3. Setting off Modifiers

Another way that sentences become more complex is by the addition of
free modifiers. Free modifiers can ordinarily be omitted without affecting the
meaning or basic structure of the sentence.

Guidelines	Examples
Words that precede the subject ❯ are potentially confusing, so they are often set off by a comma that shows where the main part of the sentence begins.	Born to wealthy parents, he was able to pursue his career without financial worries. Since the team was in last place, the attendance for the final game was less than two thousand.
When the introductory modifier is short, the comma is often omitted.	In this article I will demonstrate that we have chosen the wrong policy. At the present time the number of cigarette smokers is declining.
Certain kinds of introductory ❯ modifiers are followed by a comma even though they are short.	Thoroughly chilled, he decided to set out for home. Yes, we are prepared for any mishaps. However, it is important to understand his point of view.
Free modifiers that occur in the ❯ middle of the sentence require two commas to set them off.	It is important, however, to understand his point of view. Our distinguished colleague, the president of the guild, will be our speaker tonight.
When free modifiers occur at ❯ the end of a sentence, they should be preceded by a comma.	It is important to understand his point of view, however. She was much influenced by the impressionist painters, especially Monet and Renoir.
If the sentence can be read without pauses before and after the modifier, the commas may be omitted.	We can therefore conclude that the defendant is innocent. The applicant must understand before sending in the forms that the deposit fee is not refundable.

Guidelines	Examples
It is important to distinguish between free modifiers and other modifiers that may look very much the same but are part of the basic sentence structure. The latter should not be set off by commas.	This admirable woman, who started out on the assembly line thirty years ago, became president of the company last week. An employee who started out on the assembly line thirty years ago became president of the company last week. We congratulate the Senate whip, who organized the filibuster. We congratulate the senator who organized the filibuster.
When dates and addresses are used in sentences, each part except the first is treated as a free modifier and set off by commas. When only the month and year are given, the comma is usually omitted.	She was born on Tuesday, December 20, 1901, in a log cabin near Casey Creek, Kentucky. We took our first trip to Alaska in August 1988.
When a free modifier has internal punctuation or produces an emphatic break in the sentence, commas may not seem strong enough, and dashes can be used instead. A dash can also be used to set off a free modifier that comes at the end of a sentence.	The challenges of raising children—disciplinary, financial, emotional—are getting more formidable. These families had a median income of $55,000—$35,000 earned by the husband and $20,000 by the wife.
Parentheses provide another method for setting off extra elements from the rest of the sentence. They are used in a variety of ways.	The Federal Trade Commission (FTC) has issued regulations on the advertising of many products (see Appendix B). The community didn't feel (and why should they?) that there was adequate police protection.

4. Quotations

Quotations are used for making clear to a reader which words are the writer's and which have been borrowed from someone else.

Guidelines	Examples
" When writers use the exact words of someone else, they must use quotation marks to set " them off from the rest of the text.	In 1841, Ralph Waldo Emerson wrote, "I hate quotations. Tell me what you know."
Indirect quotations—in which writers report what someone else said without using the exact words—should not be set off by quotation marks.	Emerson said that he hated quotations and that writers should instead tell the reader what they themselves know.
When quotations are longer than two or three lines, they are often placed on separate lines. Sometimes shorter line length and/or smaller type is also used. When this is done, quotation marks are not used.	In his essay "Notes on Punctuation," Lewis Thomas* gives the following advice to writers using quotations: If something is to be quoted, the exact words must be used. If part of it must be left out because of space limitations, it is good manners to insert three dots to indicate the omission, but it is unethical to do this if it means connecting two thoughts which the original author did not intend to have tied together.
If part of a quotation is omitted, the omission must be marked ••• with points of ellipsis. When the omission comes in the middle of •••• a sentence, three points are used. When the omission included the end of one or more sentences, four points are used.	Lewis Thomas offers this advice: If something is to be quoted, the exact words must be used. If part of it must be left out . . . insert three dots to indicate the omission, but it is unethical to do this if it means connecting two thoughts which the original author did not intend to have tied together.

**New England Journal of Medicine*, Vol. 296, pp. 1103-05 (May 12, 1977). Quoted by permission.

Guidelines	Examples
[ ] When writers insert something within a quoted passage, the insertion should be set off with brackets. Insertions are sometimes used to supply words that make a quotation easier to understand.	Lewis Thomas warns that "it is unethical to [omit words in a quotation] . . . if it means connecting two thoughts which the original author did not intend to have tied together."
Writers can make clear that a mistake in the quotation has been carried over from the original by using the word *sic*, meaning "thus."	As Senator Claghorne wrote to his constituents, "My fundamental political principals [sic] make it impossible for me to support the bill in its present form."
, Text that reports the source of quoted material is usually separated from it by a comma.	Mark said, "I've decided not to apply to law school until next year." "I think we should encourage people to vote," said the mayor.
When quoted words are woven into a text so that they perform a basic grammatical function in the sentence, no introductory punctuation is used.	According to Thoreau, most of us "lead lives of quiet desperation."
( ) Quotations that are included within other quotations are set off by single quotation marks.	The witness made the same damaging statement under cross-examination: "As I entered the room, I heard him say, 'I'm determined to get even.'"
" " Final quotation marks follow other punctuation marks, except for semicolons and colons.	Ed began reading Williams's "The Glass Menagerie"; then he turned to "A Streetcar Named Desire."
Question marks and exclamation marks precede final quotation marks when they refer to the quoted words. They follow when they refer to the sentence as a whole.	Once more she asked, "What do you think we should do about this?" What did Carol mean when she said, "I'm going to do something about this"? "Get out of here!" he yelled.

5. Word-level punctuation

The punctuation covered so far is used to clarify the structure of sentences. There are also punctuation marks that are used with words.

Guidelines	Examples
, The apostrophe is used with nouns to show possession.	The company's management resisted the union's demands. She found it impossible to decipher the students' handwriting.
(1) An apostrophe plus s is added to all words—singular or plural—that do not end in -s.	the boy's hat children's literature a week's vacation
(2) Just an apostrophe is added at the end of plural words that end in -s.	the boys' hats two weeks' vacation
(3) An apostrophe plus s is usually added at the end of singular words that end in -s. Just an apostrophe is added to names of classical or biblical derivation that end in -s.	the countess's daughter Dickens's novels Achilles' heel Moses' brother
, An apostrophe is used in contractions to show where letters or numerals have been omitted.	he's four o'clock didn't readin', writin' and let's 'rithmetic Ma'am the class of '55
, An apostrophe is sometimes used when making letters or numbers plural.	45's ABC's
• A period is used to mark shortened forms like abbreviations and initials.	Prof. M. L. Smith 14 ft. 4:00 p.m. U.S.A. or USA etc.
— A hyphen is used to end a line of text when part of a word must be carried over to the next line.	. . . insta- bility
_ Hyphens are sometimes used to form compound words.	twenty-five self-confidence

Guidelines	Examples
In certain situations, hyphens are used between prefixes or suffixes and root words.	catlike *but* bull-like preschool *but* pre-Christian recover *vs.* re-cover
Hyphens are often used to indicate that a group of words is to be understood as a unit.	a scholar-athlete hand-to-hand combat
When two modifiers containing hyphens are joined together, common elements are often not repeated.	The study included fourth- and twelfth-grade students.

6. Other uses of punctuation marks

Guidelines	Examples
Commas are used to indicate that a word or words used elsewhere in the sentence have been omitted.	Our company has found it difficult to find and keep skilled workers: the supply is limited; the demand, heavy; the turnover, high.
A comma is used after the complimentary close in a letter. In a personal letter, a comma is also used after the salutation.	Very truly yours, Love, Dear Sally,
In numbers used primarily to express quantity, commas are used to divide the digits into groups of three. Commas are not ordinarily used in numbers that are used for identification.	The attendance at this year's convention was 12,347. Norma lived at 18325 Sunset Boulevard.
Quotation marks are used occasionally to indicate that a word or phrase is used in a special way. For other special uses of quotation marks, see *Italics* section below.	People still speak of "typing," even when they are seated in front of a computer screen.

Guidelines	Examples
• A colon can be used generally to call attention to what follows.	There were originally five Marx brothers: Groucho, Chico, Harpo, Zeppo, and Gummo.
	The senior citizens demanded the following: better police protection, more convenient medical facilities, and a new recreational center.
• A colon is used after the salutation in a business letter.	Dear Ms. McFadden:
	Dear Valued Customer:
	Dear Frank:
The dash can be used to indicate hesitations in speech.	"Well—uh—I'd like to try again—if you'll let me," he offered.
When a list precedes a general statement about the items listed, it is followed by a dash.	Strength, endurance, flexibility—these three goals should guide your quest for overall physical fitness.
The hyphen can be used as a substitute for *to*, with the meaning "up to and including." It should not, however, be used in conjunction with *from*.	The text of the Constitution can be found on pages 679-87.
	The period between 1890-1914 was a particularly tranquil time in Europe.
	The Civil War lasted from 1861 to 1865. (not from 1861-1865)

Note: It is important not to confuse the hyphen (-) with the dash (—), which is more than twice as long. The hyphen is used to group words and parts of words together, while the dash is used to clarify sentence structure. With a typewriter, a dash is formed by typing two successive hyphens (--). Most computer operating systems provide a method for obtaining a dash even though there is no specific dash key on the keyboard.

ITALICS

Guidelines	Examples
Titles of newspapers, magazines, and books should be put in italics. Articles, essays, stories, chapters, and poems should be enclosed in quotation marks.	*The New York Times* *Consumer Reports* Whitman's "Song of Myself"
Titles of plays and movies should be put in italics. Television and radio programs should be enclosed in quotation marks.	Shakespeare's *Hamlet* the movie *High Noon* "Sesame Street"
Titles of works of art and long musical works should be put in italics. Shorter works such as songs should be enclosed in quotation marks. When the form of a musical work is used as its title, neither italics nor quotation marks are used.	Leonardo da Vinci's *Last Supper* Handel's *Messiah* "Summertime" Beethoven's Ninth Symphony
The names of ships and airplanes should be put in italics.	the aircraft carrier *Intrepid* Lindbergh's *The Spirit of St. Louis*
Words and phrases from a foreign language should be put in italics. Accompanying translations are often enclosed in quotation marks. Words of foreign origin that have become familiar in an English context should not be italicized.	As a group, these artists are in the avant-garde. They are not, however, to be thought of as *enfants terribles,* or "terrible children," people whose work is so outrageous as to shock or embarrass.
Words used as words, and letters used as letters, should be put in italics.	I can never remember how to spell *broccoli.* Your handwriting is hard to read; the *o*'s and *a*'s look alike.
Italics are sometimes used to indicate that a word or words should be pronounced with extra emphasis.	The boss is *very* hard to get along with today. John loaned the tape to Robert, and *he* gave it to Sally.

CAPITALIZATION

Guidelines	Examples
The important words in titles are capitalized. This includes the first and last words and all other words except articles, prepositions, and coordinating conjunctions, such as *and, but,* and *or.*	*The Cat in the Hat* *Gone with the Wind*
Proper nouns—names of specific people, places, organizations, groups, events, etc.—are capitalized, as are the proper adjectives derived from them.	Martin Luther King, Jr. Civil War United States Coast Guard Canada Canadian
When proper nouns and adjectives have taken on a specialized meaning, they are often no longer capitalized.	My brother ordered a bologna sandwich and french fries.
Titles of people are capitalized when they precede the name, but not usually when they follow or when they are used alone.	Queen Victoria Victoria, queen of England the queen of England
Kinship terms are capitalized when they are used before a name or alone in place of a name. They are not capitalized when they are preceded by modifiers.	I'm expecting Aunt Alice to drop by this weekend. I forgot to call Mother on her birthday. I forgot to call my mother on her birthday.
Geographical features are capitalized when they are part of the official name. In the plural, they are capitalized when they precede names, but not when they follow.	The Pacific Ocean is the world's largest ocean. In recent years, Lakes Erie and Ontario have been cleaned up. The Hudson and Mohawk rivers are both in New York State.
Points of the compass are capitalized only when they are used as the name of a section of the country.	We've been driving east for over two hours. We visited the South last summer.

Proofreader's Marks

The marks shown below are used in (1) preparing a manuscript to be typeset or (2) proofreading or revising printed material.

The mark should be written in the margin, directly in line with the sentence or part of the text in which the change is being made, and the line of text should also be marked to indicate the exact place of the change.

When more than one change is being made in the same line, diagonal or vertical slashes are used in the margin to separate the respective marks. Marks that are actual words, such as "OK?," "run over," and "set?," as well as editorial comments or queries noted in the margin, are often circled to distinguish them from textual corrections (words to be inserted) themselves.

In practice, these marks often differ slightly from person to person. For example, some proofreaders use slash marks even when making only one correction in a line. In all cases, however, the marks must be legible and carefully placed to avoid creating uncertainty or introducing new errors.

Letters, Words, Spacing, and Queries

MARK IN MARGIN	INDICATION IN TEXT	INSTRUCTION OR COMMENT
a	Peter left town in hurry.	Insert at caret ( )
a/r	Peter left town in hury.	Insert at carets ( )
𝓎 or ૪	Joan sent me me the book.	Delete
◠	ma ke	Close up; no space
𝓎	I haven't seen the em in years.	Delete and close up
stet	They phoned both Betty and Jack	Let it stand; disregard indicated deletion or change
¶	up the river. Two years	Start new paragraph
no ¶ or run in	many unnecessary additives. The most dangerous one	No new paragraph
tr	Put the book on the table	Transpose
tr	Put the book table on the	Transpose

MARK IN MARGIN	INDICATION IN TEXT	INSTRUCTION OR COMMENT
tr	Put the table on the book.	Transpose
tr up or *tr* ↗	to Betty Steinberg, who was traveling abroad. Mrs. Steinberg, an actress.	Transpose to place indicated above
tr down or *tr* ↙	in the clutch. The final score was 6–5. He pitched the last three innings but didn't have it. ←	Transpose to place indicated below
sp	Lunch cost me 6 dollars	Spell out; use letters
fig	There were eighteen members present.	Set in figures; use numbers
#	It was a smallvillage ∧	Insert one letter space
# #	too late.After the dance ∧	Insert two letter spaces
hr #	jeroboam ∧	Insert hair space (very thin space, as between letters)
line #	Oscar Picks # This year's Academy Awards nomination.	Insert line space
eq #	Ronnie got rid of the dog	Equalize spacing between words or between lines
=	thre^e d_ays later	Align horizontally
‖	from one hand to another without spilling it	Align vertically
run over	enhance production. 2. It will	Start new line
□	□ Rose asked the price.	Indent or insert one em (space)
□□	□□The use of the Comma	Indent or insert two ems
⸠	⸠What's Ellen's last name?	Move left
⸡	April 2, 1945⸡	Move right
⎴	⎴Please go now⎴	Move up
⎵	⎵Well, that's that!⎵	Move down
⸠⸡	⸡"The Birth of Atomic Energy"⸠	Center (heading, title, etc.)
fl	⸠2. Three (3) skirts	Flush left; no indention

MARK IN MARGIN	INDICATION IN TEXT	INSTRUCTION OR COMMENT
fr	Total: $89.50 ⌐	Flush right; no indention
sent /? [the specific word that appears to be missing]	He the copy. ∧	Insert this word here?
OK? or ?	by Francis G. Kellsey. She wrote	Query or verify; is this correct?
out : see copy	the discovery of but near the hull ∧	Something left out in typesetting
set ?	arrived in 1922 wrong date and	Is this part of the copy, to be set (or a marginal note)?

Punctuation

	INDICATION IN TEXT	INSTRUCTION OR COMMENT
⊙	Christine teaches fifth ∧ grade ∧	Insert period (.)
∧̦	We expect Eileen Tom, and Ken. ∧	Insert comma (,)
∧̦	I came; I saw I conquered. ∧	Insert semicolon (;)
⊙̇	Jenny worked until 630 P.M. ∧	Insert colon (:)
=	Douglas got a two thirds majority. ∧	Insert hyphen (-)
=	Douglas got a two = thirds majority.	End-of-line hyphen is part of word
1/M	Mike then left very reluctantly. ∧	Insert one-em dash or long dash (—)
1/N	See pages 96 124. ∧	Insert one-en dash or short dash (–)
∀̆	Don't mark the authors copy. ∨	Insert apostrophe (')
∀̆	Don't mark the authors copy. ∧	Insert exclamation point (!)
!	Watch out	Insert exclamation point (!)
?	Did Seth write to you ∧	Insert question mark (?)
℃ /℃	I always liked ✓Stopping by Woods on a Snowy Evening.	Insert quotation marks (" ")

MARK IN MARGIN	INDICATION IN TEXT	INSTRUCTION OR COMMENT
ᵛ / ᵛ	She said, "Read The Raven tonight."	Insert single quotation marks (' ')
(/) ⱻ/ⱻ	Dorothy paid 8 pesos 800 centavos for it	Insert parentheses (( ))
⊏/⊐ ⱻ/ⱻ	The "portly and profane author Dickson, presumably in his cups" was noticed by nobody else.	Insert brackets ([ ])

Typographic Case, Style, and Adjustment

	INDICATION IN TEXT	INSTRUCTION OR COMMENT
ital	I've read Paradise Lost twice.	Set in *italic* (not roman) type
bf	See the definition at peace.	Set in boldface (heavier) type
lf	She repaired **the** motor easily.	Set in lightface (standard) type
rom	Gregory drove to Winnipeg.	Set in roman (not *italic*) type
cap or *caps* or *uc + lc*	the italian role in Nato	Set as CAPITAL letter(s)
sc	He lived about 350 B.C.	Set as SMALL CAPITAL letter(s)
lc or *l/c*	Arlene enjoys Reading. I do NOT.	Set in lowercase; not capitalized
u+lc or *c+lc* or *uc+lc*	STOP! STOP!	Set in uppercase and lowercase
₂	H₂O	Set as subscript; inferior figure
²	A² + B2	Set as superscript; superior figure
✕	They drove to Miami.	Broken (damaged) letter of type
wf	Turn Right	Wrong font; not the proper typeface style or size
⑤	Bert proofread the book	Turn inverted (upsidedown) letter

Dictionary of
Abbreviations

Acknowledgements

The *Random House Dictionary of Abbreviations* is derived from the large computerized database that is part of the Random House Living Dictionary Project. This abbreviations dictionary was compiled and edited by the staff of the Random House Reference Department. The staff gratefully acknowledges the valuable contributions made by Archie Hobson, Julia Penelope, Lenka Sosic, and Roger M. Stern.

Guide to Pronunciation

The symbol (ˊ), as in **moth′er**, is used to mark primary stress; the syllable preceding it is pronounced with greater prominence than the other syllables in the word. The symbol (ˈ), as in **grand′moth′er**, is used to mark secondary stress; a syllable marked for secondary stress is pronounced with less prominence than one marked (ˊ) but with more prominence than those bearing no stress mark at all.

a	act, bat	**m**	my, him	**u**	up, love
ā	able, cape	**n**	now, on	**û**	urge, burn
â	air, dare	**ng**	sing, England		
ä	art, calm			**v**	voice, live
		o	box, hot	**w**	west, away
b	back, rub	**ō**	over, no	**y**	yes, young
ch	chief, beach	**ô**	order, ball	**z**	zeal, lazy, those
d	do, bed	**oi**	oil, joy	**zh**	vision, measure
		oͦo	book, put		
e	ebb, set	**ōō**	ooze, rule	**ə**	occurs only in
ē	equal, bee	**ou**	out, loud		unaccented
					syllables and in-
f	fit, puff	**p**	page, stop		dicates the
g	give, beg	**r**	read, cry		sound of
h	hit, hear	**s**	see, miss		a *in* along
		sh	shoe, punish		e *in* system
i	if, big	**t**	ten, bit		i *in* easily
ī	ice, bite	**th**	thin, path		o *in* gallop
		th	that, other		u *in* circus
j	just, edge				
k	kept, make				
l	low, all				

A

A **1.** *Cards.* ace. **2.** adulterer; adulteress. **3.** *Electricity.* ampere; amperes. **4.** *Physics.* angstrom. **5.** answer. **6.** *British.* arterial (used with a road number to designate a major highway).

A *Symbol.* **1.** the first in order or in a series. **2.** (in some grading systems) a grade or mark, indicating the quality of a student's work as excellent or superior. **3.** (in some school systems) a symbol designating the first semester of a school year. **4.** *Music.* **a.** the sixth tone in the scale of C major or the first tone in the relative minor scale, A minor. **b.** a string, key, or pipe tuned to this tone. **c.** a written or printed note representing this tone. **d.** (in the fixed system of solmization) the sixth tone of the scale of C major; called *l a.* **e.** the tonality having A as the tonic note. **5.** *Physiology.* a major blood group, usually enabling a person whose blood is of this type to donate blood to persons of group A or AB and to receive blood from persons of O or A. **6.** (*sometimes lowercase*) the medieval Roman numeral for 50 or 500. **7.** *Chemistry.* (formerly) argon. **8.** *Chemistry, Physics.* mass number. **9.** *Biochemistry.* **a.** adenine. **b.** alanine. **10.** *Logic.* universal affirmative. **11.** *British.* a designation for a motion picture recommended as suitable for adults. **12.** a proportional shoe width size, narrower than B and wider than AA. **13.** a proportional brassiere cup size, smaller than B and larger than AA. **14.** a quality rating for a corporate or municipal bond, lower than AA and higher than BBB.

a *Measurements.* are; ares.

a *Symbol, Logic.* universal affirmative.

Å *Symbol, Physics.* angstrom.

A- atomic (used in combination): *A-bomb; A-plant.*

A. **1.** Absolute. **2.** Academy. **3.** acre; acres. **4.** America. **5.** American. **6.** angstrom. **7.** year. [from Latin *annō,* ablative of *annus*] **8.** answer. **9.** before. [from Latin *ante*] **10.** April. **11.** Artillery. **12.** Australia. **13.** Australian.

a. **1.** about. **2.** acre; acres. **3.** active. **4.** adjective. **5.** alto. **6.** ampere; amperes. **7.** year. [from Latin *annō,* ablative of *annus*] **8.** anonymous. **9.** answer. **10.** before. [from Latin *ante*] **11.** *Measurements.* are; ares. **12.** *Sports.* assist; assists. **13.** at.

AA **1.** administrative assistant. **2.** Alcoholics Anonymous. **3.** antiaircraft. **4.** author's alteration.

AA *Symbol.* **1.** a proportional shoe width size, narrower than A and wider than AAA. **2.** the smallest proportional brassiere cup size. **3.** a quality rating for a corporate or municipal bond, lower than AAA and higher than A. **4.** *Electricity.* a battery size for 1.5 volt dry cells: diameter, 0.6 in. (1.4 cm); length, 2 in. (5 cm). **5.** *British.* a designation for motion pictures certified as unsuitable for children under 14 unless accompanied by an adult. Compare **A** (def. 11), **U** (def. 5), **X** (def. 9).

A.A. **1.** Alcoholics Anonymous. **2.** antiaircraft. **3.** antiaircraft artillery. **4.** Associate in Accounting. **5.** Associate of Arts. **6.** author's alteration.

a.a. **1.** always afloat. **2.** author's alteration. Also, **aa**

AAA **1.** Agricultural Adjustment Administration. **2.** Amateur Athletic

Association. **3.** American Automobile Association. **4.** antiaircraft artillery. **5.** Automobile Association of America.

AAA *Symbol.* **1.** a proportional shoe width size, narrower than AA. **2.** the highest quality rating for a corporate or municipal bond. **3.** *Electricity.* a battery size for 1.5 volt dry cells: diameter, 0.4 in. (1 cm); length 1.7 in. (4.3 cm).

A.A.A. 1. Amateur Athletic Association. **2.** American Automobile Association. **3.** Automobile Association of America.

A.A.A.L. American Academy of Arts and Letters.

A.A.A.S. American Association for the Advancement of Science. Also, **AAAS**

A.A.E. American Association of Engineers.

A.Ae.E. Associate in Aeronautical Engineering.

A.A.E.E. American Association of Electrical Engineers.

AAES American Association of Engineering Societies.

AAF 1. Allied Air Forces. **2.** (in the U.S., formerly) Army Air Forces. Also, **A.A.F.**

A.Agr. Associate in Agriculture.

AAM air-to-air missile.

a&b assault and battery.

A&E Arts and Entertainment (a cable television station).

a&h *Insurance.* accident and health.

a&i *Insurance.* accident and indemnity.

A&M Agricultural and Mechanical (college). Also, **A and M**

A&R (in the recording industry) artists and repertory. Also, **A. & R., A-and-R**

a&r assault and robbery.

a&s *Insurance.* accident and sickness.

AAP Association of American Publishers.

A.A.P.S.S. American Academy of Political and Social Science.

a.a.r. 1. against all risks. **2.** average annual rainfall.

AARP (*pronounced as initials or* ärp) American Association of Retired Persons.

A.A.S. 1. Fellow of the American Academy. [from Latin *Academiae Americanae Socius*] **2.** American Academy of Sciences. **3.** Associate in Applied Science.

A.A.U. Amateur Athletic Union. Also, **AAU**

A.A.U.P. 1. American Association of University Professors. **2.** American Association of University Presses. Also, **AAUP**

A.A.U.W. American Association of University Women.

AB 1. *Nautical.* able seaman. **2.** airbase. **3.** airborne. **4.** *U.S. Air Force.* Airman Basic. **5.** Alberta, Canada (for use with ZIP code). **6.** antiballistic; antiballistic missile. **7.** assembly bill.

AB *Symbol, Physiology.* a major blood group usually enabling a person whose blood is of this type to donate blood to persons of type AB and to receive blood from persons of type O, A, B, or AB.

Ab *Symbol.* **1.** *Chemistry.* alabamine. **2.** *Immunology.* antibody.

ab. 1. about. **2.** *Baseball.* (times) at bat.

A.B. 1. *Nautical.* able seaman. **2.** Bachelor of Arts. [from Latin *Artium Baccalaureus*] **3.** *Baseball.* (times) at bat.

a.b. *Baseball.* (times) at bat.

ABA 1. Amateur Boxing Association.

2. American Badminton Association.
3. American Bankers Association.
4. American Bar Association.
5. American Basketball Association.
6. American Book Award. **7.** American Booksellers Association. **8.** Associate in Business Administration. Also, **A.B.A.**

abbr. I. abbreviate. **2.** abbreviated. **3.** abbreviation. Also, **abbrev.**

ABC I. American Broadcasting Company. **2.** atomic, biological, and chemical: *ABC warfare.*

A.B.C. I. Advance Booking Charter. **2.** Alcoholic Beverage Control.

abcb air-blast circuit breaker.

ABD all but dissertation: applied to a person who has completed all requirements for a doctoral degree except for the writing of a dissertation. Also, **abd.**

abd I. abdomen. **2.** abdominal.

abd. I. abdicated. **2.** abdomen. **3.** abdominal.

A.B.Ed. Bachelor of Arts in Education.

A.B.F.M. American Board of Foreign Missions.

abl. *Grammar.* ablative.

A.B.L.S. Bachelor of Arts in Library Science.

ABM antiballistic missile.

abn airborne.

ABO *Physiology.* ABO system (of blood classification).

A-bomb (ā′bom′), atomic bomb.

abp. archbishop.

abr. I. abridge. **2.** abridged. **3.** abridgment.

ABRV Advanced Ballistic Reentry Vehicle.

ABS I. *Chemistry.* ABS resin: a type of plastic. [*(a)crylanitrile, (b)utadiene,* and *(s)tyrene*] **2.** antilock braking system.

abs. I. absent. **2.** absolute. **3.** abstract.

A.B.S. I. American Bible Society. **2.** American Bureau of Shipping.

abs. re. *Law.* in the absence of the defendant. [from Latin *absente reo*]

abstr. I. abstract. **2.** abstracted.

abt. about.

abv. above.

AC I. *Real Estate.* air conditioning. **2.** *Electricity.* alternating current.

Ac *Chemistry.* **I.** acetate. **2.** acetyl.

Ac *Symbol, Chemistry.* actinium.

ac *Electricity.* alternating current.

A/C I. *Bookkeeping.* **a.** account. **b.** account current. **2.** *Real Estate.* air conditioning. Also, **a/c**

A.C. I. *Real Estate.* air conditioning. **2.** *Electricity.* alternating current. **3.** before Christ. [from Latin *ante Christum*] **4.** Army Corps. **5.** Athletic Club.

a.c. I. *Real Estate.* air conditioning. **2.** *Electricity.* alternating current. **3.** (in prescriptions) before meals [from Latin *ante cibum*].

ACA I. American Camping Association. **2.** American Canoe Association. **3.** American Casting Association.

ACAA Agricultural Conservation and Adjustment Administration.

acad. academy. Also, **Acad.**

AC and U Association of Colleges and Universities. Also, **AC&U**

acb air circuit breaker.

ACC Atlantic Coast Conference.

acc. I. accelerate. **2.** acceleration. **3.** accept. **4.** acceptance. **5.** accompanied. **6.** accompaniment. **7.** accordant. **8.** according. **9.** account. **10.** accountant. **11.** accounted. **12.** accusative.

ACCD American Coalition of Citizens with Disabilities.

accel. *Music.* accelerando.

accom accommodate.

accomp. 1. accompaniment. **2.** accomplishment.

accrd. accrued.

acct. 1. account. **2.** accountant.

accum. 1. accumulate. **2.** accumulative.

accus. accusative.

ACDA Arms Control and Disarmament Agency.

AC/DC 1. *Electricity.* alternating current or direct current. **2.** *Slang.* sexually responsive to both men and women; bisexual. Also, **A.C./D.C., ac/dc, a-c/d-c, a.c.-d.c.**

acdt accident.

ACE 1. American Council on Education. **2.** Army Corps of Engineers.

acft aircraft.

ACH automated clearinghouse.

ACh *Biochemistry.* acetylcholine.

achiev. achievement.

ack. 1. acknowledge. **2.** acknowledgment.

A.C.L.S. American Council of Learned Societies.

ACLU 1. American Civil Liberties Union. **2.** American College of Life Underwriters. Also, **A.C.L.U.**

ACM Association for Computing Machinery.

ACOC Air Command Operations Center.

ACOG American College of Obstetricians and Gynecologists.

A.C.P. American College of Physicians.

acpt. acceptance.

acq acquisition.

A.C.S. 1. Advanced Communications System. **2.** American Cancer Society. **3.** American Chemical Society. **4.** American College of Surgeons. **5.** autograph card signed. Also, **ACS**

A.C.S.C. Association of Casualty and Surety Companies.

A/cs pay. accounts payable. Also, **a/cs pay.**

A/cs rec. accounts receivable. Also, **a/cs rec.**

acst acoustic.

acsy accessory.

ACT 1. American College Test. **2.** Association of Classroom Teachers. **3.** Australian Capital Territory.

act. 1. acting. **2.** action. **3.** active. **4.** actor. **5.** actual. **6.** actuary.

actg. acting.

ACTH *Biochemistry.* a polypeptide hormone that stimulates the cortex of adrenal glands. [*a(dreno)c(ortico)t(ropic) h(ormone)*]

ACTION (ak′shən), *U.S. Government.* an independent agency that administers domestic volunteer programs. [named by analogy with the acronymic names of other agencies, but itself not an acronym]

actl actual.

ACTP American College Testing Program.

actr actuator.

actvt activate.

ACV 1. Also, **A.C.V.** actual cash value. **2.** air cushion vehicle.

ACW *Radio.* alternating continuous waves.

AD assembly drawing.

Ad Alzheimer's Disease.

a-d *Electronics.* analog-to-digital.

ad. 1. adverb. **2.** advertisement.

A.D. 1. active duty. **2.** in the year of the Lord; since Christ was born. [from Latin *annō Dominī*] **3.** art director. **4.** assembly district. **5.** assistant director. **6.** athletic director. **7.** average deviation.

a.d. 1. after date. **2.** before the day. [from Latin *ante diem*] **3.** autograph document.

ADA 1. adenosine deaminase.
2. American Dental Association.
3. American Diabetes Association
4. Americans for Democratic Action.

A.D.A. 1. American Dental Association. **2.** American Diabetes Association. **3.** Americans for Democratic Action.

ADAD (ā′dad), a coded card or other device that when inserted into a telephone allows the user to reach a number without dialing. [*a(utomatic telephone) d(ialing-) a(nnouncing) d(evice)*]

ADAMHA Alcohol, Drug Abuse, and Mental Health Administration.

A.D.B. accidental death benefit. Also, **adb.**

ADC 1. advanced developing countries. **2.** Aid to Dependent Children. **3.** Air Defense Command.

A.D.C. aide-de-camp.

ADD attention deficit disorder.

addn. addition.

addnl. additional.

ADF automatic direction finder.

ad fin. to, toward, or at the end. [from Latin *ad finem*]

ADH *Biochemistry.* antidiuretic hormone.

ADHD attention deficit hyperactivity disorder.

ad inf. to infinity; endlessly; without limit. Also, **ad infin.** [from Latin *ad infinitum*]

ad init. at the beginning. [from Latin *ad initium*]

ad int. in the meantime. [from Latin *ad interim* for the time between]

adj. 1. adjacent. **2.** adjective.
3. adjoining. **4.** adjourned.
5. adjudged. **6.** adjunct. **7.** adjust.
8. *Banking.* adjustment. **9.** adjutant.

Adj.A. Adjunct in Arts.

adjt. adjutant.

ADL Anti-Defamation League (of B'nai B'rith). Also, **A.D.L.**

ad lib. 1. at one's pleasure. **2.** *Music.* not obligatory. [from Latin *ad libitum*]

ad loc. at or to the place. [from Latin *ad locum*]

Adm. 1. admiral. **2.** admiralty. Also, **ADM**

adm. 1. administration. **2.** administrative. **3.** administrator.
4. admission.

admin. administration.

admov. *(in prescriptions)* **1.** apply. [from Latin *admovē*] **2.** let it be applied. [from Latin *admoveātur*]

ADP 1. *Biochemistry.* an ester of adenosine and pyrophosphoric acid, $C_{10}H_{12}N_5O_3H_3P_2O_7$, serving to transfer energy during glycolysis. [*a(denosine) d(i)p(hosphate)*]
2. automatic data processing.

ad part. dolent. *(in prescriptions)* to the painful parts. [from Latin *ad partēs dolentēs*]

adptr adapter.

adrs address.

ADS 1. Alzheimer's Disease Society.
2. American Dialect Society.

a.d.s. autograph document, signed.

adst. feb. *(in prescriptions)* when fever is present. [from Latin *adstante febre*]

ADTS Automated Data and Telecommunications Service.

Adv. 1. Advent. **2.** Advocate.

adv. 1. in proportion to value. [from Latin *ad valorem*] **2.** advance.
3. adverb. **4.** adverbial. **5.** adverbially.
6. adversus. **7.** advertisement.
8. advertising. **9.** adviser.
10. advisory.

ad val. in proportion to value. [from Latin *ad valorem*]

advt. advertisement.

AE 1. account executive. **2.** Actors Equity. **3.** American English.

ae. at the age of. [from Latin *aetātis*]

A.E. 1. Agricultural Engineer. **2.** Associate in Education. **3.** Associate in Engineering.

a.e. *Math.* almost everywhere.

A.E.A. 1. Actors' Equity Association. **2.** Also, **AEA** *British.* Atomic Energy Authority.

A.E. and P. Ambassador Extraordinary and Plenipotentiary.

AEC Atomic Energy Commission.

A.E.C. *Insurance.* additional extended coverage.

A.Ed. Associate in Education.

Ae.E. Aeronautical Engineer.

A.E.F. American Expeditionary Forces; American Expeditionary Force. Also, **AEF**

A.Eng. Associate in Engineering.

aeq. equal. [from Latin *aequālis*]

aero. 1. aeronautic; aeronautical. **2.** aeronautics. **3.** aerospace.

aerodyn aerodynamic.

aeron. aeronautics.

aet. at the age of. Also, **aetat.** [from Latin *aetātis*]

AEW airborne early warning.

AF 1. Air Force. **2.** Anglo-French. **3.** Asian Female.

af 1. audiofidelity. **2.** audiofrequency. **3.** autofocus.

Af. 1. Africa. **2.** African.

A.F. 1. Air Force. **2.** Anglo-French. **3.** audio frequency.

a.f. audio frequency.

A.F.A. Associate in Fine Arts.

AFAIK as far as I know.

A.F.A.M. Ancient Free and Accepted Masons.

AFB Air Force Base.

A.F.B. American Federation for the Blind.

AFBF American Farm Bureau Federation.

AFC 1. American Football Conference. **2.** American Foxhound Club. **3.** Association Football Club. **4.** automatic flight control. **5.** automatic frequency control.

AFCS automatic flight control system.

AFDC Aid to Families with Dependent Children. Also, **A.F.D.C.**

aff. 1. affairs. **2.** affirmative. **3.** affix.

afft. affidavit.

AFGE American Federation of Government Employees.

Afgh. Afghanistan. Also, **Afg.**

A1c airman, first class.

AFL 1. American Federation of Labor. **2.** American Football League.

A.F.L. American Federation of Labor. Also, **A.F. of L.**

AFL-CIO American Federation of Labor and Congress of Industrial Organizations.

AFM 1. American Federation of Musicians. **2.** audio frequency modulation.

AFP *Biochemistry.* alphafetoprotein.

Afr African.

Afr. 1. Africa. **2.** African.

A.-Fr. Anglo-French.

AFS American Folklore Society.

A.F.S. American Field Service.

AFSCME American Federation of State, County, and Municipal Employees.

AFT American Federation of Teachers. Also, **A.F.T.**

aft. afternoon.

AFTRA (af′trə), American Federation of Television and Radio Artists. Also, **A.F.T.R.A.**

Ag *Symbol, Chemistry.* silver. [from Latin *argentum*]

Ag. August.

ag. 1. agricultural. **2.** agriculture.

A.G. 1. Adjutant General. **2.** Attorney General. Also, **AG**

AGA Amateur Gymnastics Association.

AGAC American Guild of Authors and Composers.

AGC 1. advanced graduate certificate. **2.** automatic gain control. Also, **A.G.C.**

AGCA automatic ground-controlled approach.

AGCL automatic ground-controlled landing.

agcy. agency.

Ag.E. Agricultural Engineer.

A.G.E. Associate in General Education.

Agh. (in Afghanistan) afghani.

AGI 1. Also, **agi.** adjusted gross income. **2.** American Geological Institute.

agit. (in prescriptions) shake, stir. [from Latin *agitā*]

AGM air-to-ground missile.

AGMA American Guild of Musical Artists. Also, **A.G.M.A.**

agr. 1. agricultural. **2.** agriculture.

agric. 1. agricultural. **2.** agriculture.

agron. agronomy.

AGS 1. American Gem Society. **2.** American Geographical Society. **3.** American Geriatrics Society.

A.G.S. Associate in General Studies.

agst. against.

Agt. agent. Also, **agt.**

AGU American Geophysical Union.

Ah ampere-hour. Also, **a.h.**

A.H. in the year of the Hegira; since the Hegira (A.D. 622). [from Latin *annō Hejirae*]

AHA American Heart Association.

A.H.A. 1. American Historical Association. **2.** American Hospital Association.

AHAUS Amateur Hockey Association of the United States.

AHE Association for Higher Education.

A.H.E. Associate in Home Economics.

AHF *Biochemistry.* antihemophilic factor.

AHL 1. American Heritage Foundation. **2.** American Hockey League.

AHQ 1. Air Headquarters. **2.** Army Headquarters.

AHRA American Hot Rod Association.

AHS American Humane Society.

AHSA American Horse Shows Association.

AI 1. Amnesty International. **2.** artificial insemination. **3.** artificial intelligence. Also, **A.I.**

A.I.A. 1. American Institute of Architects. **2.** American Insurance Association.

A.I.C. 1. Army Intelligence Center. **2.** American Institute of Chemists.

AIChE American Institute of Chemical Engineers. Also, **A.I.Ch.E.**

AID (ād), *U.S. Government.* the division of the United States International Development Cooperation Agency that coordinates the various foreign aid programs with U.S. foreign policy. [A(gency for) I(nternational) D(evelopment)]

AID 1. American Institute of Decorators. **2.** American Institute of Interior Designers. **3.** Also, **A.I.D.** *British.* artificial insemination donor.

aid. acute infectious disease.

AIDS (ādz), Acquired Immune Deficiency Syndrome.

AILS automatic instrument landing system.

AIM (ām), American Indian Movement.

A.I.M.E. 1. American Institute of Mining Engineers. **2.** Association of the Institute of Mechanical Engineers.

A.I.M.U. American Institute of Marine Underwriters.

AInd Anglo-Indian.

AIP American Institute of Physics.

air. artist in residence.

AIS administrative and information services.

AISI American Iron and Steel Institute.

AK Alaska (for use with ZIP code).

a.k. Slang (vulgar). ass-kisser.

a.k.a. also known as: Joe Smith a.k.a. Joseph Smathers. Also, **AKA, aka**

A.K.C. American Kennel Club.

AL 1. Alabama (for use with ZIP code). **2.** Anglo-Latin.

Al Symbol, Chemistry. aluminum.

AL. Anglo-Latin.

al. 1. other things. [from Latin alia] **2.** other persons. [from Latin alii]

A.L. 1. Baseball. American League. **2.** American Legion. **3.** Anglo-Latin.

a.l. autograph letter.

Ala Biochemistry. alanine.

Ala. Alabama.

A.L.A. 1. American Library Association. **2.** Associate in Liberal Arts. **3.** Authors League of America. **4.** Automobile Legal Association.

Alas. Alaska.

Alb. 1. Albania. **2.** Albanian. **3.** Albany. **4.** Alberta.

alb. (in prescriptions) white. [from Latin albus]

ALBM air-launched ballistic missile.

alc. alcohol.

alcd alcad: aluminum clad.

ALCM air-launched cruise missile. Also, **A.L.C.M.**

Ald. alderman. Also, **ald.**

A.L.E. Insurance. additional living expense.

Alg. 1. Algerian. **2.** Algiers.

alg. algebra.

ALGOL (al′gol, -gôl), a computer language in which information is expressed in algebraic notation. [algo(rithmic) l(anguage)]

alk. 1. alkali. **2.** alkaline.

allow. allowance.

ALM audio-lingual method.

Alp. alpine.

A.L.P. American Labor Party. Also, **ALP**

alpha alphabetical.

ALS amyotrophic lateral sclerosis.

a.l.s. autograph letter, signed.

alt. 1. alteration. **2.** alternate. **3.** altitude. **4.** alto.

Alta. Alberta.

altm altimeter.

altn alternate.

altntr alternator.

altnv alternative.

altrd altered.

altrn alternation.

ALU Computers. arithmetic/logic unit.

Aly. alley.

AM 1. Electronics. amplitude modulation. **2.** Radio. a system of broadcasting by means of amplitude modulation. **3.** Asian male.

Am Symbol, Chemistry. americium.

Am. 1. America. **2.** American.

am amber.

A/m ampere per meter.

A.M. 1. before noon. [from Latin ante merīdiem] **2.** Master of Arts. [from Latin Artium Magister]

a.m. before noon.

A.M.A. 1. American Management Association. **2.** American Medical Association. **3.** American Motorcycle Association.

Amb. Ambassador. Also, **amb.**

AMC American Movie Classics (a cable channel).

A.M.D.G. for the greater glory of

God: motto of the Jesuits. Also **AMDG** [from Latin *ad majōrem Deī glōriam*]

A.M.E. 1. Advanced Master of Education. **2.** African Methodist Episcopal.

AMEDS Army Medical Service. Also, **AMedS**

Amer. 1. America. **2.** Also, **Amer** American.

AmerSp American Spanish.

AMEX (am′eks), American Stock Exchange. Also, **Amex**

am/fm (ā′em′ef′em′), (of a radio) able to receive both AM and FM stations. Also, **AM/FM**

AMG Allied Military Government.

ami acute myocardial infarction.

A.M.L.S. Master of Arts in Library Science.

amm antimissle missle.

ammo ammunition.

Amn Air Force airman.

AMNH American Museum of Natural History.

AMORC Ancient Mystic Order Rosae Crucis.

amort. amortization.

AMP *Biochemistry.* a white, crystalline, water-soluble nucleotide, $C_{10}H_{12}N_5O_3H_2PO_4$, obtained by the partial hydrolysis of ATP or of ribonucleic acid. [*a(denosine) m(ono) p(hosphate)*]

amp. *Electricity.* **1.** amperage. **2.** ampere; amperes.

AMPAS Academy of Motion Picture Arts and Sciences.

ampl amplifier.

AMS 1. Agricultural Marketing Service. **2.** American Mathematical Society. **3.** American Meteorological Society. **4.** American Musicological Society.

A.M.S. Army Medical Staff.

A.M.S.W. Master of Arts in Social Work.

AMT alternative minimum tax.

amt. amount.

A.M.T. 1. Associate in Mechanical Technology. **2.** Associate in Medical Technology. **3.** Master of Arts in Teaching.

amu atomic mass unit. Also, **AMU**

A.Mus. Associate in Music.

A.Mus.D. Doctor of Musical Arts.

AMVETS (am′vets′), an organization of U.S. veterans of World War II and more recent wars. [*Am(erican) Vet(eran)s*]

AN Anglo-Norman. Also, **A.-N.**

An *Symbol, Chemistry.* actinon.

an. 1. above named. **2.** annual. **3.** in the year. [from Latin *annō*]

A.N. 1. Anglo-Norman. **2.** Associate in Nursing.

A.N.A. 1. American Newspaper Association. **2.** American Nurses Association. **3.** Association of National Advertisers. Also, **ANA**

anal analysis.

analyt. analytical.

anat. 1. anatomical. **2.** anatomist. **3.** anatomy.

ANBS Armed Nuclear Bombardment Satellite.

ANC 1. Also, **A.N.C.** African National Congress. **2.** Army Nurse Corps.

anc automatic noise control.

anc. ancient.

andz anodize.

aner aneroid.

ANF *Biochemistry.* atrial natriuretic factor.

ANG 1. acute necrotizing gingivitis; trench mouth. **2.** Air National Guard.

ang. 1. angiogram. **2.** angle.

Angl. 1. Anglican. **2.** Anglicized.

anglr angular.

anhyd. *Chemistry.* anhydrous.

ani *Telecommunications.* automatic number identification.

anim. *Music.* animato.

anl automatic noise limiter.

anlg analog.

anlr annular.

ann. **1.** annals. **2.** annuity. **3.** years. [from Latin *annī*]

annot. **1.** annotated. **2.** annotation. **3.** annotator.

ano alphanumeric output.

anon. **1.** anonymous. **2.** anonymously.

ANPA American Newspaper Publishers Association.

ANRC American National Red Cross.

ANS American Name Society.

ans. answer.

ANSI (an′sē), American National Standards Institute.

Ant. Antarctica.

ant. **1.** antenna **2.** antonym.

ANTA (an′tə), American National Theatre and Academy.

anthol. anthology.

anthrop. **1.** anthropological. **2.** anthropology.

anthropol. anthropology.

antiq. **1.** antiquarian. **2.** antiquary. **3.** antiquity.

ANTU (an′tōō), *Trademark.* a brand of gray, water-insoluble, poisonous powder, $C_{11}H_{10}N_2S$, used for killing rodents; alpha-naphthylthiourea.

ANZUS (an′zəs), Australia, New Zealand, and the United States, especially as associated in the mutual defense treaty (**ANZUS Pact** or **ANZUS Treaty**) of 1952.

A/O **1.** account of. **2.** and others. Also, **a/o**

AOA Administration on Aging.

AOH Ancient Order of Hibernians.

aoi angle of incidence.

A-OK all OK; perfect. Also, **A-o.k.,** **A-okay.**

AOL *Computers.* America Online.

A-1 first class.

AOR **1.** advice of rights. **2.** album-oriented radio. **3.** album-oriented rock.

aor angle of reflection.

AOS **1.** American Opera Society. **2.** American Orchid Society.

A.O.U. American Ornithologists' Union.

AP **1.** adjective phrase. **2.** *Education.* Advanced Placement. **3.** Air Police. **4.** American plan. **5.** antipersonnel. Also, **A.P.**

Ap. **1.** Apostle. **2.** Apothecaries'. **3.** April.

A/P **1.** account paid. **2.** accounts payable. **3.** authority to pay or purchase. Also, **a/p**

a-p American plan.

a.p. **1.** additional premium. **2.** advanced placement. **3.** as prescribed. **4.** author's proof.

APA **1.** American Psychiatric Association. **2.** American Psychological Association.

A.P.A. **1.** American Philological Association. **2.** American Protective Association. **3.** American Protestant Association. **4.** American Psychiatric Association. **5.** American Psychological Association. **6.** Associate in Public Administration.

a-part. alpha particle; alpha particles.

APB all-points bulletin.

APC **1.** Also, **A.P.C.** *Pharmacology.* aspirin, phenacetin, and caffeine: a compound formerly used in headache and cold remedies. **2.** armored personnel carrier.

APCB Air Pollution Control Board.

aper. aperture.

APEX (ā'peks), a type of international air fare offering reduced rates for extended stays that are booked in advance. [*A(dvance) P(urchase) Ex(cursion)*]

aph. *Linguistics.* aphetic.

APHIS Animal and Plant Health Inspection Service.

API American Petroleum Institute. Also, **A.P.I.**

APL 1. allowance parts list. **2.** *Computers.* an interactive programming language. [*A P(rogramming) L(anguage)*]

APLA American Patent Law Association.

A.P.O. Army & Air Force Post Office. Also, **APO**

app. 1. apparatus. **2.** apparent. **3.** appendix. **4.** *Computers.* application. **5.** applied. **6.** appointed. **7.** approved. **8.** approximate.

appar. 1. apparent. **2.** apparently.

appd. approved.

appl. 1. appeal. **2.** applicable. **3.** application. **4.** applied.

appmt. appointment.

approp. appropriation.

approx. 1. approximate. **2.** approximately.

apprp appropriate.

apprx approximate.

appt. 1. appoint. **2.** appointed. **3.** appointment.

apptd. appointed.

appx appendix.

APR annual percentage rate. Also, **A.P.R.**

Apr. April.

aprch approach.

aprt airport.

A.P.S. 1. American Peace Society. **2.** American Philatelic Society. **3.** American Philosophical Society. **4.** American Physical Society. **5.** American Protestant Society.

A.P.S.A. American Political Science Association.

apt. apartment. Also, **apt**

apu auxiliary power unit.

apv approve.

apvd approved.

apvl approval.

apx. appendix.

AQ *Psychology.* achievement quotient.

aq. water. [from Latin *aqua*]

AQAB Air Quality Advisory Board.

aq. bull. (in prescriptions) boiling water. [from Latin *aqua bulliēns*]

aq. comm. (in prescriptions) common water. [from Latin *aqua commūnis*]

aq. dest. (in prescriptions) distilled water. [from Latin *aqua dēstillāta*]

aq. ferv. (in prescriptions) hot water. [from Latin *aqua fervēns*]

AQL acceptable quality level.

aqstn acquisition.

AR 1. annual return. **2.** Arkansas (for use with ZIP code). **3.** Army Regulation; Army Regulations. **4.** as required.

Ar Arabic.

Ar *Symbol, Chemistry.* argon.

Ar. 1. Arabic. **2.** Aramaic.

ar. 1. arrival. **2.** arrive; arrived; arrives.

A/R account receivable; accounts receivable. Also, **a/r**

A.R. 1. annual return. **2.** Army Regulation; Army Regulations.

a.r. *Insurance.* all risks.

ARA Agricultural Research Administration.

A.R.A. 1. American Railway Association. **2.** Associate of the Royal Academy.

Aram Aramaic. Also, **Aram.**

ARC (ärk), *Pathology.* AIDS-related complex.

ARC American Red Cross. Also, **A.R.C.**

Arc. arcade (approved for postal use).

arc cos *Trigonometry.* arc cosine.

arc cot *Trigonometry.* arc cotangent.

arc csc *Trigonometry.* arc cosecant.

Arch. Archbishop.

arch. 1. archaic. 2. archaism. 3. archery. 4. archipelago. 5. architect. 6. architectural. 7. architecture. 8. archive; archives.

archaeol. 1. archaeological. 2. archaeology.

Archbp. Archbishop.

archd. 1. archdeacon. 2. archduke. Also, **Archd.**

Arch. E. Architectural Engineer.

archt. architect.

ARCN *Computers.* Attached Resource Computer Network.

A.R.C.S. 1. Associate of the Royal College of Science. 2. Associate of the Royal College of Surgeons.

ard acute respiratory disease.

ARDS *Pathology.* adult respiratory distress syndrome.

arf acute respiratory failure.

Arg *Biochemistry.* arginine.

Arg. Argentina.

argus advanced research on groups under stress.

arith. 1. arithmetic. 2. arithmetical.

Ariz. Arizona.

Ark. Arkansas.

ARL Association of Research Libraries.

arl average remaining lifetime.

ARM adjustable-rate mortgage.

Arm Armenian.

Arm. 1. Armenian. 2. Armorican.

Ar.M. Master of Architecture. [from Latin *Architecturae Magister*]

aro *Commerce.* after receipt of order.

ARP *Stock Exchange.* adjustable-rate preferred.

ARR American Right to Read.

arr. 1. arranged. 2. arrangement. 3. *Music.* arranger. 4. arrival. 5. arrive; arrived; arrives.

arrgt. arrangement.

ARS 1. advanced record system. 2. Agricultural Research Service. 3. American Rescue Service. 4. American Rose Society.

ART *Linguistics.* article: often used to represent the class of determiners, including words such as *this, that,* and *some* as well as the articles *a, an,* and *the.*

art. 1. artificial. 2. artillery. 3. artist.

ARU *Computers.* audio response unit.

A.R.V. 1. AIDS-related virus. 2. American Revised Version (of the Bible).

ARVN (är′vin), (in the Vietnam War) a soldier in the army of South Vietnam. [*A(rmy of the) R(epublic of) V(iet) N(am)*]

AS 1. American Samoa (for use with ZIP code). 2. Anglo-Saxon. 3. antisubmarine.

As *Symbol, Chemistry.* arsenic.

AS. Anglo-Saxon.

A.S. 1. Anglo-Saxon. 2. Associate in Science.

A.-S. Anglo-Saxon.

ASA 1. Acoustical Society of America. 2. American Standards Association. 3. the numerical exposure index of a photographic film under the system adopted by the American Standards Association.

ASAP as soon as possible. Also, **A.S.A.P., a.s.a.p.**

ASAT (ā′sat′), antisatellite.

ASBM air-to-surface ballistic missile. Also, **A.S.B.M.**

ASC American Society of Cinematographers. Also, **A.S.C.**

ASCAP (as′kap), American Society of Composers, Authors, and Publishers.

ASCE American Society of Civil Engineers.

ASCII (as'kē), a standard code for characters stored in a computer or to be transmitted between computers. [*A(merican) S(tandard) C(ode) for I(nformation) I(nterchange)*]

ASCM antiship capable missile.

ASCP American Society of Clinical Pathologists.

ascr *Electronics.* asymmetrical semiconductor controlled rectifier.

ASCS Agricultural Stabilization and Conservation Service.

ASCU Association of State Colleges and Universities.

ASE American Stock Exchange. Also, **A.S.E.**

ASEAN Association of Southeast Asian Nations. Also, **A.S.E.A.N.**

asgd. assigned.

asgmt. assignment.

asgn assign.

ASHD arteriosclerotic heart disease.

ASI 1. *Aeronautics.* airspeed indicator. **2.** American Safety Institute.

ask amplitude shift keying.

ASL 1. American Shuffleboard League. **2.** American Sign Language. **3.** American Soccer League.

ASLA American Society of Landscape Architects.

ASM air-to-surface missile.

asm assemble.

ASME American Society of Mechanical Engineers.

ASN Army service number.

Asn *Biochemistry.* asparagine.

ASNE American Society of Newspaper Editors.

ASP American selling price.

Asp *Biochemistry.* aspartic acid.

A.S.P.C.A. American Society for the Prevention of Cruelty to Animals.

ASPCC American Society for the Prevention of Cruelty to Children.

ASR 1. airport surveillance radar. **2.** *U.S. Navy.* air-sea rescue.

asr *Teletype.* automatic send-receive.

ass. 1. assistant. **2.** association. **3.** assorted.

assn. association. Also, **Assn.**

assoc. 1. associate. **2.** associated. **3.** association.

ASSR Autonomous Soviet Socialist Republic. Also, **A.S.S.R.**

asst. 1. assistance. **2.** assistant.

asstd. assorted.

Assyr. Assyrian.

AST Atlantic Standard Time. Also, **A.S.T., a.s.t.**

astb *Electronics.* astable.

ASTM American Society for Testing Materials. Also, **A.S.T.M.**

Astronomy. 1. astronomer. **2.** astronomical. **3.** astronomy.

ASU American Students Union.

A.S.V. American Standard Version (of the Bible). Also, **ASV**

A.S.W. Association of Scientific Workers.

ASWG American Steel Wire Gauge.

asym assymmetric.

asymp *Math.* asymptote.

asyn asynchronous.

AT 1. achievement test. **2.** *Military.* antitank.

At ampere-turn.

At *Symbol, Chemistry.* astatine.

at. 1. atmosphere. **2.** atomic. **3.** attorney.

A.T. Atlantic time.

ATA Air Transport Association.

A.T.A. Associate Technical Aide.

atb *Telephones.* all trunks busy.

ATC 1. Air Traffic Control. **2.** Air Transport Command.

atch attach.

ATE equipment that makes a series

of tests automatically. [*a(utomatic) t(est) e(quipment)*]

ATF (Bureau of) Alcohol, Tobacco, and Firearms.

ATLA American Trial Lawyers Association.

ATM automated-teller machine.

atm. 1. atmosphere; atmospheres. **2.** atmospheric.

At/m ampere-turns per meter.

at. m. atomic mass.

at. no. atomic number.

ATP *Biochemistry.* an ester of adenosine and triphosphoric acid, $C_{10}H_{12}N_5O_4H_4P_3O_9$. [*a(denosine) t(ri)p(hosphate)*]

atr antitransmit-receive.

ATS *British. Military.* Auxiliary Territorial Service.

A.T.S. 1. American Temperance Society. **2.** American Tract Society. **3.** American Transport Service.

att. 1. attached. **2.** attention. **3.** attorney.

att. gen. attorney general.

attn. attention.

attrib. 1. attribute. **2.** attributive. **3.** attributively.

atty. attorney.

Atty. Gen. Attorney General.

ATV all-terrain vehicle.

at. wt. atomic weight. Also, **at wt**

AU astronomical unit.

Au *Symbol, Chemistry.* gold. [from Latin *aurum*]

au. author.

A.U. *Physics.* angstrom unit. Also, **a.u.**

A.U.A. American Unitarian Association.

A.U.C. 1. from the founding of the city (of Rome in 753? B.C.). [from Latin *ab urbe conditā*] **2.** in the year from the founding of the city (of Rome). [from Latin *annō urbis conditae*]

aud. 1. audit. **2.** auditor.

Aug. August.

aug. 1. augmentative. **2.** augmented.

AUM air-to-underwater missile.

AUS Army of the United States. Also, **A.U.S.**

Aus. 1. Austria. **2.** Austrian.

Aust. 1. Austria. **2.** Austria-Hungary. **3.** Austrian.

Austral Australian.

Austral. 1. Australasia. **2.** Australia. **3.** Australian.

auth. 1. authentic. **2.** author. **3.** authority. **4.** authorized.

Auth. Ver. Authorized Version (of the Bible).

auto. 1. automatic. **2.** automobile. **3.** automotive.

AUTODIN (ô′tō din), automatic digital network.

autoxfmr autotransformer.

AUX *Linguistics.* auxiliary verb. Also, **Aux**

aux. auxiliary; auxiliaries. Also, **aux, auxil.**

AV 1. arteriovenous. **2.** atrioventricular. **3.** audiovisual.

av 1. avenue. **2.** average. **3.** avoirdupois weight.

A-V 1. atrioventricular. **2.** audiovisual.

A/V 1. Also, **a.v.** ad valorem. **2.** audiovisual.

A.V. 1. Artillery Volunteers. **2.** audiovisual. **3.** Authorized Version (of the Bible).

A.V.C. 1. American Veterans' Committee. **2.** automatic volume control. Also, **AVC**

avdp. avoirdupois weight.

Ave. avenue. Also, **ave.**

AVF all-volunteer force.

avg. average.

avlbl available.

AVMA American Veterinary Medical Association.

avn. aviation.

avr automatic voltage regulator.

AW Articles of War.

a.w. 1. actual weight. **2.** (in shipping) all water. **3.** atomic weight. Also, **aw**

AWACS (ā′waks), a detection aircraft, fitted with radar and computers, capable of simultaneously tracking and plotting large numbers of low-flying aircraft. [A(irborne) W(arning) A(nd) C(ontrol) S(ystem)]

AWB air waybill.

AWG American Wire Gauge.

AWI Animal Welfare Institute.

AWIS Association of Women in Science.

A.W.L. absent with leave. Also, **a.w.l.**

AWOL (*pronounced as initials or* ā′wôl, ā′wol), away from military duties without permission, but without the intention of deserting. Also, **awol, A.W.O.L., a.w.o.l.** [A(bsent) W(ith)o(ut) L(eave)]

AWS American Weather Service.

AWSA American Water-Skiing Association.

ax. 1. axial. **2.** axiom.

A.Y.H. American Youth Hostels.

AZ Arizona (for use with ZIP code).

az. 1. azimuth. **2.** azure.

AZT *Pharmacology, Trademark.* azidothymidine: an antiviral drug used in the treatment of AIDS.

B

B 1. base: a semiconductor device. **2.** *Chess.* bishop. **3.** black. **4.** *Photography.* bulb. **5.** *Computers.* byte.

B *Symbol.* **1.** the second in order or in a series. **2.** (In some grading systems) a grade or mark, indicating the quality of a student's work as good or better than average. **3.** (In some school systems) a symbol designating the second semester of a school year. **4.** *Physiology.* a major blood group usually enabling a person whose blood is of this type to donate blood to persons of type B or AB and to receive blood from persons of type O or B. **5.** *Music.* **a.** the seventh tone in the scale of C major or the second tone in the relative minor scale, A minor. **b.** a string, key, or pipe tuned to this tone. **c.** a written or printed note representing this tone. **d.** (in the fixed system of solmization) the seventh tone of the scale of C major, called *ti.* **e.** the tonality

having B as the tonic note. **6.** (*sometimes lowercase*) the medieval Roman numeral for 300. **7.** *Chemistry.* boron. **8.** a proportional shoe width size, narrower than C and wider than A. **9.** a proportional brassiere cup size, smaller than C and larger than A. **10.** *Physics.* magnetic induction. **11.** bel. **12.** *Electricity.* susceptance. **13.** a designation for a motion picture made on a low budget and meant as the secondary part of a double feature. **14.** a quality rating for a corporate or municipal bond, lower than BB and higher than CCC.

b 1. *Physics.* **a.** bar; bars. **b.** barn; barns. **2.** *Computers.* bit. **3.** black.

B- *U.S. Military.* (in designations of aircraft) bomber: *B-29.*

B. 1. bachelor. **2.** bacillus. **3.** *Baseball.* base; baseman. **4.** bass. **5.** basso. **6.** bay. **7.** Bible. **8.** bolivar. **9.** boliviano. **10.** book. **11.** born.

12. breadth. **13.** British. **14.** brother. **15.** brotherhood.

b. **1.** bachelor. **2.** bale. **3.** *Baseball.* base; baseman. **4.** bass. **5.** basso. **6.** bay. **7.** billion. **8.** blend of; blended. **9.** book. **10.** born. **11.** breadth. **12.** brother. **13.** brotherhood.

BA bank acceptance.

Ba *Symbol, Chemistry.* barium.

ba. **1.** bath. **2.** bathroom.

B.A. **1.** Bachelor of Arts. [from Latin *Baccalaureus Artium*] **2.** *Theater.* bastard amber. **3.** *Baseball.* batting average. **4.** British Academy. **5.** British America. **6.** British Association (for Advancement of Science). **7.** Buenos Aires.

B.A.A. Bachelor of Applied Arts.

B.A.A.E. Bachelor of Aeronautical and Astronautical Engineering.

Bab. Babylon; Babylonia.

BAC blood-alcohol concentration: the percentage of alcohol in the bloodstream.

bact. **1.** bacterial. **2.** bacteriology. **3.** bacterium.

BAE **1.** Bureau of Agricultural Economics. **2.** Bureau of American Ethnology.

B.A.E. **1.** Bachelor of Aeronautical Engineering. **2.** Bachelor of Agricultural Engineering. **3.** Bachelor of Architectural Engineering. **4.** Bachelor of Art Education. **5.** Bachelor of Arts in Education.

B.A.Ed. Bachelor of Arts in Education.

B.A.E.E. Bachelor of Arts in Elementary Education.

B.Ag. Bachelor of Agriculture.

B.Ag.E. Bachelor of Agricultural Engineering.

B.Agr. Bachelor of Agriculture.

B.Ag.Sc. Bachelor of Agricultural Science.

Ba. Is. Bahama Islands.

B.A.Jour. Bachelor of Arts in Journalism.

BAK file (bak), *Computers.* backup file.

BAL **1.** *Chemistry.* British Anti-Lewisite: dimercaprol. **2.** *Computers.* Basic Assembly Language.

bal blood alcohol level.

Bal. Baluchistan.

bal. **1.** balance. **2.** balancing.

Balt. Baltic.

balun balanced-to-unbalanced network.

B.A.M. **1.** Bachelor of Applied Mathematics. **2.** Bachelor of Arts in Music.

B.A.Mus.Ed. Bachelor of Arts in Music Education.

B and B **1.** *Trademark.* a brand of liqueur combining Benedictine and brandy. **2.** bed-and-breakfast. Also, **B&B**

B&D bondage and discipline: used in reference to sadomasochistic sexual practices. Also, **B and D**

B&S Brown and Sharp wire gauge.

Bap. Baptist. Also, **Bapt.**

bap. baptized.

B.A.P.C.T. Bachelor of Arts in Practical Christian Training.

B.App.Arts. Bachelor of Applied Arts.

BAR Browning automatic rifle.

Bar. *Bible.* Baruch.

bar. **1.** barometer. **2.** barometric. **3.** barrel. **4.** barrister.

B.Ar. Bachelor of Architecture.

B.Arch. Bachelor of Architecture.

B.Arch.E. Bachelor of Architectural Engineering.

barit. baritone.

baro barometer.

barr. barrister.

BART (bärt), Bay Area Rapid Transit.

Bart. Baronet.

B.A.S. 1. Bachelor of Agricultural Science. **2.** Bachelor of Applied Science.

B.A.Sc. 1. Bachelor of Agricultural Science. **2.** Bachelor of Applied Science.

BASIC (bā′sik), *Computers.* a programming language that uses English words, punctuation marks, and algebraic notation. [*B(eginner's) A(ll-purpose) S(ymbolic) I(nstruction) C(ode)*]

bat. 1. battalion. **2.** battery.

BATF Bureau of Alcohol, Tobacco, and Firearms.

batt. 1. battalion. **2.** battery.

Bav. 1. Bavaria. **2.** Bavarian.

bay *Electronics.* bayonet.

bayc *Electronics.* bayonet candelabra.

bay cand dc *Electronics.* bayonet candelabra double-contact.

bay cand sc *Electronics.* bayonet candelabra single-contact.

BB a quality rating for a corporate or municipal bond, lower than BBB and higher than B.

bb. 1. ball bearing. **2.** *Baseball.* base on balls; bases on balls. **3.** bulletin board.

B/B bottled in bond.

B.B. 1. bail bond. **2.** Blue Book. **3.** B'nai B'rith. **4.** Bureau of the Budget.

b.b. 1. bail bond. **2.** baseboard.

B.B.A. 1. Bachelor of Business Administration. **2.** Big Brothers of America.

BBB Better Business Bureau.

BBB a quality rating for a corporate or municipal bond, lower than A and higher than BB.

B.B.C. British Broadcasting Corporation. Also, **BBC**

bbl. barrel.

bbq barbecue.

bbrg ball bearing.

BBS *Computers.* **1.** bulletin board service. **2.** bulletin board system.

BC 1. British Columbia, Canada (for use with ZIP code). **2.** *Scuba Diving.* buoyancy compensator.

bc 1. *Music.* basso continuo. **2.** between centers. **3.** Also, **bcc** blind carbon copy: used as a notation on the carbon copy of a letter or other document sent to a third person without the addressee's knowledge. **4.** broadcast.

B/C bills for collection.

B.C. 1. Bachelor of Chemistry. **2.** Bachelor of Commerce. **3.** bass clarinet. **4.** battery commander. **5.** before Christ (used in indicating dates). **6.** British Columbia.

BCA Boys' Clubs of America.

bcc blind carbon copy.

BCD 1. *Military.* bad conduct discharge. **2.** *Computers.* binary-coded decimal system.

B.C.E. 1. Bachelor of Chemical Engineering. **2.** Bachelor of Christian Education. **3.** Bachelor of Civil Engineering. **4.** before Christian (or Common) Era.

B.Cer.E. Bachelor of Ceramic Engineering.

bcfsk binary-coded frequency-shift keying.

bch. bunch.

B.Ch. Bachelor of Chemistry.

B.Ch.E. Bachelor of Chemical Engineering.

bci binary-coded information.

B.C.L. Bachelor of Civil Law.

bcn beacon.

BCNU *Pharmacology.* carmustine. [abbreviation of the chemical name *1,3-bis 2-chloroethyl-1-nitrosourea*]

B.Com.Sc. Bachelor of Commercial Science.

B.C.P. 1. Bachelor of City Planning. **2.** Book of Common Prayer.

B.C.S. 1. Bachelor of Chemical Science. **2.** Bachelor of Commercial Science.

Bd *Symbol.* baud.

BD. (in Bahrain) dinar; dinars.

bd. 1. board. **2.** bond. **3.** bound. **4.** bundle.

B/D 1. bank draft. **2.** bills discounted. **3.** *Accounting.* brought down.

b/d barrels per day.

B.D. 1. Bachelor of Divinity. **2.** bank draft. **3.** bills discounted.

B.D.A. 1. Bachelor of Domestic Arts. **2.** Bachelor of Dramatic Art.

bdc bottom dead center.

bde *Military.* brigade.

bd elim band elimination.

B.Des. Bachelor of Design.

bd. ft. board foot; board feet.

bdg binding.

bdgh binding head.

bdl. bundle.

bdle. bundle.

bdrm. bedroom.

bdry. boundary.

B.D.S. Bachelor of Dental Surgery.

b.d.s. (in prescriptions) twice a day. [from Latin *bis diē sūmendum*]

BDSA Business and Defense Services Administration.

Be *Symbol, Chemistry.* beryllium.

Bé. *Chemistry.* Baumé: calibrated according to a Baumé scale, used to measure specific gravity of liquids.

B/E bill of exchange. Also, **b.e.**

B.E. 1. Bachelor of Education. **2.** Bachelor of Engineering. **3.** Bank of England. **4.** bill of exchange. **5.** Board of Education.

bec. because.

B.Ed. Bachelor of Education.

B.E.E. Bachelor of Electrical Engineering.

bef. before.

B.E.F. British Expeditionary Force; British Expeditionary Forces.

Bel. 1. Belgian. **2.** Belgic. **3.** Belgium.

Belg. 1. Belgian. **2.** Belgium.

B.E.M. 1. Bachelor of Engineering of Mines. **2.** British Empire Medal.

benef. beneficiary.

Beng. 1. Bengal. **2.** Bengali.

B. Engr. Bachelor of Engineering.

B.E.P. Bachelor of Engineering Physics.

ber bit error rate.

Ber. Is. Bermuda Islands.

B.E.S. Bachelor of Engineering Science.

BEShT *Judaism.* Baal Shem-Tov.

BET Black Entertainment Television.

bet. between.

betw between.

BeV (bev), *Physics.* billion electron-volts. Also, **Bev, bev**

BEW Board of Economic Warfare.

BF black female.

bf. *Law.* brief.

B/F *Accounting.* brought forward.

B.F. 1. Bachelor of Finance. **2.** Bachelor of Forestry.

b.f. *Printing.* boldface. Also, **bf**

B.F.A. Bachelor of Fine Arts.

B.F.A.Mus. Bachelor of Fine Arts in Music.

bfo *Electronics.* beat-frequency oscillator.

bfr 1. before. **2.** buffer.

B.F.S. Bachelor of Foreign Service.

BFT biofeedback training. Also, **bft**

B.F.T. Bachelor of Foreign Trade.

bg. 1. background. **2.** bag.

B.G. 1. Birmingham gauge. **2.** brigadier general. Also, **BG**

bge beige.

bGH *Biochemistry, Agriculture.* bovine growth hormone.

Bglr. bugler.

BHA *Chemistry, Pharmacology.* a synthetic antioxidant, $C_{11}H_{16}O_2$. [*b(utylated) h(ydroxy)a(nisole)*]

BHC *Chemistry.* a crystalline, water-soluble, poisonous solid, $C_6H_6Cl_6$. [*b(enzene) h(exa)c(hloride)*]

bhd. bulkhead.

B.H.L. 1. Bachelor of Hebrew Letters. **2.** Bachelor of Hebrew Literature.

Bhn *Metallurgy.* Brinell hardness number.

bhp brake horsepower. Also, **BHP, B.H.P., b.hp., b.h.p.**

BHT *Chemistry, Pharmacology.* an antioxidant, $C_{15}H_{24}O$. [*b(utylated) h(ydroxy)t(oluene)*]

BI *Real Estate.* built-in.

Bi *Symbol, Chemistry.* bismuth.

bi bisexual.

BIA Bureau of Indian Affairs.

BiAF bisexual Asian female.

BiAM bisexual Asian male.

Bib. 1. Bible. **2.** Biblical.

bib. (in prescriptions) drink. [from Latin *bibe*]

BiBF bisexual black female.

Bibl Biblical. Also, **Bibl.**

bibl. 1. biblical. **2.** bibliographical. **3.** bibliography.

BiblHeb Biblical Hebrew.

BiBM bisexual black male.

bicarb. 1. bicarbonate. **2.** bicarbonate of soda.

B.I.D. Bachelor of Industrial Design.

b.i.d. (in prescriptions) twice a day. [from Latin *bis in diē*]

B.I.E. Bachelor of Industrial Engineering.

BiF bisexual female.

Big O *Slang.* orgasm.

BIL Braille Institute Library.

BiM bisexual male.

bin binary.

B.Ind.Ed. Bachelor of Industrial Education.

biog. 1. biographer. **2.** biographical. **3.** biography.

biol. 1. biological. **2.** biologist. **3.** biology.

BIOS (bī′ōs, -os), *Computers.* firmware that directs many basic functions of the operating system. [*B(asic) I(nput)/O(utput) S(ystem)*]

B.I.S. 1. Bank for International Settlements. **2.** British Information Services.

B.I.T. Bachelor of Industrial Technology.

BiWF bisexual white female.

BiWM bisexual white male.

B.J. Bachelor of Journalism.

Bk *Symbol, Chemistry.* berkelium.

bk 1. back. **2.** *Baseball.* balk; balks. **3.** black.

bk. 1. bank. **2.** book.

bkbndr. bookbinder.

bkcy. bankruptcy.

bkdn breakdown.

bkg. 1. banking. **2.** bookkeeping. **3.** breakage.

bkgd. background.

bklr. *Printing.* black letter.

bkpg. bookkeeping.

bkpr. bookkeeper.

bkpt. bankrupt.

bks. 1. banks. **2.** barracks. **3.** books.

bkt. 1. basket. **2.** bracket. **3.** bucket.

bl. 1. bale; bales. **2.** barrel; barrels. **3.** black. **4.** block. **5.** blue.

b/l *Commerce.* bill of lading. Also, **B/L**

B.L. 1. Bachelor of Laws. **2.** Bachelor of Letters. **3.** bill of lading.

b.l. 1. bill of lading. **2.** *Military.* breech loading.

B.L.A. 1. Bachelor of Landscape Architecture. **2.** Bachelor of Liberal Arts.

bldg. building.

Bldg.E. Building Engineer.

bldr. builder.

B.L.E. Brotherhood of Locomotive Engineers.

B.Lit. Bachelor of Literature.

B.Litt. Bachelor of Letters.

blk. 1. black. **2.** block. **3.** bulk.

blkg 1. blanking. **2.** blocking.

B.LL. Bachelor of Laws.

BLM Bureau of Land Management. Also, **B.L.M.**

blo blower.

BLS Bureau of Labor Statistics.

bls. 1. bales. **2.** barrels.

B.L.S. 1. Bachelor of Library Science. **2.** Bureau of Labor Statistics.

BLT a bacon, lettuce, and tomato sandwich. Also, **B.L.T.**

bltin built-in.

Blvd. boulevard. Also, **blvd.**

blw below.

blzd blizzard.

BM 1. basal metabolism. **2.** *Surveying.* bench mark. **3.** black male. **4.** *Informal.* bowel movement.

bm *Electricity.* break-before-make: a relay contact.

B.M. 1. Bachelor of Medicine. **2.** Bachelor of Music. **3.** British Museum.

B.Mar.E. Bachelor of Marine Engineering.

B.M.E. 1. Bachelor of Mechanical Engineering. **2.** Bachelor of Mining Engineering. **3.** Bachelor of Music Education.

B.M.Ed. Bachelor of Music Education.

B.Met. Bachelor of Metallurgy.

B.Met.E. Bachelor of Metallurgical Engineering.

BMEWS (bē myōōz′), *U.S. Military.* Ballistic Missile Early Warning System.

B.Mgt.E. Bachelor of Management Engineering.

BMI Broadcast Music, Inc.

B.Min.E. Bachelor of Mining Engineering.

BMOC big man on campus. Also, **B.M.O.C.**

BMR basal metabolic rate.

B.M.S. Bachelor of Marine Science.

B.M.T. Bachelor of Medical Technology.

B.Mus. Bachelor of Music.

B.M.V. Blessed Mary the Virgin. [from Latin *Beāta Maria Virgō*]

bn brown.

Bn. 1. Baron. **2.** Battalion.

bn. battalion.

B.N. Bachelor of Nursing.

BNA British North America. Also, **B.N.A.**

BND Germany's national intelligence service. [from German *B(undes)-n(achrichten)d(ienst)*]

bnls boneless.

bnr burner.

B.N.S. Bachelor of Naval Science.

bnsh burnish.

bnz bronze.

bo 1. blackout. **2.** *Electronics.* blocking oscillator.

B/o *Accounting.* brought over.

B.O. 1. Board of Ordnance. **2.** *Informal.* body odor. **3.** *Theater.* box office.

b.o. 1. back order. **2.** box office. **3.** branch office. **4.** broker's order. **5.** buyer's option.

BOB Bureau of the Budget.

BOD biochemical oxygen demand.

Bol. Bolivia.

bol. (in prescriptions) bolus (larger than a regular pill).

BOMFOG brotherhood of man, fatherhood of God.

BOQ *U.S. Military.* bachelor officers' quarters.

bor. borough.

bot. 1. botanic; botanical. **2.** botanist. **3.** botany. **4.** bottle.

B.O.T. Board of Trade.

BP 1. beautiful people; beautiful person. **2.** blood pressure.

bp 1. between perpendiculars. **2.** blueprint. **3.** boilerplate.

bp. 1. baptized. **2.** birthplace. **3.** bishop.

B/P *Commerce.* bills payable.

B.P. 1. Bachelor of Pharmacy. **2.** Bachelor of Philosophy. **3.** *Finance.* basis point. **4.** *Archaeology.* before the present: (in radiocarbon dating) in a specified amount of time or at a specified point in time before A.D. 1950. **5.** *Commerce.* bills payable.

b.p. 1. *Finance.* basis point. **2.** below proof. **3.** *Commerce.* bills payable. **4.** *Physics, Chemistry.* boiling point. **5.** the public good [from Latin *bonum publicum*].

bpa bandpass amplifier.

B.P.A. Bachelor of Professional Arts.

BPD barrels per day. Also, **B.P.D.**

B.P.E. Bachelor of Physical Education.

B.Pet.E. Bachelor of Petroleum Engineering.

B.Ph. Bachelor of Philosophy.

B.P.H. Bachelor of Public Health.

B.Pharm. Bachelor of Pharmacy.

B.Phil. Bachelor of Philosophy.

BPI 1. Also, **bpi** *Computers.* **a.** bits per inch. **b.** bytes per inch. **2.** Bureau of Public Inquiries.

bpl. birthplace.

B.P.O.E. Benevolent and Protective Order of Elks.

bps *Computers.* bits per second. Also, **BPS**

BR 1. *Real Estate.* bedroom. **2.** Bureau of Reclamation.

Br *Symbol, Chemistry.* bromine.

Br. 1. branch (in place names). **2.** brick. **3.** Britain. **4.** British.

br. 1. bedroom. **2.** branch. **3.** brass. **4.** brig. **5.** bronze. **6.** brother. **7.** brown.

b.r. *Commerce.* bills receivable. Also, **B.R., B/R**

Braz. 1. Brazil. **2.** Brazilian.

B.R.C.A. Brotherhood of Railway Carmen of America.

B.R.C.S. British Red Cross Society.

brdg bridge.

B.R.E. Bachelor of Religious Education.

brg bearing.

Brig. 1. brigade. **2.** brigadier.

Brig. Gen. brigadier general.

Brit. 1. Britain. **2.** British.

brk brake.

brkg breaking.

brkr *Electricity.* breaker.

brkt bracket.

brng burning.

Bros. brothers. Also, **bros.**

brs brass.

Br. Som. British Somaliland.

BR STD British Standard.

brt 1. bright. **2.** brightness.

B.R.T. Brotherhood of Railroad Trainmen.

BRV Bravo (a cable television station).

brz braze.

BS 1. Bureau of Standards. **2.** *Slang (sometimes vulgar).* bullshit.

b/s 1. bags. **2.** bales. **3.** bill of sale.

B.S. 1. Bachelor of Science. **2.** Bachelor of Surgery. **3.** bill of sale. **4.** *Slang (sometimes vulgar).* bullshit.

b.s. 1. balance sheet. **2.** bill of sale. **3.** *Slang (sometimes vulgar).* bullshit.

B.S.A. 1. Also, **B.S. Agr.** Bachelor of Science in Agriculture. **2.** Bachelor of Scientific Agriculture. **3.** Boy Scouts of America.

B.S.A.A. Bachelor of Science in Applied Arts.

B.S.Adv. Bachelor of Science in Advertising.

B.S.A.E. 1. Also, **B.S.Ae.Eng.** Bachelor of Science in Aeronautical Engineering. **2.** Also, **B.S.Ag.E.** Bachelor of Science in Agricultural Engineering. **3.** Also, **B.S.Arch.E., B.S.Arch.Eng.** Bachelor of Science in Architectural Engineering.

B.S.Arch. Bachelor of Science in Architecture.

B.S.Art.Ed. Bachelor of Science in Art Education.

B.S.B.A. Bachelor of Science in Business Administration.

B.S.Bus. Bachelor of Science in Business.

B.S.Bus.Mgt. Bachelor of Science in Business Management.

B.Sc. Bachelor of Science.

B.S.C. Bachelor of Science in Commerce.

B.S.C.E. Bachelor of Science in Civil Engineering.

B.S.Ch. Bachelor of Science in Chemistry.

B.S.Ch.E. Bachelor of Science in Chemical Engineering.

B.Sch.Music Bachelor of School Music.

B.S.Com. Bachelor of Science in Communications.

B.S.C.P. Brotherhood of Sleeping Car Porters.

B.S.D. Bachelor of Science in Design. Also, **B.S.Des.**

B.S.E. 1. Also, **B.S.Ed.** Bachelor of Science in Education. **2.** Also, **B.S.Eng.** Bachelor of Science in Engineering.

B.S.Ec. Bachelor of Science in Economics.

B.S.E.E. 1. Also, **B.S.E.Engr.** Bachelor of Science in Electrical Engineering. **2.** Bachelor of Science in Elementary Education.

B.S.El.E. Bachelor of Science in Electronic Engineering.

B.S.E.M. Bachelor of Science in Engineering of Mines.

B.S.E.P. Bachelor of Science in Engineering Physics.

B.S.E.S. Bachelor of Science in Engineering Sciences.

B.S.F. Bachelor of Science in Forestry. Also, **B.S.For.**

B.S.F.M. Bachelor of Science in Forest Management.

B.S.F.Mgt. Bachelor of Science in Fisheries Management.

B.S.F.S. Bachelor of Science in Foreign Service.

B.S.F.T. Bachelor of Science in Fuel Technology.

B.S.G.E. Bachelor of Science in General Engineering. Also, **B.S.Gen.Ed.**

B.S.G.Mgt. Bachelor of Science in Game Management.

bsh. bushel; bushels.

B.S.H.A. Bachelor of Science in Hospital Administration.

B.S.H.E. Bachelor of Science in Home Economics. Also, **B.S.H.Ec.**

B.S.H.Ed. Bachelor of Science in Health Education.

bshg bushing.

B.S.Hyg. Bachelor of Science in Hygiene.

B.S.I.E. 1. Also, **B.S.Ind.Ed.** Bachelor of Science in Industrial Education. **2.** Also, **B.S.Ind.Engr.** Bachelor of Science in Industrial Engineering.

B.S.Ind.Mgt. Bachelor of Science in Industrial Management.

B.S.I.R. Bachelor of Science in Industrial Relations.

B.S.I.T. Bachelor of Science in Industrial Technology.

B.S.J. Bachelor of Science in Journalism.

bskt. basket.

Bs/L bills of lading.

B.S.L. 1. Bachelor of Sacred Literature. **2.** Bachelor of Science in Law. **3.** Bachelor of Science in Linguistics.

B.S.L.A. and Nurs. Bachelor of Science in Liberal Arts and Nursing.

B.S.Lab.Rel. Bachelor of Science in Labor Relations.

B.S.L.Arch. Bachelor of Science in Landscape Architecture.

B.S.L.M. Bachelor of Science in Landscape Management.

B.S.L.S. Bachelor of Science in Library Science.

B.S.M. 1. Bachelor of Sacred Music. **2.** Bachelor of Science in Medicine. **3.** Bachelor of Science in Music.

B.S.M.E. 1. Bachelor of Science in Mechanical Engineering. **2.** Bachelor of Science in Mining Engineering. **3.** Also, **B.S.Mus.Ed.** Bachelor of Science in Music Education.

B.S.Met. Bachelor of Science in Metallurgy.

B.S.Met.E. Bachelor of Science in Metallurgical Engineering.

bsmt basement. Also, **Bsmt**

B.S.M.T. Bachelor of Science in Medical Technology. Also, **B.S.Med.Tech.**

B.S.N. Bachelor of Science in Nursing.

B.S.N.A. Bachelor of Science in Nursing Administration.

bsns business

BSO *Astronomy.* blue stellar object.

B.S.Orn.Hort. Bachelor of Science in Ornamental Horticulture.

B.S.O.T. Bachelor of Science in Occupational Therapy.

B.S.P. Bachelor of Science in Pharmacy. Also, **B.S.Phar., B.S.Pharm.**

B.S.P.A. Bachelor of Science in Public Administration.

B.S.P.E. Bachelor of Science in Physical Education.

B.S.P.H. Bachelor of Science in Public Health.

B.S.P.H.N. Bachelor of Science in Public Health Nursing.

B.S.P.T. Bachelor of Science in Physical Therapy. Also, **B.S.Ph.Th.**

B.S.Radio-TV. Bachelor of Science in Radio and Television.

B.S.Ret. Bachelor of Science in Retailing.

B.S.R.T. Bachelor of Science in Radiological Technology.

B.S.S. 1. Bachelor of Secretarial Science. **2.** Bachelor of Social Science.

B.S.S.A. Bachelor of Science in Secretarial Administration.

B.S.S.E. Bachelor of Science in Secondary Education.

B.S.S.S. 1. Bachelor of Science in Secretarial Studies. **2.** Bachelor of Science in Social Science.

B.S.T.&I.E. Bachelor of Science in Trade and Industrial Education.

bstb *Electricity, Electronics.* bistable.

B.S.Trans. Bachelor of Science in Transportation.

Bt. Baronet.

bt. 1. boat. **2.** bought.

B.T. 1. Bachelor of Theology. **2.** board of trade.

B.t. *Biology, Agriculture.* Bacillus thuringiensis.

B.T.Ch. Bachelor of Textile Chemistry.

B.T.E. Bachelor of Textile Engineering.

bth bathroom.

B.Th. Bachelor of Theology.

btl. bottle.

btn button.

btn. battalion.

btry. battery.

btry chgr battery charger.

B.T.U. *Physics.* British thermal unit; British thermal units. Also, **BTU, B.t.u., B.th.u., Btu**

BU *Numismatics.* brilliant uncirculated.

bu. 1. bureau. **2.** bushel; bushels.

Bulg. 1. Bulgaria. **2.** Bulgarian. Also, **Bulg**

bull. bulletin. Also, **bul.**

BUN blood urea nitrogen.

Bur. Burma.

bur. bureau.

bus. business.

bush. bushel; bushels.

B.V. 1. Blessed Virgin. [from Latin *Beāta Virgō*] **2.** farewell. [from Latin *bene valē*]

b.v. book value.

B.V.A. Bachelor of Vocational Agriculture.

B.V.D. *Trademark.* a brand of men's underwear. Also, **BVD's**

B.V.E. Bachelor of Vocational Education.

bvg beverage.

B.V.I. British Virgin Islands.

bvl bevel.

B.V.M. Blessed Virgin Mary. [from Latin *Beāta Virgō Maria*]

bvt. 1. brevet. **2.** brevetted.

BW 1. bacteriological warfare. **2.** biological warfare. **3.** (in television, motion pictures, photography, etc.) black and white.

bw *Telecommunications.* bandwidth.

BWC Board of War Communications.

BWG Birmingham Wire Gauge.

B.W.I. British West Indies.

bx base exchange. Also, **BX**

bx. box.

By *Computers.* byte.

BYOB bring your own bottle (in an invitation, to indicate that the host will not provide liquor). Also, **BYO**

byp. bypass. Also, **Byp.**

Byz. Byzantine.

Bz. benzene.

bzr buzzer.

C

C 1. cocaine. **2.** *Electronics.* collector: an electron device. **3.** *Electricity.* common (in diagrams). **4.** *Grammar.* complement. **5.** consonant. **6.** coulomb. **7.** county (used with a number to designate a county road).

C *Symbol.* **1.** the third in order or in a series. **2.** (in some grading systems) a grade or mark, indicating the quality of a student's work as fair or average. **3.** *Music.* **a.** the first tone, or keynote, in the scale of C major or the third tone in the relative minor scale, A minor. **b.** a string, key, or pipe tuned to this tone. **c.** a written or printed note representing this tone. **d.** (in the fixed system of solmization) the first tone of the scale of C major, called *do.* **e.** the tonality having C as the tonic note. **f.** a symbol indicating quadruple time and appearing after the clef sign on a musical staff. **4.** (*sometimes lowercase*) the Roman numeral for 100. **5.** Celsius. **6.** centigrade. **7.** *Electricity.* **a.** capacitance. **b.** a battery size for 1.5 volt dry cells: diameter, 1 in. (2.5 cm); length, 1.9 in. (4.8 cm). **8.** *Chemistry.* carbon. **9.** *Physics.* **a.** charge conjugation. **b.** charm. **10.** *Biochemistry.* **a.** cysteine. **b.** cytosine. **11.** Also, **C-note.** *Slang.* a hundred-dollar bill. **12.** a proportional shoe width size, narrower than D and wider than B. **13.** a proportional brassiere cup size, smaller than D and larger than B. **14.** the lowest quality rating for a corporate or municipal bond. **15.** *Computers.* a high-level programming language. **16.** coulomb.

c 1. calorie. **2.** *Optics.* candle; candles. **3.** carbohydrate; carbohydrates. **4.** (with a year) about: *c1775.* [from

Latin *circā, circiter, circum*] **5.** *Physics, Chemistry.* curie; curies. **6.** cycle; cycles.

C- *U.S. Military.* (in designations of aircraft) cargo: *C-124.*

C. 1. calorie. **2.** Cape. **3.** Catholic. **4.** Celsius. **5.** Celtic. **6.** Centigrade. **7.** College. **8.** (in Costa Rica and El Salvador) colon; colons. **9.** Congress. **10.** Conservative.

c. 1. calorie. **2.** *Optics.* candle; candles. **3.** carat. **4.** carbon. **5.** carton. **6.** case. **7.** *Baseball.* catcher. **8.** cathode. **9.** cent; cents. **10.** centavo. **11.** *Football.* center. **12.** centigrade. **13.** centime. **14.** centimeter. **15.** century. **16.** chairman; chairperson. **17.** chapter. **18.** chief. **19.** child. **20.** church. **21.** (with a year) about: *c. 1775.* [from Latin *circā, circiter, circum*] **22.** cirrus. **23.** city. **24.** cloudy. **25.** cognate. **26.** color. **27.** gallon. [from Latin *congius*] **28.** copper. **29.** copyright. **30.** corps. **31.** cubic. **32.** (in prescriptions) with. [from Latin *cum*] **33.** cycle; cycles.

C++ *Computers.* a programming language.

CA 1. cable. **2.** California (for use with ZIP code). **3.** chronological age.

Ca *Symbol, Chemistry.* calcium.

ca. 1. cathode. **2.** centiare. **3.** Also, **ca** (with a year) about: *ca. 476* B.C. [def. 3 from Latin *circā*]

C/A 1. capital account. **2.** cash account. **3.** credit account. **4.** current account.

C.A. 1. Central America. **2.** chartered accountant. **3.** *Accounting.* chief accountant. **4.** Coast Artillery. **5.** commercial agent. **6.** consular agent. **7.** controller of accounts. **8.** current assets.

CAA Civil Aeronautics Administration. Also, **C.A.A.**

CAB Civil Aeronautics Board. Also, **C.A.B.**

cab cabinet.

CAC *Real Estate.* central air conditioning.

C.A.C. Coast Artillery Corps.

CAD (kad), computer-aided design.

CAD/CAM (kad/kam/), computer-aided design and computer-aided manufacturing.

CADMAT (kad/mat), computer-aided design, manufacture, and test.

CAE computer-aided engineering.

C.A.F. 1. cost and freight. **2.** cost, assurance, and freight. Also, **c.a.f.**

CAFE (ka fā/, kə-), *n.* a U.S. standard of average fuel consumption for all the cars produced by one manufacturer in a given year. [*C(orporate) A(verage) F(uel) E(conomy)*]

C.A.G.S. Certificate of Advanced Graduate Study.

CAI computer-aided instruction; computer-assisted instruction. Also, **cai**

Cal kilocalorie.

cal 1. calibrate. **2.** calorie.

Cal. California.

cal. 1. calendar. **2.** caliber. **3.** calorie.

calc. calculate.

Calif. California.

CAM (kam), computer-aided manufacturing.

Cam. Cambridge.

cam. camber.

CAMA (kam/ə), *Telecommunications.* centralized automatic message accounting.

Camb. Cambridge.

camflg camouflage.

cAMP *Biochemistry.* cyclic AMP.

camr camera.

Can. 1. Canada. **2.** Canadian.

can. 1. canceled. **2.** canon. **3.** canto.

Canad. Canadian.

canc. 1. cancel. **2.** canceled.
3. cancellation.

cand candelabra.

C. & F. *Commerce.* cost and freight.

C&I 1. commerce and industry.
2. commercial and industrial.

c&sc *Printing.* capitals and small
capitals.

cand scr candelabra screw.

C and W country-and-western.
Also, **C&W**

CanF Canadian French.

Cant. 1. Canterbury. **2.** Cantonese.

cantil cantilever.

canv canvas.

CAP 1. Civil Air Patrol. **2.** Common
Agricultural Policy. **3.** computer-aided
publishing. **4.** *Stock Exchange.* convertible adjustable preferred (stock).
Also, **C.A.P.** (for defs. 1, 2, 4).

cap. 1. capacitance, capacitor.
2. capacity. **3.** (in prescriptions) let
the patient take. [from Latin *capiat*]
4. capital. **5.** capitalize. **6.** capitalized.
7. capital letter. **8.** chapter. [from
Latin *capitulum, caput*] **9.** computer-
aided production.

cap. moll. (in prescriptions) soft
capsule. [from Latin *capsula mollis*]

caps. 1. capital letters. **2.** (in prescriptions) a capsule [from Latin
capsula].

cap scr cap screw.

capt. *Military.* captain. Also, **CPT**

CAR computer-assisted retrieval.

car. 1. carat; carats. **2.** cargo.

carb carburetor.

Card. Cardinal.

CARE (kâr), Cooperative for American Relief Everywhere. Also, **Care**

Caricom (kar′i kom′, kâr′-), an
economic association formed in
1974 by ten Caribbean nations.
Also, **CARICOM** [*Cari(bbean)
com(munity)*]

Carol. Carolingian.

carp. carpentry.

carr carrier.

carr cur carrier current.

CAS collision-avoidance system.

cas 1. calculated airspeed. **2.** castle.

C.A.S. Certificate of Advanced
Studies.

case computer-aided support
equipment.

cas nut castle nut.

CAT 1. clear-air turbulence. **2.** *Medicine.* computerized axial tomography.

cat. 1. catalog; catalogue. **2.** catapult.
3. catechism.

cate computer-aided test equipment.

cath *Electricity.* cathode.

Cath. 1. (*often lowercase*) cathedral.
2. Catholic.

CATV community antenna television
(a cable television system).

caus. causative.

cav. 1. cavalier. **2.** cavalry. **3.** cavity.

cax community automatic exchange.

CB 1. Citizens Band (radio). **2.** *Military.* construction battalion. **3.** continental breakfast.

Cb *Symbol, Chemistry.* columbium.

cb 1. *Electronics.* common base.
2. *Telephones.* common battery.

C.B. 1. Bachelor of Surgery. [from
Latin *Chīrurgiae Baccalaureus*]
2. *British.* Companion of the Bath.

cbal counterbalance.

CBAT College Board Achievement
Test.

CBC 1. Also, **C.B.C.** Canadian Broadcasting Corporation. **2.** *Medicine.*
complete blood count.

C.B.D. 1. cash before delivery.
2. central business district.

C.B.E. Commander of the Order of
the British Empire.

C.B.E.L. Cambridge Bibliography of
English Literature. Also, **CBEL**

CBI computer-based instruction.

CBO Congressional Budget Office.

cbore counterbore.

cboreo counterbore other side.

CBS Columbia Broadcasting System.

CBT 1. Chicago Board of Trade. 2. computer-based training.

CBW chemical and biological warfare.

CC *Symbol.* a quality rating for a corporate or municipal bond, lower than CCC and higher than C.

Cc cirrocumulus.

cc 1. carbon copy. 2. close-coupled. 3. closing coil. 4. *Electronics.* common collector. 5. copies. 6. cross-couple. 7. cubic centimeter.

cc. 1. carbon copy. 2. chapters. 3. copies. 4. cubic centimeter. Also, **c.c.**

C.C. 1. carbon copy. 2. cashier's check. 3. chief clerk. 4. circuit court. 5. city council. 6. city councilor. 7. civil court. 8. company commander. 9. county clerk. 10. county commissioner. 11. county council. 12. county court. Also, **c.c.**

C.C.A. 1. Chief Clerk of the Admiralty. 2. Circuit Court of Appeals. 3. County Court of Appeals.

CCC 1. Civilian Conservation Corps. 2. Commodity Credit Corporation. 3. copyright clearance center.

CCD 1. *Electronics.* charge-coupled device. 2. Confraternity of Christian Doctrine.

ccf hundred cubic feet (used of gas).

ccg *Electricity.* constant-current generator.

C.C.I.A. Consumer Credit Insurance Association.

CCITT Consultative Committee for International Telephony and Telegraphy.

CCK *Physiology.* cholecystokinin.

C.Cls. Court of Claims.

CCM counter-countermeasures.

ccm *Electricity.* constant-current modulation.

ccn contract change notice.

cco crystal-controlled oscillator.

CCP Chinese Communist Party.

C.C.P. 1. *Law.* Code of Civil Procedure. 2. Court of Common Pleas.

CCR Commission on Civil Rights.

ccs 1. *Telephones.* common-channel signaling. 2. continuous commercial service.

cct *Electricity.* constant-current transformer.

CCTV closed-circuit television.

CCU coronary-care unit.

ccu camera control unit.

ccw counterclockwise.

CD 1. *Finance.* certificate of deposit. 2. Civil Defense. 3. Community Development. 4. compact disk.

Cd *Symbol, Chemistry.* cadmium.

cd 1. candela; candelas. 2. card. 3. circuit description. 4. cold drawn. 5. Also, **cd.** cord; cords. 6. current density.

C/D certificate of deposit. Also, **c/d**

C.D. 1. *Finance.* certificate of deposit. 2. Civil Defense. 3. civil disobedience. 4. Congressional District.

c.d. cash discount.

CDC Centers for Disease Control.

cdc cold-drawn copper.

cdel constant delivery.

cdf *Telephones.* combined distributing frame.

cdg coding.

CD-P compact disc-photographic.

cd pl cadmium plate.

Cdr. Commander. Also, **CDR**

cd rdr card reader.

cdrill counterdrill.

CD-ROM (sē′dē′rom′), a compact disk on which digitized read-only data can be stored. [*c(ompact) d(isk) r(ead-)o(nly) m(emory)*]

cds cold-drawn steel.

CDT Central daylight time. Also, C.D.T.

CDTA Capital District Transportation Authority.

cdx control-differential transmitter.

Ce *Symbol, Chemistry.* cerium.

ce 1. *Electronics.* common emitter. **2.** communications-electronics.

C.E. 1. Chemical Engineer. **2.** chief engineer. **3.** Christian Era. **4.** Church of England. **5.** Civil Engineer. **6.** common era. **7.** Corps of Engineers.

c.e. 1. buyer's risk. [from Latin *cāveat emptor* may the buyer beware] **2.** compass error.

CEA Council of Economic Advisers.

CEEB College Entrance Examination Board.

C.E.F. Canadian Expeditionary Force.

Cels. Celsius.

Celt. Celtic.

CEM communications electronics meteorological.

cem cement.

CEMA Council for Economic Mutual Assistance.

cemf counter electromotive force.

cen. 1. central. **2.** century.

cent. 1. centigrade. **2.** central. **3.** centum. **4.** century.

CEO chief executive officer. Also, C.E.O.

cephalom. cephalometry.

cer ceramic.

Cer.E. Ceramic Engineer.

cermet (sûr′met), ceramic-to-metal: a type of seal.

CERN (sârn, sûrn), European Laboratory for Particle Physics; formerly called European Organization for Nuclear Research. [from French *C(onseil) e(uropéen pour la) r(echerche) n(ucléaire)*]

cert. 1. certificate. **2.** certification. **3.** certified. **4.** certify.

certif. 1. certificate. **2.** certificated.

CETA (sē′tə), Comprehensive Employment and Training Act.

cet. par. other things being equal. [from Latin *ceteris paribus*]

CF 1. *Baseball.* center field. **2.** *Baseball.* center fielder. **3.** Christian female. **4.** Also, **cf** cubic foot; cubic feet. **5.** cystic fibrosis.

Cf *Symbol, Chemistry.* californium.

cf 1. cathode follower. **2.** center field. **3.** center fielder. **4.** centrifugal force. **5.** concrete floor.

cf. 1. *Bookbinding.* calf. **2.** *Music.* cantus firmus. **3.** compare [from Latin *confer*].

c.f. 1. *Baseball.* center field. **2.** *Baseball.* center fielder. **3.** cost and freight.

c/f *Bookkeeping.* carried forward.

C.F. cost and freight.

CFA chartered financial analyst.

CFAE contractor-furnished aircraft equipment.

cfd cubic feet per day.

CFE contractor-furnished equipment.

CFG Camp Fire Girls.

cfh cubic feet per hour.

C.F.I. cost, freight, and insurance. Also, **c.f.i.**

CFL Canadian Football League.

cfm cubic feet per minute.

CFNP Community Food and Nutrition Programs.

CFO chief financial officer. Also, C.F.O.

CFP 1. certified financial planner. **2.** contractor-furnished property.

CFR Code of Federal Regulations.

cfr crossfire.

CFS chronic fatigue syndrome.

cfs 1. cold-finished steel. **2.** cubic feet per second.

CFT *Medicine.* complement fixation test.

CFTC Commodity Futures Trading Commission.

CG Commanding General.

cg centigram; centigrams.

C.G. 1. Captain of the Guard. **2.** center of gravity. **3.** Coast Guard. **4.** Commanding General. **5.** Consul General.

c.g. 1. Captain of the Guard. **2.** center of gravity. **3.** Commanding General. **4.** Consul General.

CGA *Computers.* color graphics adapter.

cgs centimeter-gram-second (system). Also, **CGS, c.g.s.**

ch 1. case harden. **2.** *Surveying, Civil Engineering.* chain; chains. **3.** channel. **4.** chiffonier. **5.** *Electricity.* choke.

Ch. 1. Chaldean. **2.** Chaldee. **3.** *Television.* channel. **4.** chapter. **5.** Château. **6.** *Chess.* check. **7.** China. **8.** Chinese. **9.** church.

ch. 1. chair. **2.** chaplain. **3.** chapter. **4.** *Chess.* check. **5.** chief. **6.** child; children. **7.** church.

c.h. 1. candle hours. **2.** clearinghouse. **3.** courthouse. **4.** custom house.

chal challenge.

Chal. 1. Chaldaic. **2.** Chaldean. **3.** Chaldee.

Chald. 1. Chaldaic. **2.** Chaldean. **3.** Chaldee.

cham chamfer.

Chan. 1. Chancellor. **2.** Chancery. Also, **Chanc.**

chan. channel.

chanc. 1. chancellor. **2.** chancery.

chap. 1. Chaplain. **2.** chapter. Also, **Chap.**

char. 1. character. **2.** charter.

chart. (in prescriptions) paper. [from Latin *charta*]

chart. cerat. (in prescriptions) waxed paper. [from Latin *charta cērāta*]

chas chassis.

Chât. (especially in Bordeaux wines) Château.

Ch.B. Bachelor of Surgery. [from Latin *Chīrurgiae Baccalaureus*]

chc choke coil.

chd chord.

Ch.E. Chemical Engineer.

Chem. 1. chemical. **2.** chemist. **3.** chemistry.

Chem.E. Chemical Engineer.

chg. 1. change. **2.** charge. Also, **chge.**

chgov changeover.

Chin. 1. China. **2.** Chinese. Also, **Chin**

Ch. J. Chief Justice.

chk check.

chkb check bit.

chld chilled.

chm. 1. chairman. **2.** checkmate.

chmbr chamber.

chmn. chairman.

chng change.

choc. chocolate.

chp 1. chairperson. **2.** chopper.

CHQ Corps Headquarters.

chr chroma.

Chr. 1. Christ. **2.** Christian.

Chron. *Bible.* Chronicles.

chron. 1. chronicle. **2.** chronograph. **3.** chronological. **4.** chronology.

chrst characteristic.

chs. chapters.

chw chairwoman.

CI counterintelligence.

Ci curie; curies.

ci 1. cast iron. **2.** circuit interrupter.

C.I. Channel Islands.

CIA Central Intelligence Agency. Also, **C.I.A.**

Cia. Company. Also, **cia.** [from Spanish *Compaìía*]

cib. (in prescriptions) food. [from Latin *cibus*]

C.I.C. **1.** Combat Information Center. **2.** Commander in Chief. **3.** Counterintelligence Corps.

cid component identification.

C.I.D. Criminal Investigation Department (of Scotland Yard).

c.i.d. *Automotive.* cubic-inch displacement: the displacement of an engine measured in cubic inches. Also, **cid, CID**

Cie. Company. Also, **cie.** [from French *Compagnie*]

C.I.F. *Commerce.* cost, insurance, and freight (the price quoted includes the cost of the merchandise, packing, and freight to a specified destination plus insurance charges). Also, **CIF, c.i.f.**

CIM **1.** computer input from microfilm. **2.** computer-integrated manufacturing.

C. in C. Commander in Chief. Also, **C-in-C**

cine cinematographic.

C.I.O. **1.** chief investment officer. **2.** Congress of Industrial Organizations. Also, **CIO**

CIP Cataloging in Publication: a program in which a partial bibliographic description of a work appears on the verso of its title page.

cip cast-iron pipe.

Cir. circle (approved for postal use).

cir. **1.** about: *cir. 1800.* [from Latin *circā, circiter, circum*] **2.** circle. **3.** circular.

circ (sûrk), circular.

circ. **1.** about: *circ. 1800.* [from Latin *circā, circiter, circum*] **2.** circuit. **3.** circular. **4.** circulation. **5.** circumference.

circum. circumference.

CIS *Computers.* CompuServe Information Services.

C.I.S. Commonwealth of Independent States.

CISC (sisk), complex instruction set computer.

cit. **1.** citation. **2.** cited. **3.** citizen. **4.** citrate.

C.I.T. counselor in training.

ciu computer interface unit.

Civ. **1.** civil. **2.** civilian.

CJ Chief Justice.

ck. **1.** cask. **2.** check. **3.** cook. **4.** cork.

ckb cork base.

ckbd corkboard.

ckpt cockpit.

ckt circuit.

ckt brkr circuit breaker.

ckt cl circuit closing.

ckt op circuit opening.

CL common law.

Cl *Symbol, Chemistry.* chlorine.

cl **1.** center line. **2.** centiliter; centiliters. **3.** class. **4.** closed loop. **5.** closing. **6.** clutch.

cl. **1.** carload. **2.** claim. **3.** clarinet. **4.** class. **5.** classification. **6.** clause. **7.** clearance. **8.** clerk. **9.** close. **10.** closet. **11.** cloth.

C/L **1.** carload. **2.** carload lot. **3.** cash letter.

c.l. **1.** carload. **2.** carload lot. **3.** center line. **4.** civil law. **5.** common law.

CLA College Language Association.

clar. clarinet.

class. **1.** classic. **2.** classical. **3.** classification. **4.** classified.

cld. **1.** *Stock Exchange.* (of bonds) called. **2.** cleared. **3.** cooled.

cldy cloudy.

clg **1.** ceiling. **2.** cooling.

CLI cost-of-living index. Also, **cli**

clin. clinical.

clk. **1.** clerk. **2.** clock.

clkg caulking.

clkj caulked joint.

cln clean.

clnc clearance.

clnt coolant.

clo. clothing.

clos *Real Estate.* closet.

clp clamp.

clpbd *Real Estate.* clapboard.

clpr clapper.

clp scr clamp screw.

clr. 1. clear. 2. color. 3. cooler. 4. current-limiting resistor.

clrg clearing.

cls classify.

clt cleat.

clthg clothing.

CLU Civil Liberties Union.

C.L.U. Chartered Life Underwriter.

clws. clockwise.

CM 1. Christian male. 2. Common Market. 3. countermeasures.

Cm *Symbol, Chemistry.* curium.

cm 1. Also, **cm.** centimeter; centimeters. 2. *Computers.* core memory. 3. corrective maintenance.

c/m (of capital stocks) call of more.

C.M. *Roman Catholic Church.* Congregation of the Mission.

c.m. 1. church missionary. 2. common meter. 3. corresponding member. 4. court martial.

cm³ *Symbol.* cubic centimeter.

CMA Canadian Medical Association.

C.M.A. certificate of management accounting.

CMC 1. certified management consultant. 2. Commandant of the Marine Corps.

cmd *Computers.* core-memory drive.

cmd. command.

cmdg. commanding.

Cmdr. Commander.

Cmdre Commodore.

CME Chicago Mercantile Exchange.

CMEA Council for Mutual Economic Assistance. See **COMECON.**

cmf coherent memory filter.

cmflr cam follower.

C.M.G. Companion of the Order of St. Michael and St. George.

CMI computer-managed instruction. Also, **cmi**

cmil circular Military.

CML current-mode logic.

cml. commercial.

cmnt comment.

CMOS (sē′môs′, -mos′), *Electronics.* complementary metal oxide semiconductor.

CMP *Biochemistry.* cytidine monophosphate.

cmpd compound.

cmplm complement.

cmplt complete.

cmpns compensate.

cmpnt component.

cmpr compare.

cmps compass.

cmpsg compensating.

cmpsn composition.

cmpst composite.

cmpt compute.

cmptg computing.

cmptr computer.

cmrlr cam roller.

CMS *Printing.* color management system.

cms current-mode switching.

cmshft camshaft.

cmsn commission.

Cmsr Commissioner.

cmte committee.

CMV *Pathology.* cytomegalovirus.

CMYK *Computers, Printing.* cyan, magenta, yellow, black; used for color mixing for printing.

CN 1. change notice. 2. chloroacetophenone: used as a tear gas.

C/N 1. circular note. 2. credit note.

cna copper-nickel alloy.

cncl concealed.

cnctrc concentric.

cncv concave.

cnd conduit.

cndct *Electricity.* **1.** conduct. **2.** conductivity. **3.** conductor.

cnds condensate.

cndtn condition.

cnfig configuration.

CNM Certified Nurse Midwife.

CNN Cable News Network (a cable television channel).

CNO Chief of Naval Operations.

CNS central nervous system. Also, **cns**

cnsld consolidate.

cnsltnt consultant.

cnsp conspicuously.

cnstr canister.

cntbd centerboard.

cntd contained.

cntor *Electricity.* contactor.

cnvc convenience.

cnvr conveyor.

cnvt convert.

cnvtb convertible.

cnvtr converter.

cnvx convex.

CO **1.** change order. **2.** Colorado (for use with ZIP code). **3.** Commanding Officer. **4.** conscientious objector.

Co *Symbol, Chemistry.* cobalt.

co **1.** carbon monoxide. **2.** cardiac output. **3.** cutoff. **4.** cutout.

Co. **1.** Company. **2.** County. Also, **co.**

C/O **1.** cash order. **2.** *Commerce.* certificate of origin.

C/o **1.** care of. **2.** *Bookkeeping.* carried over.

c/o **1.** care of. **2.** *Bookkeeping.* carried over. **3.** cash order. **4.** consist of.

C.O. **1.** cash order. **2.** Commanding Officer. **3.** conscientious objector. **4.** correction officer.

c.o. **1.** care of. **2.** *Bookkeeping.* carried over.

COA change of address.

CoA *Biochemistry.* coenzyme A.

coam coaming.

coax (kō′aks), *Electronics.* coaxial (cable).

COBOL (kō′bôl), *Computers.* a programming language. [*Co(mmon) B(usiness-)O(riented) L(anguage)*]

coch. (in prescriptions) a spoonful. [from Latin *cochlear*]

coch. amp. (in prescriptions) a tablespoonful. [from Latin *cochlear amplum* large spoon(ful)]

coch. mag. (in prescriptions) a tablespoonful. [from Latin *cochlear magnum* large spoon(ful)]

coch. med. (in prescriptions) a dessertspoonful. [from Latin *coch-lear medium* medium-sized spoon(ful)]

coch. parv. (in prescriptions) a teaspoonful. [from Latin *cochlear parvum* little spoon(ful)]

COD. codex. Also, **cod.**

C.O.D. *Commerce.* cash, or collect, on delivery (payment to be made when delivered to the purchaser). Also, **c.o.d.**

coef coefficient.

COFC container-on-flatcar.

C of C Chamber of Commerce.

coff cofferdam.

C. of S. Chief of Staff.

cog. **1.** cognate. **2.** cognizant.

coho coherent oscillator.

COIN (koin), counterinsurgency. [*co(unter) in(surgency)*]

COL **1.** Computer-Oriented Language. Also, **col** **2.** cost of living.

Col. **1.** Colombia. **2.** Colonel. **3.** Colorado. **4.** *Bible.* Colossians.

col. **1.** (in prescriptions) strain. [from Latin *colā*] **2.** collected. **3.** collector. **4.** college. **5.** collegiate. **6.** colonial. **7.** colony. **8.** color. **9.** colored. **10.** column.

COLA (kō′lə), a clause, especially in union contracts, that grants automatic wage increases to cover the rising cost of living due to inflation. [*c(ost) o(f) l(iving) a(djustment)*]

colat. (in prescriptions) strained. [from Latin *colātus*]

colent. (in prescriptions) let them be strained. Also, **colen.** [from Latin *colentur*]

colet. (in prescriptions) let it be strained. [from Latin *colētur*]

colidar coherent light detection and ranging.

coll. 1. collateral. 2. collect. 3. collection. 4. collective. 5. collector. 6. Also, **Coll.** college. 7. collegiate. 8. colloquial. 9. (in prescriptions) an eyewash. [from Latin *collȳrium*]

collab. 1. collaboration. 2. collaborator.

collat. collateral.

colloq. 1. colloquial. 2. colloquialism. 3. colloquially.

collun. (in prescriptions) a nose wash. [from Latin *collunarium*]

collut. (in prescriptions) a mouthwash. [from Latin *collūtorium*]

collyr. (in prescriptions) an eyewash. [from Latin *collȳrium*]

Colo. Colorado.

colog *Math.* cologarithm.

color. (in prescriptions) let it be colored. [from Latin *colōrētur*]

COM (kom), 1. Comedy Central (a cable channel). 2. computer output on microfilm.

Com. 1. Commander. 2. Commission. 3. Commissioner. 4. Committee. 5. Commodore. 6. Commonwealth.

com. 1. comedy. 2. comma. 3. command. 4. commander. 5. commerce. 6. commercial. 7. commission. 8. commissioner. 9. committee. 10. common. 11. commonly. 12. communications.

comb. 1. combination. 2. combined. 3. combining. 4. combustion.

combl combustible.

comd. command.

comdg. commanding.

Comdr. commander. Also, **comdr.**

Comdt. commandant. Also, **comdt.**

COMECON (kom′i kon′), an economic association of Communist countries. Also, **Comecon, CMEA** [*Co(uncil for) M(utual) Econ(omic) Assistance)*]

COMEX (kō′meks), Commodity Exchange, New York.

Com. in Chf. Commander in Chief.

coml. commercial.

comm 1. communication. 2. commutator.

comm. 1. commander. 2. commerce. 3. commission. 4. committee. 5. commonwealth. Also, **Comm.**

comp. 1. companion. 2. comparative. 3. compare. 4. compensation. 5. compilation. 6. compiled. 7. compiler. 8. complement. 9. complete. 10. composition. 11. compositor. 12. compound. 13. comprehensive.

compander *Audio.* compressor-expander.

compar. comparative.

compass *Computers.* compiler-assembler.

compd. compound.

Comp. Gen. Comptroller General.

compl complete.

compn compensate.

compt. 1. compartment. 2. Also, **Compt.** comptroller.

comptr comparator.

Comr. Commissioner.

Com•sat (kom′sat′), *Trademark.* a privately owned corporation servicing the global communications satellite system. [*Com(munications) Sat(ellite) Corporation)*]

Con. 1. *Religion.* Conformist. 2. Consul.

con. 1. concerto. 2. conclusion. 3. connection. 4. consolidated. 5. consul. 6. continued. 7. against [from Latin *contrā*].

CONAD (kon′ad), Continental Air Defense Command.

conc. 1. concentrate. 2. concentrated. 3. concentration. 4. concerning. 5. concrete.

concl conclusion.

concr concrete.

cond. 1. condenser. 2. condition. 3. conditional. 4. conductivity. 5. conductor.

conf. 1. (in prescriptions) a confection. [from Latin *confectiō*] 2. compare. [from Latin *confer*] 3. conference. 4. confessor. 5. confidential. 6. conformance.

confed. 1. confederacy. 2. confederate. 3. confederation. Also, **Confed.**

Cong. 1. Congregational. 2. Congregationalist. 3. Congress. 4. Congressional.

cong. gallon. [from Latin *congius*]

congr congruent.

coni conical.

conj. 1. conjugation. 2. conjunction. 3. conjunctive.

conn connect, connector.

Conn. Connecticut.

conn diag connection diagram.

Cons. 1. Conservative. 2. Constable. 3. Constitution. 4. Consul. 5. Consulting.

cons. 1. consecrated. 2. conservative. 3. (in prescriptions) conserve; keep. [from Latin *conservā*] 4. consolidated. 5. consonant. 6. constable. 7. constitution. 8. constitutional.

9. construction. 10. consul. 11. consulting.

consec consecutive.

consol. consolidated.

conspec construction specification.

consperg. (in prescriptions) dust; sprinkle. [from Latin *consperge*]

Const. Constitution.

const. 1. constable. 2. constant. 3. constitution. 4. constitutional. 5. construction.

constr. 1. constraint. 2. construction. 3. construed.

cont 1. contact. 2. continue. 3. continued. 4. continuous.

Cont. Continental.

cont. 1. containing. 2. contents. 3. continent. 4. continental. 5. continue. 6. continued. 7. contra. 8. contract. 9. contraction. 10. control. 11. (in prescriptions) bruised [from Latin *contūsus*].

contd. continued.

contemp. contemporary.

contg. containing.

contin. continued.

contr. 1. contract. 2. contracted. 3. contraction. 4. contractor. 5. contralto. 6. contrary. 7. contrasted. 8. control. 9. controller.

cont. rem. (in prescriptions) let the medicines be continued. [from Latin *continuāntur remedia*]

contrib. 1. contribution. 2. contributor.

contro contracting officer.

conv. 1. convention. 2. conventional. 3. convertible. 4. convocation.

convn convection.

COO chief operating officer.

coop. cooperative. Also, **co-op.**

coord coordinate.

COP *Thermodynamics.* coefficient of performance.

Cop. 1. Copernican. 2. Coptic.

cop. **1.** copper. **2.** copyright; copyrighted.

COPD chronic obstructive pulmonary disease.

cop pl copper plate.

Cor. **1.** *Bible.* Corinthians. **2.** Coroner.

cor. **1.** corner. **2.** cornet. **3.** coroner. **4.** corpus. **5.** correct. **6.** corrected. **7.** correction. **8.** correlative. **9.** correspondence. **10.** correspondent. **11.** corresponding.

CORE (kôr, kōr), Congress of Racial Equality. Also, **C.O.R.E.**

Corn. **1.** Cornish. **2.** Cornwall.

coroll. corollary. Also, **corol.**

corp. **1.** corporal. **2.** corporation. Also, **Corp.**

corpl. corporal. Also, **Corpl.**

corpn. corporation.

corr. **1.** correct. **2.** corrected. **3.** correction. **4.** correspond. **5.** correspondence. **6.** correspondent. **7.** corresponding. **8.** corrugated. **9.** corrupt. **10.** corrupted. **11.** corruption.

correl. correlative.

corresp. correspondence.

corspnd correspond.

cort. (in prescriptions) the bark. [from Latin *cortex*]

cos *Trigonometry.* cosine.

cos. **1.** companies. **2.** consul. **3.** consulship. **4.** counties.

C.O.S. cash on shipment. Also, **c.o.s.**

cosh *Trigonometry.* hyperbolic cosine.

cot **1.** *Trigonometry.* cotangent. **2.** cotter pin.

coth *Trigonometry.* hyperbolic cotangent.

cov cutoff valve.

covers *Trigonometry.* coversed sine.

cowl cowling.

COWPS Council on Wage and Price Stability.

CP **1.** candlepower. **2.** *Pharmacology.* chemically pure.

cP *Physics.* centipoise. Also, **cp**

cp. **1.** camp. **2.** center punch. **3.** cerebral palsy. **4.** clock pulse. **5.** command post. **6.** compare. **7.** constant pressure.

C.P. **1.** Chief Patriarch. **2.** command post. **3.** Common Pleas. **4.** Common Prayer. **5.** Communist Party.

c.p. **1.** chemically pure. **2.** circular pitch. **3.** command post. **4.** common pleas.

C.P.A. **1.** certified public accountant. **2.** chartered public accountant.

CPB Corporation for Public Broadcasting. Also, **C.P.B.**

cpch prop controllable-pitch propeller.

CPCU *Insurance.* Chartered Property and Casualty Underwriter. Also, **C.P.C.U.**

cpd. compound.

CPFF cost plus fixed fee.

CPI **1.** consumer price index. **2.** cost plus incentive.

cpi characters per inch.

cpl couple.

cpl. corporal. Also, **Cpl.**

cpld coupled.

cplg coupling.

cplr coupler.

cplry capillary.

CPM **1.** *Commerce.* cost per thousand. **2.** Critical Path Method.

cpm **1.** card per minute. **2.** *Commerce.* cost per thousand. **3.** critical-path method. **4.** cycles per minute.

CP/M *Trademark.* Control Program/Microprocessors: a microcomputer operating system.

c.p.m. *Music.* common particular meter.

cpntr carpenter.

CPO chief petty officer. Also, **C.P.O.**, **c.p.o.**

CPR cardiopulmonary resuscitation.

cprs compress.

cprsn compression.

cprsr compressor.

CPS certified professional secretary.

cps 1. *Computers.* characters per second. **2.** cycles per second.

cpse counterpoise.

cpt critical-path technique.

cpt. counterpoint.

CPU *Computers.* central processing unit.

cpunch counterpunch.

CQ 1. *Radio.* a signal sent at the beginning of radiograms. **2.** *Military.* charge of quarters.

CR 1. conditioned reflex; conditioned response. **2.** consciousness-raising. **3.** critical ratio.

Cr *Symbol, Chemistry.* chromium.

cr 1. cold rolled. **2.** controlled rectifier. **3.** control relay. **4.** crystal rectifier. **5.** current relay.

cr. 1. credit. **2.** creditor. **3.** crown.

C.R. 1. Costa Rica. **2.** *Banking.* credit report.

CRC Civil Rights Commission.

crc *Computers.* cyclical redundancy check.

crclt circulate.

crcmf circumference.

crctn correction.

cre corrosion-resistant.

Cres. crescent (in addresses).

cres corrosion-resistant steel.

CRF *Biochemistry.* corticotropin releasing factor.

crg carriage.

crim. criminal.

crim. con. *Law.* criminal conversation.

criminol. 1. criminologist. **2.** criminology.

crit. 1. critic. **2.** critical. **3.** criticism. **4.** criticized.

crk crank.

crkc crankcase.

CRM counter-radar measures.

crn 1. crane. **2.** crown.

crnmtr chronometer.

cro cathode-ray oscilloscope.

CRP *Biochemistry.* C-reactive protein.

crp crimp.

crpt carpet.

crs 1. coarse. **2.** cold-rolled steel.

crs. 1. creditors. **2.** credits.

crsn corrosion.

crsv corrosive.

crsvr crossover.

CRT cathode-ray tube.

crtg 1. cartridge. **2.** crating.

crv curve.

cryo cryogenic.

crypta cryptanalysis.

crypto cryptography.

cryst. 1. crystalline. **2.** crystallized. **3.** crystallography.

Cs *Symbol, Chemistry.* cesium.

cS *Physics.* centistoke; centistokes. Also, **cs**

cs 1. case; cases. **2.** cast steel. **3.** control switch. **4.** *Computers.* core shift.

C/S cycles per second.

C.S. 1. chief of staff. **2.** Christian Science. **3.** Christian Scientist. **4.** Civil Service. **5.** Confederate States.

c.s. 1. capital stock. **2.** civil service.

CSA Community Services Administration.

C.S.A. Confederate States of America.

CSC Civil Service Commission.

csc *Trigonometry.* cosecant.

CSCE Conference on Security and Cooperation in Europe.

csch *Trigonometry.* hyperbolic cosecant.

csd *Computers.* core-shift drive.

CSEA Civil Service Employees Association.

CSF *Physiology.* cerebrospinal fluid.

csg casing.

cshaft crankshaft.

csk. 1. cask. **2.** countersink.

cskh countersunk head.

C.S.O. 1. Chief Signal Officer.
2. Chief Staff Officer. Also, **CSO**

CSP C-SPAN (a cable channel).

C-SPAN (sē′span′), Cable Satellite
Public Affairs Network (a cable
channel).

CSR 1. Certified Shorthand
Reporter. **2.** customer service representative.

csr customer signature required.

CST 1. Also, **C.S.T., c.s.t.** Central
Standard Time. **2.** convulsive shock
therapy.

cstl castellate.

CSW Certified Social Worker. Also,
C.S.W.

Cswy. causeway.

CT 1. Central time. **2.** Connecticut
(for use with ZIP code).

ct 1. control transformer. **2.** current
transformer.

Ct. 1. Connecticut. **2.** Count.

ct. 1. carat; carats. **2.** cent; cents.
3. centum; hundred. **4.** certificate.
5. county. **6.** Also, **Ct.** court.

C.T. Central time.

CTA commodities trading adviser.

C.T.A. *Law.* with the will annexed.
[from Latin *cum testāmentō annexō*]

CTC 1. centralized traffic control.
2. Citizens' Training Corps.

ctd coated.

ctf certificate.

ctg. 1. Also, **ctge.** cartage. **2.** cartridge. **3.** coating. **4.** cutting.

CTL 1. *Computers.* complementary
transistor logic. **2.** core transistor
logic.

ctlry cutlery.

ctlst catalyst.

ct/m count per minute.

ctn *Trigonometry.* cotangent.

ctn. carton.

ctnr container.

c to c center to center.

ctr. 1. center. **2.** contour. **3.** cutter.

ctrfgl centrifugal.

ctrg centering.

ctrl central.

ctrlr controller.

ctrst contrast.

CTS Cleveland Transit System.

cts. 1. centimes. **2.** cents.
3. certificates.

ct/s count per second.

ctshft countershaft.

CTU centigrade thermal unit. Also,
ctu

ctwlk catwalk.

ctwt counterweight.

cty county.

CU close-up.

Cu *Symbol, Chemistry.* copper. [from
Latin *cuprum*]

cu 1. cubic. **2.** *Electronics.* crystal unit.

Cu. cumulus.

cu. 1. cubic. **2.** cumulus.

cub. 1. cubic. **2.** cubicle.

cu. ft. cubic foot; cubic feet.

cu. in. cubic inch; cubic inches.

cuj. (in prescriptions) of which; of
any. [from Latin *cūjus*]

culv culvert.

cu m cubic meter.

cum. cumulative.

cu mm cubic millimeter.

cuo copper oxide.

cup cupboard.

cur. 1. currency. **2.** current.

cust. 1. custodian. **2.** custody.
3. customer.

cu yd cubic yard.

CV 1. cardiovascular. **2.** Also, **C.V.**
curriculum vitae.

cv 1. continuously variable. **2.** Also,
cvt. convertible. **3.** counter voltage.

CVA 1. *Pathology.* cerebrovascular accident. 2. Columbia Valley Authority.

CVD *Commerce.* countervailing duty.

CVJ *Automotive.* constant-velocity joint.

cvntl conventional.

C.V.O. Commander of the Royal Victorian Order.

cvr cover.

cvrsn conversion.

CVT continuously variable transmission.

CW 1. chemical warfare. 2. *Radio.* continuous wave.

cw 1. clockwise. 2. continuous wave.

c/w complete with.

CWA 1. Civil Works Administration. 2. Communications Workers of America.

CWO *Military.* chief warrant officer.

c.w.o. cash with order.

CWPS Council on Wage and Price Stability.

cwt hundredweight; hundredweights.

cx control transmitter.

CY calendar year.

Cy. county.

cy. 1. capacity. 2. currency. 3. cycle; cycles.

CYA *Slang (sometimes vulgar).* cover your ass.

CYC *Biochemistry.* cyclophosphamide.

cyc. cyclopedia.

cyl. 1. cylinder. 2. cylindrical.

Cym. Cymric.

CYO Catholic Youth Organization.

Cys *Biochemistry.* cysteine.

cytol. 1. cytological. 2. cytology.

C.Z. Canal Zone. Also, **CZ**

D

D 1. *Electricity.* debye. 2. deep. 3. depth. 4. *Optics.* diopter. 5. divorced. 6. Dutch.

D *Symbol.* 1. the fourth in order or in a series. 2. (in some grading systems) a grade or mark, indicating the quality of a student's work as poor or barely passing. 3. (*sometimes lowercase*) a classification, rating, or the like, indicating poor quality. 4. *Music.* **a.** the second tone in the scale of C major, or the fourth tone in the relative minor scale, A minor. **b.** a string, key, or pipe tuned to this tone. **c.** a written or printed note representing this tone. **d.** (in the fixed system of solmization) the second tone of the scale of C major, called *re*. **e.** the tonality having D as the tonic note. 5. (*sometimes lowercase*) the Roman numeral for 500. 6. *Chemistry.* deuterium. 7. *Electricity.* **a.** electric displace-

ment. **b.** a battery size for 1.5 volt dry cells: diameter, 1.3 in. (3.3 cm); length, 2.4 in. (6 cm). 8. *Biochemistry.* aspartic acid. 9. a proportional shoe width size, narrower than E and wider than C. 10. a proportional brassiere cup size, larger than C. 11. *Physics.* darcy.

D- *Symbol, Biochemistry.* (of a molecule) having a configuration resembling the dextrorotatory isomer of glyceraldehyde: always printed as a small capital, roman character (distinguished from *l-*). Cf. *d-*.

d- *Symbol, Chemistry, Biochemistry.* dextrorotatory; dextro- (distinguished from *l-*). Cf. **D-**.

D. 1. day. 2. December. 3. Democrat. 4. Democratic. 5. *Physics.* density. 6. Deus. 7. *Bible.* Deuteronomy. 8. Doctor. 9. dose. 10. Dutch.

d. 1. (in prescriptions) give. [from Latin *dā*] 2. date. 3. daughter. 4. day.

5. deceased. **6.** deep. **7.** degree. **8.** delete. **9.** *British.* pence. [from Latin *denāriī*] **10.** *British.* penny. [from Latin *denārius*] **11.** *Physics.* density. **12.** depth. **13.** deputy. **14.** dialect. **15.** dialectal. **16.** diameter. **17.** died. **18.** dime. **19.** dividend. **20.** dollar; dollars. **21.** dose. **22.** drachma.

DA 1. Department of Agriculture. **2.** *Dictionary of Americanisms.* **3.** a male hairstyle in which the hair is slicked back on both sides to overlap at the back of the head. [euphemistic abbreviation of *duck's ass*]

da *Telecommunications.* don't answer.

d-a *Electronics.* digital-to-analog.

DA. (in Algeria) dinar; dinars.

da. 1. daughter. **2.** day; days.

D/A *Commerce.* **1.** Also, **d/a.** days after acceptance. **2.** deposit account. **3.** documents against acceptance. **4.** documents for acceptance.

D.A. 1. delayed action. **2.** direct action. **3.** District Attorney. **4.** *Commerce.* documents against acceptance. **5.** *Commerce.* documents for acceptance. **6.** doesn't answer; don't answer.

DAB *Dictionary of American Biography.*

D.A.E. *Dictionary of American English.* Also, **DAE**

dag dekagram; dekagrams.

D.Agr. Doctor of Agriculture.

Dak. Dakota.

dal dekaliter; dekaliters.

dam dekameter; dekameters.

Dan. 1. *Bible.* Daniel. **2.** Also, **Dan** Danish.

D and C *Medicine.* a surgical method for the removal of diseased tissue or an early embryo from the lining of the uterus. [*d(ilation) and c(urettage)*]

D&D drug and disease free.

Danl. Daniel.

DAR Defense Aid Reports.

dar 1. *Military.* defense acquisition radar. **2.** digital audio recording.

D.A.R. Daughters of the American Revolution.

DARE (dâr), *Dictionary of American Regional English.*

DARPA (där′pə), Defense Advanced Research Projects Agency.

DAT digital audiotape.

dat. 1. dative. **2.** datum.

datacom (dā′tə kom′), data communication.

dau. daughter.

D.A.V. Disabled American Veterans. Also, **DAV**

DB *Radio and Television.* delayed broadcast.

dB *Physics.* decibel; decibels.

D.B. 1. Bachelor of Divinity. **2.** Domesday Book.

d.b. daybook.

DBA doing business as. Also, **dba, d.b.a.**

dBa decibels above reference noise, adjusted. Also, **dba**

d/b/a doing business as.

D.B.A. Doctor of Business Administration.

D.B.E. Dame Commander of the Order of the British Empire.

D.Bib. Douay Bible.

dbl. double.

dblr *Electronics.* doubler.

DBMS *Computers.* Data Base Management System.

DBS *Television.* direct broadcast satellite.

DC 1. dental corps. **2.** *Electricity.* direct current. **3.** District of Columbia (for use with ZIP code).

dc *Electricity.* **1.** Also, **d.c.** direct current. **2.** double contact.

D.C. 1. *Music.* da capo. **2.** *Dictionary of Canadianisms.* **3.** *Electricity.* direct current. **4.** District of Columbia. **5.** Doctor of Chiropractic.

dcd decode.

dcdr decoder.

DCF divorced Christian female.

D.Ch.E. Doctor of Chemical Engineering.

DCHP *Dictionary of Canadianisms on Historical Principles.*

dckg docking.

dcl door closer.

D.C.L. Doctor of Civil Law.

dclr decelerate.

DCM divorced Christian male.

D.C.M. *British.* Distinguished Conduct Medal.

D.Cn.L. Doctor of Canon Law.

DCPA Defense Civil Preparedness Agency.

D.Crim. Doctor of Criminology.

D.C.S. 1. Deputy Clerk of Sessions. **2.** Doctor of Christian Science. **3.** Doctor of Commercial Science.

DCTL *Computers.* direct-coupled transistor logic.

DD dishonorable discharge.

dd 1. *Law.* today's date. [from Latin *dē datō*] **2.** deep-drawn. **3.** degree-day. **4.** delayed delivery. **5.** delivered. **6.** *Banking.* demand draft. **7.** double deck. **8.** *Shipbuilding.* dry dock.

dd. delivered.

D/D *Commerce.* days after date.

D.D. 1. *Banking.* demand draft. **2.** Doctor of Divinity.

dda digital differential analyzer.

D-day (dē′dā′), **1.** a day set for beginning something. **2.** June 6, 1944, the day the Allies invaded W Europe. Also, **D-Day.**

DDD *Telecommunications.* direct distance dialing.

DDP *Computers.* distributed data processing.

DDR German Democratic Republic. [from German *D(eutsche) D(emokratische) R(epublik)*]

DDS *Pharmacology.* dapsone. [*d(iamino)d(iphenyl) s(ulfone)*]

D.D.S. 1. Doctor of Dental Science. **2.** Doctor of Dental Surgery.

D.D.Sc. Doctor of Dental Science.

DDT *Chemistry.* a white, crystalline, water-insoluble solid, $C_{14}H_9Cl_5$, used as an insecticide and as a scabicide and pediculicide. [*d(ichloro)d(iphenyl)t(richloroethane)*]

DE 1. Delaware (for use with ZIP code). **2.** destroyer escort.

de digital encoder.

D.E. 1. Doctor of Engineering. **2.** driver education.

DEA Drug Enforcement Administration.

Dec. December.

dec. 1. (in prescriptions) pour off. [from Latin *dēcantā*] **2.** deceased. **3.** decimal. **4.** decimeter. **5.** declension. **6.** decrease. **7.** *Music.* decrescendo.

decaf. decaffeinated.

decd. deceased.

decn decision.

decompn decompression.

decontn decontamination.

decr decrease.

ded. 1. dedicate. **2.** dedicated. **3.** deduct. **4.** deducted. **5.** deduction.

D.Ed. Doctor of Education.

de d in d (in prescriptions) from day to day. [from Latin *dē diē in diem*]

def. 1. defective. **2.** defense. **3.** definition. Also, **def**

DEFCON (def′kon), any of several alert statuses for U.S. military forces. [*def(ense readiness) con(dition)*]

defl deflect.

defs. definitions.

deg. degree; degrees.

deglut. (in prescriptions) may be swallowed; let it be swallowed. [from Latin *dēglutiātur*]

D.E.I. Dutch East Indies.

Del. Delaware.

del. 1. delegate; delegation. **2.** delete; deletion. **3.** he or she drew this [from Latin *delineavit*].

dele delete.

dely. delivery.

dem demodulator.

Dem. 1. Democrat. **2.** Democratic.

dem. 1. demand. **2.** demonstrative. **3.** demurrage.

demod (dē′mod), demodulator.

demux (dē′muks), *Telecommunications.* demultiplexer.

den denote.

Den. Denmark.

deng diesal engine.

D.Eng. Doctor of Engineering.

D.Eng.S. Doctor of Engineering Science.

dens density.

dent. 1. dental. **2.** dentist. **3.** dentistry.

dep. 1. depart. **2.** department. **3.** departs. **4.** departure. **5.** deponent. **6.** deposed. **7.** deposit. **8.** depot. **9.** deputy.

depr. 1. depreciation. **2.** depression.

dept. 1. department. **2.** deponent. **3.** deputy.

der. 1. derivation. **2.** derivative. **3.** derive. **4.** derived.

deriv. 1. derivation. **2.** derivative. **3.** derive. **4.** derived.

DES *Pharmacology.* diethylstilbestrol.

des designation.

descr 1. describe. **2.** description.

D. ès L. Doctor of Letters. [from French *Docteur ès Lettres*]

D. ès S. Doctor of Sciences. [from French *Docteur ès Sciences*]

destn destination.

DET 1. Also, **Det** *Linguistics.* determiner. **2.** *Pharmacology.* diethyltryptamine.

det. 1. detach. **2.** detachment. **3.** detail. **4.** detector. **5.** determine. **6.** (in prescriptions) let it be given [from Latin *dētur*].

Deut. *Bible.* Deuteronomy.

dev. 1. development. **2.** deviation.

devel. development.

DEW (dōō, dyōō), distant early warning.

DF divorced female.

df 1. direction finder. **2.** dissipation factor.

D/F direction finding. Also, **DF**

D.F. 1. Defender of the Faith. [from Latin *Dēfēnsor Fideī*] **2.** Distrito Federal. **3.** Doctor of Forestry.

D.F.A. Doctor of Fine Arts.

D.F.C. Distinguished Flying Cross.

dfl deflating.

D.F.M. Distinguished Flying Medal.

dfr defrost.

dft drift.

dftg drafting.

dftr deflector.

dftsp draftsperson.

dg decigram; decigrams.

D.G. 1. by the grace of God. [from Latin *Deī grātiā*] **2.** Director General.

dgr degrease.

dgs degaussing system.

dgt digit.

dgtl digital.

DH 1. *Racing.* dead heat. **2.** *Baseball.* designated hitter. Also, **dh**

DH. (in Morocco) dirham; dirhams.

D.H. 1. Doctor of Humanics. **2.** Doctor of Humanities.

DHA *Biochemistry.* an omega-3 fatty

acid present in fish oils. [*d(ocosa)-h(exaenoic) a(cid)*]

D.H.L. 1. Doctor of Hebrew Letters. **2.** Doctor of Hebrew Literature.

dhmy dehumidify.

dhw double-hung window.

dhyr dehydrator.

DI 1. Department of the Interior. **2.** drill instructor.

Di *Symbol, Chemistry.* didymium.

di. diameter. Also, **dia.**

dia. diameter. Also, **dia**

diag 1. diagonal. **2.** diagram.

Dial. 1. dialect. **2.** dialectal. **3.** dialectic. **4.** dialectical.

diaph diaphragm.

dict. 1. dictation. **2.** dictator. **3.** dictionary.

DID 1. data item description. **2.** *Telecommunications.* direct inward dialing.

dieb. alt. (in prescriptions) every other day. [from Latin *diēbus alternīs*]

dieb. secund. (in prescriptions) every second day. [from Latin *diēbus secundīs*]

dieb. tert. (in prescriptions) every third day. [from Latin *diēbus tertius*]

diel dielectric.

dif. 1. difference. **2.** different.

diff. 1. difference. **2.** different. **3.** differential.

dig. digest.

dil 1. dilute. **2.** diluted.

dim. 1. dimension. **2.** (in prescriptions) one-half. [from Latin *dīmidius*] **3.** diminish. **4.** *Music.* diminuendo. **5.** diminutive.

dimin. 1. diminish. **2.** *Music.* diminuendo. **3.** diminutive.

DIN (din), *Photography.* a designation, originating in Germany, of the speed of a particular film emulsion. [from German *D(eutsche) I(ndustrie) N(ormen)* German industrial standards (later construed as *Das ist Norm* that is (the) standard), registered mark of the German Institute for Standardization]

Din. (in Yugoslavia) dinar; dinars.

d. in p. aeq. (in prescriptions) let it be divided into equal parts. [from Latin *dīvidātur in partēs aequālēs*]

dio diode.

dioc. 1. diocesan. **2.** diocese.

diopt *Optics.* diopter.

DIP (dip), *Computers.* a packaged chip that connects to a circuit board by means of pins. [*d(ual) i(n-line) p(ackage)*]

dipl. 1. diplomat. **2.** diplomatic.

diplxr *Electronics.* diplexer.

dir. 1. direct. **2.** direction. **3.** directional. **4.** director. **5.** directory. **6.** direxit.

dir cplr *Electronics.* directional coupler.

direc. prop. (in prescriptions) with a proper direction. [from Latin *dīrectiōne prōpriā*]

DIS The Disney Channel (a cable channel).

dis. 1. distance. **2.** distant. **3.** distribute.

disassm disassemble.

disassy disassembly.

disc. 1. disconnect. **2.** discount. **3.** discovered.

disch discharge.

disp 1. dispatcher. **2.** dispenser.

displ displacement.

dist. 1. distance. **2.** distant. **3.** distinguish. **4.** distinguished. **5.** district.

Dist. Atty. district attorney.

Dist. Ct. District Court.

distn distortion.

distr. 1. distribute. **2.** distribution. **3.** distributor.

div 1. *Mathematics, Mechanics.* divergence. 2. *Music.* divisi.

Div. 1. divine. 2. divinity.

div. 1. diverter. 2. divide. 3. divided. 4. dividend. 5. division. 6. divisor. 7. divorced.

div. in par. aeq. (in prescriptions) let it be divided into equal parts. [from Latin *dīvidātur in partēs aequālēs*]

DIY *British.* do-it-yourself. Also, **D.I.Y., d.i.y.**

DIYer (dē/ī/wī/ər), *British.* do-it-yourselfer. Also, **DIY'er.**

D.J. 1. Also, **DJ, d.j.** disc jockey. 2. District Judge. 3. Doctor of Law [from Latin *Doctor Jūris*].

DJF divorced Jewish female.

DJM divorced Jewish male.

D.Journ. Doctor of Journalism.

D.J.S. Doctor of Juridical Science.

D.J.T. Doctor of Jewish Theology.

DK *Real Estate.* deck.

dk. 1. dark. 2. deck. 3. dock.

dkg dekagram; dekagrams.

dkl dekaliter; dekaliters.

dkm dekameter; dekameters.

DL diesel.

dl 1. data link. 2. daylight. 3. dead load. 4. deciliter; deciliters. 5. drawing list.

D/L demand loan.

dla data link address.

D. Lit. Doctor of Literature.

D. Litt. Doctor of Letters. [from Latin *Doctor Litterārum*]

D.L.O. dead letter office.

dlr. 1. dealer. 2. Also, **dlr** dollar.

dlrs. dollars. Also, **dlrs**

D.L.S. Doctor of Library Science.

dlvy delivery.

dlx deluxe.

dly 1. delay. 2. dolly.

DM 1. Deutsche mark. 2. divorced male.

dm 1. decimeter; decimeters. 2. demand meter.

DM. direct mail.

Dm. Deutsche mark.

DMA *Computers.* direct memory access.

dmd demodulate.

D.M.D. Doctor of Dental Medicine. [from Latin *Dentāriae Medicīnae Doctor* or *Doctor Medicīnae Dentālis*]

DMDT *Chemistry.* methoxychlor. [*d(i)m(ethoxy)d(iphenyl)-t(richloroethane)*]

D.M.L. Doctor of Modern Languages.

dmm *Electricity.* digital multimeter.

DMN *Chemistry.* dimethylnitrosamine. Also, **DMNA**

dmp *Computers.* dot-matrix printer.

dmpr damper.

dmr dimmer.

D.M.S. 1. Director of Medical Services. 2. Doctor of Medical Science.

DMSO a liquid substance, C_2H_6OS, used in industry as a solvent; proposed as an analgesic and anti-inflammatory. [*d(i)m(ethyl) s(ulf)o(xide)*]

DMT *Pharmacology.* dimethyltryptamine.

D. Mus. Doctor of Music.

DMV Department of Motor Vehicles.

dmx data multiplex.

DMZ demilitarized zone.

dn. down.

DNA *Genetics.* deoxyribonucleic acid: an extremely long macromolecule that is the main component of chromosomes and is the material that transfers genetic characteristics.

dna does not apply.

DNase (dē/en/ās, -āz), deoxyribonuclease: any of several enzymes that break down the DNA molecule. Also, **DNAase.**

D.N.B. *Dictionary of National Biography.*

DNC Democratic National Committee.

DNR 1. *Medicine.* do not resuscitate (used in hospitals and other health-care facilities). **2.** Also, **D.N.R.** do not return.

dntl dental.

do. ditto.

D/O delivery order. Also, **d.o.**

D.O. 1. Also, **DO, d.o.** direct object. **2.** Doctor of Optometry. **3.** Doctor of Osteopathy.

DOA dead on arrival. Also, **D.O.A.**

DOB date of birth. Also, **D.O.B., d.o.b.**

DOC Department of Commerce.

doc. 1. data output channel. **2.** document. **3.** Also, **doc** documentation.

DOD 1. Department of Defense. **2.** *Telecommunications.* direct outward dialing.

DOE 1. Department of Energy. **2.** Also, **d.o.e.** depends on experience; depending on experience (used in stating a salary range in help-wanted ads).

DOHC *Automotive.* double overhead camshaft.

DOI Department of the Interior.

DOJ Department of Justice.

DOL Department of Labor.

dol. 1. *Music.* dolce. **2.** dollar.

dols. dollars.

Dom. 1. Dominica. **2.** Dominican.

dom. 1. domain. **2.** domestic. **3.** dominant. **4.** dominion.

D.O.M. to God, the Best, the Greatest. [from Latin *Deō Optimō Maximō*]

d.o.m. *Slang.* dirty old man.

D.O.P. *Photography.* developing-out paper.

Dor. 1. Dorian. **2.** Doric.

DORAN (dôr′an, dōr′-), an electronic device for determining range and assisting navigation. [*Do(ppler) r(ange) a(nd) n(avigation)*]

DOS (dôs, dos), *Computers.* any of several operating systems, especially for microcomputers, that reside wholly on disk storage. [*d(isk) o(perating) s(ystem)*]

DOS Department of State.

DOT 1. Department of Transportation. **2.** *Dictionary of Occupational Titles.*

DOVAP (dō′vap), *Electronics.* a system for plotting the trajectory of a missile or other rapidly moving object by means of radio waves bounced off it. [*Do(ppler) V(elocity) a(nd) P(osition)*]

Dow. dowager.

doz. dozen; dozens.

DP 1. data processing. **2.** displaced person.

dp 1. dashpot: relay. **2.** data processing. **3.** deflection plate. **4.** depth. **5.** dial pulsing. **6.** *Baseball.* double play; double plays. **7.** *Electricity.* double-pole. **8.** dripproof.

D/P documents against payment.

D.P. 1. data processing. **2.** displaced person.

d.p. (in prescriptions) with a proper direction. [from Latin *dīrēctiōne prōpriā*]

D.P.A. Doctor of Public Administration.

DPC Defense Plant Corporation.

dpdt *Electricity.* double-pole double-throw.

dpg damping.

DPH Department of Public Health.

D. Ph. Doctor of Philosophy.

D.P.H. Doctor of Public Health.

dpi *Computers.* dots per inch.

DPL diplomat.

D.P.M. Doctor of Podiatric Medicine.

D.P.P. *Insurance.* deferred payment plan.

D.P.S. Doctor of Public Service.

dpst *Electricity.* double-pole single-throw.

dpstk dipstick.

DPT diphtheria, pertussis, and tetanus: a mixed vaccine used for primary immunization. Also, **DTP**

dpt. 1. department. **2.** deponent.

D.P.W. Department of Public Works. Also, **DPW**

dpx duplex.

DQ disqualify.

DR *Real Estate.* dining room.

Dr *Chiefly British.* Doctor.

dr 1. dead reckoning. **2.** door. **3.** *Electronics.* drain. **4.** dram; drams. **5.** drill. **6.** drive.

Dr. 1. Doctor. **2.** Drive (used in street names).

dr. 1. debit. **2.** debtor. **3.** drachma; drachmas. **4.** dram; drams. **5.** drawer. **6.** drum.

D.R. 1. Daughters of the (American) Revolution. **2.** *Navigation.* dead reckoning. **3.** Dutch Reformed.

dram detection-radar automatic monitoring.

dram. pers. *Theater.* dramatis personae.

drch. drachma; drachmas. Also, **dr.**

D.R.E. 1. Director of Religious Education. **2.** Doctor of Religious Education.

dri dead-reckoning indicator.

drsg dressing.

DRTL *Computers.* diode resistor transistor logic.

D.R.V. (on food labels) Daily Reference Value: the amount of nutrients appropriate for one day.

drvr driver.

drzl drizzle.

Ds *Symbol, Chemistry.* (formerly) dysprosium.

ds 1. diode switch. **2.** domestic service.

D.S. 1. *Music.* from the sign. [from Italian *dal segno*] **2.** Doctor of Science.

d.s. 1. daylight saving. **2.** *Commerce.* Also, **D/S** days after sight. **3.** document signed.

DSA *Medicine.* digital subtraction angiography.

dsb *Electronics.* double sideband.

dsbl disable.

DSC 1. The Discovery Channel (a cable channel). **2.** Defense Supplies Corporation.

D.Sc. Doctor of Science.

D.S.C. 1. Distinguished Service Cross. **2.** Doctor of Surgical Chiropody.

dscc dessicant.

dscont discontinue.

dscrm *Electronics.* discriminator.

dsd *Computers.* dual-scan display.

dsdd *Computers.* double-side, double-density.

dsgn design.

dshd *Computers.* double-side, high density.

dsl diesel.

dsltr desalter.

dslv dissolve.

D.S.M. 1. Distinguished Service Medal. **2.** Doctor of Sacred Music.

DSNA Dictionary Society of North America.

D.S.O. Distinguished Service Order.

dsp *Computers.* digital signal processing.

D.S.P. died without issue. [from Latin *dēcessit sine prōle*]

dspec design specification.

dspl display.

dspo disposal.

DSR *Medicine.* dynamic spatial reconstructor.

D.S.S. Doctor of Social Science.

dssd *Computers.* double-side, single-density.

DST daylight-saving time.

D.S.T. 1. daylight-saving time. **2.** Doctor of Sacred Theology.

dstlt distillate.

dstng distinguish.

DSU disk storage unit.

D. Surg. Dental Surgeon.

D.S.W. 1. Doctor of Social Welfare. **2.** Doctor of Social Work.

DT *Slang.* detective. Also, **D.T.**

dt 1. decay time. **2.** double throw.

dtd dated.

d.t.d. (in prescriptions) give such doses. [from Latin *dentur tālēs dosēs*]

D.Th. Doctor of Theology. Also, **D.Theol.**

DTL *Computers.* diode transistor logic.

dtl detail.

dtmf *Telecommunications.* dual-tone multifrequency.

DTP 1. desktop publishing. **2.** diphtheria, tetanus, and pertussis. See **DPT.**

dtrbd *Computers.* daughterboard.

dtrs distress.

d.t.'s (dē′tēz′), *Pathology.* delirium tremens.

dtv digital television.

dty cy duty cycle.

Du. 1. Duke. **2.** Dutch.

DUI driving under the influence.

dulc. (in prescriptions) sweet. [from Latin *dulcis*]

dupl duplicate.

duplxr duplexer.

dut *Electronics.* device under test.

D.V. 1. God willing. [from Latin *D(eo) v(olente)*] **2.** Douay Version (of the Bible).

dvc device.

dvl develop.

D.V.M. Doctor of Veterinary Medicine. Also, **DVM**

D.V.M.S. Doctor of Veterinary Medicine and Surgery.

dvr diver.

D.V.S. Doctor of Veterinary Surgery.

dvt deviate.

DW *Real Estate.* dishwasher.

dw 1. dishwasher. **2.** distilled water. **3.** double weight.

D/W *Law.* dock warrant.

dwg drawing.

DWI driving while intoxicated.

dwl dowel.

DWM *Slang.* dead white male.

dwn drawn.

dwr drawer.

DWT deadweight tons; deadweight tonnage.

dwt 1. deadweight tons; deadweight tonnage. **2.** pennyweight; pennyweights.

d.w.t. deadweight tons; deadweight tonnage.

DX *Radio.* distance. Also, **D.X.**

Dx diagnosis.

dx duplex.

Dy *Symbol, Chemistry.* dysprosium.

dyn 1. dynamic. **2.** *Physics.* dyne; dynes.

dyn. dynamics. Also, **dynam.**

dynm dynamotor.

dynmm dynamometer.

dynmt dynamite.

DZ drop zone.

dz. dozen; dozens.

E

E 1. east. 2. eastern. 3. English. 4. excellent. 5. Expressway.

E *Symbol.* 1. the fifth in order or in a series. 2. (in some grading systems) a grade or mark, indicating the quality of a student's work is in need of improvement in order to be passing. 3. *Music.* **a.** the third tone in the scale of C major or the fifth tone in the relative minor scale, A minor. **b.** a string, key, or pipe tuned to this tone. **c.** a written or printed note representing this tone. **d.** (in the fixed system of solmization) the third tone of the scale of C major, called *mi.* **e.** the tonality having E as the tonic note. 4. (*sometimes lowercase*) the medieval Roman numeral for 250. 5. *Physics, Electricity.* **a.** electric field. **b.** electric field strength. 6. *Physics.* energy 7. *Biochemistry.* glutamic acid. 8. *Logic.* universal negative. 9. a proportional shoe width size, narrower than EE and wider than D.

e 1. electron. 2. *Physics.* elementary charge.

E. 1. Earl. 2. Earth. 3. east. 4. Easter. 5. eastern. 6. engineer. 7. engineering. 8. English.

e. 1. eldest. 2. *Football.* end. 3. engineer. 4. engineering. 5. entrance. 6. *Baseball.* error; errors.

ea. each.

E.A.A. Engineer in Aeronautics and Astronautics.

ead. (in prescriptions) the same. [from Latin *eādem*]

EAM National Liberation Front, a Greek underground resistance movement and political coalition of World War II. [from Modern Greek *E(thnikó) A(pelevtherōtikò) M(étōpo)*]

EAP employee assistance program.

eax electronic automatic exchange.

EB Epstein-Barr (syndrome).

EBCDIC (eb'sē dik'), *n. Computers.* a code used for data representation and transfer. [*e(xtended) b(inary-) c(oded) d(ecimal) i(nterchange) c(ode)*]

EbN east by north.

EbS east by south.

EBV Epstein-Barr virus.

EC European Community.

E.C. 1. Engineering Corps. 2. Established Church.

e.c. for the sake of example. [from Latin *exemplī causā*]

ECA Economic Cooperation Administration. Also, **E.C.A.**

ECC *Computers.* error-correction code.

ecc eccentric.

Eccl. *Bible.* Ecclesiastes. Also, **Eccles.**

eccl. ecclesiastic; ecclesiastical. Also, **eccles.**

Ecclus. *Bible.* Ecclesiasticus.

ECCM *Military.* electronic countermeasures.

ecd estimated completion date.

ECF extended-care facility.

ECG 1. electrocardiogram. 2. electrocardiograph.

ech echelon.

ECL *Computers.* emitter-coupled logic.

ECM 1. electronic countermeasures. 2. European Common Market.

ecn engineering change notice.

eco 1. electron-coupled oscillator. 2. engineering change notice.

ecol. 1. ecological. 2. ecology.

E. co•li (ē' kō'lī), *Escherichia coli,* an anaerobic bacterium.

econ. 1. economic. 2. economics. 3. economy.

ecp engineering change proposal.

ecr engineering change request.

ECT electroconvulsive therapy.

ECU (ā kōō′ or, sometimes, ē′sē′y-ōō′), a money of account of the European Common Market used in international finance. [E(uropean) C(urrency) U(nit), perhaps with play on écu, an old French coin]

E.C.U. English Church Union.

ED Department of Education.

ED₅₀ ED_{50} *Pharmacology.* effective dose for 50 percent of the group.

ed. 1. edited. 2. edition. 3. editor. 4. education.

E.D. 1. Eastern Department. 2. election district. 3. *Finance.* ex dividend. 4. executive director.

EDA Economic Development Administration.

edac error detection correction.

EDB *Chemistry.* a colorless liquid, $C_2H_4Br_2$, used as an organic solvent, gasoline additive, pesticide, and soil fumigant. [e(thylene) d(i)b(romide)]

Ed.B. Bachelor of Education.

EDC European Defense Community.

Ed.D. Doctor of Education.

EDES Hellenic National Democratic army, a Greek resistance coalition in World War II. [from Modern Greek E(thnikós) D(ēmokratikós) E(llēnikós) S(yndésmos)]

edit. 1. edited. 2. edition. 3. editor.

Ed.M. Master of Education.

EDP *Computers.* electronic data processing.

eds. 1. editions. 2. editors.

Ed.S. Education Specialist.

EDT Eastern daylight time. Also, **E.D.T.**

EDTA *Chemistry., Pharmacology.* a colorless compound, $C_{10}H_{16}N_2O_8$, with a variety of medical and other uses. [e(thylene)d(iamine)t(etraacetic) a(cid)]

edtn edition.

edtr editor.

educ. 1. educated. 2. education. 3. educational.

E.E. 1. Early English. 2. electrical engineer. 3. electrical engineering.

e.e. errors excepted.

E.E. & M.P. Envoy Extraordinary and Minister Plenipotentiary.

EEC European Economic Community.

EEG 1. electroencephalogram. 2. electroencephalograph.

EENT *Medicine.* eye, ear, nose, and throat.

EEO equal employment opportunity.

EEOC Equal Employment Opportunity Commission.

eeprom *Electronics.* electronically erasable programmable read-only memory.

EER energy efficiency ratio.

ef emitter follower.

eff. 1. effect. 2. effective. 3. efficiency.

EFI electronic fuel injection.

EFL English as a foreign language.

efl 1. effluent. 2. *Photography.* equivalent focal length.

EFM electronic fetal monitor.

efph equivalent full-power hour.

EFT electronic funds transfer. Also, **EFTS**

EFTA European Free Trade Association.

EFTS electronic funds transfer system.

Eg. 1. Egypt. 2. Egyptian.

e.g. for example; for the sake of example; such as. [from Latin exemplī grātiā]

EGA *Computers.* enhanced graphics adapter.

EGmc East Germanic.

EGR *Automotive.* exhaust-gas recirculation.

EHF extremely high frequency. Also, **ehf**

EHS Environmental Health Services.

EHV extra high voltage.

E.I. 1. East Indian. **2.** East Indies.

EIA Electronic Industries Association.

E. Ind. East Indian.

EIR Environmental Impact Report.

EIS Environmental Impact Statement.

EISA *Computers.* extended industry standard architecture.

EJ (ē′jā′), **1.** electronic journalism. **2.** electronic journalist.

ejn ejection.

ejtr ejector.

EKG 1. electrocardiogram. **2.** electrocardiograph. [from German *E(lectro)k(ardio)g(ramme)*]

el. 1. electroluminescent. **2.** elevation.

E.L.A.S. Hellenic People's Army of Liberation, Greek resistance force in World War II. [from Modern Greek *E(thnikòs) L(aikòs) A(peleutherōtikòs) S(tratós)*]

elb elbow.

elctd electrode.

elctlt electrolyte; electrolytic.

elctrn electron.

elctrochem electrochemical.

Elect. 1. electric. **2.** electrical. **3.** electrician. **4.** electricity. Also, **elec.**

elek electronic.

elem. 1. element; elements. **2.** elementary.

elev. 1. elevation. **2.** elevator.

elex electronics.

ELF extremely low frequency. Also, **elf**

elim eliminate.

ELISA (i lī′zə, -sə), **1.** *Medicine.* a diagnostic test for past or current

exposure to an infectious agent, as the AIDS virus. **2.** *Biology, Medicine.* any similar test using proteins as a probe for the identification of antibodies or antigens. [*e(nzyme-) l(inked) i(mmuno)s(orbent) a(ssay)*]

elix. (in prescriptions) elixir.

Eliz. Elizabethan.

elmech electromechanical.

elng elongate.

e. long. east longitude.

elp elliptical.

elpneu electropneumatic.

elvn elevation.

EM 1. electromagnetic. **2.** electromotive. **3.** electronic mail. **4.** electron microscope. **5.** electron microscopy. **6.** end matched. **7.** Engineer of Mines. **8.** enlisted man; enlisted men.

Em *Symbol, Physical Chemistry.* emanation.

em 1. electromagnetic. **2.** enlisted men.

E.M. 1. Earl Marshal. **2.** Engineer of Mines.

e-mail (ē′māl′), electronic mail. Also, **E-mail.**

emb emboss.

embryol. embryology.

emer emergency.

E.Met. Engineer of Metallurgy.

emf electromotive force. Also, **EMF, E.M.F.,e.m.f.**

EMG 1. electromyogram. **2.** electromyograph. **3.** electromyography.

emi electromagnetic interference.

EMP *Physics.* electromagnetic pulse.

Emp. 1. Emperor. **2.** Empire. **3.** Empress.

emp. (in prescriptions) a plaster. [from Latin *emplastrum*]

e.m.p. (in prescriptions) after the manner prescribed; as directed. [from Latin ex *mōdō praescrīptō*]

empl employee.

EMS 1. emergency medical service. **2.** European Monetary System.

ems electromagnetic surveillance.

emsn emission.

EMT emergency medical technician.

emtr *Electronics.* emitter.

EMU 1. Also, **emu** electromagnetic unit; electromagnetic units. **2.** *Aerospace.* extravehicular mobility unit.

emuls. (in prescriptions) an emulsion. [from Latin *ēmulsiō*]

enam enamel.

enbl enable.

enc. 1. enclosed. **2.** enclosure. **3.** encyclopedia.

encap encapsulate.

encd encode.

encl. 1. enclosed. **2.** enclosure.

encsd encased.

ency. encyclopedia. Also, **encyc., encycl.**

end. endorsed.

ENE east-northeast. Also, **E.N.E.**

ENG *Television.* electronic news gathering.

Eng. 1. England. **2.** English.

eng. 1. engine. **2.** engineer. **3.** engineering. **4.** engraved. **5.** engraver. **6.** engraving.

enga engage.

Eng. D. Doctor of Engineering.

engr. 1. engineer. **2.** engraved. **3.** engraver. **4.** engraving.

engrg engineering.

engrv engrave.

engy energy.

enl. 1. enlarge. **2.** enlarged. **3.** enlisted.

enlg enlarge.

enrgz energize.

Ens. Ensign.

ensi (en′sē), equivalent-noise-sideband-input.

ENT *Medicine.* ear, nose, and throat.

entomol. 1. entomological. **2.** entomology. Also, **entom.**

entr 1. enter. **2.** entrance.

enum enumerate, enumeration.

env. envelope.

envr 1. environment. **2.** environmental.

EO executive order.

e.o. ex officio.

EOB Executive Office Building.

EOE 1. equal-opportunity employer. **2.** *Disparaging.* an employee who is considered to have been hired only to satisfy equal-opportunity regulations.

EOF *Computers.* end-of-file.

EOG electrooculogram.

eolm electrooptical light modulator.

eom end of message.

e.o.m. *Chiefly Commerce.* end of the month. Also, **E.O.M.**

EOP Executive Office of the President.

eot end of tape.

EP 1. European plan. **2.** extended play (of phonograph records).

Ep. *Bible.* Epistle.

EPA 1. Environmental Protection Agency. **2.** an omega-3 fatty acid present in fish oils. [e*(icosa)*p*(entaenoic)* a*(cid)*]

Eph. *Bible.* Ephesians. Also, **Ephes., Ephs.**

Epiph. Epiphany.

Epis. 1. Episcopal. **2.** Episcopalian. **3.** *Bible.* Epistle.

Episc. 1. Episcopal. **2.** Episcopalian.

Epist. *Bible.* Epistle.

epit. 1. epitaph. **2.** epitome.

EPROM (ē′prom), *Computers.* a memory chip whose contents can be erased and reprogramed. [e*(rasable)* p*(rogrammable)* r*(ead)*-o*(nly)* m*(emory)*]

EPS earnings per share.

EPT excess-profits tax.

ept external pipe thread.

epu emergency power unit.

EQ educational quotient.

eq. 1. equal. **2.** equation. **3.** equivalent.

eql equal, equally.

eqlz 1. equalize. **2.** equalizer.

eqpt. equipment.

equil equilibrium.

equip. equipment.

equiv. equivalent.

ER 1. efficiency report. **2.** emergency room.

Er *Symbol, Chemistry.* erbium.

E.R. 1. East Riding (Yorkshire). **2.** East River (New York City). **3.** King Edward. [from Latin *Edwardus Rex*] **4.** Queen Elizabeth. [from Latin *Elizabeth Regina*] **5.** emergency room.

ERA 1. Also, **era** *Baseball.* earned run average. **2.** Emergency Relief Administration. **3.** Equal Rights Amendment.

ercg erecting.

erct erection.

ERG electroretinogram.

ERIC Educational Resources Information Center.

ERISA (ə ris′ə), Employee Retirement Income Security Act.

ERP European Recovery Program. Also, **E.R.P.**

errc error correction.

erron. 1. erroneous. **2.** erroneously.

ERS Emergency Radio Service. Also, **E.R.S.**

ers 1. erase. **2.** erased.

ERTS Earth Resources Technology Satellite.

E.R.V. English Revised Version (of the Bible).

Es *Symbol, Chemistry.* einsteinium.

es electrostatic.

E.S. Education Specialist.

ESA European Space Agency.

Esc. (in Portugal and several other nations) escudo; escudos.

esc. 1. escape. **2.** escrow.

escl escalator.

esct escutcheon.

Esd. *Bible.* Esdras.

ESDI (es′dē), *Computers.* enhanced small device interface.

ESE east-southeast. Also, **E.S.E.**

esk engineering sketch.

Esk. Eskimo.

ESL English as a second language.

ESOL (ē′sôl, es′əl), English for speakers of other languages.

ESOP (ē′sop), a plan under which a company's stock is acquired by its employees or workers. [E(mployee) S(tock) O(wnership) P(lan)]

ESP extrasensory perception.

esp. especially.

espec. especially.

ESPN the Entertainment Sports Network (a cable channel).

Esq. Esquire. Also, **Esqr.**

ESR 1. erythrocyte sedimentation rate: the rate at which red blood cells settle in a column of blood, serving as a diagnostic test. **2.** electron spin resonance.

ess electronic switching system.

EST Eastern Standard Time. Also, **E.S.T.,e.s.t.**

est. 1. established. **2.** estate. **3.** estimate. **4.** estimated. **5.** estuary.

estab. established.

Esth. 1. *Bible.* Esther. **2.** Esthonia.

esu electrostatic unit.

Et *Symbol, Chemistry.* ethyl.

E.T. 1. Eastern time. **2.** extraterrestrial. Also, **ET**

e.t. electrical transcription.

E.T.A. estimated time of arrival. Also, **ETA**

et al. (et al′, äl′, ôl′), **1.** and elsewhere. [from Latin *et alibī*] **2.** and
others. [from Latin *et aliī*]

etc. et cetera.

E.T.D. estimated time of departure.
Also, **ETD**

Eth. Ethiopia.

ethnog. ethnography.

ethnol. 1. ethnological. **2.** ethnology.

ethol. ethology.

ETI extraterrestrial intelligence.

eti elapsed-time indicator.

ETO (in World War II) European
Theater of Operations. Also, **E.T.O.**

e to e end to end.

etr estimated time of return.

Etr. Etruscan.

ETS *Trademark.* Educational Testing
Service.

et seq. *plural* **et seqq., et sqq.** and
the following. [from Latin *et sequēns*]

et seqq. and those following. Also,
et sqq. [from Latin *et sequentēs, et
sequentia*]

et ux. *Chiefly Law.* and wife. [from
Latin *et uxor*]

ETV educational television.

etvm electrostatic transistorized
voltmeter.

ety. etymology.

etym. 1. etymological. **2.** etymology.
Also, **etymol.**

Eu *Symbol, Chemistry.* europium.

Eur. 1. Europe. **2.** European.

eV *Physics.* electron-volt. Also, **ev**

E.V. English Version (of the Bible).

EVA *Aerospace.* extravehicular activity.

evac evacuation.

eval evaluation.

evap. 1. evaporate. **2.** evaporation.

evg. evening.

evm electronic voltmeter.

evom electronic voltohmmeter.

EW 1. electronic warfare. **2.** enlisted
women.

Ex. *Bible.* Exodus.

ex. 1. examination. **2.** examined.
3. example. **4.** except. **5.** exception.
6. exchange. **7.** excursion. **8.** exe-
cuted. **9.** executive. **10.** express.
11. extra.

exam. 1. examination. **2.** examined.
3. examinee. **4.** examiner.

Exc. Excellency.

exc. 1. excellent. **2.** except.
3. exception. **4.** he or she printed
or engraved (this). [from Latin *excudit*] **5.** excursion.

exch. 1. exchange. **2.** exchequer.
Also **Exch.**

excl., 1. exclamation. **2.** excluding.
3. exclusive.

exclam. 1. exclamation.
2. exclamatory.

excsv excessive.

exctr exciter.

excud. he or she printed or
engraved (this). [from Latin *excudit*]

Ex. Doc. executive document.

exec. 1. executive. **2.** executor.

exer exercise.

exh 1. exhaust. **2.** exhibit.

ex int. *Stock Exchange.* ex interest.

ex lib. from the library of. [from
Latin *ex libris*]

Exod. *Bible.* Exodus.

ex off. by virtue of office or position. [from Latin *ex officio*]

exor. executor.

exp 1. expand. **2.** expansion. **3.** experiment. **4.** expose. **5.** expulsion.

exp. 1. expenses. **2.** experience.
3. expired. **4.** exponential.
5. export. **6.** exported. **7.** exporter.
8. express.

exped expedite.

expen expendable.

exp jt expansion joint.

expl 1. explain. **2.** explanation.

expld explode.

expln explosion.

expnt 1. exponent. 2. exponential.

expo exposition.

expr express.

expsr exposure.

expt. experiment.

exptl. experimental.

Expy. expressway.

exr. executor.

exstg existing.

ext. 1. extension. 2. exterior.

3. external. 4. extinct. 5. extinguish. 6. extra. 7. extract.

extd. 1. extended. 2. extrude.

extm extreme.

extn. 1. extension. 2. external.

extnr extinguisher.

extr. 1. exterior. 2. extract.

eylt eyelet.

eypc eyepiece.

Ez. *Bible.* Ezra. Also, **Ezr.**

Ezek. *Bible.* Ezekiel.

F

F 1. Fahrenheit. 2. female. 3. *Genetics.* filial. 4. firm. 5. franc; francs. 6. French.

F *Symbol.* 1. the sixth in order or in a series. 2. (in some grading systems) a grade or mark that indicates academic work of the lowest quality; failure. 3. *Music.* **a.** the fourth tone in the scale of C major or the sixth tone in the relative minor scale, A minor. **b.** a string, key, or pipe tuned to this tone. **c.** a written or printed note representing this tone. **d.** (in the fixed system of solmization) the fourth tone of the scale of C major, called *fa.* **e.** the tonality having F as the tonic note. 4. (*sometimes lowercase*) the medieval Roman numeral for 40. 5. *Math.* **a.** field. **b.** function (of). 6. (*sometimes lowercase*) *Electricity.* farad. 7. *Chemistry.* fluorine. 8. (*sometimes lowercase*) *Physics.* **a.** force. **b.** frequency. **c.** fermi. 9. *Biochemistry.* phenylalanine.

f 1. firm. 2. *Photography.* f-number. 3. *Music.* forte.

f *Symbol, Optics.* focal length.

F- *Military.* (in designations of aircraft) fighter: *F-105.*

F. 1. Fahrenheit. 2. February. 3. Fellow. 4. (in Hungary) forint; forints. 5. franc; francs. 6. France.

7. French. 8. Friday.

f. 1. (in prescriptions) make. [from Latin *fac*] 2. farad. 3. farthing. 4. father. 5. fathom. 6. feet. 7. female. 8. feminine. 9. (in prescriptions) let them be made. [from Latin *fīant*] 10. (in prescriptions) let it be made. [from Latin *fiat*] 11. filly. 12. fine. 13. fluid (ounce). 14. folio. 15. following. 16. foot. 17. form. 18. formed of. 19. franc. 20. from. 21. *Math.* function (of). 22. (in the Netherlands) guilder; guilders.

f/ *Photography.* f-number. Also, **f/, f:**

fa 1. final assembly. 2. forced air.

FAA Federal Aviation Administration.

F.A.A.A.S. 1. Fellow of the American Academy of Arts and Sciences. 2. Fellow of the American Association for the Advancement of Science.

fab fabricate.

fabx fire alarm box.

fac. 1. facsimile. 2. factor. 3. factory. 4. faculty.

facil facility.

F.A.C.P. Fellow of the American College of Physicians. Also, **FACP**

FACS 1. *Biology.* fluorescence-activated cell sorter. 2. Also, **F.A.C.S.** Fellow of the American College of Surgeons.

facsim. facsimile.

FAdm Fleet Admiral.

Fahr. Fahrenheit (thermometer). Also, **Fah.**

F.A.L.N. Armed Forces of National Liberation: a militant underground organization whose objective is independence for Puerto Rico. Also, **FALN** [from Spanish *F(uerzas) A(rmadas de) L(iberación) N(acional)*]

FAM The Family Channel (a cable television station).

fam. **1.** familiar. **2.** family.

F.A.M. Free and Accepted Masons. Also, **F. & A.M.**

F. & T. *Insurance.* fire and theft.

FAO Food and Agriculture Organization.

F.A.Q. *Australian.* fair average quality. Also, **f.a.q.**

f/a ratio fuel-air ratio.

FAS **1.** fetal alcohol syndrome. **2.** Foreign Agricultural Service.

F.A.S. *Commerce.* free alongside ship: without charge to the buyer for goods delivered alongside ship. Also, **f.a.s., fas**

FASB Financial Accounting Standards Board.

fath. fathom.

fax (faks), facsimile.

f.b. **1.** freight bill. **2.** *Sports.* fullback.

F.B.A. Fellow of the British Academy.

FBI *U.S. Government.* Federal Bureau of Investigation.

fbk firebrick.

fbm foot board measure.

FBO for the benefit of. Also, **F/B/O**

fbr fiber.

fbrbd fiberboard.

FC foot-candle; footcandles. Also, **fc**

fc **1.** *Computers.* ferrite core. **2.** file cabinet. **3.** fire control.

f.c. **1.** *Baseball.* fielder's choice. **2.** *Printing.* follow copy.

FCA Farm Credit Administration.

FCC *U.S. Government.* Federal Communications Commission.

fcg facing.

FCIA Foreign Credit Insurance Association.

FCIC Federal Crop Insurance Corporation.

fcp. foolscap.

fcr fuse current rating.

fcs. francs.

fcsg focusing.

fcsle forecastle.

fctn function.

fctnl functional.

fcty factory.

fcy. fancy.

fd feed.

F.D. **1.** Defender of the Faith. [from Latin *Fidei Defensor*] **2.** fire department. **3.** focal distance.

fdb field dynamic braking.

fdbk feedback.

fdc **1.** fire department connection. **2.** *Computers.* floppy-disk controller.

fdd *Computers.* floppy-disk drive.

fddl frequency-division data link.

Fdg *Banking.* funding.

FDIC Federal Deposit Insurance Corporation.

fdm frequency-division multiplex.

fdn foundation.

fdp *Hardware.* full dog point.

FDR Franklin Delano Roosevelt.

fdr **1.** feeder. **2.** finder. **3.** fire door.

fdry foundry.

fd svc food service.

fdx *Telecommunications.* full duplex.

Fe *Symbol, Chemistry.* iron. [from Latin *ferrum*]

fe. he or she has made it. [from Latin *fecit*]

FEB Fair Employment Board.

Feb. February.

Fed. Federal.

fed. 1. federal. **2.** federated. **3.** federation.

fedn. federation.

Fed. Res. Bd. Federal Reserve Board.

Fed. Res. Bk. Federal Reserve Bank.

felr feeler.

FeLV feline leukemia virus.

fem. 1. female. **2.** feminine.

FEMA Federal Emergency Management Agency.

FEPA Fair Employment Practices Act.

FEPC Fair Employment Practices Commission.

FERA Federal Emergency Relief Administration.

FERC Federal Energy Regulatory Commission.

FET 1. *Banking.* federal estate tax. **2.** *Electronics.* field-effect transistor.

F.E.T. Federal Excise Tax.

fext fire extinguisher.

ff 1. flip-flop. **2.** folios. **3.** (and the) following (pages, verses, etc.). **4.** *Music.* fortissimo.

FFA Future Farmers of America.

F.F.A. *Commerce.* free from alongside (ship). Also, **f.f.a.**

FFC 1. Foreign Funds Control. **2.** free from chlorine.

F.F.I. free from infection.

ffilh *Hardware.* flat fillister head.

ffrr full frequency-range recording.

F.F.V. First Families of Virginia.

ffwd fast forward.

f.g. *Basketball, Football.* field goal; field goals.

fgd forged.

fgn. foreign.

FGP Foster Grandparent Program.

FGT federal gift tax.

fgy foggy.

FH *Pathology.* familial hypercholesterolemia.

fh fire hose.

FHA 1. Farmers' Home Administration. **2.** Federal Housing Administration. **3.** Future Homemakers of America.

FHLB Federal Home Loan Bank.

FHLBA Federal Home Loan Bank Administration.

FHLBB Federal Home Loan Bank Board.

FHLBS Federal Home Loan Bank System.

FHLMC Federal Home Loan Mortgage Corporation.

FHWA Federal Highway Administration.

fhy fire hydrant.

F.I. Falkland Islands.

FIA Federal Insurance Administration.

fict. fiction.

fid. fiduciary.

FIDO (fī′dō), *Aeronautics.* a system for evaporating the fog above airfield runways. [*f(og) i(nvestigation) d(ispersal) o(perations)*]

FIFO (fī′fō), *n.* **1.** *Commerce.* first-in, first-out. **2.** *Computers.* a storage and retrieval technique, in which the first item stored is also the first item retrieved.

fig. 1. figurative. **2.** figuratively. **3.** figure; figures.

FIIG (fig), Federal Item Identification Guide.

fil 1. filament. **2.** *Hardware.* fillister.

filh *Hardware.* fillister head.

filt. (in prescriptions) filter. [from Latin *filtrā*]

Fin. 1. Finland. **2.** Finnish.

fin. 1. finance. **2.** financial. **3.** finish.

fin. sec. financial secretary.

F.I.O. *Commerce.* free in and out: a term of contract in which a ship charterer pays for loading and unloading.

FIT *Banking.* Federal Insurance Tax.

fk fork.

FL 1. Florida (for use with ZIP code). **2.** foreign language.

fL *Optics.* foot-lambert.

fl 1. *Sports.* flanker. **2.** flashing. **3.** flat. **4.** flush. **5.** focal length.

Fl. 1. Flanders. **2.** Flemish.

fl. 1. floor. **2.** florin; florins. **3.** flourished. [from Latin *flōruit*] **4.** fluid. **5.** (in the Netherlands) guilder; guilders. [from Dutch *florin*]

Fla. Florida.

flav. (in prescriptions) yellow. [from Latin *flāvus*]

F.L.B. Federal Land Bank.

fld. 1. field. **2.** fluid.

fldg folding.

fl dr fluid dram; fluid drams.

fldt floodlight.

fldxt (in prescriptions) fluidextract. [from Latin *fluidextractum*]

FLETC Federal Law Enforcement Training Center.

flex flexible.

flg 1. flange. **2.** flooring.

flh flathead.

fll frequency-locked loop.

flld full load.

flm flame.

flmb flammable.

flmt flush mount.

fln fuel line.

FLOPS (flops), *Computers.* floating-point operations per second.

flor. flourished. [from Latin *flōruit*]

flot flotation.

fl. oz. fluid ounce; fluid ounces.

flr 1. failure. **2.** filler. **3.** floor.

FLRA Federal Labor Relations Authority.

flrt flow rate.

flry flurry.

flt 1. flashlight. **2.** flight. **3.** float.

fltg floating.

fltr 1. filter. **2.** flutter.

fluor fluorescent.

flusoch fluted socket head.

flv flush valve.

flw flat washer.

flwp followup.

flywhl flywheel.

FM 1. Federated States of Micronesia (approved for postal use). **2.** *Electronics.* frequency modulation: a method of impressing a signal on a radio carrier wave. **3.** *Radio.* a system of radio broadcasting by means of frequency modulation.

Fm *Symbol, Chemistry.* fermium.

fm 1. *Symbol, Physics.* femtometer. **2.** field manual.

fm. 1. fathom; fathoms. **2.** from.

f.m. (in prescriptions) make a mixture. [from Latin *fiat mistūra*]

FMB Federal Maritime Board.

FMC Federal Maritime Commission.

FMCS Federal Mediation and Conciliation Service.

fmcw frequency-modulated continuous wave.

F.Mk. finmark; Finnish markka. Also, **FMk**

fmla formula.

fmr former.

fmw *Computers.* firmware.

fn footnote.

fnd found.

FNMA Federal National Mortgage Association.

fnsh finish.

fo. 1. *Electricity.* fast-operate: a type of relay. **2.** foldout. **3.** folio.

F.O. 1. field officer. **2.** foreign office. **3.** *Military.* forward observer.

f.o.b. *Commerce.* free on board: without charge to the buyer for goods placed on board a carrier at the point of shipment. Also, **F.O.B.**

FOBS fractional orbital bombardment system. Also, **F.O.B.S.**

foc focal.

F.O.E. Fraternal Order of Eagles.

FOIA Freedom of Information Act.

fol. 1. folio. 2. (in prescriptions) a leaf. [from Latin *folium*] 3. followed. 4. following.

foll. following.

For. Forester.

for. 1. foreign. 2. forester. 3. forestry.

F.O.R. *Commerce.* free on rails. Also, **f.o.r.**

fort. 1. fortification. 2. fortified.

FORTRAN (fôr'tran), *Computers.* a programming language used mainly in science and engineering. [*for(mula) tran(slation)*]

F.O.S. *Commerce.* 1. free on station. 2. free on steamer. Also, **f.o.s.**

F.O.T. *Commerce.* free on truck. Also, **f.o.t.**

fouo for official use only.

4WD four-wheel drive.

fp 1. faceplate. 2. *Music.* forte-piano. 3. *Football.* forward pass.

F.P. *Physics.* foot-pound; foot-pounds.

f.p. 1. fireplug. 2. foolscap. 3. foot-pound; foot-pounds. 4. *Music.* forte-piano. 5. freezing point. 6. fully paid.

FPC 1. Federal Power Commission. 2. fish protein concentrate.

FPHA Federal Public Housing Authority.

Fpl *Real Estate.* fireplace.

fpl fire plug.

fpm feet per minute. Also, **ft/min, ft./min.**

FPO *Military.* 1. field post office. 2. fleet post office.

fprf fireproof.

fps 1. Also, **ft/sec** feet per second. 2. *Physics.* foot-pound-second.

f.p.s. 1. Also, **ft./sec.** feet per second. 2. *Physics.* foot-pound-second. 3. frames per second.

fpsps feet per second per second. Also, **ft/s²**

FPT freight pass-through.

fpt female pipe thread.

FR 1. *Real Estate.* family room. 2. freight release.

Fr *Symbol, Chemistry.* francium.

fr 1. failure rate. 2. *Electricity.* fast release: a type of relay. 3. field reversing.

Fr. 1. Father. 2. franc; francs. 3. France. 4. *Religion.* frater. 5. Frau: the German form of address for a married woman. 6. French. 7. Friar. 8. Friday.

fr. 1. fragment. 2. franc; francs. 3. from.

frac fractional.

frag fragment.

F.R.A.S. Fellow of the Royal Astronomical Society.

FRB 1. Federal Reserve Bank. 2. Federal Reserve Board. Also, **F.R.B.**

frbd freeboard.

FRC Federal Radio Commission.

FRCD *Finance.* floating-rate certificate of deposit.

F.R.C.P. Fellow of the Royal College of Physicians.

F.R.C.S. Fellow of the Royal College of Surgeons.

freq. 1. frequency. 2. frequent. 3. frequentative. 4. frequently.

freqm frequency meter.

frequ frequency.

fres fire-resistant.

F.R.G. Federal Republic of Germany.

F.R.G.S. Fellow of the Royal Geographical Society.

Fri. Friday.

frict friction.

Fris. Frisian. Also, **Fris**

Frl. Fräulein: the German form of address for an unmarried woman.

frm frame.

FRN *Finance.* floating-rate note.

frnc furnace.

frng fringe.

front. frontispiece.

frpl *Real Estate.* fireplace.

FRS Federal Reserve System.

Frs. Frisian.

frs. francs.

F.R.S. Fellow of the Royal Society.

F.R.S.L. Fellow of the Royal Society of Literature.

F.R.S.S. Fellow of the Royal Statistical Society.

frt. 1. freight. **2.** front.

frwk framework.

frz freeze.

frzr freezer.

FS Federal Specification.

fs 1. field service. **2.** fire station. **3.** functional schematic.

f.s. foot-second; foot-seconds.

FSA Farm Security Administration

fsbl 1. feasible. **2.** fusible.

fsc full scale.

FSH *Biochemistry.* follicle-stimulating hormone.

fsk frequency-shift keying.

FSLIC Federal Savings and Loan Insurance Corporation.

fsm field-strength meter.

FSN Federal Stock Number.

FSO foreign service officer.

FSR Field Service Regulations.

fssn fission.

fstnr fastener.

fsz full size.

FT full time.

Ft. (in Hungary) forint; forints.

ft. foot; feet.

ft^3 *Symbol.* cubic foot; cubic feet.

FTC *U.S. Government.* Federal Trade Commission.

ftc fast time constant.

ftd fitted.

ftg 1. fitting. **2.** footing.

fth. fathom; fathoms. Also, **fthm.**

ft./hr. feet per hour.

fthrd female thread.

ft-L *Optics.* foot-lambert.

ft-lb *Physics.* foot-pound.

ft./min. feet per minute.

FTP *Computers.* File Transfer Protocol.

ft-pdl *Physics.* foot-poundal.

ft./sec. feet per second.

FTZ free-trade zone.

fu fuse.

fuhld fuseholder.

ful fulcrum.

fund fundamental.

funl funnel.

fur. furlong; furlongs.

furl. furlough.

furn 1. furnish. **2.** furniture.

fuslg fuselage.

fut. future.

fv flux valve.

f.v. on the back of the page. [from Latin *foliō versō*]

FVC *Medicine.* forced vital capacity.

FWA Federal Works Agency.

FWD 1. Also, **4WD** four-wheel drive. **2.** front-wheel drive.

fwd. 1. foreword. **2.** forward.

F.W.I. French West Indies.

fwv full wave.

Fwy. freeway.

FX foreign exchange.

fx. 1. fracture. **2.** fractured.

fxd fixed.

fxtr fixture.

FY fiscal year.

FYI for your information.

fz fuze.

G

G **1.** *Slang.* grand: one thousand dollars. **2.** (*sometimes lowercase*) *Aerospace.* gravity: a unit of acceleration.

G **1.** gay. **2.** *Psychology.* general intelligence. **3.** German. **4.** good.

G *Symbol.* **1.** the seventh in order or in a series. **2.** *Music.* **a.** the fifth tone in the scale of C major or the seventh tone in the relative minor scale, A minor. **b.** a string, key, or pipe tuned to this tone. **c.** a written or printed note representing this tone. **d.** (in the fixed system of solmization) the fifth tone of the scale of C major, called *sol.* **e.** the tonality having G as the tonic note. **3.** (*sometimes lowercase*) the medieval Roman numeral for 400. **4.** *Electricity.* **a.** conductance. **b.** gauss. **5.** *Physics.* constant of gravitation; law of gravity. **6.** *Biochemistry.* **a.** glycine. **b.** guanine. **7.** a rating assigned to a motion picture by the Motion Picture Association of America indicating that the film is suitable for general audiences, or children as well as adults.

g **1.** *Psychology.* general intelligence. **2.** good. **3.** gram; grams. **4.** *Electronics.* grid.

g *Symbol, Physics.* **1.** acceleration of gravity. **2.** gravity.

G. **1.** General. **2.** German. **3.** (in Haiti) gourde; gourdes. **4.** (*specific*) gravity. **5.** Gulf.

g. **1.** gauge. **2.** gender. **3.** general. **4.** generally. **5.** genitive. **6.** going back to. **7.** gold. **8.** grain; grains. **9.** gram; grams. **10.** *Sports.* guard. **11.** *British.* guinea; guineas. **12.** gun.

GA **1.** Gamblers Anonymous. **2.** General American. **3.** general of the army. **4.** Georgia (for use with ZIP code).

Ga *Symbol, Chemistry.* gallium.

Ga. Georgia.

G.A. **1.** General Agent. **2.** General Assembly. **3.** Also, **g.a., G/A** *Insurance.* general average.

G.A.A. Gay Activists' Alliance.

GABA (gab′ə), *Biochemistry.* a neurotransmitter of the central nervous system that inhibits excitatory responses. [g(*amma-*)a(*mino*)b(*utyric*) a(*cid*)]

G/A con. *Insurance.* general average contribution.

G/A dep. *Insurance.* general average deposit.

GAE General American English.

GAI guaranteed annual income.

Gal. *Bible.* Galatians.

gal. gallon; gallons.

gal/h *Symbol.* gallons per hour.

gall gallery.

gal/min *Symbol.* gallons per minute.

gals. gallons.

gal/s *Symbol.* gallons per second.

galv galvanic.

galvnm galvanometer.

galvs galvanized steel.

galy galley.

GAM **1.** graduate in Aerospace Mechanical Engineering. **2.** ground-to-air missile.

G&AE *Accounting.* general and administrative expense.

G and T gin and tonic. Also, **g and t**

GAO General Accounting Office.

GAPL Ground-to-Air Data Link.

gar. garage. Also, **gar**

G.A.R. Grand Army of the Republic.

gas gasoline.

GASP Gravity-assisted Space Probe.

GAT **1.** *Military.* Ground Attack Tactics. **2.** Ground-to-Air Transmitter.

GATT (gat), General Agreement on Tariffs and Trade.

G.A.W. guaranteed annual wage.

gaz. 1. gazette. 2. gazetteer.

GB 1. *Computers.* gigabyte: 1000 megabytes. 2. *Finance.* Gold Bond. 3. (on CB radio) good-bye. 4. Great Britain.

Gb *Electricity.* gilbert.

G.B. Great Britain.

G.B.E. Knight Grand Cross of the British Empire or Dame Grand Cross of the British Empire.

GBF gay black female.

gbg garbage.

GBM gay black male.

GBO *Commerce.* goods in bad order.

GBS *Radiography.* Gall Bladder Series.

Gc 1. gigacycle; gigacycles. 2. gigacycles per second.

GCA Girls' Clubs of America.

g-cal gram calorie. Also, **g-cal.**

G.C.B. Grand Cross of the Bath.

GCC Gulf Cooperation Council.

G.C.D. 1. *Math.* greatest common denominator. 2. greatest common divisor. Also, **g.c.d.**

GCE *British.* General Certificate of Education.

G.C.F. *Math.* greatest common factor; greatest common divisor. Also, **g.c.f.**

GCG *Military.* Guidance Control Group.

G.C.M. *Math.* greatest common measure. Also, **g.c.m.**

GCPS gigacycles per second. Also, **Gc/s, Gc/sec**

GCR *Military.* ground-controlled radar.

G.C.T. Greenwich Civil Time.

GCU *Aerospace.* Ground Control Unit.

GD 1. *Real Estate.* garbage disposal. 2. General Delivery.

Gd *Symbol, Chemistry.* gadolinium.

gd. 1. good. 2. guard.

G.D. 1. Grand Duchess. 2. Grand Duke.

Gde. (in Haiti) gourde; gourdes.

GDI *Slang.* God Damned Independent.

gdlk grid leak.

Gdn guardian.

gdn garden.

gdnc guidance.

Gdns. gardens.

GDP gross domestic product.

GDR German Democratic Republic. Also, **G.D.R.**

gds. goods.

GE *Medicine.* gastroenterology.

Ge *Symbol, Chemistry.* germanium.

g.e. *Bookbinding.* gilt edges.

GEB Guiding Eyes for the Blind.

geb. born. [from German *geboren*]

GED 1. general educational development. 2. general equivalency diploma.

GEF 1. Gauss Error Function. 2. *Military.* ground equipment failure.

GEM giant earth mover.

Gen. 1. *Military.* General. 2. Genesis. 3. Geneva.

gen. 1. gender. 2. general. 3. generator. 4. genitive. 5. genus.

genit. genitive.

genl general.

Genl. General.

Gen. Mtg. *Banking.* general mortgage.

Gent. gentleman; gentlemen. Also, **gent.**

Geo. George.

geod. 1. geodesy. 2. geodetic.

geog. 1. geographer. 2. geographic; geographical. 3. geography.

geol. 1. geologic; geological. 2. geologist. 3. geology.

geom. 1. geometric; geometrical. 2. geometry.

GEOS Geodetic Earth Orbiting Satellite.

Ger. 1. German. **2.** Germany.

ger. 1. gerund. **2.** gerundive.

Gestapo (gə stä′pō), the German secret police under Hitler. [from German Ge(heime) Sta(ats)po(lizei) secret state police]

GeV Physics. gigaelectron volt. Also, **Gev**

GF gay female.

gfci ground-fault circuit interrupter.

GFE government-furnished equipment.

GFR German Federal Republic.

G.F.T.U. General Federation of Trade Unions.

GG 1. gamma globulin. **2.** great gross.

GGR great gross.

GH growth hormone.

GHA Greenwich hour angle.

GHF gay Hispanic female.

GHM gay Hispanic male.

GHz Physics. gigahertz; gigahertzes.

GI (jē′ī′), a member of the U.S. armed forces, especially an enlisted soldier. Also, **G.I.** [originally abbreviation of galvanized iron, used in U.S. Army bookkeeping in entering articles (e.g., trash cans) made of it; later extended to all articles issued (as an assumed abbreviation of government issue) and finally to soldiers themselves]

Gi Electricity. gilbert; gilberts.

gi. gill; gills.

G.I. 1. galvanized iron. **2.** gastrointestinal. **3.** general issue. **4.** government issue. Also, **GI, g.i.**

Gib. Gibraltar.

GIGO (gī′gō), Computers. a rule of thumb stating that when faulty data are fed into a computer, the information that emerges will also be faulty. [g(arbage) i(n) g(arbage) o(ut)]

GILMER guardian of impressive letters and master of excellent replies.

GIRLS (gûrlz), Generalized Information Retrieval and Listing System.

GI's (jē′īz′), **the GI's,** Slang. diarrhea. Also, **G.I.'s, G.I.s** [probably for GI shits]

GJ Informal. grapefruit juice.

GJF gay Jewish female.

GJM gay Jewish male.

Gk Greek. Also, **Gk.**

Gl Symbol, Chemistry. glucinum.

gl gold.

gl. 1. glass; glasses. **2.** gloss.

g/l grams per liter.

GLB gay, lesbian, bisexual.

glb Math. greatest lower bound.

Gld. guilder; guilders.

GLF Gay Liberation Front.

Gln Biochemistry. glutamine.

GLO Slang. get the lead out.

gloss. glossary.

GLOW Gross Lift-Off Weight.

GLP Gross Lawyer Product.

glpg glowplug.

glsry glossary.

Glu Biochemistry. glutamic acid.

glv globe valve.

Gly Biochemistry. glycine.

glyc. (in prescriptions) glycerite. [from Latin glyceritum]

glycn glycerine.

glz glaze.

GM 1. gay male. **2.** General Manager. **3.** General Medicine. **4.** Greenwich Meridian.

gm. 1. gram; grams. **2.** guided missile.

G.M. 1. General Manager. **2.** Grand Marshal. **3.** Grand Master. Also, **GM**

G.M.&S. general, medical, and surgical.

GMAT 1. Trademark. Graduate Management Admissions Test. **2.** Greenwich Mean Astronomical Time.

GMB *British.* Grand Master of the Bath.

gmbl gimbal.

Gmc Germanic. Also, **Gmc.**

GMP *Biochemistry.* a ribonucleotide constituent of ribonucleic acid. [g(uanosine) m(ono)p(hosphate)]

GMT Greenwich Mean Time. Also, **G.M.T.**

gmtry geometry.

gmv guaranteed minimum value.

GMW gram-molecular weight.

gn green.

G.N. Graduate Nurse.

gnd *Electricity.* ground.

GNI *Economics.* Gross National Income.

gnltd granulated.

GNMA Government National Mortgage Association.

GNP gross national product. Also, **G.N.P.**

GnRH gonadotropin releasing hormone.

G.O. **1.** general office. **2.** general order. Also, **g.o.**

GOES Geostationary Operational Environmental Satellite.

G.O.K. *Medicine.* God Only Knows.

GOO Get Oil Out.

G.O.P. Grand Old Party (an epithet of the Republican party since 1880). Also, **GOP**

Goth. Gothic. Also, **Goth, goth.**

Gov. governor.

gov. **1.** government. **2.** governor.

Govt. government. Also, **govt.**

GP **1.** Galactic Probe. **2.** General Purpose.

gp **1.** general purpose. **2.** glide path.

gp. group. Also, **Gp.**

G.P. **1.** General Practitioner. **2.** General Purpose. **3.** Gloria Patri. **4.** Graduate in Pharmacy. **5.** Grand Prix.

GPA grade point average.

gpad gallons per acre per day.

gpcd gallons per capita per day.

gpd gallons per day.

gph **1.** gallons per hour. **2.** graphite.

gpi ground-position indicator.

gpib *Computers.* general-purpose interface bus.

gpm **1.** gallons per mile. **2.** gallons per minute.

G.P.O. **1.** general post office. **2.** Government Printing Office. Also, **GPO**

GPRF gay Puerto Rican female.

GPRM gay Puerto Rican male.

GPS *Aerospace, Navigation.* Global Positioning System.

gps gallons per second.

GPU General Postal Union; Universal Postal Union .

GPU (gā′pā′ōō′, jē′pē′yōō′), (in the Soviet Union) the secret-police organization (1922–23) functioning under the NKVD. Also, **G.P.U.** [from Russian G(osudárstvennoe) p(olitích-eskoe) u(pravlénie) state political directorate]

GQ General Quarters.

gr **1.** gear. **2.** grain. **3.** gram; grams. **4.** gross.

Gr. **1.** Grecian. **2.** Greece. **3.** Greek.

gr. **1.** grade. **2.** grain; grains. **3.** gram; grams. **4.** grammar. **5.** gravity. **6.** great. **7.** gross. **8.** group.

G.R. King George. [from Latin *Geōrgius Rēx*]

grad. **1.** *Math.* gradient. **2.** graduate. **3.** graduated.

gram. **1.** grammar. **2.** grammarian. **3.** grammatical.

gran **1.** granite. **2.** granular; granulated.

GRAS (gras), generally recognized as safe: a status label assigned by the FDA to a listing of substances not known to be hazardous and thus approved for use in foods.

Gr. Br. Great Britain. Also, **Gr. Brit.**

grbx gearbox.

grd 1. grind. **2.** guard.

grdl griddle.

grdtn graduation.

GRE Graduate Record Examination.

GRF growth hormone releasing factor.

GRI Government Reports Index.

gro. gross.

grom grommet.

grp group.

grph graphic.

grs grease.

grshft gearshaft.

grtg grating.

grtr grater.

GRU (in the former Soviet Union) the Chief Intelligence Directorate of the Soviet General Staff, a military intelligence organization founded in 1920 and functioning as a complement to the KGB. Also, **G.R.U.** [from Russian *G(lávnoe) r(azvédyvatel'noe) u(pravlénie)*]

Grv. grove.

grv groove.

gr. wt. gross weight.

GS 1. General Schedule (referring to the Civil Service job classification system). **2.** general staff. **3.** German silver.

gs ground speed.

G.S. 1. general secretary. **2.** general staff. Also, **g.s.**

GSA 1. General Services Administration. **2.** Girl Scouts of America. Also, **G.S.A.**

G.S.C. General Staff Corps.

GSE ground-support equipment.

Gsil German silver.

gskt gasket.

GSL Guaranteed Student Loan.

G spot (jē'spot'), Gräfenberg spot: a patch of tissue in the vagina pur-

portedly excitable and erectile. Also, **G-spot.**

GSR 1. galvanic skin reflex. **2.** galvanic skin response.

gsr glide slope receiver.

GST Greenwich Sidereal Time.

G-suit (jē'sōōt'), *Aerospace*. anti-G suit: a flier's or astronaut's suit. Also, **g-suit.** [*g(ravity) suit*]

GT 1. Game Theory. **2.** gigaton; gigatons. **3.** grand theft **4.** *Automotive.* grand touring: a car type.

gt. 1. gilt. **2.** great. **3.** (in prescriptions) a drop [from Latin *gutta*].

Gt. Br. Great Britain. Also, **Gt. Brit.**

g.t.c. 1. good till canceled. **2.** good till countermanded. Also, **G.T.C.**

gtd. guaranteed.

GTG ground-to-ground.

GTO *Automotive.* Gran Turismo Omologato: a car style (grand touring).

GTP *Biochemistry.* an ester that is an important metabolic cofactor and precursor in the biosynthesis of cyclic GMP. [*g(uanosine) t(ri)p(hosphate)*]

gtrb gas turbine.

GTS gas turbine ship.

gtt. (in prescriptions) drops. [from Latin *guttae*]

GU 1. genitourinary. **2.** Guam (for use with ZIP code).

guar guarantee.

GUGB the Chief Directorate for State Security: the former Soviet Union's secret police organization (1934–1941) functioning as part of the NKVD. Also, **G.U.G.B.** [from Russian *G(lávnoe) u(pravlénie) g(osudárstvennoĭ) b(ezopásnosti)*]

GUI (gōō'ē), *Computers.* graphical user interface.

Gui. Guiana.

Guin. Guinea.

gun. gunnery.

GUT *Physics.* grand unification theory.

gut gutter.

g.v. 1. gravimetric volume. **2.** giga-volt; gigavolts.

gvl gravel.

GVW gross vehicle weight; gross vehicular weight.

GW gigawatt; gigawatts. Also, **Gw**

GWF gay white female.

GWh Gigawatt-hour.

GWM gay white male.

Gy *Physics.* gray: a measure of radiation absorption.

gy gray.

GYN 1. gynecological. **2.** gynecologist. **3.** gynecology. Also, **gyn.**

gyp gypsum.

GySgt *Marine Corps.* gunnery sergeant.

GZ ground zero.

H

H 1. hard. **2.** *Grammar.* head. **3.** *Electricity.* henry. **4.** *Slang.* heroin. **5.** high.

H *Symbol.* **1.** the eighth in order or in a series. **2.** (*sometimes lowercase*) the medieval Roman numeral for 200. **3.** *Chemistry.* hydrogen. **4.** *Biochemistry.* histidine. **5.** *Physics.* **a.** enthalpy. **b.** horizontal component of the earth's magnetic field. **c.** magnetic intensity. **6.** *Music.* the letter used in German to indicate the tone B.

H¹ *Symbol, Chemistry.* protium. Also, **¹H, Hᵃ**

H² *Symbol, Chemistry.* deuterium. Also, **²H, Hᵇ**

H³ *Symbol, Chemistry.* tritium. Also, **³H, Hᶜ**

h hard.

h *Symbol, Physics.* Planck's constant.

H. (in prescriptions) an hour. [from Latin *hōra*]

h. 1. harbor. **2.** hard. **3.** hardness. **4.** heavy sea. **5.** height. **6.** hence. **7.** high. **8.** *Baseball.* hit; hits. **9.** horns. **10.** hour; hours. **11.** hundred. **12.** husband. Also, **H.**

Ha *Symbol, Chemistry.* hahnium.

ha hectare; hectares.

h.a. 1. *Gunnery.* high angle. **2.** in this year [from Latin *hōc annō*].

Hab. *Bible.* Habakkuk.

HAC House Appropriations Committee.

Hag. *Bible.* Haggai.

Hal *Chemistry.* halogen.

H&A Health and Accident.

haust. (in prescriptions) draught. [from Latin *haustus*].

Haw. Hawaii.

HAWK (hôk), **1.** have alimony, will keep. **2.** Homing All the Way Killer (small missile).

haz hazardous.

Hb *Symbol, Biochemistry.* hemoglobin.

h.b. *Sports.* halfback.

H.B.M. His Britannic Majesty; Her Britannic Majesty.

HBO Home Box Office (a cable television channel).

H-bomb (āch′bom′), hydrogen bomb.

HBP high blood pressure.

HBV hepatitis B.

H.C. 1. Holy Communion. **2.** House of Commons.

h.c. for the sake of honor. [from Latin *honōris causā*]

hce human-caused error.

H.C.F. *Math.* highest common factor. Also, **h.c.f.**

hCG human chorionic gonadotropin.

H.C.M. His Catholic Majesty; Her Catholic Majesty.

H. Con. Res. House concurrent resolution.

HCR highway contract route.

hcs high-carbon steel.

hd. 1. hand. **2.** hard. **3.** head.

h.d. 1. heavy duty. **2.** (in prescriptions) at bedtime [from Latin *hōra decubitūs*]

hdbk. handbook.

hdcp handicap.

hdd *Computers*. hard-disk drive.

hdg heading.

hdkf. handkerchief.

HDL high-density lipoprotein.

hdl handle.

hdlg handling.

hdlng headlining.

hdn harden.

hdns hardness.

H. Doc. House document.

HDPE high-density polyethylene.

hdqrs. headquarters.

hdr header.

hdshk *Computers*. handshake.

hdst headset.

HDTV high-definition television.

hdw. hardware. Also, **hdwe, hdwr.**

hdwd hardwood.

hdx *Telecommunications*. half duplex.

HE high explosive. Also, **he**

He *Symbol, Chemistry*. helium.

H.E. 1. high explosive. **2.** His Eminence. **3.** His Excellency; Her Excellency.

HEAO High Energy Astrophysical Observatory.

Heb Hebrew.

Heb. 1. Hebrew. **2.** *Bible*. Hebrews. Also, **Hebr.**

herp. herpetology. Also, **herpet.**

herpetol. 1. herpetological. **2.** herpetology.

het heterodyne.

HETP *Chemistry*. hexaethyl tetraphosphate.

HEW Department of Health, Education, and Welfare.

hex. 1. *Math*. hexadecimal (number system). **2.** hexagon. **3.** hexagonal.

hex hd hexagonal head.

hex soch hexagonal socket head.

HF 1. high frequency. **2.** Hispanic female.

Hf *Symbol, Chemistry*. hafnium.

hf. half.

hf. bd. *Printing*. half-bound.

hfe human-factors engineering.

HG 1. High German. **2.** *British*. Home Guard.

Hg *Symbol, Chemistry*. mercury. [from Latin *hydrargyrum*, from Greek *hydrárgyros* literally, liquid silver]

hg hectogram; hectograms.

H.G. 1. High German. **2.** His Grace; Her Grace.

hGH human growth hormone.

hgr hanger.

hgt. height.

hgwy. highway.

H.H. 1. His Highness; Her Highness. **2.** His Holiness.

hhd hogshead; hogsheads.

HH.D. Doctor of Humanities.

HHFA Housing and Home Finance Agency.

H-hour (āch′ouər′, -ou′ər), the time, usually unspecified, set for the beginning of a planned attack.

HHS Department of Health and Human Services.

HI Hawaii (for use with ZIP code).

H.I. 1. Hawaiian Islands. **2.** *Meteorology*. heat index.

HIF human-initiated failure.

hi-fi (hī′fī′), high fidelity. Also, **hi fi**

H.I.H. His Imperial Highness; Her Imperial Highness.

H.I.M. His Imperial Majesty; Her Imperial Majesty.

Hind Hindustani.

Hind. 1. Hindi. **2.** Hindu. **3.** Hindustan. **4.** Hindustani.

hint high intensity.

HIP (āch′ī′pē′ or, sometimes, hip), Health Insurance Plan.

hipar high-power acquisition radar.

hipot high potential.

His Biochemistry. histidine.

hist. 1. histology. 2. historian. 3. historical. 4. history.

HIV human immunodeficiency virus; AIDS virus.

H.J. here lies. [from Latin hīc jacet]

H.J. Res. House joint resolution.

H.J.S. here lies buried. [from Latin hīc jacet sepultus]

HK Hong Kong.

hksw Telephones. hookswitch.

hl 1. haul. 2. hectoliter; hectoliters.

H.L. House of Lords.

HLA Immunology. human leukocyte antigen.

HLBB Home Loan Bank Board.

hlcl helical.

hlcptr helicopter.

hldg holding.

hldn holddown.

hldr holder.

hll Computers. high-level language.

hlpr helper.

HLTL Computers. high-level transistor logic.

HLTTL Computers. high-level transistor-transistor logic.

HM Hispanic male.

hm hectometer; hectometers.

H.M. Her Majesty; His Majesty.

hma Computers. high-memory area.

HMAS Her Majesty's Australian Ship; His Majesty's Australian Ship.

hmc harmonic.

HMCS Her Majesty's Canadian Ship; His Majesty's Canadian Ship.

hmd humidity.

HMF Her Majesty's Forces; His Majesty's Forces.

HMMV humvee: a military vehicle.

Also, **HMMWV.** [H(igh)-M(obility) M(ultipurpose) W(heeled) V(ehicle)]

HMO health maintenance organization.

hmr hammer.

H.M.S. 1. Her Majesty's Service; His Majesty's Service. 2. Her Majesty's Ship; His Majesty's Ship.

hnd cont hand control.

hndrl handrail.

hndst handset.

hndwl handwheel.

hng hinge.

hntg hunting.

HO (hō), (in police use) habitual offender.

Ho Symbol, Chemistry. holmium.

ho. house.

H.O. 1. Head Office. 2. Home Office.

HOLC Home Owners' Loan Corporation. Also, **H.O.L.C.**

Hon. 1. Honorable. 2. Honorary.

hon. 1. honor. 2. honorable. 3. honorably. 4. honorary.

Hond. Honduras.

hor. 1. horizon. 2. horizontal. 3. horology.

hor. interm. (in prescriptions) at intermediate hours. [from Latin hōrā intermediīs]

horol. horology.

hor. som. (in prescriptions) at bedtime. [from Latin hōrā somnī at the hour of sleep]

hort. 1. horticultural. 2. horticulture.

hor. un. spatio (in prescriptions) at the end of one hour. [from Latin hōrae ūnius spatiō]

horz horizontal.

Hos. Bible. Hosea.

hosp. hospital.

HOV high-occupancy vehicle.

hp 1. high pass. 2. horsepower.

H.P. 1. Electricity. high power. 2. high

pressure. **3.** horsepower. Also, **h.p., HP**

HPER Health, Physical Education, and Recreation.

hpot helical potentiometer.

hps high-pressure steam.

HPV human papilloma virus.

H.Q. headquarters. Also, **h.q., HQ**

HR 1. *Baseball.* home run; home runs. **2.** House of Representatives.

Hr. Herr: the German form of address for a man.

hr. hour; hours. Also, **h.**

H.R. House of Representatives. Also, **HR**

h.r. *Baseball.* home run; home runs. Also, **hr**

HRA Health Resources Administration.

H-R diagram *Astronomy.* Hertzsprung-Russell diagram.

H.R.E. 1. Holy Roman Emperor. **2.** Holy Roman Empire.

H. Rept. House report.

H. Res. House resolution.

hrg hearing.

H.R.H. His Royal Highness; Her Royal Highness.

H.R.I.P. here rests in peace. [from Latin *hīc requiēscit in pāce*]

hrs. 1. hot-rolled steel. **2.** hours.

hrzn horizon.

HS 1. *Medicine.* Herpes Simplex. **2.** laid here. [from Latin *Hic sītus*]

hs high speed.

H.S. 1. High School. **2.** *British.* Home Secretary.

h.s. 1. in this sense. [from Latin *hōc sensū*] **2.** (in prescriptions) at bedtime. [from Latin *hōrā somnī* at the hour of sleep]

hse house.

hsg housing.

H.S.H. His Serene Highness; Her Serene Highness.

hshld household.

HSI heat stress index.

H.S.M. His Serene Majesty; Her Serene Majesty.

hss high-speed steel.

HST Hawaii Standard Time. Also, **H.S.T., h.s.t.**

hsth hose thread.

HSV-1 herpes simplex virus: usually associated with oral herpes. Also, **HSV-I.**

HSV-2 herpes simplex virus: usually causing genital herpes. Also, **HSV-II.**

HT 1. *Sports.* halftime. **2.** halftone. **3.** Hawaii time. **4.** *Electricity.* high tension. **5.** high tide. **6.** at this time. [from Latin *hōc tempōre*] **7.** under this title. [from Latin *hōc titulō*]

ht. height.

h.t. at this time. [from Latin *hōc tempōre*]

htd heated.

htg heating.

HTLV *Pathology.* human T-cell lymphotropic virus.

HTLV-1 *Pathology.* human T-cell lymphotropic virus type 1. Also, **HTLV-I.**

HTLV-2 *Pathology.* human T-cell lymphotropic virus type. Also, **HTLV-II.**

HTLV-3 *Pathology.* human T-cell lymphotropic virus type 3; AIDS virus. Also, **HTLV-III.**

HTML *Computers.* HyperText Markup Language.

htr heater.

Hts. Heights.

ht tr heat-treat.

HUAC (hyōō′ak), House Un-American Activities Committee.

HUD (hud), Department of Housing and Urban Development.

HUM humanities.

huricn hurricane.

husb. husbandry.

H.V. 1. high velocity. **2.** Also, **h.v., hv** high voltage. **3.** high volume.

HVAC heating, ventilating, and air conditioning.

HVDC high-voltage direct current.

HVP hydrolyzed vegetable protein. Also, **H.V.P.**

hvps high-voltage power supply.

hvy. heavy.

HW 1. half wave. 2. *Real Estate.* hardwood. 3. high water. 4. hot water (heat).

HWM high-water mark. Also, **H.W.M., h.w.m.**

hwy highway. Also, **Hwy, hwy.**

hy. *Electricity.* (formerly) henry.

hyb hybrid.

hyd. 1. hydrant. 2. hydraulics. 3. hydrostatics.

hydm hydrometer.

hydr hydraulic.

hydraul. hydraulics.

hydrelc hydroelectric.

HYDROPAC (hī′drə pak′), an urgent warning of navigational dangers in the Pacific Ocean, issued by the U.S. Navy Hydrographic Office.

hydros. hydrostatics.

hyp. 1. hypotenuse. 2. hypothesis. 3. hypothetical.

hypoth. 1. hypothesis. 2. hypothetical.

Hz hertz; hertzes.

I

I interstate (used with a number to designate an interstate highway): *I-95.*

I *Symbol.* 1. the ninth in order or in a series. 2. (*sometimes lowercase*) the Roman numeral for 1. 3. *Chemistry.* iodine. 4. *Biochemistry.* isoleucine. 5. *Physics.* isotopic spin. 6. *Electricity.* current. 7. *Logic.* particular affirmative.

i Symbol, Math. 1. the imaginary number. 2. a unit vector on the *x*-axis of a coordinate system.

I. 1. Independent. 2. Indian. 3. Iraqi. 4. Island; Islands. 5. Isle; Isles. 6. Israeli.

i. 1. imperator. 2. incisor. 3. interest. 4. intransitive. 5. island. 6. isle; isles.

IA Iowa (for use with ZIP code).

ia 1. immediately available. 2. impedance angle. 3. international angstrom.

Ia. Iowa.

i.a. in absentia.

IAAF International Amateur Athletic Federation.

IAB 1. Industry Advisory Board. 2. Inter-American Bank.

IAC Industry Advisory Commission.

IACA Independent Air Carriers Association.

IACB International Association of Convention Bureaus.

IADB 1. Inter-American Defense Board. 2. Inter-American Development Bank.

IAEA International Atomic Energy Agency.

IAG International Association of Gerontology.

IAIA Institute of American Indian Arts.

IAMAW International Association of Machinists and Aerospace Workers.

IAS 1. *Aeronautics.* indicated air speed. 2. Institute for Advanced Study.

ias indicate airspeed.

IAT international atomic time.

IATA International Air Transport Association.

IATSE International Alliance of Theatrical Stage Employees (and Moving Picture Machine Operators of the U.S. and Canada).

iaw in accordance with.

ib. 1. in the same book, chapter, page, etc. [from Latin *ibidem*] **2.** instruction book.

IBA 1. Independent Bankers Association. **2.** International Bar Association.

IBC 1. International Broadcasting Corporation. **2.** international business company.

IBD inflammatory bowel disease.

IBEW International Brotherhood of Electrical Workers.

IBF international banking facilities.

ibid. (ib′id), in the same book, chapter, page, etc. [from Latin *ibidem*]

IBR infectious bovine rhinotracheitis.

I.B.T.C.W.H. International Brotherhood of Teamsters, Chauffeurs, Warehousemen, and Helpers of America.

IC 1. immediate constituent. **2.** *Computers, Electronics.* integrated circuit. **3.** intensive care.

I.C. Jesus Christ. [from Latin *I(ēsus) C(hrī̆stus)*]

ICA 1. International Communication Agency (1978–82). **2.** International Cooperation Administration.

ICAO International Civil Aviation Organization.

icas intermittent commercial and amateur service.

ICBM intercontinental ballistic missile. Also, **I.C.B.M.**

ICC Indian Claims Commission.

I.C.C. 1. International Control Commission. **2.** Interstate Commerce Commission. Also, **ICC**

Icel. 1. Iceland. **2.** Icelandic. Also, **Icel**

ICF *Physics.* inertial confinement fusion: an experimental method for producing controlled thermonuclear energy.

ICJ International Court of Justice.

ICM Institute of Computer Management.

icm 1. intercom. **2.** intercommunication.

ICR 1. Institute of Cancer Research. **2.** Institute for Cooperative Research.

ICRC International Committee of the Red Cross.

icrm ice cream.

ICS International College of Surgeons.

ICSE International Committee for Sexual Equality.

ICSH *Biochemistry, Pharmacology.* interstitial-cell stimulating hormone.

ICU intensive care unit.

icw interrupted continuous wave.

ID (ī′dē′), a means of identification, as a card or bracelet.

ID 1. Idaho (for use with ZIP code). **2.** Also, **i.d., id** inside diameter.

id 1. inside diameter. **2.** internal diameter.

ID. (in Iraq) dinar; dinars.

Id. Idaho.

id. idem: the same as previously given.

I.D. 1. identification. **2.** identity. **3.** *Military.* Infantry Division. **4.** Intelligence Department.

IDA 1. Industrial Development Agency. **2.** Institute for Defense Analysis.

IDB 1. Industrial Development Board. **2.** industrial development bond.

IDE *Computers.* integrated drive electronics: hard-drive interface.

ident 1. identical. **2.** identification.

idf *Telephones.* intermediate distributing frame.

IDP 1. integrated data processing. **2.** International Driving Permit.

IDR 1. Institute for Dream Research. **2.** international drawing rights.

idrty indirectly.

idx index.

IE Indo-European.

I.E. 1. Indo-European. 2. Industrial Engineer.

i.e. that is. [from Latin *id est*]

IEC International Electrotechnical Commission.

I.E.E.E. (ī′ trip′əl ē′), Institute of Electrical and Electronics Engineers. Also, **IEEE**

IEP Individualized Educational Program.

IES Illuminating Engineering Society.

if 1. inside frosted (of a light bulb). 2. intermediate frequency.

IFA *Medicine.* immunofluorescence assay.

IFALP International Federation of Air Line Pilots Associations.

IFC 1. International Finance Corporation. 2. International Fisheries Commission 3. International Freighting Corporation.

IFF 1. *Military.* Identification, Friend or Foe: a system to distinguish between friendly and hostile aircraft. 2. Institute for the Future.

iff *Math.* if and only if.

IFIP (if′ip), International Federation for Information Processing.

I.F.L.W.U. International Fur and Leather Workers' Union.

IFN *Biochemistry, Pharmacology.* interferon.

ifr instrument flight rules.

IFS International Foundation for Science.

I.F.S. Irish Free State.

IG *Electronics.* ignitor: an electron device.

Ig *Immunology.* immunoglobulin.

I.G. 1. Indo-Germanic. 2. Inspector General.

IgA *Immunology.* immunoglobulin A.

IgE *Immunology.* immunoglobulin E.

IGFET insulated-gate field-effect transistor.

IgG *Immunology.* immunoglobulin G.

IgM *Immunology.* immunoglobulin M.

ign. 1. ignition. 2. unknown [from Latin *ignōtus*].

igt ingot.

IGY International Geophysical Year.

IHL International Hockey League.

ihp indicated horsepower. Also, **IHP**

IHS 1. Jesus. [from Latin, from Greek: partial transliteration of the first three letters of *Iēsoûs* Jesus] 2. Jesus Savior of Men. [from Latin *Iēsus Hominum Salvātor*] 3. in this sign (the cross) shalt thou conquer. [from Latin *In Hōc Signō Vincēs*] 4. in this (cross) is salvation. [from Latin *In Hōc Salūs*]

IL Illinois (for use with ZIP code).

Il *Symbol, Chemistry.* illinium.

il. 1. illustrated. 2. illustration.

ILA 1. International Law Association. 2. International Longshoremen's Association. Also, **I.L.A.**

ILAS Instrument Landing Approach System.

I.L.G.W.U. International Ladies' Garment Workers' Union. Also, **ILGWU**

Ill. Illinois.

ill. 1. illustrated. 2. illustration. 3. illustrator. 4. most illustrious [from Latin *illustrissimus*].

illum illuminate.

illus. 1. illustrated. 2. illustration. Also, **illust.**

ILO International Labor Organization. Also, **I.L.O.**

I.L.P. Independent Labour Party.

ILS 1. *Aeronautics.* instrument landing system. 2. Integrated Logistic Support.

ILTF International Lawn Tennis Federation.

I.L.W.U. International Longshoremen's and Warehousemen's Union.

im intermodulation.

I.M. Isle of Man.

imag imaginary.

IMCO Inter-Governmental Maritime Consultive Organization.

imd intermodulation distortion.

IMF International Monetary Fund. Also, **I.M.F.**

imit. 1. Also, **imit** imitation. **2.** imitative.

immed immediate.

immunol. immunology.

IMP *Bridge.* international match point.

Imp. 1. Emperor. [from Latin *Imperātor*] **2.** Empress. [from Latin *Imperātrīx*]

imp. 1. impact. **2.** imperative. **3.** imperfect. **4.** imperial. **5.** impersonal. **6.** implement. **7.** import. **8.** important. **9.** imported. **10.** importer. **11.** imprimatur. **12.** in the first place. [from Latin *imprīmīs*] **13.** imprint. **14.** improper. **15.** improved. **16.** improvement.

impd impedance.

imper. imperative.

imperf. imperfect.

impers. impersonal.

impf. imperfect.

imp. gal. imperial gallon.

impl implement.

implr impeller.

imprg impregnate.

imprl imperial.

improv 1. improvement. **2.** improvisation.

imprsn impression.

impv. imperative.

imrs immersion.

IN Indiana (for use with ZIP code).

In *Symbol, Chemistry.* indium.

in. inch; inches.

in³ *Symbol.* cubic inch; cubic inches.

INA 1. international normal atmosphere. **2.** Israeli News Agency.

inbd inboard.

Inc. incorporated.

inc. 1. engraved. [from Latin *incīsus*] **2.** inclosure. **3.** included. **4.** including. **5.** inclusive. **6.** income. **7.** incorporated. **8.** increase. **9.** incumbent.

incand incandescent.

incin incinerator.

incl. 1. inclosure. **2.** including. **3.** inclusive.

incln inclined.

incls inclosure.

incm incoming.

incmpl incomplete.

incnd incendiary.

incog incognito.

incoh incoherent.

incor. 1. Also, **incorp.** incorporated. **2.** incorrect.

incorr. incorrect. Also, **incor.**

incpt intercept.

incr. 1. increase. **2.** increased. **3.** increasing. **4.** increment.

incrt increment.

IND *Pharmacology.* investigative new drug.

Ind. 1. India. **2.** Also, **Ind** Indian. **3.** Indiana. **4.** Indies.

ind. 1. independence. **2.** independent. **3.** index. **4.** indicate. **5.** indicated. **6.** indicative. **7.** indicator. **8.** indigo. **9.** indirect. **10.** industrial. **11.** industry.

in d. (in prescriptions) daily. [from Latin *in diēs*]

I.N.D. in the name of God. [from Latin *in nōmine Deī*]

Ind.E. Industrial Engineer.

indef. indefinite.

indep independent.

indic. 1. indicating. **2.** indicative. **3.** indicator.

individ. individual. Also, **indiv.**

indl industrial.

indn induction.

indt indent.

indtry industry.

induc. induction.

indus. 1. industrial. **2.** industry.

indv individual.

INF European-based U.S. nuclear weapons that were capable of striking the Soviet Union and Soviet ones that could hit Western Europe. [I(ntermediate-range) N(uclear) F(orces)]

inf 1. *Math.* greatest lower bound. [from Latin *infimum*] **2.** infinite. **3.** infinity.

Inf. 1. infantry. **2.** infuse [from Latin *infunde*].

in f. in the end; finally. [from Latin *in fine*]

infin. infinitive.

info (in′fō), information.

INH *Pharmacology, Trademark.* a brand of isoniazid.

inher. inheritance.

in. Hg *Meteorology.* inch of mercury.

init. Also, **init** initial.

inject. (in prescriptions) an injection. [from Latin *injectiō*]

inl inlet.

in loc. cit. in the place cited. [from Latin *in locō citātō*]

in mem. in memoriam.

inn. *Sports.* inning.

inop inoperative.

inorg. inorganic.

INP International News Photos.

inp input.

inq inquiry.

inr inner.

I.N.R.I. Jesus of Nazareth, King of the Jews. [from Latin *Iēsūs Nazarēnus, Rēx Iūdaeōrum*]

INS 1. Immigration and Naturaliza-

tion Service. **2.** Also, **I.N.S.** International News Service. **3.** Integrated Navigation System.

ins. 1. inches. **2.** *Chiefly British.* inscribed. **3.** inside. **4.** inspector. **5.** insulated. **6.** insurance. **7.** insure.

in./sec. inches per second.

insep. inseparable. Also, **insep**

insol. insoluble.

insp. 1. inspection. **2.** inspector.

inst. 1. instant. **2.** instantaneous. **3.** Also, **Inst.** institute. **4.** Also, **Inst.** institution. **5.** instructor. **6.** instrument. **7.** instrumental.

instl 1. install. **2.** installation.

instm instrumentation.

instr. 1. instruct. **2.** instructor. **3.** instrument. **4.** instrumental.

insuf insufficient.

insul 1. insulate. **2.** insulation.

int. 1. intelligence. **2.** interest. **3.** interim. **4.** interior. **5.** interjection. **6.** internal. **7.** international. **8.** interpreter. **9.** interval. **10.** intransitive.

intchg interchangeable.

intcom intercommunication.

intcon interconnection.

integ 1. integral. **2.** integrate.

integrg integrating.

intel intelligence.

INTELSAT (in tel′sat′, in′tel-), International Telecommunications Satellite Consortium.

inten intensity.

Intens *Grammar.* intensifier. Also, **intens**

intens. 1. intensifier. **2.** intensive.

inter. 1. intermediate. **2.** interrogation. **3.** interrogative.

interj. interjection.

internat. international.

Interpol (in′tər pōl′), International Criminal Police Organization.

interrog. 1. interrogation. **2.** interrogative.

intfc *Computers.* interface.

intk intake.

intl 1. internal. 2. Also, **intnl.** international.

intlk interlock.

intlz initialize.

intmd intermediate.

intmt intermittent.

intpr interpret.

intr 1. interior. 2. intransitive. 3. introduce. 4. introduced. 5. introducing. 6. introduction. 7. introductory.

intrans. intransitive.

in trans. in transit. [from Latin *in trānsitū*]

Int. Rev. Internal Revenue.

intrf interference.

intrg interrogate.

intro introduction.

intrpl interpolate.

intrpt interrupt.

intsct intersect.

intstg interstage.

intvl interval.

inv. 1. he or she invented it. [from Latin *invenit*] 2. invented. 3. invention. 4. inventor. 5. inventory. 6. investment. 7. invoice.

invs inverse.

invt. 1. inventory. 2. invert.

invtr inverter.

Io *Symbol, Chemistry.* ionium.

Io. Iowa.

I/O 1. inboard-outboard. 2. Also **i/o** *Computers.* input/output.

I.O. indirect object. Also, **IO, i.o.**

IOC International Olympic Committee. Also, **I.O.C.**

I.O.F. Independent Order of Foresters.

IOM interoffice memo.

I.O.O.F. Independent Order of Odd Fellows.

IOU a written acknowledgment of a debt, especially an informal one. Also, **I.O.U.** [representing *I owe you*]

IPA 1. International Phonetic Alphabet. 2. International Phonetic Association. 3. International Press Association. Also, **I.P.A.**

IPB illustrated parts breakdown.

i.p.h. 1. *Printing.* impressions per hour. 2. inches per hour. Also, **iph**

IPI International Patent Institute.

IPL information processing language. Also, **ipl**

IPM integrated pest management.

ipm inches per minute. Also, **i.p.m.**

IPO initial public offering.

ipr inches per revolution. Also, **i.p.r.**

ips inches per second. Also, **i.p.s.**

IQ *Psychology.* intelligence quotient.

i.q. the same as. [from Latin *idem quod*]

IR 1. information retrieval. 2. infrared. 3. intelligence ratio.

Ir Irish.

Ir *Symbol, Chemistry.* iridium.

ir 1. infrared. 2. insulation resistance.

Ir. 1. Ireland. 2. Irish.

I.R. 1. immediate reserve. 2. infantry reserve. 3. intelligence ratio. 4. internal revenue.

IRA 1. individual retirement account. 2. Irish Republican Army. Also, **I.R.A.**

IRB 1. Industrial Relations Bureau. 2. industrial revenue bond.

IRBM intermediate range ballistic missile. Also, **I.R.B.M.**

IRC 1. Internal Revenue Code. 2. International Red Cross.

Ire. Ireland.

IRO 1. International Refugee Organization. 2. International Relief Organization.

IRQ *Computers.* interrupt request.

irreg. 1. irregular. 2. irregularly.

irrglr irregular.

IRS Internal Revenue Service.

Is. **1.** *Bible.* Isaiah. **2.** Island; Islands. **3.** Isle; Isles.

is. **1.** island; islands. **2.** isle; isles.

ISA Instrument Society of America.

Isa. *Bible.* Isaiah.

ISBA International Seabed Authority.

ISBN International Standard Book Number.

ISDN integrated-services digital network.

isgn insignia.

isl. **1.** island. **2.** isle. Also, **Isl.**

isln isolation.

isls. islands. Also, **Isls.**

ISO **1.** incentive stock option. **2.** in search of. **3.** *Photography.* International Standardization Organization.

iso isometric.

isol isolate.

isos isosceles.

ISR Institute for Sex Research.

Isr. **1.** Israel. **2.** Israeli.

iss issue.

ISSN International Standard Serial Number.

IST **1.** insulin shock therapy. **2.** International Standard Thread (metric).

Isth. isthmus. Also, **isth.**

ISV International Scientific Vocabulary.

It Italian.

It. **1.** Italian. **2.** Italy.

I.T.A. Initial Teaching Alphabet. Also, **i.t.a.**

Ital. **1.** Italian. **2.** Italic. **3.** Italy.

ital. **1.** italic; italics. **2.** italicized.

ITC **1.** International Trade Commission. **2.** investment tax credit.

ITO International Trade Organization.

ITU International Telecommunication Union.

I.T.U. International Typographical Union.

ITV instructional television.

IU **1.** immunizing unit. **2.** Also, **I.U.** international unit.

IUD intrauterine device.

IUS *Rocketry.* inertial upper stage.

IV (ī′vē′), *Medicine.* an intravenous device.

IV *Medicine.* **1.** intravenous. **2.** intravenous drip. **3.** intravenous injection. **4.** intravenously.

I.V. initial velocity.

i.v. **1.** increased value. **2.** initial velocity. **3.** invoice value.

IVF in vitro fertilization.

I.W. Isle of Wight.

i.w. **1.** inside width. **2.** isotopic weight.

IWC International Whaling Commission.

I.W.W. Industrial Workers of the World. Also, **IWW**

J

J **1.** *Cards.* jack. Also, **J**. **2.** Jewish. **3.** *Physics.* joules.

J *Symbol.* **1.** the tenth in order or in a series, or, when *I* is omitted, the ninth. **2.** (*sometimes lowercase*) the medieval Roman numeral for 1. **3.** *Physics.* angular momentum.

j *Symbol.* **1.** *Math.* a unit vector on the y-axis of a coordinate system. **2.** *Engineering.* the imaginary number square root of minus one.

J. **1.** *Cards.* jack. Also, **J** **2.** Journal. **3.** Judge. **4.** Justice.

JA **1.** joint account. **2.** Joint Agent. **3.** Judge Advocate. **4.** Junior Achievement. Also, **J.A.**

Ja. January.

J.A.C. Junior Association of Commerce.

J.A.G. Judge Advocate General. Also, **JAG**

Jam. Jamaica.

Jan. January.

Jap. 1. Japan. **2.** Japanese.

Japn. 1. Japan. **2.** Japanese. Also, **Japn**

Jas. *Bible.* James.

Jav. Javanese.

jb junction box.

JC 1. junior college. **2.** juvenile court.

J.C. 1. Jesus Christ. **2.** Julius Caesar. **3.** *Law.* jurisconsult. [from Latin *jūris cōnsultus*]

J.C.B. 1. Bachelor of Canon Law. [from Latin *Jūris Canonicī Baccalaureus*] **2.** Bachelor of Civil Law. [from Latin *Jūris Civilis Baccalaureus*]

J.C.C. Junior Chamber of Commerce.

J.C.D. 1. Doctor of Canon Law. [from Latin *Jūris Canonicī Doctor*] **2.** Doctor of Civil Law. [from Latin *Jūris Civilis Doctor*]

JCI Jaycees International.

JCL *Computers.* job control language.

J.C.L. Licentiate in Canon Law. [from Latin *Jūris Canonicī Licentiātus*]

J.C.S. Joint Chiefs of Staff. Also, **JCS**

jct. junction. Also, **jctn.**

JD *Informal.* **1.** juvenile delinquency. **2.** juvenile delinquent.

JD. (in Jordan) dinar; dinars.

J.D. 1. *Astronomy.* Julian Day. **2.** Doctor of Jurisprudence; Doctor of Law. [from Latin *Jūris Doctor*] **3.** Doctor of Laws. [from Latin *Jūrum Doctor*] **4.** Justice Department. **5.** *Informal.* **a.** juvenile delinquency. **b.** juvenile delinquent.

JDC Juvenile Detention Center.

JDL Jewish Defense League.

Je. June.

Jer. 1. *Bible.* Jeremiah. **2.** Jersey.

JFET (jā′fet), junction field-effect transistor.

JFK John Fitzgerald Kennedy.

jg junior grade. Also, **j.g.**

JHS IHS (defs. 1, 2).

J.H.S. junior high school.

JJ. 1. Judges. **2.** Justices.

jk jack.

jkt jacket.

jl journal.

Jl. 1. Journal. **2.** July.

jn join.

Jno. John.

jnr. junior.

jnt. joint.

Jo. Bapt. John the Baptist.

JOBS (jobz), Job Opportunities in the Business Sector.

Jo. Div. John the Divine.

Jo. Evang. John the Evangelist.

Josh. *Bible.* Joshua.

jour. 1. journal. **2.** journeyman.

journ. journalism.

JP 1. jet propulsion. **2.** Justice of the Peace.

J.P. Justice of the Peace. Also, **j.p.**

JPEG (jā′peg), Joint Photographic Experts Group.

Jpn. 1. Japan. **2.** Japanese. Also, **Jpn**

Jr. 1. Journal. **2.** Junior.

jr. junior.

JRC Junior Red Cross.

JSC Johnson Space Center.

J.S.D. Doctor of the Science of Law; Doctor of Juristic Science.

jt. joint.

Ju. June.

Jud. *Bible.* **1.** Judges. **2.** Judith (Apocrypha).

jud. 1. judge. **2.** judgment. **3.** judicial. **4.** judiciary.

Judg. *Bible.* Judges.

Jul. July.

Jun. 1. June. **2.** Junior.

Junc. Junction. Also, **junc.**

Jur. D. Doctor of Law. [from Latin *Jūris Doctor*]

jurisp. jurisprudence. Also, **juris.**

Jur. M. Master of Jurisprudence.

just. justification.

juv. juvenile.

JV 1. joint venture. **2.** junior varsity. Also, **J.V.**

jwlr. jeweler.

J.W.V. Jewish War Veterans.

Jy jansky; janskies.

Jy. July.

K

K 1. *Chess.* king. **2.** *Physics.* Kelvin. **3.** the number 1000: *The salary is $20K.* [abbreviation of *kilo-*] **4.** *Electronics.* cathode. **5.** *Music.* Köchel listing. **6.** kindergarten: *a K-12 boarding school.* **7.** *Real Estate.* kitchen.

K *Symbol.* **1.** the eleventh in order or in a series, or, when *I* is omitted, the tenth. **2.** *Chemistry.* potassium. [from Latin *kalium*] **3.** *Computers.* **a.** the number 1024 or 2^{10}. **b.** kilobyte. **4.** *Baseball.* strikeout; strikeouts. **5.** *Physics.* kaon. **6.** *Biochemistry.* lysine.

K *Ecology.* carrying capacity.

k *Symbol.* **1.** *Math.* a vector on the z-axis, having length 1 unit. **2.** *Physics.* Boltzmann constant.

K. 1. kip; kips (monetary unit). **2.** Knight. **3.** (in Malawi or Zambia) kwacha.

k. 1. *Electricity.* capacity. **2.** karat. **3.** kilogram; kilograms. **4.** kindergarten. **5.** *Chess.* king. **6.** knight. **7.** knot. **8.** kopeck.

kA *Electricity.* kiloampere; kiloamperes.

Kan. Kansas. Also, **Kans., Kas.**

KB 1. *Chess.* king's bishop. **2.** *Computers.* kilobyte; kilobytes.

Kb *Computers.* kilobit; kilobits.

kB *Computers.* kilobyte; kilobytes.

kb kilobar; kilobars.

K.B. 1. King's Bench. **2.** Knight Bachelor.

kbar (kā/bär), kilobar; kilobars.

K.B.E. Knight Commander of the British Empire.

KBP *Chess.* king's bishop's pawn.

kc 1. kilocycle; kilocycles. **2.** kilocurie; kilocuries.

K.C. 1. Kansas City. **2.** King's Counsel. **3.** Knight Commander. **4.** Knights of Columbus.

K.C.B. Knight Commander of the Bath.

kCi kilocurie; kilocuries.

K.C.M.G. Knight Commander of the Order of St. Michael and St. George.

Kčs. koruna; korunas. [from Czech *k(oruna) č(esko)s(lovenská)*]

kc/s kilocycles per second. Also, **kc/sec**

K.C.S.I. Knight Commander of the Order of the Star of India.

K.C.V.O. Knight Commander of the (Royal) Victorian Order.

KD 1. kiln-dried. **2.** Also, **k.d.** *Commerce.* knocked-down.

KD. (in Kuwait) dinar; dinars.

Ken. Kentucky.

kG kilogauss; kilogausses.

kg kilogram; kilograms.

kg. 1. keg; kegs. **2.** kilogram; kilograms.

K.G. 1. Knight of the Garter. **2.** (in police use) known gambler.

KGB Committee for State Security: the intelligence and internal-security agency of the former Soviet Union. Also, **K.G.B.** [from Russian *K(omitét) g(osudárstvennoĭ) b(ezopásnosti)*]

kgf kilogram-force.

kg-m kilogram-meter; kilogram-meters.

KGPS kilograms per second. Also, **kgps**

Kh Knoop hardness.

Khn Knoop hardness number.

kHz kilohertz.

Ki. *Bible.* Kings.

KIA killed in action. Also, **K.I.A.**

KIAS knot indicated airspeed.

kil. kilometer; kilometers.

kip-ft one thousand foot-pounds.

KISS (kis), keep it simple, stupid.

K.J.V. King James Version (of the Bible).

K.K.K. Ku Klux Klan. Also, **KKK**

KKt *Chess.* king's knight.

KKtP *Chess.* king's knight's pawn.

kl kiloliter; kiloliters. Also, **kl.**

km kilometer; kilometers.

km. **1.** kilometer; kilometers. **2.** kingdom.

kMc kilomegacycle; kilomegacycles.

km/sec kilometers per second.

KN *Chess.* king's knight.

kn knot; 1 nautical mile.

kn. (in Germany and Austria) kronen.

KNP *Chess.* king's knight's pawn.

kn sw knife switch.

Knt. Knight.

KO (kā′ō′, kā′ō′), *Slang.* a knockout, especially in boxing. Also, **ko, K.O., k.o., kayo.** [*k(nock) o(ut)*]

K. of C. Knights of Columbus.

K. of P. Knights of Pythias.

kop. kopeck.

KP *Chess.* king's pawn.

K.P. **1.** *Military.* kitchen police. **2.** Knight of the Order of St. Patrick. **3.** Knights of Pythias.

kpc kiloparsec; kiloparsecs.

kph kilometers per hour. Also, **k.p.h.**

KR *Chess.* king's rook.

Kr *Symbol, Chemistry.* krypton.

Kr. **1.** (in Sweden and the Faeroe Islands) krona; kronor. **2.** (in Iceland) króna; krónur. **3.** (in Denmark and Norway) krone; kroner.

kr. **1.** (in Germany and Austria) kreutzer. **2.** (in Sweden and the Faeroe Islands) krona; kronor. **3.** (in Iceland) króna; krónur. **4.** (in Denmark and Norway) krone; kroner.

KRP *Chess.* king's rook's pawn.

krs (in Turkey) kurus.

krsn kerosene.

KS Kansas (for use with ZIP code).

ksi one thousand pounds per square inch. [*k(ilo)* + *s(quare) i(nch)*]

ksr *Telecommunications.* keyboard send and receive.

Kt *Chess.* knight. Also, **Kt.**

Kt. knight.

kt. **1.** karat; karats. **2.** kiloton; kilotons. **3.** knot; knots.

K.T. **1.** Knights Templars. **2.** Knight of the Order of the Thistle.

Kt. Bach. knight bachelor.

kV kilovolt; kilovolts. Also, **kv**

K.V. *Music.* Köchel-Verzeichnis, the chronological listing of Mozart's works.

kVA kilovolt-ampere; kilovolt-amperes. Also, **kva**

kVAhm kilovolt-ampere hour meter.

kW kilowatt; kilowatts. Also, **kw.**

kWh kilowatt-hour. Also, **kwhr, K.W.H.**

KWIC (kwik), of or designating an alphabetical concordance of the principal terms in a text showing every occurrence of each term surrounded by a few words of the context. [*k(ey)-w(ord)-i(n) c(ontext)*]

kwy keyway.

KY Kentucky (for use with ZIP code).

Ky. Kentucky.

kybd keyboard.

kypd keypad.

L

L **1.** *Optics.* lambert; lamberts. **2.** language. **3.** large. **4.** Latin. **5.** left. **6.** length. **7.** *British.* pound; pounds. [from Latin *lībra*] **8.** long: denoting a size longer than regular, esp. for suits and coats. **9.** longitude. **10.** *Theater.* stage left.

L *Symbol.* **1.** the 12th in order or in a series, or, if *I* is omitted, the 11th. **2.** (*sometimes lowercase*) the Roman numeral for 50. **3.** *Electricity.* inductance. **4.** *Physics.* kinetic potential. **5.** *Biochemistry.* leucine. **6.** *Economics.* liquid assets. **7.** liter; liters.

l **1.** large. **2.** liter; liters. **3.** long.

L- **1.** *Chemistry.* levo-. **2.** *U.S. Military.* (in designations of light aircraft) liaison: *L-15.*

L- *Symbol, Biochemistry.* (of a molecule) having a configuration resembling the levorotatory isomer of glyceraldehyde: printed as a small capital, roman character. Compare **l-.**

l- *Symbol, Optics, Chemistry, Biochemistry.* levorotatory; levo-. Compare **L-.**

L. **1.** Lady. **2.** Lake. **3.** large. **4.** Latin. **5.** latitude. **6.** law. **7.** left. **8.** (in Honduras) lempira; lempiras. **9.** (in Romania) leu; lei. **10.** (in Bulgaria) lev; leva. **11.** book. [from Latin *liber*] **12.** Liberal. **13.** (in Italy) lira; lire. **14.** place. [from Latin *locus*] **15.** Lord. **16.** Low. **17.** lumen. **18.** *Theater.* stage left.

l. **1.** large. **2.** latitude. **3.** law. **4.** leaf. **5.** league. **6.** left. **7.** length. **8.** *plural* **ll.,** line. **9.** link. **10.** (in Italy) lira; lire. **11.** liter; liters. **12.** long.

LA Louisiana (for use with ZIP code).

La *Symbol, Chemistry.* lanthanum.

La. Louisiana.

l/a letter of authority.

L.A. **1.** Latin America. **2.** Law Agent. **3.** Library Association. **4.** Local Agent. **5.** Los Angeles.

Lab. **1.** Laborite. **2.** Labrador.

lab. **1.** labor. **2.** laboratory. **3.** laborer.

LAC leading aircraftsman.

LACW leading aircraftswoman.

LAD language acquisition device.

LaF Louisiana French.

lag lagging.

LAK cell *Immunology.* lymphokine-activated killer cell.

Lam. *Bible.* Lamentations.

lam. laminated.

LAN (lan), local area network.

lang. language.

laq lacquer.

laser (lā′zər), *Electronics.* light amplification by stimulated emission of radiation.

LASH (lash), an ocean-going vessel equipped with special cranes and holds for lifting and stowing cargo-carrying barges. [*l(ighter) a(board) sh(ip)*]

Lat. Latin.

lat. latitude.

latl lateral.

lau laundry.

LAV lymphadenopathy-associated virus.

lav lavatory.

LAWN (lôn), local-area wireless network.

lb *Telecommunications.* local battery.

lb. *plural* **lbs., lb,** pound. [from Latin *lībra,* plural *lībrae*]

L.B. **1.** landing barge. **2.** light bomber. **3.** bachelor of letters; bachelor of literature. [from Latin *Litterārum Baccalaureus; Līterārum Baccalaureus*] **4.** local board.

lb. ap. *Pharmacology.* pound apothecary's.

L bar. angle iron. Also, **L beam.**

lb. av. pound avoirdupois.

lbf *Physics.* pound-force.

LBJ Lyndon Baines Johnson.

lbl label.

LBO *Finance.* leveraged buyout.

lbr lumber.

lbry library.

lb. t. pound troy.

lbyr labyrinth.

LC 1. inductance-capacitance. **2.** landing craft.

L/C letter of credit. Also, **l/c**

L.C. Library of Congress.

l.c. 1. left center. **2.** letter of credit. **3.** in the place cited. [from Latin *locō citātō*] **4.** *Printing.* lowercase.

l.c.a. lowercase alphabet.

LCD *Electronics.* liquid-crystal display.

L.C.D. *Math.* least common denominator; lowest common denominator. Also, **l.c.d.**

L.C.F. *Math.* lowest common factor. Also, **l.c.f.**

L chain *Immunology.* light chain.

LCI *Military.* a type of landing craft used in World War II. [*L(anding) C(raft) I(nfantry)*]

lcl local.

L.C.L. *Commerce.* less than carload lot. Also, **l.c.l.**

L.C.M. least common multiple; lowest common multiple. Also, **l.c.m.**

LCR inductance-capacitance-resistance.

LCT *Military.* a type of landing craft used in World War II. [*L(anding) C(raft) T(ank)*]

LD 1. praise (be) to God. [from Latin *laus Deō*] **2.** learning disability. **3.** learning-disabled. **4.** lethal dose. **5.** long distance (telephone call). **6.** Low Dutch.

LD. (in Libya) dinar; dinars.

Ld. 1. limited. **2.** Lord.

ld 1. leading. **2.** line drawing.

ld. load.

L.D. Low Dutch.

LD₅₀ *Pharmacology.* median lethal dose.

LDC less developed country. Also, **L.D.C.**

ldg. 1. landing. **2.** loading.

LDH *Biochemistry.* lactate dehydrogenase.

LDL *Biochemistry.* low-density lipoprotein.

ldmk landmark.

Ldp. 1. ladyship. **2.** lordship.

LDPE *Chemistry.* low-density polyethylene.

ldr ladder.

L.D.S. 1. Latter-day Saints. **2.** praise (be) to God forever. [from Latin *laus Deō semper*] **3.** Licentiate in Dental Surgery.

l.e. *Football.* left end.

lect. 1. lecture. **2.** lecturer.

LED *Electronics.* light-emitting diode.

legis. 1. legislation. **2.** legislative. **3.** legislature.

LEM (lem), lunar excursion module.

LEP 1. *Physics.* large electron-positron collider. **2.** limited English proficiency.

Lett. Lettish.

Lev. *Bible.* Leviticus.

lex. 1. lexical. **2.** lexicon.

LF 1. *Baseball.* left field. **2.** *Baseball.* left fielder. **3.** low frequency.

lf 1. *Baseball.* left field. **2.** *Baseball.* left fielder. **3.** *Printing.* lightface. **4.** line feed.

l.f. *Baseball.* **1.** left field. **2.** left fielder.

lfb *Sports.* left fullback.

LG Low German. Also, **L.G.**

lg. 1. large. **2.** length. **3.** long.

l.g. *Football.* left guard.

lgc logic.

lge. large. Also, **lge**

L. Ger. 1. Low German. **2.** Low Germanic.

LGk Late Greek. Also, **LGk, L.Gk.**

lgsltd legislated.

lgsltr legislature.

lgstcs logistics.

lgth. length.

LH *Biochemistry, Physiology.* luteinizing hormone.

lh *Sports.* left halfback.

l.h. 1. left hand; left-handed. **2.** lower half. Also, **L.H.**

l.h.b. *Sports.* left halfback.

L.H.D. 1. Doctor of Humane Letters. **2.** Doctor of Humanities. [from Latin *Litterārum Humāniōrum Doctor*]

lhdr left-hand drive.

Li *Symbol, Chemistry.* lithium.

li *Surveying.* link; links.

L.I. 1. *British.* light infantry. **2.** Long Island.

Lib. Liberal.

lib. 1. book. [from Latin *liber*] **2.** librarian. **3.** library.

lic. 1. license. **2.** licensed.

Lieut. lieutenant.

Lieut. Col. lieutenant colonel.

Lieut. Comdr. lieutenant commander.

LIF Lifetime (a cable television channel).

LIFO (lī′fō), **1.** *Commerce.* last-in, first-out. **2.** *Computers.* a data storage and retrieval technique, in which the last item stored is the first item retrieved. [*l(ast) i(n) f(irst) o(ut)*]

lim. limit.

lin. 1. lineal. **2.** linear. **3.** liniment.

lin ft linear foot; linear feet.

liq. 1. liquid. **2.** liquor. **3.** (in prescriptions) solution. [from Latin *liquor*]

LISP (lisp), *Computers.* a programming language that processes data in the form of lists. [*lis(t) p(rocessing)*]

Lit. (in Italy) lira; lire.

lit. 1. liter; liters. **2.** literal. **3.** literally. **4.** literary. **5.** literature.

Lit.B. Bachelor of Letters; Bachelor of Literature. [from Latin *Lit(t)erārum Baccalaureus*]

Lit.D. Doctor of Letters; Doctor of Literature. [from Latin *Lit(t)erārum Doctor*]

Lith. 1. Lithuania. **2.** Also, **Lith** Lithuanian.

lith. 1. lithograph. **2.** lithographic. **3.** lithography.

lithol. lithology.

Litt. B. Bachelor of Letters; Bachelor of Literature. [from Latin *Lit(t)erārum Baccalaureus*]

Litt. D. Doctor of Letters; Doctor of Literature. [from Latin *Lit(t)erārum Doctor*]

Litt.M. Master of Letters. [from Latin *Lit(t)erārum Magister*]

Lk. *Bible.* Luke.

lkd locked.

lkg looking.

lkge linkage.

lknt locknut.

lkr locker.

LL 1. Late Latin. **2.** Low Latin. Also, **L.L.**

ll. 1. lines. **2.** low level.

l.l. 1. in the place quoted. [from Latin *locō laudātō*] **2.** loose-leaf.

L. Lat. 1. Late Latin. **2.** Low Latin.

LLB Little League Baseball.

LL.B. Bachelor of Laws. [from Latin *Lēgum Baccalaureus*]

LL.D. Doctor of Laws. [from Latin *Lēgum Doctor*]

LL.M. Master of Laws. [from Latin *Lēgum Magister*]

llti long lead-time item.

LM (often lem), lunar module.

lm 1. list of material. **2.** *Optics.* lumen; lumens.

L.M. 1. Licentiate in Medicine. **2.** Licentiate in Midwifery. **3.** Lord Mayor.

lm-hr *Optics.* lumen-hour; lumen-hours.

LMT local mean time.

lmtr limiter.

lm/W *Symbol.* lumen per watt.

Ln. lane.

ln logarithm (natural).

lndry rm *Real Estate.* laundry room.

LNG liquefied natural gas.

lnrty linearity.

lntl lintel.

LO lubrication order.

loc. locative.

loc. cit. (lok′ sit′), in the place cited. [from Latin *locō citātō*]

loep list of effective pages.

lof local oscillator frequency.

log. logarithm.

logamp logarithmic amplifier.

LOGO (lō′gō), *Computers.* a programming language widely used to teach children how to use computers. [from Greek *lógos* word, spelled as if an acronym]

lon. longitude.

Lond. London.

long. 1. longitude. **2.** longitudinal.

L.O.O.M. Loyal Order of Moose.

LOP *Navigation.* line of position.

loq. he speaks; she speaks. [from Latin *loquitur*]

loran (lôr′an, lōr′-), *Electronics.* long-range navigation.

lo-res (lō′rez′), *Computers.* low-resolution.

lot. (in prescriptions) a lotion. [from Latin *lōtiō*]

lox (loks), liquid oxygen.

LP long-playing: a phonograph record played at 33 1/3 r.p.m.

L.P. *Printing.* **1.** long primer. **2.** low pressure. Also, **l.p.**

LPG liquefied petroleum gas. Also called **LP gas.**

LPGA Ladies Professional Golf Association.

lphldr lampholder.

lpm *Computers.* lines per minute. Also, **LPM**

LPN licensed practical nurse.

lprsvr life preserver.

L.P.S. Lord Privy Seal.

lptv low-power television.

lpw lumen per watt.

LQ letter-quality.

lqp *Computers.* letter-quality printer.

LR 1. *Real Estate.* living room. **2.** long range. **3.** lower right.

Lr *Symbol, Chemistry.* lawrencium.

L.R. Lloyd's Register.

LRAM long-range attack missile.

LRBM long-range ballistic missile.

lrg. large.

LRT light-rail transit.

LS 1. left side. **2.** letter signed. **3.** library science. **4.** lightship.

ls loudspeaker.

L.S. 1. Licentiate in Surgery. **2.** Linnaean Society. **3.** Also, **l.s.** the place of the seal, as on a document [from Latin *locus sigilli*].

LSA 1. Leukemia Society of America. **2.** Linguistic Society of America.

LSAT *Trademark.* Law School Admission Test.

lsb 1. least significant bit. **2.** lower sideband.

l.s.c. in the place mentioned above. [from Latin *locā suprā citātō*]

LSD 1. *U.S. Navy.* a seagoing amphibious ship capable of carrying and launching assault landing craft. [*l(anding) s(hip) d(eck)*] **2.** *Pharmacology.* lysergic acid diethylamide: a powerful psychedelic drug. **3.** *Math.* least significant digit.

L.S.D. *British.* pounds, shillings, and

pence. Also, **£.s.d., l.s.d.** [from Latin *librae, solidī, dēnāriī*]

LSI *Electronics.* large-scale integration.

LSM a type of military landing ship. [*l(anding) s(hip) m(edium)*]

L.S.S. Lifesaving Service.

LST an oceangoing military ship, used for landing troops and heavy equipment on beaches. [*l(anding) s(hip) t(ank)*]

l.s.t. local standard time.

lt **1.** Also, **lt.** light. **2.** *Electricity.* low-tension.

Lt. lieutenant.

L.T. **1.** long ton. **2.** *Electricity.* low-tension.

l.t. **1.** *Football.* left tackle. **2.** local time. **3.** long ton.

LTA (of an aircraft) lighter-than-air.

Lt. Col. Lieutenant Colonel. Also **LTC**

Lt. Comdr. Lieutenant Commander. Also, **Lt. Com.**

Ltd. limited. Also, **ltd, ltd.**

ltg lighting.

Lt. Gen. Lieutenant General. Also, **LTG**

Lt. Gov. Lieutenant Governor.

L.Th. Licentiate in Theology.

lthr leather.

Lt. Inf. *Military.* light infantry.

LTJG *U.S. Navy.* Lieutenant Junior Grade.

LTL *Commerce.* less-than-truckload lot.

LTR long-term relationship.

ltr. **1.** letter. **2.** lighter.

ltrprs letterpress.

lt-yr light-year; light-years.

lub *Math.* least upper bound.

lub. **1.** lubricant. **2.** lubricating. **3.** lubrication.

lubo lubricating oil.

lubt lubricant.

luf lowest usable frequency.

LULAC League of United Latin-American Citizens.

lum luminous.

Luth. Lutheran.

Lux. Luxembourg.

LV. (in Bulgaria) lev; leva.

lv. **1.** leave; leaves. **2.** (in France) livre; livres.

lvl level.

LVN licensed vocational nurse.

lvr **1.** lever. **2.** louver.

LW low water.

l/w lumen per watt; lumens per watt.

l.w.m. low water mark.

lwop leave without pay.

lwp leave with pay.

lwr lower.

LWV League of Women Voters. Also, **L.W.V.**

lwyr lawyer.

lx *Optics.* lux.

lyr layer.

lyt layout.

LZ landing zone.

M

M **1.** mach. **2.** *Music.* major. **3.** male. **4.** married. **5.** Medieval. **6.** medium. **7.** mega-: one million [from Greek *mégas* large, great] **8.** Middle. **9.** modal auxiliary. **10.** modifier. **11.** *Economics.* monetary aggregate. **12.** *British.* motorway (used with a road number).

M *Symbol.* **1.** the thirteenth in order or in a series, or, when *I* is omitted, the twelfth. **2.** (*sometimes lowercase*) the Roman numeral for 1,000. **3.** *Electricity.* magnetization. **4.** *Biochemistry.* methionine.

m **1.** *Physics.* mass. **2.** *Finance.* (of bonds) matured. **3.** medieval.

4. medium. **5.** meter; meters.
6. middle. **7.** *Music.* minor.

m *Symbol, Electricity.* magnetic pole strength.

M- *U.S. Military.* (used to designate the production model of military equipment, as the M-1 rifle.)

m- *Chemistry.* meta-: least hydrated (of a series); designating the meta position in the benzene ring.

M. 1. Majesty. **2.** Manitoba. **3.** (in Finland) markka; markkaa. **4.** Marquis. **5.** *Music.* measure. **6.** medicine. **7.** medium. **8.** meridian. **9.** noon. [from Latin *merīdiēs*] **10.** Monday. **11.** *plural* **MM.** Monsieur. **12.** mountain.

m. 1. male. **2.** (in Germany) mark; marks. **3.** married. **4.** masculine. **5.** *Physics.* mass. **6.** medium. **7.** noon. [from Latin *merīdiēs*] **8.** meter. **9.** middle. **10.** mile. **11.** minute. **12.** (in prescriptions) mix. [from Latin *misce*] **13.** modification of. **14.** *Physics, Math.* modulus. **15.** molar. **16.** month. **17.** moon. **18.** morning. **19.** mouth.

m³ *Symbol.* cubic meter.

MA 1. Massachusetts (for use with ZIP code). **2.** *Psychology.* mental age.

mA *Electricity.* milliampere; milliamperes.

ma master.

M.A. 1. Master of Arts. [from Latin *Magister Artium*] **2.** *Psychology.* mental age. **3.** Military Academy.

MAA master-at-arms.

M.A.Arch. Master of Arts in Architecture.

MAb *Immunology.* monoclonal antibody.

mac maintenance allocation chart.

Mac. *Bible.* Maccabees.

M.Ac. Master of Accountancy.

Macc. *Bible.* Maccabees.

Maced. Macedonia.

Mach *Physics.* mach number.

mach. 1. machine. **2.** machinery. **3.** machinist.

MAD (mad), Mutual Assured Destruction.

Mad. Madam.

MADD (mad), Mothers Against Drunk Driving.

Madm. Madam.

M.A.E. 1. Master of Aeronautical Engineering. **2.** Master of Art Education. **3.** Master of Arts in Education.

M.A.Ed. Master of Arts in Education.

M.Aero.E. Master of Aeronautical Engineering.

mag. 1. magazine. **2.** magnet. **3.** magnetic. **4.** magnetism. **5.** magneto. **6.** magnitude. **7.** (in prescriptions) large. [from Latin *magnus*]

magamp magnetic amplifier.

M.Ag.Ec. Master of Agricultural Economics.

M.Ag.Ed. Master of Agricultural Education.

magn *Electronics.* magnetron.

magtd magnitude.

mah mahogany.

maint maintenance.

Maj. Major.

Maj. Gen. Major General.

Mal. *Bible.* **1.** Malachi. **2.** Malayan.

M.A.L.D. Master of Arts in Law and Diplomacy.

malf malfunction.

M.A.L.S. 1. Master of Arts in Liberal Studies. **2.** Master of Arts in Library Science.

mam milliammeter.

Man. 1. Manila. **2.** Manitoba.

man. manual.

manf manifold.

MAO *Biochemistry.* monoamine oxidase.

MAOI *Biochemistry.* monoamine oxidase inhibitor.

MAO inhibitor *Biochemistry.* monoamine oxidase inhibitor.

MAP modified American plan.

MAPI *Computers.* Messaging Application Programming Interface.

Mar. March.

mar. 1. maritime. 2. married.

M.A.R. Master of Arts in Religion.

MARC (märk), a standardized system developed by the Library of Congress for producing and transmitting records. [*ma(chine) r(eadable) c(atologing)*]

March. Marchioness.

M.Arch. Master of Architecture.

M.Arch.E. Master of Architectural Engineering.

Mar.E. Marine Engineer.

marg. 1. margin. 2. marginal.

Mar.Mech.E. Marine Mechanical Engineer.

Marq. 1. Marquess. 2. Marquis.

MARS (marz), 1. Military Affiliated Radio System. 2. multiple-access retrieval system.

mas. masculine.

masc. masculine.

maser (māʹzər), *Electronics.* microwave amplification by stimulated emission of radiation.

MASH (mash), mobile army surgical hospital.

mas. pil. (in prescriptions) a pill mass. [from Latin *massa pilulāris*]

Mass. Massachusetts.

mat. 1. *Ecclesiastical.* matins. 2. *Finance.* maturity.

M.A.T. Master of Arts in Teaching.

Mat.E. Materials Engineer.

math 1. mathematical. 2. mathematics.

matl material.

MATS (mats), Military Air Transport Service.

Matt. *Bible.* Matthew.

MATV master antenna television system.

MAX Cinemax (a cable television channel).

max. maximum.

MB 1. Manitoba, Canada (for use with ZIP code). 2. *Computers.* megabyte; megabytes.

Mb *Computers.* megabit; megabits.

mb *Physics.* 1. millibar; millibars. 2. millibarn; millibarns.

M.B. *Chiefly British.* Bachelor of Medicine. [from Latin *Medicinae Baccalaureus*]

M.B.A. Master of Business Administration. Also, **MBA**

mbb *Electricity.* make-before-break.

mbd (of oil) million barrels per day.

MBE Multistate Bar Examination.

M.B.E. Member of the Order of the British Empire.

mbl mobile.

Mbm one thousand feet, board measure.

mbm *Computers.* magnetic bubble memory.

MBO management by objective.

mbr member.

MBTA Massachusetts Bay Transportation Authority.

MByte *Computers.* megabyte: one million bytes.

MC 1. Marine Corps. 2. master of ceremonies. 3. Medical Corps. 4. Member of Congress.

Mc 1. *Physics, Chemistry.* megacurie; meg-acuries. 2. *Electricity.* megacycle.

mC 1. *Electricity.* millicoulomb; millicoulombs. 2. *Physics, Chemistry.* millicurie; millicuries.

mc 1. *Electricity.* megacycle. 2. *Optics.* meter-candle. 3. *Physics, Chemistry.* millicurie; millicuries. 4. *Electricity.* momentary contact.

M.C. 1. Master Commandant.

2. master of ceremonies. **3.** Medical Corps. **4.** Member of Congress. **5.** Member of Council. **6.** *British. Military Cross.*

MCAT Medical College Admission Test.

M.C.E. Master of Civil Engineering.

Mcf one thousand cubic feet. Also, **mcf, MCF**

Mcfd thousands of cubic feet per day.

M.Ch.E. Master of Chemical Engineering.

MChin Middle Chinese.

mchry machinery.

mCi *Physics, Chemistry.* millicurie; millicuries.

M.C.J. Master of Comparative Jurisprudence.

mcm 1. *Computers.* magnetic-core memory. **2.** thousand circular mils.

MCP male chauvinist pig.

M.C.P. Master of City Planning.

M.C.R. Master of Comparative Religion.

mcw *Electronics.* modulated continuous wave.

MD 1. Maryland (for use with ZIP code). **2.** Doctor of Medicine. [from Latin *Medicīnae Doctor*] **3.** Middle Dutch. **4.** months after date. **5.** muscular dystrophy.

Md *Music.* right hand. [from Italian *mano destra* or French *main droite*]

Md *Symbol, Chemistry.* mendelevium.

md mean deviation.

Md. Maryland.

M/D months after date. Also, **m/d**

M.D. 1. Doctor of Medicine. [from Latin *Medicīnae Doctor*] **2.** Middle Dutch.

MDA *Pharmacology.* an amphetamine derivative, $C_{10}H_{13}NO_2$. [*m(ethylene) d(ioxy)a(mphetamine)*]

MDAA Muscular Dystrophy Association of America.

MDAP Mutual Defense Assistance Program.

M.Des. Master of Design.

mdf *Telephones.* main distributing frame.

mdl 1. middle. **2.** minimum detectable level. **3.** module.

Mdlle. Mademoiselle.

mdm medium.

Mdm. Madam.

MDMA an amphetamine derivative, $C_{11}H_{15}NO_2$. [*m(ethylene) d(ioxy)m(eth)a(mphetamine)*]

Mdme. Madame.

mdn median.

mdnt. midnight.

mdnz modernize.

MDR minimum daily requirement.

mdse. merchandise.

MDT 1. mean downtime. **2.** Also, **M.D.T.** Mountain Daylight Time.

ME 1. Maine (for use with ZIP code). **2.** Middle East. **3.** Middle English.

Me *Chemistry.* methyl.

Me. Maine.

M.E. 1. (*often lowercase*) managing editor. **2.** Master of Education. **3.** Master of Engineering. **4.** Mechanical Engineer. **5.** Medical Examiner. **6.** Methodist Episcopal. **7.** Middle English. **8.** Mining Engineer.

meas. 1. measurable. **2.** measure. **3.** measurement.

mech. 1. mechanical. **2.** mechanics. **3.** mechanism.

med. 1. medical. **2.** medicine. **3.** medieval. **4.** medium.

M.Ed. Master of Education.

Medit. Mediterranean.

Med.Sc.D. Doctor of Medical Science.

MEG *Medicine.* magnetoencephalogram.

meg 1. *Electricity.* megacycle. **2.** megohm; megohms.

MEGO (mē′gō), my eyes glaze over.

MEK *Chemistry.* methyl ethyl ketone.

mem. 1. member. **2.** memoir. **3.** memorandum. **4.** memorial. **5.** memory.

M.Eng. Master of Engineering.

M.E.P. Master of Engineering Physics.

m.e.p. mean effective pressure.

M.E.P.A. Master of Engineering and Public Administration.

mEq milliequivalent.

mer. 1. meridian. **2.** meridional.

merc. 1. mercantile. **2.** mercurial. **3.** mercury.

Messrs. (mes′ərz), plural of **Mr.**

Met *Biochemistry.* methionine.

met. 1. metal. **2.** metallurgical. **3.** metaphor. **4.** metaphysics. **5.** meteorology. **6.** metropolitan.

metal. 1. metallurgical. **2.** metallurgy.

metall. 1. metallurgical. **2.** metallurgy.

metaph. 1. metaphysical. **2.** metaphysics.

metaphys. metaphysics.

Met.E. metallurgical engineer.

meteor. 1. meteorological. **2.** meteorology.

meteorol. 1. Also, **metrl** meteorological. **2.** meteorology.

Meth. Methodist.

MeV (mev), *Physics.* million electron volts; megaelectron volt. Also, **Mev, mev**

Mex. 1. Mexican. **2.** Mexico.

MexSp Mexican Spanish.

mez mezzanine.

MF 1. married female. **2.** medium frequency. **3.** Middle French.

mF *Electricity.* millifarad; millifarads.

mf 1. medium frequency. **2.** microfilm. **3.** *Electricity.* millifarad; millifarads.

mf. 1. *Music.* mezzo forte. **2.** *Electricity.* microfarad.

m/f male or female: used especially in classified ads. Also, **M/F**

M.F. 1. Master of Forestry. **2.** Middle French.

MFA Museum of Fine Arts.

M.F.A. Master of Fine Arts.

mfd. manufactured.

mfg. manufacturing.

m/f/h male, female, handicapped: used especially in classified ads. Also, **M/F/H**

M.F.H. master of foxhounds.

MFlem Middle Flemish.

MFM *Computers.* modified frequency modulation: hard-drive interface.

M.For. Master of Forestry.

mfr. 1. manufacture. **2.** manufacturer.

M.Fr. Middle French.

M.F.S. 1. Master of Food Science. **2.** Master of Foreign Service. **3.** Master of Foreign Study.

mfsk multiple-frequency shift-keying.

M.F.T. Master of Foreign Trade.

MG 1. machine gun. **2.** major general. **3.** military government. **4.** *Pathology.* myasthenia gravis.

Mg *Music.* left hand. [from French *main gauche*]

Mg *Symbol, Chemistry.* magnesium.

mg 1. milligram; milligrams. **2.** motor-generator.

mGal milligal; milligals.

MGB the Ministry of State Security in the U.S.S.R. (1946–53). [from Russian, for *Ministérstvo gosudárstvennoï bezopásnosti*]

mgd. millions of gallons per day.

mgf magnify.

MGk. Medieval Greek. Also, **MGk**

mgl mogul.

mgmt management.

mgn 1. magneto. **2.** margin.

MGr. Medieval Greek.

mgr. 1. manager. **2.** Monseigneur. **3.** Monsignor. Also, **Mgr.**

mgt. management.

MGy Sgt master gunnery sergeant.

MH Marshall Islands (approved for postal use).

mH *Electricity*. millihenry; millihenries. Also, **mh**.

M.H. Medal of Honor.

M.H.A. Master in Hospital Administration; Master of Hospital Administration.

MHC *Biochemistry*. major histocompatibility complex.

MHD *Physics*. magnetohydrodynamics.

mhd 1. magnetohydrodynamic. **2.** masthead.

M.H.E. Master of Home Economics.

MHG Middle High German. Also, **M.H.G.**

M.H.R. Member of the House of Representatives.

M.H.W. mean high water. Also, **MHW, mhw, m.h.w.**

MHz megahertz. Also, **mhz**

mHz millihertz.

MI Michigan (for use with ZIP code).

MI *Pathology*. myocardial infarction.

mi mile; miles.

mi. 1. mile; miles. **2.** *Finance*. mill; mills.

M.I. 1. Military Intelligence. **2.** Mounted Infantry.

MIA *Military*. missing in action.

M.I.A. 1. Master of International Affairs. **2.** *Military*. missing in action.

mic 1. micrometer. **2.** microphone.

Mic. *Bible*. Micah.

Mich. 1. Michaelmas. **2.** Michigan.

MICR *Electronics*. magnetic ink character recognition.

micr microscope.

micros. microscopy.

Mid. Midshipman.

mid. middle.

M.I.D. Master of Industrial Design.

midar (mī′där), microwave detection and ranging.

MIDI (mid′ē), *Electronics*. Musical Instrument Digital Interface.

MIDN Midshipman.

Midn. Midshipman.

M.I.E. Master of Industrial Engineering.

MiG (mig), any of several Russian fighter aircraft. Also, **Mig, MIG** [named after Artem *Mi(koyan)* and Mikhail *G(urevich)*, aircraft designers]

mil. 1. military. **2.** militia.

milit. military.

M.I.L.R. Master of Industrial and Labor Relations.

MIL-STD military standard.

min minim; minims.

min. 1. mineralogical. **2.** mineralogy. **3.** minim. **4.** minimum. **5.** mining. **6.** minor. **7.** minuscule. **8.** minute; minutes.

M.Ind.E. Master of Industrial Engineering.

Min.E. Mineral Engineer.

mineral. 1. mineralogical. **2.** mineralogy.

Mining Eng. Mining Engineer.

Minn. Minnesota.

mintr miniature.

MIP monthly investment plan.

MIPS (mips), *Computers*. million instructions per second: a measure of computer speed.

mir mirror.

MIr. Middle Irish. Also, **M.Ir.**

MIRV (mûrv), multiple independently targetable reentry vehicle. Also, **M.I.R.V.**

MIS 1. management information system. **2.** *Electronics*. metal-insulated semiconductor.

misc. 1. miscellaneous. **2.** miscellany.

Misc. Doc. miscellaneous document.

Miss. Mississippi.

miss. 1. mission. **2.** missionary.

mist. (in prescriptions) a mixture. [from Latin *mistūra*]

MITC mortgage investment tax credit.

mitt. (in prescriptions) send. [from Latin *mitte*]

mixt. mixture.

M.J. Master of Journalism.

mk. 1. (in Germany) mark. **2.** (in Finland) markka.

mkr marker.

MKS meter-kilogram-second. Also, **mks**

MKSA meter-kilogram-second-ampere. Also, **mksa**

mkt. market.

mktg. marketing.

ML Medieval Latin. Also, **M.L.**

mL *Optics.* millilambert; millilamberts.

ml milliliter; milliliters.

ml. 1. mail. **2.** milliliter; milliliters.

MLA Modern Language Association.

M.L.A. 1. Master of Landscape Architecture. **2.** Modern Language Association.

M.L.Arch. Master of Landscape Architecture.

MLB Maritime Labor Board.

MLD 1. median lethal dose. **2.** minimum lethal dose.

mldg. molding.

MLF Multilateral Nuclear Force.

MLG. Middle Low German. Also, **M.L.G.**

Mlle. Mademoiselle. Also, **Mlle**

Mlles. Mesdemoiselles.

MLR minimum lending rate.

MLS *Real Estate.* Multiple Listing Service.

M.L.S. Master of Library Science.

MLU *Psycholinguistics.* mean length of utterance.

MLW mean low water.

MM married male.

mM millimole; millimoles.

mm millimeter; millimeters.

MM. Messieurs.

mm. 1. *Music.* measures. **2.** thousands. [from Latin *millia*] **3.** millimeter; millimeters.

M.M. 1. Master Mason. **2.** Master Mechanic. **3.** Master of Music.

mm³ *Symbol.* cubic millimeter.

MMA Metropolitan Museum of Art.

Mme. Madame.

M.M.E. 1. Master of Mechanical Engineering. **2.** Master of Mining Engineering. **3.** Master of Music Education.

Mmes. Mesdames.

M.Met.E. Master of Metallurgical Engineering.

mmf *Electricity.* magnetomotive force. Also, **m.m.f.**

M.Mgt.E. Master of Management Engineering.

mm Hg millimeter of mercury. Also, **mmHg**

mmho *Electricity.* millimho; millimhos.

MMPI *Psychology.* Minnesota Multiphasic Personality Inventory.

M.M.Sc. Master of Medical Science.

MMT 1. *Astronomy.* Multiple Mirror Telescope. **2.** *Chemistry.* $C_9H_7MnO_3$, a gasoline additive. [*m(ethylcyclopentadienyl) m(anganese) t(ricarbonyl)*]

mmu memory-management unit.

M.Mus. Master of Music.

M.Mus.Ed. Master of Music Education.

MN Minnesota (for use with ZIP code).

Mn *Symbol, Chemistry.* manganese.

mn main.

M.N. Master of Nursing.

M.N.A. Master of Nursing Administration.

M.N.A.S. Member of the National Academy of Sciences.

mncpl municipal.

M.N.E. Master of Nuclear Engineering.

mnfrm *Computers.* mainframe.

mng managing.

Mngr. Monsignor.

mngr. manager.

mnl manual.

Mnr. manor.

mnrl mineral.

M.N.S. Master of Nutritional Science.

mnstb *Electronics.* monostable.

M.Nurs. Master of Nursing.

MO **1.** method of operation. **2.** Missouri (for use with ZIP code). **3.** mode of operation. **4.** modus operandi.

Mo *Symbol, Chemistry.* molybdenum.

Mo. **1.** Missouri. **2.** Monday.

mo. month. Also, **mo**

M.O. **1.** mail order. **2.** manually operated. **3.** Medical Officer. **4.** method of operation. **5.** mode of operation. **6.** modus operandi. **7.** money order.

m.o. **1.** mail order. **2.** modus operandi. **3.** money order.

mod **1.** *Computers.* magneto-optical drive. **2.** model. **3.** modification. **4.** modulator.

modem (mō′dəm, -dem), an electronic device that makes possible the transmission of data to or from a computer via telephone or other communication lines. [*mo(dulator)-dem(odulator)*]

MODFET (mod′fet′), *Electronics.* modulation-doped field effect transistor.

ModGk Modern Greek. Also, **Mod. Gk., Mod. Gr.**

ModHeb Modern Hebrew. Also, **Mod. Heb.**

modif. modification.

mod. praesc. (in prescriptions) in the manner prescribed; as directed.

[from Latin *modō praescrīptō*]

Moham. Mohammedan.

M.O.I. *British.* **1.** Ministry of Information. **2.** Ministry of the Interior.

mol *Chemistry.* mole.

mol. **1.** molecular. **2.** molecule.

mol. wt. molecular weight.

mom momentary.

m.o.m. middle of month.

MOMA (mō′mə), Museum of Modern Art.

Mon. **1.** Monday. **2.** Monsignor.

mon. **1.** monastery. **2.** monetary. **3.** monitor. **4.** monument.

mono monophonic.

Mons. Monsieur.

Mont. Montana.

MOPED (mō′ped), motor-assisted pedal cycle.

M.Opt. Master of Optometry.

MOR *Music.* middle-of-the-road.

mor. morocco.

more dict. (in prescriptions) in the manner directed. Also, **mor. dict.** [from Latin *mōre dictū*]

more sol. (in prescriptions) in the usual manner. Also, **mor. sol.** [from Latin *mōre solitō*]

morphol. morphology.

mort morse taper.

MOS *Electronics.* metal oxide semiconductor.

mos. **1.** months. **2.** mosaic.

MOSFET (mos′fet′), *Electronics.* metal oxide semiconducter field-effect transistor.

MOST (mōst), *Electronics.* metal-oxide-semiconductor transistor.

mot motor.

MP **1.** Military Police. **2.** Military Policeman. **3.** Mounted Police. **4.** Northern Mariana Islands (approved for postal use).

mp **1.** melting point. **2.** melting pot. **3.** *Music.* mezzo piano.

M.P. 1. Member of Parliament. **2.** Metropolitan Police. **3.** Military Police. **4.** Military Policeman. **5.** Mounted Police.

m.p. 1. melting point. **2.** (in prescriptions) in the manner prescribed; as directed. [from Latin *modō praescrīptō*]

M.P.A. 1. Master of Professional Accounting. **2.** Master of Public Administration. **3.** Master of Public Affairs.

MPAA Motion Picture Association of America.

MPB Missing Persons Bureau.

MPC Multimedia PC: a system conforming to specifications covering audio, video, and other multimedia components, and able to run multimedia software.

M.P.E. Master of Physical Education.

MPEG (em′peg), Motion Picture Experts Group.

MPers Middle Persian.

mpg miles per gallon. Also, **mi/gal., m.p.g., M.P.G., MPG**

mph miles per hour. Also, **mi/h., m.p.h., MPH**

M.Ph. Master of Philosophy.

M.P.H. Master of Public Health.

M.Pharm. Master of Pharmacy.

mpl maintenance parts list.

mpt male pipe thread.

MR 1. motivation research. **2.** Moral Re-Armament. Also, **M.R.**

mR *Physics.* milliroentgen; milliroentgens. Also, **mr**

Mr. (mis′tər), *plural* **Messrs.** (mes′ə-rz). mister: a title of respect prefixed to a man's name or position: *Mr. Lawson; Mr. President.*

MRA Moral Re-Armament.

MRBM medium-range ballistic missile. Also, **mrbm**

M.R.E. Master of Religious Education.

mrg mooring.

MRI *Medicine.* **1.** Also called **NMR.** magnetic resonance imaging. **2.** magnetic resonance imager.

mRNA *Genetics.* messenger RNA.

M.R.P. Master in Regional Planning; Master of Regional Planning.

Mrs. (mis′iz, miz′iz), *plural* **Mmes.** (mā däm′, -dam′). a title of respect prefixed to the name of a married woman: *Mrs. Jones.*

MRV *Military.* multiple reentry vehicle. Also, **M.R.V.**

MS 1. Mississippi (for use with ZIP code). **2.** motorship. **3.** multiple sclerosis.

ms millisecond; milliseconds.

MS., *plural* **MSS.** manuscript.

Ms. (miz), *plural* **Mses.** (miz′əz). a title of respect prefixed to a woman's name or position: unlike *Miss* or *Mrs.,* it does not depend upon or indicate her marital status.

ms., *plural* **mss.** manuscript.

M/S 1. *Commerce.* months after sight. **2.** motorship.

m/s meter per second; meters per second.

M.S. 1. mail steamer. **2.** Master of Science. **3.** Master in Surgery. **4.** motorship.

m.s. 1. *Grammar.* modification of the stem of. **2.** *Commerce.* months after sight.

M.S.A. Master of Science in Agriculture.

M.S.A.E. Master of Science in Aeronautical Engineering.

M.S.A.M. Master of Science in Applied Mechanics.

M.S.Arch. Master of Science in Architecture.

MSAT Minnesota Scholastic Aptitude Test.

M.S.B.A. Master of Science in Business Administration.

M.S.B.C. Master of Science in Building Construction.

M.S.Bus. Master of Science in Business.

MSC Manned Spacecraft Center.

M.Sc. Master of Science.

M.Sc.D. Doctor of Medical Science.

M.S.C.E. Master of Science in Civil Engineering.

M.S.Ch.E. Master of Science in Chemical Engineering.

M.Sc.Med. Master of Medical Science.

M.S.Cons. Master of Science in Conservation.

M.S.C.P. Master of Science in Community Planning.

mscr machine screw.

MSD 1. mean solar day. 2. *Math.* most significant digit.

M.S.D. 1. Doctor of Medical Science. 2. Master of Science in Dentistry.

M.S.Dent. Master of Science in Dentistry.

MS DOS (em′es′ dôs′, -dos′), *Trademark.* a microcomputer operating system. Also, **MS-DOS**

M.S.E. 1. Master of Science in Education. 2. Master of Science in Engineering.

msec millisecond; milliseconds.

m/sec meter per second; meters per second.

M.S.Ed. Master of Science in Education.

M.S.E.E. Master of Science in Electrical Engineering.

M.S.E.M. 1. Master of Science in Engineering Mechanics. 2. Master of Science in Engineering of Mines.

M.S.Ent. Master of Science in Entomology.

M.S.F. Master of Science in Forestry.

M.S.F.M. Master of Science in Forest Management.

M.S.For. Master of Science in Forestry.

MSG monosodium glutamate.

msg. message.

M.S.Geol.E. Master of Science in Geological Engineering.

M.S.G.M. Master of Science in Government Management.

M.S.G.Mgt. Master of Science in Game Management.

msgr messenger.

Msgr. 1. Monseigneur. 2. Monsignor.

M.Sgt. master sergeant.

MSH 1. *Biochemistry.* melanocyte-stimulating hormone; melanotropin: a hormone that causes dispersal of the black pigment melanin of melanocytes. 2. *Mineralogy.* Mohs scale.

M.S.H.A. Master of Science in Hospital Administration.

M.S.H.E. Master of Science in Home Economics. Also, **M.S.H.Ec.**

M.S.Hort. Master of Science in Horticulture.

M.S.Hyg. Master of Science in Hygiene.

MSI *Electronics.* medium-scale integration.

M.S.J. Master of Science in Journalism.

mskg masking.

msl missile.

M.S.L. 1. Master of Science in Linguistics. 2. Also, **m.s.l.** mean sea level.

msly mostly.

M.S.M. 1. Master of Sacred Music. 2. Master of Science in Music.

M.S.M.E. Master of Science in Mechanical Engineering.

M.S.Met.E. Master of Science in Metallurgical Engineering.

M.S.Mgt.E. Master of Science in Management Engineering.

M.S.N. Master of Science in Nursing.

msnry masonry.

msp *Printing.* manuscript page.

M.S.P.E. Master of Science in Physical Education.

M.S.P.H. Master of Science in Public Health.

M.S.Phar. Master of Science in Pharmacy. Also, **M.S.Pharm.**

M.S.P.H.E. Master of Science in Public Health Engineering.

M.S.P.H.Ed. Master of Science in Public Health Education.

MSS. manuscripts. Also, **MSS, Mss, mss.**

M.S.S. 1. Master of Social Science. 2. Master of Social Service.

M.S.Sc. Master of Social Science.

M.S.S.E. Master of Science in Sanitary Engineering.

MST 1. mean solar time. 2. Mountain Standard Time.

M.S.T. 1. Master of Science in Teaching. 2. Also, **m.s.t.** Mountain Standard Time.

mstr moisture.

MSTS *U.S. Military.* Military Sea Transportation Service.

M.S.W. 1. Master of Social Welfare. 2. Master of Social Work or Master in Social Work. Also, **MSW**

MT 1. mean time. 2. mechanical translation. 3. *Physics.* megaton; megatons. 4. Montana (for use with ZIP code). 5. Mountain time.

mt mount.

Mt. 1. mount: *Mt. Rainier.* 2. Also, **mt.** mountain.

M.T. 1. metric ton. 2. Also, **m.t.** Mountain time.

MTA Metropolitan Transit Authority.

MTBF mean time between failures.

MTBI mean time between incidents.

MTCF mean time to catastrophic failure.

mtchd matched.

mtd 1. mean temperature difference. 2. mounted.

mtg. 1. meeting. 2. mortgage. 3. mounting. Also, **mtg**

mtge. mortgage.

M.Th. Master of Theology.

mthbd *Computers.* motherboard.

mthd method.

MTI *Electronics.* moving target indicator. Also, **mti**

mtn 1. motion. 2. mountain.

MTO *Military.* (in World War II) Mediterranean Theater of Operations.

MTR mean time to restore.

mtr 1. magnetic tape recorder. 2. meter (instrument).

Mt. Rev. Most Reverend.

mtrg metering.

MTS *Broadcasting.* multichannel television sound.

Mts. mountains. Also, **mts.**

MTTF mean time to failure.

MTTFF mean time to first failure.

MTTM mean time to maintain.

MTTR mean time to repair.

mtu magnetic tape unit.

MTV Music Television (a cable television channel).

mtx matrix.

MUF material unaccounted for.

muf 1. maximum usable frequency. 2. muffler.

mult 1. multiple. 2. multiplication.

multr multiplier.

mun. 1. municipal. 2. municipality.

munic. 1. municipal. 2. municipality.

M.U.P. Master of Urban Planning.

Mus. Muslim.

mus 1. museum. 2. music. 3. musical. 4. musician.

Mus.B. Bachelor of Music. Also, **Mus. Bac.** [from Latin *Mūsicae Baccalaureus*]

Mus.D. Doctor of Music. Also, **Mus.Doc., Mus.Dr.** [from Latin *Mūsicae Doctor*]

Mus.M. Master of Music. [from Latin *Mūsicae Magister*]

mut. 1. mutilated. **2.** mutual.

muw music wire.

mux (muks), *Electronics.* **1.** multiplex. **2.** multiplexer.

MV 1. main verb. **2.** *Electricity.* megavolt; megavolts. **3.** motor vessel.

Mv *Symbol, Chemistry.* mendelevium.

mV *Electricity.* millivolt; millivolts.

mv 1. mean variation. **2.** *Electronics.* multivibrator.

m.v. 1. market value. **2.** mean variation. **3.** *Music.* mezza voce.

mvbl movable.

M.V.Ed. Master of Vocational Education.

mvg moving.

MVP Most Valuable Player. Also, **M.V.P.**

mvt movement.

MW *Electricity.* megawatt; megawatts.

mW *Electricity.* milliwatt; milliwatts.

mw medium wave.

M.W.A. Modern Woodmen of America.

MWG music wire gauge.

mwo modification work order.

mwp maximum working pressure.

M.W.T. Master of Wood Technology.

mwv maximum working voltage.

MX missile experimental: a ten-warhead U.S. intercontinental ballistic missile.

Mx *Electricity.* maxwell; maxwells.

mxd mixed.

mxg mixing.

mxr mixer.

mxt mixture.

mycol. mycology.

M.Y.O.B. mind your own business.

myth. 1. mythological. **2.** mythology.

mythol. 1. mythological. **2.** mythology.

N

N 1. *Physics.* newton; newtons. **2.** north. **3.** northern.

N *Symbol.* **1.** the 14th in order or in a series, or, when *I* is omitted, the 13th. **2.** (*sometimes lowercase*) the medieval Roman numeral for 90. **3.** *Chemistry.* nitrogen. **4.** *Biochemistry.* asparagine. **5.** *Math.* an indefinite, constant whole number, esp. the degree of a quantic or an equation, or the order of a curve. **6.** *Chess.* knight. **7.** *Printing.* en. **8.** *Chemistry.* Avogadro's number. **9.** neutron number.

n *Symbol.* **1.** *Physics.* neutron. **2.** *Optics.* index of refraction.

n- *Chemistry.* an abbreviated form of *normal*, used in the names of hydrocarbon compounds.

N. 1. Nationalist. **2.** Navy. **3.** New. **4.** Noon. **5.** *Chemistry.* normal (strength solution). **6.** Norse.

7. north. **8.** northern. **9.** *Finance.* note. **10.** November.

n. 1. name. **2.** born. [from Latin *nātus*] **3.** nephew. **4.** *Commerce.* net. **5.** neuter. **6.** new. **7.** nominative. **8.** noon. **9.** *Chemistry.* normal (strength solution). **10.** north. **11.** northern. **12.** *Finance.* note. **13.** noun. **14.** number.

NA 1. not applicable. **2.** not available.

Na *Symbol, Chemistry.* sodium. [from Latin *natrium*]

n/a 1. no account. **2.** not applicable.

N.A. 1. National Army. **2.** North America. **3.** not applicable. **4.** *Microscopy.* numerical aperture.

NAA National Aeronautic Association.

NAACP National Association for the Advancement of Colored People. Also, **N.A.A.C.P.**

NAB 1. Also, **N.A.B.** National Association of Broadcasters. **2.** New American Bible.

NACA National Advisory Committee for Aeronautics. Also, **N.A.C.A.**

NAD *Biochemistry.* a coenzyme, $C_{21}H_{27}N_7O_{14}P_2$, involved in many cellular oxidation-reduction reactions. [n(icotinamide) a(denine) d(inucleotide)]

N.A.D. National Academy of Design.

NADH *Biochemistry.* an abbreviation for the reduced form of NAD in electron transport reactions. [NAD + H, for hydrogen]

NADP *Biochemistry.* a coenzyme, $C_{21}H_{28}N_7O_{17}P_3$, similar in function to NAD. [n(icotinamide) a(denine) d(inucleotide) p(hosphate)]

NAFTA (naf′tə), North American Free Trade Agreement. Also, **Nafta.**

Nah. *Bible.* Nahum.

NAHB National Association of Home Builders.

NAM National Association of Manufacturers. Also, **N.A.M.**

nar narrow.

narc. narcotics.

N.A.S. 1. National Academy of Sciences. **2.** naval air station. Also, **NAS**

NASA (nas′ə), National Aeronautics and Space Administration.

NASCAR (nas′kär), National Association for Stock Car Auto Racing. Also, **N.A.S.C.A.R.**

NASD National Association of Securities Dealers. Also, **N.A.S.D.**

NASDAQ (nas′dak, naz′-), National Association of Securities Dealers Automated Quotations.

nat. 1. national. **2.** native. **3.** natural. **4.** naturalist.

natl. national.

NATO (nā′tō), an organization formed in 1949, comprising the 12 nations of the Atlantic Pact together with Greece, Turkey, and the Federal Republic of Germany, for the purpose of collective defense. [N(orth) A(tlantic) T(reaty) O(rganization)]

naut. nautical.

nav. 1. naval. **2.** navigable. **3.** navigation.

Nav. Arch. Naval Architect.

Nav. E. Naval Engineer.

navig. navigation.

NAVSAT (nav′sat′), navigational satellite.

NB 1. New Brunswick, Canada (for use with ZIP code). **2.** Also, **N.B.** note well; take notice. [from Latin *nota bene*]

Nb *Symbol, Chemistry.* niobium.

nb *Telecommunications.* narrowband.

N.B. New Brunswick.

NBA 1. National Basketball Association. **2.** Also, **N.B.A.** National Book Award. **3.** National Boxing Association.

nba narrowband amplifier.

NBC National Broadcasting System.

NbE north by east.

NBIOS *Computers.* network basic input-output system.

nbr number.

NBS National Bureau of Standards. Also, **N.B.S.**

NbW north by west.

NC 1. National coarse (a thread measure). **2.** no change. **3.** no charge. **4.** North Carolina (for use with ZIP code). **5.** numerical control. **6.** *Military.* Nurse Corps.

nc 1. no connection. **2.** *Electricity.* normally closed (of contacts).

n/c no charge.

N.C. 1. no charge. **2.** North Carolina.

NCA 1. National Council on the Aging. **2.** National Council on the Arts.

nca nickel-copper alloy.

NCAA National Collegiate Athletic Association. Also, **N.C.A.A.**

N.C.C. National Council of Churches. Also, **NCC**

NCCJ National Conference of Christians and Jews.

ncd no can do.

N.C.O. Noncommissioned Officer.

NCTE National Council of Teachers of English.

ND North Dakota (for use with ZIP code).

Nd *Symbol, Chemistry.* neodymium.

nd *Stock Exchange.* (especially of bonds) next day (delivery).

n.d. no date.

NDAC National Defense Advisory Commission.

N.Dak. North Dakota. Also, **N.D.**

nde near-death experience.

ndf *Photography.* neutral-density filter.

ndro nondestructive readout.

NDSL National Direct Student Loan.

ndt nondestructive testing.

NE 1. Nebraska (for use with ZIP code). **2.** northeast. **3.** northeastern.

Ne *Symbol, Chemistry.* neon.

N.E. 1. naval engineer. **2.** New England. **3.** northeast. **4.** northeastern.

n.e. 1. northeast. **2.** northeastern.

N.E.A. 1. National Education Association. **2.** National Endowment for the Arts. Also, **NEA**

Neb. Nebraska.

NEbE northeast by east.

NEbN northeast by north.

Nebr. Nebraska.

NEC National Electrical Code.

nec necessary.

n.e.c. not elsewhere classified.

N.E.D. *New English Dictionary.* Also, **NED**

NEF National extra fine (a thread measure).

neg. 1. Also, **neg** negative. **2.** negatively.

NEH National Endowment for the Humanities.

Neh. *Bible.* Nehemiah.

nem. con. no one contradicting; unanimously. [from Latin *nemine contradicente*]

nem. diss. no one dissenting; unanimously. [from Latin *nemine dissentiente*]

N. Eng. Northern England.

NEP (nep), New Economic Policy. Also, **Nep, N.E.P.**

NES New England Sports Network (a cable television channel).

n.e.s. not elsewhere specified. Also, **N.E.S.**

NESC National Electrical Safety Code.

NET National Educational Television.

Neth. Netherlands.

n. et m. (in prescriptions) night and morning. [Latin *nocte et mane*]

neurol. neurology; neurological.

neut. 1. neuter. **2.** neutral.

Nev. Nevada.

Newf. Newfoundland.

NF 1. National fine (a thread measure). **2.** *Pharmacology.* National Formulary. **3.** Newfoundland, Canada (for use with ZIP code). **4.** no funds. **5.** Norman French.

nf *Telecommunications.* noise figure.

n/f no funds. Also, **N/F**

N.F. 1. no funds. **2.** Norman French.

NFC National Football Conference.

NFD. Newfoundland. Also, **Nfd., Nfld.**

NFL National Football League.

NFS not for sale. Also, **N.F.S.**

NG 1. *Chemistry.* nitroglycerin. **2.** *Anatomy.* nasogastric.

ng nanogram; nanograms.

N.G. 1. National Guard. **2.** New Guinea. **3.** no good.

n.g. no good.

NGC *Astronomy.* New General Catalogue: a catalog of clusters, nebulae, and galaxies published in 1888.

NGF nerve growth factor.

NGk New Greek. Also, **N.Gk.**

NGNP nominal gross national product.

NGS National Geodetic Survey.

NGU *Pathology.* nongonococcal urethritis.

NH New Hampshire (for use with ZIP code).

nh nonhygroscopic.

NHA National Housing Agency. Also, **N.H.A.**

nha next higher assembly.

N. Heb. New Hebrides.

NHG New High German. Also, **NHG., N.H.G.**

NHI *British.* National Health Insurance.

NHL National Hockey League.

NHS 1. *British.* National Health Service. **2.** National Honor Society.

NHSC National Highway Safety Council.

NHTSA National Highway Traffic Safety Administration.

Ni *Symbol, Chemistry.* nickel.

N.I. Northern Ireland.

NIA 1. National Intelligence Authority. **2.** Newspaper Institute of America.

NIH National Institutes of Health.

NIK Nickelodeon (a cable television channel).

NIMBY (*usually* nim′bē), not in my backyard. Also, **Nimby.**

NIMH National Institute of Mental Health.

NiMH *Electricity.* nickel-metal hydride (battery).

nip nipple.

ni. pr. (in prescriptions) unless before. [from Latin *nisi prius*]

NIRA National Industrial Recovery Act. Also, **N.I.R.A.**

NIST (nist), National Institute of Standards and Technology.

NIT National Invitational Tournament.

NJ New Jersey (for use with ZIP code).

N.J. New Jersey.

NKGB in the U.S.S.R., a secret-police organization (1941–46). [from Russian *N(aródnyĭ) k(omissariát) g(osudárstvennoĭ) b(ezopásnosti)* People's Commissariat for State Security]

nkl nickel.

NKVD in the U.S.S.R., a secret-police organization (1934–46). [from Russian *N(aródnyĭ) K(omissariát) V(nútrennikh) D(el)* People's Commissariat of Internal Affairs]

NL 1. Also, **NL.** New Latin; Neo-Latin. **2.** night letter.

nl nonleaded (of gasoline).

N.L. 1. *Baseball.* National League. **2.** New Latin; Neo-Latin.

n.l. 1. *Printing.* new line. **2.** *Law.* it is not allowed. [from Latin *non licet*] **3.** *Law.* it is not clear or evident. [from Latin *non liquet*]

N. Lat. north latitude. Also, **N. lat.**

N.L.F. National Liberation Front.

nlnr nonlinear.

NLRB National Labor Relations Board. Also, **N.L.R.B.**

NM 1. New Mexico (for use with ZIP code). **2.** *Grammar.* noun modifier.

nm 1. nanometer; nanometers. **2.** nautical mile. **3.** nonmetallic.

N.M. New Mexico. Also, **N. Mex.**

nmag nonmagnetic.

NMI no middle initial. Also, **nmi**

nmi *Symbol.* nautical mile.

nmlz normalize.

NMN no middle name.

NMR 1. *Physics.* nuclear magnetic

resonance. **2.** *Medicine.* magnetic resonance imaging.

nmr no maintenance required.

NMSQT National Merit Scholarship Qualifying Test.

NMSS National Multiple Sclerosis Society.

N.M.U. National Maritime Union. Also, **NMU**

NNE north-northeast. Also, **N.N.E.**

NNP net national product.

NNW north-northwest. Also, **N.N.W.**

No *Symbol, Chemistry.* nobelium.

no *Electricity.* (of contacts) normally open.

no. 1. north. **2.** northern. **3.** number. Also, **No.**

N/O *Banking.* registered.

NOAA National Oceanic and Atmospheric Administration.

N.O.C. *Insurance.* not otherwise classified.

n.o.i.b.n. not otherwise indexed by name.

nol. pros. *Law.* unwilling to prosecute. [from Latin *nolle prosequi*]

nom. *Grammar.* nominative.

Nom. Cap. *Finance.* nominal capital.

nomen nomenclature.

noncom. noncommissioned.

nonflm nonflammable.

non obst. *Law.* notwithstanding. [from Latin *non obstante*]

non pros. *Law.* a judgment against a plaintiff who does not appear in court. [from Latin *non prosequitur* he does not pursue]

non rep. (in prescriptions) do not repeat. [from Latin *non repetatur* it is not repeated]

non seq. *Logic.* a conclusion which does not follow from the premises. [from Latin *non sequitur* it does not follow]

nonstd nonstandard.

nonsyn nonsynchronous.

NOP not our publication. Also, **N.O.P.**

Nor. 1. Norman. **2.** North. **3.** Northern. **4.** Norway. **5.** Norwegian.

nor. 1. north. **2.** northern.

NORAD (nôr′ad), a joint U.S.-Canadian air force command. [*Nor(th American) A(ir) D(efence Command)*]

norm normal.

Norw. 1. Norway. **2.** Norwegian.

NOS *Computers.* network operating system.

nos. numbers. Also, **Nos.**

n.o.s. not otherwise specified.

NOTA none of the above.

Nov. November.

nov. novelist.

NOW (nou), **1.** National Organization for Women. **2.** *Banking.* negotiable order of withdrawal.

noz nozzle.

NP 1. National pipe (a thread measure). **2.** noun phrase. **3.** nurse-practitioner.

Np *Physics.* neper; nepers.

Np *Symbol, Chemistry.* neptunium.

N.P. 1. new paragraph. **2.** *Law.* nisi prius. **3.** no protest. **4.** notary public.

n.p. 1. net proceeds. **2.** new paragraph. **3.** *Law.* nisi prius. **4.** no pagination. **5.** no place of publication. **6.** no protest. **7.** notary public.

NPK *Horticulture.* nitrogen, phosphorus, and potassium.

npl nameplate.

npn negative-positive-negative (transistor).

n.p. or d. no place or date.

NPR National Public Radio. Also, **N.P.R.**

nprn neoprene.

NPT 1. National (taper) pipe thread. **2.** Nonproliferation Treaty.

n.p.t. normal pressure and temperature. Also, **npt**

nr I. negative resistance. **2.** nuclear reactor.

NRA I. National Recovery Administration: a former federal agency (1933–36). **2.** National Recreation Area. **3.** National Rifle Association. Also, **N.R.A.**

NRAB National Railroad Adjustment Board.

NRC I. National Research Council. **2.** Nuclear Regulatory Commission.

NROTC Naval Reserve Officer Training Corps. Also **N.R.O.T.C.**

NRPB National Resources Planning Board.

NRTA National Retired Teachers Association.

nrtn nonreturn.

nrvsbl nonreversible.

nrz nonreturn-to-zero.

NS I. not sufficient (funds). **2.** Nova Scotia, Canada (for use with ZIP code). **3.** nuclear ship.

Ns *Meteorology.* nimbostratus.

ns I. Also, **nsec** nanosecond; nanoseconds. **2.** nonserviceable.

N.S. I. New Style. **2.** Nova Scotia.

n.s. not specified.

NSA I. National Security Agency. **2.** National Shipping Authority. **3.** National Standards Association. **4.** National Student Association. Also, **N.S.A.**

NSC I. National Safety Council. **2.** National Security Council.

NSF I. National Science Foundation. **2.** not sufficient funds. Also, **N.S.F.**

N/S/F not sufficient funds.

N.S.P.C.A. National Society for the Prevention of Cruelty to Animals.

N.S.P.C.C. National Society for the Prevention of Cruelty to Children.

n.s.p.f. not specifically provided for.

NSU *Pathology.* nonspecific urethritis; nongonococcal urethritis.

N.S.W. New South Wales.

NT I. New Testament. **2.** Northwest Territories, Canada (for use with ZIP code).

Nt *Symbol, Chemistry.* niton.

nt *Physics.* nit; nits.

N.T. I. New Testament (of the Bible). **2.** Northern Territory. **3.** Northwest Territories.

ntc negative temperature coefficient.

NTIA National Telecommunications and Information Administration.

ntp normal temperature and pressure.

nts not to scale.

NTSB National Transportation Safety Board.

ntwk network.

nt. wt. net weight. Also, **ntwt**

nuc nuclear.

NUCFLASH (nook'flash', nyook'-), a report of highest precedence notifying the president or deputies of an accidental or unauthorized nuclear-weapon launch or of a nuclear attack. [*nuc(lear) flash*]

NUL National Urban League. Also **N.U.L.**

Num. *Bible.* Numbers.

num. I. number. **2.** numeral; numerals.

numis. I. numismatic. **2.** numismatics. Also, **numism.**

N.U.T. *British.* National Union of Teachers.

N.U.W.W. *British.* National Union of Women Workers.

NV Nevada (for use with ZIP code).

N/V *Banking.* no value.

NW I. net worth. **2.** northwest. **3.** northwestern. Also, **N.W., n.w.**

NWbW northwest by west.

NWC *Military.* National War College.

NWLB National War Labor Board.

NWS National Weather Service.

nwt nonwatertight.

n. wt. net weight.

N.W.T. Northwest Territories.

NY New York (for use with ZIP code).

N.Y. New York.

NYA National Youth Administration. Also, **N.Y.A.**

N.Y.C. New York City. Also, **NYC**

NYCSCE New York Coffee, Sugar, and Cocoa Exchange.

nyl nylon.

NYME New York Mercantile Exchange.

NYP not yet published. Also, **N.Y.P.**

NYSE New York Stock Exchange. Also, **N.Y.S.E.**

N.Z. New Zealand. Also, **N. Zeal.**

O 1. Old. **2.** *Grammar.* object.

O *Symbol.* **1.** the fifteenth in order or in a series. **2.** the Arabic cipher; zero. **3.** (*sometimes lowercase*) the medieval Roman numeral for 11. **4.** *Physiology.* a major blood group, usually enabling a person whose blood is of this type to donate blood to persons of group O, A, B, or AB and to receive blood from persons of group O. **5.** *Chemistry.* oxygen. **6.** *Logic.* particular negative.

0. 1. Ocean. **2.** (in prescriptions) a pint. [from Latin *octārius*] **3.** octavo. **4.** October. **5.** Ohio. **6.** Old. **7.** Ontario. **8.** Oregon.

o. 1. pint. [from Latin *octārius*] **2.** *Printing.* octavo. **3.** off. **4.** old. **5.** only. **6.** order. **7.** *Baseball.* out; outs.

OA office automation.

oa overall.

o/a 1. on account. **2.** on or about.

OAO *U. S. Aerospace.* Orbiting Astronomical Observatory.

OAP *British.* old-age pensioner.

OAPC Office of Alien Property Custodian.

OAS Organization of American States.

O.A.S.I. Old Age and Survivors Insurance.

OAU Organization of African Unity. Also, **O.A.U.**

OB 1. Also, **ob** *Medicine.* **a.** obstetri-

cal. **b.** obstetrician. **c.** obstetrics. **2.** off Broadway. **3.** opening of books. **4.** ordered back. **5.** outward bound.

ob. 1. he died; she died. [from Latin *obiit*] **2.** incidentally. [from Latin *obiter*] **3.** oboe. **4.** *Meteorology.* observation.

O.B. 1. opening of books. **2.** ordered back. Also, **O/B**

obb. *Music.* obbligato.

obdt. obedient.

O.B.E. 1. Officer (of the Order) of the British Empire. **2.** Order of the British Empire.

OB-GYN *Medicine.* **1.** obstetrician-gynecologist. **2.** obstetrics-gynecology.

obit. obituary.

obj. 1. object. **2.** objection. **3.** objective.

objv objective.

obl. 1. oblique. **2.** oblong.

oblg 1. obligate. **2.** obligation. **3.** oblige.

obs. 1. observation. **2.** observatory. **3.** obsolete. Also, **Obs.**

obsl obsolete.

obstet. 1. obstetric. **2.** obstetrics.

obstn obstruction.

obsv observation.

OBulg. Old Bulgarian. Also, **OBulg**

obv obverse.

oc outside circumference.

Oc. ocean. Also, **oc.**

o/c overcharge.

O.C. *Philately.* original cover.

o.c. **1.** *Architecture.* on center. **2.** in the work cited. [from Latin *opere citātō*]

occ. **1.** occasional. **2.** occasionally. **3.** occident. **4.** occidental. **5.** occupation. **6.** occupy.

occas. **1.** occasional. **2.** occasionally.

OCD Office of Civil Defense.

OCDM Office of Civil and Defense Mobilization.

ocld oil-cooled.

OCR *Computers.* **1.** optical character reader. **2.** optical character recognition.

OCS **1.** *Military.* officer candidate school. **2.** Old Church Slavonic. **3.** outer continental shelf.

ocsnl occasional.

Oct. October.

oct. **1.** octagon. **2.** octavo.

octl octal.

octn octane.

OD an overdose of a drug, especially a fatal one.

OD **1.** officer of the day. **2.** Old Dutch. **3.** Ordnance Department. **4.** outside diameter.

od **1.** on demand. **2.** outside diameter. **3.** outside dimensions. **4.** *Banking.* overdraft. **5.** *Banking.* overdrawn.

OD. Old Dutch.

O.D. **1.** Doctor of Optometry. **2.** (in prescriptions) the right eye. [from Latin *oculus dexter*] **3.** officer of the day. **4.** Old Dutch. **5.** (of a military uniform) olive drab. **6.** ordinary seaman. **7.** outside diameter. **8.** *Banking.* overdraft. **9.** *Banking.* overdrawn.

o.d. **1.** (in prescriptions) the right eye. [from Latin *oculus dexter*] **2.** olive drab. **3.** on demand. **4.** outside diameter.

odom odometer.

odpsk oil dipstick.

ODT Office of Defense Transportation.

OE Old English. Also, **OE.**

Oe *Electricity.* oersted; oersteds.

O.E. **1.** Old English. **2.** *Commerce.* omissions excepted.

o.e. *Commerce.* omissions excepted. Also, **oe**

OEC Office of Energy Conservation.

OECD Organization for Economic Cooperation and Development.

OED *Oxford English Dictionary.* Also, **O.E.D.**

OEEC Organization for European Economic Cooperation.

OEM original equipment manufacturer.

OEO Office of Economic Opportunity.

OES **1.** Office of Economic Stabilization. **2.** Order of the Eastern Star.

OF Old French. Also, **OF.**, **O.F.**

of outside face.

ofc office.

ofcl official.

ofcr officer.

ofl offline.

OFlem Old Flemish. Also, **OFlem.**

ofltr oil filter.

O.F.M. Order of Friars Minor (Franciscan). [from Latin *Ordō Frātrum Minōrum*]

OFr. Old French. Also, **OFr**

OFris. Old Frisian. Also, **OFris**

oft outfit.

OG officer of the guard.

O.G. **1.** officer of the guard. **2.** *Architecture.* ogee. **3.** *Philately.* See **o.g.** (def. 1).

o.g. **1.** Also, **O.G.** *Philately.* original gum: the gum on the back of a stamp when it is issued. **2.** *Architecture.* ogee.

OGO *U.S. Aerospace.* Orbiting Geophysical Observatory.

OGPU (og′pōō), (in the U.S.S.R.) the government's secret-police organization (1923–1934). Also, **Ogpu.** Cf. **KGB.** [from Russian *Ógpu,* for *Ob´´edinënnoe gosudárstvennoe politícheskoe upravlénie* Unified State Political Directorate]

ogr *Telephones.* outgoing repeater.

ogt *Telephones.* outgoing trunk.

OH Ohio (for use with ZIP code).

OHC *Automotive.* overhead camshaft.

OHG Old High German. Also, **OHG., O.H.G.**

O.H.M.S. On His Majesty's Service; On Her Majesty's Service.

OI opportunistic infection.

OIC officer in charge.

OIcel Old Icelandic.

OIr Old Irish. Also, **OIr.**

OIt Old Italian.

OJ *Informal.* orange juice. Also, **O.J., o.j.**

OJT on-the-job training. Also, **O.J.T.**

OK Oklahoma (for use with ZIP code).

OK (ō′kā′, ō′kā′, ō′kā′), all right; permissible or acceptable; satisfactory or under control. Also, **O.K., okay** [initials of a facetious folk phonetic spelling, e.g., *oll* or *orl korrect* representing *all correct,* first attested in Boston, Massachusetts, in 1839, then used in 1840 by Democrat partisans of Martin Van Buren during his election campaign, who allegedly named their organization, the *O.K. Club,* in allusion to the initials of *Old Kinderhook,* Van Buren's nickname, derived from his birthplace *Kinderhook,* New York]

Okla. Oklahoma.

OL Old Latin. Also, **OL.**

Ol. (in prescriptions) oil. [from Latin *oleum*]

O.L. 1. Also, **o.l.** (in prescriptions) the left eye. [from Latin *oculus laevus*] **2.** Old Latin.

Old Test. Old Testament (of the Bible).

OLE *Computers.* object linking and embedding.

OLG Old Low German. Also, **O.L.G.**

OLLA Office of Lend Lease Administration.

olvl oil level.

Om. (formerly, in East Germany) ostmark.

O.M. *British.* Order of Merit.

OMA orderly marketing agreement.

OMB Office of Management and Budget. Also, **O.M.B.**

OMBE Office of Minority Business Enterprise.

omn. bih. (in prescriptions) every two hours. [from Latin *omnī bihōriō*]

omn. hor. (in prescriptions) every hour. [from Latin *omnī hōra*]

omn. man. (in prescriptions) every morning. Also, **omn man** [from Latin *omnī māne*]

omn. noct. (in prescriptions) every night. Also, **omn noct** [from Latin *omnī nocte*]

omn. quadr. hor. (in prescriptions) every quarter of an hour. Also, **omn quadr hor** [from Latin *omnī quadrante hōrae*]

ON 1. Also, **ON., O.N.** Old Norse. **2.** Ontario, Canada (for use with ZIP code).

ONF Old North French.

ONFr. Old North French.

ONI Office of Naval Intelligence.

ONR Office of Naval Research.

Ont. Ontario.

O.O.D. 1. officer of the deck. **2.** officer of the day.

OOG *Computers.* object-oriented graphics.

OOP *Computers.* object-oriented programming.

OOT out of town. Also, **O.O.T.**

OP observation post. Also, **O.P.**

op (op), a style of abstract art. [from *op(tical)*]

Op. *Music.* opus.

op. 1. opera. **2.** operation. **3.** opposite. **4.** opus.

O.P. 1. observation post. **2.** *British Theater.* opposite prompt. **3.** Order of Preachers (Dominican). [from Latin *Ōrdō Praedicātōrum*] **4.** out of print. **5.** *Distilling.* overproof.

o.p. out of print.

OPA Office of Price Administration: the federal agency (1941–46) charged with regulating rents and the distribution and prices of goods during World War II.

opa opaque.

op. cit. (op′ sit′), in the work cited. [from Latin *opere citātō*]

OPEC (ō′pek), an organization founded in 1960 of nations that export large amounts of petroleum, to establish oil-exporting policies and set prices. [*O(rganization of) P(etroleum) E(xporting) C(ountries)*]

Op-Ed (op′ed′), a newspaper page devoted to signed articles of varying viewpoints. [*op(posite) ed(itorial page)*]

OPer. Old Persian.

OPers Old Persian.

ophthal. 1. ophthalmologist. **2.** ophthalmology.

OPM 1. Office of Personnel Management. **2.** operations per minute. **3.** *Slang.* other people's money.

opn operation.

opnr opener.

Opp. *Music.* opuses. [from Latin *opera*]

opp. 1. opposed. **2.** opposite.

opp hnd opposite hand.

OPr Old Provençal.

opr 1. operate. **2.** operator.

oprg operating.

oprs oil pressure.

OPruss Old Prussian.

OPS Office of Price Stabilization. Also, **O.P.S.**

opt 1. optical. **2.** optimum.

optl optional.

opty opportunity.

OR 1. *Law.* on (one's own) recognizance. **2.** operating room. **3.** operations research. **4.** Oregon (for use with ZIP code). **5.** owner's risk.

or outside radius.

O.R. 1. *Military.* orderly room. **2.** owner's risk.

O.R.C. Officers' Reserve Corps.

orch. orchestra.

ord. 1. Also, **ord** order. **2.** ordinal. **3.** ordinance. **4.** ordinary. **5.** ordnance.

ordn. ordnance.

Ore. Oregon.

Oreg. Oregon.

orf orifice.

org. 1. organic. **2.** organization. **3.** organized.

orig. 1. origin. **2.** original. **3.** originally.

orn orange.

ornith. 1. ornithological. **2.** ornithology.

ornithol. 1. ornithological. **2.** ornithology.

ORT Registered Occupational Therapist.

Orth. Orthodox.

orth. 1. orthopedic **2.** orthopedics.

ORuss Old Russian

ORV off-road vehicle.

OS 1. Old Saxon. **2.** *Computers.* operating system.

Os *Symbol, Chemistry.* osmium.

O/S (of the calendar) Old Style.

o/s 1. (of the calendar) Old Style. **2.** out of stock. **3.** *Banking.* outstanding.

O.S. 1. (in prescriptions) the left eye. [from Latin *oculus sinister*] **2.** Old Saxon. **3.** Old School. **4.** old series. **5.** (of the calendar) Old Style. **6.** ordinary seaman.

o.s. 1. (in prescriptions) the left eye. [from Latin *oculus sinister*] **2.** ordinary seaman.

O.S.A. Order of St. Augustine.

O.S.B. Order of St. Benedict.

osc oscillator.

OSD Office of the Secretary of Defense.

O.S.D. Order of St. Dominic.

O.S.F. Order of St. Francis.

OSFCW Office of Solid Fuels Coordinator for War.

OSHA (ō′shə, osh′ə), the division of the Department of Labor that sets and enforces occupational health and safety rules. [*O(ccupational) S(afety and) H(ealth) A(dministration)*]

osl oil seal.

osmv *Electronics.* one-shot multivibrator.

OSO *U.S. Aerospace.* Orbiting Solar Observatory.

OSP died without issue. [from Latin *obiit sine prōle*]

OSp Old Spanish.

OSRD Office of Scientific Research and Development.

OSS Office of Strategic Services: a U.S. government intelligence agency during World War II. Also, **O.S.S.**

OT 1. occupational therapist. **2.** occupational therapy. **3.** *Bible.* Old Testament. **4.** overnight telegram. **5.** overtime.

O.T. Old Testament (of the Bible).

o.t. overtime.

OTA Office of Technology Assessment.

OTB offtrack betting.

OTC 1. Also, **O.T.C.** Officers' Training Corps. **2.** over-the-counter.

OTS Officers' Training School. Also, **O.T.S.**

OU (in prescriptions) **1.** both eyes. [from Latin *oculi uterque*] **2.** each eye. [from Latin *oculus uterque*]

out 1. outlet. **2.** output.

outbd outboard.

outg outgoing.

ov over.

ovbd overboard.

ovh oval head.

ovhd overhead.

ovhl overhaul.

OV language (ō′vē′), *Linguistics.* a type of language that has direct objects preceding the verb. [*O(bject)-V(erb)*]

ovld overload.

ovp oval point.

ovrd override.

ovsz oversize.

ovtr overtravel.

ovv overvoltage.

OW Old Welsh.

OWI 1. Office of War Information: the U.S federal agency (1942–45) charged with disseminating information about World War II. **2.** operating (a motor vehicle) while intoxicated.

Ox. Oxford. [from Latin *Oxonia*]

oxd oxidized.

Oxon. 1. Oxford. [from Latin *Oxonia*] **2.** of Oxford. [from Latin *Oxoniēnsis*]

oz. ounce; ounces. [abbreviation of Italian *onza*]

oz. av. ounce avoirdupois.

ozs. ounces.

oz. t. ounce troy.

P

P 1. (as a rating of student performance) passing. **2.** *Chess.* pawn. **3.** *Electronics.* plate. **4.** poor. **5.** *Grammar.* predicate. **6.** Protestant.

P *Symbol.* **1.** the 16th in order or in a series, or, when *I* is omitted, the 15th. **2.** (*sometimes lowercase*) the medieval Roman numeral for 400. **3.** *Genetics.* parental. **4.** *Chemistry.* phosphorus. **5.** *Physics.* **a.** power. **b.** pressure. **c.** proton. **d.** space inversion. **e.** poise. **6.** *Biochemistry.* proline.

p 1. penny; pence. **2.** *Music.* softly. [from Italian *piano*]

P- *Military.* (in designations of aircraft) pursuit: *P-38.*

p- *Chemistry.* designating the 1, 4 position on the benzene ring. [from Greek *para-* beside, by, beyond]

P. 1. pastor. **2.** father. [from Latin *Pater*] **3.** peseta. **4.** peso. **5.** post. **6.** president. **7.** pressure. **8.** priest. **9.** prince. **10.** progressive.

p. 1. page. **2.** part. **3.** participle. **4.** past. **5.** father. [from Latin *pater*] **6.** *Chess.* pawn. **7.** penny; pence. **8.** per. **9.** *Grammar.* person. **10.** peseta. **11.** peso. **12.** *Music.* softly. [from Italian *piano*] **13.** pint. **14.** pipe. **15.** *Baseball.* pitcher. **16.** pole. **17.** population. **18.** after. [from Latin *post*] **19.** president. **20.** pressure. **21.** purl.

PA 1. paying agent. **2.** Pennsylvania (for use with ZIP code). **3.** physician's assistant. **4.** press agent. **5.** public-address system.

Pa *Physics.* pascal; pascals.

Pa *Symbol, Chemistry.* protactinium.

Pa. Pennsylvania.

P.A. 1. Also, **PA** Parents' Association. **2.** *Insurance.* particular average. **3.** passenger agent. **4.** *Military.* post adjutant. **5.** power of attorney. **6.** press agent. **7.** public-address system. **8.** publicity agent. **9.** purchasing agent.

p.a. 1. participial adjective. **2.** per annum. **3.** press agent.

p.-a. public-address system.

PABA (pä′bə), *Chemistry, Biochemistry.* a crystalline solid, $C_7H_7NO_2$, used especially in pharmaceuticals. [*p(ara-)a(mino)b(enzoic) a(cid)*]

PABX *Telephones.* an automatically operated PBX. Also, **pabx** [*p(rivate) a(utomatic) b(ranch) ex(change)*]

PAC (pak), political action committee.

Pac. Pacific.

P.A.C. political action committee.

pacm pulse amplitude code modulation.

PaD Pennsylvania Dutch; Pennsylvania German.

p. ae. (in prescriptions) equal parts. [from Latin *partēs aequālēs*]

PaG Pennsylvania German.

Pak. Pakistan.

PAL (pal), a special air service offered by the U.S. Postal Service for sending parcels. [*P(arcel) A(ir) L(ift)*]

PAL Police Athletic League. Also, **P.A.L.**

Pal. Palestine.

pal. 1. paleography. **2.** paleontology.

paleog. paleography.

paleon. paleontology.

paleontol. paleontology.

PAM 1. *Aerospace.* payload assist module. **2.** Also, **pam** *Telecommunications.* pulse amplitude modulation.

pam. pamphlet.

pamfm pulse amplitude modulation frequency modulation.

Pan (pan), an international distress signal used by shore stations to inform a ship, aircraft, etc., of something vital to its safety or that of one of its passengers. Also, **pan.**

pan panoramic.

Pan. Panama.

P. and L. profit and loss. Also, **P. & L., p. and l.**

par precision-approach radar.

par. 1. paragraph. **2.** parallel. **3.** parenthesis. **4.** parish.

para paragraph.

Para. Paraguay.

par. aff. (in prescriptions) to the part affected. [from Latin *pars affecta*]

paren parenthesis.

Parl. 1. Parliament. **2.** Parliamentary. Also, **parl.**

parl. proc. parliamentary procedure.

parsec (pär'sek'), *Astronomy*. parallax second.

part. 1. participial. **2.** participle. **3.** particular.

part. adj. participial adjective.

part. aeq. (in prescriptions) equal parts. [from Latin *partes aequales*]

part. vic. (in prescriptions) in divided doses. [from Latin *partibus vicibus*]

pas public address system.

pass. 1. passage. **2.** passenger. **3.** here and there throughout. [from Latin *passim*] **4.** passive.

PAT 1. *Football*. point after touchdown; points after touchdown. **2.** *Banking*. preauthorized automatic transfer.

pat. 1. patent. **2.** patented.

patd. patented.

path. 1. pathological. **2.** pathology.

pathol. 1. Also, **pathol** pathological. **2.** pathology.

Pat. Off. Patent Office.

pat. pend. patent pending. Also, **patpend**

P.A.U. Pan American Union.

PAX *Telephones*. private automatic exchange.

PAYE 1. pay as you enter. **2.** pay as you earn.

PB power brakes.

Pb *Symbol, Chemistry*. lead. [from Latin *plumbum*]

pb pushbutton.

P.B. 1. British Pharmacopoeia. [from Latin *Pharmacopoeia Britannica*] **2.** Prayer Book.

p.b. *Baseball*. passed ball; passed balls.

PBA 1. Professional Bowlers Association. **2.** Public Buildings Administration.

P.B.A. Patrolmen's Benevolent Association.

PBB *Chemistry*. any of the highly toxic and possibly carcinogenic aromatic compounds consisting of two benzene rings in which bromine takes the place of two or more hydrogen atoms. [*p(oly)b(rominated) b(iphenyl)*]

pbd pressboard.

PBK Phi Beta Kappa.

pblg publishing.

pblr publisher.

PBS Public Broadcasting Service.

PBX a manually or automatically operated telephone facility that handles communications within an office, office building, or organization. [*P(rivate) B(ranch) Ex(change)*]

PC 1. Peace Corps. **2.** personal computer. **3.** politically correct. **4.** printed circuit. **5.** professional corporation.

pc 1. *Astronomy*. parsec. **2.** parts catalog. **3.** *Physics, Chemistry*. picocurie; picocuries.

pc. 1. piece. **2.** prices.

P/C 1. petty cash. **2.** price current. Also, **p/c**

P.C. 1. Past Commander. **2.** *British.* Police Constable. **3.** politically correct. **4.** Post Commander. **5.** *British.* Prince Consort. **6.** *British.* Privy Council. **7.** professional corporation.

p.c. 1. percent. **2.** petty cash. **3.** postal card. **4.** (in prescriptions) after eating; after meals. [from Latin *post cibōs*] **5.** price current. **6.** printed circuit.

PCB a family of highly toxic chemical compounds consisting of two benzene rings in which chlorine takes the place of two or more hydrogen atoms. [*p(oly)c(hlorinated) b(iphenyl)*]

pcb *Electronics.* printed-circuit board.

pcf pounds per cubic foot.

pchs purchase.

pchsg purchasing.

pcht parchment.

PCI *Computers.* peripheral component interconnect.

pci pounds per cubic inch.

PCL *Computers.* Printer Control Language.

pcl pencil.

PCM 1. *Computers.* plug-compatible manufacturer. **2.** Also, **pcm** *Telecommunications.* pulse code modulation.

PCMCIA Personal Computer Memory Card International Association.

pcmd pulse code modulation digital.

pcmfm pulse code modulation frequency modulation.

PCNB *Chemistry.* a crystalline compound, $C_6Cl_5NO_2$, used as a herbicide and insecticide. [*p(enta)c(hloro)n(itro)b(enzene)*]

PCP 1. *Slang.* phencyclidine; an anaesthetic drug [perhaps *p(hen)c(yclidine)* + *(peace) p(ill)*, an earlier designation] **2.** *Pathology.* pneumocystis pneumonia.

pct. percent. Also, **pct**

pctm pulse count modulation.

PCV *Automotive.* positive crankcase ventilation.

pcv pollution-control valve.

Pd *Symbol, Chemistry.* palladium.

pd pitch diameter.

pd. paid.

P.D. 1. per diem. **2.** Police Department. **3.** *Insurance.* property damage.

p.d. 1. per diem. **2.** potential difference.

PDA *Computers.* personal digital assistant.

PDB *Chemistry.* a crystalline solid, $C_6H_4Cl_2$, used especially as a moth repellent. [*p(ara-)d(ichloro)b(enzene)*]

Pd.B. Bachelor of Pedagogy.

Pd.D. Doctor of Pedagogy.

pdl 1. *Computers.* page description language. **2.** poundal.

pdm pulse duration modulation.

Pd.M. Master of Pedagogy.

pdmfm pulse duration modulation frequency modulation.

P.D.Q. *Informal.* immediately; at once. Also, **PDQ** [*p(retty) d(amn) q(uick)*]

PDR Physicians' Desk Reference.

pdr powder.

PDT Pacific daylight time. Also, **P.D.T.**

PE Prince Edward Island, Canada (for use with ZIP code).

pe probable error.

p/e price-earnings ratio. Also, **P/E, PE, P-E, p-e**

P.E. 1. Petroleum Engineer. **2.** physical education. **3.** Presiding Elder. **4.** printer's error. **5.** *Statistics.* probable error. **6.** Professional Engineer. **7.** Protestant Episcopal.

p.e. printer's error.

pec photoelectric cell.

ped. 1. pedal. **2.** pedestal. **3.** pedestrian.

Ped.D. Doctor of Pedagogy.

P.E.Dir. Director of Physical Education.

P.E.F. *Insurance.* personal effects floater.

P.E.I. Prince Edward Island.

pelec photoelectric.

pem *Computers.* preemptive multitasking.

pen penetration.

Pen. peninsula. Also, **pen.**

P.E.N. International Association of Poets, Playwrights, Editors, Essayists, and Novelists.

Penn. Pennsylvania. Also, **Penna.**

Pent. Pentecost.

Per. 1. Persia. **2.** Persian.

per. 1. percentile. **2.** period. **3.** person.

per an. per annum.

perc percussion.

perf. 1. perfect. **2.** perforated. **3.** performance.

perf. part. perfect participle.

perh. perhaps.

perm 1. permanent. **2.** permission.

permb permeability.

perp. perpendicular.

per pro. *Law.* by one acting as an agent; by proxy. Also, **per proc.** [from Latin *per procurationem*]

Pers Persian.

Pers. 1. Persia. **2.** Persian.

pers. 1. person. **2.** personal. **3.** personnel.

persp perspective.

PERT (pûrt), a management method of controlling and analyzing a system or program. [*P(rogram) E(valuation and) R(eview) T(echnique)*]

pert. pertaining.

PET (pet), *Medicine.* positron emission tomography.

Pet. *Bible.* Peter.

pet. petroleum.

Pet.E. Petroleum Engineer.

PETN *Chemistry, Pharmacology.* a crystalline, explosive solid,

$C_5H_8N_4O_{12}$. [*p(enta)e(rythritol) t(etra)n(itrate)*]

petro petroleum.

petrog. petrography.

petrol. petrology.

pF *Electricity.* picofarad; picofarads.

pf power factor.

pf. 1. perfect. **2.** (in Germany) pfennig. **3.** *Music.* pianoforte; piano. **4.** *Finance.* (of stock) preferred. **5.** proof.

p.f. *Music.* louder. [from Italian *più forte*]

Pfc. *Military.* private first class. Also, **PFC**

PFD personal flotation device.

pfd. preferred. Also, **pfd**

pfg. (in Germany) pfennig.

PFM *Telecommunications.* pulse frequency modulation. Also, **P.F.M.**

PG *Informal.* pregnant.

PG parental guidance: a rating assigned to a motion picture by the Motion Picture Association of America. [*p(arental) g(uidance) advised*]

pg 1. picogram; picograms. **2.** pulse generator.

Pg. 1. Portugal. **2.** Also, **Pg** Portuguese.

pg. page.

P.G. 1. Past Grand. **2.** paying guest. **3.** Postgraduate. **4.** Also, **p.g.** *Informal.* pregnant.

PGA 1. Also, **P.G.A.** Professional Golfers' Association. **2.** *Biochemistry.* folic acid [*p(teroyl) + g(lutamic) a(cid)*].

pga *Computers.* pin-grid array.

pgmt pigment.

Ph *Chemistry.* phenyl.

pH *Chemistry.* the symbol for the logarithm of the reciprocal of hydrogen ion concentration in gram atoms per liter, used to express the acidity or alkalinity of a solution.

ph *Optics.* phot; phots.

ph. **1.** phase. **2.** phone.

P.H. Public Health.

PHA Public Housing Administration.

Phar. **1.** pharmaceutical. **2.** pharmacology. **3.** pharmacopoeia. **4.** pharmacy. Also, **phar.**

Phar.B. Bachelor of Pharmacy.

Phar.D. Doctor of Pharmacy.

pharm. **1.** pharmaceutical. **2.** pharmacology. **3.** pharmacopoeia. **4.** pharmacy.

Pharm.D. Doctor of Pharmacy.

Pharm.M. Master of Pharmacy.

Ph.B. Bachelor of Philosophy. [from Latin *Philosophiae Baccalaureus*]

Ph. C. Pharmaceutical Chemist.

Ph.D. Doctor of Philosophy. [from Latin *Philosophiae Doctor*]

Phe *Biochemistry.* phenylalanine.

P.H.E. Public Health Engineer.

phen phenolic.

Ph. G. Graduate in Pharmacy.

phh phillips head.

Phil. **1.** *Bible.* Philemon. **2.** Philip. **3.** *Bible.* Philippians. **4.** Philippine.

phil. **1.** philosophical. **2.** philosophy.

Phila. Philadelphia.

Philem. *Bible.* Philemon.

Phil. **1.** Philippine Islands.

philol. **1.** philological. **2.** philology.

philos. **1.** philosopher. **2.** philosophical. **3.** philosophy.

Ph.L. Licentiate in Philosophy.

phm **1.** phantom. **2.** phase modulation.

Ph.M. Master of Philosophy.

phofl photoflash.

phon. phonetics.

phonet. phonetics.

phono phonograph.

phonol. phonology.

phos phosphate.

phot. **1.** photograph. **2.** photographer. **3.** photographic. **4.** photography.

photog. **1.** photographer. **2.** photographic. **3.** photography.

photom. photometry.

phr. phrase.

phren. **1.** phrenological. **2.** phrenology.

phrenol. **1.** phrenological. **2.** phrenology.

phrm pharmacy.

phrmcol pharmacological.

PHS Public Health Service. Also, **P.H.S.**

phsk phase-shift keying.

phys. **1.** physical. **2.** physician. **3.** physics. **4.** physiological. **5.** physiology.

phys. chem. physical chemistry.

phys ed (fiz′ ed′), *Informal.* physical education. Also, **phys. ed.**

phys. geog. physical geography.

physiol. **1.** physiological. **2.** physiologist. **3.** physiology.

PI **1.** *Law.* personal injury. **2.** politically incorrect. **3.** principal investigator. **4.** private investigator. **5.** programmed instruction.

Pi. (in Turkey and other countries) piaster. Also, **pi.**

P.I. **1.** Philippine Islands. **2.** Also, **p.i.** private investigator.

p.i. politically incorrect.

pias. (in Turkey and other countries) piaster.

PID *Pathology.* pelvic inflammatory disease.

PIE Proto-Indo-European.

PIK payment in kind. Also, **p.i.k.**

pil. (in prescriptions) pill. [from Latin *pilula*]

PIM personal information manager.

pim pulse-interval modulation.

PIN (pin), *Computers.* a number assigned to an individual, used to establish identity in order to gain access to a computer system. [p(ersonal) i(dentification) n(umber)]

pin positive-intrinsic-negative transistor.

PINS (pinz), a person of less than 16 years of age placed under the jurisdiction of a juvenile court. [P(erson) I(n) N(eed of) S(upervision)]

PIO *U.S. Military.* **1.** public information office. **2.** public information officer.

PIRG Public Interest Research Group.

piv peak inverse voltage.

pizz. *Music.* pizzicato.

p.j.'s (pē′jāz′), *Informal.* pajamas. Also, **P.J.'s**

pjtr projector.

PK 1. personal knowledge **2.** psychokinesis.

pk. 1. pack. **2.** park. **3.** Also, **pk** peak. **4.** peck; pecks.

pkg. package.

pkt. 1. packet. **2.** pocket.

PKU *Pathology.* phenylketonuria.

pkwy. parkway.

PL Public Law.

pl 1. parts list. **2.** place. **3.** plain. **4.** plug. **5.** private line.

pl. 1. Also, **Pl.** place. **2.** plate. **3.** plural.

P/L profit and loss.

P.L. Poet Laureate.

PLA People's Liberation Army.

PLAM price-level adjusted mortgage.

plat. 1. plateau. **2.** platinum. **3.** platoon.

PLC *British.* public limited company.

plc power-line carrier.

pld payload.

plf pounds per linear foot.

plf. plaintiff. Also, **plff.**

plk *Machinery.* pillowblock.

pll 1. pallet. **2.** *Electronics.* phase-locked loop.

plmg plumbing.

plmr plumber.

pln plane.

plnm plenum.

plnr planar.

plnt planet.

plnty planetary.

PLO Palestine Liberation Organization.

plo phase-locked oscillator.

PL/1 *Computers.* programming language one.

plq plaque.

PLR Public Lending Right.

plr 1. pillar. **2.** pliers. **3.** puller.

plrs *Navigation.* pelorus.

plrt polarity.

pls. 1. please. **2.** pulse.

PLSS portable life support system.

plstc plastic.

plt 1. pilot. **2.** plant.

pltf platform.

pltg 1. planting. **2.** plating.

PLU price lookup.

plu. plural.

plupf. pluperfect. Also, **plup.**, **pluperf.**

plur. 1. plural. **2.** plurality.

plywd plywood.

Plz. plaza.

plzd polarized.

PM preventive maintenance.

Pm *Symbol, Chemistry.* promethium.

pm 1. permanent magnet. **2.** *Computers.* primary memory. **3.** *Electronics.* pulse modulation.

pm. premium.

P.M. 1. Past Master. **2.** Paymaster. **3.** p.m. **4.** Police Magistrate. **5.** Postmaster. **6.** post-mortem. **7.** Prime Minister. **8.** Provost Marshal.

p.m. after noon. [from Latin *post merīdiem*]

pmflt pamphlet.

P.M.G. 1. Paymaster General. **2.** Postmaster General. **3.** Provost Marshal General.

pmk. postmark.

P.M.L. *Insurance.* probable maximum loss.

PMLA Publications of the Modern Language Association of America. Also, **P.M.L.A.**

PMS 1. *Printing.* Pantone matching system. **2.** premenstrual syndrome.

PMT premenstrual tension.

pmt. payment.

PN 1. please note. **2.** promissory note. **3.** psychoneurotic.

pn 1. part number. **2.** please note. **3.** promissory note.

P/N promissory note. Also, **p.n.**

pneum. 1. Also, **pneu** pneumatic. **2.** pneumatics.

pnh pan head.

pnl panel.

pnld paneled.

pnlg paneling.

pnnt pennant.

pnp positive-negative-positive transistor.

pnt paint.

pntgn pentagon.

pnxt. he or she painted it. [from Latin *pinxit*]

PO purchase order.

Po *Symbol, Chemistry.* polonium.

po. *Baseball.* put-out; put-outs.

p/o part of.

P.O. 1. parole officer. **2.** petty officer. **3.** postal (money) order. **4.** post office.

p.o. (in prescriptions) by mouth. [from Latin *per ōs*]

POA primary optical area.

POB post-office box. Also, **P.O.B.**

POC port of call.

pocul. (in prescriptions) a cup. [from Latin *pōculum*]

POD port of debarkation.

p.o.'d (pē′ōd′), *Slang.* angry or annoyed. [*p(issed) o(ff)*]

P.O.D. 1. pay on delivery. **2.** Post Office Department.

POE 1. port of embarkation. **2.** port of entry. Also, **P.O.E.**

poet. 1. poetic; poetical. **2.** poetry.

POGO (pō′gō), Polar Orbiting Geophysical Observatory.

POL petroleum, oil, and lubricants.

Pol. 1. Poland. **2.** Also, **Pol** Polish.

pol. 1. political. **2.** politics.

polit. econ. political economy.

pol. sci. political science.

polstr polystyrene.

polthn polyethylene.

poly. polytechnic.

POP proof-of-purchase.

pop. 1. popular. **2.** popularly. **3.** population.

P.O.P. 1. printout paper. **2.** point-of-purchase.

p.o.p. point-of-purchase.

p.o.r. pay on return.

Port. 1. Portugal. **2.** Portuguese.

pos. 1. position. **2.** positive. **3.** possession. **4.** possessive.

P.O.S. point-of-sale; point-of-sales. Also, **POS**

posn position.

poss. 1. possession. **2.** possessive. **3.** possible. **4.** possibly.

POSSLQ (pos′əl kyōō′), either of two persons, one of each sex, who share living quarters but are not related by blood, marriage, or adoption: a categorization used by the U.S. Census Bureau. [*p(erson of the) o(pposite) s(ex) s(haring) l(iving) q(uarters)*]

postop (pōst′op′), postoperative. Also, **post-op.**

pot. *Electricity.* **1.** potential. **2.** potentiometer.

POTS (pots), *Telecommunications.* plain old telephone service.

POV *Motion Pictures.* point of view: used especially in describing a method of shooting a scene or film.

POW prisoner of war. Also, **P.O.W.**

PP 1. parcel post. **2.** prepositional phrase.

pp *Radio.* push-pull.

pp. 1. pages. **2.** past participle. **3.** *Music.* pianissimo. **4.** privately printed.

p-p peak-to-peak.

P.P. 1. parcel post. **2.** parish priest. **3.** past participle. **4.** postpaid. **5.** prepaid.

p.p. 1. parcel post. **2.** past participle. **3.** per person. **4.** postpaid.

PPA *Pharmacology.* a substance, $C_9H_{13}NO$, used as an appetite suppressant. [*p(henyl)p(ropanol)a(mine)*]

PPB 1. Also, **P.P.B.** *Publishing.* paper, printing, and binding. **2.** provisioning parts breakdown.

ppb *Publishing.* **1.** paper, printing, and binding. **2.** parts per billion. Also, **p.p.b.**

ppd. 1. postpaid. **2.** prepaid.

p.p.d.o. per person, double occupancy.

PPE *British.* philosophy, politics, and economics.

P.P.F. *Insurance.* personal property floater.

PPH paid personal holidays. Also, **P.P.H.**

pph. pamphlet.

PPI *Pharmacology.* **1.** patient package insert. **2.** Also, **ppi** *Electronics.* plan position indicator. **3.** producer price index.

ppl. participle.

ppll programmable phase-locked loop.

PPLO *Pathology.* pleuropneumonia-like organism.

PPM 1. *Computers.* pages per minute. **2.** Also, **ppm** *Telecommunications.* pulse position modulation.

ppm 1. *Computers.* pages per minute: a measure of the speed of a page printer. **2.** parts per million. **3.** pulse per minute.

p.p.m. parts per million. Also, **P.P.M., ppm, PPM**

PPO preferred-provider organization.

ppp 1. peak pulse power. **2.** *Music.* pianississimo; double pianissimo.

ppr. 1. paper. **2.** Also, **p.pr.** present participle.

pps pulse per second.

P.P.S. a second or additional postscript. Also, **p.p.s.** [from Latin *post postscríptum*]

ppt. *Chemistry.* precipitate. Also, **ppt**

ppv *Television.* pay-per-view. Also, **p.p.v., PPV, P.P.V.**

PQ Quebec, Canada (for use with ZIP code).

p.q. previous question.

PR 1. payroll. **2.** percentile rank. **3.** public relations. **4.** *Slang (often disparaging and offensive).* Puerto Rican. **5.** Puerto Rico (for use with ZIP code).

Pr Provençal.

Pr *Symbol, Chemistry.* praseodymium.

Pr. 1. (of stock) preferred. **2.** Priest. **3.** Prince. **4.** Provençal.

pr. 1. pair; pairs. **2.** paper. **3.** power. **4.** preference. **5.** (of stock) preferred. **6.** present. **7.** price. **8.** priest. **9.** *Computers.* printer. **10.** printing. **11.** pronoun.

P.R. 1. parliamentary report. **2.** Roman people. [from Latin *populus Rōmānus*] **3.** press release. **4.** prize ring. **5.** proportional representation. **6.** public relations. **7.** Puerto Rico.

p.r. public relations.

PRA Public Roads Administration.

prand. (in prescriptions) dinner. [from Latin *prandium*]

prblc parabolic.

PRC 1. Also, **P.R.C.** People's Republic of China. **2.** Postal Rate Commission.

prcht parachute.

prcs process.

prcsr processor.

prcst precast.

prdn production.

prdr producer.

P.R.E. Petroleum Refining Engineer.

prec. 1. preceded. **2.** preceding.

precdg preceding.

precp precipitation.

pred. predicate.

pref. 1. preface. **2.** prefaced. **3.** prefatory. **4.** preference. **5.** preferred. **6.** prefix. **7.** prefixed. Also, **pref**

prefab prefabricated.

prelim. preliminary.

prem. premium.

pre•op (prē′op′), preoperative; preoperatively. Also, **pre′-op′.**

prep. 1. preparation. **2.** preparatory. **3.** prepare. **4.** preposition.

Pres. 1. Presbyterian. **2.** President.

pres. 1. present. **2.** presidency. **3.** president.

Presb. Presbyterian.

Presbyt. Presbyterian.

prescr prescription.

pres. part. present participle.

press pressure.

pret. *Grammar.* preterit.

prev. 1. previous. **2.** previously.

PRF 1. Puerto Rican female. **2.** Also, **prf** *Telecommunications.* pulse repetition frequency.

prf. proof. Also, **prf**

prfm performance.

prfrd *Printing.* proofread.

prfrdg *Printing.* proofreading.

prfrdr proofreader.

prft press fit.

prfx prefix.

prgm program.

prgmg *Computers.* programming.

prgmr *Computers.* programmer.

pri primary.

prin. 1. principal. **2.** principally. **3.** principle.

print. printing.

priv. 1. private. **2.** *Grammar.* privative.

priv. pr. privately printed.

prl parallel.

PRM Puerto Rican male.

prm pulse rate modulation.

prm. premium.

prmtr parameter.

prn pseudorandom noise.

p.r.n. (in prescriptions) as the occasion arises; as needed. [from Latin *prō rē nāta*]

prntg printing.

PRO public relations officer. Also, **P.R.O.**

Pro *Biochemistry.* proline.

prob. 1. probable. **2.** probably. **3.** problem.

prob cse probable cause.

proc. 1. procedure. **2.** proceedings. **3.** process. **4.** proclamation. **5.** proctor.

Prod. *Computers.* Prodigy.

prod. 1. produce. **2.** produced. **3.** producer. **4.** product. **5.** production.

Prof. Professor.

Prof. Eng. Professional Engineer.

Prog. Progressive.

prog. 1. progress. **2.** progressive.

proj project.

PROM (prom), *Computers.* a memory chip whose contents can be programmed by a user or manufacturer. Also, **prom** [*p(rogrammable) r(ead)-o(nly) m(emory)*]

prom. promontory.

pron. I. *Grammar.* pronominal.
2. pronoun. 3. pronounced.
4. pronunciation.

prop. I. properly. 2. property.
3. proposition. 4. proprietary.
5. proprietor.

propr. proprietor.

pros. I. *Theater.* proscenium.
2. prosody.

Pros. Atty. prosecuting attorney.

prot protective.

Prot. Protestant.

pro tem. for the time being. [from
Latin *pro tempore*]

Prov. I. Provençal. 2. Provence.
3. *Bible.* Proverbs. 4. Province.
5. Provost.

prov. I. province. 2. provincial.
3. provisional. 4. provost.

prox. the next month. [from Latin
proximo]

prp. I. present participle. 2. purpose.

prphl peripheral.

prpsl proposal.

prs. pairs.

prsrz pressurize.

PRT personal rapid transit.

prt print.

prtg printing.

prtl partial.

prtr printer.

Prus. I. Prussia. 2. Prussian. Also,
Pruss., Pruss

prv peak reverse voltage.

prvw preview.

prx prefix.

PS I. *Linguistics.* phrase structure.
2. power steering.

ps picosecond; picoseconds.

Ps. *Bible.* Psalm; Psalms. Also, **Psa.**

ps. I. pieces. 2. pseudonym.

P.S. I. passenger steamer. 2. permanent secretary. 3. postscript. 4. Privy
Seal. 5. *Theater.* prompt side. 6. Public School.

p.s. postscript.

PSA I. *Medicine.* prostatic specific
antigen. 2. public service
announcement.

Psa. *Bible.* Psalms.

p's and q's manners; behavior; conduct. [perhaps from some children's
difficulty in distinguishing the two
letters]

PSAT Preliminary Scholastic Aptitude
Test.

PSB *Printing.* prepress service bureau.

PSC Public Service Commission.

PSD prevention of significant deteri-
oration: used as a standard of measurement by the U.S. Environmental
Protection Agency.

PSE Pidgin Sign English.

psec picosecond; picoseconds. Also,
ps

pseud. I. pseudonym.
2. pseudonymous.

psf pounds per square foot. Also,
p.s.f.

PSG I. platoon sergeant. 2. *Medicine.*
polysomnogram.

psgr passenger.

psi pounds per square inch. Also, **p.s.i.**

psia pounds per square inch, absolute.

psid pounds per square inch,
differential.

psig pounds per square inch, gauge.

psiv passive.

psm prism.

psnl personal.

PSRO Professional Standards Review
Organization. Also, **P.S.R.O.**

P.SS. postscripts. Also, **p.ss.** [from
Latin *postscrīpta*]

PST Pacific Standard Time. Also,
P.S.T., p.s.t.

pst paste.

pstl pistol.

pstn piston.

psvt *Metallurgy.* passivate.

psvtn preservation.

psych. 1. psychological. 2. psychologist. 3. psychology.

psychoanal. psychoanalysis.

psychol. 1. psychological. 2. psychologist. 3. psychology.

Pt *Symbol, Chemistry.* platinum.

pt 1. patient. 2. pint; pints.

Pt. 1. point. 2. port.

pt. 1. part. 2. payment. 3. pint; pints. 4. point. 5. port. 6. *Grammar.* preterit.

P/T part-time. Also, **p/t**

P.T. 1. Also, **PT** Pacific time. 2. Also, **PT** part-time. 3. physical therapy. 4. physical training. 5. postal telegraph. 6. post town. 7. pupil teacher.

p.t. 1. Pacific time. 2. past tense. 3. post town. 4. for the time being [from Latin *pro tempore*].

PTA 1. Also, **P.T.A.** Parent-Teacher Association. 2. Philadelphia Transportation Authority.

Pta. peseta.

PTC *Biochemistry.* phenylthiocarbamide.

ptc positive temperature coefficient.

ptd painted.

ptfe polytetrafluoroethylene.

ptg. printing.

ptl patrol.

ptly partly.

PTM *Telecommunications.* pulse time modulation. Also, **ptm**

ptn 1. partition. 2. pattern.

PTO 1. Parent-Teacher Organization. 2. Patent and Trademark Office. 3. *Machinery.* power takeoff.

P.T.O. 1. Parent-Teacher Organization. 2. Also, **p.t.o.** please turn over (a page or leaf).

pts. points.

PTSD posttraumatic stress disorder.

PTT Post, Telegraph, and Telephone (the government-operated system, as in France or Turkey).

ptt push-to-talk.

PTV public television.

Pty *Australian.* proprietary.

pty party.

Pu *Symbol, Chemistry.* plutonium.

pu 1. Also, **p/u** pick up. 2. power unit. 3. purple.

pub. 1. public. 2. publication. 3. published. 4. publisher. 5. publishing.

publ. 1. public. 2. publication. 3. publicity. 4. published. 5. publisher.

pubn publication.

PUC Public Utilities Commission. Also, **P.U.C.**

P.U.D. pickup and delivery.

pul pulley.

pulsar (pul′sär), pulsating star.

pulv. (in prescriptions) powder. [from Latin *pulvis*]

punc. punctuation.

PUVA (pōō′və), *Medicine.* a therapy for psoriasis combining the drug psoralen and ultraviolet light. [*p(soralen)* + *UV-A* ultraviolet light of a wavelength between 320 and 400 nanometers]

pv 1. *Finance.* par value. 2. plan view.

PVA polyvinyl acetate.

PVC polyvinyl chloride. Also, **pvc**

pvnt prevent.

pvntv preventive.

pvt. private.

PW Palau (approved for postal use).

pw 1. plain washer. 2. pulse width.

PWA 1. person with AIDS. 2. Also, **P.W.A.** Public Works Administration.

P wave a longitudinal earthquake wave that is usually the first to be recorded by a seismograph. [*p(rimary) wave*]

pwb printed-wiring board.

P.W.D. Public Works Department. Also, **PWD**

pwm pulse-width modulation.

pwr power.

pwt pennyweight. Also, **pwt.**

pwtr pewter.

PX post exchange.

P.X. please exchange.

pxt. he or she painted it. [from Latin *pinxit*]

pymt. payment.

PYO pick your own.

pyr pyramid.

Q

Q 1. quarterly. 2. *Cards, Chess.* queen.

Q *Symbol.* 1. the 17th in order or in a series, or, when *I* is omitted, the 16th. 2. (*sometimes lowercase*) the medieval Roman numeral for 500. 3. *Biochemistry.* glutamine. 4. *Physics.* heat. 5. *Thermodynamics.* a unit of heat energy, equal to 10^{18} British thermal units (1.055×10^{21} joules). 6. *Electronics.* the ratio of the reactance to the resistance of an electric circuit or component. 7. *Biblical Criticism.* the symbol for material common to the Gospels of Matthew and Luke that was not derived from the Gospel of Mark.

Q. 1. quarto. 2. Quebec. 3. Queen. 4. question. 5. (in Guatemala) quetzal; quetzals.

q. 1. farthing. [from Latin *quadrāns*] 2. quart; quarts. 3. query. 4. question. 5. quintal. 6. *Bookbinding.* quire.

QA quality assurance.

Q and A (kyōō′ ən ā′, ənd), *Informal.* an exchange of questions and answers. Also, **Q&A**

QB 1. *Football.* quarterback. 2. *Chess.* queen's bishop.

Q.B. *British Law.* Queen's Bench.

q.b. *Football.* quarterback.

QBP *Chess.* queen's bishop's pawn.

Q.C. 1. quality control. 2. Quartermaster Corps. 3. Queen's Counsel. Also, **QC**

QCD *Physics.* quantum chromodynamics.

q.d. (in prescriptions) every day. [from Latin *quāque diē*]

qdisc quick disconnect.

qdrnt quadrant.

qdrtr quadrature.

q.e. which is. [from Latin *quod est*]

QED *Physics.* quantum electrodynamics.

Q.E.D. which was to be shown or demonstrated (used especially in mathematical proofs). [from Latin *quod erat dēmōnstrandum*]

Q.E.F. which was to be done. [from Latin *quod erat faciendum*]

Q.F. quick-firing.

Q fever *Pathology.* an acute, influenza-like disease caused by rickettsia. [abbreviation of *query*]

q.h. (in prescriptions) each hour; every hour. [from Latin *quāque hōrā*]

q.i.d. (in prescriptions) four times a day. [from Latin *quater in diē*]

QKt *Chess.* queen's knight.

QKtP *Chess.* queen's knight's pawn.

ql. quintal.

q.l. (in prescriptions) as much as is desired. [from Latin *quantum libet*]

QLI quality-of-life index. Also, **qli**

qlty. quality.

QM 1. Also, **Q.M.** Quartermaster. 2. *Physics.* quantum mechanics.

q.m. (in prescriptions) every morning. [from Latin *quoque matutino*]

QMC *Military.* Quartermaster Corps. Also, **Q.M.C.**

QMG Quartermaster-General. Also, **Q.M.G., Q.M.Gen.**

QN *Chess.* queen's knight.

q.n. (in prescriptions) every night. [from Latin *quoque nocte*]

QNP *Chess.* queen's knight's pawn.

QP *Chess.* queen's pawn.

q.p. (in prescriptions) as much as you please. Also, **q. pl.** [from Latin *quantum placet*]

Qq. *Bookbinding.* quartos.

qq. questions.

qq. v. (in formal writing) which (words, things, etc.) see. [from Latin *quae vidē*]

QR *Chess.* queen's rook.

qr. **1.** farthing. [from Latin *quadrāns*] **2.** quarter. **3.** *Bookbinding.* quire.

QRP *Chess.* queen's rook's pawn.

qry quarry.

q.s. **1.** (in prescriptions) as much as is sufficient; enough. [from Latin *quantum sufficit*] **2.** quarter section.

QSO *Astronomy.* quasi-stellar object.

QSS *Astronomy.* quasi-stellar radio source.

qstn question.

qt. **1.** quantity. **2.** *plural* **qt., qts.** quart.

q.t. *Informal.* quiet. Also, **Q.T.**

qto. *Bookbinding.* quarto.

qtr. **1.** quarter. **2.** quarterly.

qty quantity.

qu. **1.** quart. **2.** quarter. **3.** quarterly. **4.** queen. **5.** query. **6.** question.

quad quadrilateral.

quad. **1.** quadrant. **2.** quadratic.

quadr quadruple.

qual. **1.** qualification. qualify. **2.** qualitative; quality.

quant. quantitative.

quar. **1.** quarter. **2.** quarterly.

quart. **1.** quarter. **2.** quarterly.

quasar (kwā′zär), *Astronomy.* quasi-stellar radio source.

quat. (in prescriptions) four. [from Latin *quattuor*]

Que. Quebec.

ques. question.

quin quintuple.

quinq. (in prescriptions) five. [from Latin *quīnque*]

quint. (in prescriptions) fifth. [from Latin *quīntus*]

quor. (in prescriptions) of which. [from Latin *quōrum*]

quot. **1.** quotation. **2.** quotient. Also, **quot**

quotid. (in prescriptions) daily. [from Latin *quotīdiē*]

q.v. **1.** (in prescriptions) as much as you wish. [from Latin *quantum vīs*] **2.** *plural* **qq.v.** (in formal writing) which see. [from Latin *quod vidē*]

QWERTY (kwûr′tē, kwer′-), of or pertaining to a keyboard having the keys in traditional typewriter arrangement, with the letters *q, w, e, r, t,* and *y* being the first six of the top row of alphabetic characters, starting from the left side.

R

R **1.** *Chemistry.* radical. **2.** *Math.* ratio. **3.** regular: suit or coat size. **4.** *Electricity.* resistance. **5.** restricted: a rating assigned to a motion picture by the Motion Picture Association of America indicating that children under the age of 17 will not be admitted unless accompanied by an adult. **6.** *Theater.* stage right. **7.** *Physics.* roentgen. **8.** *Chess.* rook.

R *Symbol.* **1.** the 18th in order or in a series, or, when *I* is omitted, the 17th. **2.** (*sometimes lowercase*) the medieval Roman numeral for 80. **3.** *Biochemistry.* arginine. **4.** *Physics.* universal gas constant. **5.** registered trademark: written as superscript ® following a name registered with the U.S. Patent and Trademark Office.

r **1.** radius. **2.** *Commerce.* registered. **3.** *Electricity.* resistance. **4.** *Physics.* roentgen. **5.** royal. **6.** (in Russia) ruble. **7.** *Baseball.* run; runs. **8.** (in India, Pakistan, and other countries) rupee.

r *Ecology.* the theoretical intrinsic rate of increase of a population; Malthusian parameter.

R. **1.** rabbi. **2.** radical. **3.** radius. **4.** railroad. **5.** railway. **6.** (in South Africa) rand; rands. **7.** Réaumur (temperature). **8.** Also, **R** (in prescriptions) take. [from Latin *recipe*] **9.** rector. **10.** redactor. **11.** queen. [from Latin *regina*] **12.** Republican. **13.** response. **14.** king. [from Latin *rex*] **15.** river. **16.** road. **17.** royal. **18.** (in Russia) ruble. **19.** (in India, Pakistan, and other countries) rupee. **20.** *Theater.* stage right.

r. **1.** rabbi. **2.** railroad. **3.** railway. **4.** range. **5.** rare. **6.** *Commerce.* received. **7.** recipe. **8.** replacing. **9.** residence. **10.** right. **11.** rises. **12.** river. **13.** road. **14.** rod. **15.** royal. **16.** rubber. **17.** (in Russia) ruble. **18.** *Baseball.* run; runs. **19.** (in India, Pakistan, and other countries) rupee.

RA regular army.

Ra *Symbol, Chemistry.* radium.

R.A. **1.** rear admiral. **2.** regular army. **3.** *Astronomy.* right ascension. **4.** royal academician. **5.** Royal Academy.

R.A.A.F. Royal Australian Air Force.

rab rabbet.

rad **1.** *Math.* radian; radians. **2.** radiation absorbed dose. **3.** radio. **4.** radius.

rad. **1.** *Math.* radical. **2.** Also, **rd** *Chemistry.* radium. **3.** radius. **4.** radix.

radar (rā/där), radio detection and ranging.

RADINT radar intelligence.

RAdm rear admiral. Also, **RADM**

radn radiation.

rad opr radio operator.

RAF Royal Air Force. Also, **R.A.F.**

rall. *Music.* rallentando.

RAM (ram), volatile computer memory available for creating, loading, or running programs and for the temporary storage and manipulation of data. [*r(andom)-a(ccess) m(emory)*]

RAM reverse annuity mortgage.

R.A.M. Royal Academy of Music.

R&B rhythm-and-blues. Also, **r&b, R and B**

R&D research and development. Also, **R and D**

R&E research and engineering.

R. & I. **1.** king and emperor. [from Latin *Rēx et Imperātor*] **2.** queen and empress. [from Latin *Rēgīna et Imperātrix*]

R and R **1.** rest and recreation. **2.** rest and recuperation. **3.** rest and rehabilitation. **4.** rock-'n'-roll. Also, **R&R**

raser (rā/zər), radio-frequency amplification by stimulated emission of radiation.

RATO (rā/tō), *Aeronautics.* rocket-assisted takeoff.

RB **1.** *Sports.* right back. **2.** *Football.* right fullback. **3.** *Football.* running back.

Rb *Symbol, Chemistry.* rubidium.

RBC red blood cell.

R.B.I. *Baseball.* run batted in; runs batted in. Also, **RBI, rbi, r.b.i.**

rbr rubber.

RC resistance-capacitance.

rc remote control.

R.C. **1.** Red Cross. **2.** Reserve Corps. **3.** Roman Catholic. Also, **RC**

R.C.A.F. Royal Canadian Air Force. Also, **RCAF**

RCB **1.** Retail Credit Bureau. **2.** *Football.* right cornerback.

RCC Rape Crisis Center.
R.C.Ch. Roman Catholic Church.
rcd. received.
rcdr recorder.
rcht ratchet.
rcl recall.
rclm reclaim.
R.C.M.P. Royal Canadian Mounted Police. Also, **RCMP**
rcn recreation.
R.C.N. Royal Canadian Navy. Also, **RCN**
rcndt recondition.
R.C.P. Royal College of Physicians.
rcpt. 1. receipt. 2. receptacle.
rcptn reception.
R.C.S. Royal College of Surgeons.
Rct 1. receipt. 2. *Military.* recruit. Also, **rct**
RCTL resistor-capacitor-transistor logic.
rcv receive.
rcvd received.
rcvg receiving.
rcvr receiver.
RD 1. Registered Dietician. 2. rural delivery.
Rd *Symbol, Chemistry.* (formerly) radium.
rd 1. read. 2. rod; rods.
Rd. Road.
rd. 1. rendered. 2. road. 3. rod; rods. 4. round.
R/D *Banking.* refer to drawer.
R.D. 1. registered dietitian. 2. Rural Delivery.
RDA 1. (not in technical use) recommended daily allowance. Compare **U.S. RDA.** 2. recommended dietary allowance. Also, **R.D.A.**
RdAc *Symbol, Chemistry.* radioactinium.
RD&D research, development, and demonstration.
RD&E research, development, and engineering.

rdc reduce.
rdcr reducer.
RDD *Marketing.* random digit dialing.
RDF 1. Also, **rdf** radio direction finder. 2. rapid deployment force.
rdg 1. reading. 2. rounding.
rdh round head.
rdl radial.
rdm recording demand meter.
rdout readout.
rdr 1. radar. 2. reader.
RDS *Pathology.* respiratory distress syndrome.
rdsd roadside.
RDT&E research, development, testing, and engineering.
rdtr radiator.
RDX a white, crystalline explosive, $C_3H_6N_6O_6$. [*R(esearch) D(epartment) (E)x(plosive)*, referring to such a department in Woolwich, England]
Re *Symbol, Chemistry.* rhenium.
Re. (in India, Pakistan, and other countries) rupee. Also, **re.**
R/E real estate. Also, **RE**
R.E. 1. real estate. 2. Reformed Episcopal. 3. *Football.* right end. 4. Right Excellent.
r.e. *Football.* right end.
REA Rural Electrification Administration. Also, **R.E.A.**
Rear Adm. Rear Admiral.
reasm reassemble.
reassy reassembly.
Réaum. Réaumur (temperature).
reb. *Basketball.* rebounds.
rec. 1. receipt. 2. (in prescriptions) fresh. [from Latin *recēns*] 3. recipe. 4. record. 5. recorder. 6. recording. 7. recreation.
recalc recalculate.
recd. received. Also, **rec'd.**
recip. 1. reciprocal. 2. reciprocity.
recirc recirculate.

recit. *Music.* recitative.

recl reclose.

recm recommend.

recog recognition.

recon reconnaissance.

recpt receipt.

Rec. Sec. Recording Secretary. Also, **rec. sec.**

rect. 1. receipt. **2.** rectangle. **3.** rectangular. **4.** (in prescriptions) rectified. [from Latin *rēctificātus*] **5.** rectifier. **6.** rector. **7.** rectory.

redupl. reduplication.

ref. 1. referee. **2.** reference. **3.** referred. **4.** refining. **5.** reformation. **6.** reformed. **7.** *Music.* refrain. **8.** refund. **9.** refunding.

Ref. Ch. Reformed Church.

ref des reference designation.

refl. 1. reflection. **2.** reflective. **3.** reflex. **4.** reflexive.

Ref. Pres. Reformed Presbyterian.

refr 1. refrigerate. **2.** refrigerator.

Ref. Sp. reformed spelling.

refs. req. references required.

Reg. 1. regiment. **2.** queen [from Latin *rēgīna*].

reg. 1. regent. **2.** regiment. **3.** region. **4.** register. **5.** registered. **6.** registrar. **7.** registry. **8.** regular. **9.** regularly. **10.** regulation. **11.** regulator.

regd. registered.

regen regenerate.

regr. registrar.

regt. 1. regent. **2.** regiment.

reinf reinforce.

REIT (rēt), real-estate investment trust.

rej reject.

rel. 1. relating. **2.** relative. **3.** relatively. **4.** released. **5.** religion. **6.** religious.

relig. religion.

rel. pron. relative pronoun.

REM (rem), rapid eye movement.

rem (rem), *Nucleonics.* the quantity of ionizing radiation whose biological effect is equal to that produced by one roentgen of x-rays. [r(oentgen) e(quivalent in) m(an)]

rem remainder.

remitt. remittance.

rep (rep), *Physics.* a unit proposed but not adopted as a supplement to roentgen for expressing dosage of ionizing radiation. [r(oentgen) e(quivalent) p(hysical)]

Rep. 1. Representative. **2.** Republic. **3.** Republican.

rep. 1. repair. **2.** repeat. **3.** (in prescriptions) let it be repeated. [from Latin *repetātur*] **4.** report. **5.** reported. **6.** reporter.

repl. 1. replace. **2.** replacement.

repr. 1. represented. **2.** representing. **3.** reprint. **4.** reprinted.

repro 1. reproduce. **2.** reproduction.

rept. report.

Repub. 1. Republic. **2.** Republican.

req. 1. Also, **req** request. **2.** require. **3.** Also, **reqd** required. **4.** requisition.

reqn requisition.

reqt requirement.

RES *Immunology.* reticuloendothelial system.

res 1. resistance. **2.** resistor. **3.** resume.

res. 1. research. **2.** reserve. **3.** residence. **4.** resident; residents. **5.** residue. **6.** resigned. **7.** resolution.

resc rescind.

resid residual.

resln resolution.

resn resonant.

resp. 1. respective. **2.** respectively. **3.** respelled; respelling. **4.** respondent.

Res. Phys. Resident Physician.

restr. 1. restaurant. **2.** restorer.

ret. **1.** retain. **2.** retired. **3.** return. **4.** returned.

retd. **1.** retained. **2.** retired. **3.** returned.

retn retain.

retr retract.

retro **1.** retroactive. **2.** retrograde.

Rev. *Bible.* **1.** Revelation; Revelations. **2.** Reverend.

rev. **1.** revenue. **2.** reverse. **3.** review. **4.** reviewed. **5.** revise; revised. **6.** revision. **7.** revolution. **8.** revolving.

Rev. Stat. Revised Statutes.

Rev. Ver. Revised Version (of the Bible).

rew rewind.

RF **1.** radiofrequency. **2.** *Baseball.* right field; right fielder.

rf *Baseball.* right field; right fielder.

R.F. Reserve Force.

r.f. **1.** range finder. **2.** rapid-fire. **3.** reducing flame. **4.** *Baseball.* right field; right fielder.

R.F.A. Royal Field Artillery.

r.f.b. *Sports.* right fullback. Also, **R.F.B.**

RFC Reconstruction Finance Corporation.

rfc radio-frequency choke.

R.F.D. rural free delivery. Also, **RFD**

RFE Radio Free Europe. Also, **R.F.E.**

rfgt refrigerant.

RFI radio frequency interference.

RFLP (rif′lip′), restriction fragment length polymorphism: a fragment of DNA used to trace family relationships. Also called **riflip.**

rflx reflex.

RFQ *Commerce.* request for quotation.

r.g. *Football.* right guard.

RGB *Television.* red-green-blue.

rgd rigid.

rglr regular.

rglt regulate.

rgltd regulated.

rgltr regulator.

RGNP real gross national product.

rgtr register.

RH *Meteorology.* relative humidity. Also, **rh**

Rh **1.** *Physiology.* Rh factor. **2.** *Metallurgy.* Rockwell hardness.

Rh *Symbol, Chemistry.* rhodium.

R.H. Royal Highness.

r.h. right hand. right-handed.

r.h.b. *Football.* right halfback. Also, **RHB, R.H.B.**

rhd railhead.

rheo rheostat.

RHIP rank has its privileges.

Rhn *Metallurgy.* Rockwell hardness number.

Rho. Rhodesia. Also, **Rhod.**

rhomb **1.** rhombic. **2.** rhomboid.

RI Rhode Island (for use with ZIP code).

R.I. **1.** Queen and Empress. [from Latin *Rēgīna et Imperātrīx*] **2.** King and Emperor. [from Latin *Rēx et Imperātor*] **3.** Rhode Island.

R.I.B.A. Royal Institute of British Architects.

RICO (rē′kō), Racketeer Influenced and Corrupt Organizations Act.

RIF (rif), **1.** *Military.* a reduction in the personnel of an armed service or unit. **2.** a reduction in the number of persons employed, especially for budgetary reasons. [*R(eduction) I(n) F(orce)*]

R.I.I.A. Royal Institute of International Affairs.

RIP *Computers.* raster image processor.

R.I.P. **1.** may he or she rest in peace. [from Latin *requiēscat in pāce*] **2.** may they rest in peace. [from Latin *requiēscant in pāce*] Also, **RIP**

RISC (risk), *Computers.* reduced instruction set computer.

rit. *Music.* ritardando. Also, **ritard.**
riv. river.
RJ *Military.* road junction.
rkt rocket.
RL resistance-inductance.
RLB *Football.* right linebacker.
RLC resistance, inductance, capacitance.
rlct *Electricity.* reluctance.
rld rolled.
R.L.D. retail liquor dealer.
rlf relief.
RLL *Computers.* run-length limited.
R.L.O. returned letter office.
rloc relocate.
rlr roller.
rlse release.
rlt relate.
rltn relation.
rltv relative.
rlv relieve.
rlxn relaxation.
rly relay.
RM (in Germany) reichsmark.
rm range marks.
rm. **1.** ream. **2.** room.
r.m. (in Germany) reichsmark.
R.M.A. *British.* **1.** Royal Marine Artillery. **2.** Royal Military Academy.
R.M.C. *British.* Royal Military College.
rmd remedy.
rmdr remainder.
rms *Math.* root mean square. Also, **r.m.s.**
R.M.S. **1.** Railway Mail Service. **2.** *British.* Royal Mail Service. **3.** *British.* Royal Mail Steamship.
rmt remote.
rmv remove.
rmvbl removable.
Rn *Symbol, Chemistry.* radon.
rn **1.** radio navigation. **2.** rain.
R.N. **1.** registered nurse. **2.** *British.* Royal Navy.
RNA *Genetics.* ribonucleic acid.

R.N.A.S. *British.* Royal Naval Air Service.
RNase (är′en′ās, -āz), *Biochemistry.* ribonuclease. Also, **RNAase** (är′e-n′ā′ās, -āz).
RNC Republican National Committee.
rnd. round.
rndm random.
rng range.
rnge range.
rngg ringing.
rngr *Telephones.* ringer.
rnl renewal.
RNP *Biochemistry.* a nucleoprotein containing RNA. [*r(ibo)n(ucleo)p(rotein)*]
R.N.R. *British.* Royal Naval Reserve.
rnwbl renewable.
R.N.W.M.P. *Canadian.* Royal Northwest Mounted Police.
rnwy runway.
rny rainy.
RO. (in Oman) rial omani.
ro. **1.** *Bookbinding.* recto. **2.** roan. **3.** rood.
R.O. **1.** Receiving Office. **2.** Receiving Officer. **3.** Regimental Order. **4.** *British.* Royal Observatory.
ROA *Accounting.* return on assets.
ROE *Accounting.* return on equity.
R.O.G. *Commerce.* receipt of goods. Also, **ROG, r.o.g.**
ROI return on investment. Also, **R.O.I.**
ROK Republic of Korea.
ROM (rom), computer memory in which program instructions, operating procedures, or other data are permanently stored. [*r(ead)-o(nly) m(emory)*]
Rom. **1.** Roman. **2.** Romance. **3.** Romania. **4.** Romanian. **5.** Romanic. **6.** *Bible.* Romans. Also, **Rom** (for defs. 2, 5).

rom. *Printing.* roman.

Rom. Cath. Roman Catholic.

Rom. Cath. Ch. Roman Catholic Church.

RONA *Accounting.* return on net assets.

R.O.P. run-of-paper: a designation specifying that the position of a newspaper or magazine advertisement is to be determined by the publisher.

R.O.R. *Law.* released on own recognizance.

ROS *Computers.* read only storage.

ROT rule of thumb.

rot. 1. rotating. **2.** rotation.

R.O.T.C. (är′ō tē sē′, rot′sē), Reserve Officers Training Corps. Also, **ROTC**

rotr rotator.

Roum. 1. Roumania. **2.** Roumanian.

ROW right of way.

RP 1. *Linguistics.* Received Pronunciation. **2.** repurchase agreement. **3.** *Pathology.* retinitis pigmentosa.

Rp. (in Indonesia) rupiah; rupiahs.

R.P. 1. Reformed Presbyterian. **2.** Regius Professor.

RPG role-playing game.

rpg *Basketball.* rebounds per game.

rplr repeller.

rplsn repulsion.

rplt repellent.

rpm revolutions per minute. Also, **r/min.,r.p.m.**

R.P.O. Railway Post Office. Also, **RPO**

RPQ request for price quotation.

rpr repair.

rprt report.

rps revolutions per second. Also, **r.p.s., r/s**

rpt. 1. repeat. **2.** report.

rptn repetition.

rptr repeater.

RPV *Military.* remotely piloted vehicle.

rpvntv rust preventive.

R.Q. *Physiology.* respiratory quotient.

R.R. 1. railroad. **2.** Right Reverend. **3.** rural route.

RRM renegotiable-rate mortgage.

rRNA *Biochemistry.* ribosomal RNA.

R.R.R. return receipt requested (used in registered mail). Also, **RRR**

RRT rail rapid transit.

R.R.T. registered respiratory therapist.

Rs. 1. (in Portugal) reis. **2.** (in India, Pakistan, and other countries) rupees.

R.S. 1. Recording Secretary. **2.** Reformed Spelling. **3.** Revised Statutes. **4.** Royal Society.

r.s. right side.

RSA Republic of South Africa.

rsc rescue.

rsch research.

RSE Received Standard English.

RSFSR Russian Soviet Federated Socialist Republic. Also, **R.S.F.S.R.**

rslvr resolver.

rspd respond.

rsps response.

rspsb responsible.

rspv 1. respective. **2.** responsive.

rsrc resource.

rss root sum square.

rst restore.

rstg roasting.

rstr 1. *Electronics.* raster. **2.** restrain. **3.** restrict.

RSV Revised Standard Version (of the Bible).

rsv reserve.

RSVP (used on invitations) please reply. Also, **R.S.V.P., rsvp, r.s.v.p.** [from French r(épondez) s('il) v(ous) p(laît)]

rsvr reservoir.

RSWC right side up with care.

RT radiotelephone.

rt. 1. rate. **2.** right.

r.t. *Football.* right tackle.

rtcl reticle.

rte. route. Also, **Rte.**

RTF *Genetics.* resistance transfer factor; R factor.

rtf *Computers.* rich-text format.

rtg rating.

Rt. Hon. Right Honorable.

RTL resistor transistor logic.

rtn return.

rtng retaining.

rtnr retainer.

rtr rotor.

rtrv retrieve.

rtry rotary.

Rts. *Finance.* rights.

rtty radio teletypewriter.

rtw ready-to-wear.

rtz return-to-zero.

Ru *Symbol, Chemistry.* ruthenium.

Rum. 1. Rumania. **2.** Also, **Rum** Rumanian.

Rus. 1. Russia. **2.** Russian.

Russ. 1. Russia. **2.** Russian. Also, **Russ**

RV 1. recreational vehicle. **2.** Revised Version (of the Bible).

rv rear view.

rvam reactive volt-ampere meter.

rvlg revolving.

rvlv revolve.

rvm reactive voltmeter.

RVN Republic of Vietnam.

rvrb reverberation.

rvs 1. reverse. **2.** revise.

rvsbl reversible.

rvs cur reverse current.

rvsn revision.

RVSVP (used on invitations) please reply quickly. Also, **R.V.S.V.P., rvsvp, r.v.s.v.p.** [from French *r(épondez) v(ite) s('il) v(ous) p(laît)*]

rvw review.

R/W right of way.

r/w read/write. Also, **r-w**

R.W. 1. Right Worshipful. **2.** Right Worthy.

Rwy. Railway.

Rx 1. prescription. **2.** (in prescriptions) take. [from Latin, representing an abbreviation of *recipe*] **3.** (in India, Pakistan, and other countries) tens of rupees.

Ry. Railway.

S

S 1. *Baseball.* sacrifice. **2.** satisfactory. **3.** Saxon. **4.** sentence. **5.** short. **6.** *Electricity.* siemens. **7.** signature. **8.** single. **9.** small. **10.** soft. **11.** *Music.* soprano. **12.** South. **13.** Southern. **14.** state (highway). **15.** stimulus. **16.** *Grammar.* subject.

S *Symbol.* **1.** the 19th in order or in a series, or, when *I* is omitted, the 18th. **2.** (*sometimes lowercase*) the medieval Roman numeral for 7 or 70. **3.** second. **4.** *Biochemistry.* serine. **5.** *Thermodynamics.* entropy. **6.** *Physics.* strangeness. **7.** *Chemistry.* sulfur.

s 1. satisfactory. **2.** signature. **3.** small.

4. soft. **5.** *Music.* soprano. **6.** south. **7.** stere.

s *Symbol.* second.

S. 1. Sabbath. **2.** Saint. **3.** Saturday. **4.** Saxon. **5.** (in Austria) schilling; schillings. **6.** School. **7.** Sea. **8.** Senate. **9.** September. **10.** *British.* shilling; shillings. **11.** (in prescriptions) **a.** mark; write; label. [from Latin *signa*] **b.** let it be written. [from Latin *signētur*] **12.** Signor: an Italian form of address for a man. **13.** Small. **14.** Socialist. **15.** Society. **16.** Fellow. [from Latin *socius*] **17.** (in Peru) sol. **18.** South. **19.** Southern. **20.** (in Ecuador) sucre; sucres. **21.** Sunday.

s. 1. saint. **2.** school. **3.** second.
4. section. **5.** see. **6.** series. **7.** *British.*
shilling; shillings. **8.** sign. **9.** signed.
10. silver. **11.** singular. **12.** sire.
13. small. **14.** society. **15.** son.
16. south. **17.** southern. **18.** species.
19. statute. **20.** steamer. **21.** stem.
22. stem of. **23.** substantive.

Sa *Symbol, Chemistry.* (formerly)
samarium.

Sa. Saturday.

S/A *Banking.* survivorship agreement.

S.A. 1. Salvation Army. **2.** seaman
apprentice. **3.** South Africa. **4.** South
America. **5.** South Australia. **6.** corporation [from French *société ano-
nyme* or Spanish *sociedad anónima*].

s.a. 1. semiannual. **2.** sex appeal.
3. without year or date. [from Latin
sine annō] **4.** subject to approval.

S.A.A. Speech Association of America.

Sab. Sabbath.

SAC (sak), Strategic Air Command.
Also, **S.A.C.**

SAD seasonal affective disorder.

SADD Students Against Drunk
Drivers.

S.A.E. 1. self-addressed envelope.
2. Society of Automotive Engineers.
3. stamped addressed envelope.
Also, **SAE; s.a.e.** (for defs. 1, 3).

SAF single Asian female.

saf safety.

S. Afr. 1. South Africa. **2.** South
African.

S. Afr. D. South African Dutch. Also,
SAfrD

SAG (sag), Screen Actors Guild.

sal. hist. salary history.

SALT (sôlt), Strategic Arms Limita-
tions Treaty.

Salv. Salvador.

SAM, (sam), **1.** shared-appreciation
mortgage. **2.** single Asian male.
3. surface-to-air missile. **4.** Space

Available Mail: a special air service
for sending parcels to overseas
members of the armed forces.

Sam. *Bible.* Samuel.

S. Am. 1. South America. **2.** South
American.

S. Amer. 1. South America. **2.** South
American.

Saml. Samuel.

san sanitary.

sand. sandwich.

S.&F. *Insurance.* stock and fixtures.

S and H shipping and handling
(charges). Also, **S&H**

S&L *Banking.* savings and loan association. Also, **S and L**

S and M sadomasochism; sadism
and masochism. Also, **S&M, s&m**

S.&M. *Insurance.* stock and machinery.

S&P Standard & Poor's.

s. & s.c. (of paper) sized and supercalendered.

SANE (sān), a private nationwide
organization in the U.S. that oppos-
es nuclear testing and advocates
international peace. [official shorten-
ing of its by-name *Committee for a
Sane Nuclear Policy*]

Sans. Sanskrit.

Sansk. Sanskrit.

Sar. Sardinia.

S.A.R. 1. South African Republic.
2. Sons of the American Revolution.

SASE self-addressed stamped envelope. Also, **sase, S.A.S.E., s.a.s.e.**

Sask. Saskatchewan.

SAT *Trademark.* Scholastic Aptitude
Test.

Sat. 1. Saturday. **2.** Saturn.

sat. 1. satellite. **2.** saturate.
3. saturated.

SATB *Music.* soprano, alto, tenor,
bass.

satcom communications satellite.

Sax. 1. Saxon. **2.** Saxony.

Sb *Symbol, Chemistry.* antimony. [from Latin *stibium*]

sb 1. service bulletin. **2.** sideband. **3.** *Optics.* stilb. **4.** stove bolt.

sb. *Grammar.* substantive.

S.B. 1. Bachelor of Science. [from Latin *Scientiae Baccalaureus*] **2.** South Britain (England and Wales).

s.b. *Baseball.* stolen base; stolen bases.

SBA Small Business Administration. Also, **S.B.A.**

SbE south by east.

SBF single black female.

SBIC Small Business Investment Company.

SBLI Savings Bank Life Insurance.

SBM single black male.

SBN *Publishing.* Standard Book Number.

sbstr *Electronics.* substrate.

SbW south by west.

SC 1. security council. **2.** signal corps. **3.** South Carolina (for use with ZIP code). **4.** SportsChannel New England (a cable television channel). **5.** supreme court.

Sc *Symbol, Chemistry.* scandium.

sc solar cell.

Sc. 1. Scotch. **2.** Scotland. **3.** Scots. **4.** Scottish.

sc. 1. scale. **2.** scene. **3.** science. **4.** scientific. **5.** namely. [from Latin *scilicet*, contraction of *scire licet* it is permitted to know] **6.** screw. **7.** scruple. **8.** he or she carved, engraved, or sculpted it. [from Latin *sculpsit*]

S.C. 1. Sanitary Corps. **2.** Security Council (of the U.N.). **3.** Signal Corps. **4.** South Carolina. **5.** Staff Corps. **6.** Supreme Court.

s.c. *Printing.* **1.** small capitals. **2.** supercalendered.

Scan. Scandinavia.

Scand Scandinavian.

Scand. 1. Scandinavia. **2.** Scandinavian.

s. caps. *Printing.* small capitals.

scav scavenge.

Sc.B. Bachelor of Science. [from Latin *Scientiae Baccalaureus*]

Sc.B.C. Bachelor of Science in Chemistry.

Sc.B.E. Bachelor of Science in Engineering.

scd specification control drawing.

Sc.D. Doctor of Science. [from Latin *Scientiae Doctor*]

Sc.D.Hyg. Doctor of Science in Hygiene.

Sc.D.Med. Doctor of Medical Science.

scdr screwdriver.

sce source.

SCF single Christian female.

scf standard cubic foot.

scfh standard cubic feet per hour

scfm standard cubic feet per minute.

sch socket head.

Sch. (in Austria) schilling; schillings.

sch. 1. schedule. **2.** school. **3.** schooner.

SCHDM schematic diagram.

sched. schedule.

schem schematic.

Sch.Mus.B. Bachelor of School Music.

sci. 1. science. **2.** scientific.

SCID *Pathology.* severe combined immune deficiency.

sci-fi (sī′fī′), science fiction.

scil. to wit; namely. [from Latin *scilicet*]

SCLC Southern Christian Leadership Conference. Also, **S.C.L.C.**

sclr scaler.

SCM single Christian male.

Sc.M. Master of Science. [from Latin *Scientiae Magister*]

scn specification change notice.

scng scanning.

scnr scanner.

S. Con. Res. Senate concurrent resolution.

SCORE (skôr), Service Corps of Retired Executives.

Scot 1. Scots. 2. Scottish.

Scot. 1. Scotch. 2. Scotland. 3. Scottish.

ScotGael Scots Gaelic.

SCOTUS Supreme Court of the United States. Also, **SCUS**

SCR *Electronics.* semiconductor controlled rectifier.

scr. 1. screw. 2. scruple.

Script. 1. Scriptural. 2. Scripture.

scrn screen.

SCS Soil Conservation Service.

SCSI (skuz/ē), a standard for computer interface ports. [*s(mall) c(omputer) s(ystem) i(nterface)*]

sctd scattered.

sctrd scattered.

scty security.

SCU Special Care Unit.

scuba (skōō/bə), self-contained underwater breathing apparatus.

sculp. 1. sculptor. 2. sculptural. 3. sculpture. Also, **sculpt.**

SD 1. sea-damaged. 2. South Dakota (for use with ZIP code). 3. *Statistics.* standard deviation. 4. the intelligence and counterespionage service of the Nazi SS [from German *S(icherheits)d(ienst)*].

sd side.

sd. sound.

S/D 1. school district. 2. *Commerce.* sight draft.

S.D. 1. doctor of science. [from Latin *Scientiae Doctor*] 2. sea-damaged. 3. senior deacon. 4. South Dakota. 5. special delivery. 6. *Statistics.* standard deviation.

s.d. 1. without fixing a day for further action or meeting. [from Latin *sine die*] 2. *Statistics.* standard deviation.

S.D.A. Seventh Day Adventists.

S. Dak. South Dakota.

sdg siding.

SDI Strategic Defense Initiative.

sdl saddle.

sdn sedan.

S. Doc. Senate document.

SDR *Banking.* special drawing rights. Also, **S.D.R.**

sdr sender.

SDS Students for a Democratic Society.

SE 1. southeast. 2. southeastern. 3. *Football.* split end. 4. Standard English. Also, **S.E.**

Se *Symbol, Chemistry.* selenium.

se special equipment.

SEATO (sē/tō), Southeast Asia Treaty Organization (1954–1977).

SEbE southeast by east.

SEbS southeast by south.

SEC Securities and Exchange Commission. Also, **S.E.C.**

sec 1. *Trigonometry.* secant. 2. second. 3. section.

sec¹ *Symbol, Trigonometry.* arc secant.

sec. 1. second. 2. secondary. 3. secretary. 4. section. 5. sector. 6. according to [from Latin *secundum*].

sech *Math.* hyperbolic secant.

sec. leg. according to law. [from Latin *secundum lēgem*]

secs. 1. seconds. 2. sections.

sect. 1. section. 2. sector.

secy secretary. Also, **sec'y**

SEE Signing Essential English.

seg segment.

seismol. 1. seismological. 2. seismology.

SEIU Service Employees International Union.

sel. 1. select. 2. selected. 3. selection; selections. 4. selectivity. 5. selector.

selsyn self-synchronous.

SEM 1. *Optics.* scanning electron microscope. 2. shared equity mortgage.

Sem. 1. Seminary. 2. Semitic. Also, **Sem**

sem. 1. semicolon. 2. seminar. 3. seminary.

semicnd semiconductor.

semih. (in prescriptions) half an hour. [from Latin *sēmihōra*]

sen. 1. senate. 2. senator. 3. senior. Also, **sen**

sens 1. sensitive. 2. sensitivity.

SEP simplified employee pension.

Sep. 1. September. 2. *Bible.* Septuagint.

sep. 1. *Botany.* sepal. 2. separable. 3. separate. 4. separated. 5. separation.

Sept. 1. September. 2. *Bible.* Septuagint.

seq 1. sequence. 2. sequential.

seq. 1. sequel. 2. the following (one). [from Latin *sequēns*] 3. that which follows. [from Latin *sequitur*]

seqq. the following (ones). [from Latin *sequentia*]

Ser *Biochemistry.* serine.

ser. 1. serial. 2. series. 3. sermon.

Serb. 1. Serbia. 2. Serbian.

serno serial number.

serr serrate.

serv. service.

SES socioeconomic status.

sess. session.

setg setting.

SETI search for extraterrestrial intelligence.

setlg settling.

sew sewer.

SF 1. *Baseball.* sacrifice fly. 2. science fiction. 3. single female. 4. *Finance.* sinking fund.

sf 1. science fiction. 2. *Music.* sforzando.

s-f science fiction.

S.F. 1. San Francisco. 2. senior fellow.

Sfc *Military.* sergeant first class.

sfm surface feet per minute.

SFr. (in Switzerland) franc; francs. Also, **Sfr.**

sft shaft.

sftw software.

sfx suffix.

sfz *Music.* sforzando.

SG 1. senior grade. 2. Secretary General. 3. Solicitor General. 4. Surgeon General.

sg *Grammar.* singular. Also, **sg.**

s.g. specific gravity.

sgd. signed.

sgl single.

SGML *Computers.* Standard Generalized Markup Language.

SGO Surgeon General's Office.

Sgt. Sergeant.

Sgt. Maj. Sergeant Major.

sh 1. sheet. 2. shower. 3. shunt.

s/h 1. shipping/handling. 2. shorthand.

SHA *Navigation.* sidereal hour angle.

Shak. Shakespeare.

Shaks. Shakespeare.

SHAPE (shāp), Supreme Headquarters Allied Powers, Europe. Also, **Shape.**

shcr shipping container.

SHF 1. single Hispanic female. 2. Also, **shf** superhigh frequency.

shl shellac.

shld shield.

shldr shoulder.

shltr shelter.

SHM single Hispanic male.

S.H.M. *Physics.* simple harmonic motion. Also, **s.h.m.**

SHO Showtime (a cable channel).

shp shaft horsepower. Also, **SHP, S.H.P., s.hp., s.h.p.**

shpng shipping.

shpt. shipment.

sht. sheet.

shtc short time constant.

shtdn shutdown.

shtg. shortage.

shthg sheathing.

shv sheave.

shwr shower.

SI International System of Units. [from French S(ystème) I(nternationale d'unités)]

Si Symbol, Chemistry. silicon.

S.I. Staten Island.

SIC Standard Industrial Classification: a system used by the federal government to classify business activities.

Sic. 1. Sicilian. 2. Sicily.

SIDS (sidz), sudden infant death syndrome.

SIG special-interest group.

Sig. 1. (in prescriptions) write; mark; label: indicating directions to be written on a package or label for the use of the patient. [from Latin signā] 2. let it be written. [from Latin signētur] 3. Signore; Signori: the Italian form of address for a man.

sig. 1. signal. 2. signature. 3. signore; signori: an Italian form of address for a man.

sil silence.

sils silver solder.

sim. 1. similar. 2. simile. 3. simulator.

simlt simultaneous.

SIMM (sim), Computers. single inline memory module.

sing. singular.

sinh Math. hyperbolic sine.

SINS (sinz), Navigation. a gyroscopic device indicating the exact speed and position of a vessel. [s(hip's) i(nertial) n(avigation) s(ystem)]

SIOP (sī'op), (formerly) the secret U.S. contingency plan for waging a

nuclear war with the Soviet Union. [s(ingle) i(ntegrated) o(perations) p(lan)]

SIP (sip), 1. Computers. single inline package. 2. supplemental income plan.

sit situation.

SI units International System of Units.

S.J. Society of Jesus.

S.J.D. Doctor of Juridical Science. [from Latin Scientiae Jūridicae Doctor]

SJF single Jewish female.

SJM single Jewish male.

S.J. Res. Senate joint resolution.

SK Saskatchewan, Canada (for use with ZIP code).

sk. 1. sack. 2. sink. 3. sketch.

sklt skylight.

sks seeks.

Skt Sanskrit. Also, **Skt., Skr., Skrt.**

skt 1. skirt. 2. socket.

sktd skirted.

SL source language.

sl sliding.

s.l. 1. Also, **sl.** salvage loss. 2. Bibliography. without place (of publication). [from Latin sine locō]

SLA Special Libraries Association.

S. Lat. south latitude.

Slav Slavic. Also, **Slav.**

slbl soluble.

SLBM 1. sea-launched ballistic missile. 2. submarine-launched ballistic missile. Also, **S.L.B.M.**

slc slice.

SLCM sea-launched cruise missile. Also, **S.L.C.M.**

sld Electricity. single-line diagram.

sld. 1. sailed. 2. Also, **sld** sealed.

sldr solder.

SLE Pathology. systemic lupus erythematosus.

slfcl self-closing.

slfcln self-cleaning.

slfcntd self-contained.

slfprop self-propelled.

slftpg self-tapping.

SLIC (Federal) Savings and Loan Insurance Corporation. Also, **S.L.I.C.**

SLMA Student Loan Marketing Association.

slp slope.

S.L.P. Socialist Labor Party.

SLR *Photography.* single-lens reflex camera.

sls sales.

slt sleet.

sltd slotted.

slv sleeve.

slvg 1. salvage. **2.** sleeving.

slvt solvent.

SM 1. service mark. **2.** single male.

Sm *Symbol, Chemistry.* samarium.

sm some.

sm. small.

S-M 1. Also, **S and M.** sado-masochism. **2.** sadomasochistic. Also, **s-m, S/M, s/m**

S.M. 1. Master of Science. [from Latin *Scientiae Magister*] **2.** sergeant major. **3.** State Militia.

SMA Surplus Marketing Administration.

s-mail (es′māl′), snail mail.

smat see me about this.

S.M.B. Bachelor of Sacred Music.

sm. c. small capital; small capitals. Also, **sm. cap.** or **sm. caps**

SMD *Pathology.* senile macular degeneration.

S.M.D. Doctor of Sacred Music.

smk smoke.

sml small.

smls seamless.

S.M.M. Master of Sacred Music.

S.M.O.M. Sovereign and Military Order of Malta.

SMPTE Society of Motion Picture and Television Engineers.

SMS Synchronous Meteorological Satellite.

SMSA Standard Metropolitan Statistical Area.

smy summary.

SN 1. Secretary of the Navy. **2.** serial number.

Sn *Symbol, Chemistry.* tin. [from Latin *stannum*]

sna•fu (sna foo′, snaf′oo), situation normal, all fouled up.

SNCC (snik), a U.S. civil-rights organization formed by students and active especially during the 1960s. [*S(tudent) N(onviolent) C(oordinating) C(ommittee)*]

snd sound.

SNG synthetic natural gas.

snkl snorkel.

snl standard nomenclature list.

sno 1. snow. **2.** stock number.

snr 1. signal-to-noise ratio. **2.** sonar.

sns sense.

snsr sensor.

sntr *Metallurgy.* sintered.

sntzd sensitized.

sny sunny.

SO *Baseball.* strikeout; strikeouts.

so *Electricity.* slow operate (a relay type).

So. 1. South. **2.** Southern.

s/o shipping order.

S.O. 1. Signal Officer. **2.** Special Order. **3.** Standing Order.

s.o. 1. seller's option. **2.** shipping order.

S.O.B. 1. (*sometimes lowercase*) *Slang.* son of a bitch. **2.** Senate Office Building. Also, **SOB**

Soc. 1. socialist. **2.** (*often lowercase*) society. **3.** sociology.

socd source control drawing.

sociol. 1. sociological. **2.** sociology.

socn source control number.

SOF sound on a film.

S. of Sol. *Bible.* Song of Solomon.

sol 1. solenoid. **2.** solid.

Sol. 1. Solicitor. **2.** Song of Solomon.

sol. 1. soluble. **2.** solution.

S.O.L. *Slang.* **1.** strictly out (of) luck. **2.** *Vulgar.* shit out (of) luck. Also, **SOL**

soln solution.

som start of message.

sonar (sō′när), sound navigation ranging.

SOP Standard Operating Procedure; Standing Operating Procedure. Also, **S.O.P.**

sop. soprano.

SOS 1. the letters represented by the radio telegraphic signal (••• --- •••) used as an internationally recognized call for help. **2.** *Slang.* creamed chipped beef on toast. [s(hit) o(n a) s(hingle)]

s.o.s. (in prescriptions) if necessary. [from Latin *sī opus sit*]

SOV language *Linguistics.* a type of language that has basic subject-object-verb order.

Sov. Un. Soviet Union.

SP 1. Shore Patrol. **2.** Specialist. **3.** Submarine Patrol.

sp 1. spare. **2.** special-purpose. **3.** speed

Sp. 1. Spain. **2.** Spaniard. **3.** Also, **Sp** Spanish.

sp. 1. space. **2.** special. **3.** species. **4.** specific. **5.** specimen. **6.** spelling. **7.** spirit.

S.P. 1. Shore Patrol. **2.** Socialist party. **3.** Submarine Patrol.

s.p. without issue; childless. [from Latin *sine prōle*]

Sp. Am. 1. Spanish America. **2.** Spanish American.

Span. 1. Spaniard. **2.** Spanish.

SPAR (spär), (during World War II) a woman enlisted in the women's reserve of the U.S. Coast Guard. Also, **Spar.** [from Latin *S(emper) par(ātus)* "Always ready" the Coast Guard motto]

SpAr Spanish Arabic.

spat silicon precision alloy transistor.

S.P.C.A. Society for the Prevention of Cruelty to Animals.

S.P.C.C. Society for the Prevention of Cruelty to Children.

spchg supercharge.

spcl special.

spcr spacer.

SPDA single-premium deferred annuity.

sp. del. special delivery.

spdl spindle.

spdom speedometer.

spdt sw single-pole double-throw switch.

spec. 1. special. **2.** specially. **3.** specifically. **4.** specification. **5.** specimen.

specif. 1. specific. **2.** specifically.

SPECT (spekt), *Medicine.* single photon emission computed tomography.

Sp.Ed. Specialist in Education.

SPF sun protection factor.

spg spring.

sp. gr. specific gravity. Also, **spg.**

spher spherical.

sp.ht. *Physics.* specific heat.

spkl sprinkler.

spkr speaker.

spkt sprocket.

splc splice.

splt spotlight.

spltr splitter.

sply supply.

spmkt supermarket.

spnr spanner.

spp. species.

sp/ph split/phase.

sppl spark plug.

S.P.Q.R. the Senate and People of

Rome. Also, **SPQR** [from Latin *Senātus Populusque Rūmānus*]

spr spring.

S.P.R. Society for Psychical Research.

sprdr spreader.

SPRF single Puerto Rican female.

sprl spiral.

SPRM single Puerto Rican male.

sprt support.

spst sw single-pole single-throw switch.

spt. seaport.

spvn supervision.

Sq. 1. Squadron. **2.** Square (of a city or town).

sq. 1. sequence. **2.** the following; the following one. [from Latin *sequēns*] **3.** squadron. **4.** square.

sqdn squadron.

sq. ft. square foot; square feet.

sq. in. square inch; square inches.

sq. km square kilometer; square kilometers.

SQL *Computers.* structured query language.

sq. m square meter; square meters.

sq. mi. square mile; square miles.

sq. mm square millimeter; square millimeters.

sqq. the following; the following ones. [from Latin *sequentia*]

sq. r. square rod; square rods.

sq. rt. square root.

SQUID (skwid), *Medicine.* superconducting quantum interference device.

sq. yd. square yard; square yards.

SR *Postal Service.* star route.

Sr *Symbol, Chemistry.* strontium.

sr 1. selenium rectifier. **2.** shift register. **3.** *Electricity.* slow release (a relay type). **4.** *Geometry.* steradian.

Sr. 1. Senhor: a Portuguese form of address for a man. **2.** Senior. **3.** Señor: a Spanish form of address

for a man. **4.** Sir. **5.** *Ecclesiastical.* Sister [from L *Soror*].

S-R stimulus-response.

S.R. Sons of the Revolution.

s.r. semantic reaction.

Sra. 1. Senhora: a Portuguese form of address for a woman. **2.** Señora: a Spanish form of address for a woman.

SRAM short-range attack missile.

SRB solid rocket booster.

SRBM short-range ballistic missile.

srch search.

S. Rept. Senate report.

S. Res. Senate resolution.

srng syringe.

SRO 1. single-room occupancy. **2.** standing room only. Also, **S.R.O.**

SRS air bag. [*s(upplemental) r(estraint) s(ystem)*]

Srta. 1. Senhorita: a Portuguese form of address for a girl or unmarried woman. **2.** Señorita: a Spanish form of address for a girl or unmarried woman.

srvln surveillance.

SS 1. an elite military unit of the Nazi party. [from German *S(chutz)s(taffel)*] **2.** *Baseball.* shortstop. **3.** social security. **4.** steamship. **5.** *Football.* strong safety. **6.** supersonic.

ss 1. same size. **2.** (in prescriptions) a half. Also, **ss.** [from Latin *sēmis*] **3.** single-shot.

SS. 1. Saints. [from Latin *sānctī*] **2.** See **SS** (def. 1). **3.** See **ss.** (def. 1).

ss. 1. to wit; namely (used especially on legal documents, to verify the place of action). [from Latin *scīlicet*] **2.** sections. **3.** *Baseball.* shortstop.

S.S. 1. See **SS** (def. 1). **2.** (in prescriptions) in the strict sense. [from Latin *sēnsū strictō*] **3.** steamship. **4.** Sunday School.

SSA **I.** Social Security Act. **2.** Social Security Administration.

SSAE stamped self-addressed envelope.

SSB **I.** Selective Service Board. **2.** Social Security Board.

ssb single sideband.

SSBN the U.S. Navy designation for the fleet ballistic missile submarine. [S(trategic) S(ubmarine) B(allistic) N(uclear)]

SSC Banking. small-saver certificate.

S.Sc.D. Doctor of Social Science.

sscr setscrew.

S.S.D. Most Holy Lord: a title of the pope. [from Latin Sānctissimus Dominus]

S.S.D. Doctor of Sacred Scripture. [from Latin Sacrae Scrīptūrae Doctor]

ssdd Computers. single-side, double-density.

SSE south-southeast. Also, **S.S.E.,** **s.s.e.**

sse solid-state electronics.

ssf saybolt second furol.

ssfm single-sideband frequency modulation.

sshd Computers. single-side, high-density.

SSI **I.** Electronics. small-scale integration: the technology for concentrating semiconductor devices in a single integrated circuit. **2.** Supplemental Security Income.

S sleep slow-wave sleep.

SSM surface-to-surface missile.

ssm **I.** single-sideband modulation. **2.** solid-state materials.

SSN Social Security number.

SSPE Pathology. subacute sclerosing panencephalitis.

SSR Soviet Socialist Republic. Also, **S.S.R.**

ssr solid-state relay.

SSS Selective Service System.

sssd Computers. single-side, single-density.

SST supersonic transport.

ssu saybolt second universal.

SSW south-southwest. Also, **S.S.W.,** **s.s.w.**

ST Real Estate. septic tank.

St Physics. stoke.

st **I.** sawtooth. **2.** stere.

St., **I.** Saint. **2.** statute; statutes. **3.** Strait. **4.** Street.

st. **I.** stanza. **2.** state. **3.** statute; statutes. **4.** Printing. let it stand. [from Latin stet] **5.** stitch. **6.** British. stone (weight). **7.** strait. **8.** street.

s.t. short ton.

Sta. **I.** Saint. [from Italian or Spanish Santa] **2.** Station.

sta. **I.** station. **2.** stationary.

stab. **I.** stabilization. **2.** stabilizer. **3.** stable.

stacc. Music. with disconnected notes. [from Italian staccato]

START (stärt), Strategic Arms Reduction Talks.

stat (stat), Medicine. immediately. [from Latin statim]

stat. **I.** (in prescriptions) immediately. [from Latin statim] **2.** statuary. **3.** statue. **4.** status. **5.** statute.

S.T.B. **I.** Bachelor of Sacred Theology. [from Latin Sacrae Theologiae Baccalaureus] **2.** Bachelor of Theology. [from Latin Scientiae Theologicae Baccalaureus]

stbd. starboard.

stbln stabilization.

stby standby.

STC Society for Technical Communication.

stc sensitivity time control.

stch stitch.

STD sexually transmitted disease.

std. standard. Also, **std**

S.T.D. Doctor of Sacred Theology.

[from Latin *Sacrae Theologiae Doctor*]

stdy steady.

stdzn standardization.

Ste. (referring to a woman) Saint. [from French *Sainte*]

sten stencil.

steno. 1. stenographer. 2. stenographic. 3. stenography. Also, **stenog.**

ster. sterling.

stereo. stereotype.

St. Ex. Stock Exchange.

stg. 1. stage. 2. sterling.

stge. storage.

stif stiffener.

stk. stock.

stl 1. steel. 2. studio-transmitter link.

S.T.L. Licentiate in Sacred Theology.

STM scanning tunneling microscope.

stm 1. steam. 2. storm.

S.T.M. Master of Sacred Theology.

stmt statement.

stmy stormy.

stng sustaining.

STOL (es′tôl′), a convertiplane that can become airborne after a short takeoff run and has forward speeds comparable to those of conventional aircraft. [*s(hort) t(ake)o(ff and) l(anding)*]

stor storage.

STP 1. standard temperature and pressure. 2. *Slang.* a potent long-acting hallucinogen. [def. 2 probably after *STP*, trademark of a motor-oil additive]

stp stamp.

stpd stripped.

stpg stepping.

stpr *Telephones.* stepper.

str 1. straight. 2. strength.

str. 1. steamer. 2. strait. 3. *Music.* string; strings.

strat strategic.

stratig. stratigraphy.

strato stratosphere.

strg 1. steering. 2. strong.

strk stroke.

strl structural.

strln streamline.

strm 1. storeroom. 2. stream.

strn strainer.

sttg starting.

sttr stator.

stud. student.

STV subscription television; pay television.

stv satellite television.

Su. Sunday.

SUB supplemehtal unemployment benefits.

sub. 1. submissive. 2. subordinated. 3. subscription. 4. substitute. 5. suburb. 6. suburban. 7. subway.

subassy subassembly.

subch. subchapter.

subj. 1. subject. 2. subjective. 3. subjectively. 4. subjunctive.

submin subminiature.

subq subsequent.

subsc subscription.

subst. 1. *Grammar.* substantive. 2. substantively. 3. substitute.

substa substation.

subtr subtract.

suc 1. succeeding. 2. successor.

suct suction.

suf sufficient.

suf. suffix. Also, **suff.**

Suff. 1. Suffolk. 2. *Ecclesiastical.* suffragan.

suff. 1. sufficient. 2. suffix.

Suffr. *Ecclesiastical.* suffragan.

SUM surface-to-underwater missile.

Sun. Sunday. Also, **Sund.**

sup. 1. superior. 2. superlative. 3. supine. 4. supplement. 5. supplementary. 6. supply. 7. above. [from Latin *supra*]

super. 1. superintendent.
2. superior.

superl. superlative.

supp. 1. supplement. 2. supplementary. Also, **suppl.**

Supp. Rev. Stat. Supplement to the Revised Statutes.

supr. 1. superior. 2. suppress.
3. supreme.

supra cit. cited above. [from Latin *supra citato*]

supsd supersede.

Supt. superintendent. Also, **supt.**

supv supervise.

supvr. supervisor.

surf surface.

surg. 1. surgeon. 2. surgery. 3. surgical.

surv. 1. survey. 2. surveying.
3. surveyor.

survey. surveying.

susp suspend.

Sv *Physics.* sievert; sieverts.

S.V. Holy Virgin. [from Latin *Sāncta Virgō*]

s.v. 1. under the word (or heading). [from Latin *sub verbo*] 2. under the word. [from Latin *sub voce*]

SV 40 *Microbiology.* simian virus 40. Also, **SV-40, SV40**

svc. service. Also, **svce.**

SVGA *Computers.* super video graphics adapter.

svgs. savings.

SVO language *Linguistics.* a type of language that has basic subject-verb-object word order.

svr (of weather) severe.

S.V.R. (in prescriptions) rectified spirit of wine (alcohol). [from Latin *spīritus vīnī rēctificātus*]

SVS still-camera video system.

SW 1. shipper's weight. 2. southwest.
3. southwestern.

sw 1. short wave. 2. single weight.
3. switch.

Sw. 1. Sweden. 2. Swedish. Also, **Swed**

S/W *Computers.* software.

S.W. 1. South Wales. 2. southwest.
3. southwestern.

S.W.A. South West Africa.

Swab. 1. Swabia. 2. Swabian.

S.W.A.K. sealed with a kiss. Also, **SWAK** (swak).

SWAT (swot), a special section of some law enforcement agencies trained and equipped to deal with especially dangerous or violent situations. Also, **S.W.A.T.** [*S(pecial) W(eapons) a(nd) T(actics)*]

Swazil. Swaziland.

swbd switchboard.

SWbS southwest by south.

SWbW southwest by west.

SWC Southwest Conference.

Swed. 1. Sweden. 2. Swedish.

SWF single white female.

swg sewage.

S.W.G. standard wire gauge.

swgr switchgear.

Swit. Switzerland.

Switz. Switzerland.

SWM single white male.

SWP Socialist Workers Party.

swp sweep.

swr *Electronics.* standing-wave ratio.

Swtz. Switzerland.

swvl swivel.

sxs *Telephones.* step-by-step: switching system.

syll. 1. syllable. 2. syllabus.

sym. 1. symbol. 2. *Chemistry.* symmetrical. 3. symphony. 4. symptom.

symm symmetrical.

symp symposium.

syn. 1. synonym. 2. synonymous.
3. synonymy. 4. synthetic.

sync 1. synchronize. 2. synchronous.

synd. 1. syndicate. 2. syndicated.

synop. synopsis.

synth synthetic.

synthzr synthesizer.

syr *Pharmacology.* syrup.

Syr. 1. Syria. **2.** Syriac. **3.** Syrian.

SYSOP (sis′op′), systems operator.

syst. system. Also, **sys**

sz. size.

T

T 1. tablespoon; tablespoonful.
2. tera-; one trillion of a base unit.
3. *Electricity,* tesla; teslas. **4.** *Physics.*
temperature. **5.** time. **6.** (*sometimes
lowercase*) T-shirt.

T *Symbol.* **1.** the 20th in order or in a
series, or, when *I* is omitted, the
19th. **2.** (*sometimes lowercase*) the
medieval Roman numeral for 160.
3. surface tension. **4.** *Biochemistry.*
a. threonine. **b.** thymine. **5.** *Photography.* T number. **6.** *Physics.* **a.** tau
lepton. **b.** time reversal. **7.** the
launching time of a rocket or
missile.

T₁ *Biochemistry.* triiodothyronine.

T₂ *Biochemistry.* thyroxine.

t *Statistics.* **1.** a random variable having Student's t distribution. **2.** the
statistic employed in Student's t-test.

T- *U.S. Military.* (in designations of aircraft) trainer: *T-11.*

t- *Chemistry.* tertiary.

T. 1. tablespoon; tablespoonful.
2. Territory. **3.** Thursday. **4.** Township. **5.** Tuesday.

t. 1. *Football.* tackle. **2.** taken from.
3. *Commerce.* tare. **4.** teaspoon; teaspoonful. **5.** temperature. **6.** in the
time of. [from Latin *tempore*]
7. *Music.* tenor. **8.** *Grammar.* tense.
9. territory. **10.** time. **11.** tome.
12. ton. **13.** town. **14.** township.
15. transit. **16.** *Grammar.* transitive.
17. troy.

TA 1. transactional analysis. **2.** transit
authority.

Ta *Symbol, Chemistry.* tantalum.

t-a *Immunology.* toxin-antitoxin.

tab 1. tabular. **2.** tabulate.

tab. 1. tables. **2.** (in prescriptions)
tablet. [from Latin *tabella*]

tac tactical.

TACAN (tə kan′), tactical air
navigation.

tach tachometer.

T/Agt transfer agent. Also, **T. Agt.**

tal. (in prescriptions) such; like this.
[from Latin *tālis*]

TAN (tan), tax-anticipation note.

tan *Trigonometry.* tangent.

tan¹ *Trigonometry.* arc tangent.

T&A 1. *Slang.* tits and ass. **2.** tonsillec-
tomy and adenoidectomy. Also,
T and A

t&a tonsils and adenoids.

T&E travel and entertainment. Also,
T and E

Tang. Tanganyika.

tanh *Math.* hyperbolic tangent.

TAP Trans-Alaska Pipeline.

TAR (tär), terrain-avoidance radar.

tas true airspeed.

Tasm. Tasmania.

TAT *Psychology.* Thematic Appercep-
tion Test.

taut. *Logic.* tautological; tautology.

TB 1. technical bulletin. **2.** *Baseball.*
a. times at bat. **b.** total bases.
3. *Boxing.* total bouts. **4.** treasury
bill. **5.** tubercle bacillus. **6.** tuberculosis. Also **T.B.**

Tb 1. tubercle bacillus.
2. tuberculosis.

Tb *Symbol, Chemistry.* terbium.

tb terminal board.

T/B title block.

t.b. 1. tablespoon. **2.** tablespoonful.

3. *Bookkeeping.* trial balance.

4. tubercle bacillus. **5.** tuberculosis.

T.B.A. to be announced. Also, **TBA, t.b.a.**

TBD to be determined.

TBI *Automotive.* throttle-body injection.

T-bill (tē′bil′), a U.S. Treasury bill.

tblr tumbler.

tblsht troubleshoot.

T.B.O. *Theater.* total blackout.

T-bond (tē′bond′), a U.S. Treasury bond.

TBS 1. *Nautical.* talk between ships: a radiotelephone for short-range communication between vessels. **2.** Turner Broadcasting System (a cable television channel).

tbs. tablespoon; tablespoonful.

TC 1. Teachers College. **2.** technical circular. **3.** Trusteeship Council (of the United Nations).

Tc *Symbol, Chemistry.* technetium.

tc 1. thermocouple. **2.** time constant.

TCA *Chemistry.* trichloroacetic acid.

TCB taking care of business.

TCBM transcontinental ballistic missile.

TCDD *Pharmacology.* dioxin.

TCE *Chemistry.* trichloroethylene.

tchr. teacher.

tci terrain-clearance indicator.

TCL transistor-coupled logic.

TCP/IP *Computers.* Transfer Control Protocol/Internet Protocol.

TCS traffic control station.

TCTO time-compliance technical order.

TD 1. technical directive. **2.** *Football.* touchdown; touchdowns. **3.** trust deed.

td time delay.

T/D *Banking.* time deposit.

T.D. 1. Traffic Director. **2.** Treasury Department.

tdc 1. *Electricity.* time-delay closing (of contacts). **2.** top dead center.

TDD telecommunications device for the deaf.

tdg twist drill gauge.

TDI temporary disability insurance.

TDL tunnel-diode logic.

TDM *Telecommunications.* time-division multiplex. Also, **tdm**

tdm tandem.

TDN totally digestible nutrients. Also, **t.d.n.**

tdo *Electricity.* time-delay opening (of contacts).

TDOS tape disk operating system.

TDRS Tracking and Data Relay Satellite.

t.d.s. (in prescriptions) to be taken three times a day. [from Latin *ter die sumendum*]

TDTL tunnel-diode transistor logic.

TDY temporary duty.

TE *Football.* tight end.

Te *Symbol, Chemistry.* tellurium.

te thermoelectric.

T/E table of equipment.

tech. 1. technic. **2.** technical. **3.** technology.

technol. technology.

tech. sgt. technical sergeant.

TEE Trans-Europe Express. Also, **T-E-E**

TEFL teaching English as a foreign language.

TEL *Chemistry.* tetraethyl lead.

tel. 1. telegram. **2.** telegraph. **3.** telephone.

telecom telecommunications.

teleg. 1. telegram. **2.** telegraph. **3.** telegraphy.

teleph. telephony.

telesat (tel′ə sat′), telecommunications satellite.

temp. 1. temperature. **2.** temporary. **3.** in the time of [from Latin *tempore*].

ten. 1. tenor. 2. *Music.* tenuto.

Tenn. Tennessee.

TENS (tenz), *Medicine.* a self-operated portable device used to treat chronic pain by sending electrical impulses through electrodes placed over the painful area. [*t(ranscutaneous) e(lectrical) n(erve) s(timulator)*]

TEPP *Chemistry.* tetraethyl pyrophosphate.

ter tertiary.

term. 1. terminal. 2. termination.

terr. 1. Also, **Ter** terrace. 2. territorial. 3. territory.

terz terrazzo.

TESL teaching English as a second language.

TESOL (tē'sôl, tes'əl), 1. teaching English to speakers of other languages. 2. Teachers of English to Speakers of Other Languages.

Test. Testament.

test. 1. testator. 2. testimony.

tetfleyne tetrafluoroethylene.

Teut. 1. Teuton. 2. Teutonic.

TeV *Physics.* trillion electron-volts. Also, **Tev, tev.**

Tex. 1. Texan. 2. Texas.

t/f true/false.

TFE *Chemistry.* tetrafluoroethylene; Teflon.

TFN till further notice.

tfr. transfer.

TFT thin-film transistor.

TFX *Military.* (in designations of aircraft) tactical fighter experimental.

TG 1. transformational-generative (grammar). 2. transformational grammar.

tg *Trigonometry.* tangent.

t.g. *Biology.* type genus.

TGG transformational-generative grammar.

TGIF *Informal.* thank God it's Friday. Also, **T.G.I.F.**

tgl toggle.

tgn *Trigonometry.* tangent.

tgt target.

TGV a high-speed French passenger train. [from French *t(rain à) g(rande) v(itesse)* high-speed train]

Th. Thursday.

T.H. Territory of Hawaii.

Th 227 *Symbol, Chemistry.* radioactinium. Also, **Th-227**

Thai. Thailand.

Th.B. Bachelor of Theology. [from Latin *Theologicae Baccalaureus*]

THC *Pharmacology.* a compound, $C_{21}H_{30}O_2$, the active component in cannabis preparations. [*t(etra)h(ydro) c(annabinol)*]

thd 1. thread. 2. total harmonic distortion.

Th.D. Doctor of Theology. [from Latin *Theologicae Doctor*]

theat. 1. theater. 2. theatrical.

theol. 1. theologian. 2. theological. 3. theology.

theor. 1. theorem. 2. theoretical.

theos. 1. theosophical. 2. theosophy.

therm. thermometer.

thermodynam. thermodynamics.

Thes. *Bible.* Thessalonians. Also, **Thess.**

T.H.I. temperature-humidity index. Also, **thi**

thkf *Electronics.* thick film.

thkns thickness.

thm *Physics.* therm.

Th.M. Master of Theology.

thml thermal.

thmom thermometer.

thms *Electronics.* thermistor.

thnf *Electronics.* thin film.

thnr thinner.

Thr *Biochemistry.* threonine.

thr threshold.

3b *Baseball.* 1. third base. 2. triple (3-base hit).

thrmo thermostat.

throt throttle.

thrt throat.

thstm thunderstorm.

Thu. Thursday.

Thurs. Thursday.

thwr thrower.

thyr *Electronics.* thyristor.

THz terahertz.

Ti *Symbol, Chemistry.* titanium.

TIA *Medicine.* transient ischemic attack.

TIAA Teachers Insurance and Annuity Association of America.

t.i.d. (in prescriptions) three times a day. [from Latin *ter in diē*]

tif telephone interference factor.

Tim. *Bible.* Timothy.

TIN (tin), taxpayer identification number.

tinct. *Pharmacology.* tincture.

tip. truly important person.

TIROS (tī′rōs), television and infrared observation satellite.

Tit. *Bible.* Titus.

tit. title.

TKO *Boxing.* technical knockout. Also, **T.K.O.**

tkt. ticket.

TL 1. target language. **2.** trade-last. **3.** truckload.

Tl *Symbol, Chemistry.* thallium.

TL. (in Turkey) lira; liras.

T/L time loan.

T.L. 1. Also, **t.l.** trade-last. **2.** *Publishing.* trade list.

TLC tender loving care. Also, **T.L.C., t.l.c.**

tlg telegraph.

tlld total load.

tlmy telemetry.

t.l.o. *Insurance.* total loss only.

TLR *Photography.* twin-lens reflex camera.

tlscp telescope.

TM 1. technical manual. **2.** trademark. **3.** Transcendental Meditation.

Tm *Symbol, Chemistry.* thulium.

t.m. true mean.

tmbr timber.

TMC The Movie Channel (a cable television channel).

tmd timed.

TMF The Menninger Foundation.

tmfl time of flight.

tmg timing.

TMI Three Mile Island.

TMJ *Anatomy.* temporomandibular joint.

TML 1. *Chemistry.* tetramethyllead. **2.** three-mile limit.

TMO telegraph money order.

tmpl template.

TMV tobacco mosaic virus.

TN 1. technical note. **2.** Tennessee (for use with ZIP code).

Tn *Symbol, Chemistry.* thoron.

tn. 1. ton. **2.** tone. **3.** town. **4.** train.

TNB *Chemistry.* trinitrobenzene, especially the 1,3,5- isomer.

TNF *Biochemistry.* tumor necrosis factor.

tng 1. tongue. **2.** training.

tnk trunk.

tnl tunnel.

TNN The Nashville Network (a cable television channel).

tnpk. turnpike.

tnsl tensile.

tnsn tension.

TNT 1. *Chemistry.* a crystalline solid, $C_7H_5N_3O_6$, a high explosive. Also, **tnt, T.N.T.** [*t(ri)n(itro)t(oluene)*] **2.** Turner Network Television (a cable television channel).

tntv tentative.

TO technical order.

T/O table of organization.

T.O. telegraph office. Also, **TO**

t.o. 1. turnover. **2.** turn over.

TOA time of arrival.

Tob. *Bible.* Tobit.

TOEFL (tō′fəl), Test of English as a Foreign Language.

TOFC trailer-on-flatcar.

tol tolerance.

tonn. tonnage.

TOP temporarily out of print.

topog. 1. topographical. **2.** topography.

torentl torrential.

torndo tornado.

TOS tape operating system.

tot. total.

TOW (tō), a U.S. Army antitank missile, steered to its target by two thin wires connected to a computerized launcher. [*t(ube-launched,) o(ptically-guided,) w(ire-tracked missile)*]

tox. toxicology.

tp. 1. telephone. **2.** test point. **3.** township. **4.** troop.

t.p. 1. title page. **2.** *Surveying.* turning point.

TPA *Biochemistry.* tissue plasminogen activator.

TPC The Peace Corps.

tpd 1. tapped. **2.** tons per day.

tpg tapping.

tph tons per hour.

tpi 1. teeth per inch. **2.** turns per inch.

tpk. turnpike. Also, **Tpk**

tpl triple.

tpm tons per minute.

TPN *Medicine.* total parenteral nutrition.

TPR *Medicine.* temperature, pulse, respiration.

tpr 1. taper. **2.** teleprinter.

tptg tuned-plate tuned-grid.

t quark *Physics.* top quark.

TR technical report.

tr. 1. *Commerce.* tare. **2.** tincture.

3. trace. **4.** train. **5.** transaction. **6.** *Grammar.* transitive. **7.** translated. **8.** translation. **9.** translator. **10.** transpose. **11.** transposition. **12.** treasurer. **13.** *Music.* trill. **14.** troop. **15.** trust. **16.** trustee.

T.R. 1. in the time of the king. [from Latin *tempore rēgis*] **2.** Theodore Roosevelt. **3.** tons registered. **4.** trust receipt.

TRA Thoroughbred Racing Association.

TRACON (trā′kon), terminal radar approach control.

trad. tradition; traditional.

traj trajectory.

tranfd. transferred.

trans. 1. transaction; transactions. **2.** transfer. **3.** transferred. **4.** transformer. **5.** transit. **6.** *Grammar.* transitive. **7.** translated. **8.** translation. **9.** translator. **10.** transparent. **11.** transportation. **12.** transpose. **13.** transverse.

transa transaction.

transl. 1. translated. **2.** translation. **3.** translator.

transp transparent.

trav. 1. traveler. **2.** travels.

trb treble.

trd tread.

treas. 1. treasurer. **2.** treasury. Also, **Treas.**

treasr. treasurer.

TRF *Biochemistry.* thyrotropin-releasing factor.

trf 1. transfer. **2.** tuned radio frequency.

trfc traffic.

TRH *Biochemistry.* thyrotropin-releasing hormone.

trh truss head.

trib. tributary.

trid. (in prescriptions) three days. [from Latin *trīduum*]

trig. 1. trigger. **2.** trigonometric. **3.** trigonometrical. **4.** trigonometry.

trip. 1. triple. **2.** triplicate.

trit. *Pharmacology.* triturate.

trk 1. track. **2.** truck.

trkg tracking.

Trl. (used in addresses) trail.

trlg trailing.

trlr trailer.

trly trolley.

TRM trademark.

trm training manual.

trmr trimmer.

trn train.

tRNA *Genetics.* transfer RNA.

trnbkl turnbuckle.

trnd turned.

trngl triangle.

trnr trainer.

trnspn transportation.

trntbl turntable.

TRO *Law.* temporary restraining order.

troch. (in prescriptions) troche; tablet or lozenge.

trop. 1. tropic. **2.** tropical.

tropo troposphere.

Trp *Biochemistry.* tryptophan.

trp *Military.* troop.

trq torque.

trsbr transcriber.

trscb transcribe.

trtd treated.

trtmt treatment.

trun trunnion.

trx triplex.

TS 1. tool shed. **2.** top secret. **3.** Also, **t.s.** *Slang (vulgar).* tough shit. **4.** transsexual. Also, **T.S.**

T.Sgt. technical sergeant.

TSH *Biochemistry.* thyroid-stimulating hormone.

tsi tons per square inch.

TSO time-sharing option.

TSP *Chemistry.* sodium phosphate.

tsp. 1. teaspoon. **2.** teaspoonful.

TSR a computer program with any of several ancillary functions, usually held resident in RAM for instant activation while one is using another program. [*t(erminate and) s(tay) r(esident)*]

TSS *Pathology.* toxic shock syndrome.

tsteq test equipment.

tstg testing.

tstr tester.

tstrz transistorize.

TSWG Television and Screen Writers' Guild.

TT Trust Territories.

TTL transistor-transistor logic.

ttl total.

TTL meter *Photography.* through-the-lens meter.

TTS teletypesetter.

TTY teletypewriter.

Tu *Chemistry.* (formerly) thulium.

Tu. Tuesday.

T.U. 1. thermal unit. **2.** toxic unit. **3.** Trade Union. **4.** Training Unit.

t.u. trade union.

Tue. Tuesday.

tun tuning.

Tun. Tunisia.

tung tungsten.

tur turret.

turb turbine.

turbo alt turbine alternator.

turbo gen turbine generator.

Turk. 1. Turkey. **2.** Also, **Turk** Turkish.

TV 1. Also, **tv** television. **2.** transvestite.

TVA 1. tax on value added: a sales tax imposed by member nations of the Common Market on imports from other countries. **2.** Tennessee Valley Authority.

tvi television interference.

tvl travel.

tvlg traveling.

tvlr traveler.

tvm transistor voltmeter.

TVP *Trademark.* a brand of textured soy protein.

tw typewriter.

T.W.I.M.C. to whom it may concern.

2b *Baseball.* **1.** double (2-base hit). **2.** second base.

2WD two-wheel drive.

twp. township. Also, **Twp.**

twr tower.

twt traveling-wave tube.

TWU Transport Workers Union of America.

TWX (*often* twiks), a teletypewriter service operating in the United States and Canada. [*t(eletype)w(riter) (c)x(change service)*]

twy taxiway.

TX Texas (for use with ZIP code).

txtl textile.

Ty. Territory.

typ. **1.** typical. **2.** typographer. **3.** typographic; typographical. **4.** typography.

typo. **1.** typographer. **2.** typographic; typographical. **3.** typographical error. **4.** typography.

typog. **1.** typographer. **2.** typographic; typographical. **3.** typography.

typstg typesetting.

typw. **1.** typewriter. **2.** typewritten.

tyvm thank you very much.

U

U *Symbol.* **1.** the 21st in order or in a series, or, when *I* is omitted, the 20th. **2.** *Chemistry.* uranium. **3.** *Biochemistry.* uracil. **4.** *Thermodynamics.* internal energy. **5.** *British.* a designation for motion pictures determined as being acceptable for viewing by all age groups. **6.** kosher certification.

u (unified) atomic mass unit.

U. **1.** uncle. **2.** and. [from German *und*] **3.** uniform. **4.** union. **5.** unit. **6.** united. **7.** university. **8.** unsatisfactory. **9.** upper.

u. **1.** and. [from German *und*] **2.** uniform. **3.** unit. **4.** unsatisfactory. **5.** upper.

U.A.E. United Arab Emirates. Also, **UAE**

UAM underwater-to-air missile.

u. & l.c. *Printing.* upper and lower-case.

U.A.R. United Arab Republic.

UART (yōō′ärt), *Computers.* universal asynchronous receiver-transmitter.

UAW United Automobile Workers. Also, **U.A.W.**

U.B. United Brethren.

ubl unbleached.

U.C. **1.** Upper Canada. **2.** under construction. **3.** undercover.

u.c. **1.** *Music.* una corda; with the soft pedal depressed. **2.** *Printing.* upper case.

ucc Universal copyright convention.

UCR Uniform Crime Report.

U.C.V. United Confederate Veterans.

U/D under deed.

u.d. (in prescriptions) as directed. [from Latin *ut dictum*]

UDAG (yōō′dag), a federal program providing funds to local governments or private investors for urban redevelopment projects. [*U(rban) D(evelopment) A(ction) G(rant)*]

UDC Universal Decimal Classification.

U.D.C. United Daughters of the Confederacy.

udtd updated.

U.F.C. United Free Church (of Scotland).

UFD user file directory.

UFO (yōō′ef′ō′ *or, sometimes,* yōō′fō), unidentified flying object.

UFT United Federation of Teachers. Also, **U.F.T.**

UFW United Farm Workers of America.

ugnd underground.

UHF ultrahigh frequency. Also, **uhf**

UHT ultrahigh temperature.

UI unemployment insurance.

u.i. as below. [from Latin *ut infra*]

UIT unit investment trust.

UJT unijunction transistor.

U.K. United Kingdom.

UL Underwriters' Laboratories (used especially on labels for electrical appliances approved by this safety-testing organization).

ULCC a supertanker with a dead-weight capacity of over 250,000 tons. [*u(ltra) l(arge) c(rude) c(arrier)*]

ulf ultralow frequency.

ULMS underwater long-range missile system.

ULSI *Computers.* ultra large-scale integration.

ult. 1. Also, **ult** ultimate. **2.** ultimately. **3.** Also, **ulto.** the last month. [from Latin *ultimo*]

umbc umbilical cord.

Umbr. Umbrian.

UMT universal military training.

umus unbleached muslin.

UMW United Mine Workers.

UN 1. unified. **2.** Also, **U.N.** United Nations.

un union.

unan. unanimous.

unauth unauthorized.

UNC 1. Unified coarse (a thread measure). **2.** Also, **U.N.C.** United Nations Command.

unc. *Numismatics.* uncirculated.

UNCF United Negro College Fund.

UNCIO United Nations Conference on International Organization.

unclas unclassified.

uncond unconditional.

und under.

undc undercurrent.

undef undefined.

undetm undetermined.

undf underfrequency.

undld underload.

undv undervoltage.

UNEF 1. Unified extra-fine (a thread measure). **2.** United Nations Emergency Force.

UNESCO (yōō nes′kō), United Nations Educational, Scientific, and Cultural Organization.

UNF Unified fine (a thread measure).

unfin unfinished.

ung. (in prescriptions) ointment. [from Latin *unguentum*]

ungt. (in prescriptions) ointment. [from Latin *unguentum*]

Unh *Symbol, Chemistry, Physics.* unnilhexium.

UNICEF (yōō′nə sef′), United Nations Children's Fund. [*U(nited) N(ations) I(nternational) C(hildren's) E(mergency) F(und)* (an earlier official name)]

unif uniform.

unifet unipolar field-effect transistor.

Unit. Unitarian.

Univ. 1. Universalist. **2.** University.

univ. 1. universal. **2.** universally. **3.** university.

UNIVAC (yōō′ni vak′), Universal Automatic Computer.

unk unknown.

unl unloading.

unlim unlimited.

unlkg unlocking.

unmkd unmarked.

unmtd unmounted.

Unp *Symbol, Chemistry, Physics.* unnilpentium.

Unq *Symbol, Chemistry, Physics.* unnilquadium.

unrgltd unregulated.

UNRRA (un′rə), United Nations Relief and Rehabilitation Administration. Also, **U.N.R.R.A.**

UNRWA United Nations Relief and Works Agency.

uns unserviceable.

UNSC United Nations Security Council.

unstpd. unstamped.

untrtd untreated.

u/o used on.

up. 1. underproof (alcohol). **2.** Also, **upr** upper.

U.P. Upper Peninsula (of Michigan).

UPC Universal Product Code.

updt update.

UPI United Press International. Also, **U.P.I.**

uprt upright.

UPS 1. *Computers.* uninterruptible power supply. **2.** *Trademark.* United Parcel Service.

UPSW Union of Postal Service Workers.

UPU Universal Postal Union.

U.P.W.A. United Packinghouse Workers of America.

upwd upward.

UR unsatisfactory report.

ur urinal.

Ur. Uruguay.

URE Undergraduate Record Examination.

urol. 1. urological. **2.** urologist. **3.** urology.

Uru. Uruguay.

US 1. *Psychology.* unconditioned stimulus. **2.** *Photography.* Uniform Systems: lens-stop marking. **3.** United States. **4.** United States highway (used with a number): *US 66.*

U.S. 1. Uncle Sam. **2.** United Service. **3.** United States.

u.s. 1. where mentioned above.

[from Latin *ubi suprā*] **2.** as above: a formula in judicial acts, directing that what precedes be reviewed. [from Latin *ut suprā*]

USA 1. United States of America. **2.** United States Army. **3.** USA Network (a cable television channel). **4.** United Steelworkers of America.

U.S.A. 1. Union of South Africa. **2.** United States of America. **3.** United States Army.

USAEC United States Atomic Energy Commission.

U.S.A.F. United States Air Force. Also, **USAF**

USAFI United States Armed Forces Institute.

U.S.A.F.R. United States Air Force Reserve. Also, **USAFR**

USAID United States Aid for International Development.

USAR United States Army Reserve.

usb upper sideband.

USBC United States Bureau of the Census.

USBLS United States Bureau of Labor Statistics.

USBP United States Border Patrol.

U.S.C. 1. United States Code. **2.** United States of Colombia. Also, **USC**

U.S.C.A. United States Code Annotated. Also, **USCA**

U.S.C.&G.S. United States Coast and Geodetic Survey.

USCC United States Chamber of Commerce.

USCG United States Coast Guard. Also, **U.S.C.G.**

USCRC 1. United States Citizens Radio Council. **2.** United States Civil Rights Commission.

USCS United States Civil Service.

U.S.C. Supp. United States Code Supplement.

USDA United States Department of Agriculture. Also, **U.S.D.A.**

USDE 1. United States Department of Education. **2.** United States Department of Energy.

USDHEW United States Department of Health Education and Welfare.

USDHUD United States Department of Housing and Urban Development.

USDI United States Department of the Interior.

USDJ United States Department of Justice.

USDL United States Department of Labor.

USDT United States Department of Transportation.

USECC United States Employees' Compensation Commission.

USES United States Employment Service. Also, **U.S.E.S.**

USG United States Gauge.

U.S.G.A. United States Golf Association. Also, **USGA**

USGPO United States Government Printing Office.

USGS United States Geological Survey.

USHA United States Housing Authority. Also, **U.S.H.A.**

USIA United States Information Agency. Also, **U.S.I.A.**

USIS United States Information Service. Also, **U.S.I.S.**

USITC United States International Trade Commission.

U.S.L.T.A. United States Lawn Tennis Association. Also, **USLTA**

USM 1. underwater-to-surface missile. **2.** United States Mail. **3.** United States Marines. **4.** United States Mint. Also, **U.S.M.**

U.S.M.A. United States Military Academy. Also, **USMA**

USMC 1. United States Marine Corps. **2.** United States Maritime Commission. Also, **U.S.M.C.**

USMS United States Maritime Service.

USN United States Navy. Also, **U.S.N.**

USNA 1. United States National Army. **2.** United States Naval Academy. Also, **U.S.N.A.**

USNG United States National Guard. Also, **U.S.N.G.**

USNR United States Naval Reserve. Also, **U.S.N.R.**

USO United Service Organizations. Also, **U.S.O.**

USOC United States Olympic Committee.

U.S.P. United States Pharmacopeia. Also, **U.S. Pharm.**

uspd underspeed.

USPHS United States Public Health Service. Also, **U.S.P.H.S.**

USPO 1. United States Patent Office. **2.** United States Post Office. Also, **U.S.P.O.**

USPS United States Postal Service. Also, **U.S.P.S.**

USR United States Reserves. Also, **U.S.R.**

USRC United States Reserve Corps. Also, **U.S.R.C.**

U.S. RDA *Nutrition.* United States recommended daily allowance.

U.S.S. 1. United States Senate. **2.** United States Service. **3.** United States Ship. **4.** United States Steamer. **5.** United States Steamship. Also, **USS**

U.S.S.B. United States Shipping Board. Also, **USSB**

U.S.S.Ct. United States Supreme Court.

U.S.S.R. Union of Soviet Socialist Republics. Also, **USSR**

U.S.S.S. United States Steamship. Also, **USSS**

USTA United States Trademark Association.

USTC United States Tariff Commission.

USTS United States Travel Service: part of the Department of Commerce.

usu. 1. usual. 2. usually.

U.S.V. United States Volunteers. Also, **USV**

USW ultrashort wave.

usw and so forth; etc. Also, **u.s.w.** [from German *und so weiter*]

USWAC United States Women's Army Corps.

usz undersize.

UT 1. Also, **u.t.** universal time. 2. Utah (for use with ZIP code).

Ut. Utah.

U/T under trust.

UTC universal time coordinated.

utend. (in prescriptions) to be used. [from Latin *ūtendum*]

UTI urinary tract infection.

util 1. Also, **util.** utility. 2. utilization.

utn utensil.

U.T.W.A. United Textile Workers of America. Also, **UTWA**

UUM underwater-to-underwater missile.

UV ultraviolet. Also, **U.V.**

UV filter *Photography.* ultraviolet filter.

UVM universal vendor marking.

U/W under will.

U/w underwriter. Also, **u/w**

u/w used with.

uwtr underwater.

ux. *Chiefly Law.* wife. [from Latin *uxor*]

V

V 1. vagabond. 2. variable. 3. *Math.* vector. 4. velocity. 5. verb. 6. victory. 7. *Electricity.* volt; volts. 8. volume. 9. vowel.

V *Symbol.* 1. the 22nd in order or in a series, or, when *J* is omitted, the 21st. 2. (*sometimes lowercase*) the Roman numeral for five. 3. *Chemistry.* vanadium. 4. *Biochemistry.* valine. 5. *Physics.* electric potential. 6. (especially during World War II) the symbol of Allied victory.

v 1. variable. 2. velocity. 3. *Crystallography.* vicinal. 4. victory. 5. *Electricity.* volt; volts. 6. voltage.

V. 1. valve. 2. Venerable. 3. verb. 4. verse. 5. version. 6. versus. 7. very. 8. Vicar. 9. vice. 10. see. [from Latin *vidē*] 11. Village. 12. violin. 13. Virgin. 14. Viscount. 15. vision. 16. visual acuity. 17. *Grammar.* vocative. 18. voice. 19. volume.

v. 1. valve. 2. (in personal names) van. 3. vector. 4. vein. 5. ventral. 6. verb. 7. verse. 8. version. 9. *Printing.* verso. 10. versus. 11. very. 12. vicar. 13. vice. 14. see. [from Latin *vidē*] 15. village. 16. violin. 17. vision. 18. *Grammar.* vocative. 19. voice. 20. volt. 21. voltage. 22. volume. 23. (in personal names) von.

VA 1. Veterans Administration. 2. Virginia (for use with ZIP code). 3. Also, **va** *Electricity.* volt-ampere; volt-amperes.

Va. Virginia.

V.A. 1. Veterans Administration. 2. Vicar Apostolic. 3. Vice-Admiral. 4. (Order of) Victoria and Albert. 5. visual aid.

v.a. 1. verb active. 2. *Grammar.* verbal adjective.

vac. 1. vacant. 2. vacation. 3. vacuum.

vacc. vaccination.

V. Adm. Vice-Admiral.

Val *Biochemistry.* valine.

val. 1. valentine. 2. valley. 3. valuation. 4. value. 5. valued.

valdtn validation.

vam voltammeter.

var. 1. variable. 2. variant. 3. variation. 4. variety. 5. variometer. 6. various.

varhm var-hour meter.

variac (vâr′ē ak′), variable-voltage transformer.

varistor (vâr′ə stər), voltage-variable resistor.

varitran (vâr′ə tran′), variable-voltage transformer.

VAT (vē′ā′tē′, vat), value-added tax.

Vat. Vatican.

v. aux. auxiliary verb.

vb. 1. verb. 2. verbal.

VBE vernacular black English.

vbtm verbatim.

VC 1. venture capital. 2. Vietcong. 3. vital capacity.

V.C. 1. venture capital. 2. Veterinary Corps. 3. Vice-Chairman. 4. Vice-Chancellor. 5. Vice-Consul. 6. Victoria Cross. 7. Vietcong.

vcl vehicle centerline.

vco voltage-controlled oscillator.

VCR videocassette recorder.

vctr vector.

VD venereal disease. Also, **V.D.**

vd void.

v.d. various dates.

V-Day (vē′dā′), a day of final military victory. [*V(ictory) Day*]

V.D.M. Minister of the Word of God. [from Latin *Verbī Deī Minister*]

vdr voltage-dependent resistor: varistor.

VDT *Computers.* 1. video display terminal. 2. *Chiefly British.* visual display terminal.

VDU *Computers.* visual display unit.

V-E Day (vē′ē′), May 8, 1945, the day of victory in Europe for the Allies. [*V(ictory in) E(urope) Day*]

veg. vegetable.

veh vehicle.

vel. *Printing.* 1. vellum. 2. velocity.

Ven. 1. Venerable. 2. Venice.

Venez. Venezuela.

vent. 1. ventilate. 2. ventilation. 3. ventilator. 4. venture.

ver. 1. verse; verses. 2. version.

verif verification.

vers. *Trigonometry.* versed sine.

verst versatile.

vert. 1. vertebra. 2. vertebrate. 3. vertical.

vet. 1. veteran. 2. veterinarian. 3. veterinary.

vet. med. veterinary medicine.

vet. sci. veterinary science.

VF 1. *Botany.* a designation applied to various plant varieties, indicating resistance to verticillium wilt and fusarium wilt. 2. *Numismatics.* very fine. 3. *Television.* video frequency. 4. visual field. 5. voice frequency.

vf 1. variable frequency. 2. voice frequency.

vfc voice-frequency carrier.

VFD volunteer fire department.

vfo variable-frequency oscillator.

VFR visual flight rules.

V.F.W. Veterans of Foreign Wars of the United States. Also, **VFW**

VG very good.

V.G. Vicar-General.

v.g. for example. [from Latin *verbī gratiā*]

VGA *Computers.* video graphics adapter.

VHF very high frequency. Also, **vhf, V.H.F.**

VHS *Trademark.* Video Home System: a format for recording and playing VCR tape, incompatible with other formats.

VI Virgin Islands (for use with ZIP code).

Vi *Symbol, Chemistry.* virginium.

vi variable interval.

V.I. 1. Vancouver Island. **2.** Virgin Islands.

v.i. 1. intransitive verb. **2.** see below. [from Latin *vidē infrā*]

Via. viaduct (in addresses).

vib vibration.

Vic. 1. Vicar. **2.** Vicarage. **3.** Victoria.

vic. vicinity.

vice pres. vice president. Also, **Vice Pres.**

Vict. 1. Victoria. **2.** Victorian.

vid. 1. see. [from Latin *vide*] **2.** Also, **vid** video.

vidf video frequency.

vil. village.

v. imp. verb impersonal.

VIN vehicle identification number.

vin. (in prescriptions) wine. [from Latin *vīnum*]

VIP (vē′ī′pē′), *Informal.* very important person. Also, **V.I.P.**

Virg. Virginia.

v. irr. irregular verb.

Vis. 1. Viscount. **2.** Viscountess. **3.** vista (in addresses).

vis. 1. visibility. **2.** visual.

visc viscosity

Visc. 1. Viscount. **2.** Viscountess.

Visct. 1. Viscount. **2.** Viscountess.

VISTA (vis′tə), a national program in the U.S., sponsored by ACTION, for sending volunteers into poor areas to teach various job skills. [*V(olunteers) i(n) S(ervice) t(o) A(merica)*]

vitr vitreous.

viz. (used to introduce examples, etc.) namely. [from Latin *videlicet*]

VJ (vē′jā′), *Informal.* **1.** Also, **V.J.** video jockey. **2.** a video journalist.

V-J Day (vē′jā′), August 15, 1945, the day Japan accepted the Allied surrender terms. [*V(ictory over) J(apan) Day*]

VL Vulgar Latin.

v.l. variant reading. [from Latin *varia lectio*]

VLA *Astronomy.* Very Large Array.

vla very low altitude.

VLBI *Astronomy.* very long baseline interferometry.

VLCC a supertanker with a deadweight capacity of up to 250,000 tons. [*V(ery) L(arge) C(rude) C(arrier)*]

VLDL *Biochemistry.* very-low-density lipoprotein.

VLF very low frequency. Also, **vlf**

vlmtrc volumetric.

vlr very long range.

VLSI *Electronics.* very large scale integration: the technology for concentrating many thousands of semiconductor devices on a single integrated circuit.

vm velocity modulation.

V.M.D. Doctor of Veterinary Medicine. [from Latin *Veterināriae Medicīnae Doctor*]

v.n. verb neuter.

vo. *Printing.* verso.

V.O. very old (used especially to indicate the age of whiskey or brandy, usually 6 to 8 years old).

VOA 1. Also, **V.O.A.** Voice of America. **2.** Volunteers of America.

voc. *Grammar.* vocative.

vocab. vocabulary.

voc. ed. vocational education.

vodat (vō′dat), voice-operated device for automatic transmission.

vogad (vō′gad), voice-operated gain-adjusting device.

vol. 1. volcano. **2.** volume. **3.** volunteer.

VO language *Linguistics.* a type of language that has direct objects following the verb. [*V(erb)-O(bject)*]

vom volt-ohm-milliammeter.

VOR *Navigation.* omnirange. [*v(ery high frequency) o(mni) r(ange)*]

vordme vhf omnirange distance-measuring equipment.

vou. voucher.

VOX (voks), a device in certain types of telecommunications equipment, that converts an incoming voice or sound signal into an electrical signal. [acronym from *voice-operated keying*, altered to conform to Latin *vōx* voice]

vox pop. the voice of the people. [from Latin *vox populi*]

VP 1. verb phrase. 2. Also, **vp, v-p** vice president.

vp vapor pressure.

V.P. Vice President. Also, **V. Pres.**

v.p. passive verb. [from Latin *verbum passīvum*]

vprs voltage-regulated power supply.

vprz vaporize.

VR 1. virtual reality. 2. voltage regulator.

vr 1. variable response. 2. voltage regulator.

V.R. Queen Victoria. [from Latin *Victōria Rēgīna*]

v.r. reflexive verb. [from Latin *verbum reflexīvum*]

V region *Immunology.* variable region.

V. Rev. Very Reverend.

vrfy verify.

vris *Electricity.* varistor.

VRM variable-rate mortgage.

vs. 1. verse. 2. versus.

V.S. Veterinary Surgeon.

v.s. see above. [from Latin *vide supra*]

vsb vestigial sideband.

vsbl visible.

vsd variable-speed drive.

vsm vestigial-sideband.

V. S. O. (of brandy) very superior old.

VSO language *Linguistics.* a type of language that has basic verb-subject-object word order.

V.S.O.P. very superior old pale (used especially to indicate a type of aged brandy).

VSR very special reserve (a classification of fortified wines).

vss. versions.

vstbl vestibule.

vstm valve stem.

V/STOL (vē′stôl′), *Aeronautics.* vertical and short takeoff and landing.

VSWR *Electronics.* voltage standing-wave ratio. Also, **vswr**

VT Vermont (for use with ZIP code).

Vt. Vermont.

v.t. transitive verb. [from Latin *verbum trānsitīvum*]

V.T.C. 1. Volunteer Training Corps. 2. voting trust certificate.

Vte. Vicomte.

Vtesse. Vicomtesse.

VT fuze a variable time fuze.

vtm voltage-tunable magnetron.

VTO *Aeronautics.* vertical takeoff.

VTOL (vē′tôl′), *Aeronautics.* a convertiplane capable of taking off and landing vertically, having forward speeds comparable to those of conventional aircraft. [*v(ertical) t(ake)o(ff and) l(anding)*]

VTR *Television.* videotape recorder.

vtvm vacuum-tube voltmeter.

vu *Audio.* volume unit. Also, **VU**

Vul. Vulgate (bible).

vulc vulcanize.

Vulg. Vulgate (bible).

vulg. 1. vulgar. 2. vulgarly.

VU meter a meter used with sound-reproducing or recording equipment that indicates average sound levels.

vv. 1. verses. 2. violins.

v.v. vice versa.

V. V. O. (of brandy) very, very old.

V. V. S. (of brandy) very very superior.

V.W. Very Worshipful.

W

W 1. watt; watts. **2.** west. **3.** western. **4.** white. **5.** wide. **6.** widowed. **7.** width. **8.** withdrawn; withdrew. **9.** withheld.

W Symbol. **1.** the 23rd in order or in a series, or, when I is omitted, the 22nd. **2.** Chemistry. tungsten. [from German Wolfram] **3.** Biochemistry. tryptophan.

w 1. Baseball. walk. **2.** watt; watts. **3.** withdrawn; withdrew. **4.** withheld.

W. 1. Wales. **2.** warden. **3.** warehouse. **4.** Washington. **5.** watt; watts. **6.** Wednesday. **7.** weight. **8.** Welsh. **9.** west **10.** western. **11.** width. **12.** Physics. work.

w. 1. warden. **2.** warehouse. **3.** water. **4.** watt; watts. **5.** week; weeks. **6.** weight. **7.** west. **8.** western. **9.** wide. **10.** width. **11.** wife. **12.** with. **13.** won. **14.** Physics. work. **15.** wrong.

w/ with.

WA 1. Washington (for use with ZIP code). **2.** Banking. withholding agent.

W.A. 1. West Africa. **2.** Western Australia. **3.** Marine Insurance. with average.

WAAC (wak), **1. a.** Women's Army Auxiliary Corps: founded during World War II. **b.** a member of the Women's Army Auxiliary Corps. **2.** British. **a.** Women's Army Auxiliary Corps: founded in 1917. **b.** a member of the Women's Army Auxiliary Corps. Also, **W.A.A.C.**

WAAF Women's Auxiliary Air Force.

waf width across flats.

W. Afr. 1. West Africa. **2.** West African.

WAFS Women's Auxiliary Ferrying Squadron. Also, **W.A.F.S.**

WAIS (wās for def. 1), **1.** Wechsler Adult Intelligence Scale. **2.** Computers. wide-area information server.

WAIS-R (wās′är′), Wechsler Adult Intelligence Scale-Revised.

Wal. 1. Wallachian. **2.** Walloon.

WAM wraparound mortgage.

WAN (wan), wide-area network.

w. & f. (in shipping) water and feed.

WAP Women Against Pornography.

war. warrant.

warrty. warranty. Also, **warr**

Wash. Washington.

WASP (wosp), **1.** Sometimes Disparaging and Offensive. white Anglo-Saxon Protestant. Also, **Wasp 2.** a member of the Women's Air Force Service Pilots (in World War II).

WATS (wots), a bulk-rate long-distance telephone service. [W(ide) A(rea) T(elecommunications) S(ervice)]

WAVAW Women Against Violence Against Women.

Wb Electricity. weber; webers.

wb 1. wet bulb. **2.** workbench.

W/B waybill. Also, **W.B.**

w.b. 1. warehouse book. **2.** water ballast. **3.** waybill. **4.** westbound.

WBA World Boxing Association.

wba wideband amplifier.

wbfp Real Estate. wood-burning fireplace.

wbg webbing.

WbN west by north.

WbS west by south.

WC water closet.

W.C. 1. water closet. **2.** west central.

w.c. 1. water closet. **2.** without charge.

W.C.T.U. Women's Christian Temperance Union.

WD wiring diagram.

wd 1. Stock Exchange. when distrib-

uted. **2.** width. **3.** wind. **4.** wood.
5. word.

wd. 1. ward. **2.** word.

W/D *Banking.* withdrawal.

w/d withdrawn.

W.D. War Department.

WDC War Damage Corporation.

wdg winding.

wdo window.

wea weather.

WEAL Women's Equity Action
League.

Wed. Wednesday.

West. western. Also, **west.**

Westm. Westminster.

WF 1. wind force. **2.** withdraw
failing.

wf *Printing.* wrong font. Also, **w.f.**

wfr wafer.

WFTU World Federation of Trade
Unions. Also, **W.F.T.U.**

wg 1. waveguide. **2.** wing.

W.G. 1. water gauge. **2.** *Commerce.*
weight guaranteed. **3.** wire gauge.
Also, **w.g.**

W. Ger. 1. West Germanic. **2.** West
Germany.

WGmc West Germanic. Also, **W.
Gmc.**

WH *Banking.* withholding. Also, **w/h**

Wh watt-hour; watt-hours. Also, **wh,
whr**

WHA World Hockey Association.

whf. wharf.

whl wheel.

WHO World Health Organization.

whr. watt-hour; watt-hours.

whse. warehouse. Also, **whs.**

whsle. wholesale.

whs. stk. warehouse stock.

wht white.

WI Wisconsin (for use with ZIP
code).

wi *Stock Exchange.* when-issued.
Also, **w.i.**

W.I. 1. West Indian. **2.** West Indies.

WIA *Military.* wounded in action.

wid. 1. widow. **2.** widower.

WIMP (wimp), *Physics.* any of a
group of weakly interacting elementary particles characterized by relatively large masses. [W(eakly) I(nter-
acting) M(assive) P(article)]

WIP 1. work in process. **2.** work in
progress. Also, **W.I.P.**

wip work in progress.

Wis. Wisconsin. Also, **Wisc.**

WISC (wisk), Wechsler Intelligence
Scale for Children.

WISC-R (wisk/är/), Wechsler Intelligence Scale for Children-Revised.

Wisd. *Bible.* Wisdom of Solomon.

wk. 1. week. **2.** work.

wkg working.

wkly. weekly.

wks workshop.

wl wavelength.

WLB War Labor Board.

wlb wallboard.

wld welded.

WLF Women's Liberation Front.

w. long. west longitude.

Wm. William.

w/m *Commerce.* weight and/or measurement.

WMC War Manpower Commission.

wmgr worm gear.

wmk. watermark.

WMO World Meteorological Organization.

wmwhl wormwheel.

wnd wound.

wndr winder.

WNW west-northwest.

WO 1. wait order. **2.** War Office.
3. Warrant Officer. Also, **W.O.**

w/o without.

w.o.b. *Commerce.* washed overboard.

w.o.c. without compensation.

WP word processing.

wp waste pipe.

wp. *Baseball.* wild pitch; wild pitches.

W.P. 1. weather permitting. **2.** wire payment. **3.** working pressure. Also, **WP, w.p.**

WPA Work Projects Administration: a former federal agency (1935–43), originally, Works Progress Administration.

WPB War Production Board. Also, **W.P.B.**

WPBL Women's Professional Basketball League.

wpg waterproofing.

WPI wholesale price index.

wpm words per minute.

wpn weapon.

WPPSI (wip′sē), Wechsler Preschool and Primary Scale of Intelligence.

wps words per second.

Wr *Medicine.* Wassermann reaction.

wr 1. washroom. **2.** wrench. **3.** writer.

w.r. 1. warehouse receipt. **2.** *Insurance.* war risk.

WRA War Relocation Authority.

WRAC *British.* Women's Royal Army Corps. Also, **W.R.A.C.**

WRAF (raf), *British.* Women's Royal Air Force. Also, **W.R.A.F.**

wrb wardrobe.

wrk work.

wrkg wrecking.

wrn warning.

wrngr wringer.

W.R.N.S. *British.* Women's Royal Naval Service.

wrnt. warrant.

wrpg warping.

W.R.S.S.R. White Russian Soviet Socialist Republic.

W-R star *Astronomy.* Wolf-Rayet star.

wrtr writer.

WS weapon system.

W.S. West Saxon.

WSA War Shipping Administration.

wshg washing.

wshld windshield.

wshr washer.

WSW west-southwest.

wt. weight.

WTA 1. Women's Tennis Association. **2.** World Tennis Association.

wtd wanted.

wtg 1. waiting. **2.** weighting.

wtr water.

wtrprf waterproof.

wtrtt watertight.

wtrz winterize.

WV West Virginia (for use with ZIP code).

W.Va. West Virginia.

wvfm waveform.

W.V.S. *British.* Women's Voluntary Service.

WW 1. World War. **2.** *Real Estate.* wall-to-wall. Also, **W/W**

ww 1. wirewound. **2.** *Stock Exchange.* with warrants (offered to the buyer of a given stock or bond).

WWI World War I.

WWII World War II.

w/wo with or without.

WWW *Computers.* World Wide Web (part of Internet).

WY Wyoming (for use with ZIP code).

Wy. Wyoming.

Wyo. Wyoming.

WYSIWYG (wiz′ē wig′), *Computers.* of, pertaining to, or noting a screen display that shows text exactly as it will appear in printed output. [*w(hat) y(ou) s(ee) i(s) w(hat) y(ou) g(et)*]

X

X 1. experimental. **2.** extra. **3.** extraordinary.

X *Symbol.* **1.** the 24th in order or in a series, or, when *I* is omitted, the 23rd. **2.** (*sometimes lowercase*) the Roman numeral for 10. **3.** Christ. **4.** Christian. **5.** cross. **6.** *Electricity.* reactance. **7.** *Slang.* a ten-dollar bill. **8.** (in the U.S.) a rating of the Motion Picture Association of America for movies with subject matter that is suitable for adults only. **9.** (in Great Britain) a designation for a film recommended for adults only. **10.** a person, thing, agency, factor, etc., of unknown identity. **11.** *Chemistry.* (formerly) xenon.

x 1. *Finance.* without. [from Latin *ex*] **2.** excess. **3.** *Stock Exchange.* **a.** (of stock trading) ex dividend; without a previously declared dividend. **b.** (of bond trading) ex interest; without accrued interest. **4.** experimental. **5.** extra.

x *Symbol.* **1.** an unknown quantity or a variable. **2.** (used at the end of letters, telegrams, etc., to indicate a kiss.) **3.** (used to indicate multiplication) times: $8 \times 8 = 64$. **4.** (used between figures indicating dimensions) by: $3' \times 4'$. **5.** power of magnification: *a 50x telescope.* **6.** (used as a signature by an illiterate person.) **7.** cross. **8.** crossed with. **9.** (used to indicate a particular place or point on a map or diagram.) **10.** out of; foaled by: *Flag-a-way x Merrylegs.* **11.** (used to indicate choice, as on a ballot, examination, etc.) **12.** (used to indicate an error or incorrect answer, as on a test.) **13.** *Math.* (in Cartesian coordinates) the x-axis.

14. *Chess.* captures. **15.** a person, thing, agency, factor, etc., of unknown identity.

xarm crossarm.

xbar *Telephones.* crossbar.

xbra crossbracing.

xbt *Telecommunications.* crossbar tandem.

xc *Stock Exchange.* without coupon. Also, **xcp**

X-C cross-country.

xcl *Insurance.* excess current liabilities.

xconn *Telephones.* cross-connection.

xcvr transceiver.

xcy cross-country.

xd *Stock Exchange.* ex dividend. See **x** (def. 3a). Also, **xdiv.**

xdcr transducer.

Xe *Symbol, Chemistry.* xenon.

XF *Numismatics.* extra fine.

xfmr *Electronics.* transformer.

xfr transfer.

xhair crosshair.

xhd crosshead.

xhvy extra heavy.

x in *Stock Exchange.* ex interest. See **x** (def. 3b).

xing crossing.

XL 1. extra large. **2.** extra long.

xmsn transmission.

xmt transmit.

xmtd *Electronics.* transmitted.

xmtg *Electronics.* transmitting.

xmtr *Electronics.* transmitter.

Xn. Christian.

Xnty. Christianity.

xpl explosive.

xpndr transponder.

x pr *Stock Exchange.* without privileges.

xprt transport.

xpt *Electricity.* crosspoint.

xptn transportation.

XQ cross question. Also, **xq**

xr *Stock Exchange.* ex rights; without rights.

xref cross reference.

XS extra small.

xsect cross section.

xstg extra strong.

xstr transistor.

Xt. Christ.

xtal *Electronics.* crystal.

xtalk *Telephones.* crosstalk.

Xtian. Christian.

xtlo crystal oscillator.

Xty. Christianity.

xvs transverse.

XX powdered sugar.

XXL extra, extra large.

XXXX confectioners' sugar.

xya *Math.* x-y axis.

xyv *Math.* x-y vector.

Y

Y (wī), *Informal.* YMCA, YWCA, YMHA, or YWHA.

Y (in Japan) yen.

Y *Symbol.* **1.** the 25th in order or in a series, or, when *I* is omitted, the 24th. **2.** (*sometimes lowercase*) the medieval Roman numeral for 150. **3.** (*sometimes lowercase*) *Electricity.* admittance. **4.** *Chemistry.* yttrium. **5.** *Biochemistry.* tyrosine.

y *Symbol, Math.* **1.** an unknown quantity. **2.** (in Cartesian coordinates) the y-axis.

y. **1.** yard; yards. **2.** year; years.

YA young adult.

YAG (yag), a synthetic yttrium aluminum garnet, used for infrared lasers and as a gemstone. [*y(ttrium) a(luminum) g(arnet)*]

yap young aspiring professional.

Yb *Symbol, Chemistry.* ytterbium.

Y.B. yearbook. Also, **YB**

Y.C.L. Young Communist League.

ycw you can't win.

YD. (in the People's Democratic Republic of Yemen) dinar; dinars.

yd. yard; yards.

yd³ *Symbol.* cubic yard.

yds. yards.

yel yellow.

yeo. yeomanry.

YHA Youth Hostels Association.

YHVH *Judaism.* a transliteration of the Tetragrammaton, the four-letter name of God. Also, **YHWH, JHVH, JHWH** [from Hebrew *yhwh* God]

YIG (yig), a synthetic yttrium iron garnet, used in electronics in filters and amplifiers. [*y(ttrium) i(ron) g(arnet)*]

YMCA Young Men's Christian Association. Also, **Y.M.C.A.**

Y.M.Cath.A. Young Men's Catholic Association.

YMHA Young Men's Hebrew Association. Also, **Y.M.H.A.**

y.o. year old; years old.

y.o.b. year of birth. Also, **YOB**

Y.P.S.C.E. Young People's Society of Christian Endeavor.

yr. **1.** year; years. **2.** your.

yrbk. yearbook.

yrs. **1.** years. **2.** yours.

YT Yukon Territory, Canada (for use with ZIP code).

Y.T. Yukon Territory.

YTD *Accounting.* year to date.

Yugo. Yugoslavia.

yuppie (yup/ē), (*sometimes capital*) a young, ambitious, educated city dweller who has a professional career and an affluent lifestyle. Also, **yuppy.** [*y(oung) u(rban) p(rofessional)* + -*ie*]

YWCA Young Women's Christian Association. Also, **Y.W.C.A.**

YWHA Young Women's Hebrew Association. Also, **Y.W.H.A.**

Z

Z **1.** *Astronomy.* zenith distance. **2.** zone.

Z *Symbol.* **1.** the 26th in order or in a series, or, when *I* is omitted, the 25th. **2.** (*sometimes lowercase*) the medieval Roman numeral for 2000. **3.** *Chemistry, Physics.* atomic number. **4.** *Electricity.* impedance.

z zone.

z *Symbol, Math.* **1.** an unknown quantity or variable. **2.** (in Cartesian coordinates) the z-axis.

z. zero.

Z⁰ *Symbol, Physics.* Z-zero particle.

ZBB zero-base budgeting.

Zech. *Bible.* Zechariah.

ZEG zero economic growth.

Zeph. *Bible.* Zephaniah.

ZI *Military.* Zone of the Interior.

ZIF (zif), *Computers.* zero insertion force.

ZIP code (zip), *Trademark.* a system used to facilitate delivery of U.S. mail, consisting of five or nine digits. [*Z(one) I(mprovement) P(lan)*]

ZIP + 4 (zip′ plus′ fôr′, fōr′), a ZIP code of nine digits.

Zn *Symbol, Chemistry.* zinc.

zn zone.

zod. zodiac.

zof zone of fire.

zoochem. zoochemistry.

zool. **1.** zoological. **2.** zoologist. **3.** zoology.

ZPG zero population growth.

Zr *Symbol, Chemistry.* zirconium.

ZZ zigzag approach.

zz zigzag.

Zz. ginger. Also, **zz.** [from Latin *zingiber*]